THE WHOLE MAN

Psychology

Books by the Same Author

THE SCIENCE OF CORRECT THINKING

REALITY AND THE MIND

THE DOMAIN OF BEING

FROM AETHER TO COSMOS

GOD AND HIS CREATURES

MAN AND MORALS

THE WHOLE MAN

PSYCHOLOGY

CELESTINE N. BITTLE, O.F.M. Cap.

THE BRUCE PUBLISHING COMPANY
MILWAUKEE

Nihil obstat: Ignatius McCormick, O.F.M.Cap.
August 28, 1943

Nihil obstat: Thomas Aquinas Heidenreich, O.F.M.Cap., Ph.D.
September 13, 1943

Imprimi potest: Clement Neubauer, O.F.M.Cap., Minister Provincial
September 20, 1943

Nihil obstat: H. B. Ries, Censor librorum
Imprimatur: ✠ Moyses E. Kiley, Archiepiscopus Milwaukiensis
August 16, 1944

made in the u. s. a.

(11/62)

AUTHOR'S PREFACE

This book is intended as a text on philosophical psychology for the undergraduate student. It should give him a fairly thorough acquaintance with this department of philosophy.

Since psychology is here treated as a department of philosophy, only those facts and laws of scientific psychology have been incorporated into the text which have a bearing on the philosophical understanding of the ultimate nature of man. Precise laboratory techniques, statistical tables, and mathematical formulae have therefore been omitted as irrelevant to the purpose in view. A general survey of the positive findings of scientific research suffices as a background for the student who is taking an elementary course in philosophical psychology. The scientific material, however, could not be eliminated entirely, because in most cases the undergraduate approaches psychology without any preliminary knowledge of the pertinent scientific facts. Just what scientific data should be taken into the text, is a debatable question; the author hopes he has struck a satisfactory medium.

Bearing the mental equipment of the undergraduate in mind, so that he will derive the greatest benefit from the text, special attention has been given to the arrangement of the material and to the form of its presentation.

Many psychologists overemphasize the distinctness of the mental functions of man and underemphasize the fundamental unity of man. As a consequence of this attitude man appears as an aggregate of functions and processes. In reality, of course, man is an integral organism expressing himself as a unit in many ways, and the student should never lose sight of this important fact. The integrality of man as an organism consisting of diversified structures, powers, and functions operating as a unit is the leading theme stressed throughout the book. This thought is brought home to the student in the treatment of *The Whole Man* as a vegetant-sentient-rational being.

Some might question the position of the chapters on consciousness and extranormal mental states in the general arrangement of the material in the book. One must remember, however, that consciousness is an over-all mental state affecting every sensory and rational phenomenon; as such, consciousness cannot be properly understood until all the sensory and rational functions have been described and discussed. Similarly, the extranormal states of hypnosis, clairvoyance, telepathy, etc., cannot be appreciated in their true significance until the normal sensory and rational states have been described and discussed.

Again, some instructors will miss an extensive treatment of aristotelian hylomorphism in connection with the problem of the union of body and soul. From a psychological standpoint, it is necessary to prove the existence or nonexistence of a vital principle or soul in the human organism. The theory of hylomorphism, however, is a general interpretation of the constitution of all natural bodies, inorganic and organic, and belongs properly to cosmology. The author has treated the theory extensively in his "From Aether to Cosmos," and there seemed no need to repeat the matter in this book.

As for the form of presentation, it has been the endeavor of the author to use nontechnical language wherever possible and advisable, with copious examples and explanations to clarify the meaning of obscure terms or facts. While this method tends to make the style somewhat diffuse, the method should enable the student to grasp the difficult subject matter more fully and effectively, and that, after all, is the purpose of every basic text.

It is the fond hope of the author that his psychology text will receive the same kindly acceptance that was accorded his texts in logic, epistemology, ontology, and cosmology.

C. N. Bittle, O.F.M.Cap.

December 8, 1944

CONTENTS

THE WHOLE MAN

Psychology

CHAPTER I

NATURE AND SCOPE OF PSYCHOLOGY

TO JUDGE from the frequency of the use of the term in ordinary conversation, in magazine articles, and in books, there is hardly any form of human endeavor to which the term 'psychology' is not applied. People speak of the 'psychology' of education, of business, of war, of social classes, of religion, of adolescence, of crime, of individualism, of dictatorship, of football, of labor unions, of fashion, and so on. Needless to say, such an application of the term is very broad and loose.

For the psychologist and philosopher, psychology is a special department of human knowledge, a *science*. As such, it has its own proper *subject matter* and its own proper *method of investigation*. It is a science in the strict sense of the word, different from other departments of human knowledge. Unfortunately, however, there is perhaps no other science in which such a divergence of views exists as to what is the proper subject matter and the proper method of investigation as in psychology. The reason for this situation is twofold. On the one hand, man, who is the main object of investigation, is so complex a being, that psychologists cannot seem to agree as to how much of his being shall be included in the general subject matter of psychology. On the other hand, psychologists are greatly influenced in their decision by the particular type of philosophy which they uphold; it makes a considerable difference, for instance, whether they are materialists or idealists in their outlook on the world.

Subject Matter of Psychology

Considered from the standpoint of its etymological derivation, *psychology* (Gr., ψυχή, soul, and λόγος, discourse, treatise) is the *science of the soul.* Now, the soul, or psyche, is considered to be that in virtue of which an organism lives, the principle of life in plants, animals, and men. Aristotle, the greatest of the Greek philosophers, already conceived it in this manner, namely, as the principle giving life to the body of the organism. Viewed this way, the subject matter of psychology is everything that pertains to the *life of the organism,* whether it be a plant, an animal, or a man. Psychology, therefore, should investigate vegetative, sensory, and rational phenomena as found in plant life, animal life, and human life. Some authors do this, but their number is small.

Most modern psychologists balk at defining psychology as 'the science of the soul.' They consider the 'soul' as a reality which smacks of theology; at best, they contend, its existence cannot be presupposed, and it should, therefore, be excluded as the proper subject matter of psychology. Many prefer to define psychology as the *science of the mind.* The 'mind' is the seat or principle of such phenomena as seeing, hearing, feeling, desiring, thinking, and willing; in other words, the mind is generally understood to be the ultimate principle or, as others prefer to view it, the sum-total of all the powers, processes, and states found in the sensory and rational life of man. Vegetative functions are not 'mental,' and their investigation does not belong to psychology. Hence, only the 'mental' phenomena characteristic of *animal* and *human* life should be included in the study of psychology.

Others object to the term 'mind.' The term seems to imply something which is the underlying 'bearer' of mental phenomena; it would be merely another name for the questionable reality of a 'soul.' Hence, they prefer to speak of psychology as the *science of consciousness* or *of the conscious states.* Since some psychologists are convinced that both animals and men possess consciousness, the mental life of *animals* and *human beings* are the subject matter of psychology. Not all, however, agree with this. They maintain that it is impossible for us to know whether animals are really 'conscious.' Consequently, psychology should restrict itself to the study of the conscious states of *man*. But even this is not entirely satisfactory. Many vital activities of man belong to the 'mental' order, though they are performed subconsciously or unconsciously, as will be seen later; these belong properly, they claim, to the field of psychological investigation. There is, then, no definite agreement among professional psychologists as to the exact subject matter of their science.

Among professional philosophers, too, one finds a division of opinion on this score. Those of the older school of thought were inclined to look upon psychology as the *philosophy of organic life;* correspondingly, they included the nature of plants, of animals, and of men as integral parts of the subject matter of psychology. Modern philosophers, however, restrict their investigations to the *nature of man*. If they bring the vegetative life of the plant and the sensory life of the animal within the scope of their studies, it is for the purpose of comparison, in order to illustrate some point in connection with the life of man. Most authors omit the discussion of vegetative functions almost entirely, stressing the *sensory* and *rational* activities of man as the proper field of psychological research. And so it has come to pass that psychology, in its historical development, has narrowed down its subject matter to a great extent.

One must distinguish between two types of psychology—*scientific* psychology and *philosophic* psychology. The attitude of science and of philosophy toward psychological problems is quite different.

Psychology as Science and Philosophy

When we speak of *scientific psychology,* or psychology as a 'science,' we place it on a par with other positive and exact sciences, such as physics, chemistry, astronomy, biology, etc. It is then considered as a department of knowledge which seeks to discover all pertinent facts by means of observation and experiment, to describe these facts in their proper order, and to establish the general laws according to which these facts occur. Science, so far as possible, uses quantitative measurements in all its findings and formulates its laws in terms of quantitative measurements.

It is characteristic of the scientific attitude to investigate phenomena by means of immediate observation and controlled experiments, so that everything is based on experience and not on speculative reasoning. The scientist does not inquire into the hidden 'nature' of things; he is satisfied to analyze the phenomena, classify them, and determine their *proximate causes.* Applying these principles of scientific research to psychology, the scientist examines the mental phenomena of sensations, perceptions, emotions, acts of the intellect and will, and so forth, and endeavors to reduce them to their simplest and most fundamental elements or laws. That is why scientific psychology is also called *empirical* and *experimental* psychology.

Philosophical psychology, or psychology as 'philosophy,' is a branch or department of philosophy and takes its place beside the departments of logic, epistemology, cosmology, ontology, theodicy, and ethics. Philosophy is the science of beings in their *ultimate reasons, causes, and principles,* acquired by the aid of human reason alone. Philosophy endeavors to penetrate beyond the surface of phenomena and uncover the nature and essence which gives rise to such phenomena; thereby it hopes to understand and explain things in a more thorough and satisfying manner. Philosophy accepts the legitimate findings of scientific (empirical, experimental) psychology and then pushes its investigation still farther into the regions of the unknown, thereby attempting to widen the boundary line of knowledge. Philosophic psychology is thus the extension and completion of scientific psychology.

The scientific psychologist touches many vital problems which he refuses to discuss; the philosophic psychologist finds these problems to be of absorbing interest and cannot resist the desire to solve them. The scientist takes life for granted. But what is life? Whence does it originate? Is it fundamentally distinct from the chemical elements that constitute the body? Is it merely a peculiar kind of material force? Is it the result of a substantial principle? Experimental psychology makes a special study of man's mind in all its moods, states, and operations. However, what is 'mind'? Is it material or immaterial? Is there such a thing as a 'soul'? If the soul exists, is it mortal or immortal? Is there an essential distinction between man and the brute? And what is the origin and destiny of man? No one can say that such problems are unimportant; on the contrary, the solution of these and similar problems are of tremendous importance to man.

The philosopher has no quarrel with the scientist. Both are driven in their research by the same unquenchable thirst for knowledge. If the scientist wishes to restrict the subject matter of his science to the immediately observable phenomena of mental life and their proximate causes, that is his privilege. The philosopher, however, wishes to disclose, if possible, the unobservable *nature* of man manifested by mental phenomena. Who would dispute the right of the philosophic psychologist to delve into the nature of man through the use of his reasoning powers? Reason is just as much an instrument of knowledge as are the senses. In fact, more so. The scientific psychologist, when he makes an experiment with a subject, uses his senses as instruments of experience to find out the facts of mental life occurring in the subject; and he also utilizes the knowledge of mental facts occurring in his own person. Facts, however, need *interpretation;* they are not self-explanatory. And he interprets these facts by means of his 'reason.' Reason, therefore, is indispensable for the proper understanding of all facts, even in scientific psychology. Hence, the philosophic psychologist is justified in his endeavor to go beyond the limits of scientific psychology by using the powers of speculative or deductive reason for the solution of the deeper problems cast to the surface by scientific investigation.

Man is simply not satisfied with an analysis and classification of the proximate causes of mental facts. The deeper problems of psychology demand a solution, and man cannot help inquiring into the *ultimate causes* which lie behind and beyond the proximate causes. Among all the objects in the universe, the object of greatest interest to man is *man*. The scientific psychologist should refrain from investigating these ultimate realities in man's being, but the philosophic psychologist must use every means at his disposal in the attempt to arrive at a solution of the fundamental problems which lie in the core of man's innermost nature. He hopes to achieve success in his undertaking by bringing these problems before the piercing scrutiny of reason. Because reason plays such a dominant part in this research into the mysterious nature of man's mental life, philosophic psychology is frequently referred to as *rational psychology*. Strictly speaking, the terms 'empirical psychology' and 'rational psychology' are misnomers. Both types of psychology are based on experience and as such are 'empirical'; both use reason and as such are 'rational.' It would be better to drop the terms 'empirical' and 'rational' psychology and speak only of 'scientific' and 'philosophic' psychology.

The Method of Psychology

The *general method* employed by psychology in its investigation can be summarized in three words: *observe, assume,* and *prove*. It is the method employed by every science.

When a problem presents itself to the psychologist, he must first seek to marshal all the available facts pertinent to the subject matter under investigation. He submits them to careful 'observation,' either by means of personal experience or by means of experiments with various kinds of appropriate instruments. These facts are carefully analyzed, described, and classified. He then makes an 'assumption' or 'hypothesis' as to the possible causes which produce them and the laws which govern their operation; this assumption or hypothesis is provisional in character and subject to revision and modification.

If the hypothesis, when applied to more and more cases of a similar character, gives a good explanation of all the facts, it becomes a 'theory.' The theory becomes a 'law' when it is able to explain invariably all cases, even the apparent exceptions, because a complete explanation is 'proof' that the original assumption or hypothesis is the correct explanation of the phenomena in question.

The procedure just described is termed *induction* or *analysis,* and it is defined as the legitimate inference of universal laws from individual cases. It passes from the particular to the universal, from the complex to the simple, from the phenomena to the underlying general law, from the effect to the cause. The natural sciences are predominantly inductive and analytic in their method of research. The reverse method is *deduction* or *synthesis.* It is defined as the legitimate inference from the more general to the less general, from a law or principle to a particular instance falling under the law or principle. It proceeds from the universal to the particular, from the simple to the complex, from the logical whole to the logical part, from the general law to the individual cases, from the cause to the effect. The mathematical and philosophical sciences are predominantly deductive and synthetic in their method. No science, however, is exclusively inductive or deductive. Both methods must be used, depending on the circumstances. Psychology, in its empirical and experimental portions, uses the inductive method, while it uses the deductive method largely in its philosophical portions.

There is a *special method* employed by psychology, and it is twofold in character: subjective and objective.

The *subjective* method is that of *introspection.* Introspection is the method of studying mental phenomena by means of the internal observation of experience on the part of the individual person. Conscious mental states exist in the mind, and they can be observed and examined only by the mind turning its attention upon its own states. This immediate observation and examination of one's own internal mental states and activities is what is meant by 'introspection.' I alone am capable of knowing what sensations, emotions, ideas, and volitions are present in my mind, so far as actual observation is concerned. Even when the scientific psychologist makes use of instruments and other experimental devices, in the final analysis he must rely on introspection, because he must interpret the facts in the conscious mental acts of his own mind.

The *objective* method is the method employed to gain information about the mental states and processes of man through means other than introspection. More is needed for the building of a science than the information acquired from a single individual's mental experiences; this personal information must be supplemented by data obtained from outside sources.

Among these outside sources, a few are of special value to the psychologist. First of all, he can study the information of *other minds,* whether communicated to him in spoken or written words, and thereby compare their observations and experiences with those of his own mind obtained through introspection. The study of the various *languages* may contribute appreciable data, because language is the external expression of mental processes and ideas. *Animal psychology,* too, can be very helpful. Animals, as will be established later, are sensory beings pure and simple, while man is partly sensory and partly rational. The study of animal behavior should enable us to draw a sharper line of distinction between the sensory and rational activities and powers in man; the knowledge gained should assist us indirectly in acquiring a better knowledge of man himself. There are many things in *biology* and *physiology* which are useful in understanding the psychical activities in man, because sensory functions are vital processes depending on specific organs. Man has a body as well as a mind, and the two are closely united in everything man does. An extensive knowledge of the nervous system should be a considerable aid in acquiring a better knowledge of how man's mind can come into contact with the physical world. *Abnormal psychology,* since it is based on pathological conditions, shows by contrast what the normal conditions are. Oftentimes, the absence of a particular function, because of disease, enables us to distinguish clearly between one mental power and another. *Psychiatry,* especially, throws a strong light on many psychical processes. Information of a most valuable kind is obtained from the experimental science of *psycho-physics,* that branch of psychology which studies the relations between mental and physical processes by investigating the response to stimuli and the perception of physical magnitudes. Such experiments are conducted in various psychological laboratories.

No single method is perfect. The combination of various methods, so far as they can be applied, will enable the psychologist to arrive at a substantial body of facts which can be molded into a real and reliable science.

Psychology and Cognate Sciences

It is usual to distinguish between the 'material' and the 'formal' object of a science. The *material object* of a science is the general object with which it occupies itself in its investigation. The *formal object* of a science is that special phase or aspect of the general object which forms the subject matter peculiar to this particular science and which distinguishes it from all other sciences.

The 'material' object may be the same for a number of sciences. The bodies existing in the world are the material object of the sciences of astronomy, physics, chemistry, crystallography, etc.; each of these sciences, however, studies the same bodies from its own characteristic standpoint. Organisms, or living bodies, are the material object of biology, botany, zoology, and psychology; nevertheless, these sciences are distinct from one another, because each one views and treats this general object under a different aspect. The various sciences thus have much in common, but they also differ among themselves. It is necessary, therefore, to distinguish psychology from a number of kindred sciences.

Among the *natural* sciences which have much in common with psychology we find biology and physiology. There is, however, a difference. *Biology* treats of life in general, as found in all organisms; psychology treats mainly of the 'mental' life of organisms, particularly of man. *Physiology* studies the functions of life present in the organs, tissues, and cells of living beings, exclusive of mental functions; psychology studies the mental life of organisms, while physiological matters are brought into the discussion only incidentally.

Among the *philosophical* departments, logic, epistemology, cosmology, and ethics have a certain kinship with psychology. Due to their formal object, however, they are distinct sciences. *Logic* examines the intellectual activities of the human mind from the standpoint of correct thinking; psychology studies the entire field of human mental states and activities, including sensation, perception, emotion, intellection, and volition. *Epistemology* is concerned with the validity or truth-value of human knowledge; psychology, with the nature of the human mind and its various operations. *Cosmology* investigates the constitution of bodies in so far as they are natural physical bodies; psychology treats of the human body only in so far as it is an integral part of the nature of man. *Ethics* examines human actions as qualified by the attributes of right or wrong and thus restricts itself to voluntary actions; psychology examines human action in all its manifestations of mental life.

We thus see that the same material object is the general subject matter of a number of sciences, making them more or less related. From the standpoint of their formal object, however, they vary to a considerable degree.

The Whole Man

The confusion of opinions about the proper 'subject matter' of psychology makes it difficult to formulate an exact definition of psychology. Everything depends on the viewpoint of the individual psychologist or of the school of psychology to which he belongs. No matter what viewpoint anyone takes, there is bound to be objections against it from many sides.

There is also a difference of opinion as to the proper 'method' to be employed in psychological investigations. The school of *behaviorism* claims that introspection is not a legitimate method. It rejects or ignores 'mind' and 'consciousness' altogether and contends that psychology should restrict itself exclusively to the study of the external behavior of animals and men. This is an extreme view which is rapidly passing out of the picture of psychology. Most modern psychologists admit that the objective method of studying behavior can and does contribute valuable data, but they are convinced that introspection must always be the main method of psychological investigation.

Notwithstanding this confusion, the psychologists of all shades agree, both in theory and in practice, that the *chief purpose* of psychology is the better understanding of *man*. Historically, psychology had its origin in the study of man as a part of philosophy; only in relatively recent times has psychology divorced itself from the philosophical study of man in general and become a science in its own right. It was a misfortune that a sharp line of demarkation was drawn through man's being, separating body and mind in such a fashion that they were considered to be opposing realities. This division should never have been made.

Irrespective of all philosophical theories, man is a *single, unitary being*. He is a single, unitary, *living* being. And it is the distinctive feature of man that he comprises within his being the vegetative functions of plant life, the sensory functions of animal life, and the intellectual and volitional activities of rational life. Though we observe in man three distinct types of life, these three types are merged together into an *integral organism* which assimilates, grows, senses, feels, thinks, and wills. Man, as each of us knows from personal experience, is *one*.

Psychology, as a branch of philosophic science, should not cut man into segments and study one or the other segment exclusively. To treat man in this manner is to do violence to man as an integral organism. *The whole man* should be studied in all the phases of his life and being. Only in this way will it be possible to obtain a full and comprehensive knowledge of what man really is, and that should be the ultimate purpose of the psychological study of man.

Philosophy seeks to bring every kind of being within the scope of its investigation. Cosmology treats mainly of inorganic beings. *Organisms,* beings endowed with organic life, should be treated in a special department of philosophy, because inorganic and organic substances are the two natural divisions of bodies existing in the universe. The organisms are represented by the three great classes, plants, animals, and men. In as much, however, as man possesses the vegetative life of plants and the sensory life of animals, it is logical to include the peculiarities of their type of life in the treatment of man as the embodiment of all three types of life in a single organism. Man, especially in his mental life, will be the *chief object* of psychological investigation, but plant life and animal life should not be pushed aside entirely.

Hence, *the whole man,* both in his activities and in his fundamental nature, is here proposed as the *primary object* of study for the psychologist who is also a philosopher. As for the *method* of investigation, any and all methods are acceptable, provided they furnish us with data which throw light on man's complex being and enable us to grasp in some measure the workings of his inner constitution. The modern scientific psychologists will in all probability disagree with us. In as much, however, as these same psychologists cannot agree among themselves as to what should be considered the proper subject matter and method of psychology, we feel justified in taking the position here indicated.

If we now attempt a *definition* of psychology, we may define psychology as the *philosophic science of the life of the human organism.* It is a 'science,' i.e., a reasoned body of truths arranged into a system of knowledge. It is a 'philosophic science,' i.e., a science which, based on the established findings of empirical and experimental psychology, draws conclusions as to the ultimate principles, reasons, and causes which account for the proximate causes of phenomena. It is the philosophic science of 'the life of the human organism,' i.e., it studies the life of the whole man as an organism, especially in its sensory and rational features, so as to arrive at an understanding of the inner constitution and nature of man.

In using the terms 'life' and 'organism,' we accept them in the meaning given to them in the biological sciences. This meaning is, of course, only provisional for the present. Everybody admits the fact that man, like the plant and animal, is an 'organism' and that he possesses 'life.' The precise philosophical meaning of these terms will become clearer in the course of our study.

The Value of Psychology

Without question, man is the noblest and most intelligent being on earth and, so far as we are able to judge, in the universe. Since every kind of knowledge is of value in some form or other, the knowledge of man should be the most valuable of all. It should be far more valuable than the knowledge of nonliving beings and of plants and animals. Hence, psychology is more important than chemistry, physics, mathematics, astronomy, geology, biology, botany, and zoology, and other natural sciences. We are speaking here, of course, of the knowledge about created things in the visible universe.

Psychology studies the *knowledge process* step by step in its development, from the reaction of the sense organs to the external stimuli, in its passage through the internal senses, and in its transition over into the intellect, until it reaches its completion in the formation of ideas, judgments, and acts of reasoning. The various *mental powers* active in the acquisition of sensory and intellectual knowledge will be studied in detail. A knowledge of these powers will be of great value for all the *sciences,* because they are the result of the knowledge process of man's mind. Similarly, such an acquaintance with the knowledge process and the powers of the human mind is essential to the entire system of *education,* for without it proper methods of education cannot be devised.

The psychological study of the *will* and of voluntary action is of paramount value for *law, ethics,* and *sociology.* Our treatment of individual responsibility, of domestic and social relations, and of international rights and duties will have to undergo essential modifications, if we must come to the decision that the human will is not truly free.

From a *personal* standpoint, the question of the existence, spirituality, and immortality of the *individual soul* is of vital interest to everyone, depending on whether the question must be answered in the affirmative or negative, because the answer will influence the direction of each one's entire life.

The first part of the book follows the general lines of empirical and experimental research. The second part seeks to determine the ultimate nature of man as an organism.

Summary of Chapter I

Psychology is a *science,* with its own proper subject matter and method of investigation.

1. *Subject Matter of Psychology.* Etymologically, psychology means 'the science of the soul.' Many modern psychologists look upon psychology as 'the science of the mind'; others, as 'the science of consciousness.'

Among philosophers, some consider psychology to be 'the philosophy of organic life,' including within its subject matter the life of plants, animals, and men. Others restrict the subject matter to the nature of man in his vegetative, sensory, and rational life. Some restrict it entirely to man's sensory and rational life.

2. *Psychology as Science and Philosophy.* As a science, in the modern sense of 'scientific psychology,' it analyzes mental phenomena, classifies them, and determines their *proximate causes.* 'Philosophical psychology' seeks to penetrate beyond the surface of phenomena to the *ultimate reasons, principles, and causes,* so as to uncover the nature and essence which gives rise to such phenomena.

Scientific psychology is also termed 'empirical' and 'experimental,' while philosophic psychology is often called 'rational.'

3. *The Method of Psychology.* The *general* method employed is induction, or analysis, and deduction, or synthesis. Both must be used, but scientific psychology is predominantly inductive and analytic, while philosophical psychology is largely deductive and synthetic.

The *special method* is twofold, subjective and objective. The *subjective* method of *introspection* studies mental phenomena by means of the internal observation of experience on the part of the individual person. The *objective* method seeks information about the mental states of man through means other than introspection. Such pertinent information is supplied by other minds, languages, animal psychology, biology, physiology, abnormal psychology, psychiatry, and psycho-physics.

4. *Psychology and Cognate Sciences.* We must distinguish between the 'material' and the 'formal' object of a science. The *material* object is the general object with which it occupies itself; the *formal* object is that special phase or aspect of the general object which forms the subject matter peculiar to this science and which distinguishes it from all other sciences. Since the material object may be common to a number of sciences, psychology is related to the natural sciences of biology and physiology and to the philosophical sciences of logic, epistemology, cosmology, and ethics. It differs from them, however, in its formal object.

5. *The Whole Man.* The *chief purpose* of psychology is the better understanding of *man.* Man is an *integral organism,* comprising within his being vegetative, sensory, and rational life. Hence, *the whole man* is here proposed as the primary object of study. We may therefore *define* psychology as *the philosophic science of the life of the human organism.*

6. *The Value of Psychology.* The study of the knowledge process and of man's mental powers is of value for all sciences and for the entire system of education. The study of the will

is of paramount value for law, ethics, and sociology. The question of the existence, spirituality, and immortality of the individual soul is of vital interest to everyone.

Readings

Maher, Michael, *Psychology,* Ch. I, II. — Brennan, Robert E., *General Psychology,* pp. 3–28. — Woodworth, Robert S., *Experimental Psychology,* Ch. I.

CHAPTER II

MAN: AN ORGANISM

MAN is an organism. Literally, an 'organism' is a being which consists of, or possesses, organs, and by an 'organ' we understand a part or structure adapted for the performance of some specific function or functions. Biologically, an *organism* is an individual constituted to carry on the activities of life by means of parts or organs more or less separate in function but mutually dependent. It is in this biological sense that man is an 'organism.'

Man is, therefore, a living bodily being, just as a plant or an animal is said to be a living bodily being. Men, animals, and plants form the three great kingdoms of living beings in our universe, so far as our knowledge goes, and, since they possess life, they are radically distinguished from inanimate, or nonliving, beings, such as chemical elements and chemical compounds.

All these types of being have much in common. Chemical functions are found in plants, animals, and men; the functions of plants are found in animals and men; and the functions of animals are found in men. It will be advisable, therefore, to analyze and compare these various types of being, in a factual manner, and thereby obtain at least a summary knowledge of man as an organism.

Living and Nonliving Matter

It is not our purpose here to introduce a philosophical discussion on the difference between living and nonliving matter. The difference between these two types of being is recognized by all to be a fact beyond dispute. Without going into elaborate details, the *main characteristics of living matter* are as follows:

First, *organization*. Living matter is organized. Living beings possess organs or structural parts distinct from one another, each of which has a specific function to perform. Organization is found in unicellular as well as in multicellular plants and animals. An amoeba, for example, possesses diverse structures within its single cell-body, and these various structures (organs, organelles) perform diverse functions.

Second, *irritability*. Living matter responds to changes in the environment (such changes are called 'stimuli') by change in shape, production or cessation of movement, or other activities of their organs or parts. Living matter does not receive the influences of surrounding objects and energies in a passive manner, but reacts to them in a specific way, each plant and animal reacting differently to the same stimulus.

Third, *metabolism*. In biology and physiology 'metabolism' is the technical term which designates the processes in plant and animal cells involved in the construction and destruction of living tissue during the course of the activities of life; it consists of the chemical changes occurring in living cells, by which the energy is furnished for carrying on vital activities and new material is assimilated for the maintenance and repair of the individual plant or animal. The essential processes of life are produced in and by the 'protoplasm.' Protoplasm is the physical basis of life. It is the essential substance constituting the body and nucleus of the cells of plants and animals. Ordinarily, protoplasm is a practically colorless, semifluid substance, filling the body of the cell and containing a large amount of water in which fine granules are suspended. Its physical structure is not well known, though it is now recognized by all biologists to be heterogeneous in character and is considered to be different in different types of cells and in different types of organisms. Chemically, it is an extremely complex compound, the composition of which is still obscure.

Metabolism has a twofold aspect. The one is constructive, and is termed 'assimilation' or 'anabolism'; the other is destructive, and is called 'disassimilation' or 'katabolism.' *Anabolism* is a synthesis, a building up of the living protoplasm through the absorption of nutritive materials and the changing of these materials into the living substance of the cell; the simple elements are thereby united into complex organic compounds, and in this chemical process energy is stored for future use. *Katabolism* is a destruction, a breaking down of the protoplasmic material; the protoplasm is decomposed and oxidized, the energy necessary for the activities of life is thereby liberated, and the waste is excreted. In this double process, therefore, dead matter is first changed into living substance, and then living substance is changed back again into dead matter.

Fourth, *growth* and *reproduction*. By 'growth' we understand the progressive development of a cell, organ, or organism from its earliest stages to full maturity. No cell, or organ, or organism comes into existence complete and fully matured in size and structure. It develops gradually through the intussusception of nutritive material. By 'reproduction' we understand the process by means of which cells produce new cells and plants and animals produce new plants and animals of the same kind. Even in the case of new plants and new animals, however, they originate from single cells, so that all reproduction is ultimately a matter of cell reproduction. Ordinary cell reproduction in multicellular plants and animals (for example, in a tree or a cat) is simply 'growth' of the individual. In unicellular plants and animals (for example, in a gloeocapsa or an amoeba) this cell reproduction always results in the generation of a new individual. In the higher forms of plants and animals the reproduction of new individuals requires specialized cells whose sole function is the generation of offspring. All reproduction, whether of cells in ordinary growth or of individuals through generation, is thus the result of some form of cell division. In order to grasp the significance of these facts, it is necessary to understand the nature of the cell and of cell division.

Notwithstanding their many differences, all cells have certain features in common, which makes them fundamentally alike. It is thus possible to give a diagrammatic representation of a *generalized cell.*

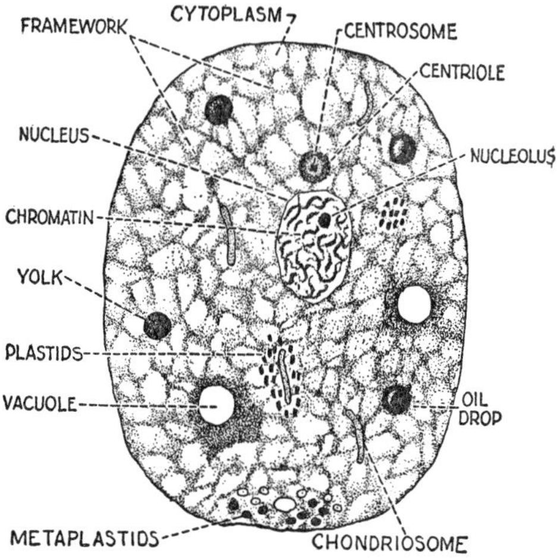

Fig. 1. Generalized Cell.

The two main parts are the nucleus and the cytoplasm. The *cytoplasm* is the protoplasmic body of the cell, as distinguished from the nucleus. — The *nucleus* with its contents is the essential organ of the activities of metabolism, growth, and reproduction of the cell; in most cases, the nucleus is a well-defined body, but in some types of cells its contents are distributed throughout the cytoplasm. — The *nucleolus* is a small nucleus usually found within the body of the regular nucleus. — *Chromatin* is a deeply staining nuclear material which is the physical basis of heredity; it appears in the nucleus as a network of irregular arrangement. — The *framework* is a sort of semisolid protoplasmic network distributed throughout the cytoplasm of the cell. — *Vacuoles* are cavities or vesicles containing a watery fluid. — *Plastids* are small bodies of specialized protoplasm, active in metabolic changes. — *Metaplastids* are lifeless undigested particles or waste material. — A *chondriosome* is a semifluid body. — *Oil drops* and *yolk globules* are nutritive material. — The *centriole* is a specialized mass of protoplasm which develops into an aster or starlike figure in cell division. — The *centrosome* is a minute protoplasmic body lying in the centriole.

Not all cells contain all the parts shown in the illustration. Essential, however, to every cell is the *nucleus;* it is the bearer of vital activity, and without it the cell would die. Among the structural elements of the nucleus, the 'chromatin' material plays an important part in the life cycle of the cell. When a cell is about to divide, whether for the purpose of growth or of generation, this chromatin material assembles itself into a strip or thread and then breaks up into separate particles called 'chromosomes.' These chromosomes contain the 'genes' which are the main factors in heredity. During cell division, each chromosome splits evenly into two portions, temporarily doubling the number of chromosomes; one half remains with the parent cell, the other half goes to the daughter cell. Since the total number of chromosomes is constant and specific for each type of plant or animal (for example, the drosophila, or fruit fly, has eight chromosomes in each cell), every cell in the body has the same number of chromosomes. The entire process of cell division is termed *mitosis* ('the formation and movement of threads') or *karyokinesis* ('movement of the nucleus'). (See Fig. 2.)

In the *generation* of new individuals, a portion of the parent's body is separated or set aside, and this portion then develops into the offspring. When the offspring originates from a single parent, it is an 'asexual' reproduction; examples are cleavage ('fission') and budding ('gemmation'). Most multicellular plants and animals, however, especially those of a higher type, generate their offspring by means of 'sexual' reproduction, in which the new individual originates from the union of the female egg cell and the male sperm cell; these sex or germ cells are called 'gametes.' If these eggs and sperms retained their full number of chromosomes and passed them on to their offspring, the latter would have a double number of chromosomes in each body cell. Thus, the first drosophila, or fruit fly, would transmit 16 chromosomes to its offspring; the second generation would receive 32; the next, 64; and so forth. In the long run this would be disastrous to the individuals and the species. As a matter of fact, of course, this

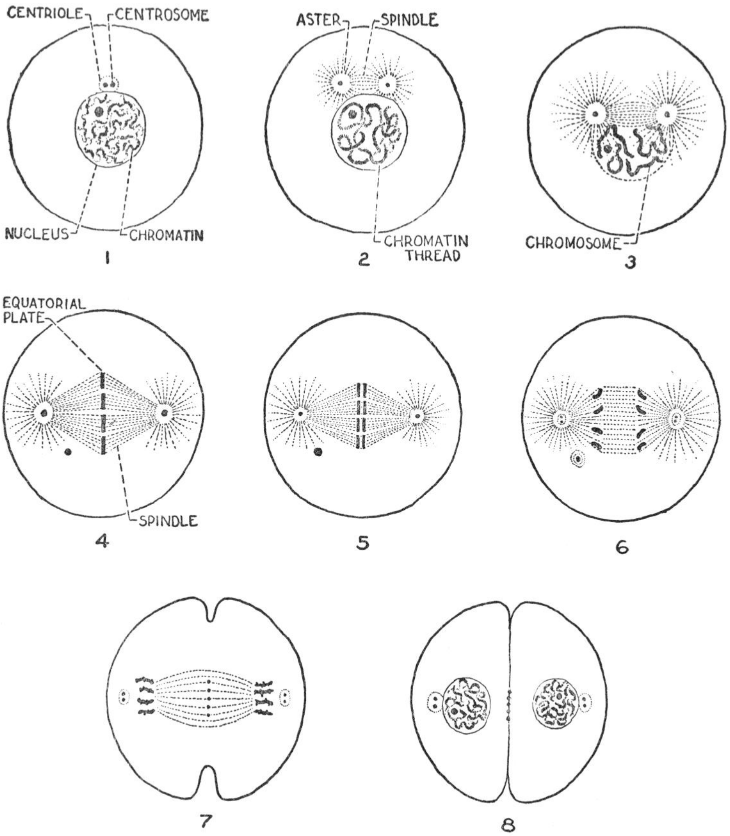

Fig. 2. Mitosis, or Cell Division.

1. The cell in its resting stage. — 2. The beginning of mitosis. The two centrosomes separate and move apart, each enclosed in an aster or starlike figure. A spindle of protoplasmic filaments is formed between the two asters. The chromatin arranges itself into a thread. — 3. The chromatin thread breaks up into loops, the chromosomes. — 4. The chromosomes are caught up by the spindle and arranged circularly in the equatorial plate. — 5. The chromosomes divide longitudinally, doubling their number. — 6. One half of the chromosomes are drawn toward one aster, the second half toward the other aster. — 7. The cell body begins to divide. — 8. The chromosomes dissolve into chromatin. The cell body has undergone a complete division, so that the original cell now consists of two daughter cells. — For the sake of simplification, the diagram represents but four chromosomes.

multiplication of chromosomes does not occur. It is avoided by a particular kind of cell division in the gametes, called 'maturation division.' In maturation division one half of the

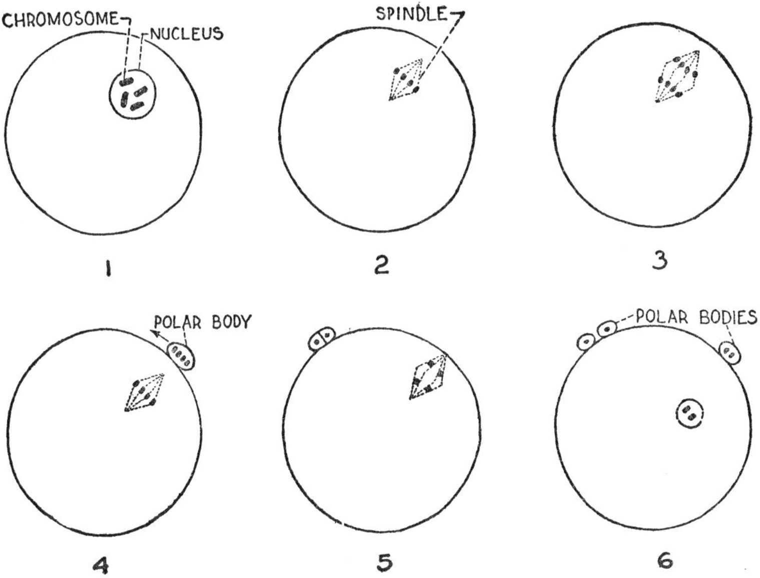

Fig. 3. Maturation Division of Gamete or Germ Cell.

1. The germ nucleus moves toward the periphery of the cell. — 2. The chromosomes arrange themselves into a spindle. — 3. The chromosomes divide. — 4. One half (4) of the chromosomes pass out through the cell wall and form the first polar body. — 5. A new spindle is formed. The remaining chromosomes arrange themselves in pairs. — 6. One pair of chromosomes passes out and forms the second polar body. Only two chromosomes (one half of the original number) are left in the mature gamete. — For the sake of simplification, the diagram represents but four chromosomes.

number of chromosomes of the germ cell pass out of the body of the cell and form a so-called 'polar body.' In this manner the number of the chromosomes of both the egg cell and the sperm cell of the parents is halved; and when these two cells unite to constitute the fertilized ovum, the original number of chromosomes is restored, so that the first cell of the offspring contains the same number as the cells of the

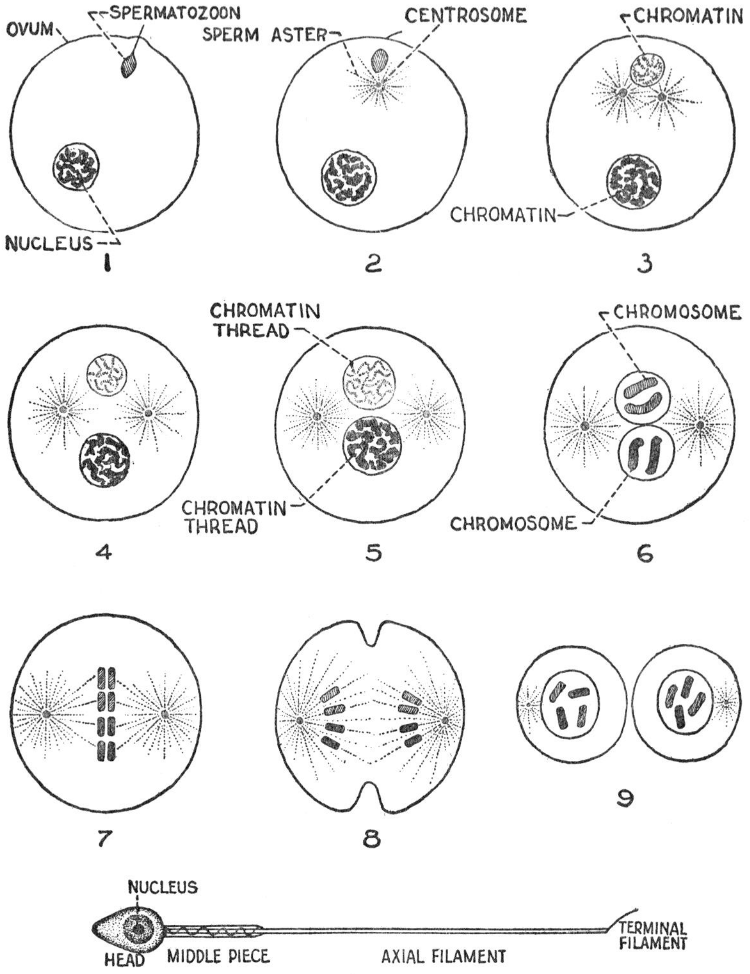

Fig. 4. Fertilization.

1. The spermatozoon (sperm, male gamete) enters ovum (female germ cell, female gamete). — 2. The centrosome of the spermatozoon becomes visible. An aster is formed. The head of the sperm cell swells, and the nucleus of the ovum grows larger. — 3. The chromatin framework of the sperm nucleus becomes visible. The centrosome doubles. — 4. The centrosomes move apart, each to opposite sides of the cell. The

parent bodies. From this point on, the first cell of the offspring divides and multiplies according to the process of ordinary mitosis. (See Figs. 3 and 4.)

Fifth, *individuality*. Every organic being consists of heterogeneous parts — elements, chemical compounds, cells, tissues, organelles, and organs. Each part has its own peculiar function. All parts and all functions, however, are not there for their own sake, but for the sake of the organism as a whole; they are mutually dependent and conspire toward the welfare of the individual plant and animal as a totality, a unit. It is the individual which counts, not so much the parts. All functions are, strictly speaking, functions of the individual, and the parts and organs are merely the means through which the individual carries out its varied activities. The individual plant and animal is, in all truth, much more than the sum of the parts which make up its body. This distinctive and constant individuality is the reason why scientists are able to make such a complete classification of plants and animals into varieties, species, genera, etc.

These are the main characteristics of living substance in general. Nothing similar to organization, irritability, metabolism, growth, reproduction, and individuality is found among the combinations of elements and compounds in inorganic nature.

---

chromatin material of the sperm nucleus has completed its framework stage. — 5. The nuclei of the spermatozoon and of the ovum are now equal in size and condition. — 6. The chromosomes are formed in the two nuclei, alike in number. (The chromosomes of the spermatozoon nucleus are shaded, while those of the ovum are in solid black.) — 7. The spindle is complete, and the chromosomes divide longitudinally and equally. — 8. Four chromosomes (two paternal and two maternal) move toward the left aster, and four to the right aster. The cell body begins to divide. — 9. The division is complete. Two cells are formed, each containing four chromosomes (two paternal and two maternal), the original number found in each of the ordinary body cells (somatic cells). Multiplication of cells now occurs through regular mitosis. — For the sake of simplification, the diagram represents but four chromosomes.

The Cell and the Crystal

Some have argued that the cell is but a type of crystal, or, at any rate, that the crystal is so similar to the cell that there is no fundamental difference between them. A resemblance exists, but it is altogether superficial. A comparison between the crystal and a unicellular plant, which is the lowest form of life, should prove fruitful in establishing the *great difference* between living and nonliving matter.

First of all, the *composition* of crystals is very different from that of cells. The material of crystals consists either of pure elements (for example, carbon or sulphur) or of chemical compounds which are found everywhere in nature (for example, sodium chloride or potassium sulphate); and the whole crystal is composed entirely of such elements and compounds. Not so the cell. There is a considerable diversity of material in the cells; organic compounds of various types are present; and this material is not distributed uniformly throughout the body of the cell, but is different in different parts.

Then, there is a difference of *structure*. A crystal is formed by the symmetrical juxtaposition of the atoms and molecules along geometrical lines and sharp angles; it is a latticework, each part of which is a constant repetition of every other part; and it is characterized by extreme rigidity. The cell, however, possesses a body made up of distinct parts, heterogeneous in structure, none of which is a mechanical repetition of another; its nucleus manifests great complexity of structural detail; the protoplasm shows a manifold differentiation; the entire cell material is relatively soft, pliable, and rounded in contour.

Again, the *growth* of a cell is radically diverse from that of a crystal. A crystal grows through the mere superposition of layer upon layer of identical material upon the outside surface, leaving the interior of the crystal untouched and unchanged. The cell, on the other hand, grows by means of intussusception and assimilation of foreign material, and this material is broken down and remade into organic compounds, the like of which is found nowhere in nature except in the organism.

Furthermore, there is a difference of *activity*. The only activity which occurs in a crystal is the atomic and molecular activity which builds the crystal and retains its geometrical shape; the crystal as a whole has no activity. The cell, however, is definitely active throughout the period of its existence; metabolic changes take place at all times. The cell reproduces itself, giving rise to new cells and to new individuals, something a crystal never does. The cell produces many by-products, such as alkaloids, essential oils, and many other organic substances, while the crystal never produces anything.

Finally, the *duration in existence* is totally different for the crystal and the cell. The crystal is a rigid and permanent thing and, if left to itself, will remain indefinitely in existence as a crystal; some crystals are, without doubt, thousands and probably millions of years old. A crystal can be dissolved and recrystallized, and this reversible process can be repeated times without number. The cell, as a cell, has a definite span of existence; after a certain length of time, it ceases to exist of its own accord and decomposes.

A superficial comparison might show a resemblance between a crystal and a cell, but a closer scrutiny reveals the fact that they are totally different: the crystal is simply dead matter, while the cell is a living being.

Man: A Vegetant Organism

Plant life is the lowest form of life known on the globe. Negatively, a plant is a living being devoid of cognition; no organs, which might serve for perception, are discernible, and no functions manifest real knowledge of any kind. Positively, a plant is an organism which possesses the functions of *nutrition, growth,* and *propagation.* Although the plant has many diversified functions, they are subservient to these three, which are characteristic of a plant as such. Since nutrition, growth, and propagation are vegetative activities, a plant is a vegetant organism pure and simple.

Man, too, is a *vegetant organism,* because man, like a plant, feeds himself, grows, and propagates.

The *elements* used in the process of human nutrition, in the main, are: oxygen (O), hydrogen (H), carbon (C), nitrogen (N), iron (Fe), calcium (Ca), sulphur (S), phosphorus (P), magnesium (Mg), sodium (Na), chlorine (Cl), manganese (Mn), copper (Cu), and potassium (K); some others are also found occasionally. These elements and their compounds serve a double purpose in the organism: the production of energy and the maintenance of the various tissues and organs throughout the body. These elements, when used as food by man, come in the form of *organic compounds* and are supplied by plants and animals. The three main groups of food substances are the carbohydrates, the proteins, and the fats. Certain mineral substances, too, are necessary, and also vitamins and hormones.

Before these organic substances can be used for energy or maintenance, they must be broken down and transformed through chemical change. This transformation is carried out in the *gastro-intestinal tract* through the agency of various secretions, elaborated by the salivary glands and the glands of the stomach, of the liver, of the pancreas, and of the intestinal walls. The enzymes, present in these secretions, perform an important function in this connection. They are organic catalysts. A catalyst is a substance which by its mere presence among other substances changes the rate of chemical reactions, without itself undergoing a change in the process. Some organic compounds are manufactured by chemists in the laboratory, but such reactions are obtained only by using high temperatures and pressures; in the organisms the enzymes bring about such reactions with utmost ease and speed. The chemist, for example, cannot change glucose to galactose, but the body does this readily with the help of enzymes. The action of enzymes is specific for certain types of substance; they may either decompose or synthesize compounds.

After the transformation of the food is complete, it is ready to be assimilated. *Resorption* occurs primarily in the small intestine. The liquified food particles, now broken down into very small molecules, pass through the intestinal wall. Most of this material is carried by the portal vein to the liver and from there by means of the hepatic veins to the inferior *vena cava,* near the right auricle of the heart, where it enters the blood stream; the rest is carried by the lymph channels through the thoracic duct to the subclavian vein, where it also enters the blood stream. In this manner the food particles become a part of the blood, flow to the heart, and are pumped to all tissues of the body. Each cell, tissue, and organ then assimilates whatever it needs for its own particular purpose.

Until an organism reaches the full stature of its maturity, it is in a condition of *growth.* Man, too, as a vegetant organism, is subject to growth. He begins life as a single cell, the fertilized ovum, which normally attaches itself to the wall of the uterus of the mother, and then receives nourishment from the maternal blood. During the period of gestation, practically all the members and organs of the child are completely formed. Man's body is thus 'fearfully and wonderfully made,' before it sees the light of day in birth. The body continues to grow and develop until the early twenties. During all this time the ordinary processes of life continue uninterruptedly: energy is stored, used, and restored in an endless cycle; cells and tissues are built, torn down, and rebuilt in unceasing activity; and all the while the growth of the body goes forward to full maturity. From that point on maintenance of bodily structure is the chief function of metabolism.

Reproduction in man, as in all living beings, is a marvel of activity and structural design. The conception of the child occurs when the gametes or germ cells, namely the female ovum and the male sperm, fuse so as to bring about a union of the chromosomes of the two gametes. The specific number of chromosomes in the somatic, or body, cells of man is 48. In order that the child, beginning life with the fecundated ovum, have this same number of chromosomes in each cell of its body, it is obviously necessary that the number of chromosomes in the parent germ-cells be reduced to one half, or 24. This is accomplished in each by means of a maturation division.

Maturation division takes place in both gametes, but not in the same manner. The female germ cell possesses 46 ordinary chromosomes and a special pair called 'X' chromosomes; the male germ cell contains, besides the 46 ordinary chromosomes, a pair consisting of one 'X' chromosome and a much smaller one designated the 'Y' chromosome. In the development of the *male* gamete, maturation division proceeds in the following manner. Forty-six chromosomes form 23 pairs of chromosomes, but the 'X' and 'Y' chromosomes do not form a real pair. The 23 pairs divide vertically (not longitudinally, as in ordinary cell-division); 'X' and 'Y' remained unchanged. The male gamete now divides into two cells, one cell having 23 chromosomes and the 'X' chromosome and the other 23 chromosomes and the 'Y' chromosome. These two cells again divide, but this time the chromosomes divide longitudinally without pairing. We now have four cells, and the result of this division is: two cells each possessing 23 ordinary chromosomes and an 'X' chromosome, and two other cells possessing 23 ordinary chromosomes and a diminutive 'Y' chromosome. Of these four sperm cells one develops and grows to full size to become the spermatozoon, or mature male fecundating cell, while the other three degenerate and disappear. The *female* ovum also undergoes a maturation division, in order to reduce the 48 chromosomes to 24; however, no further division takes place, and the result will always be that the mature ovum contains 23 ordinary chromosomes and one 'X' chromosome.

Since every female has an 'XX' pair of chromosomes in its cells and every male an 'XY' pair of chromosomes in its cells, biologists have constructed a theory to determine the sex of the child. The surviving spermatozoon may contain either an 'X' or 'Y' chromosome. Depending on the nature of this chromosome, the child will be either female or male: if it is an 'X' sperm, it will be a daughter; if a 'Y,' a son.

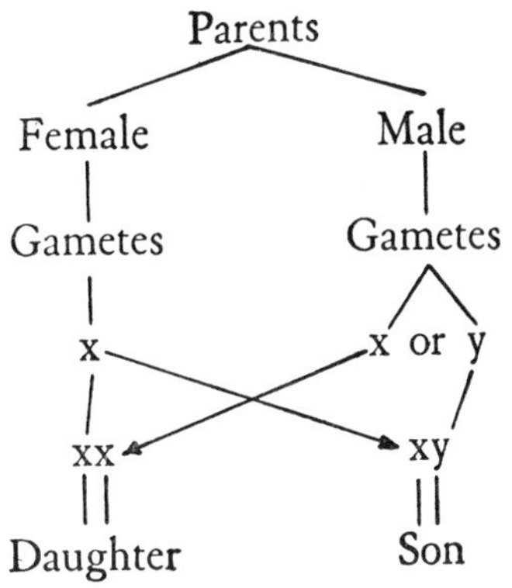

According to this theory, it will be seen, the sex of the child is already determined at conception; later developments merely bring out the characteristics of the respective sexes.

These are, in basic outline, the chief features of life in man as a vegetant organism. In reality, of course, the vegetative activities taking place in man's body are immensely varied and complex.[1]

Man: A Sentient Organism

An animal is radically different from a plant, both anatomically and functionally. A plant is restricted in its functions to the vegetative activities of nutrition, growth, and reproduction. The animal body exercises these activities, modified to suit its type, but over and above these vegetative activities it possesses a *nervous system* of some sort with an activity peculiarly its own. Man is an *animal organism* and as such has a nervous system and performs nervous functions.

The *basic unit* of the nervous system is the neuron, or nerve cell. The neuron has a number of parts. The 'cell body' consists of nerve protoplasm and takes care of the nutrition of the entire neuron. The 'nucleus,' like the nucleus of every other kind of cell, has its location in the cell body and is the functional center of all nerve activity in the neuron; it also is the

[1] For a detailed description of these activities, the student should read some standard book on human physiology.

bearer of the specific characteristics of the neuron. The 'axon' is a prolongation of the body of the nerve cell, typically single and long, terminating in short branches relatively far from the cell body; the axon, together with its coverings, forms the nerve fiber, and the axon is the axis cylinder of such a nerve fiber. The 'dendrites' are protoplasmic structural processes of the neuron; they branch repeatedly and taper rapidly, terminating near the cell body. As a rule, dendrites conduct nerve impulses toward the cell body, while axons conduct nerve impulses away from the cell body. The 'end brushes' are the many minute fibrils which extend from the axons. The 'neurilemma' is the outer sheath enclosing a nerve fiber. Some axons are enveloped in a sheath of myelin, or fatty tissue, and this is called the 'medullary sheath' or 'myelin sheath.'

Every nerve cell, or neuron, possesses the properties of *excitability* and *conductivity*. The nerve tissue is 'excitable' or 'irritable,' that is to say, it has the property to react to a stimulus; and a stimulus is the influence of free energy (chemical, thermal, radiant, mechanical) applied to irritable tissue. In response to a stimulus, an impulse is transmitted along the nerve fiber; the property of a nerve fiber to transmit such an impulse is termed 'conductivity.' This impulse may travel from the periphery inward to the central portion of the neuron; then we speak of a 'receptor neuron,' and such fibers are 'sensory' or 'afferent' fibers. Or, the impulse may travel from the central portion of the neuron to the periphery; this is an 'effector neuron,' and fibers of this type are 'motor' or 'efferent' fibers. Since the nerve impulse can travel in only one direction, depending on whether a nerve fiber is of the

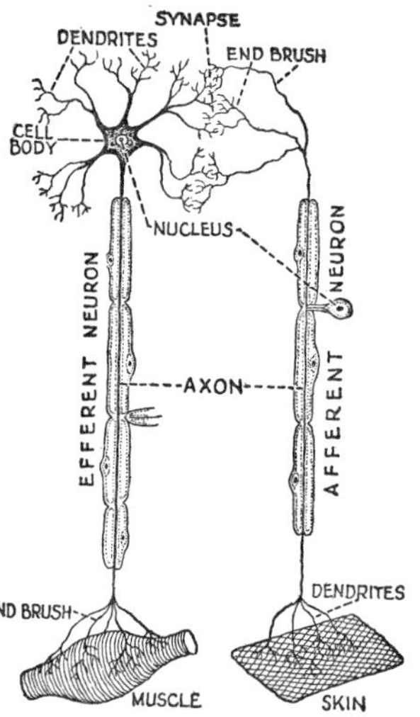

Fig. 5. Synapse of Afferent (Sensory) Neuron and Efferent (Motor) Neuron.

afferent or efferent type, nerves are said to possess 'polarity.' The endings of afferent nerves, specially adapted to the reception of peripheral stimuli, are called 'receptors'; if these endings terminate in definite organic structures, such as the eye or ear, they are termed 'receptor' or 'sense organs.' The endings of efferent nerves terminate in glands or muscular tissue, effecting a stimulation there, and such nerve endings are styled 'effector organs.'

Every neuron is a distinct anatomical unit; hence, nerve cells, in relation to each other, are not continuous, but contiguous. Contact with other neurons is made by junctions or *synapses,* and the stimulation of one neuron by another is through the synapse from end brush to dendrites. The synapse is therefore defined as the place at which a nervous impulse passes from the axon of one neuron to the dendrites of another. Whether or not an impulse shall pass from one neuron to another depends on the momentary state of the synapse. It is assumed that the resistance to the conductivity of the nerve impulse is greater in the synapse than in the neuron, and this resistance varies with conditions. Since the axons act as a stimulating apparatus and the dendrites as a receiving apparatus, the nerve impulse can travel only in one direction, namely, from axon to dendrite; this is the so-called *Law of Forward Conduction.* Whenever a neuron is stimulated, it either does not respond at all, or it responds with the maximum output of which it is capable, no matter what the strength of the stimulus; this is the *All-or-None Law* of nerve activity.

The rate of speed with which the impulse travels through a nerve is about 100 meters per second. The nature of the *nerve impulse* is not definitely known. All nerve action, however, is accompanied by *electro-chemical* phenomena. For this reason many biologists consider the nerve impulse to be entirely and solely electro-chemical in nature, in the sense that chemical changes in the tissues produce electrical pulsations of varying frequency and regularity in the nerve fiber. It must be noted, however, that the rate of speed of the nerve impulse, being far below the speed of electricity, militates against such a view. Whatever the nature of the impulse itself, electrical phenomena are always present. Attaching the two electrodes of a galvanometer to a nerve fiber and stimulating the nerve end, the needle of the instrument swings first to one side and then to the other; this fact indicates that an electrical current has passed. At the same time it is noticed that the active part of the nerve tissue is electro-negative, as compared with the part which is inactive. The frequency of these pulsations differs with the intensity of the stimulation, but all have the same magnitude in a given fiber. These pulsations are called 'action currents' or 'action potentials' of the nerve.

After a nerve has been stimulated, a certain interval of time must elapse before another reaction can set in, just as if the nerve were a battery that had been discharged and must recuperate by recharging. During the period of recuperation the nerve resists stimulation, and this period is styled the 'refractory phase.' When this refractory phase is passed, there follows a brief period, called the 'phase of hyperexcitability,' in which the nerve reacts to a stimulus of minor strength. From a *chemical* standpoint, nerves in action consume oxygen, give off carbon dioxide, and produce heat. Nerves, therefore, become fatigued through activity and demand rest periods after prolonged stimulation.

While it is true that each neuron, or nerve cell, is a physiological unit, independent of the other neurons, it is also true that these neurons do not stand and operate in isolation. By means of synaptic junction points the nerve impulses travel over a multitude of paths from fiber to fiber. In this manner the nerves together form a complete and integral *nerve system.* Spread throughout the whole extent of the body, fibers form nerves, nerves combine into trunklines, trunklines unite into minor systems, and minor systems merge into one grand system which services the entire sentient organism. In man there are two main systems of nerves: the *cerebrospinal system* and the *autonomic system.* Since the student should have at least a rudimentary knowledge of these systems, a summary of their structures and functions will be given in the next chapter.

Nerve action culminates in *sense knowledge.* This kind of cognition is a property of animal life. The animal organism possesses certain structures which mediate a knowledge of the conditions within the animal body itself and of conditions and things external to the body. Such structures are termed sense organs or 'receptors.' Various *types of sense knowledge* occur in man.

Man, by means of the *tactual* or *somesthetic* sense, experiences pressure, temperature, pain, hunger, thirst, nausea, bodily equilibrium, bodily movements, and combinations of these states. The knowledge acquired thereby enables him to safeguard the health and integrity of his body. Since the messages are conveyed by the nerve fibers connected with end-organs located in the skin, in the viscera, and in the muscles, joints, and tendons, man obtains a fairly accurate mental picture of the relative position and condition of his members. The sense of *taste* acquaints him with the savors of various objects, and the sense of *smell* with their odorous qualities. While a certain amount of pleasure is derived from taste and smell, fundamentally these senses are protective in character; they enable man to recognize and distinguish things which are useful or harmful for his well-being. Through the sense of *hearing* man perceives sounds emanating from objects in the outside world. Distant objects hereby come within the range of man's cognitive powers. Some sounds have a purely natural significance, such as the voice of wind and water, the calls of birds and animals; others receive a meaningful significance through man's own contriving, like the music of an orchestra, a song, or human speech. Perhaps the most distinctively external cognitive sense of man is that of *sight.* Practically the whole world becomes a picture book to man's mind through his eyes. He sees the colored panorama of the earth by means of his unaided sight, while with the aid of microscope and telescope he penetrates into the mysteries of the infinitesimally small and of the immeasurably vast.

Besides these so-called 'external' senses, man has *internal senses*. His *central* or *synthetic* sense combines the data of the various external senses into a composite perception. Not only does he experience the activity of the separate senses, but he can localize them in his body. He perceives the yellowish color and spherical shape of a certain object with his eyes, feels its soft and rough texture with his hands, tastes its sweet flavor with his palate, and smells its fragrant odor with his nostrils; his central sense unites these distinct and mutually independent data into a harmonious sensory whole and calls this thing of diversified qualities an 'orange.' Even when the objects which stimulate his senses are absent, he can make them present again in an image within his mind, reproducing in an imaginal way their many qualities by means of his *imagination*. Past events are recalled and recognized as past, so that their exact position in time and place is located and dated; recognition is the work of his *sensory memory*. Finally, man experiences certain unlearned tendencies or drives or dispositions toward or away from certain specific objects or activities in given situations; these drives are the *instincts,* and they are directed mainly toward the preservation of the individual and of the race.

Appetition is the second main activity of man's sensory life as an animal organism. It follows sensory knowledge. Man does not only 'know' objects in a sensory way; he also desires them and strives for them, fears them and flees from them, loves them and hates them. Emotional states, such as joy, sadness, hope, despair, courage, and anger, are involved in appetition; also feelings, as pleasure and displeasure.

There is a very important point to be noted in this connection. Man's body consists ultimately of ordinary chemical elements and compounds. But his body is not just a mass of lifeless, inert chemicals, because these elements and compounds are transformed into living, organized materials which thereby become an integral part of the body in its vegetative functions of nutrition, growth, and reproduction. Nor do the vegetative functions run an independent course in man's body, as if man as a vegetative being and as a sensory being performed vegetative and sensory functions separately along parallel lines. On the contrary, the vegetative organs not only carry out their proper functions of nutrition, growth, and reproduction like a plant, but also build, feed, repair, and reproduce nerves, nerve tissues, and organs of the body as a sentient organism. On their part, the nerves, nerve tissues, and organs stimulate and control the vegetative organs in their respective functions for the general welfare of the body as a unified whole. And the same chemical elements that are utilized in the vegetative organs and functions are also utilized in the sensory organs and functions. Man is, therefore, *one being with an integration* of materials, structures, and functions, with activities of a chemical, vegetative, and sensory character, all welded into a *vital unit organism.*

Man: A Rational Organism

Man is a *rational organism.* Man is 'rational,' because he possesses reason. Rationality, in man, implies *cognitive* and *appetitive* powers.

Intellectual cognition manifests itself in a threefold function: the formation of ideas, of judgments, and inferences.

Ideas are the intellectual representations of things. Ideas of things are quite different from the sense images of these same things. Sense images are concrete, particularized, individualized; ideas are abstract, generalized, universalized. An example will clarify this. I see a man and note that he is tall and slender, has a height of six feet two inches, weighs 190 pounds, with a white skin, brown eyes, and brown hair. All these features and attributes are concrete, particularized, individualized; and they are different for different human beings. On the other hand, my idea of 'man' is that he is a 'bodily, living, sentient, rational substance'; in other words, this man is a 'rational animal,' and the definition fits not only this man but every human being, whether infant or adult, whether male or female, whether white or black, whether tall or short, whether heavy or light, etc. Ideas are, therefore, class ideas, universals. The sense perceives a man in all his *concrete individuality,* with all the peculiar traits and characteristics which make him to be 'this' man and differentiate him as an individual from every other. The intellect, however, in its idea apprehends him in those essential attributes which he has *in common* with all other human beings, leaving aside all the individualizing and differentiating marks peculiar to himself, so that the content of the idea is *universal,* applicable to the individual and the whole class of individuals.

A *judgment* is an act of the intellect affirming or denying one idea of another. I compare, for example, the idea 'tree' with the idea 'plant' and recognize the fact that they agree; I then pass the affirming judgment, 'A tree is a plant.' Or, I compare the idea 'tree' with the idea 'animal' and see that they disagree; thereupon I pronounce their disagreement in the judgment, 'A tree is not an animal.' If my affirmation or denial in the judgment corresponds to reality, it is a true judgment; if not, it is false. Judgments, therefore, contain *truth or error.* Just as ideas are intellectual representations of 'things,' so judgments are intellectual representations of 'facts': they claim to express the truth about reality as it actually is in itself.

A *reasoning* process or *inference* is used when the mind does not perceive the agreement or disagreement between two ideas by a direct comparison of the two, so that it can make an immediate judgment about them. In order to judge that 'The sky is cloudy,' all that is necessary is that I look at the heavens and see the clouds. 'Can diamonds burn?' Looking at a diamond, or comparing the ideas 'diamond' and 'burn,' will not settle the question. If, however, I can bring in a third known idea with which, upon comparison, I find the two ideas to agree, then I am justified in saying that they agree with each other. Casting about for an idea which could mediate between the ideas 'diamond' and 'burning,' I find that 'carbon' is the substance of which diamonds are made and also that carbon burns. I now argue: 'Carbon is combustible; a diamond is carbon; therefore, a diamond is combustible.' Inference or reasoning is defined as the mental process by which, from certain truths already known, the mind passes to another truth distinct from these but necessarily following from them.

Volition is another phase of man's rational life. *Rational appetition* follows intellectual knowledge, just as sense appetition follows sense knowledge. The power of rational appetition is called the *will,* and the exercise of this power is *volition* or *willing.*

It is characteristic of human volition that an intellectual *motive* must precede its exercise. The intellect views a certain object or course of action under the aspect of something 'good.' This 'good' to be acquired is the motive which influences the will to determine itself to act. We experience the fact of *choosing* in the exercise of our will. There is the choice between action and nonaction, between one type of good and another type of good, and between various sets of means to attain the same end. The good desired may belong to the physical order, as food and sense pleasure; but it may also belong to the intellectual and moral order, as truth and virtue. One of the most important features of rational volition is that of *moral right* and *moral wrong* and the consciousness of personal *responsibility* in choosing between the two. It is the conviction of mankind that the will possesses the liberty of self-determination in such matters, so that man is said to have a *free will.*

Man: An Integral Organism

Man is a living being or organism. He is, similar to the plant, a vegetant organism. He is, similar to the animal, a sentient organism. He is also — and this is a prerogative peculiar to himself — a rational organism. From each viewpoint, he possesses distinct types of functions. It would, however, be a serious error to draw too sharp a line of demarkation between these types of functions, so as to consider man as a composite being consisting of three organisms somehow united into one. On the contrary, man is an *integral organism,* a single unitary substance which possesses vegetative, sensory, and rational functions.

It has already been pointed out that the selfsame substance performs vegetative and sensory functions. The nerves and senses support and control the vegetative organs in their functions, and the vegetative organs supply the foods which nourish and sustain the nervous system. And so, too, the same organism, which is both vegetant and sentient, is, in the case of man, also rational. There is a complete *integration* of the three types of life — vegetative, sensory, and rational — in man as a single organism.

That man is not three organisms united into one, but a single integral organism with three distinct types of vital functions, is evident from the testimony of our *consciousness.* Nothing is clearer to us than the facts manifested to us by our consciousness. Man is aware that he has a 'body' and a 'mind.' He is aware that he has intellectual knowledge and rational volition. He is aware that he has perceptions of sight, hearing, etc., and that he has sense appetitions and emotions and feelings. Finally, he is conscious of *self,* of his own *Ego,* in all these functions, and he recognizes his own self as the *subject* of these functions, as the *agent* who performs them and in whom they occur. He is also aware that these functions differ among themselves, while he, in whom they take place and in whom they inhere as their subject, is *integrally one and indivisible.* These facts are expressed by him in phrases which leave no place for doubt, like the following: 'I think,' 'I will,' 'I see,' 'I hear,' 'I feel,' 'I am hungry,' 'I experience pain,' 'I have pleasure,' 'I eat,' 'I am growing,' 'I am losing weight,' 'I am healthy,' 'I am ill,' 'I walk,' 'I am lying down,' and so forth. The same Ego, therefore, considers itself to be the one underlying subject of vegetative, sensory, and rational functions.

It is most important to bear the integrality of man in mind during all subsequent discussions. It will be necessary to treat of the various mental activities of man as if they were isolated entities; but one must never lose sight of the fact that all are *interconnected* and *mutually interdependent,* and that they are merely various closely related functions of one being, one substance, namely, of man as an *integral organism.*

Summary of Chapter II

Man is an *organism,* i.e., an individual constituted to carry on the activities of life by means of parts or organs more or less separate in function but mutually dependent.

1. *Living and Nonliving Matter.* There is a fundamental difference between living and nonliving beings. Living substance manifests *organization, irritability, metabolism, growth, reproduction,* and *individuality.* None of these features are found in nonliving matter.

The Cell and the Crystal. Though there exists a superficial resemblance between them, they differ radically in *composition, structure,* method of *growth, activity,* and natural *duration in existence.*

2. *Man: A Vegetant Organism.* Like the plant, man feeds himself, grows, and propagates. *Nutrition* is the preparation and assimilation of nourishing materials in the gastro-intestinal tract. Until he reaches the full stature of maturity he is in a condition of *growth;* growth takes place through the multiplication of the cells through mitosis. The *reproduction* of man by propagation occurs when the gametes or germ cells, after a maturation division has reduced the number of chromosomes by one half, unite to form the fertilized ovum.

3. *Man: A Sentient Organism.* The animal, as distinct from the plant, has a *nervous system* with *sensory functions.* The basic unit of the nervous system is the 'neuron'; it possesses excitability and conductivity. There are 'sensory' or 'afferent' nerves, and also 'motor' or 'efferent' nerves. The endings of afferent nerves, terminating in definite organic structures for reception of external stimuli, are called 'receptors' or 'sense organs' (eyes, ears, etc.). In man there are two main systems of nerves: the *cerebrospinal* system and the *autonomic* system.

Sense Knowledge and Appetition. There are various *types*

of sense knowledge in man: tactual or somesthetic, taste, smell, hearing, sight; central or synthetic sense, imagination, memory, and instinct. *Appetition* is the striving toward or away from objects. It is accompanied by various emotions and feelings.

4. *Man: A Rational Organism.* Rationality implies intellectual cognition and rational appetition. *Intellectual cognition* manifests itself in a threefold function: the formation of ideas, of judgments, and of inferences. The power of *rational appetition* is the 'will,' and the exercise of this power is 'volition' or 'willing.' The object of the will is the 'good.' An important feature of rational appetition is that of 'moral good' and 'moral wrong' and the consciousness of 'personal responsibility.' This is based on the conviction of mankind that man has a 'free will' possessing the liberty of self-determination.

5. *Man: An Integral Organism.* Man is a living being or organism. He is, similar to the plant, a vegetant organism. He is, similar to the animal, a sentient organism. He is also a rational organism. He is, however, not three organisms somehow united into one, but an *integral organism,* a single unitary substance which possesses vegetative, sensory, and rational functions.

Readings

Harmon, Francis L., *Principles of Psychology,* pp. 17–44. — Brennan, R. E., *Thomistic Psychology,* Ch. 3 and 4. — Windle, Bertram C. A., *What is Life?* Ch. II–V. — Eulenburg-Wiener, Renée von, *Fearfully and Wonderfully Made,* Ch. I, II. — Hauber, U. A., and O'Hanlon, M. Ellen, *Biology,* Ch. XIV, XXVII, XXXII.

CHAPTER III

THE NERVOUS SYSTEM

PSYCHOLOGY is mainly interested in the mental life of man, whether it be on the intellectual or sensory level. Since the intellectual operations are based to a very great extent on the sense operations, and since the latter are dependent on the nervous system, it is imperative to give at least a cursory description of the nervous system.

The latter consists of two main subsystems: the *cerebrospinal* system and the *autonomic* system. Though independent of each other to a certain degree, they are organically one.

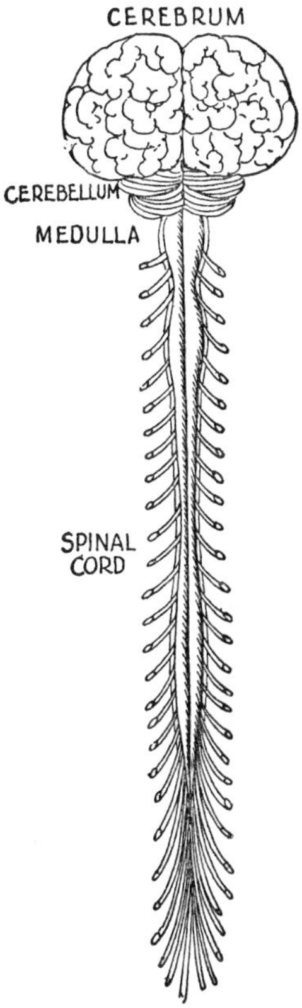

Fig. 6. Cerebrospinal Nervous System.

The figure shows the relative position of its major parts.

The Spinal Cord

The *spinal cord* is a mass of neurons and nerve fibers, enclosed in the skeletal housing of the vertebral column or spine, and extends from about the base of the skull to the end of the spine. The brain and adjacent organs are but the natural extension and amplification of the cord.

Through indentations on the ventral and the dorsal side, the cord is divided into two connected segments, the *right and left segments.* The inside of each segment consists of gray matter containing the nerve cells, while on the outside each segment consists of white matter composed of bundles of nerve fibers emanating from the cells.

Two *pairs* of nerves emerge from the cord between each of the vertebrae, one from the right side and one from the left. One part of such a pair comes from the dorsal side, and the other part from the ventral side, of the cord; both parts unite, after going separately a short distance, to form a single bundle of fibers. The part emerging from the dorsal side of the cord consists of *afferent* (sensory) nerves; the ventral part consists

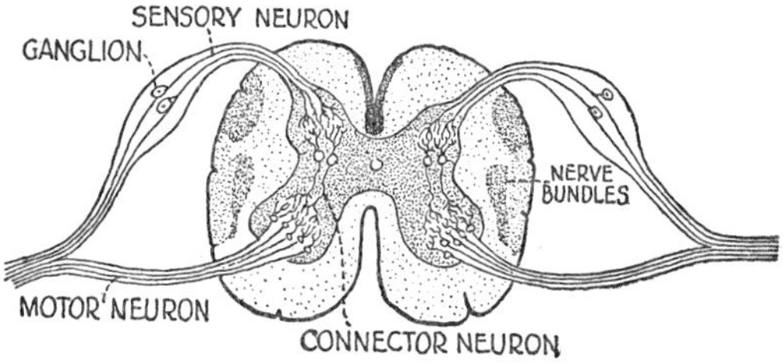

Fig. 7. Cross Section of the Spinal Cord.

of *efferent* (motor) nerves. After uniting into a single bundle, the afferent and efferent nerves travel together to various parts of the body and then separate to terminate in their respective organs. There are thus two opposing *conduction paths* from the periphery of the body (i.e., the region in which nerves terminate) to the spinal cord, and *vice versa:* afferent (sensory) nerves send impulses (sensory messages) from the peripheral organs to the spinal cord, and efferent (motor) nerves send impulses (motor messages) from the spinal cord to the peripheral organs. The *intercommunication center* is the cord itself, where a synaptical contact is made between the sensory and motor nerves. The two sets of fibers (afferent and efferent), upon juncture in the spinal cord, are also in contact with all other fibers of the spinal column and of the brain by means of *connecting* fibers extending from the brain down the entire length of the spinal cord.

The cell bodies of the efferent (motor) nerves are located in

the ventral horns of the cord. The afferent (sensory) nerves show a marked difference in this respect; their cell bodies are not located in the cord itself, but are massed together as *ganglia* outside the cord and at a short distance from it.

The *function* of the cord is clear. It serves as a communication center between receptors and effectors coming from, and leading to, the various parts of the body, and also between them and the higher centers of knowledge and control situated in the brain. A linkage is thus established between the autonomic and cerebrospinal systems.

The Autonomic System

As the name indicates, this system of nerves is 'independent,' 'a law unto itself,' 'self-acting.' While it is not true that this system is completely independent of the central nervous system as a whole, its independence of function is sufficient to warrant the name. The connection between this system and the spinal cord and brain is mainly indirect. The *autonomic system* is that part of the peripheral nervous system regulating responses not directly under voluntary control, especially responses concerned with digestive, circulatory, respiratory, and reproductive activities.

Numerous ganglia of this system are connected with the central nervous system through the mediation of *preganglionic fibers* or *white rami;* they are medullated neurons, and their cell bodies are located in the brain stem and cord. Other fibers are the *postganglionic fibers* or *gray rami;* they are unmedullated neurons, whose cell bodies are located in the autonomic ganglia, and whose fibers activate various organs in the body. These fibers are efferent, not afferent, in their functions.

The autonomic system is made up of two mutually antagonistic sections: The *sympathetic* (vegetative, visceral) system and the *parasympathetic* system. The sympathetic system is situated in the thoracic and lumbar regions. The parasympathetic consists of two parts: the *cranial,* located in the cranial or head portion of the spine, and the *sacral,* located in the sacral or extreme lower portion of the spine. (See Fig. 8.) It will be noted that the sympathetic and the parasympathetic systems send fibers to the same visceral and glandular organs;

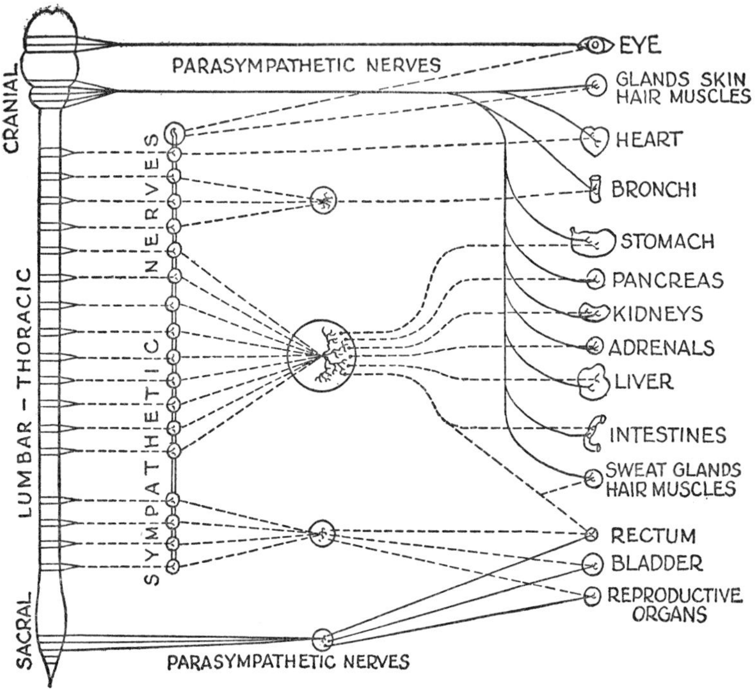

Fig. 8. Diagram of the Sympathetic and Parasympathetic Nervous System.

they also innervate the smooth (nonvoluntary) muscles of the body. While the one type of fibers acts as an 'accelerator' for some organs, the other type acts as a 'retarder' or 'brake' for the same organs, depending on whether the one type or the other is in the ascendency. Under normal conditions, each type has the dominant control over certain portions of the bodily mechanism, but gives way to the other type under particular circumstances. Ordinarily, the activities of both systems are balanced, so that their co-ordination provides a stable, harmonious functioning of the entire organism.

The *parasympathetic* or *craniosacral* section of the autonomic system regulates the digestive and eliminative processes and the reproductive functions. These operations are accompanied by the more gentle states of feeling and emotion. The *cranial* fibers affect the pupil and lens of the eyes, the circulation in the head glands, the secretions of saliva and gastric juices; they retard heart action, promote the contraction of bronchial tubes, and in general stimulate the muscles of the alimentary tract in their regular functions. The *sacral* fibers control the processes of the rectum, the bladder, and the generative organs in their nonvoluntary functions. The parasympathetic nerves are dominant when the organism is mostly in a state of repose.

The *sympathetic* section of the autonomic system is more in the nature of an 'emergency' mechanism, when danger is imminent or when injury has been sustained, and its operations are accompanied by strong emotions and feelings. In the presence of danger the organism must either flee or fight; in either case energy must be released freely and liberally, and fatigue products must be eliminated quickly. This condition demands that certain processes be accelerated, that endocrine secretions be poured into the blood stream, and that the blood itself flow rapidly and fully to the peripheral organs, leaving the digestive processes in abeyance for the time being. The effects of the sympathetic, therefore, involve the following phenomena: the heart movement is accelerated, the bronchioles of the lungs are dilated in order to furnish a larger supply of oxygen through deeper breathing, the smooth muscles of the intestinal organs are slowed down in their action and their blood vessels are constricted, the secretion of adrenalin and the secretions of the sweat glands are noticeably increased, and sugar is released from the liver and discharged into the blood for the production of more energy.

The autonomic system is made up of nerve fibers and ganglia. Two chains of ganglia, like strings of beads, lie on either side of the spine, interconnected among themselves and also connected with the spinal cord. From both these trunks of ganglia fibers ramify to the periphery, some uniting in other ganglia before reaching the visceral organs and others going directly to their destination.

Emotional states greatly influence the activities of the sympathetic and parasympathetic sections of the autonomic nervous system. On the other hand, such activities, when pronounced, are reflected in various moods of a psychic character.

The Brain Stem

The *brain stem* is a prolongation and amplification of the spinal cord. It comprises a number of distinct organs. Starting from the upper end of the spinal cord and ascending into the skull to the brain proper, these organs are: the medulla, the pons, the cerebellum, the midbrain, and the thalamus.

The *Medulla Oblongata* or *Bulb* begins just above the first spinal nerve and is an enlargement of the spinal cord. The medulla is about two and one half centimeters in length. Structurally it is similar to the cord, except for the fact that it contains much more gray matter or nerve nuclei than the cord, due to the origin of a number of nerve tracts in the medulla itself. These tracts lead outwardly to peripheral receptors and effectors and upwardly to higher centers of the brain. Some ascending nerve paths of the cord pass through the medulla to upper portions of the brain; others end in the medulla and form synaptic junction points with centers located here. The medulla, therefore, acts to a great extent as a relay center between cord and brain. It is also the main 'decussation' or crossing point of the sensory and motor paths which come from below and enter the brain. Fibers from the left side of the body cross over to the right hemisphere of the cerebrum (large brain), while fibers from the right side cross over to the left hemisphere. Some nerves, however, such as the facial nerves, enter the brain above the medulla and do not decussate. It thus happens that an injury to the left hemisphere will paralyze the left side of the face and the right side of the body. The medulla plays an important part in regulating the rhythmic processes of circulation, digestion, respiration, etc., and it also serves as the correlating center for reflexes between certain sense organs and muscles.

The *Pons Varolii* (named after Varolio, an anatomist living in the 16th century) is a further enlargement of the brain stem, situated immediately above the medulla. It consists of the projection fibers which pass through the medulla upward to the large brain (cerebrum) and also of a large number of commissural or connecting fibers which lead to the two hemispheres of the small brain (cerebellum). For a long time it was assumed that the function proper to the pons was to serve as a connection between the two hemispheres of the cerebellum; hence the name 'pons' or 'bridge.' The function of the pons is more extensive. It has a role in the innervation of autonomic nerves and also in the innervation of the facial muscles. Most important is its function of linking the cerebellum with the controlling centers of the cerebrum.

The *cerebellum* is located above the medulla and behind the pons. It is divided into two parts, called the 'hemispheres,' by a medial fissure, and it is composed of gray and white matter. The gray matter contains the cell bodies; the white matter, the axons. The gray matter is situated at the outer surface or 'cortex' of the cerebellum, while the white matter is inside and underneath. The cortex has numerous fissures and convolutions. The cerebellum receives sensory impulses from the tendons, muscles, and joints of the body, and also from the organs of postural equilibrium located in the inner ear. It is thus the center, to a large degree, of equilibrium reactions and of co-ordination in the execution of complex movements which require training and skill. Its general function, therefore, is muscular tonus and co-ordination. The activities of the cerebellum do not enter consciousness.

The *Midbrain* and *Thalamus* occupy the topmost position of the brain stem and are thus located in the center of the entire brain between the hemispheres of the cerebrum. The *midbrain,* the smallest portion of the brain in man, has four 'colliculi' or protuberances on its dorsal side and cerebral 'peduncles' or fiber bundles on its ventral side. The interior portion of the midbrain is composed of numerous nuclei and is called the 'tegumentum.' The colliculi probably control auditory and visual reflexes. In general, the midbrain is concerned with instinctive bodily impulses of various kinds. The *thalamus,*

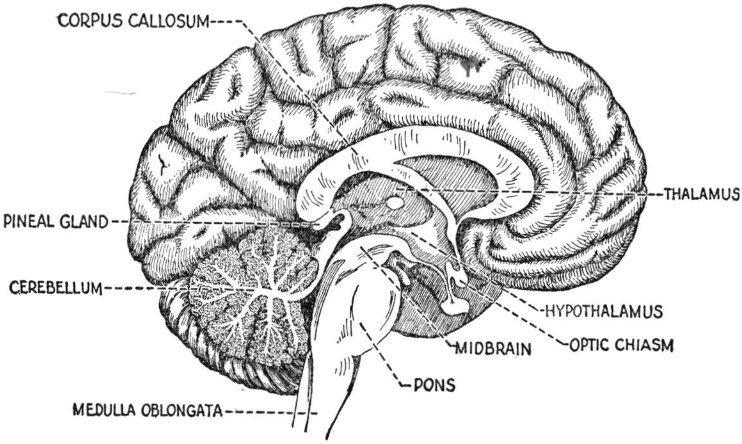

Fig. 9. Mesial Section of the Human Brain.

a bilateral organ with parts to the right and left of the stem, has three distinct portions, the dorsal thalamus, the hypothalamus, and the subthalamus. The dorsal thalamus is a center for the reception and relay of sensory impulses; its nuclei are associated with all the sense organs (smell, probably, excepted), passing their impulses on to the cerebral centers. Not much is known of the functions of the hypothalamus and subthalamus, but they are probably of a motor or efferent character. The general function of the thalamus seems to be the regulation of reflex connections for emotional responses through association with visceral reactions. Many authorities consider the thalamus to be the primary center of pain sensitivity.

The brain stem, as will be seen from these few remarks, is an important complexus of organs. Its position between the spinal cord and the cerebrum is indicative of its function in the general scheme of the nervous system as a whole; it is a midway station for sensory and motor impulses traveling to and from the cerebrum from all parts of the body.

The Cerebrum

The *cerebrum,* or large brain, is the structure of the central nervous system which lies above the brain stem. It represents the final enlargement and amplification of the spinal cord and brain stem and fills out the greatest portion of the skull. More nerve matter is found in the cerebrum than in all the rest of the body. Its weight is approximately 50 ounces, consisting of nerve nuclei, dendrites, and axons. It is estimated that the number of neurons in the cerebrum runs literally into the billions.

The full number of neurons or nerve cells is already present *at birth.* Many of these, however, are not fully developed, but are embryonic in character; these embryonic neurons are called *neuroblasts.* The neuroblasts must be developed into mature neurons before they can function as integral parts of the nervous system. No doubt much of this development occurs as the result of the natural growth of the organism; but it is very probable that development of neuroblasts into neurons also results from the conscious effort of mental activity, and this development proceeds up to middle life and even far beyond. The number of neuroblasts, however, is so large that only a portion of them reach maturity in any human being.

The *structure* of the cerebrum is very complicated. It consists of *gray* and *white* matter. The gray matter is composed of nerve cells and forms the outer surface of the cerebrum; this outer surface is termed the *cortex,* and its depth does not exceed 4mm. The white matter is composed of nerve fibers and forms the tissue beneath the cortex. The cortex has a remarkably large surface area (about 20,000 sq. mm.), because it is furrowed by many fissures (sulci) and convolutions (gyri), which provide a maximum of area in a minimum of space.

There are three relatively large and important *fissures.*

The *median* fissure divides the entire cerebrum from front to back, and the two resulting symmetrical halves are the right and left 'hemispheres.' The fissure of *Sylvius* extends horizontally just above the ear. The fissure of *Rolando,* or central fissure, begins at the center on top and runs downwards and laterally in front of the fissure of Sylvius. This division enables us to distinguish four roughly definable regions or *lobes:* frontal, parietal, occipital, and temporal. The *frontal* lobe is situated in front of the Rolandic fissure; the *parietal* lobe, immediately behind the Rolandic fissure; the *occipital* lobe, at the back of the cerebrum; the *temporal* lobe, below the fissure of Sylvius.

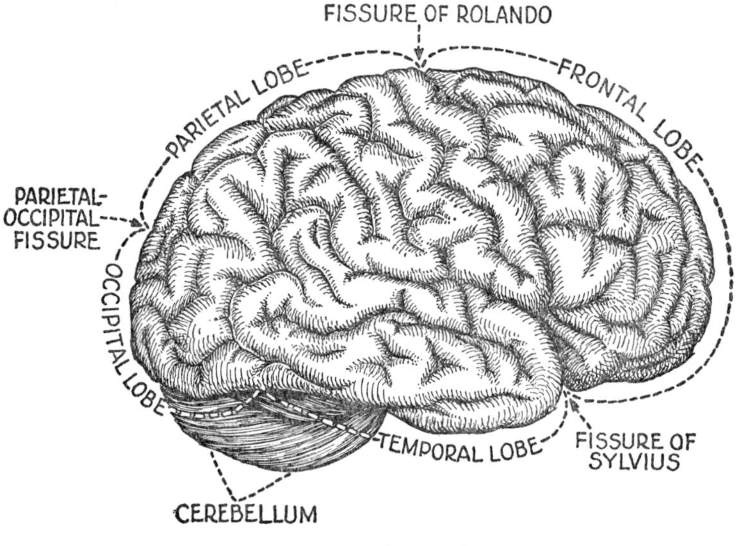

Fig. 10. Side View of the Right Hemisphere of the Human Brain.

The cerebral *cortex* or *neo-pallium,* as it is also called, consists of a number of *layers* in its structure of gray matter. These layers are not actually separated from one another; they form an uninterrupted mass of cells, but these cells are of different kinds, and a stratification among them is noticeable. The outermost layer is composed of terminal filaments, dendrites, and nerve cell bodies; then follows a layer of pyramidal cells (cells which have the shape of 'pyramids'); then, a granular layer; the latter is followed by a layer of large pyramidal cells; and, finally, situated at the bottom of the cortex, a layer of cells of various sizes and shapes, called polymorphic cells. The layers above the granular section are presumably associated with psychic functions, and those below with organic functions.

Three types of nerve fibers are found in the brain. There are various motor and sensory areas in each of the cerebral hemispheres. Masses of nerve fibers reach out in complicated patterns, connecting all such areas with one another. These fibers are the *association* fibers. The two hemispheres are symmetrical in structure, each practically a duplicate of the other. They do not act in isolation, but in conjunction; and, in order to effect this conjunction, the motor and sensory areas of the one hemisphere are interconnected by fibers with the

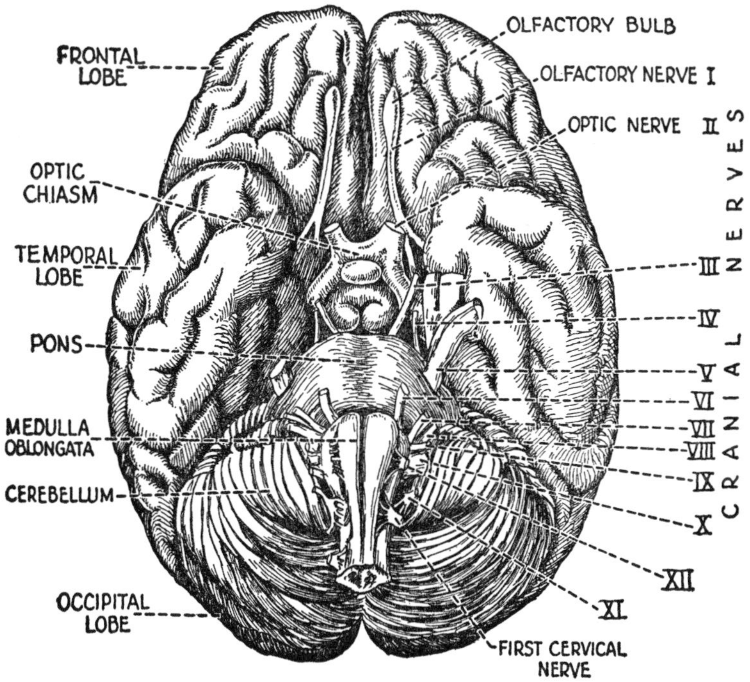

Fig. 11. Bottom View of the Human Brain.

corresponding motor and sensory areas of the other hemisphere. Such fibers are called the *commissural* fibers. Where they meet in crossing, a dense body or mass of fibers is formed between the hemispheres, serving as a sort of bridge, and this mass of fibers is termed the 'corpus callosum.' A third type consists of the fibers of *sensory* and *motor nerves*. The sensory nerves come from the spinal cord and brain stem and ascend into the cerebrum, making connections between the sense organs and the cortex. The motor nerves leave the cortex and descend into the brain stem and spinal cord, and from there pass out to the musculature. These ascending and descending nerve fibers are the *projection* fibers. Not all fibers pass down into the spinal cord; some of them, the twelve cranial nerves, leave the base of the brain directly and terminate in various parts of the head. Among them are the nerves of smell, sight, and hearing.

The structure of the cerebrum indicates very plainly that it is a marvelously complicated mechanism of nerve cells and fibers, designed as the supreme organ of co-ordination and correlation for the entire organism. And such is, indeed, its purpose and function.

Localization of Function

It has always been known that injuries to the brain affect sense knowledge and motor reactions. Gradually the fact was recognized that definite areas of the cerebrum control definite functions. The phrenologists used this fact to develop the theory that every function is located in a specific area of the brain. While this theory of *phrenology* has been definitely disproved, it is true that certain *areas* of the brain are the *localization centers* for sensory and motor functions. It would be erroneous, however, to locate such functions exclusively in these centers or areas. The structure of the brain, with its many sensory and motor nerves connecting various parts of the cortex, in itself is a strong presumptive argument that such functions are distributed, even though certain areas are the regular centers of control. The fact is now established that oftentimes, when a part of the brain is damaged, another area will take over the functions usually controlled by the part that has suffered injury. The cerebrum thus acts as an *integrating organ of co-ordinated function,* each part being involved to a certain degree in the functioning of every other part.

The actual centers of sensory and motor functions comprise a relatively small portion of the total area of the cortex. The major portion of the cortex is apparently concerned with the co-ordination and association of sensory and motor impulses and with the mental processes of conscious knowledge and behavior.

The *functional* areas of the brain (see Fig. 12) are fairly well known. In the main, they are as follows. The frontal lobe contains the *motor area.* It is located anterior to the central fissure of Rolando. Beginning from the top of the cerebrum

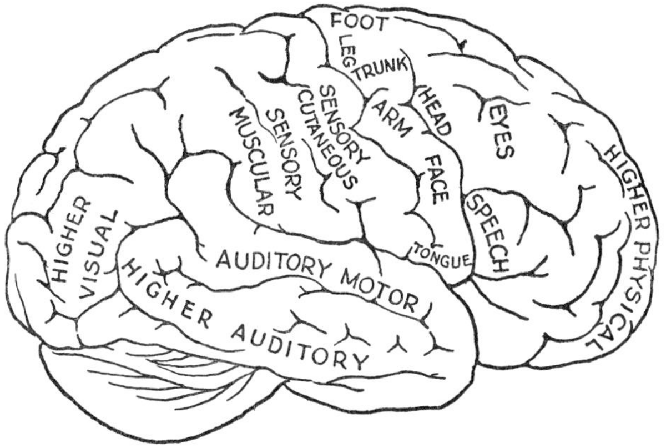

Fig. 12. Diagram of the Right Hemisphere With Localization Areas.

and moving downward, toward the ear, we encounter the motor centers, respectively, of the legs, the trunk, the arms, the head, and the tongue and mouth. Immediately posterior to the central fissure lies the *somesthetic area* which responds to sensory impulses emanating from various conditions of the body in general. The *visual area* is located in the occipital lobe or rear portion of the cortex. The *auditory area* is situated in the temporal lobe, below the fissure of Silvius. The *olfactory* and *gustatory areas* (smell and taste) have their general location centrally at the base of the brain. All these motor and sensory areas merge into *association areas;* the function of the latter consists in the correlation of the impulses received in the various motor and sensory areas, thereby enabling the brain to effect complex responses involving intelligent and adaptable activities.

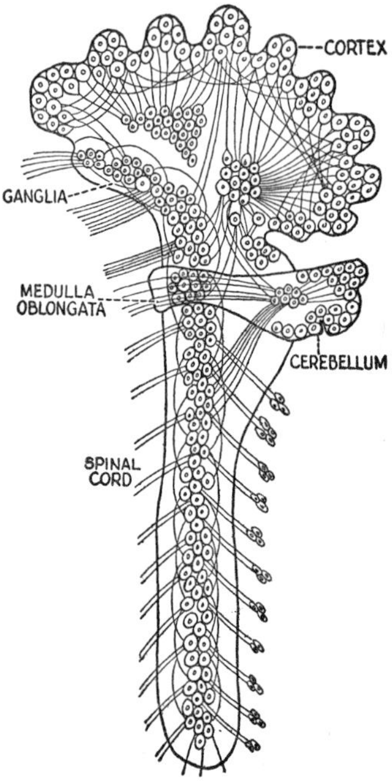

Fig. 13. Diagram of Cerebrospinal Function.

(After Mercier). The figure shows the general paths of the sensory and motor nerves.

Cerebrospinal Function

The cerebrum is the organ which is the physical and neural instrument of activities which result in *conscious* sensory and motor behavior. Of all the complex activities which occur in the brain, only a minimum actually enters into consciousness; most functions are performed without our being aware of their existence.

We open our eyes, for example, and see a building. The light rays reflected by the building enter the eyes, fall upon the retina, and there activate the receptor cells. The stimulus inaugurates a nerve impulse which travels along the optic nerve to the visual center of the cortex, and the end result of the process is the perception of the building. It is this end product which becomes conscious to the mind; the intermediary process remains unconscious throughout. And if we desire to move the eyes, so as to see another object, we consciously and deliberately direct the movements of the eyes toward the object we wish to see. Somehow, then, we are able to stimulate the motor center which controls the muscles regulating the movement of the eyes. But how we are capable of selecting and stimulating the right cortical cells, and how the motor impulse travels from the cortex to the muscles, turning the eyes in a definite direction, we do not know; the process itself does not become conscious. A large amount of neural activity must take place in the brain between the start and finish of an apparently simple function, but we are unaware of its presence.

Consciousness is a *state of the mind* in which *we are aware of our experiences,* and these experiences may pertain to motor, sensory, or rational functions. Items of conscious experience, for example, are the facts that I am walking, moving my arms, seeing the objects situated along the street, feeling the cold, thinking about the weather, desiring a ride in an automobile, etc., and I am presently aware of these items of experience. It is when I am wide awake and know what is happening to me and around me, that I am said to 'be conscious' or to 'have consciousness' of something.

Many functions of man are subject to conscious control; many are not subject to conscious control at all; and many are subject to conscious and unconscious control.

The higher funtions, those of a *rational* character, are always subject to *conscious* control. To this category belong the formation of ideas and judgments, and the acts of reasoning and volition. How far these operations may be dependent on neural and cortical conditions, need not concern us at present. It is sufficient to state that they are under direct conscious control. Many *sensory* activities are also under direct or indirect conscious control. The sense organs, when exposed to a stimulus, will always react to the stimulus, irrespective of our wishes and desires; the open eye, for instance, cannot but respond to the stimulus of light, and the ear must hear the loud report of a gun discharged in its vicinity. We have, however, conscious control over the organs of sense to a certain extent, in as much as we can direct these organs toward, or away from, definite stimuli. We can, for example, turn the eyes in this or that direction or close them entirely; we can sniff a flower or clamp the nose with our fingers; we can pinch our skin and feel the pain or refrain from such an action.

There are two kinds of muscles in the body, the smooth and the striped. The smooth are not under conscious control; the striped are. We are capable of intentionally flexing the arm or leg, turning the head, bending the body, manipulating an object, etc. All complex actions which require skill and are the result of 'learning' are consciously controlled actions. Such are walking, swimming, dancing, playing a musical instrument, writing, speaking, operating a machine, and so forth. Practice may make such activities semi-automatic, but they are always, in the last instance, under conscious control.

A large number of actions and functions in the human body are *not under conscious control.* Many of these never enter consciousness at all. Such actions and functions are usually controlled by the *brain stem* and *spinal cord.* If connecting fibers extend from the nerve centers of the stem and cord to the cortex of the cerebrum, we will, or at least may, become conscious of their presence; otherwise not. We are never conscious, for example, of the contraction of the iris of the eye under the stimulus of a bright light, nor are we aware of the modification of the curvature of the lens of the eye in focusing. On the other hand, if someone tickles us, we respond by shrinking away from the stimulation, but we are conscious of the process. Such actions are 'reflexes.'

Reflex Actions

A *reflex action,* or a *reflex,* is an *act performed automatically and involuntarily, as a response to a stimulus, by a partial mechanism of the nervous system.* The stimulus excites an afferent nerve; the impulse is transmitted along the afferent nerve fiber to a motor center, either by means of a synaptic connection, or by means of a single connecting fiber or a series of connecting fibers; the motor center is stimulated; the motor impulse travels along the efferent nerve fiber to a gland or muscle; upon reaching the gland or muscle, the end organ responds with the performance of its characteristic function. This sequence of neural activity is the so-called 'reflex arc.'

Reflexes are not learned; they are a *native endownment* of the organism's nervous system. Hence, they are inherited, and not the result of experience or practice or habit; they are localized in a definite set of nerves; they are not dependent on the action of the will, but on the influence of external stimuli. How little, at times, reflexes are dependent even on the life of the organism as a whole, can be seen in a disemboweled and decapitated frog; an electrical stimulus will induce a reflex action in the legs.

There are various *kinds* of reflexes. Some are *motor* reflexes, others *secretory*. 'Motor reflexes' have to do with contractions of the muscles. If I touch unknowingly a hot object with my hand, the hand jerks back automatically; if a bright light strikes the eyes, the pupils contract automatically. Here we have two distinct types of motor reflexes. The muscles of the hand and arm are striped muscles and as such are under conscious control, so that I can flex the arm and hand voluntarily; under the conditions just mentioned, however, the action is an involuntary reflex action. In the case of the pupillary light reflex, however, the muscles involved are smooth muscles and beyond the direct control of the will; the action of the pupils is always a reflex. 'Secretory reflexes' control glands and their secretions. When food is placed into the mouth, saliva is released; and when the food passes into the stomach, juices flow from the gastric glands. A few reflexes are *cortical*. Their centers lie in the cortex of the cerebrum; such are the reflex actions of coughing and sneezing. Most reflexes, however, as was stated above, are controlled by the *spinal cord* and the *brain stem*. A typical example of the former is the knee-jerk, effected by striking the tendon of the muscle just below the knee. The normal rhythm of the heart beat is an example of the latter. Besides the reflexes which induce a movement, there are *inhibitory reflexes* which stop a movement or hinder it from occurring. By relaxing the diaphragm one can often stop the hiccough reflexes, and by

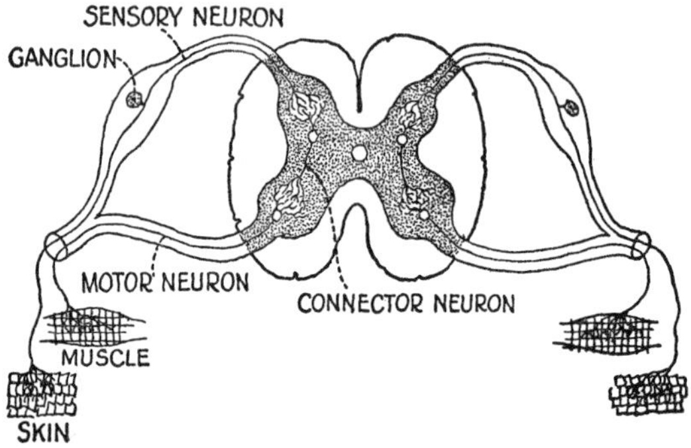

Fig. 14. Reflex Action in the Spinal Cord.

painfully pressing the upper lip against the teeth one can inhibit the tendency to sneeze. We have already noted how the sympathetic and parasympathetic sections of the autonomic nervous system counteract each other. Again, many reflexes are *regulative,* while others are *protective.* The entire autonomic system can be viewed as a vast system of motor and secretory reflexes, designed to regulate the processes of digestion, circulation, respiration, generation, and excretion; and many of its functions are also protective in character, as can be seen when germs and dangerous elements enter the organism and are destroyed or eliminated. The closing of the eye lids when objects approach and the shedding of tears when a dust particle enters the eye, are instances of protective reflexes; so, too, are vomiting, coughing, withdrawal of the foot when stepping on a piece of glass, etc.

While reflexes are by nature automatic and involuntary, an *indirect conscious control* is possible, both in a *facilitating* and *inhibiting* manner. In many instances relaxing a muscle tends to interfere with the usual reflex; holding the leg out straight makes the knee-jerk reflex almost impossible. Similarly, concentrated attention upon the expected reflex, e.g., the knee-jerk, inhibits the action. Contrariwise, conscious attention may reinforce or inhibit a reflex, as in coughing, sneezing, swallowing, vomiting, and so on; we can check or facilitate these reflexes to some degree according to our desire. We can also offset one type of reflex by counter-stimulation, as when we stop a spasm of sneezing by rubbing the nose or inhibit the winking reflex of the eyelids by holding the eyes wide open. Sometimes the forceful contraction of the muscles will prevent a reflex; thus, although normally the hand would reflexly withdraw upon contact with a hot object, we can force the hand to grasp the object firmly, thereby hindering the withdrawal reflex from operating.

Conditioned Reflexes

A *conditioned reflex* is the *reflex response of a neural mechanism to a stimulus which has been substituted for the natural stimulus normally evoking this particular reflex action.* An example will make this rather technical definition clearer.

The natural stimulus for the secretion of saliva is the presence of food in the mouth; the secretion of the saliva under such circumstances is a natural reflex of the neural mechanism in the presence of the food. This reflex, however, can also be evoked by a stimulus which, as such, bears no resemblance to food but is substituted for it. Some food is placed before a hungry dog. A bell is sounded for a few seconds, and then the food is given to the dog. After a short interval the process is repeated. This bell-and-food combination, after being made a dozen or two dozen times, has the peculiar effect that the saliva in the dog's mouth will begin to flow at the sound of the bell. Continuing the procedure for some days, it is observed that the saliva is secreted, even though no food is present, simply at the sound of the bell. Normally and naturally, the sound of a bell is not a stimulus for effecting the reflex action of salivation. Under the conditions given, however, it becomes a substitute stimulus for the presence of food in the mouth, so that the dog reacts as if he had taken food. The reflex of salivation is now 'conditioned' to the sound of the bell, and we have a 'conditioned reflex' in place of the natural or unconditioned reflex in the presence of food.

Pavlov began his experiments on the conditioned reflex around 1900, and since that time scores of psychologists have continued the work and extended the field of research among animals and men. A number of interesting facts were disclosed.

Conditioned reflexes can be acquired quite *naturally* through the *experience of life*. Through experience the animal soon learns to associate the sight of food with its taste. After a while, the sight alone is sufficient to elicit the salivation reflex. We say that the sight of food 'makes our mouth water.' Whether acquired through natural or artificial association, conditioned reflexes will readily sink into a state of *suspension* or *extinction*, if the natural stimulus, for which it is substituted, remains absent for any length of time. Thus, in the bell reflex mentioned above, if food is withheld from the dog through a number of experiments with the sounding bell, the amount of flowing saliva decreases gradually, until it reaches zero. In the animal's mind the bell stimulus is no longer associated with food, and the salivation response ceases. Then, if food is again given with the bell stimulus, the conditioned reflex receives a quick *restoration* to its full vigor. If the experiments of the conditioned reflex are omitted for a prolonged period, the animal simply reverts to the normal procedure of the natural stimulus, and the conditioned reflex is lost entirely. Such experiments show that the conditioned reflex is nothing more than a *temporary adjustment* to environmental circumstances; as the circumstances change, the conditioned reflexes change.

Almost *any kind* of stimulus can be substituted for the natural stimulus in conditioning a reflex. Various kinds of auditory, visual, and tactual stimuli have been used, and all have been successful. The main thing, of course, is that a combination or association must be established between the natural and the conditioning stimulus.

It is remarkable to what a degree a *differentiation* between stimuli of the same kind can be maintained by animals in their conditioned reflexes. Animals, for example, soon learn to differentiate between the sound of one bell and the sound of another, if the one stimulus is reinforced with food and the other not. If the reinforcement by food was delayed for a regular interval of time after the stimulus was given, say for a minute or so, the animal learned to adjust himself to the situation, so that the salivation reflex was delayed accordingly.

Conditioned reflexes have also been established in *human beings*. Experiments have been successfully performed on *infants* with a feeding bottle and a light or sound stimulus. As early as the third month of life, children distinguished between one sound and another. *S. P. Marquis* (1931) was successful in his attempts to bring about a conditioned reflex in newborn children after a few days, by using a buzzer signal just prior to feeding; at the sound of the buzzer the infants immediately commenced the oral movements of sucking. In *adults* the conditioned reflex is far more difficult to recognize, due to the conscious co-operation of the subject. Many experiments have been made, attempting to condition the reflexes of salivation, hand-withdrawal through shock, winking of the eyelid, and knee-jerk. Quite a number of psychologists are convinced that conditioned eyelid and knee-jerk reflexes have been obtained. Others are not so sure. A reflex is almost always the response of a partial neural mechanism controlled by some lower motor center. The eyelid and knee-jerk responses due to conditioning, however, seem to lack the sharp, quick, spontaneous throw so characteristic of the natural reflex. Apparently, then, there is a certain amount of cortical participation in the new response; and, if that is the case, it would be more of an indication that the organism, through its higher centers, has learned to adjust itself to a new situation. In the case of human adults, therefore, it is still not clear whether true conditioned reflexes can be obtained. If consciousness and volition play a part in the final results of the response, it can hardly be a reflex action in the strict sense of the word.

Watson and the *behaviorists* generally look upon these and similar experiments as showing that all human behavior can be explained in terms of conditioned and unconditioned reflexes. According to them, a study of reflexes is the proper study of psychology; consciousness can be eliminated as a factor in human behavior, and introspection should be omitted as a legitimate method of investigation in studying mental phenomena. A conditioned reflex of the iris of the eye seemed particularly important to Watson as strengthening the foundation of behaviorism, because this would show that such a muscle, which is definitely not under voluntary control, could be positively conditioned in its reflex without the influence of conscious activity. *Cason* made experiments on this pupillary reflex with a light-and-bell combination and found that the pupil contracted more under the stimulus of this combination than under the stimulus of light alone. However, as T. V. Moore points out, "a pupillary reaction, in spite of its involuntary character, is nevertheless indirectly subject to voluntary control. Every act of attention dilates the pupil. Every emotion does the same. Looking at a far point dilates it; looking at a near point or wrinkling the forehead contracts it. It is very likely that, as Hamel suggested, many of the experiments that were supposed to demonstrate conditioned pupillary reactions merely manifested the effect of apprehension on the size of the pupil."[1] And thus we see that conscious factors influenced the action of the pupil throughout the experiments, contrary to the supposition of Watson. Hence, consciousness cannot be eliminated as a factor in human behavior on the basis of conditioned reflexes.

Conscious factors are also present in animal experiments. It is difficult in many instances to distinguish between a true reflex controlled solely by an unconscious motor center and

[1] *Dynamic Psychology*, 2nd ed. (Lippincott, 1926), p. 70.

a sequence of behavior due to the conscious recognition of the necessity of an adjustment to new circumstances. After all, even a dog has reactions which manifest a conscious knowledge of his surroundings. If, then, he obtains food at the sound of a bell, he comes to expect this food at the sound, and this conscious expectation causes the saliva to flow; this reaction will continue until he realizes, after a change in the experiment, that food is no longer forthcoming at the sound of the bell, and then the flow of saliva progressively decreases and eventually ceases altogether. The *apprehension* and *expectation* of food are conscious, psychic factors which must not be overlooked in these experiments. They rob the conditioned reflex of much of its mystery, and they show what little support behaviorists can derive for their theory from conditioned reflexes.

Our brief description of the nervous system and its functions in the human organism emphasizes the fact that man is a unit, a completely *integrated organism*. The complexity of the nervous system in its structural details and in its functions is beyond conception and description. Nevertheless, every single part, both in structure and function, is linked with every other part so intimately and effectively, that the result is a unified totality of marvelous compactness and activity.

Summary of Chapter III

The *nervous system* of man consists of two main subsystems: The *cerebrospinal* and the *autonomic*.

1. *The Spinal Cord.* It is a mass of neurons and nerve fibers, enclosed in the skeletal housing of the spine, and extends from about the base of the skull to the sacral region. The inside of the spinal cord consists of gray matter containing the nerve cells; the outside consists of bundles of nerve fibers. Two pairs of nerves emerge from both sides of the cord between each of the vertebrae. *Afferent* nerves emerge from the dorsal side, *efferent* nerves from the ventral side.

Connecting fibers unite these nerves among themselves and also with the brain.

2. *The Autonomic System.* It is that part of the peripheral nervous system regulating responses concerned especially with digestive, circulatory, respiratory, and reproductive activities. It is composed of two mutually antagonistic sections: the *sympathetic* (vegetative, visceral) and the *parasympathetic.* The latter section consists of two parts, the 'cranial' and the 'sacral.' The sympathetic section is more in the nature of an 'emergency' mechanism.

3. *The Brain Stem.* It is a prolongation of the spinal cord and is situated at the upper end of the cord. It comprises the *medulla oblongata* or bulb, the *pons,* the *cerebellum,* the *midbrain,* and the *thalamus.*

4. *The Cerebrum.* The cerebrum is the final enlargement of the spinal cord and brain stem. The *cortex* is the outer surface and consists of gray matter, i.e., nerve cells; the inner portion consists of white matter, i.e., nerve fibers. The brain is furrowed by many fissures and convolutions. Three fissures are large: the median fissure, the fissure of Silvius, and the fissure of Orlando. *Three types of nerve fibers* are found in the brain: sensory and motor fibers, association fibers, and commissural fibers. The cerebrum is the supreme organ of co-ordination and correlation for the organism.

5. *Localization of Function.* Certain areas of the brain are the localization centers for sensory and motor functions. The frontal lobe contains the motor areas. The somesthetic area lies behind the central fissure. The visual area is located in the occipital lobe. The auditory area lies in the temporal lobe. The olfactory and gustatory areas are situated centrally at the base of the brain. All these motor and sensory areas merge into association areas.

6. *Cerebrospinal Function.* The cerebrum is the organ which is the physical and neural instrument of activities which result in *conscious* sensory and motor behavior. *Consciousness* is a state of the mind in which we are aware of our experiences, and these experiences may refer to motor, sensory, or rational

functions. Conscious control originates in the cerebrum. Many actions and functions are not under control, and these are usually controlled by the brain stem and the spinal cord.

7. *Reflex Actions.* A reflex action, or *reflex,* is an act performed automatically and involuntarily, as a response to a stimulus, by a partial neural mechanism of the nervous system. Reflexes are an inherited native endowment of the organism's nervous system.

There are various *kinds* of reflexes: motor and secretory; inhibitory; regulative and protective; cortical and those controlled by the brain stem and spinal cord. Over many of the reflexes we have an *indirect* conscious control.

8. *The Conditioned Reflexes.* A conditioned reflex is the reflex response of a neural mechanism to a stimulus which has been substituted for the natural stimulus normally evoking this particular reflex action. Example: the salivary reflex evoked at the sound of a bell associated with food. Such reflexes can be suspended, extinguished, and restored. They are a *temporary adjustment* to environmental circumstances. Conditioned reflexes have been experimentally established in infants; in adults the success is doubtful, due to the conscious factors of adjustment.

Behaviorism hails these experiments as showing that all human behavior can be explained in terms of conditioned and unconditioned reflexes, thereby eliminating consciousness as a factor in human behavior. Their view is wrong, because both men and animals are conditioned in their reflexes through apprehension and expectation, and these are psychic factors.

Readings

Harmon, F. L., *Principles of Psychology,* Ch. 3. — Eulenburg-Wiener, R. von, *Fearfully and Wonderfully Made,* Ch. XXV, XXVI. — Woodworth, R. S., *Experimental Psychology,* Ch. V. — Moore, Thomas V., *Dynamic Psychology,* Part II.

Chapter IV

THE SOMESTHETIC SENSES

TO PSYCHOLOGY, the biological and physiological processes, even those of the nervous system, are of only secondary importance. Of primary importance are the *mental processes.* Man is a sentient organism. The term 'sentient' implies 'sensing,' and sensing has to do with sense cognition, sense knowledge. Sense cognition is followed by sense appetition, sense striving. These are the *two main types* of sense function: *sense cognition* and *sense appetition.* In these psychology is vitally interested, and they will be discussed in the following chapters.

Sense cognition is the first main phase of man's mental life which the psychologist and philosopher is called upon to investigate. Sense cognition is mediated through various bodily structures called the *receptors* or *sense organs.* Through these man obtains a knowledge of conditions present in his own body and in the world around him. The receptors are activated by stimuli which impinge on them and thereby convey information to the mind by means of the act of sensation.

Sensation and Perception

By a *sense* we understand *a specialized mechanism or function* by virtue of which an animal organism is *receptive* and *responsive to a certain class of physical stimuli, resulting in knowledge of some sort.* By *sensation* we understand *a conscious experience aroused by the stimulation of an organ of sense.* Certain receptor nerves terminate in specialized organic structures, like the ear, the eye, etc., peculiarly adapted to receive the excitation of a definite stimulus. The physical stimulus which arouses the sense organ to activity may be mechanical motion, heat, sound, light, electricity, or a chemical reaction. The stimulus itself, therefore, is some form of energy and resides in, and proceeds from, some object.

The *process of sensation* is as follows. On the *physical* level there is the stimulus. Aether vibrations, for example, affect the eye; air waves affect the ear. The stimulus now produces effects in the terminal elements of the receptor nerves, and these effects are *physiological* and *neurological;* a nerve impulse is set up and travels along the sensory nerves up to their respective center in the cortex of the brain. In the cortex the process ends on the *psychological* or *mental* level; man's consciousness is modified, so that he has a conscious experience of the stimulation of the organ of sense. He experiences, for example, color and sound in a conscious manner; in other words, he has a 'sensation' of color and sound. It is essential to the concept of 'sensation' that the final result be a *conscious* experience, a modification of consciousness. Not all sensory impulses have this final result. In very many instances these impulses remain on the purely neurological level, traveling only as far as the spinal cord or brain stem, where they are shunted over to a motor center; the result, then, is a motor reflex which does not enter consciousness at all, and such a response is not a 'sensation.'

Depending on the attributes of the stimulus, a sensation also has various recognizable *attributes.* One of them is 'quality.' Color, for example, has a particular shade; sound has a particular tone. There is also 'intensity.' There is a more-or-less in the brilliance of color, in the loudness of a sound. Another attribute is 'duration.' A flash of lightning is not seen as long as the light of the desk lamp while reading; the report of a pistol is heard for a shorter period of time than the noonday whistle of a near-by factory. Quality, intensity, and duration are common attributes of all sensations. Primarily, these are the attributes of the stimuli; however, in as much as sensations are directly dependent on the stimuli, they are also the attributes of the sensations themselves.

The student must distinguish well between *sensation* and *perception.* In common parlance the distinction is seldom made, but modern psychologists are very emphatic on this point. 'Sensation' has just been defined. By *perception* we understand *the cognizing of the object which produces the sensation.* Sensation has reference solely to the stimulus; perception has reference always to the object furnishing the stimulus. In sensation I become conscious of the stimulation of a sense organ purely as such; in perception I become conscious of the object presently and actively engaged in the stimulation of a sense organ. Consider the following situation. There is a green blotter on my desk, and on the blotter is a sheet of white paper. In the dark I see nothing; but as soon as I turn on the light, I begin to see. Just what do I see? From the standpoint of a 'sensation,' I am conscious of seeing a patch of 'white' and a patch of 'green'; the stimulus of light has produced in me the conscious experience of 'white' and 'green.' From the standpoint of 'perception' I see 'an oblong sheet of white paper against the background of a green blotter.' In this process of perception, therefore, I refer the sensation 'white' and 'green' to the 'paper' and the 'blotter' and include also the 'relation' of the one to the other. The mere fact of seeing 'white' and 'green' does not tell me at all that they refer to 'paper' and a 'blotter'; that knowledge was acquired before through some other process of knowing, and so I now refer the 'white' and 'green' to these known objects in the present act of sight. Another illustration. Someone holds an object to my nose, requesting me to smell, and asks "What do you smell?" If I answer, "Something fragrant," I declare my sensation; but if I answer "A rose," I declare my perception. A final illustration: If through my hearing I am aware 'of sounds following one another,' I have merely a sensation; if, on hearing these same sounds, I am aware of 'hearing a robin sing,' I connect the sensation with the object furnishing the stimulus and have the far more complex perception.

Perceptions always involve past sensations of the same and of different kinds and combine them in the *recognition of the object* which caused them. The stimuli come from objects and thereby convey to the mind items of information regarding the objects themselves. It is the inherent purpose of stimuli to acquaint us with these objects, whether these objects are *within* our own organism or are *external* to our body. Hence, we seldom stop at the primitive experience of the sensation itself, but immediately pass on to the experience of the object causing the sensation. Thus, we rarely speak of merely 'an ache' but of 'a stomach ache,' and we are practically never conscious only of a patch of 'blue' but rather of a 'bluebird.' In everyday life, therefore, we occupy ourselves with perceptions, not with pure sensations. The ordinary man is not interested in sensations as such; since, however, perceptions are elaborations of sensations and sensations are the underlying units of perception, the research psychologist is interested in the fundamental distinction between the two kinds of mental experiences. The student should know the distinction.

The Senses

Man possesses a number of senses. A classification can be made according to a variety of standpoints. A classification, based on common experience and in vogue for over 2000 years, is the division of the senses into *external* and *internal*. The 'external' senses were subdivided into sight, hearing, taste, smell, and touch; the 'internal' senses, into the central sense, imagination, sense memory, and instinct.

Modern psychology accepts the external senses as enumerated, but insists that the sense of 'touch' really is composed of a number of distinct senses, namely, the sense of warmth, of cold, of pressure, of pain, the kinesthetic sense, the visceral sense, and the static sense. Of these, only the sense of pressure should properly be designated the sense of 'touch.' As a matter of mere convenience and methodology, these senses are often grouped together under special headings; there is, however, no uniform practice among psychologists in this regard. Usually, this entire 'touch' group is referred to as the *somesthetic* or *body senses,* or still more simply as the somesthetic or body sense. The senses of warmth and cold are often spoken of as the 'temperature sense.' Again, the senses of pressure, pain, and temperature are called the 'cutaneous' or 'skin senses,' while the visceral, kinesthetic, and static senses are termed the 'intraorganic senses.'

Another classification of the external senses is based on the *origin of the stimulus,* consideration being given to the *kind of objects* of which they convey information. Viewed from this standpoint, psychologists speak of *exteroceptive, interoceptive,* and *proprioceptive senses.* An 'exteroceptive sense' is one which is activated by stimuli orginating outside the organism. The senses which belong to this class are sight, hearing, taste, smell, the senses of warmth, cold, pressure, and pain; their stimuli originate from objects which lie outside the organism itself. An 'interoceptive' sense is one which is activated by stimuli originating within the viscera and within the vestibule of the internal ear. The visceral and static senses belong to this class. The 'proprioceptive' sense is the sense which is activated by stimuli originating within the organism by movement or tension in its own tissues. This is the kinesthetic sense.

For the purpose of correlation and clarification, the different classes of senses can be ordered as follows:

External Senses

Somesthetic (Touch)	Intra-organic	Kinesthetic	Proprioceptive
		Visceral	Interoceptive
		Static	
	Cutaneous	Pain	Exteroceptive
		Pressure	
		Cold	
		Warmth	
Smell			
Taste			
Hearing			
Sight			

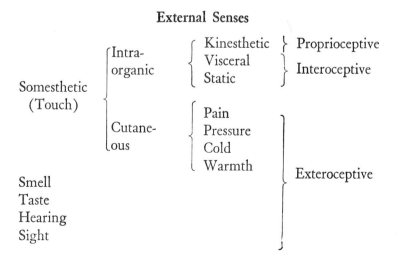

Internal Senses

Central or synthetic sense
Imagination
Sensory memory
Instinct

The main division of the senses into 'external' and 'internal' is named this way in deference to history, because these are the designations handed down through the centuries. The terms, however, must not be taken too literally. In particular, the term 'external' is to some extent a misnomer. The intraorganic senses are not really 'external' or 'exteroceptive,' because their stimuli originate within the organism itself; for this reason they should, perhaps, be classified as 'internal.' Nevertheless, we retain the nomenclature for want of more appropriate terms.

After these preliminary definitions and classifications, it will now be necessary to study the senses and their functions more in detail. Since the intellect depends, as will be shown later, on the internal senses for the preparation of its material and the internal senses depend on the external senses for the preparation of their data, the logical procedure will be to begin with the external senses. Among the external senses the element of cognition is expressed in unequal measure—most in sight and hearing, less in taste and smell, least in the somesthetic senses. Beginning with the lowest and progressing upward to the highest, the *somesthetic* senses will be considered first in the order of treatment. They are the subject matter of this chapter.

The Cutaneous or Skin Senses

A number of the somesthetic or body senses are located in the *skin region*. The skin is the protective covering of the human body and is composed of two main layers: the outer skin or *epidermis* and, underneath the epidermis, the *dermis* or *corium*. These layers rest on a tissue of *subcutaneous fat*. This region is the seat of the sense organs grouped together under the term 'cutaneous senses,' namely, the senses of *pressure, pain, warmth,* and *cold.*

Experimental research in psychological laboratories soon brought out the fact that stimuli applied to the skin did not evoke the same response over all areas. It also brought out the very important fact that the different responses represented sensations of totally different types, so that a number of senses had to be accepted instead of the one general sense of 'touch.' It is now generally recognized that the sensations of pressure, pain, warmth, and cold originate in structurally different parts or organs. Just what these organs were, remained obscure for a long time; and even to this day physiologists and psychologists are still much in doubt as to the exact nature of the organs and their function.

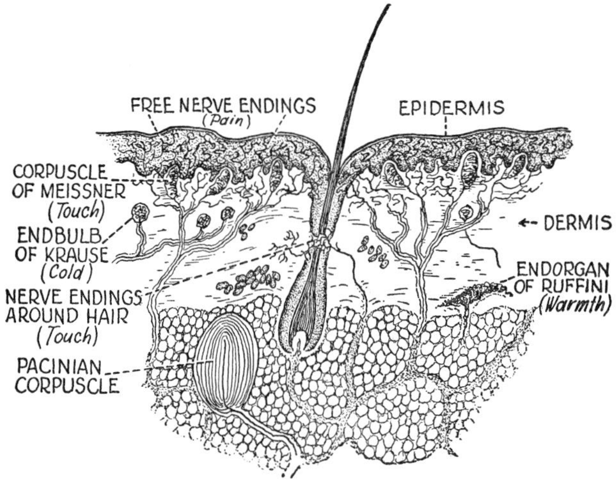

Fig. 15. Cross Section of the Skin.
Various organs of the cutaneous senses are shown.

The skin contains various types of nerve endings associated with the cutaneous sensations. Some of these have a distinctive anatomical structure. There are *capsules* or sheaths of fatty tissue, richly supplied with minute blood vessels and a network of nerve endings. Prominent among these capsulated organs are the *Pacinian* and *Meissner corpuscles,* the *Krause bulbs,* and the *end organs or Ruffini.* The *hair follicles* also play their part in cutaneous sensation. The root of the hair is encircled by numerous nerve endings. Most frequently present throughout the skin area of the body are *free nerve endings.* They are the terminal branches of nerves and have no specific organic structures as receptor organs; they themselves receive the stimuli and transmit the sensory impulse. These nerves are distributed quite freely in the skin, but the distribution is rather uneven for the individual types. It is the presence or absence of one or the other of these types of nerve endings in definite skin areas which has enabled experimenters to connect them with certain types of sensations. The *method* commonly employed is the use of a stylus or bristle, applied point by point to a localized area of skin surface. This punctiform method of investigation brought out the startling fact that the skin is not uniformly sensitive, but consists of *sensitive spots.* These spots differ in the character of their sensitivity, so that we are able to distinguish pressure spots, warmth spots, cold spots, and pain spots.

The Sense of Pressure

During the years from 1883 to 1885 three physiologists, Donaldson, Blix, and Goldscheider, proved by experimental evidence that the sensations of pressure, warmth, and cold resided in spots or points of the skin. A decade later (1894) von Frey furnished the proof that the pressure and pain senses were distinct and were localized in different spots. Beginning with the fact that light pressure or contact does not elicit the sensation of pain, while strong pressure does, he drew the conclusion that the phenomenon could be explained only on the grounds that pressure and pain were separate senses and responded to different stimuli. He thereupon engaged in a series of systematic experiments to prove his hypothesis. He used as his investigating instruments straight hairs, graduated according to thickness and strength, and measured their pressure on the skin by a delicate balance scale. The standard used was the gram per square millimeter. His computations showed that pressure and pain have different thresholds, the threshold for pressure being the lower and that for pain the higher. He also discovered that some areas of the skin are sensitive to pressure only, while others are sensitive to pain only. He thus proved his hypothesis.

Experiments show that a considerable *variation* exists in the sensitivity of the skin toward pressure. The tip of the tongue and the tips of the fingers are very sensitive; the abdomen and the back of the forearm possess a much reduced sensitivity; the thickened skin of the soles of the feet has very little sensitivity. Much depends on the thickness of the skin and the number of pressure or touch spots in a particular region. This number differs appreciably in different parts of the body. It is estimated that there are approximately 5 to 10 pressure or touch spots per square centimeter, as an average, on the arm or leg, 30 on the chest, 50 on the forehead, 100 on the lips and fingertips, and 120 on the ball of the thumb. A few restricted areas seem to lack pressure spots almost entirely; such is the case with the mucous membrane lining the inner surface of the eyelids, which is extremely sensitive to pain but scarcely registers pressure at all. On the hairy portions of the body, the pressure or touch spots are located to windward of each hair, that is to say, close over the hair follicle.

The *stimulus* for pressure sensation is anything which, upon contact, alters the even surface of the skin. Pushing against the skin, or lifting it, or bending it aside, is a stimulus exciting the pressure sense. Any such modification of the surface must affect adjacent and underlying tissues and thereby stimulate the pressure receptors.

It is certain that the hair follicles serve as the receptors of pressure in those parts of the body where hair is present. However, not all parts are covered with hair, though they are sensitive to pressure; for example, the lips, the tongue, the palm of the hand. It is fairly certain that the *Meissner* corpuscles and perhaps also the *free nerve endings* serve as pressure organs in these and other portions of the skin.

Some interesting *phenomena* are associated with the experience of pressure. In some instances, depending on the region stimulated, pressure is experienced as a mere 'contact,' in others more distinctly as 'pressure,' and again in others as a 'tickle.' Another phenomenon is that of 'adaptation.' When a stimulus is applied steadily to the pressure organs, they adapt themselves to the situation, and the sensation of pressure gradually fades and then vanishes. When the stimulus is changed, the sensation reappears. Such experiences are common. After a brief period of time, we no longer feel the clothes on our body, or the hat on our head, or the shoe on our foot, even though they fit tightly and press with some force against the skin; we become insensitive to the pen or cigarette held quietly between the fingers; we do not notice the pressure of the chair on which we are sitting or of the bed on which we are lying, until we change our posture. The sensation of pressure and touch is diminished or ceases temporarily.

The Sense of Pain

Of all the cutaneous sensations, that of pain is the one most unpleasant and most dreaded. More than any other, the pain sense serves as a protection safeguarding the integrity of the organism against injurious agencies. The presence of pain is always a warning signal.

The *stimulus* producing the sensation of pain is some object or condition which injures or nearly injures nerve tissue. The pain *receptors* are undoubtedly the 'free nerve endings.' They are known to be present wherever pain is felt. These free-branching nerve endings are distributed over the entire surface of the body, and pain can be elicited everywhere. In the center of the cornea of the eye the only sensation present is that of pain, and in this area we find only free nerve endings. From these facts of distribution physiologists conclude that the free nerve ends are the true pain receptors. Notwithstanding its great physiological importance, the pain sense is the most primitive of all, because it lacks anything resembling an 'organ' proper, consisting merely of the terminal branches of nerves.

This very lack of structural specialization, however, makes the pain sense peculiarly adapted to report injuries, because even a pin prick or slight scratch of the epidermis will immediately attack the tissue of the nerve endings themselves.

As for the *distribution* of the pain spots, they are more numerous than those of the other cutaneous senses. This distribution is, like that of the other sensitive spots, uneven in the different portions of the body; much depends, too, on the constitution of the individual. In general, though, the respective areas of the skin are practically the same in all human beings, so that it is possible to give a statistical average of the number of pain spots present in a particular region of the skin. Taking as a standard the number of spots per square centimeter, it has been estimated that there are about 45 pain spots on the tip of the nose, 60 on the ball of the thumb, and close to 200 on the back of the hand, the chest, and the inner forearm. Kiesow states that a small patch of membrane, situated opposite the second molar tooth on the inner surface of the cheek, is entirely devoid of pain spots.

One of the *phenomena* of pain sensation is its 'latent period.' It takes more time to arouse this sensation than it does in the case of the other cutaneous senses, and it also takes more time for the effect to disappear. The pain sense is relatively slow in its operation. The pressure sense is relatively fast, and this difference in reaction time is another indication that these senses are distinct. The pain sense possesses a certain amount of 'adaptation' to the steady application of a stimulus, demanding intervals for recovery to full efficiency. From a psychological standpoint, the 'quality' of pain varies from a sharp sting to a dull ache. Pain originating from the internal organs of the body is always pathological in character.

Contrary to what might be expected, there are no sensitive spots for pleasure, although pleasure is usually considered to be the counterpart of pain as much as cold is the counterpart of warmth. Evidently, then, pleasure is a condition of the organism totally different from that of pain. Pleasure will be considered in a later chapter.

The Temperature Sense

Physiologists and psychologists often speak of the 'temperature sense' in the singular, as if there were but a single sense for warmth and cold; then again, they often refer to the 'sense of warmth' and the 'sense of cold,' as if they were two separate senses. Many, perhaps most, of these scientists favor the two-sense view, but there is always a note of uncertainty in their expression.

Up to date, the *experimental evidence* is neither clear nor conclusive, notwithstanding the great amount of research work done in the laboratories. It has been found that the cold spots of the skin far outnumber the warmth spots; and it has also been discovered that there are regions where cold spots are present while warmth spots are absent, and vice versa. There is also good evidence in support of the view that the cold receptors are close to the skin surface, while the warmth receptors lie deeper; when the skin is cocainized, the cold sensation disappears first and the warmth sensation later. This evidence argues for the two-sense view.

Offsetting this evidence is the fact that these spots do not seem to be stable; the location and the number of spots shift about to a certain extent from experiment to experiment with the same subject. Besides, when the stimulus is increased, namely, by using a somewhat warmer or colder stimulus than was used before, the number of sensitive spots is also increased; this fact does not seem to conform with the theory of fixed receptors of warmth and cold with a punctate form of distribution. It may be, of course, that some spots are more sensitive than others, and that an increase of the stimulus produces its effect over a wider area with a corresponding involvement of more spots.

If it were possible to identify definitely two distinct types of receptor organs for the sensations of cold and warmth, the problem would be solved. Investigators associate the sensation of cold with the *end bulbs of Krause* and the sensation of warmth with the *end organs of Ruffini.* There is some experimental evidence which points to these structures as being the organs of cold and warmth, but this evidence is also not conclusive. Von Frey had already observed that the conjunctiva of the eye is very sensitive to cold, and this area abounds with the Krause bulbs. Strughold and Karbe, using a very ingenious method of mapping the cold spots, confirmed the findings of von Frey; every cold spot of the conjunctiva was found to correspond to a Krause bulb located at the spot. There is thus little doubt that the Krause end bulbs are cold receptors or at least are associated with them. The problem, however, is still left unsolved. Cold spots are very numerous in the skin and are freely distributed over the entire surface of the body; and yet, despite repeated efforts, investigators have failed to discover the presence of these end bulbs in the skin where the cold spots are located.

Another phenomenon which seems to militate against the two-sense theory is the fact that very intense stimulation of the temperature spots is sensed as a 'burning.' It is commonly known that contact with an extremely cold object is experienced as a 'burning' sensation and not as cold. If the cold and warmth receptors were specifically distinct as senses, this fact is, to say the least, disturbing.

Due to these apparently conflicting facts, some scientists look for the true stimulus source of cold and warmth in the *blood vessels.* A 'dilation' of the vessels would be the stimulus for the sensation of warmth, a 'constriction' of the vessels for that of cold, and a 'spastic constriction' the stimulus of the burning sensation which is aroused by extreme excitation. There is, however, little positive evidence for this theory.

And so there is still uncertainty whether we have a single common temperature sense or a distinct sense for warmth and another for cold. Future investigation may settle the question. Leaving this matter aside, we will now give our attention to factual information concerning the sensations of warmth and cold.

The *distribution* of the cold and warmth spots is rather variable. The cold spots far outnumber the warmth spots, considered as a whole, although in some restricted areas the warmth spots predominate. Striking an average from the results obtained by a number of investigators, von Stramlik[1] gives the following averages per square centimeter of skin surface. Cold spots: forehead, 8; tip of nose, 13; chest, 9; volar side of forearm, 6; back of hand, 7. Warmth spots: forehead, 6; tip of nose, 1.0; chest, .3; volar side of forearm, .4; back of hand, .5. Sommer estimated that the entire body surface contains about 250,000 cold spots and 30,000 warmth spots, with an average of 12–13 cold spots and 1–2 warmth spots per square centimeter.

Warmth and cold have no absolute values, but are relative in character. Whether a *thermal stimulus* will or will not arouse the sensations of warmth and (or) cold, depends upon the temperature of the skin to which it is applied. If the temperature of the stimulus is higher than that of the skin, it is experienced as 'warmth'; if the temperature of the stimulus is lower, it is experienced as 'cold'; and if the temperature of the stimulus is the same as that of the skin, neither warmth nor cold is experienced. Warmth and cold are simply modalities which are relative to the temperature of an organism. The skin temperature is termed *physiological zero,* because that is the temperature to which the organism is 'indifferent.' Various portions of the skin may have different physiological zeros, in as much as one portion may be warmer or colder than another. On a very cold day the physiological zero of the exposed parts, such as the hands and face, will be lowered with respect to the covered parts; on a very hot day, or when exposed to a fire, it will be raised. It then happens that the same thermal stimulus will be experienced as warm and cold when applied to different parts of the skin.

One of the phenomena connected with the temperature sense is that of *paradoxical cold* and *paradoxical warmth.* Of the two,

[1] See R. S. Woodworth, *Experimental Psychology* (Holt, 1938), p. 457.

paradoxical cold is obtained more frequently. Paradoxical cold results under a special set of conditions when a hot stimulus is applied to the skin and there arouses, not a sensation of warmth, but a sensation of cold instead. If a temperature of 45° C. is applied for a short time to the front of the forearm and then a contact is made with a stimulus of 48° C., a sensation of cold will be experienced. The explanation given is, that the warmth receptors have adapted themselves to the temperature of 45° C. and do not respond immediately to the increased temperature of the second stimulus; the cold receptors, however, are able to respond to this stimulus by a cold sensation, since they have not been weakened by the temperature stimulus of 45° C. and can respond in full force.

The *reaction time* for the sensations of cold and warmth is different. When a cold spot is stimulated, the sensation in all its intensity is experienced at once, but the sensation of warmth reaches its full intensity only gradually. This difference in reaction time probably receives its explanation in the fact (if it is a fact) that the warmth receptors are situated in the deeper tissues.

The sensation of *heat* (not mere warmth) is peculiar. The stimulation of warmth spots alone will never arouse the sensation of heat. Intense stimulation will produce the sensation of warmth or pain (pain will ensue, because of the injury to nerve tissue), but not 'heat.' In order that 'heat' be experienced, it is necessary that both warmth and cold spots be present in the stimulated area. It is therefore assumed that heat is not a simple sensation, but a blended sensation of warmth and cold resulting from the simultaneous stimulation of adjacent warmth and cold spots. That it is a blended sensation is born out by the heat-grill experiment. The grill consists of small tubes placed in parallel a few millimeters apart, warm and cold water alternating in the parallel tubes, so that warm stimuli affect warmth spots and cold stimuli affect cold spots in the same general area. Although no real heat is applied in this experiment, the subject, by placing his hand or forearm on the grill, soon experiences 'heat' without pain. Psychologists call this 'synthetic heat,' in contrast to real heat. When 'burning heat' is experienced, due to the application of an extremely hot or cold stimulus, pain receptors are also involved in the stimulus pattern.

Adaptation to stimuli is noticeable to a marked degree in the temperature sense. Under steady stimulation of moderate warmth or cold the skin adapts itself by a corresponding shift of the physiological zero. The surface temperature of the exposed parts of the body is usually between 30–32° C. (86–90° F.). If the left hand is placed in a jar of water with a temperature of 20° C. and the right hand in water of 40° C., the left hand will at first have the sensation of cold and the right hand of warmth; soon, however, both hands will have no sensation of cold or warmth at all, because of adaptation to the two temperatures. On placing both hands then in a jar of water with a temperature of 30° C., the sensation for the left hand will be that of warmth and for the right that of cold: the same temperature appears cold and warm at the same time. The *limit of adaptation,* according to experimenters, ranges from about 16° C. to about 40–42° C. As a rule, adaptation is impossible below this minimum and above this maximum temperature; in other words, in most individuals, anything below 16° C. will always be experienced as cold and anything above 42° C. as warm, without a physiological zero being established.

This description concludes our examination of the cutaneous senses of pressure, pain, cold, and warmth. They are *exteroceptive* senses. Next in line among the somesthetic senses are the *intraorganic senses.*

The Visceral Senses

There are two main types of intraorganic senses, the interoceptive and the proprioceptive. Two kinds of senses are *interoceptive:* the *visceral* senses and the *static* sense. They are called 'interoceptive,' because in their case the stimulus is not furnished by objects outside the organism but by organs lying far beneath the skin in the *interior* of the body. Through them we become aware of sensations aroused by stimuli originating within the body itself. One set of stimuli has its source in the *viscera,* or, generally speaking, in the vegetative organs. Sensations arising from this set of stimuli acquaint us with the condition of our internal organs. The senses mediating these sensations are termed the *visceral senses.* The other set of stimuli has its source in the inner ear. Sensations produced by this set make us conscious of the equilibrium present or absent in the position of our body; hence the term *static* sense. The visceral senses will be described first.

Perhaps the best way to treat the visceral senses is to describe the *various kinds of visceral sensations.* 'Visceral sensations' are those which are aroused through changes of the inner organs and have the purpose of acquainting us with the condition of our organism, particularly with *the disturbed functions of vegetative life.* These sensations are many and diverse.

Some pertain to the musculature. Among these may be mentioned the sensation of fatigue, of freshness, of strength, of weakness, of relief after bodily strain in work, etc.

Others pertain to the nutrition system. The sensations of hunger and thirst stand out prominently. *Hunger* comes from the need of solid food. It is localized in the mouth, the throat, and the stomach. It manifests itself as a sort of dull pressure in the region of the stomach, but it may eventually turn into a painful sensation. *Thirst* is a sensation expressing the need of fluids in the system and is localized in the soft palate. It is assumed that a deficiency of lymph causes the membrane of the palate to shrink, thereby causing a stimulation of touch corpuscles present in that region. *Nausea* is a pronounced disgust or loathing of food, often accompanied by the vomiting reflex; nausea is primarily localized in the throat.

Functional disturbances of the *digestive* tract manifest themselves in a variety of sensations, ranging all the way from the dull discomfiture of a general malaise to the sharp, spastic pains of griping, etc. These sensations may be only generally localized in the abdomen or sharply localized in a definite area, depending on the affected organs and the degree of functional disturbance. When the organs perform their operations in a normal manner, we are unconscious of their presence.

Then, there are sensations arising in connection with the *respiratory* and *circulatory* systems. In violent exertion, we experience a constriction of the chest; in asthmatic conditions, a sensation of suffocation; after shock or a fast run, a painful contraction of the heart, etc. Associated with the functioning of the circulatory sensations are shuddering, itch, 'goose flesh,' and tingling, etc.; these are blended sensations in which pressure, pain, and other sensations are mixed.

In general, it should be noted that the organic sensations convey *little cognitive information,* but involve strong feelings. Their purpose is the *protection* of the organism in its vital functions, demanding imperatively our attention so as to obtain a correction of functional or organic disorders. Hence, pressure, pain, warmth (fever), and cold (chills) play such an important part in the pattern of visceral sensations.

For a long time the opinion was prevalent that the internal organs are insensitive to external stimuli. This belief was based on the statement of surgeons. Even severe handling of the internal organs do not seem to produce any definite sensory reactions. However, experimentation under favorable conditions shows that sensibility to chemical, thermal, mechanical, and electrical stimuli is present, and positive reactions result in practically all regions, if not to all stimuli, then at least to some. Exact localization is usually difficult to determine, since the vegetative organs as a whole have only a very indirect connection with the conscious centers of the cortex.

It is very *doubtful* whether any *special senses* participate in visceral sensations. No unusual anatomic structures have been discovered so far which might be construed as being new sensory organs, different from those already described in cutaneous reactions. Apparently, the receptors of pressure, pain, cold, and warmth combine in the viscera in various patterns and thus give rise to different visceral sensations.

The Static Sense

The *static sense* is an intraorganic sense, the end organs of which lie in the internal ear and are stimulated by the pull of gravity and by head movements. It is also termed the 'labyrinthine,' 'vestibular,' and 'equilibrium' sense. The name 'static' or 'equilibrium' sense is used, because this sense acquaints us with the position of our body in rest and motion. The name 'labyrinthine' or 'vestibular' sense is used, because the 'labyrinth' and 'vestibule' refer to the internal ear where this sense is located.

The *organ* of the static sense consists of a number of specialized parts: the *semicircular canals, ampullae, utricle,* and *saccule.* The semicircular canals are filled with a liquid and stand roughly in the directions of three planes placed at right angles to one another, like the floor and the two joined walls of a room. At the base of each canal the structure bulges out into a vase-like formation, the ampulla. A vestibule or chamber unites the canals in the region of the ampullae. The ampullae have cells with hair-like endings which are mechanically stimulated by the pressure of the liquid, or endolymph, present in the canals and ampullae. The utricle and saccule contain otoliths which are minute crystals of carbonate of lime. The entire structure is frequently called the 'labyrinth.'

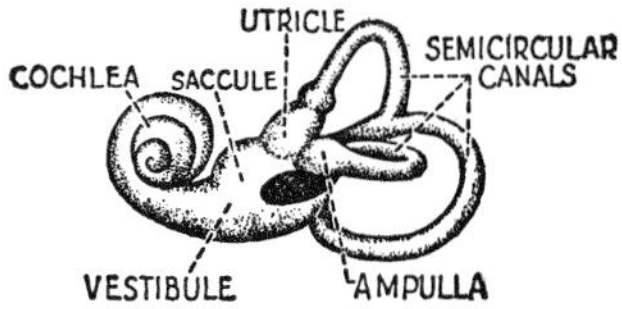

Fig. 16. Vestibular Organ of the Static Sense.

The *functions* of these parts are presumed to be as follows. The *semicircular canals* are directly concerned with *rotary movements of the head* and indirectly thereby also with rotary movements of the body, provided the head and body act as a unit and have the same movement without changing their position relative to each other. No matter in what plane the head rotates, the liquid of one or the other of the canals will be affected by the movement. The liquid, or endolymph, presses against the cell hairtips of the ampulla, bending them out of their normal position. These hairtips stimulate the receptor cells in which they are rooted, and these receptor cells respond with a nerve impulse which results in the sensation of rotary movement. As the rotary movement continues, the endolymph adjusts itself, and the hairtips return to their normal position, the stimulation ceasing. As for the functions of the *otoliths,* it is assumed that an inclination of the head in any direction causes these little stony particles to sag and thereby bend the hairs in which they are embedded, producing a stimulation of the receptor cells. This stimulation continues as long as the head (and body) deviates from its normal *position.* The static sense, therefore, is a sense of positional equilibrium and orientation in head movements.

The position of the vestibular organ in the interior of the head makes experimental *verification* of these assumptions very difficult. Whatever evidence there is, confirms the assumptions. Pressure on the canals, anesthetization, inflammation, resection, partial or total destruction of the labyrinth, etc., show effects of interference with the equilibrium of the bodily members just as happens in change of movement and position. An example. When normal people rotate around the axis of their body and come to a stop, they experience the illusion of rotation for some time and have the feeling of dizziness. Those deafmutes, however, whose vestibular organ is destroyed, experience no dizziness after rotary movement and proceed to walk without the staggering gait observed in normal people; on the other hand, it is claimed that they lack the sense of orientation when immersed under water with closed eyes. Ordinarily, like other people, deafmutes are able to know and maintain their body positions through visual cues, body pressure from surrounding objects (e.g., the pressure of the earth against their feet when standing, or the pressure of the bed against their body when lying down), and gravitational pull. When these factors are more or less neutralized (as through immersion under water with closed eyes), their sense of positional equilibrium is lacking, due to the absence of the vestibular organ. When the otoliths of a fish have been removed, it also lacks body equilibrium and is indifferent to position.

Impulses from the vestibular organ are transmitted to reflex centers of the brain stem and cerebellum, producing compensatory adjustments of the head and limbs and oscillatory movements of the eyes (nystagmus). 'Sea-sickness,' 'train-sickness,' 'car-sickness,' 'elevator-sickness,' and 'plane-sickness' are visceral reflex reactions sometimes originating from vestibular impulses. A considerable amount of *adaptation* is possible, as can be seen in the case of acrobats, whirling dancers, and aviators; they adjust themselves quickly after violent movements.

The Kinesthetic Sense

The last of the somesthetic senses is the *kinesthetic sense.* It mediates sensations of the *position* and of the active and passive *movements* of the *bodily members* in relation to one another. By 'active' movements are meant movements of our limbs which we execute voluntarily, through our own effort; by 'passive' movements, those movements of our limbs executed through someone else, as when someone lifts our hand without active participation or resistance on our part.

A number of different *sensations* must be considered with reference to the kinesthetic sense. There are sensations with regard to the *position* of the members in bodily *posture.* We know, for example, even without looking, whether the arm is raised or lowered, whether our knees are flexed or straight, whether our fingers are clenched or relaxed, etc. Again, we experience sensations acquainting us with the *movements* of our limbs. In passive movements these sensations are localized apparently in the joints; in active movements they are localized more in the tensed muscles. Then, we have the sensation of *resistance.* In pushing against a solid wall, we not only experience touch and pressure on the surface of the hand, but also resistance in the joints of the hand, elbow, and shoulder. Finally, there is the sensation of *weight,* localized in the joints, tendons, and muscles.

Sensations seem necessary for *voluntary* movements. Such movements are apparently impossible whenever sensations are excluded. In the cases of organic loss of sensibility, where no sensory impulses reach the cortex of the cerebrum from the limbs themselves, patients cannot voluntarily move these limbs, even though the motor centers and nerves be intact, nor are they conscious of any passive movements executed by others. But if they can see their limbs, they can perform voluntary movements without any difficulty, provided the motor centers and nerves be intact. In normal persons such movements are possible even with the eyes closed. These facts indicate that in normal, voluntary movements sensory impulses must travel from the muscles to the brain in order that such movements can be executed.

There is uncertainty in the minds of physiologists as to the particular *organ* which serves as the reception for kinesthetic stimuli. For a long time the *muscles* were considered to be the anatomical substrate for this sense, and accordingly it was named the 'muscle sense.' This view, at least in this exclusive and simple form, had to be abandoned. In some pathological cases, where the muscles had degenerated and were totally inactive, the patients preserved the sensations of posture and resistance and recognized the passive movements of their limbs. The muscle, as such, therefore, is not the organ of the kinesthetic sense. Others sought to reduce the kinesthetic sensations to *skin pressure* or to the *feeling of innervation* of the muscles. It was found, however, that the pressure sense could be destroyed, while the sensations of active and passive movement continued. The feeling of the innervation of the muscles in movements is, no doubt, an important factor in the normal sensing of voluntary movements, but it can hardly be the true kinesthetic sense. Some patients, after an accident, were able to execute movements correctly as ordered, but they did not know, unless they looked, whether they had actually made the movements. They innervated their muscles and were aware of the feeling of innervation, yet they were unaware of the movements themselves.

Perhaps the fundamental form of sensation concerning the position and movement of our members is that of *muscular tension.* Pressure, touch, and the feeling of innervation no doubt play an important part in normal kinesthetic sensation, but there are two structures which seem to have a special significance in this connection: the *muscle spindles and the end organs of Golgi.*

The *muscle spindle* is a capsulated bundle of muscle fibers (Weissmann fascicle) located in a muscle close to where the fibers of this muscle pass over into tendinous fibers. The capsule is connected with the tissue of the muscle by an outer layer of connective tissue. Besides the motor nerves which terminate in motor plates on the muscle fibers, a set of sensory nerves enter the spindle and coil around the muscle fibers of the spindle. Any contraction of the ordinary muscle is thus bound to stimulate these nerves of the capsulated muscle spindle and transmit a sensory impulse. The tendons possess similar spindle-shaped structures, the *end organs of Golgi.* Their function must be the same as those of the muscle spindles. There are, then, two special structures in the muscles and tendons situated where they are capable of localizing sensations of position, movement, resistance, etc. The neuro-muscular end organs of the muscle spindles register muscular contraction and thereby enable us to experience the position of our members. The neuro-tendinous end organs of Golgi register intense muscular effort, acquainting us with the resistance offered by objects.

Besides these two special structures, numerous *corpuscles of Ruffini* are located around the tendons, the capsules of the joints, and the periosteum (membrane of connective tissue investing the bones), while *corpuscles of Pacini* are present around the joints. The former probably react to tension, and the latter to pressure. It would therefore seem that they also play a part in the general pattern of kinesthetic sensations as a whole, though a minor one, whereas the muscle spindles and the tendon spindles have the major roles.

The kinesthetic receptors are termed *proprioceptive,* because they are activated by stimuli produced within the organism by movement or tension in its own tissues.

Kinesthetic sensations are very important for the performance of properly co-ordinated bodily movements. Impairment brings on serious disturbances. Ataxia, or the inability to co-ordinate voluntary movements, is an abnormal condition due to impairment of kinesthetic function.

All the somesthetic senses — pressure, pain, temperature, visceral, static, and kinesthetic — have as their primary purpose the *protection and well-being of the organism as a whole.* None of these senses acts as an isolated sensory unit. Their functions are interrelated and interdependent. They serve the organism in performing the normal activities of its vital organs and in safeguarding its integrity against injurious influences from within and from without; at the same time they convey much information about the environment in which man lives. The somesthetic senses show that man is an *integral organism.*

Summary of Chapter IV

Sense cognition is mediated through various bodily structures called the *receptors* or *sense organs.*

1. *Sensation and Perception.* A *sense* is a specialized mechanism or function by virtue of which an animal organism is receptive and responsive to a certain class of physical stimuli, resulting in knowledge of some sort. *Sensation* is a conscious experience aroused by the stimulation of an organ of sense. *Perception* is the cognizing of the object which produces the sensation.

2. *The Senses.* The *internal senses* are the central or synthetic sense, imagination, sense memory, and instinct. The *external senses* are sight, hearing, taste, smell, and the somesthetic senses. The somesthetic senses are the cutaneous senses of pressure, pain, warmth, and cold, and the intraorganic senses, i.e., the visceral sense, static sense, and kinesthetic sense. Sight, hearing, taste, smell, warmth, cold, pressure, and pain are *exteroceptive;* the visceral and static senses are *interoceptive;* and the kinesthetic sense is *proprioceptive.*

3. *The Cutaneous or Skin Senses.* The cutaneous senses are located in the skin region, and they are the senses of pressure, pain, warmth, and cold. The skin contains various types of nerve endings associated with the cutaneous sensations: *capsules, Pacinian* and *Meissner corpuscles, Krause bulbs,* and the *end organs of Ruffini.*

4. *The Sense of Pressure.* The stimulus is anything which, upon contact, alters the even surface of the skin. Hair follicles serve as receptors of touch and pressure; most likely also Meissner corpuscles and perhaps free nerve endings.

5. *The Sense of Pain.* The stimulus is some object which injures or nearly injures nerve tissue. The pain receptors are the free nerve endings.

6. *The Temperature Sense.* It is still somewhat uncertain whether this is a single sense or whether there is a distinct sense of warmth and a distinct sense of cold. Most probably they are separate and distinct senses. Investigators associate the sensation of cold with the Krause bulbs and that of warmth with the end organs of Ruffini; others look for the true stimulus source in the blood vessels. The sensation of 'heat' results from the stimulation of adjacent warmth and cold spots.

6. *The Visceral Senses.* The visceral senses and the static sense are *interoceptive.* The *visceral senses* have the source of their stimuli in the viscera or vegetative organs. There are several kinds of visceral *sensations:* some pertain to the musculature, some to the nutrition system, some to the digestive tract, and some to the respiratory and circulatory systems. It is doubtful whether any special senses participate in visceral sensations; apparently, the receptors of pressure, pain, cold, and warmth combine in various patterns and thus give rise to visceral sensations.

8. *The Static Sense.* It is an intraorganic sense, the end organs of which lie in the internal ear and are stimulated by the pull of gravity and by head movements. The *organ* consists of the semicircular canals, ampullae, utricle, and saccule. The canals, with their endolymph, acquaint us with the *rotary movements* of the head. The utricle and saccule, with their otoliths, ac-

quaint us with any deviations of the head and body from their normal *positions.* The static sense is a sense of positional equilibrium and orientation in head movements.

9. *The Kinesthetic Sense.* It mediates sensations of the *position* and of the active and passive *movements of the bodily members.* We also experience sensations of resistance and weight. The *organs* are probably muscle spindles and tendon spindles. Corpuscles of Ruffini and Pacini, in all probability, also play a part in these sensations.

Readings

Harmon, F. L., *Principles of Psychology,* Ch. 5. — Moore, T. V., *Cognitive Psychology,* Part III, Ch. I and *Dynamic Psychology,* Part VI, Ch. V. — Woodworth, R. S., *Experimental Psychology,* Ch. XIX.

CHAPTER V

SMELL, TASTE, HEARING

SMELL and taste are 'chemical senses' because they are activated by chemical stimuli. They are also reckoned, together with the somesthetic senses, among the 'lower' senses, while hearing and sight belong to the 'higher.' Smell and taste have more of a nutritive value, while hearing and sight have more of a cognitive value, and nutrition is of a lower order than cognition. Since the logical procedure is to pass from the lower to the higher, smell and taste must be discussed first, then hearing and sight.

The Sense of Smell

Smell is the sense by which *certain properties of bodies* (called their smell, odor, or scent) *become known through the stimulation of receptors responsive to chemical substances in a gaseous form or to minute particles which reach them normally from a distance and in low concentration.*

The *organ* of smell is a brown-yellow spot of the mucous membrane of the nose, about the size of a ten-cent piece, situated in a little pocket above the ordinary nostril chamber and connected with it through a narrow cleft. Its location places it apart from any direct contact with the inhaled and exhaled air and protects it against dust, insects, etc., and also against sudden changes of temperature. Odorous particles mingle with the air and are inhaled into the nostrils through breathing; they then reach the olfactory spot through diffusion or through eddies in the air currents produced by sniffing. Foods and liquids taken into the mouth also give off odorous particles which are exhaled with the breath; a part or all of this exhaled breath is forced up into the nasal cavities from the rear of the mouth, and in this manner the olfactory receptors are stimulated by the odor of foods and liquids. The *receptors* are nerve cells situated within the membrane of the olfactory spot; slender nerve endings (dendrites) reach out from the cells peripherally to the membrane surface, while axons of the cells extend inward to the olfactory bulb at the base of the brain, where connections are made with the olfactory center in the cerebrum.

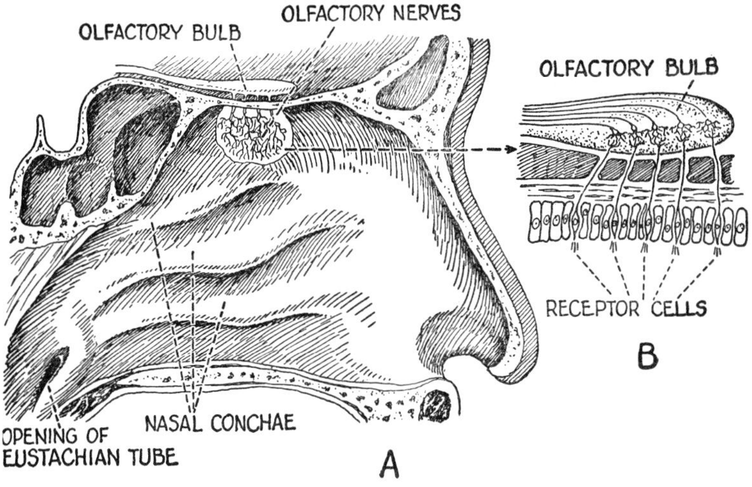

Fig. 17. Organ of Smell.

A. Relative position of the olfactory organ and the nasal cavity. — B. Enlarged cross section of the receptor cells.

The *stimulus* for the sense of smell is a *gas* in which odorous *particles* are suspended. Formerly it was thought by some that objects send off vibrations to the nose and thereby produce the sensation of smell; and the reason for this view was the alleged fact that certain strongly odorous substances, such as musk, apparently lost no weight even over long periods of time. It is now known that minute particles are released from such substances at all times. The vibration theory has received a positive refutation through the fact that a complete stoppage of the nasal cavities excludes completely the sensation of smell, although vibrations may still reach the interior of the nose. It is now universally accepted that solids and fluids must volatilize before their odorous qualities can be sensed. Usually the minute particles thus liberated mix with gaseous air and thus influence the sense organ. E. H. Weber filled the nasal cavities completely with eau de cologne and experienced no sensation of smell; eau de cologne must volatilize and diffuse into the air before it can act as a stimulus.

Some vapors and gases are odorous; others are not. It seems that the *chemical constitution* of a substance and the *specific receptivity* of the receptor cells determine whether a particular substance can arouse a sensation of smell and what kind of smell. The pure elements, with the exception of the halogens (fluorine, chlorine, bromine, iodine), are nonodorous. Most odorous substances are *carbon compounds*. It is estimated that only sixteen elements enter into combinations which emit odors perceptible to man. Arranged according to the chemical families to which they belong, these are: hydrogen; carbon, silicon; nitrogen, phosphorus, arsenic, antimony, bismuth; oxygen, sulphur, selenium, tellurium; fluorine, chlorine, bromine, iodine. Similar compounds within a chemical family usually possess similar odorous qualities. The quality of a substance, determining whether or not it can act as a stimulus for smell, depends apparently upon the atomic or molecular grouping of a substance. In accordance with this view, some scientists have proposed the theory that *electronic oscillation* is the stimulus for the sense of smell; thus Haycraft, Heyninx, and Zwaardemaker. This theory is interesting, but as yet it lacks experimental verification to a considerable degree. It is plausible that the organ of smell is a *composite organ,* consisting of different types of cells with specific reactions. Rollett induced a total anosmia (lack of the sense of smell) in himself; as the anosmia waned, smell revived gradually and that in a very definite order. Similarly, when the organ of smell becomes fatigued through overstimulation from a particular odor and responds sluggishly, it will also respond sluggishly to odors related to the first. Partial destruction of the sense of smell occurs, so that certain types of odors are eliminated while others can still be sensed.

Concerning the *classification of odors,* no system has been devised which gives complete satisfaction. Linnaeus (1756) was the first to make an attempt at a scientific classification. He enumerated *seven* fundamental types of odors: aromatic (typical: carnation), fragrant (lily), ambrosial (musk), alliaceous (garlic), hircine (valerian), repulsive (some bugs), nauseous (rotten meat). Zwaardemaker (1925) added two classes to the list of Linnaeus, placing 'ethereal' odors at the head before the aromatic odors and 'empyreumatic' odors after the alliaceous; ether is an example of the ethereal group, and roasted coffee of the empyreumatic group. He also subdivided the various classes and endeavored to find a place for the odorous compounds of organic chemistry. The four at the beginning of the list are 'nutritive' odors, the rest 'decomposed' odors. Henning (1924), after extensive experiments with no less than 415 odorous substances, arrived at the following classification:

Fragrant — heliotrope, etc.	Spicy — cloves, etc.
Fruity — apple, etc.	Putrid — carrion, etc.
Resinous — turpentine, etc.	Burned — coffee, etc.

Much experimentation with odors has been done, and some phenomena are noteworthy. *Fatigue,* with *adaptation* to the stimulus, is common. Continued exposure to the same stimulus weakens the sensation, if the stimulus is strong; if the stimulus is a mild odor, sensation usually disappears completely. The *mixture* of odor stimuli produces diverse results. In most cases, one experiences a blend of odors; the components are individually perceptible, though the total impression is unitary. In the case of a great dissimilarity between two component stimuli, the usual experience is to sense first the one, then the other, successively. Another phenomenon which occurs, according to some investigators but denied by others, is *compensation* or *neutralization*. Some stimuli, when combined, simply cancel out each other. It is claimed that the stimuli of caoutchouc and wax or paraffin neutralize each other.

One often speaks of odors which are 'sweet,' 'sour,' 'pungent, 'bitter,' etc. These are, in all probability, not qualities of odors as such. End organs for pressure, pain, cold, and warmth are located in the nostrils and in the rear portion of the mouth, and it is obvious that they, too, are stimulated by odorous gases; combined sensations are the result. If the sense of taste is eliminated, chloroform no longer smells 'sweet'; and if the sense of smell is eliminated, the sweetness of chloroform remains. Taste and smell, due to the close proximity of their end organs and the similarity of their stimulation as chemical senses, are intimately connected in function, so that the stimulus of the one is frequently referred to the other. In ordinary life, it is practically impossible to separate the two.

The Sense of Taste

Taste is the sense by which certain *qualities* (taste, savor, flavor) *of soluble substances become known by contact with a particular set of epithelial end organs (taste buds) located mainly in the papillae of the tongue.*

The *organs* of taste are the *taste buds,* and they are present in great numbers in pimplelike protuberances called papillae. These papillae are found mainly on the tip, sides, and rear portion of the tongue, but some also in the soft palate and in the throat; the middle portion of the tongue is devoid of taste sensitivity.

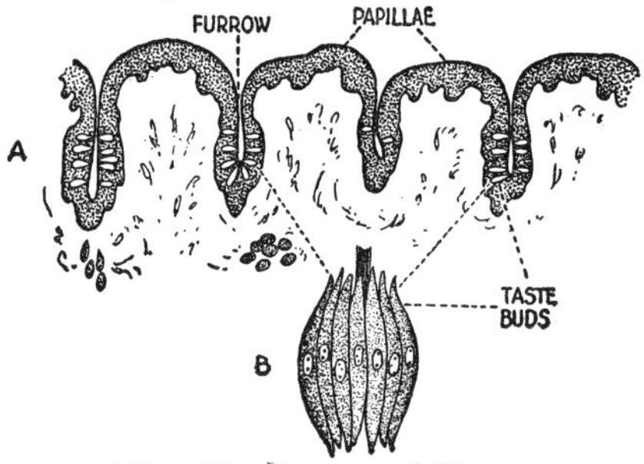

Fig. 18. Organ of Taste.

A. Cross section of the tongue.—
B. Taste bud (greatly enlarged).

The *stimuli* are chemical substances which must be *soluble* to some extent; insoluble substances are tasteless. Vapors and gases can be tasted; ordinarily, however, substances enter the mouth in a solid or fluid condition. Upon contact with the tongue, particles in solution seep down from the surface of the tongue through little crevices or canals into the interior of the taste buds and there stimulate the actual *taste cells.* Pressure of the tongue against the roof of the mouth facilitates stimulation by forcing the solution into the taste buds. The brushlike endings of the sensory nerves in the taste buds carry the impulse along the lingual and glossopharyngeal nerves to the gustatory center of the brain.

As in the case of the sense of smell, the sensations of taste very rarely appear alone; they are mixed with those of smell and with those of the cutaneous senses. It is difficult to eliminate these extraneous components; but when they are eliminated, it is found that the *number of sensations* is no more than four: *sour, salty, sweet,* and *bitter.* Such, at least, is the general opinion today. There are not even subgroups or variations of these four. Substances of the same concentration always have the same sour, salty, sweet, or bitter taste, whatever happens to be the flavor of these particular substances. When we speak of a 'hot,' 'cool,' 'pungent,' 'astringent,' taste, etc., one or the other or several of the cutaneous senses are certain to be involved as component factors.

The *localization* of the various tastes shows that they are distributed unevenly. While some papillae respond only to sour or to bitter or to sweet, others respond to two or three kinds of stimuli, and many to all four. Definite areas of the tongue are more sensitive to one kind of stimulus than to another. Experimentation proves that sensitivity to sweet is strongest at the tip of the tongue and decreases gradually in strength toward the back; the sensitivity to bitter is strongest in the rear portion of the tongue and becomes gradually weaker toward the front; the sensitivity to sour is strongest at the edges in the middle of the tongue and weakest toward the front and back; sensitivity to a salty flavor is strongest toward the front and side areas of the tongue. One kind of taste is independent of the other because one kind can be impaired and even lost without affecting the others.

This evidence seems to warrant the conclusion that there are *four types of receptors* in the sense of taste, so that certain receptor cells in the papillae respond only to certain stimuli. Many physiologists assume that the hydrogen ion is the stimulating agent in the sour taste, and the anion in the salty taste, while sweet and bitter substances react with the lipoid (fatlike) substance present in the taste cells. It is a probable theory that the four principal tastes are the result of a chemical reaction between four receptive substances in the cells and the sapid substances placed upon the tongue. That the physiological process is chemical in nature, is without doubt; but the exact details of the process are still very obscure.

Adaptation is a common phenomenon in taste sensations, as everyday experience proves. A sweet solution tastes sweetest at first contact; afterward it tastes less sweet. The concentration of a solution must be increased many times after adaptation before the sensation can be aroused again. Adaptation varies. It is least in the case of sour and salty solutions, greater in the case of bitter, and greatest in the case of sweet.

Individually and in their combination, the senses of smell and taste enable us to recognize many properties of substances and thereby the substances themselves. Their primary purpose is obviously to supply us with the necessary cues to distinguish between what is good or harmful for the organism in the line of food and drink. Bitter substances, for instance, have lower threshold values than sweet; that is to say, it takes a much smaller amount of bitter than of sweet substances in order to arouse sensation. The majority of bitter substances are alkaloids and therefore frequently poisonous, while sweet substances are usually energy giving and as such beneficial. We shun the bitter and crave the sweet; the difference in threshold value thus manifests biological purposiveness.

The Sense of Hearing

Hearing is the sense by which the *vibrations of certain media acting upon the ear become known as sounds.* The human ear is a marvelous neural mechanism. Consider a symphony orchestra with its manifold types of instruments, its constantly progressing and changing melodies, its shifting keys and chords, its harmonies and dissonances, its slow and rushing tempos, its whispering pianissimos and thundering fortissimos — the ear is capable of detecting, distinguishing, and analyzing all these confusing factors with a nicety and assurance that is truly amazing. A minute piece of organic structure in the head thus reacts selectively to a veritable flood of intermingling air waves emanating from vibrating bodies. It is but natural, therefore, that physicists have made an intensive study of sound waves, that anatomists have subjected the ear to a thorough microscopical examination, that physiologists have endeavored to trace the function of hearing from start to finish, and that psychologists have conducted innumerable experiments in auditory sensation and perception.

Since the ear is the organ of hearing and hearing is the power or act of detecting sound, it is important to understand precisely what is meant by *sound,* because the physicist and the psychologist attach a different meaning to the term 'sound.' To the *psychologist* 'sound' is a *sensation* caused by the stimulation of the auditory nerves and the auditory center of the brain. To the *physicist* 'sound' is a form of *vibrational energy* transmitted through an elastic medium (e.g., air) in external nature. The physicist considers 'sounds' to be identical with the 'vibrations' in so far as they proceed from a vibrating or 'sounding' body and travel through a medium, irrespective of whether or not they are heard by an ear. The psychologist, on the other hand, considers 'sound' to be identical with the 'conscious experience of tonal qualities' resulting from the stimulation of the neural mechanism of the organ of hearing, after the stimulus (the sound wave of the physicist) has acted upon the organ. The viewpoint of the physicist is that of one studying the external objective *agent* which eventually arouses the sensation of hearing, while the viewpoint of the psychologist is that of one examining the internal subjective act of *conscious response* to this external objective agent. Both viewpoints are legitimate. In order to avoid a confusion of ideas, however, it is well to know this difference in meaning. In the following discussion both meanings occur, and the context shows which of the two is intended at the moment.

It will be necessary to touch on the main features brought to light on the mechanism of the *human ear,* on the nature of *physical sound,* and on the *relationship between the two.*

The Human Ear

The *organ* of hearing is the *ear.* In man the ear consists of three distinct parts: the *outer* ear, the *middle* ear, and the *inner* ear.

The *outer ear* of man is designed to collect sound waves and transmit them to the middle ear. One part of the outer ear is the shell-like or trumpet-like structure, called the *pinna* or *auricle,* which extends outward from the side of the head. Man has muscles in his ears which indicate that he was able at one time, no doubt in the far past, to move them for directional purposes. In the vast majority of human beings these muscles are atrophied, so that the external ears are of little use. More important for hearing is the canal, or *external auditory meatus,* which leads into the interior of the head and permits the air waves to come into contact with the ear drum. The *ear drum,* or *tympanic membrane,* is a membrane which stretches across the external meatus like the head of a drum and thus closes off the inner end of the external meatus and separates it from the middle ear.

The *middle ear* is an air-filled cavity within the skull, situated immediately behind the tympanic membrane. This membrane, therefore, is the end of the external ear and the beginning of the middle ear. The air waves, passing along the external auditory meatus, strike against the tympanic membrane and produce vibrations in it which correspond to the vibrations in the air. From the tympanic membrane these vibrations are now carried forward by *three small bones,* or *ossicles,* across the cavity of the middle ear. The first of these bones is the

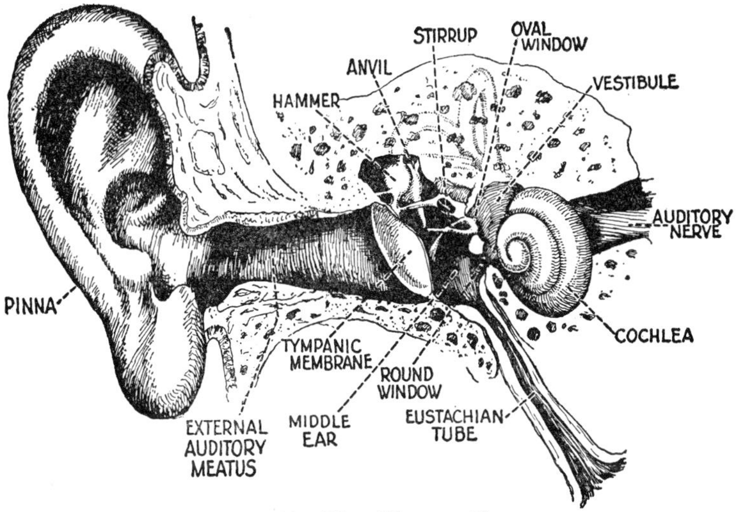

Fig. 19. The Human Ear.

hammer, or *malleus.* The handle of the malleus extends down toward the center of the tympanic membrane, where it is permanently attached. The second bone is the *anvil,* or *incus,* which is attached to the head of the hammer. The incus has a tapering prolongation, the lower extremity of which is attached to the *stirrup,* or *stapes,* the third bone in the series. The stirrup, on its part, is attached to the membrane of the *oval window,* or *fenestra ovalis,* of the internal ear. The arrangement and articulation of these three small bones is an ingenious contrivance of levers, to transmit the vibrations of the tympanic membrane across the space of the middle ear to the inner ear and also to absorb any injurious shocks. The inner ear, the real organ of hearing, is a delicate mechanism. The tympanum is often exposed to explosive shocks of excessively strong air waves, so that a direct contact between the tympanum and the inner ear might do serious harm. The ossicles act as shock absorbers, while serving as vibration communicators between the tympanum and the inner ear. In order to equalize the air pressure on both sides of the tympanic membrane and thus protect it against rupturing, a tubal opening connects the middle ear with the posterior portion of the nasal cavity; this opening is the 'eustachian tube.'

By means of the three ossicles, vibrations reach the *inner ear.* The inner ear contains a number of structures: the semicircular canals, the vestibule, and the cochlea. The semicircular canals have nothing to do with the sense of hearing, but are a part of the static sense; the cochlea belongs exclusively to the sense of hearing; the vestibule belongs to the static sense, but it also has an important function in connection with hearing.

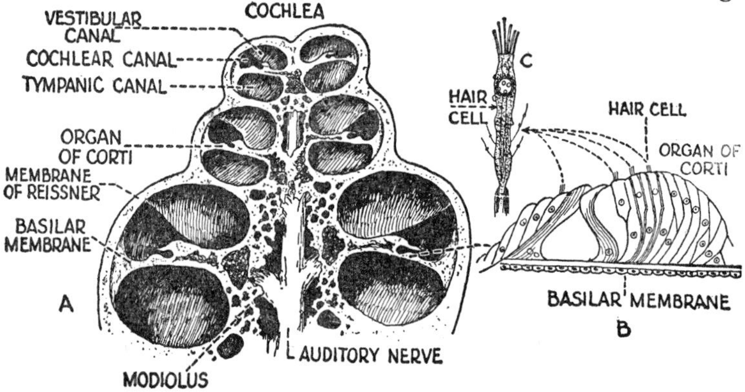

Fig. 20. Cross Section of the Organ of Hearing.

A. Cross section of the cochlea (enlarged). — B. Cross section of the organ of Corti (greatly enlarged). — C. Receptor cell (very much enlarged).

The inner ear is completely surrounded by the bone structure of the head, except for a portion of the vestibule which borders on, and is exposed to, the cavity of the middle ear. All the organs of the inner ear are enclosed in a bony casing. The casing is pierced in the region of the middle ear by two openings which are covered by membranes: the 'oval window' or *fenestra ovalis,* just mentioned, and the 'round window' or *fenestra rotunda.* The purpose of these two membrane-covered openings will soon be described.

The *cochlea* contains the real organ of hearing. It is a bony casing or housing, shaped spirally like a snail's shell; hence the name. Its spiral has two and one half turns and is built around a conical bony core, the *modiolus.* The cochlea is divided throughout its entire length into two main sections by means of the *basilar membrane* which stretches transversely across the cochlear cavity from the modiolus to the outer casing. The two channels formed thereby are the *vestibular canal* and the *tympanic canal.* The vestibular canal ends at the 'oval window,' while the tympanic canal terminates at the 'round window.' At the upper end or apex of the cochlea, both canals are in communication with each other through a small opening, the 'helicotrema.' The vestibular and tympanic canals are filled with a fluid called *perilymph.* The function of this fluid is evident. When the stirrup communicates its vibrations to the membrane of the 'oval window,' this membrane, in turn, relays the vibrations to the perilymph of the vestibular canal; through the helicotrema these vibrations pass over into the tympanic canal; in this manner the vibrations travel from the base of the cochlea to the apex and from the apex back to the base and to the membrane of the 'round window.' Since liquids are practically incompressible, the membrane of the 'round window' must equalize the pressure exerted upon the membrane of the 'oval window' by the vibrating stirrup bone. The minute vibrations are thus transmitted through the perilymph with full vigor.

There is, however, a *third canal* in the cochlea, the most important of the three canals. It is triangular in shape and is formed by the *membrane of Reissner.* This membrane runs from the cochlear casing at an angle to the basilar membrane, near the point where the basilar membrane is joined to the modiolus. The base of the triangle is thus the bony casing of the cochlea, and the two sides of the triangle, converging to a point near the modiolus, are the basilar membrane and the membrane of Reissner. A part of the vestibular canal is thus cut off to form this third canal, the *cochlear canal* or *ductus cochlearis*. Its location is between the vestibular canal and the tympanic canal, and it, too, runs through the entire length of the spiral. The cochlear canal is filled with a liquid called the *endolymph*, the purpose of which is to take up the vibrations transmitted through the perilymph to the Reissner membrane and carry them to the 'organ of Corti.'

The Organ of Corti

The *organ of Corti* is the *neurological organ of hearing*. It is to the ear what the retina is to the eye. All the structures described so far are accessory structures leading the vibrations of the sonorous bodies to the actual organ of hearing, the organ of Corti.

The organ of Corti is situated *on the basilar membrane* in the cochlear canal. Transverse fibers, estimated at about 24,000, are stretched across the basilar membrane; they vary in length, the longest being about three times the length of the shortest. The organ of Corti is microscopical in size. In it are found the *receptor cells* of hearing, resting on the transverse fibers of the basilar membrane. These cells are 'hair cells'; that is to say, certain hairlike terminations protrude from them, and these 'hairs' are embedded in the *tectorial membrane* which extends out into the endolymph nearly halfway across the canal. Whatever vibrations pass through the endolymph bend these 'hairs' back and forth. In this manner the vibrations act as a stimulus for the hair cells; a nerve impulse is produced in the nerves terminating in the cells; these auditory nerves pass through the modiolus, make their exit at the base of the cochlear spiral, form the eighth cranial nerve, and go to the midbrain and from there to the superior gyrus of the cerebral cortex. The result of this nerve impulse is the *sensation of sound*.

From this description of the outer, middle, and inner ear it is obvious that the air vibrations, taken up by the outer ear, never reach the cochlea and the organ of Corti. The air vibrations become vibrations of the ear drum; these become vibrations of the three ossicles, the hammer, anvil, and stirrup; these become vibrations of the membrane of the oval window; these become vibrations of the perilymph in the vestibular and tympanic canals; these become vibrations of the membrane of Reissner; these become vibrations of the endolymph of the cochlear canal; and these vibrations are the proximate stimulus for the receptor cells of the organ of Corti. While the air vibrations are the normal ones to start the chain of vibrations which eventually lead to the hearing of sound, they are not strictly necessary. People whose outer or middle ear is very defective can hear if the vibrations are transmitted to the cochlea through the bones of the head. Vibrations are necessary for hearing, but they need not be vibrations of air.

Sound as Sensation

Upon stimulation of the receptor cells in the organ of Corti, the nerve impulse produced there travels up to the auditory center of the cerebrum. We now *consciously experience sound;* this conscious experience of sound is what is meant by the sensation of sound or *sound as sensation.* In considering sound sensation, we are not interested in the type of vibration which acted as the stimulus for arousing the receptor cells, but merely in our conscious experience which is the end result of this stimulation; in other words, we are interested in the conscious effect, not in the physical cause.

Viewed from this standpoint, we are conscious of *two main kinds* of sounds: *tones* and *noises.* There is a fundamental difference between the two kinds, although we usually encounter a mixture of both. As given in our subjective experience, 'tones' are something clear, musical, agreeable, while 'noises' are more or less harsh, unmusical, disagreeable. One need but think of the preliminary tuning-up exercises of a band just prior to playing, and the actual rendition of a concert piece, in order to understand the difference between 'noises' and 'tones.'

Sounds, considered psychologically, have *three chief characteristics:* pitch, loudness, and timbre.

Pitch. The pitch of a sound is designated by the expressions *high* and *low.* These expressions are metaphors taken from spatial dimensions; we have no literally direct terms to designate 'pitch' as a sound quality. The expressions, however, are apt enough. No doubt, the terms 'high' and 'low,' as applied to the psychological experience of sound, have their origin in the association with volume and dimension. There is something broad, voluminous, massive, dark about the 'low' sounds; sounds lose more and more of this character as the scale advances, until they become thin, sharp, light, bright in the 'high' sounds. The progress from the bottom to the top of the scale of sounds resembles the ascent from the deep broad lowlands of the valleys to the high narrow tip of a mountain peak. Some such association probably prompted the selection of the terms 'low' and 'high' as analogically descriptive of the pitch of sounds.

Sounds having a definite, well marked pitch are called *tones.* Sounds produced by musical instruments and, as a rule, by the animal voice, are tones. Not always, however; a sneeze, a cough, the bark of a dog, and the roar of a lion are noises. *Noises* also have pitch. An exploding firecracker has a higher pitch than a bomb. Language appropriately describes the difference of pitch in noises by means of words: squeak, slither, blare, rattle, noise, shot, roar, rumble, boom.

The *range* of the human ear and its *selective discrimination* of pitch is remarkable. Sensitivity differs in individuals to some extent, but the average person is capable of distinguishing about 20,000 different tones. Pitch sensitivity is a native endowment, but attention and practice sharpen the acuity of discrimination; it is best in the middle section of the scale, and not so good in the lower and higher sections.

Loudness. Loudness, like pitch, is unidimentional; that is to say, it is progressive in character, beginning with sounds so weak as to be barely audible and increasing in strength until sounds of maximum intensity are reached.

Timbre. Timbre, or tone color, is that quality which *distinguishes tones of the same pitch,* when produced by different voices or instruments. For example, when instruments are being tuned for a concert piece, the pianist will strike a certain note on the piano. This same note will then be played by other musicians on the violin, the clarinet, the flute, the trumpet, the oboe, etc. The pitch of the tone is the same for all the instruments; yet this same tone is characteristically different for each instrument. And if a number of singers give voice to this same note, it will be noticed that their tones are individually different. A musician can always recognize the type of instrument by its tonal quality. It is this tonal quality which is designated as tone color or timbre. In the description of tones, words like 'soft,' 'metallic,' 'wooden,' 'mellow,' 'thin,' 'full,' 'hollow,' 'sweet,' 'clanging,' etc., express timbre.

Timbre is the result of a *fundamental tone* combined with harmonic *partials* or *overtones.* Tones as we hear them are practically never simple, pure tones, but tones compounded of a dominant (fundamental) tone and a number of other tones (partials or overtones) which have a definite harmonic relation to the dominant tone. Close attention to tones as emitted by various instruments enables a trained listener to pick out the fundamental and also the distinctive overtones, although in normal experience, leaving critical analysis aside, the tone as a whole is sensed as a *unit.* The number and strength of the partials, therefore, determine mostly the timbre of a voice or instrument. Various kinds of *harmonic analyzers* have been devised to discover the overtones accompanying the fundamental tone; these analyzers show that the timbre of instruments depends on the number and strength of the overtones. Over 40 partials can be detected in the low notes of a piano, and in the clarinet some of the partials constitute about 60 per cent of the tone. The timbre of the same instrument changes considerably in the low, middle, and high registers. Timbre, then, is a matter of overtone structure more than anything else.

Sound as Vibration

So far we have considered sound as a psychological experience, as sensation. Sound, however, has a *physical cause;* it is not something purely subjective. The physical correlate of the sensation of sound is the *vibration* of air or of some other medium. Such vibrations determine the pitch, the intensity, and the timbre of the sounds we hear, because they are the *physical stimulus* of the organ of hearing, and sensation is a conscious response to a physical stimulus.

From the standpoint of physics, *sound* is a form of vibration, a *wave motion in an elastic medium.* The sound wave is a *longitudinal vibration,* the particles of the medium moving back and forth, not in a curve, but in a straight line. In air, which is the common medium of physical sound, this wave is produced by a condensation and rarefaction of the air. The waves proceed from the sounding body in all directions, so that they represent an ever-widening sphere. Sound waves travel through the air with the speed of about 1100 feet per second, depending on the density of the air. They follow one another at a certain *frequency,* and by 'frequency' we mean the number of vibrations per second. The *energy* of the stimulus determines the *amplitude* of the *vibration,* and that is its *intensity.*

Psychologically, sounds are experienced as having pitch, loudness, and timbre. Since sensation is the conscious response to a physical stimulus, and since the physical stimulus is the sound wave or vibration, what in the stimulus corresponds to pitch, loudness, and timbre? To put it in a different way: How do sound waves or vibrations produce the pitch, loudness, and timbre of sounds as experienced in sensation?

Pitch and Sound Waves. Extensive experimental research has established the fact that *pitch* is determined by the *vibration rate* or *frequency.* A low rate produces low sounds; a high rate, high sounds. Middle C, for example, has a vibration rate of 260 vibrations per second; this rate is expressed in a different manner by saying that the frequency of these waves is 260 cycles per second. The octave below middle C has a rate of 130 vibrations per second, and the octave above a rate of 520. The lowest sound still audible by the human ear has about 16 to 20 vibrations, while the highest has about 20 to 21,000 vibrations per second. Individuals differ, of course, in sensitivity, and absolute figures are thus impossible; the figures given are those of the most reliable authorities. Young persons have a larger range than older persons. Sensitivity is not uniform in all registers, so far as the distinction of differences in tones is concerned; it is finest in the middle registers, where sounds have a vibration rate of from approximately 1000 to 5000 per second. Many persons are able to distinguish tones with a difference of only four vibrations, and a trained ear can notice the difference between half a vibration and even less. A semitone is one twelfth of an octave and has about 16 vibrations at middle C; this interval is relatively large and is easily distinguishable. It is claimed that in the middle octave as many as 1000 tones can be discerned as to pitch, at least by very keen ears.

Loudness and Sound Waves. The *loudness* of tones is dependent on the *amplitude* or *intensity* (energy) of the vibration. The vibration rate or frequency of a sound wave remains the same at all times, unless impeded in some way, and the pitch, therefore, also remains the same. The amplitude or energy of a sound wave does not remain the same; unless reinforced constantly, energy is gradually used up, so that the amplitude decreases as time goes on. Thus, a tuning fork whose note is middle C will always give off this tone, because its vibration rate or frequency is always 260 cycles per second as long as it vibrates; its amplitude or energy, however, diminishes gradually, and the tone becomes weaker and weaker in loudness, until it finally ceases altogether. The greater the amplitude of the sound wave, therefore, the louder the tone; the smaller the amplitude, the weaker the tone.

Pitch is determined by frequency, vibration rate; loudness, by amplitude, intensity, energy. It would be erroneous, however, to give an absolute value to this rule. The organ of hearing is not a machine which responds mechanically to a mechanical stimulus. Hearing is the function of a living organ, and this function modifies to some extent the operation of the rule. Since the sensitivity of the organ of hearing is finest in the middle range (1000 to 5000 vibrations per second) and weaker in the low and high ranges, sound waves in the low and high ranges must have greater energy than in the middle range in order that the sounds be equally loud to the ear. The voice of a soprano will appear louder than that of a bass singer, even though the intensity of both voices be the same. Similarly, octaves have the ratio of one to two as to frequency; psychologically, in the low and high registers, the octaves seem to have a smaller span than in the middle region of the musical scale. The semitones represent the same interval in all octaves, and this interval should be heard as the same in every octave; but that is not the case. If two adjacent keys are struck successively at the lower and upper end of the keyboard of a piano and then in the middle of the keyboard, the interval between the semitones in the middle register will appear greater than that of the semitones at both ends. Pitch and loudness, therefore, are not rigidly determined by the frequency and amplitude of the vibrations, but depend to some extent on the unequal sensitivity of the ear.

Timbre and Sound Waves. Timbre, as was said before, is a mixture or blending of a fundamental and overtones. In sounds produced by musical instruments these overtones stand in a harmonic relation to the fundamental, namely, in the ratio of 1, 2, 3, 4, etc. The reason is the fact that a sounding body vibrates not only as a whole but also in its parts. When a violinist draws the bow over a string, the string vibrates as a whole, and that gives rise to the *fundamental.* But the string also vibrates by halves, quarters, eighths, etc., each part having its own frequency relative to the others; these vibrating parts thus give rise to *partials* or *overtones.* These overtones also have *different intensity quantities;* some are stronger, some weaker. Frequency means pitch; intensity means loudness.

It is the blending of these overtones of different pitch and intensity with the fundamental of the string as a whole which constitutes the timbre of the violin. The material and construction of the instrument as a *resonator* for the tones contribute greatly to this timbre, because the body of the instrument vibrates also in its own peculiar manner, damping some tones and reinforcing others. The tuning fork, being so simple in construction, emits a relatively simple and pure tone.

Noises and Sound Waves. That noises and tones are not essentially different is clear from the fact that tones are present in all noises. Noises are combinations of tones; these tones can be separated through sound filters and eliminated individually. Being combinations of tones, noises consist of a number of fundamentals with their respective partials; this combination brings about a *conflict of frequencies and amplitudes* among the component tones which affects the ear disagreeably because of interference among their proper ratios. Noises are somewhat in the nature of timbre, except that the parts are combined in a disharmonious whole; hence some instruments, particularly drums and certain horns, are more noisy than musical.

The Musical Scale. A 'tone' is a sound with a well-marked or definite pitch. A *musical tone* is one which has a definite harmonic relation to other tones, so that it can be combined with them into harmonies and melodies. A *harmony* is the simultaneous combination of musical tones which gives pleasure to the listener. A *melody* is the rhythmical succession of single musical tones arranged into a pleasing unity. A *musical scale* is a graduated series of tones, ascending or descending in order of pitch according to a specified scheme of their intervals. The typical interval scheme of the modern scale of music is the octave. In the 'chromatic' scale there are twelve equal steps or intervals (semitones) between a keynote and its octave, based on the frequency of the sound waves. It is indifferent what particular vibration be chosen as a keynote; but once a keynote has been selected, the intervals progress in a definite ratio of vibrations up to the octave. By international agreement the tone of 440 cycles (vibrations) per second is designated as *a′*. Since the octave above a chosen keynote stands to this keynote in a frequency ratio of 2 to 1, it is obvious that the vibration rate of this octave must be 880 per second. By multiplying 440 by 1.059 and dividing the product by the twelfth root of 2, we arrive at the vibration rate of each of the twelve semitones in this octave. In order that tones be 'musical,' so that they can be combined in harmonic relations with one another, they must be 'spaced' or separated from one another by definite distances in the scale. Because of this fact, only about 85 tones are available for musical purposes, so that there are only 7, or at the most 8, octaves in the musical tone system which can be effectively used by musicians.

Theories of Hearing

A relationship undoubtedly exists between physical sound waves and the pitch, loudness, and timbre of sounds as experienced in the organ of hearing. From time to time theories have been advanced attempting to explain this relationship.

The Resonance Theory. This theory is associated with the name of the eminent scientist *Helmholtz*. To him and his followers the basilar membrane of the cochlea, with its more than 20,000 transverse fibers, is similar to a piano with its many strings. When the damper is lifted and a note is sung into the piano, this note is an air wave compounded of many frequencies, and each string which corresponds to one of these frequencies will vibrate. In this manner the fundamental and partials of the voice tone is reproduced through *resonance* in the strings of the piano. In an analogical fashion the fibers of the basilar membrane are individually attuned to the frequencies of the sound waves, each to its proper frequency. The membrane is narrowest at the base of the cochlea and widest at the apex; it is therefore assumed that the 'resonators' for the high sounds are at the base and those for the low sounds at the apex. The vibrations communicated to the endolymph thus affect the transverse fibers and stimulate the 'hair cells' attached to them, and the impulse is transmitted from each cell through a conducting nerve fiber to the brain. Pitch would be explained by the rate of vibrations, loudness by their energy, and timbre by the complex of vibrations of the sound waves producing a similar effect in the transverse fibers.

Evidence of a sort for the resonance theory is found in the cases of *tone deafness* due to *localized injury* in the organ of Corti. Injuries make people deaf to tones of a certain frequency band, depending on the region affected. On the other hand, objection is raised against the theory on the basis of the *microscopical dimensions* of the transverse fibers; it is difficult to understand how a correspondence can exist between the relatively large sound waves and the infinitesimal fibers.

The Sound-Pattern Theory. In this theory, the basilar membrane as a whole reacts to the incoming vibrations in such a manner that it vibrates in patterns which correspond to the *sound patterns.* Accordingly, some sections of the membrane vibrate while others are at rest, and the type of vibration varies in the different sections, so that the neural current is the exact counterpart of the sound pattern.

Considering the rapid changes which occur in the sound patterns of, let us say, a spirited concert piece, it seems doubtful whether the *refractory phase* of a nerve impulse (see p. 34) would permit such rapid changes and impulses without serious interference. To offset this difficulty, some adherents of the sound-pattern theory, especially *Wever* and *Bray,* contend that it is not necessary to suppose that the single nerve fiber responds to every successive wave, but only, perhaps, alternately or at certain intervals. To use the analogy of a company of soldiers firing their rifles, certain squads may fire a volley in rotation instead of the entire company firing at once. This so-called *volley theory* is based on the plausible assumption that the refractory phase is not the same for all nerve fibers, so that some fibers can transmit the impulse while others are in their refractory phase.

Neither the resonance theory nor the sound-pattern theory seems capable of explaining all the facts. Perhaps neither is an adequate interpretation of hearing. On the other hand, the two theories are not mutually exclusive in their main features, and it is possible that both contain elements of truth which can be united in a serviceable theory. Some psychologists favor the view that a composite theory, combining the resonance and sound-pattern ideas, is the best.

Smell, taste, and hearing are important senses. They convey to the organism many items of information concerning things as they exist for themselves. These senses, like the somesthetic senses, enable man to make a *proper adjustment to his environment,* and this is the main purpose of the cognitive element in sense function.

One important fact should be noted. There is *no mechanical point-for-point correspondence* between sense and stimulus. The senses are *selective* in their response to possible stimuli. Taste, for example, responds in just four ways to the manifold chemical properties of things; pitch and loudness are not mechanical reproductions of the frequency and amplitude of sound waves. Vital function is thus seen to be distinct from mere physical action. Furthermore, these senses, especially the closely co-operating smell and taste, plainly show again that man is an *integral organism,* because their functions are not isolated activities but are subservient to the welfare of the organism as a whole.

Summary of Chapter V

Smell and taste belong to the 'lower' senses, hearing and sight to the 'higher'; the former are nutritive, the latter are more cognitional in character.

1. *The Sense of Smell.* It is the sense by which certain properties (smell, odor, scent) become known through the stimulation of receptors responsive to chemical substances in a gaseous form or to minute particles which reach them normally from a distance and in low concentration. The *organ* of smell is a small brown-yellow spot of the mucous membrane of the

nose. The *stimuli* are odorous particles which enter the nostrils through the breathing in of some form of gas in which the particles are suspended. The odorous quality of substances depend on the chemical constitution of the substances and on the specific receptivity of the receptor cells.

Among the many *classifications* of odors, the following is the one generally accepted: fragrant, fruity, resinous, spicy, putrid, burned.

2. *The Sense of Taste.* It is the sense by which certain qualities (taste, savor, flavor) of soluble substances become known by contact with a particular set of epithelial end organs (taste buds) located mainly in the papillae of the tongue. The *organs* of taste are the taste buds. The *stimuli* are chemical substances in solution. The *kinds* of taste are four: sour, salty, sweet, and bitter. In all probability there are four types of receptors corresponding to these four kinds of taste.

3. *The Sense of Hearing.* It is the sense by which the vibrations of certain media acting upon the ear become known as sounds.

'Sound' has two distinct meanings: physical and psychological. *Physical sound* means the vibrations emanating from a vibrating body. *Psychological sound* means the conscious experience of tonal qualities after the organ of hearing has become activated by the stimulus of the vibrations.

4. *The Human Ear.* The ear is the *organ* of hearing. In man it consists of three parts. The *outer* ear consists of the auricle and the external auditory meatus. The *middle* ear consists of the tympanic membrane and the three ossicles. The *inner* or internal ear consists of the vestibule and the cochlea. This latter contains three canals: the tympanic, vestibular, and cochlear canals.

5. *The Organ of Corti.* It is situated on the basilar membrane. Transverse fibers are stretched across this membrane, containing the 'hair cells' which are the receptors.

6. *Sound as Sensation.* There are two main kinds of sound: tones and noises. Sounds have three chief characteristics: *pitch, loudness, and timbre.*

7. *Sound as Vibration.* Physically, sound is a *vibration* or wave motion in an elastic medium. As such it has 'frequency' (vibration rate) and 'amplitude' (intensity, energy). Frequency determines the pitch; amplitude, the loudness. Timbre is the result of the vibrations of a sounding body which vibrates as a whole and in its parts, giving rise to a fundamental and partials (overtones). *Noises* consist of a number of fundamentals and their overtones mutually interfering. *Tones* have a definite fundamental. A *musical scale* is a graduated series of tones, ascending or descending in order of pitch according to a specified scheme of their intervals.

8. *Theories of Hearing.* In the *resonance theory* of Helmholtz the transverse fibers of the basilar membrane of the cochlea are assumed to be individually attuned to the frequencies of the sound waves, each to its proper frequency, similar to the strings of a piano. According to the *sound-pattern theory,* the basilar membrane as a whole vibrates in patterns which correspond to the sound patterns. This theory has been modified by *Wever* and *Bray,* who contend that single nerve fibers need not respond to every successive wave, but only, perhaps, alternately or at certain intervals; this is the *volley theory.* Neither theory seems to be satisfactory in every respect.

Readings

Woodworth, R. S., *Experimental Psychology,* Ch. XX, XXI. — Harmon, F. L., *Principles of Psychology,* Ch. 6. — Gruender, Hubert, *Experimental Psychology,* Ch. V.

CHAPTER VI

SIGHT

SIGHT is the noblest of the external senses. More than the others, it brings the mind into cognitional contact with the world. Unaided sight spreads before us in vivid clarity the colors and shapes of objects in our immediate vicinity. Aided by the instrumentalities of telescope and microscope, it penetrates the vast immensity of the starry heavens and the infinitesimal recesses of subvisible bodies. Distances measured in light years and in microns are thus brought within the field of vision.

Sight apparently has the marvelous power of perceiving things at a distance without the necessity of any physical contact. The eye, small though it is in comparison to the objects it beholds, seems capable of encompassing the whole world. Little wonder, then, that physiologists and psychologists have given so much attention to the miracle of sight. Much has been discovered concerning sight through scientific research.

The Organ of Sight

Sight is the sense which is *responsive to the stimuli of radiant energy or light.* The *organ* of vision is the *eye.* Its general shape is that of a sphere. It is the only sensory organ with a mechanism which prevents the normal stimulus from affecting the receptors, namely, the eyelid. An ingenious arrangement of muscles enables us to turn the eyeball to the right, the left, up, down, in a circle, and at various directional angles.

The eye itself consists of a number of distinct structures. The outer part of the eyeball is composed of *three layers of tissue:* the sclerotic, the choroid, and the retina. The *sclerotic* is the dense, tough, opaque, white coat or covering which encases the eyeball on the outside, except for the front part (the cornea). The *choroid* is a membrane containing numerous blood vessels and large branched pigment cells, situated next to the sclerotic on the inside of the eyeball. The *retina* is a membrane lining the posterior chamber of the eye next to the choroid; it contains the receptors and is the immediate seat of vision.

At the front of the eyeball the sclerotic is modified into the transparent *cornea.* The cornea is like the segment of a sphere attached to the eyeball. It is transparent, so that light rays can enter the eye. It consists of layers of interlacing fibers, united by a cementing substance. Beneath it is a limpid fluid, called the *aequeous humor.* Just as the cornea is an extension of the sclerotic, the *iris* is an extension of the choroid. It is an opaque, muscular, contractile membrane, perforated by an opening, the *pupil.* The anterior portion of the iris is colored, and this coloring is different in different individuals; the posterior surface is pigmented, so as to exclude all light except through the pupillary opening. The iris acts as a diaphragm, contracting when light is dim, so that the pupil becomes enlarged, and relaxing when light is strong, so that the pupil becomes smaller. This action is reflex (the 'pupillary reflex') and adjusts the eye automatically to the quantity of light necessary for accurate vision.

The cornea refracts the rays of light, but it is nonadjustive. In order that the rays be refracted according to the distance of the objects seen, a transparent biconvex body, the *crystalline lens,* is suspended by a ring of ligaments immediately behind the iris. It consists of concentric lamellae or plates composed of slender, curved, rod-like cells. The lens is elastic to some extent, so that its curvature can become more spherical or more flattened, depending on the relaxation or contraction of the *ciliary muscles* which control the ligaments holding the lens in place. By means of this varying curvature the rays of light are focused on the retina. The chamber of the eyeball, situated between the lens and the retinal layer, is the *fundus,* and it is filled with a clear, colorless, transparent jelly-like substance, the *vitreous humor.* The latter is enclosed by a membrane, called the *hyaloid membrane.*

The eye, as will be noted, is constructed very much like a photographic camera. It consists of a focusing apparatus (cornea, iris, lens), a dark chamber (fundus, choroid), and a sensitive plate or film (retina).

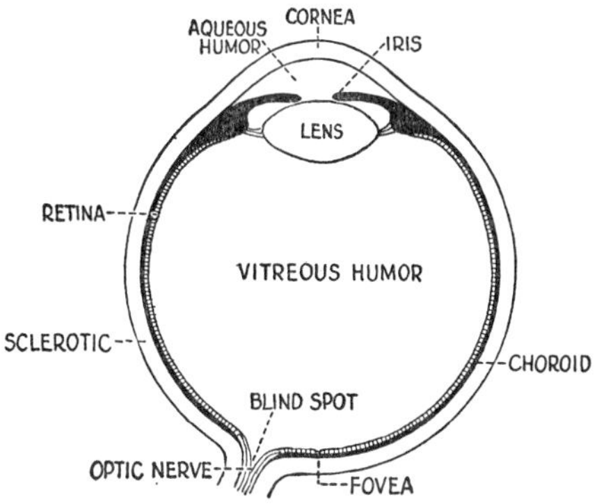

Fig. 21. Diagram of the Human Eye.

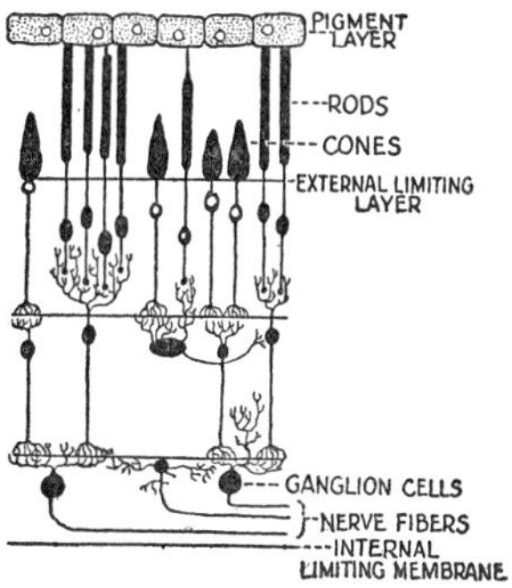

Fig. 22. Cross Section of the Human Retina.

The *retina* is the seat of vision. A number of distinguishable *layers* compose the retina. Beginning with the retinal surface in contact with the vitreous humor and ending with the surface resting on the choroid, these layers succeed one another in the following order: the inner limiting membrane, separating the retina from the vitreous humor; a layer of branches of the optic nerve, together with blood vessels and ganglion cells; the inner reticular layer of fibers; the inner nuclear layer; the outer reticular layer; the outer nuclear layer; the outer limiting membrane; the rods and cones; and, finally, a layer of pigment cells, next to the choroid. The retina forms the innermost lining of the eyeball and is not more than five tenths millimeter in thickness. Toward the center of the posterior surface of the retina is a small yellow spot, called the *macula lutea,* and in it is located the *fovea,* a small depression or shallow pit, which is the area of acute vision. The retinal nerves unite into a bundle and emerge from the retina a short distance from the macula lutea on the nasal side of the eyeball, thereby forming the *blind spot* where no vision is possible.

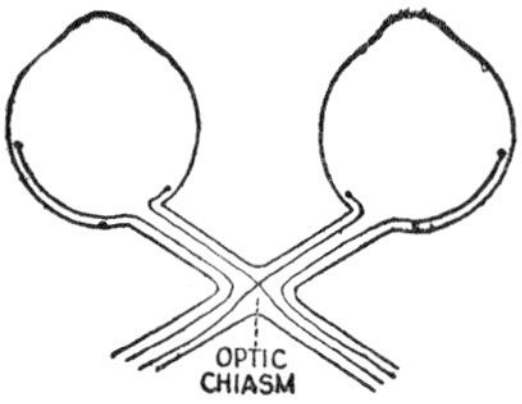

Fig. 23. Diagram of the Optic Chiasm.

A *partial decussation* of the optic nerves occurs where the nerves of the two eyes meet. This decussation is termed the *optic chiasm* (from the Greek letter 'chi,' χ, which it resembles). The result of this chiasm or partial decussation is that the nerves of the nasal half of the right eye and of the outer half of the left eye meet and travel to the left hemisphere of the brain, while the nerves of the nasal half of the left eye and of the outer half of the right eye meet and travel to the right hemisphere. Hence, any object to the right of the eyes will throw its image on the left half of the retina of each eye and be perceived by or in the left hemisphere of the cerebral cortex; reversely, the impulses originating from an object to the left of both eyes will travel to the right hemisphere. The terminal branches of the retinal nerves spread out over the entire retina, so that each point of the retina has a nerve. Each nerve goes to a ganglion in the superior colliculus of the midbrain, and from these ganglia nerves proceeed to the visual center of the occipital cortex of the cerebrum. In this manner every point of the retina is connected with a corresponding point in the cortex of the brain.

While it is commonly stated that the retina (in conjunction, of course, with the brain) is the seat of vision, in the retina itself the *rods* and *cones* are the *receptors*. They are called 'rods' and 'cones' because of their shape, the rods being more long and slender, while the cones are more short and conical. Contrary to what one might expect, the rods and cones are not placed at the top of the retinal layer next to the vitreous humor, but at the bottom near the choroid. In consequence of this arrangement, light rays must pass through all the retinal layers before reaching these receptors. The function of the rods and cones will be explained presently.

Light Rays as Stimulus

The *stimulus* of sight is *radiant energy.* Ordinarily, the radiant energy of the sun is the stimulus; but star light and artificial lights are also stimuli which normally activate the organ of vision.

Light emanates from luminous bodies in the form of *photons,* and photons are particles or corpuscles approximately the size of electrons. Notwithstanding this fact, light also manifests itself as a form of *electromagnetic wave* propagated through the hypothetical aether. How to harmonize this double phenomenon of light, is one of the great problems of modern physics.[1] Since we are not concerned here with the physical problem of the constitution of light, we will follow the usual procedure of treating light as a wave.

The vibrations of light waves are transverse to the direction of their propagation, and the speed of their transmission is about 186,300 miles per second. The wave lengths of light are measured in millimicrons, i.e., in millionths of a millimeter, of which the symbol is $m\mu$. Not all wave lengths emitted by radiant bodies affect the retina and stimulate it to vision. Ultraviolet rays are shorter than $400m\mu$, and ultrared rays are longer than $800m\mu$, but neither are visible. The range of the visible spectrum lies roughly between wave lengths of $386m\mu$ and $800m\mu$. If one passes a ray of sunlight through a prism, one disperses this light into rays according to their wave length and the spectral colors appear: red ($760m\mu$) is at one end of the spectrum, violet ($400m\mu$) at the other end, yellow ($580m\mu$), and green ($530m\mu$), and blue ($480m\mu$) in between. Intermediate wave lengths give various shades of these colors. When the stimulus consists of a ray of one wave length, one frequency, it is said to be a *homogeneous ray* of light. Most rays, however, are *mixtures* of various wave lengths.

[1] See the author's *From Aether to Cosmos* (Bruce, 1941), pp. 58–64.

The white light of the sun has a maximum mixture, as the prismatic colors reveal.

A *physical object* is *colored,* when it emits, transmits, or reflects all or some of the rays of light. In this sense, a body is 'white,' when it absorbs none of the solar rays but reflects them all diffusely; a body is 'black,' when it absorbs all rays and reflects none; a body is 'blue,' when it absorbs selectively a portion of the rays and diffusely reflects the others, among which the 'blue rays' predominate. The *color of an object,* therefore, from the standpoint of the physicist, is that property of an object, due to its atomic and molecular constitution, which enables it to emit, transmit, or reflect all or some of the rays of light capable of stimulating the retina to sensation. Viewed this way, objects possess *physical color,* irrespective of whether or not they ever affect an organ of sight, because the physicist considers 'color' to be identical with electromagnetic aether *vibrations* in so far as they are *capable* of becoming the stimulus activating the retina. Strictly speaking, then, a 'black body' is devoid of all physical color, because it absorbs all light rays, so that no light is emitted or reflected.

Like sound, light waves have *length, frequency,* and *amplitude.* Differences in these magnitudes bring about differences in the waves. The hue or color depends mainly on the wave length, while brightness or brilliance depends mainly on the amplitude of the wave.

Color as Sensation

The *psychologist* has only a secondary interest in the physical vibrations or light waves which produce vision. His primary interest lies in the *conscious reaction* or *sensation of sight* evoked by the action of the physical stimulus on the organ of vision. His field of investigation, therefore, is *visual experience,* namely, color as it appears in visual sensation.

All in all, there are more than 30,000 distinguishable colors. Viewed from the standpoint of psychological experience, we have *achromatic* and *chromatic* sensations. In 'achromatic' sensations we experience 'white,' 'black,' and the intermediate 'grays.' There are about 700 different shades of gray between pure white and complete black. They differ from one another in brightness. In 'chromatic' sensations we experience what we ordinarily call 'colors,' namely, blue, green, yellow, red. Although the term 'achromatic' means 'non-colored,' psychologically 'white,' 'gray,' and 'black' are experienced as 'colors,' just as much as 'blue,' 'green,' etc. We therefore divide visual sensations into experiences of *neutral* (achromatic) and *chromatic colors.*

If we now classify *psychological colors,* we find that we have *six psychologically primary colors.* There are two neutral colors, white and black. The grays are intermediates of white and black. And there are four chromatic colors, red, yellow, green, and blue. All other colors are shades or blends of these four. We have here one of the great differences between physics and psychology. According to physics, neither 'white' nor 'black' is a distinctive color. 'White' has no specific wave length in the spectrum; it is a mixture of the wave lengths of various colors. 'Black' has no wave length at all which could be said to correspond to it. In psychological experience, however, both 'white' and 'black' are colors as distinctive as any of the chromatic colors. 'Black' is not the same as 'colorless' in our experience; distilled water and a clear pane of glass are 'colorless,' but coal and the printed words of this page are decidedly 'colored.'

Chromatic colors have *three attributes* or characteristics: hue, saturation, and brightness. By *hue* we understand that attribute of a color which we designate by naming it 'red,' 'blue,' etc., distinguishing it thereby from the neutral colors. Although this is a roundabout way of describing a 'hue,' we cannot do better, because the sensation of color is an ultimate datum of experience and such a datum is incapable of strict definition. It is much easier to point to a stick of sealing wax and say 'This is red' and to the sky and say 'That is blue,' and it is this characteristic of 'red' and 'blue,' etc., which we mean by 'hue.' The solar spectrum shows us a series of hues in various shades from violet to red. *Saturation* is the amount of hue present in a given chromatic color. There are, for example, many shades of red, but some shades contain more 'redness' than others; 'pink,' for example, is less saturated than 'cardinal red,' because there is more white and less red in the former than in the latter. We might say that hues, so far as saturation is concerned, run from 'dull' or 'pale' to 'vivid'; 'pink' is a pale or dull red, while 'cardinal' is a vivid red. By *brightness* or *brilliance* we mean that attribute of hues which enable us to place them in a series progressing from 'light' to 'dark.' All hues of the solar spectrum can be placed in such a series, and a series can also be made of any particular hue in its various shades. In the spectrum, for example, yellow is the brightest hue and blue the darkest. In the entire series of green hues, nile green is very bright and bottle green is very dark. Among the *neutral* colors, white represents extreme brightness and black extreme darkness; the grays occupy a middle place in brightness between them.

There are a number of *phenomena* in connection with color which deserve special consideration. They give us a better insight into the *psychology of vision* as such. In general, it is true, of course, to say that the sensation of vision depends on the stimulus and varies with the stimulus. Sensation, however, depends also on the *peculiar sensitivity of the receptor organ,* and this vital factor produces phenomena which cannot be explained on the basis of physical light waves alone. Some of these phenomena will be treated in the sections following.

Rod and Cone Vision

The rods and cones are the *receptor cells* which receive the stimulus of light and react to it. Sight, therefore, has a *duplex apparatus.* According to the theory of *Von Kries,* the rods and cones differ fundamentally in function, and at present no one seriously doubts the truth of the theory. The theory states that the *rods* are the receptors for *achromatic vision.* The rods are sensitive only to the white-gray-black series; they are insensitive to chromatic colors or hues, such as red, green, etc. On the other hand, the *cones* are the receptors for *chromatic vision*. They respond to the different wave lengths of light by sensations of chromatic colors or hues (red, yellow, brown, indigo, etc.), and thus are the receptors for what is commonly called 'color vision.'

There is good *evidence* in support of the difference between rod and cone vision. The fovea, which is the area of the retina where chromatic vision is most noticeable, contains closely packed cones, but no rods. From the fovea outward, rods begin to occur in the retina and increase in number toward the periphery, while the cones decrease steadily in proportion, until at the extreme periphery the retina contains rods almost exclusively. It is a known fact, however, that the extreme periphery of the retina responds only with sensations of the white-gray-black series but not with sensations of the chromatic-color series. Again, people who are devoid of cones entirely in their retina are totally color-blind and see all things in the neutral shades of white-gray-black, just as in an ordinary photograph; in order to see objects, these persons must turn their eyes slightly sideways, so as to focus the light away from the fovea to the rods of the periphery. Finally, nocturnal animals, like owls, bats, and others, have eyes which possess mostly rods and few cones, because in the dim night light objects are not seen in chromatic colors but in gray and black or, as it is called, in 'rod-white.'

The *stimulus threshold* is lower for the rods than the cones so that the rods will respond to dim or faint light where the cones of the fovea will not respond at all. The cones are, therefore, 'night blind,' while the rods are able to respond to the dim light of the moon and stars. We can see a faint star in the heavens, not by looking at it directly, but by looking slightly to the right or left of it, because then the light strikes the rods situated in the periphery and away from the central or foveal portion of the retina. A simple *experiment* will show that the rods and cones produce their own particular subjective effect in the perceiver. Place three electric lamps (preferably with carbon filaments) in a row, connected together in one circuit and standing about a yard apart. Decrease the current until the filaments barely glow. Stand in such a position that only the center bulb is seen in the line of direct vision, while the two outer bulbs are seen by oblique vision only. In a darkened room the center bulb will now appear with a red glow, while the two outer bulbs will show the 'rod-white' luminosity. No matter how quickly you shift your gaze from one lamp to the other, only the one directly viewed will be red; the other two will immediately change to 'rod-white.' You perceive the lamp as 'red' when its rays fall upon the cones, and as neutral 'rod-white' when its rays enter the eyes obliquely and fall upon the rods. The cones, therefore, are the organ of high intensity or *photopic vision,* while the rods are the organ of low intensity or *scotopic vision.* The cones are adapted for daylight and brightness and the rods for twilight and relative darkness.

Color Mixture

By *color mixture* we mean the stimulation of the same retinal spot by light rays of different wave length. These rays may be applied to the retinal spot simultaneously or in rapid succession; the result is the same. Color mixing is important to psychology because of the fact that many diverse physical stimuli will produce the selfsame color sensation, which again proves that there is no point-for-point correspondence between physical stimulus and conscious response. There are *three laws of color mixture.* It should be borne in mind that these laws apply solely to lights, not to pigments.

The First Law. It concerns the *complementary* colors and is formulated in two parts. The *first* part reads: "For every long wave of visible spectrum a definite short wave can be found so that when the two waves are mixed in appropriate proportions, each component of the mixture will neutralize the chromatic effect of the other and the sensation of neutral white will arise." The *second* part reads: "If the relative strength of the two components is not appropriately adjusted, the neutralization of one component is incomplete and the result of such a mixture is the sensation of an unsaturated color whose tone is determined by that of the stronger component."

This law expresses the general fact that two homogeneous light waves, one of long wave length and one of short wave length, when stimulating the same retinal spot, will not produce the sensation of their respective normal hues, but will produce a sensation of *white* (or gray). The wave lengths which produce the sensation of white are said to be *complementary colors.* The effect does not depend entirely on the specific wave lengths, but depends somewhat on the individual differences of the observers. In his own case, *Helmholtz* determined the complementary colors as follows, the numbers indicating the wave lengths of the homogeneous colors in Angstrom units:

Color	*Complementary Color*	
Red (656.2)	Green Blue (492.1)	
Orange (607.7)	Blue (489.7)	
Gold (585.3)	Blue (485.4)	RESULT
Gold (573.9)	Blue (482.1)	IN
Yellow (567.1)	Indigo Blue (464.5)	WHITE
Yellow (564.4)	Indigo Blue (461.8)	
Green Yellow (563.6)	Violet (433)	

The Second Law. It concerns *intermediate* colors and reads: "When two waves are combined which separately arouse color sensations whose tones are not complementary to each other, the result of such a mixture is the sensation of an intermediate color." According to this law, non-complementary pairs of wave lengths, when mixed, will result in color sensations of intermediate hue and brightness. Color mixtures of this type give rise to such colors as orange, yellow-green, green-blue, greenish-yellow, red-yellow, pink, lake, rose, tan, lilac, etc. For example, by mixing red and yellow in different proportions, we obtain vermillion, orange, and gold; red and yellow are non-complementary hues, and their mixture will never give white or gray. By mixing green and red lights we obtain a yellow hue.

The Third Law. It concerns the *substitution* of colors in mixtures containing more than two components and it reads: "If a definite mixture of lights has the color of a definite other light, then this mixture can be substituted for it, whenever this other light is required as a component in some other mixture." An illustration will make the meaning of this law clearer. Yellow, for example, is one of the spectral colors resulting from a homogeneous ray of light with a wave length of 567mμ. But yellow also results from a definite mixture of red and green lights. Now, yellow and indigo blue lights, when mixed, give white. Instead of homogeneous yellow (y), we can substitute red and green lights $(r + g)$ and mix them with indigo blue light (i.b.), and by means of this double mixture we obtain white (W). We thus have the formula $(r + g) + \text{i.b.} = W$, and that is the same formula as $y + \text{i.b.} = W$.

Pigments do not behave like lights in mixing. Yellow and blue pigments give rise to a green color in mixture, but yellow and blue lights give rise to a sensation of white. Yellow pigment absorbs certain wave lengths, including blue; it then reflects diffusely some wave lengths, including green, but the light which is predominantly reflected is yellow. Blue pigment absorbs certain wave lengths, including yellow; it then reflects diffusely some wave lengths, including green, but the light which is predominantly reflected is blue. Then, when blue and yellow pigments are mixed, the blue pigment absorbs the yellow, and the yellow pigment absorbs the blue; the green rays, however, are still reflected by both, and so the mixture of both pigments results in green color. It will thus be seen that the mixture of *lights* is a matter of *addition* of wave-length stimuli, while the mixture of *pigments* is a matter of *subtraction* or double absorption of wave-length stimuli. Hence the difference.

Color Contrast

A psychological phenomenon somewhat similar to color mixing is that of *color contrast.* By color contrast we mean the *difference in the appearance of colors* brought about by the stimulation of adjacent sets of rods and cones in the retina. When one set of rods and cones is stimulated by certain kinds and amounts of lights or colors and the adjacent set of rods and cones is stimulated by different kinds and amounts of lights or colors, then these different stimulations bring about a condition in which the affected sets mutually modify each other to such an extent that the colors change their appearance in some measure. These changes in appearance are sometimes quite pronounced. The effect of color contrast seems to be mainly the result of *physiological inhibition.* The stimulation of one area of the retina inhibits, either partially or completely, the effect produced in the other, and the result is a change in the appearance of a definite color.

The student can observe the effects of *simultaneous contrast* by means of a simple experiment. Take sheets of colored paper of as many hues as you can procure — white, black, red, yellow, green, blue, and intermediate colors. From each sheet cut out a piece two inches square, to be used as a background. Then cut out small pieces about half an inch square from each sheet, so that you will have a small piece of the same color to place in the center of each background. Now place a small piece of yellow paper against the larger background of white, black, red, blue, etc., preferably in the center of the background. Arrange the backgrounds with the yellow pieces in a series, side by side, on a table in good light, and compare the yellow pieces one with the other. Note the *different shades* of yellow which now appear against the various backgrounds. Do the same with pieces of blue, green, etc., placing them on the same backgrounds. The apparent change in color for pieces taken from the same sheet of paper is rather remarkable. Though they all have the same color in the sense that they reflect the same wave length, the psychological effect, due to simultaneous contrast in adjacent retinal areas, has changed the sensation of color considerably for the individual pieces.

Against a green background gray appears tinged with red, blue seems purplish, and yellow becomes more like orange. The laws of color mixture apply here, so that contrast effects tend toward the complementary colors of the contrasting colors; a green background, for example, induces a sensation of red in the color placed within its field. That is why it is unwise to select colored fabrics under artificial light; artificial light is usually yellowish and that produces color contrast.

Afterimages

Adaptation is a common phenomenon of vision. Prolonged stimulation of the same retinal area by a uniform stimulus decreases its effectiveness and makes this area more sensitive to the stimulus of the opposite color. *Successive contrast* results.

One type of successive contrast is the *afterimage*. Afterimages are sensations occurring after the stimuli causing them have ceased. They are of two kinds: negative and positive. A visual afterimage is *negative* or *complementary,* when a dark image is replaced by a light image, or a light by a dark, or the color of the original sensation by its complementary color. A visual afterimage is *positive,* when it preserves the color or shade of the original sensation.

Afterimages or aftersensations occur because it takes a certain amount of time for the visual apparatus to reach the height of its response to the stimulus, and it also takes some time for the apparatus to lose the effect of the stimulus. In consequence of this *after-lag* the response continues for a time after the stimulus has ceased. If someone swings a torch in a circle at night, the after-lag of the response produces the sensation of a fiery ring. Motion pictures make the impression of continuous action, although there is a lightless interval between the individual pictures thrown on the screen, because the response of the retina, due to after-lag, persists after the picture has been removed from the screen and thus bridges the gap of the dark interval between one picture and another; if the dark interval is too long, we observe a flicker. We notice the same phenomenon in an electric lamp using alternating current; the light appears constant and continuous. In such instances we still have the *original response,* not an afterimage. This after-lag of the original response does not last longer than half a second after the stimulus has ceased. That a certain *aftereffect* still persists in the retina after the original response has faded out, is observed in the fact that afterimages can be seen after a blank interval following the original response and its after-lag.

The student can easily demonstrate to himself the existence of positive and negative afterimages. Place a sheet of white paper used for typewriting and a piece of black or very dark cloth of about the same size side by side on a table. Look for a second or two directly at an exposed electric lamp, one with clear glass. Then turn your eyes to the paper and to the dark cloth, blinking the eyelids at the same time. You will see the outline of the filament loop of the lamp, now bright like the original (positive afterimage), now in its complementary color (negative afterimage). On a dark field the image will in all probability be positive, if you look at the field without blinking, and on a light field it is likely to be negative; the effect, however, depends on a number of circumstances. After a while these afterimages become weaker and weaker and then disappear entirely. Afterimages can, of course, be produced in many ways. A simple method is to look at a black or white or colored object with a fixed gaze for about half a minute and then turn the eyes upon a background of medium gray, and a negative afterimage will appear. These images are *subjective* in character, because they follow the movement of the eyes in any direction, after the eyes have ceased looking at the original object. As a rule, we do not see afterimages in the daytime, because bright light blots them out; however, if we look at the setting sun and then look at other objects with a flat surface, we obtain after-images of the sun, because the sun is brighter than these surfaces.

Color Blindness

Color blindness is another interesting phenomenon of vision. By *color blindness* we understand the partial or total inability to distinguish or recognize chromatic colors. It is an abnormality of vision in which certain colors drop out of the spectrum for the individual observer or all things are seen in neutral colors. Color blindness is adjudged an 'abnormal' condition in the visual mechanism because ninety-five per cent of persons see all the chromatic colors of the spectrum.

Color blindness assumes different forms. According to physics, there are *three primary colors:* red, green, and blue. The proper mixture of these will produce any hue. The ability to see these primaries equally well constitutes normal vision and is termed *trichromatism* (three-color vision); a normal person is said to be a 'trichromat.'

Partial color blindness is dichromatism, and it exists in two forms: red-green blindness, or blue-yellow blindness. In red-green blindness these two colors appear as gray. This type of color blindness may follow one of two patterns. It may be red blindness, in which the brightest part of the spectrum is in the normal yellow-green, and the red end of the spectrum is invisible; this is called *protanopia.* Or it may be green blindness, in which case the brightest part of the spectrum is the normal yellow; this is *deuteranopia.* In *blue-yellow* blindness, the second form of dichromatism, blue and yellow appear gray, while red and green, or blue-green, are distinguished; this type is termed *tritanopia.* About four per cent of males are protanopes or deuteranopes; color blindness is seldom found among women. Tritanopia, or blue-yellow blindness, is extremely rare. Much of the data concerning partial color blindness have been gathered from the experiences of persons who had trichromatic vision and then, through disease or injury, had become color-blind. One or the other case is on record where a person was normal in one eye and color-blind in the other.

Total color blindness, or *monochromatism,* is relatively rare. Persons afflicted with this form of color blindness are unable to see any colors of the spectrum; they see all objects in neutral tones of white-gray-black, as in an ordinary photograph. Though their vision is deprived of all chromatic color perception, they are able to distinguish differences in brightness.

Color weakness is not color blindness. Persons who are color weak see all chromatic colors and can distinguish them, but some colors need a *stronger* stimulus than others in order to be seen. Red and green light, for example, produce the sensation of yellow, when properly mixed; but a red-weak person needs more red, and a green-weak person needs more green, in order to obtain the yellow which a normal person sees.

Since the receptors of chromatic color vision are the cones of the retina, color blindness and also color weakness presupposes some defect in the cones. And since in dichromatism the vision of one or the other color is missing, while vision for the rest is unimpaired, one must assume that the defect responsible for color blindness is present in practically all the cones of the eye or eyes. Just what this defect could be, is difficult to say. An adequate explanation of color blindness is a crucial test for a good theory of vision.

Binocular Vision

Man's two eyes are placed in such a position that both look forward. The object seen is observed from two divergent angles; and thus the field for each eye is slightly different, and the fovea of one eye receives an optical image which differs to some extent from that of the other. It would seem that man should see two distinct fields and two distinct objects. When normal eyes, however, are directed toward an object, they see but a *single object and a single field.* What is the explanation?

There is a *correspondence* between the *retinal points* of

one eye and those of the other. The fovea, where focusing occurs, is a relatively small area, and it is assumed that here the correspondence is rather close. Due to the decussation of the optic nerves, the foveal points are connected with each hemisphere of the brain, so that the two foveas act as a single organ of vision. The result is a *single cortical response* to the two overlapping retinal fields, termed *binocular fusion.* Fusion occurs only when the rays of the field or of an object are focused on the foveas in a practically identical manner.

We can and do see *double images* of the same field or object when the two foveas are out of alignment. With both eyes open, look at some object, say a book, and then press a finger against one eyeball, thereby pushing this eyeball out of its normal position with respect to the other; you will see two images of the book, one stationary (in the stationary eye) and one moving (in the eye moving under the pressure of the finger). Even in ordinary vision we see double images. Focus your eyes on an object about five or six feet away, and then place your extended index finger directly in the line of vision about six inches in front of your eyes while they remain focused on the distant object; you will have a single image of the distant object, but a double image of your finger, and you will be able to see the distant object (or field) *through* the images of your finger. If you focus your eyes on a near object, the distant object will appear double. Be sure that you do not shift the focus of your eye in this experiment. Ordinarily, of course, we never notice these double images, although they are always present, because we concentrate our attention upon the object in focus and neglect the rest of the field. It is only at the focal point of the fovea that the two optical images are practically identical and are thus capable of fusion. In the outlying areas of the retina the rays of light will not converge to a point, but cross, and throw the image of the object or field on different retinal areas, thus producing the vision of a double object or field.

Binocular rivalry occurs, when each eye, separately and simultaneously, sees colors or objects or figures which are very different in appearance. Under such conditions, at first there is a response only to one field: the image of one field is seen, that of the other is suppressed and invisible. Then a shift occurs, in which the latter field, at first invisible, now become visible. After an interval the fields are again reversed, and this alternation of the two fields continues back and forth. It is as if a 'rivalry' existed between the two eyes. When complementary colors are used in these experiments, some observers experience only a rivalry; others, however, experience *psychological fusion* according to the laws of color mixture. In the case of fusion of complementary colors, this fusion cannot occur in the retinas themselves, because each retina is stimulated by a single wave length of light. The fusion can only occur in the midbrain or in the cortex; and in all probability the response is in the cortex of the cerebrum. If this interpretation is correct, it is an indication that the *cortical* response has more to do with actual color sensation and general vision than is usually supposed. The shift of fields in binocular rivalry seems to receive its explanation in *adaptation* or *fatigue*. The neural mechanism responding to the one field gradually suffers fatigue, whereupon the other field forces itself into the foreground, only to be replaced after a while by the first field; the process repeats itself alternately through fatigue and recuperation.

Behaviorism and Color Vision

It is an axiom of *behaviorism* that an *exact correlation* exists between *stimulus* and *response;* the response is the exact physiological counterpart of the stimulus. If we know the stimulus (cause), we also know what response (effect) will follow; and if we know the response (effect), we also know the stimulus (cause) which produced it. Applied to physiological optics, this axiom means that, if we know the wave length, amplitude, and form of the light wave, we can predict what sensation of color will ensue. Facts, however, show that the *behaviorists are in error.*

Different stimuli produce the same sensation. Given certain stimuli of light waves, we cannot predict automatically the sensation which will follow; introspection shows that the response may be different from what the behavioristic axiom would indicate. Mixing wave lengths 656 and 567 (red and yellow) should give a blend of the two, namely 612 (orange); and it does. Then mixing yellow and indigo-blue should give a blend of these two, and so should the mixing of red and green-blue; but it does not, because these are complementary colors, and complementary colors give white (or gray), which has no resemblance to the colors which act as stimulus. All complementary colors act in this manner.

Simultaneous contrast shows that the sensations of color change, even though the kind and amount of wave lengths emitted or reflected to the retina remain unchanged. Hence, from the nature of the stimulus we cannot predict the character of the sensation.

The *sensation of black,* which is just as characteristic as white or blue, etc., should be impossible in the theory of behaviorism, because no light waves reach the retina from a 'black' object. 'Black' is an indirect effect of light, arising under simultaneous or successive contrast; but it is real enough, as we can readily observe by reading the print of a book. The mere absence of the stimulus, therefore, will not enable the behaviorists to account for the sensation of 'black.'

The *negative afterimage* are genuine phenomena of mental life; yet, since they are 'negative' in character, no objective method of behaviorism can detect their existence. They are perceivable by no one but the sentient individual, and he alone can describe their properties through introspection.

Visual Space

What we see in vision is not the retinal image, nor the electromagnetic waves of light, nor color mixing, nor simply patches of color. These realities, of course, are present and play their respective parts in vision and without them vision would be impossible. What we actually see in vision are *objects, things:* human beings, animals, plants, buildings, vehicles, fields, clouds, sky, etc. When we designate the objects of vision in this fashion, we are not speaking of visual sensations but of *visual perceptions.*

We apparently see things in definite *places;* they are a certain *distance* away, both in relation to ourselves and to other things; they have a definite *size* and *shape;* they are composed of *parts* spread out in the *three spatial dimensions* of length, height, and depth. In other words, we have a perception of visual space in three dimensions. If we inquire into *how* this perception is acquired, we are confronted with a rather complicated problem.

Colored surface in two dimensions is an immediate visual experience. Any seen object or patch of color shows that it is spread out in height and length; we cannot see a mathematical point. In any seen object or patch of color, we can intuitively distinguish 'right' and 'left,' 'up' and 'down'; consequently, we distinguish concrete parts of surfaces. We cannot see an object or patch of color, if they lie within the bounds of the visual field, without seeing their general shape; colored surfaces have limits of extension which involve shape, and 'shape' or 'form' is thus concretely given with the vision of colored surfaces, as anyone can observe by looking at a landscape or series of buildings. Even relative size is concretely given with colored surfaces; looking at an archery target, we see that the outer rings are relatively larger than the inner rings.

Depth in space, the third dimension, is not an immediate experience, but a matter of perception and judgment. We have become so accustomed to interpret the visual image in three dimensions, it seems that depth in space is also a datum of immediate experience. Distance and depth are rather a matter of *interpretative judgment,* and that is acquired through learning.

Merely looking at the heavens gives us no indication of the absolute size and distance of the sun, moon, and stars. History proves this; it is only through astronomical calculations that these things are now known to us. Perspective seemingly enables us to observe depth in space directly; that this judgment is erroneous, is clearly shown in stereopticon views, where flat pictures have apparent depth. The futile graspings of infants at objects which they see indicates that distance in space and absolute size are not directly given in visual images. More valuable evidence is derived from the experiences of persons who, blind from birth, had received their sight in later years, so that they were able to give a rational account of their new experiences. There was no experience of depth in space, and everything was seen in a flat side-by-sideness in two dimensions.

How do we learn to interpret our visual images as to *depth* and *distance in space?* Why are we so certain that there is a *third dimension?* A number of factors are involved in this process of interpretation.

In this respect the *tactual sense* is a great aid to sight. By means of the tactual sense, we experience *double contact* in our own body; that is to say, by passing our hands over our body, a contact is established between the hands and the body, hands and body both experiencing sensations of touch. In this manner we soon learn the general contour of our body, the relative position of the various members, and their relative size with respect to one another. We also learn that the various members are distinct from one another; hand, leg, foot, arm, trunk, head, etc., are not the same, and yet they are all *parts* of our own organism and belong to our body. When we grasp a pencil or an apple we obtain a rough estimate of size, shape, etc.; most of all, however, we perceive that they do not belong to our being, but are totally different from our self. We have the same experience when we touch a tree, a desk, a building, or some other person. By *combining sight and touch* we learn to distinguish ourselves and other beings, some of which are similar to our being (other persons) and others dissimilar (pencil, apple, tree, building, etc.).

From here to the *perception of depth* in space is but a short step in experimental learning. Through contact with an object by the hand or body, we experience pressure and kinesthetic sensations; through sight we see the contact made. We notice, however, that we do not always obtain sensations of contact, even though in the visual image the hand seems to touch the object. We then stretch out the hand to make contact; even this does not suffice at times, and then we walk toward the object. When we finally reach the object and touch it, our visual and tactual images again coincide. Our body thereby becomes a standard of measurement, and we thus learn two very important facts: *depth and distance in space* and the *measurement* of this depth and distance in space in terms of a standard of measurement. We now realize through progressive experience that some objects are near and some are far.

Having established the fact of depth and distance through the combined data of sight and touch, we begin to observe *many criteria in the visual image* itself which can be utilized effectively in gauging the size and distance of objects in space.

Light and *shadow* are criteria of distance and depth in space. There are 'cast shadows' and 'attached shadows.' When a light is thrown onto an object, the object casts a shadow onto the ground or onto another object. The light on a contoured object, i.e., an object not entirely flat, does not cover the object evenly; some parts are highlighted, and others are shaded or in shadow, and this type of shadow appears attached to the object itself. If we know the source and direction of the light, we can form a fairly accurate estimate of depth and distance. The cast shadows reveal the relative distances in space between one object and another, while the attached shadows reveal the three dimensions of a particular object taken alone.

Perspective is another criterion. 'Linear perspective' reveals distance by the apparent reduction in the size of known objects. A horse, a man, and an automobile, for example, seem to become larger as they approach, and smaller as they go away from us; we can gauge the distance in space by the apparent size. In 'detail perspective,' an object loses more and more of its distinctness in line and shape as the distance from the observer increases. Knowing these items from close observation, their progressive diminution in distinctness becomes a criterion of distance. Due to 'aerial perspective,' it is noticeable that familiar objects lose color tone, vividness, and brightness as they recede into the distance. 'Movement perspective' is another criterion. Watch a speedy airplane close overhead and note how fast it cuts through space; but as it circles around in the distance, it almost seems to stand still, although its speed is still the same. These various types of perspective, therefore, are cues to distance and depth in space.

In binocular vision of a nearby object, the *angular difference* of the two overlapping optical fields also reveals depth in space with regards to the shape of the object, because we thereby see 'around the corner' of an object. The stereoscope is based on this fact.

Another factor which assists us in gauging distance is the *focusing of the eyes* by means of the muscles of the eyes. When we look at an object which is very close, it appears blurred in outline and detail, and the muscles are strained in the attempt to make the eyes converge sufficiently for accurate focusing. When we look at a remote object, convergence and muscular strain are absent.

Experience teaches us to make use of a *combination of tactile and visual cues* in order to estimate the relative size of objects and their distance and depth in space. Training and learning, together with association, enable us to interpret these cues so proficiently that we have the impression that the perception of the third dimension is directly given in our visual image.

Two opposing theories of visual space deserve mention: *nativism* and *empiricism*. The nativists claim that our perceptions of space are the result of a native or constitutional property of vision itself, independent of learning and interpretation. The empiricists claim that our perceptions of space are entirely and exclusively a matter of experiential education;

due to the kinesthetic sensations accompanying the movements of the eye in vision, we obtain cues or 'local signs' which enable us to pass a judgment on the direction and distance of objects in space.

The *nativists* advance a number of facts in support of their theory. Spatial dimensions are given directly in the perception of colored surfaces. Chicks just out of the egg pick at grain particles with unerring accuracy and follow the movements of a worm or insect without difficulty. Similar incidents are reported about other animals, and they seem to indicate a congenital faculty of space perception. Examples from animal life, however, are inconclusive, because it could be that the sense of smell has more to do with their actions than sight. While the nativists are correct in stating that spatial dimensions are necessarily involved in colored surfaces, it does not follow that the perception of the third dimension is also an immediate datum of visual experience; the perception of the third dimension, as we have shown, is rather a matter of interpretation based on the sense of touch and on various cues of the visual image.

The *empiricists* also advance certain facts in support of their view. They refer particularly to the cases where persons, blind from birth, have received sight. Cheselden, Wardrop, and Franz reported such cases more than a century ago, and many cases of a similar kind have been described since. Such persons have no perception of distance or depth in space and must learn to interpret their visual images. They have, however, an immediate vision of the two dimensions of length and height. It is the contention of the empiricists that the sense of sight has no native capacity of recognizing extension in any manner. In order to see a circle or triangle, the eye must follow the lines of these figures, and the eye itself must move in the form of a circle or triangle. From these muscular sensations, through experience and association, we gradually acquire the notion of extension and three-dimensional space. These muscular movements of the eyes thus become the 'local signs' whereby we judge distance. Lotze (1817–1881) was a prominent exponent of the 'local sign' theory. Empiricists are wrong in attributing our judgments about dimensions to the muscular sensations of the eye following the lines of figures, etc. Were their contention correct, we would have no notion what a circle, triangle, or other mathematical figure is like, because photographic reproductions of the eye movements show they are jerky and irregular and never describe anything like the smooth lines observed in the contour of any object or figure. Eye movements form one of the criteria of distance and size, but they play only a minor part; criteria present in the visual image itself, as mentioned above, play the major part in space perception.

These facts concerning vision, furnished by the physicists, physiologists, and psychologists, are very informative. The *fundamental purpose* of the sense of sight, as of the other external senses, is the *adjustment* of the organism to its surroundings. As a living being living in a world of manifold objects, man must be able to find his way about among them. All the senses serve as channels of information regarding these objects, so that man can protect, preserve, and develop his being as an *integral organism.*

One fact stands out prominently, as we look back over these various senses: Sense function is a type of activity far superior to that of physical or chemical substances, and sense function cannot be explained in terms of physical or chemical action and reaction.

The information assembled by the external senses is passed on to the *internal senses;* these must now be examined.

Summary of Chapter VI

More than any other sense, sight brings the mind into *cognitional contact* with the world.

1. *The Organ of Sight.* It is the eye. The *eye* consists of a number of distinct parts: the sclerotic, the choroid, the retina, the cornea, the iris, the lens, the aequeous and vitreous

humors. The *retina,* which is the seat of vision, is composed of various layers of tissue. Its *rods* and *cones* are the receptors.

2. *Light Rays as Stimulus.* Light appears as photons and also as electromagnetic waves. The range of the visible spectrum lies between wave lengths of 386mμ and 800 mμ. Light waves have length, frequency, and amplitude.

3. *Color as Sensation.* In *achromatic* sensations we experience white, black, and gray; in *chromatic* sensations, red, blue, green, yellow, and intermediate hues. There are *six psychological primaries:* white, black, red, green, yellow, and blue. Chromatic colors have *three attributes:* hue, saturation, and brightness.

4. *Rod and Cone Vision.* The rods are the receptors for achromatic, low intensity, scotopic vision; the cones are the receptors for chromatic, high intensity, photopic vision. The organ of sight, therefore, is a duplex apparatus.

5. *Color Mixture.* By this we mean the stimulation of the same retinal spot by light rays of different wave length. There are *three laws* of color mixture. The first concerns complementary colors; the second concerns intermediate colors; the third concerns the substitution of colors in mixtures containing more than two colors.

6. *Color Contrast.* By this is meant the difference in the appearance of colors brought about by the stimulation of adjacent sets of rod and cones. Contrast seems to be mainly the result of partial or complete physiological *inhibition. Simultaneous* contrast can be observed by placing a piece of colored paper against variously colored backgrounds.

7. *Afterimages.* Afterimages are sensations occurring after the stimuli causing them have ceased. They are *negative* or *complementary,* when a dark image is replaced by a light image, or a light by a dark, or the color of the original sensation by its complementary color. They are *positive,* when they preserve the color or shade of the original sensation. Afterimages are subjective.

8. *Color Blindness.* This is the partial or total inability to distinguish or recognize chromatic colors. *Dichromatism* or

partial color blindness exists in two forms: red-green and blue-yellow blindness. In *monochromatism* or *total* color blindness a person sees all things in the neutral colors of white-gray-black.

9. *Binocular Vision.* The optical fields of both eyes, though slightly different, are seen as a *single field,* due to binocular fusion in consequence of a single cortical response. When the two fields are focused on the fovea in a practically identical manner, fusion occurs; otherwise we see double images. Binocular *rivalry* occurs, when each eye, separately and simultaneously, see colors or objects or figures very different in appearance. When complementary colors are used, *psychological fusion* may occur according to the laws of color mixture.

10. *Behaviorism and Color Vision.* In accordance with this theory, an exact correlation must exist between stimulus and response. Such an exact correlation does not exist in color vision. Different stimuli produce the same sensation. In simultaneous contrast the sensations of color change, though the kind and amount of wave lengths remain unchanged. The sensation of black is not properly accounted for. Afterimages are subjective in character.

11. *Visual Space.* Colored surface in *two dimensions,* length and height, is an immediate visual experience; visual experience also includes the intuitive distinction of concrete parts, shape, and relative size. *Depth in space,* or the third dimension, is a matter of perception and judgment. The combination of *touch and sight* assists us in interpreting the visual image with respect to depth in space. Thereupon certain *criteria* in the visual image enable us to gauge depth: light and shadow, perspective, angular difference of the optical fields in binocular vision, and the muscular movements of the eyes in focusing.

Nativism attributes perception of space to a native or constitutional property of vision itself. The theory, however, is wrong in including the direct perception of the third dimension, depth in space. *Empiricism* attributes it entirely and exclusively to experiential education, in which the kinesthetic sensations of eye movements furnish us with 'local signs.' This theory overlooks the fact that the visual image itself furnishes criteria of visual space and that the vision of colored surfaces gives two dimensions immediately.

Readings

Harmon, F. L., *Principles of Psychology,* Ch. 7.—Gruender H., *Experimental Psychology,* Ch. III, IV, VI, VII.—Woodworth, R. S., *Experimental Psychology,* Ch. XXII, XXIII, XXVI.—Helmholtz, H. L. F., *Physiological Optics.*—Hering, E., *Grundzüge der Lehre vom Lichtsinn.*—Ladd-Franklin, C., *Color and Color Theories.*

Chapter VII

CENTRAL OR SYNTHETIC SENSE

INFORMATION concerning conditions in man's own organism and in the outside world comes to the mind through the channels of the external senses — sight, hearing, taste, smell, and the somesthetic senses. This information comes piecemeal. Each sense resembles a brook, and each item of sensation resembles a drop of water carrying a bit of information in solution, and through these diverse sources an enormous amount of information flows into the common reservoir of the brain.

These bits of information do not remain isolated, nor do they mingle indiscriminately into a jumbled mass of heterogeneous items. They are analyzed, sifted, sorted, arranged, and combined into meaningful wholes; they are stored away, capable of being recalled for future use, ready to be compared and combined with further information received from the vital sources of the senses as time goes on. This process of elaboration is carried out by the *internal senses* — the *central sense, imagination, sensory memory,* and *instinct.* These will now be discussed.

The Central Sense

We may define the *central sense* as the mental *power to consciously perceive, distinguish, and synthesize the objects and operations of the presently active external senses.* From Aristotle down through the Middle Ages and up to our own day, this power has been termed the *common sense* (*sensus communis*). While the name is accurate enough in its technical meaning, the English language unfortunately uses the expression 'common sense' more frequently to designate things totally different. Sometimes 'common sense' is used to mean plain good judgment; again it is used to mean the intuitive judgment of mankind relative to certain fundamental principles; and it is also used to designate the unscientific and unreflective opinions of common people who lack an extensive education. Because of these various meanings, it seems unwise to apply the term 'common sense' to the internal sense in question. T. V. Moore employs the term *synthetic sense.* We prefer the term *central sense,* because it is general enough to include all the functions proper to this sense, without any danger of confusing it with other mental powers. In as much, however, as Moore's term is apt and expressive, it may be advisable to speak of this power either as the 'central' or 'synthetic sense.'

The central or synthetic sense has a *double function.* When the external senses react to a stimulus, so that the eye sees and the ear hears, etc., the central sense perceives and distinguishes the various sense qualities presented, combines them, and refers them to the *one object* from which the stimuli originate. This is the objective phase of the function of the central sense. There is, however, also a subjective phase to its function. By means of the central sense we *become aware of the acts of sensation* present in the various external senses, such as the act of seeing and the act of hearing, etc.; and we also become aware of their differences as acts of sensations, so that we know that the act of seeing is not the act of hearing, etc. Viewed from the standpoint of this latter function, the central or synthetic sense is termed *sensory consciousness.*

Existence of the Central Sense

Introspection proves that we have the ability to *distinguish* between the *qualities* perceived by the various external senses. The eye, of course, can distinguish between white and black, between red and green; taste can distinguish between bitter and sour and sweet and salty; smell can distinguish between fruity and fragrant and fetid odors; hearing can distinguish between high and low notes, between a cacophonous noise and a clear tone; and the somesthetic senses can distinguish between the different sense qualities in their particular field. But one sense knows nothing of what is registered by another sense: sight knows nothing of sound, hearing knows nothing of color or flavor or odor or cold or pain, etc. We distinguish, however, between these various sense qualities and the sensations they produce in us. For example, we distinguish between the whiteness, roughness, and sweetness of sugar; between the shape, the tone, and the touch of a violin; between the blackness, the odor, and the disagreeable taste of tar; between the sharpness, the temperature of a needle, and the pain caused by its puncture, and so on.

Introspection also proves that we *combine* these different sense qualities and refer them to the *same object.* I take a certain thing between my fingers, and it is hard and square to the touch; I look at it and see that it is white; I taste it, and it is sweet. The fingers know nothing of its color or taste; the eye knows nothing of its hardness or taste; the tongue knows nothing of its hardness or color. Yet I make a synthesis of these irreducible qualities, refer them to the same object, and call it 'sugar.' I look at my desk and see a pencil; it is yellow and slender, and I take it and strike it against the desk, hearing a sharp sound. These are sensations of sight, touch, and hearing. I refer them all to the one same pencil, and I perceive that they all belong together, simultaneously, to the same object. What makes the synthesis of these heterogeneous items? Since the single senses respond only to their own stimuli, no single external sense nor combination of senses can effect the synthesis. There must exist, therefore, a *central sense* to which the single senses relay their information; this central sense, upon receipt of the data of the separate senses, distinguishes between them, combines them, and then refers them to the one concrete object from which the various stimuli originate.

That this analysis and synthesis of sensations and their objects is not an intellectual operation, but the activity of a sensory power, is shown by the fact that *brutes possess this ability.* Consider the actions of a dog. Suppose the dog is in one room, and his master is in the adjoining room behind the closed door. If the master calls the dog by name, the dog will prick up his ears and listen; he recognizes his master's voice. Not seeing his master, he runs about; coming to the door, he sniffs and recognizes the odor peculiar to his master. If the master now opens the door, the dog runs to him without hesitation, even if other persons are also present. The dog knows that he hears his master, but he also knows that he does not see him; he recognizes the fact that the sound and odor are those of his master, but he also knows that he lacks the sight of his master; and when he sees him, he combines sound and odor and sight and refers them to the same object, his master. The dog, therefore, makes a concrete distinction between the various sensations and their objects and synthesizes them into a concrete whole. A lion does not bite so eagerly into the neck of a zebra because the zebra has a striped hide or emits a certain odor or utters a peculiar sound. The lion kills the zebra because the zebra tastes so delicious. But the lion knows that objects of such a shape and color, emitting such an odor, and uttering such a sound, have a delicious flavor. The lion thus distinguishes between these sensations and the sense qualities and refers them all to one object. Such examples could be multiplied indefinitely. They show that animals possess a central or synthetic sense.

In a similar manner, it can be shown that men and brutes possess *sensory consciousness,* so that they are aware of their sensations and of the sense qualities present in the sensations.

If I take a bell in my hand and ring it, I not only see its shape and color, perceive its hardness and temperature, and hear the sound of its ringing, but I am aware of the fact that I see the shape and color, perceive its hardness and temperature, and hear its sound. I have such an experience every time I pay attention to my senses and their operations and attempt to discover, for example, how acute my hearing is by listening to the tick of a watch, how sharp my eyesight is by reading a distant sign, how delicate my touch is by fingering weights when blindfolded, etc. In such cases I not only have sensations but 'become aware' of them. It is obvious, however, that the eye is not conscious of its seeing, nor the ear of its hearing, nor the finger of its touching, etc. Much less can the eye be conscious of the hearing of the ear or of the touching of the fingers; and the same must be said of each of the external senses with respect to the sensations of the others. Still, the awareness of the operations and qualities present in the senses, singly and conjointly, is a fact. Since this awareness cannot be attributed to the external senses themselves, we must admit the presence of a central or synthetic sense which is conscious of these senses, their operations and sense objects.

Brutes, too, possess sensory consciousness. They seek to alleviate pain, hunger, thirst, sex urge, etc. If they were not conscious of these things, how could they seek to alleviate them? They look at a wounded foot and lick it; if they were not conscious of the pain, they would not act in this manner. They manifest signs of pleasure, fear, and anger. Scratch a dog under the chin, or stroke the back of a cat; they give every indication of pleasure and of being aware of the pleasurable feeling. When the master approaches the dog with a whip, the dog slinks away or crouches at the feet of the master; he shows fear of the whipping and is conscious of the anticipated pain to be received from the blow. When the dog and the cat collide, they jump apart, face each other, the dog barking and the cat spitting, ready to fight; they are angry, and they are conscious of the fact that they stand in the face of an attacking foe. None of these actions have any meaning except under the supposition that animals are conscious of objects and of their own sensory reactions in a concrete manner.

Animals exhibit curiosity in their surroundings, and that presupposes consciousness. One of the most comical scenes to witness is the first acquaintance of a dog with a live frog. Curiosity prompts the dog to investigate this object. He walks up to the frog, inquisitive but cautious, eyes it uncertainly, and then sniffs it. When the frog, frightened, leaps through the air, the dog is visibly perturbed, jumps away, stops, stares at the strange creature, hesitates, barks, quiets down, and then, perhaps, approaches it again with the slowness and deliberation of a very mystified observer. Who would say that he is not conscious of the frog and his own perceptions in its presence? Or, if a squirrel is near, toss a piece of candy on the ground, and watch its antics. Curiosity urges the squirrel to examine the object, while fear of the human being holds it in check. It approaches stealthily, stops, flashes its tail, and then scampers away in fright. The action is repeated from a different angle of approach a number of times, but every time the squirrel comes a trifle closer, until at last it can smell the candy and give it a tentative nibble; if the taste is agreeable, it will grab the candy in its paws, put it between its jaws, and rush away to enjoy the morsel in safety and leisure. The squirrel most assuredly is conscious of the object perceived and of its acts of perception. Animals show curiosity by turning their head to hear better, by looking fixedly at objects to see better, by approaching objects to smell them better, and so forth. Such actions show that they are conscious of the sensations present in their sense organs and of the objects presented by them.

The mere fact that men and brutes have *different senses* makes a central or synthetic sense a necessity, for they would be useless without it. It would be useless for an animal, whether man or brute, to see food, if the animal were not conscious that it is food. The animal could not strive to relieve the sensation of hunger by taking food, if it did not experience hunger consciously as its own hunger. It is obvious that men and brutes do not experience sensations as detached, isolated, unconsciously received processes, but are aware of the presence of these processes as their own in a concrete sensory manner. The fact, however, necessitates a central or synthetic sense capable of distinguishing and synthesizing the data presented by the separate external senses, because otherwise there would be no *common bond* which would enable us to compare, distinguish, and unite them into concrete wholes. It is precisely because of this common bond that the philosophers of old termed this sense the 'common sense.'

Gestalt and Synthetic Sense

The *associationism* of Hume, which has dominated modern psychology to a great extent, was frankly sensationalistic. According to Hume, there are just two fundamental elements which enter into the fabric of human knowledge, 'impressions' and 'ideas'; translated into the terms of modern psychology, these are 'sensations' and 'mental images.' The 'ideas' (images) are but faint replicas of 'impressions' (sensations), and these are all we can and do know. They are simple, discrete components which are combined and recombined in various ways according to the laws of association. Hume insisted that they are isolated, discrete 'existences' or elements, and the mind cannot perceive any connection between them, nor can it combine them into higher units or organized wholes; this theory follows logically from his doctrine that the mind of man is not a distinct entity but merely "a heap of perceptions."

The philosophy of Gestalt (a German word for 'form' or 'shape' or 'configuration') is in opposition to this 'atomistic' concept of Hume and his followers. The more recent School of Gestalt was founded by M. Wertheimer, K. Koffka, and W. Köhler about the year 1912. For the isolated, discrete psychic elements of sensationalism and associationism they substituted 'organized wholes,' 'configuration,' 'Gestalt.' In this view the whole is not a mere sum of the discrete parts, but something over and above the sum of the parts; the whole is prior to its component parts; the parts derived their character from the whole, not the whole from the parts. Wertheimer expresses the essence of the Gestalt theory in this manner: "There are wholes, the behavior of which is not determined by that of their individual elements, but where the part-processes are themselves determined by the intrinsic nature of the whole."[1]

Applied to sensory experiences, this principle implies that we do not build up a percept, like a mosaic, by putting together

[1] Willis D. Ellis, *A Source Book of Gestalt Psychology* (Harcourt, Brace and Co., 1938), p. 2.

the individual sensory elements, so that the whole-properties are a mere summation of the part-properties; on the contrary, what we perceive primarily are the wholes and their properties, and then first analysis will reveal the parts of wholes. For example, I see a house. From the standpoint of *sensations,* there may be one hundred and twenty distinct sensations of brightness and shades of color in my total impression of the house. But that is not what I actually *see;* what I see is the 'house' as a 'whole-complex,' and the component parts with their brightness and color properties are but 'parts-of-the-whole-house,' if they are noticed at all. Again, when I behold a city scene, the 'whole view' is what I behold first and primarily, and then I notice streets, houses, lawns, trees, automobiles, people, etc., as subsidiary wholes and parts; but I am never aware of a million and more discrete sensations which through addition make up the total scene as a result of their combination.

Such 'wholes' contain more than the mere sum of all the parts, as paradoxical as this may seem. If I take nine distinct tones of different pitch and place them in a definite sequence, the result, let us say, is a 'melody.' I can arrange them in a different sequence, and the result is a different melody. I can rearrange them again, and now there is no melody at all. In every case, the sensations are the same as to kind and number. 'Melody,' therefore, is more than the mere summation of these nine sensations; it is the 'form' or 'configuration' of the nine tones as a unit or whole which constitutes melody, and that is something over and above the single tones as discrete elements. The 'form' or 'configuration' of the melody becomes still clearer, when we take the melody and transpose it into different keys; we now have totally different sets of nine tones, yet we recognize the 'melody' without difficulty as being the same in every key. We thus see that it is the *form,* the *configuration* of the melody as a whole or unit which determines the nature of the tones as component parts of the melody, and not the nature of the single tones as sensation elements which determine the nature of the melody as a whole. The same is true of the call of a robin, the song of a bob-o-link, the trill of a wren, the hoot of an owl, the moo of a cow, the whinny of a horse, the bray of a mule, the howl of a wolf, the trumpeting of an elephant, etc.; they are perceived as configured wholes and are recognized as such, not as so many separate sensations arising from air vibrations added together to make a numerical total. A symphony by Bach is more than the mere sum of all the separate notes, and a painting by Raphael is more than the juxtaposition of so many particles of paint and daubs of color; the symphony and painting as configured or structuralized wholes are what I perceive, and the separate parts have importance only in so far as they are integral portions of the whole.

The advocates of the Gestalt theory are certainly correct, when they claim that our percepts are configured wholes and not mere aggregates of elements of sensation. Sensory configuration is a fact, as the above-mentioned instances prove. Perhaps the best proof is found in the case of persons afflicted with cataract from birth and then operated on later in life, because their first acquaintance with visual perception is uninfluenced by past experience.

When conditions were exceptionally favorable, it was invariably found that these patients perceived *objects* and *scenes* as whole-complexes. Trees were seen as trees, houses as houses, streets as streets, persons as persons; but they were *not recognized as such* until they were manipulated or brought into relation with past experiences in some way. These patients could see that a cube was different from a sphere, but they did not know which was the cube and which the sphere until placed in their hand. After a walk through the village, a patient of Dufour remarked that he had seen 'many beautiful things,' but he did not know what they were because he had not been told. We thus see that *configuration* is given immediately in visual perception. *Interpretation,* however, is an intellectual process. The visual picture of individual objects and scenes is clear and precise, but it has no *meaning* until connected with the data of other senses, especially with the data of touch and hearing; only after this connection is made, it is possible to interpret the picture and recognize the objects for what they really are.

Experiences of this kind make it clear that things are not perceived as a mere aggregate of disparate visual, auditory, or tactual sensations, but as individual objects, as *configured wholes;* the component parts are present and are also perceived, but as constituents in a secondary manner. *Sensory synthesis* must always be present, because the whole-complex must be seen in relation to its parts, and the parts must be seen in relation to the whole-complex, and because the data of the various senses must be combined into a *perceptual whole.* Only then, after this sensory synthesis is effected, can the intellect proceed to interpret the configured whole and give it meaning. A sensory synthesis, however, demands a special sensory power capable of holding apart and combining the various sensory items. This sensory power is the *central* or *synthetic sense.* Gestaltists do not admit the existence of a central or synthetic sense, though it follows logically from the facts of their theory. They realize, however, the necessity of a sensory synthesis, and so E. M. v. Hornbostel, for example, argues for *the unity of the senses.*[2] He does not claim that all the senses are really only one sense, but he stresses the point (unduly, it is true) that the properties of one sense quality are often applied to another sense-quality on the basis of *similarity.* The point is worthy of consideration.

We always speak of tones as 'high' or 'low' in the scale; we also speak of tones as 'warm,' 'cold,' 'sharp,' 'dull,' 'bright,' 'dark,' 'heavy,' 'light,' and so forth. Similarly, we designate colors as 'warm,' 'cold,' 'loud,' 'quiet,' 'soft,' 'hard,' and so on. In this manner we express the fact that we recognize a definite similarity between the qualities of one sense and those of another, although the sense qualities in themselves are radically different. There is more to this transfer of properties than fanciful language. The basis for this transfer of properties lies in the operation of the *central* or *synthetic sense.* This internal sense

[2] Erich M. v. Hornbostel, "The Unity of the Senses," in *A Source Book of Gestalt Psychology,* pp. 210–216.

is the common receptacle for the sensations mediated by all the external senses; it holds them apart and yet holds them together, discriminating betwen them and synthesizing them. The mind notes similarities which at first are not obvious, but which are there fundamentally nevertheless. Language reveals the presence of these similarities in the sensory field of the various senses. Only on the supposition of the existence of a central or synthetic sense does this remarkable feature receive a satisfactory explanation.

The facts brought forth by the psychology of Gestalt in this connnection are not really new; they were known in principle by Aristotle and the Schoolmen. They verify the aristotelian-scholastic concept of the central sense.

Pathology and Central Sense

T. V. Moore[3] has shown that *pathological conditions of the brain,* with their attending disturbances, definitely prove the existence of a central or synthetic sense. When such conditions prevail, the afflicted persons lose to some extent the power to synthesize the sensory data into a perceptual whole, even though the single items are all perceived as present.

In the *visual* presentation of an object, we first perceive it as a confused whole and then differentiate the details; we then reform the details into a meaningful whole. For example, we first see an object in a general way as a human person; we then note the details of this person as to color, stature, gait, voice, etc.; we finally reform these details and recognize this person as 'John Jones.' In the case of cerebral disturbances, such as lesions through injury or disease, the power of sensory synthesis is impaired, although the ordinary sensory and intellectual abilities are intact.

Lissauer (1890) describes the case of a man who had injured his head in a fall. He could match colors placed before him, but he made frequent errors when asked to pick out a color

---

[3] *Cognitive Psychology* (Lippincott, 1939), Part III, Ch. II, III, IV.

by name. He could draw the figure of a watch set before him, but he was incapable of identifying and recognizing either the watch or the drawing; if he took the watch in his hand or listened to it tick, he recognized and named it immediately. When told to draw a figure from memory, he would draw a few strokes, ponder, make a few more strokes somewhere, attempt to group them, etc. The drawing had no meaning for him. Sometimes he recognized a picture as a whole, for instance, an animal, but could not distinguish the head from the tail. He also recognized a bust picture of Bismarck, but was unable to point out correctly the eyes, the ears, etc.

To a normal person the synthesizing of the various items presented in a picture or drawing, if it is not too extensive or complicated in details, is a relatively easy matter; but to a person suffering from a cerebral disturbance of some sort, it is difficult or even impossible. In order that such a synthesis be effective, it is necessary that the main items be held together in the span of conscious perception long enough for the concrete relations of the parts to become apparent to the observer. The focus of attention passes from one item to the other, but the single items attended to must not fade from consciousness during the successive phases of focusing. Such a fading, however, is precisely what may, and often does, happen in the case of cerebral disturbance; persons afflicted in this manner cannot retain the impressions long enough to make the necessary comparison and synthesis. One patient, for example, was capable of recognizing the single objects and persons in a comparatively simple picture and describe each one separately, but could not hold the items together in consciousness so as to give a correct interpretation of the picture as a whole. Others are able to interpret a single picture, but are unable to interpret a series of pictures in continuity, as in a comic strip. The 'interpretation,' of course, is a function of the intellect. That the intellect failed, however, to make the interpretation, was not the fault of the intellect as such, but the fault of the sensory mechanism furnishing the items for interpretation. That the sensory mechanism is at fault can be observed in those cases where the brain recovers from the injury or disturbance; as the condition gradually clears, synthesis also improves. In some instances patients of this kind return almost to normal. The synthetic function, therefore, is a sensory function dependent on the cerebral centers and their neural associations.

Inability to synthesize *tactual* sensations has also been observed. Dejerine (1906) had a patient who, when a key was placed in his right hand, did not know what it was, although he could give a rather accurate description of it. It was described as "a fairly long object, thin, hard, that has a hole at one end." When it was placed in his left hand, he recognized it immediately and said it was "a key." When the touch spots are insensitive to vibration, because the stimuli, due to some cerebral condition retarding perception, are too slow in reaching consciousness, patients are unable to distinguish between the feel of wool and the feel of glass, etc. Even when capable of recognizing the primary qualities of an object by touch, some persons are unable to recognize the object itself by means of tactile sensations; in other words, the perception of tactile qualities is normal, but they lack the power of synthesizing the perceived data into an integrated perceptual whole.

The lack of perceptual synthesis has also been observed in *taste*. To recognize an object of taste, a combination of the qualities of taste, smell, temperature, touch, and kinesthesis is required; taste alone merely reveals the qualities of sweet, bitter, sour, and salty, without identifying the object itself. One woman patient could readily distinguish the four flavors, but did not know what she was eating.

These and similar pathological cases show clearly that the data of the separate external senses are insufficient to account for the sensory synthesis which occurs in our normal mental life. Over and above the functions of the external senses themselves there must exist the function of a super-sense intimately connected with the brain. If the function of this super-sense is impaired through cerebral injury or disturbance, normal sensory synthesis is slowed down or partially lost. This super-sense is the central or synthetic sense.

The Nature of the Central Sense

The central sense, it should be clear from what has been stated about its function, is really the *root* and *principle* of the external senses. The external senses are in the nature of instrumental causes in the service of the central sense as the principal cause. The central sense operates through the external senses, collecting divergent data from each of them and synthesizing these data into perceptual wholes, or precepts, so that the organism can know and recognize the single *objects* more or less in their entirety. While the single senses perceive specific sense qualities (proper sensibles), the central sense becomes aware of these qualities and also of the general qualities of bodies based on extension (common sensibles). These common sensibles are movement, rest, figure, magnitude, and number. Our perception of visual space, especially of the third dimension, is mainly the result of the synthetic operation of the central sense using the data supplied by the special senses.

If we now inquire into the *nature* and the *organ* of the central sense, we immediately become involved in difficulties. *Aristotle*[4] had already realized the problem.

The central sense must be a sensory power, because it is concerned with sense objects; besides, brutes possess this power, and they are restricted to sense perceptions. Aristotle pointed out that if one person sensed the 'whiteness' of an object (say, sugar) and another person its 'sweetness,' there would be no possibility for them to compare their sensations and combine them in a common percept. The same difficulty, however, seems to arise, if we assume that the central sense is a distinct power residing in a *special organ*. We must bear in mind that this organ would perceive not only the sense *objects* of all the special senses (color, sound, flavor, odor, warmth, cold, pain, etc.) but also the *percipient acts* of sensations (seeing, hearing, tasting, etc.). An organ, however, being material, must consist of parts; every part would perceive the act of sensation and the

[4] *On the Soul,* Book III, Chap. 2, 426 b.

corresponding object of a particular external sense. We have here practically the case of the two individual persons of whom Aristotle speaks, since each separate part of the organ corresponds to such an individual person; and under such circumstances the comparison, discrimination, and synthesis of the sense objects into a perceptual whole would remain unexplained.

The eye sees color, but it does not see itself see; the ear hears sound, but it does not hear itself hear. No sense perceives its own act of sensation, because that would be a *reflex knowledge* of itself which, as we will see later, is impossible to a material organ. It follows, of course, that a central or synthetic sense is necessary, but the acceptance of a central or synthetic sense does not solve the difficulties.

D. Card. Mercier,[5] the eminent Belgian philosopher, finds *three serious difficulties* in the assumption that the central sense is a distinct power or faculty with a special organ. The *first* is, that we have two distinct senses perceiving the same proper sense qualities. The eye and the central sense would perceive color, the ear and the central sense would perceive sound, the tongue and the central sense would perceive flavor, and so on. The *second* is, that it would be necessary to ascribe to the central sense such totally disparate things as the perception of color and the perception of seeing the color, the perception of sound and the perception of hearing the sound, the perception of flavor and the perception of tasting the flavor, and so forth. The objects of sense and the acts of sensation are so entirely different in character, that it is difficult to understand how they can stimulate one and the same power and organ into activity. The *third* difficulty is, that the same central sense would become active through the perception of formally diverse objects like color, sound, odor, taste, pressure, warmth, pain, etc. Why all the special external senses, if one sense and one organ can perceive them all?

Mercier is of the opinion that these difficulties can be avoided by assuming that the central sense is *not a special power* or faculty *with a special organ* determined to the *one specific*

[5] *Psychologie* (11th ed., 1923), marg. nn. 100–102.

activity of discrimination and synthesis. No special organ is required. Synthesis would occur though the functioning of the *cerebral centers* of the single external senses connected with one another by *association fibers.* His *explanation* then is as follows:

When I grasp a bell and ring it, I have sensations of touch, pressure, temperature, sight, and sound. Each sensation goes to its respective cerebral center. The simultaneousness of these sensations produces in the cerebrum a *simultaneous reaction* which presents itself psychologically as a *synthesis* of the sensations of touch, pressure, temperature, sight, and sound, and in this manner the object, the bell, is apprehended in its various qualities as a *perceptual whole.* What more is needed?

Each kind of sensation leaves a cerebral *image* of its sense quality behind in its respective cerebral center, and all centers are united through association fibers. As a consequence, the visual image of the bell will recall the image of its ringing, its hardness, its temperature, etc.; so, too, the image of the ringing of the bell will recall its shape, etc. If, however, one of these centers should be destroyed or impaired, the cerebral image of this center will also be destroyed or impaired, so that this particular image drops out of the association either entirely or in part. It then happens that persons will not be able to recognize objects by sight or touch or hearing, and so forth, because of a lack of cerebral synthesis. Psychic blindness, psychic deafness, and similar perceptual abnormalities result from such a lack of cerebral synthesis.

In as much as no special structure or cerebral center has been discovered which could be assigned definitely to the central or synthetic sense as the seat of its function, it seems very reasonable to ascribe the central sense and its function to the *brain as a whole,* operating through its centers and association tracks.

Sensory Consciousness

Mercier's explanation of the central sense's function of *consciousness* is also interesting.

We perceive the percipient act of sight, hearing, and of the other special senses. When an external sense is activated to sensation, the muscular apparatus serving this sense contracts and produces *muscular* or *kinesthetic sensations*. This muscular sensation, which is the same everywhere, is really what we call sensory *consciousness*.

As *proof* for his contention, Mercier adduces certain facts. The exercise of an external sense is always *accompanied* by muscular exertion and sensation. In order to see properly, we turn the head and the eyes, fix the focal point and the ocular axis; in order to hear properly, we turn the head in the direction of the sound and strain the ears; in order to taste and smell properly, we move the tongue about and inhale the air through the nose; in order to 'feel' properly, we manipulate an object. In other words, to apprehend an object clearly with our senses, we must accommodate the organ to the object by means of muscular movements. There is thus a permanent *connection* and *association* between these muscular sensations and the exercise of the sense organs, and the result is the inner perception or 'consciousness' that sensation takes place in a special organ.

Attention to these muscular sensations, as we know, strengthens the consciousness of perceptions. Lack of attention, or the concentration of attention on one type of perception, impedes the consciousness of entire sets of perceptions. Many soldiers, in the heat of battle, fail to notice minor wounds and experience no pain for a while. Absorption in a problem makes us oblivious of street noises.

According to Mercier's theory, then, consciousness does not manifest to us an internal perception of the *act* of perception strictly as such. We see or hear or taste or smell or feel something and at the same time have the 'feeling of activity' through muscular sensation. The sentient subject simply perceives *simultaneously a sense object* (color, sound, flavor, etc.) and the *muscular sensation of activity*.

Mercier's theory of sensory consciousness is ingenious, but it does *not* seem very *satisfactory*. For one thing, the sensations of some external senses are not accompanied by muscular sensations. Such are the sensations of the touch, temperature, and pain spots; they can be aroused by very slight punctiform stimulation, when the muscles are completely relaxed and inactive. The end organs for these sensations are distributed profusely throughout the skin, even in areas where muscle and tendon spindles (the organs of muscular sensation) are not present; one need but mention, for example, the cornea of the eye with its sensitivity to pain. Under such circumstances, we should not be conscious of these sensations; as a matter of fact, however, we are. Again, when the sensory nerves leading from the muscles of a part of the body are severed, muscular sensations from that part of the body are no longer experienced; but other sensations may still be normal and are consciously apprehended as occurring in that part. Finally, the muscular or kinesthetic sense is one of the external senses, on a level with the senses of sight, hearing, touch, temperature, pain, and the others; as such, this sense is no different from the others. Hence, we are also *conscious of muscular sensations,* as we can easily observe, if we flex our arms or lift a weight. Consciousness, then, cannot be identical with the muscular sensation of activity, but must be something over and above it; otherwise we would be obliged to assume that this second consciousness would thus be the muscular sensation of a muscular sensation.

Mercier's theory, that the synthesizing function of the central sense should be attributed to the brain and its associated centers, is reasonable, and many philosophers hold the same view. His theory of sensory consciousness, however, seems to run counter to observed facts.

Tilmann Pesch,[6] the prominent neo-scholastic, claims that *concomitant consciousness,* or *apperception,* is an essential phase of every act of cognition and therefore also of the function of sensory perception. Every act of cognition (and sensation is such an act) reveals not only the *object which* is presented but also the *subject to whom* the object is presented. Just as it is essential to the act of knowledge (here sensation) that it manifest the thing to the knower, so it is also essential to the

[6] *Institutiones Psychologicae* (Herder, 1898), Vol. II, nn. 474 et 574.

act of knowledge to manifest *itself* secondarily and, so to say, 'obliquely' to the knowing (sentient) subject; concomitant consciousness consists precisely in this 'experiential manifestation.' Sensation would not be an act of knowledge, of cognition, if the sentient subject were not aware (conscious) of the knowledge obtained through sensation; and since the knowledge of sensation is negotiated to the subject through the 'act' of sensation, the sentient subject becomes simultaneously, concretely and concomitantly, aware (conscious) of the act itself. It follows, then, that 'consciousness' is *not a specific function* of the central sense at all, but is an *essential property of all cognitive functions* of whatever kind.

Obviously, of course, some ultimate principle of unity is demanded to link the cerebral centers and their separate functions and data together. This principle must be the *unitary nature* of the percipient subject, based upon a single *vital principle* of sentiency which is predominantly active in the centralizing organ of the brain.

Summary of Chapter VII

The internal senses are: The central or synthetic sense, imagination, sensory memory, and instinct. This chapter deals with the central sense.

1. *The Central Sense.* It is also called the 'common sense' and the 'synthetic sense,' and is defined as the mental *power to consciously perceive, distinguish, and synthesize the objects and operations of the presently active external senses.* A double function is ascribed to it: It perceives and distinguishes the sense qualities presented, combines them, and refers them to one object; it also makes us aware of the percipient acts of sensation. In this latter capacity it is termed 'sensory consciousness.'

2. *Existence of the Central Sense.* Introspection shows that we *distinguish* between the 'whiteness' and 'sweetness' and 'hardness' of sugar, etc.; also, that we *combine* them and refer them to the same object. Since the single senses respond only to their respective stimuli (the eye to light, the ear to sound, etc.)

and not to those of other senses, they cannot make the synthesis; a central or synthetic sense is required. Brutes also possess a central sense, as their actions show.

Introspection also reveals that we are *conscious* of the percipient acts of sensation; we not only see, hear, etc., but are aware that we see, hear, etc. Brutes, too, have this consciousness.

The fact that we have different *kinds* of senses, makes a central, synthetic sense necessary, otherwise our mental life would consist of a mass of isolated, unrelated sensations.

3. *Gestalt and Synthetic Sense.* For the isolated discrete psychic elements of sensationalism and associationism, Gestaltists substitute 'organized wholes,' 'configurations,' 'Gestalt.' The whole is prior to the parts; the parts derive their character from the whole, not the whole from the parts. What we perceive primarily are the wholes and their properties, and then first will analysis reveal the parts of the wholes. Much experimental evidence is adduced to prove the truth of this fundamental fact of mental life.

Sensory synthesis must always be present in the perception of configured wholes. Such a sensory synthesis, however, demands a special sensory power capable of holding apart and combining the various sensory items. This sensory power is the *central* or *synthetic sense.*

4. *Pathology and the Central Sense.* Due to cerebral disturbances and lesions, the power of sensory synthesis is impaired or partially lost, although the ordinary sensory and intellectual abilities are intact. Hence, the data of the separate external senses are insufficient to account for sensory synthesis. The central sense in such cases is impaired.

5. *Nature of the Central Sense.* If one assumes that the central sense is a distinct power residing in a special organ, grave difficulties are encountered, because one part of the organ would presumably perceive one thing, and another part another thing; and thus a synthesis seems impossible.

Mercier is of the opinion that the simultaneousness of the sensations produces in the cerebrum a simultaneous reaction which presents itself psychologically as a synthesis; hence, the central or synthetic sense and its functions should be ascribed to the brain as a whole. This is a reasonable theory.

6. *Sensory Consciousness.* Sense consciousness, Mercier contends, is nothing more than the muscular sensation which accompanies seeing, hearing, etc. Tilmann Pesch insists that consciousness is an essential phase of every act of cognition, including sensation, otherwise sensation would not be 'cognition'; hence, consciousness is not a specific function of the central sense at all.

The functions of the central sense ultimately demand a *vital principle* as the principle of unity.

Readings

Maher, M., *Psychology,* Ch. V, toward end. — Moore, T. V., *Cognitive Psychology,* Part III, Ch. II, III, IV. — Aristotle, *On the Soul,* Book III, Ch. 3. — Gaffney, Mark A., *The Psychology of the Interior Senses,* Ch. II. — Ellis, Willis D., *A Source Book of Gestalt Psychology.*

CHAPTER VIII

IMAGINATION

WE HAVE now advanced one step farther in following the progressive stages of human knowledge. Objects stimulate the various sense organs into activity. These organs transmit nerve impulses to the brain, and the organism responds with the sensations appropriate to the stimuli. Sensations reveal a number of qualities, such as color, sound, flavor, warmth, cold, and so on. Then the internal central or synthetic sense combines these different sense qualities into a perceptual whole by referring them to the same object. This meaningful impression of the object obtained by the use of the senses is called the *percept.* The percept, therefore, is the sensory representation of the object as it appears to the activated senses and the central sense.

It is the purpose of this entire process to make us acquainted with the *objects* existing in the world in which we live. This purpose, however, would be only incompletely realized, if the impression of these objects would disappear when the objects themselves disappear, because then we could have *no abiding knowledge* of them. One of two things is necessary, if we are to have an abiding knowledge of objects: either the objects must remain present to our senses all the time, or we must have internal images of the objects present in us all the time. The first alternative is practically impossible and, as a matter of fact, does not occur. The second alternative, therefore, is a natural necessity, and nature has provided for this requirement of knowledge in the internal sense of *imagination.*

The Concept of Imagination

The *imagination* can be defined as the *power to form mental images or phantasms of perceived objects, together with the ability to reproduce these images or phantasms even in the absence of the perceived objects.*

The term 'image' or 'phantasm' must be taken broadly so as to include the representations of all the senses. We can imagine the color and shape of a rose (visual image), the fragrance of an orange (olfactory image), the taste of sugar (gustatory image), the tickle of a feather (touch image), the weight of steel (pressure image), the song of a canary (auditory image), the temperature of the yearly seasons (warmth and cold image), the misery of an operation (pain image), the strain of running (kinesthetic image), the sensation of falling (static image), the ache of hunger (visceral image).

The *differences between percepts and phantasms* or images are noteworthy. Upon comparison, we find that percepts are vivid and strong; phantasms are pale and weak. One need but look at a street scene, in order to observe the vividness and strength of the visual picture; the same view, as reproduced by the imagination with closed eyes, is extremely pale and weak. Percepts are unchangeable for the will; phantasms are changeable. So long as the stimuli reach the senses, they produce their effects, and our will can do nothing to alter them; the imagination, however, is dependent on the direction of the will, so that the will can decide what phantasms shall remain present or be eliminated. When we listen to a song on the radio, we hear the melody just as it is rendered by the singer; but when we imagine a song, we can change the melody at any point and even stop it entirely. Percepts possess clarity and fulness of detail; phantasms are vague and indistinct. Look at a bouquet of flowers and note the clarity and fullness of detail in shapes and colors; then close your eyes and imagine the same bouquet, and the details give way to vague and indistinct impressions.

These characteristics of percepts and phantasms are indicative of the *difference between the central sense and the imagination.* The central sense receives its data from the external senses and is directly dependent on the stimulation of these senses in its own proper function; hence, it never operates except when the external senses function, and it occupies itself exclusively with the objects presented by these senses. The imagination receives its data from the central or synthetic sense and then forms phantasms of the objects, and these phantasms can be revived even when the originals, the objects, are absent; the imagination, therefore, does not occupy itself with the objects, but with images in so far as they are representations of these objects. The causes which produce the percepts exist outside of us, as a rule, and are beyond our control; but the causes which produce the phantasms exist entirely within us and are, to a great extent, subject to our control. Because of these conditions, the percepts come into existence as items in a series fixed according to time and place, following the spatio-temporal order of the physical stimuli; but the representations of the imagination, being derived from the stored-up images always present after their formation, are capable of being evoked, separated, or combined in various ways and can be arranged in a series totally different from that in which the original perceptions occurred. The products of the central or synthetic sense are *presentations* of immediately present objects; the products of the imagination are *re-presentations* of these objects in the form of phantasms.

Imaginal activity thus reveals three distinct features of the imagination: *formation* and *conservation* of the images of sense objects; *reproduction* of the images; *construction* of the images into new combinations. We therefore speak of the 'conservatory' imagination, the 'reproductive' imagination, and the 'constructive' imagination. In speaking in this manner, we do not mean to imply that there are three distinct imaginations in man; there is but one imagination with three phases to its normal activity.

The Conservatory Imagination

Somehow or other, we *conserve* the 'images' or 'phantasms' of previous sensations and perceptions in our imagination; or, at any rate, we conserve something which the imagination elaborates into 'images.' Our daily experience proves that we are able to revive these images, not only once but hundreds of times. The ability to revive them presupposes the conservation of these images or of something which gives rise to them.

Certain *ultra-spiritualist* philosophers, such as Herbart, Sir William Hamilton, and others, look upon the conservation of images as taking place in the *mind* or *soul alone,* independent of neurological processes and of the brain; brain and nerve substance have nothing to do with the conservation of images. If this theory were true, a number of facts are unintelligible. Drowsiness retards the revival of images; tea, coffee, and some drugs increase the flow of images, while other drugs decrease their flow; in old age the conservation of images is weaker than in youth; diseases and injuries of the brain blot out entire sections of kindred images producing psychic blindness, psychic deafness, etc., leaving others intact and revivable; tumors of the brain often disturb imaginal functioning, and the functioning sometimes returns to normal after removal of the tumor; fatigue interferes with the retention of impressions. Facts of this nature show definitely that the conservation of images is not a purely psychic process, but is dependent at least to some extent on physiological conditions and neurological processes, especially those of the brain.

Materialistic psychologists and philosophers, among whom are Bain, Spencer, Ribot, and many others, place the conservation of images on a purely *neurological* basis. Cerebral processes alone are involved in conservation. These psychologists and philosophers differ in the details of the theory, but the general view is that the sensory impulses produce a modification in the tissue of the fibers and cells of the brain. Ribot, for example, assumes a definite modification of neural elements. The molecules of a nerve cell are forced by the nerve impulse to oscillate in a particular manner and do not return to their original condition; a repetition of this process tends to fix the molecules in this state of modified action; a number of such neural elements become connected through dynamic association, and thus entire events are recorded. Others look for the trace of the images in the grooving of pathways through groups of neurons and fibers brought on by repeated stimulation; the neural mechanism would be something like a new engine which must be 'broken in' and then runs smoothly, because it is grooved in a definite direction.

That some sort of modification of the nerve substance actually occurs and plays a part in the conservation of images, is undoubtedly correct. But that such neurological processes should be accepted as the complete explanation of the conservation of images, is an *inadequate theory,* because it is too *mechanistic* and ignores the *psychical features* of the images.

To say that sense perception leaves in the cerebrum a *weak representation,* a *faded copy,* or a *vestige,* is merely a restatement of the problem. What sort of a weak representation or faded copy of a color, a sound, a flavor, or of a pain can exist in the brain? If present, would we not be conscious of them? Our experience is to the effect that we can revive such images, sometimes voluntarily and sometimes involuntary, but they are not present *as images* until revived.

We can, and probably must, admit that some sort of image *trace* or, as Wundt terms it, '*functional disposition* of the nervous substance' remains in the neural elements after sense perception. More, however, is required. 'Traces,' 'dispositions,' 'oscillations,' or 'grooved pathways' of nerve tissue and cells are *not images.* What similarity is there between these things and the imaginal phantasms representing the Battle of Pearl Harbor, an Army and Navy football game, a morning in the Alps, the Bay of Naples, the bustle and hubbub of the port of Hong Kong, the death scene of a dear relative, the rhapsody of a symphonic orchestra, or the misery of a painful illness? Most of the events and scenes relived with the greatest vividness in our imagination have occurred *only once,* and thus a repeated stimulation of the same cells never took place to produce a modification of molecular grouping or grooved pathways of functional dispositions. Furthermore, when we look at a scene, the visual image covers the entire retina; looking at other scenes immediately after, we cover the same retinal elements with new visual images; and this process occurs hundreds of times in succession. One set of brain cells certainly does not select the impulses of one retinal image and conserve its trace exclusively, and another set the trace of another image, and so forth with the retinal images of all the successive visual impressions. The *same cerebral cells* receive the nerve impulses of a *multitude of visual images;* and since there is no reason to assume a preferential selection of traces on the part of the cerebral cells, these traces should overlap and interfere with each other, something like multiple exposures on the same photographic plate. No such confusion of images, however, takes place, because each scene or event can be reproduced *as a whole.* Again, if an identical tone is sounded, say, four times in succession, the impulses should reach the same cerebral spot along the same fibers, leaving a single reinforced trace or groove, and one should be able to revive only a single image of this tone; as a matter of fact, however, our imagination revives the whole event as a tone sounded four times.

The simple fact is that neural modifications of the cerebrum can no more be the full and exclusive explanation of the conservation of phantasms than the activations of sensory nerve terminals by physical stimuli are the full and exclusive explanation of the original perceptions of which the phantasms are the imaginal representations. Just as there is more to a perception than the molecular vibration of a nerve cell, so there is more to a phantasm than the molecular modification of a brain cell. Perceptions and imaginal phantasms involve the mental element of *conscious cognition,* and conscious cognition is something *psychic,* not purely physical; there is a *meaning* in what we perceive and imagine, but there is no meaning in the molecular oscillations of brain cells or in the grooved pathways of cerebral substance concerning whose existence we are totally unconscious.

The ultra-spiritualistic and materialistic theories are oversimplified extremes. Perceptions and phantasms are neither purely psychical nor purely physiological, but *psycho-physiological.* Cortical centers and cortical cells are necessary conditions for the conservation of phantasms, as is evident from the fact that injury to certain cortical centers makes the storage and revival of imaginal phantasms at times impossible. On the other hand, phantasms have a cognitional element which is truly psychical in character, and as such they demand a mind or psyche capable of cognition as distinct from mere neurological function. The psychical and physiological features of the phantasm and its 'trace' are interdependent, because man is a *psycho-physiological organism.* The phantasmal 'trace,' or whatever it is that is stored and conserved, must, therefore, also be psycho-physiological.

What, then, precisely is this 'trace' or 'vestige' or 'disposition' which underlies the phantasm or image of the conservatory imagination? Frankly speaking, we do not know. Something of the sort must be assumed to exist and be conserved; otherwise we cannot explain how the phantasms can arise after the actual perceptions have disappeared, sometimes even after the lapse of decades. It is likely that the phantasmal trace is such that a direct examination of its nature either by introspection or by experimental methods is not possible. And so the workings of the conservatory imagination may never actually become known.

The Reproductive Imagination

The *reproductive imagination* is the imagination in so far as it has the power of forming phantasms of objects and events which have been previously perceived. It should be noted very carefully that what are reproduced here in phantasmal forms are objects and events *as they have been perceived* at one time or other in actual experience, though at present they are no longer before the senses. It is not necessary that they be recognized as having been previously experienced; 'recognition' is a function of memory.

Just as we do not know exactly how the phantasmal trace is stored by the conservatory imagination, so we do not know how the reproductive imagination elaborates the phantasms from these traces. Someone says 'Times Square in New York,' and there rises up within our imagination the visual phantasm of this famous triangular thoroughfare with its crowds, theaters, stores, and bright lights. Someone mentions 'Lohengrin,' and the auditory phantasm of the wedding march begins to unfold in stately rhythm. Someone speaks of 'army grub,' and the gustatory and olfactory phantasm of corned beef and canned salmon assail the consciousness of the former soldier. And so with other experiences of the past. How are these phantasms evoked and evolved? The inner mechanism is hidden in the recesses of the mind.

Through experience we know that our imaginal phantasms are not isolated fragments of mental phenomena; they are *associated* with one another. The reproduction of related phantasms is called *association,* and the principles which condition the reproduction of a related set of phantasms are called the *Laws of Association.* That reason and will exert a powerful influence on the reproduction of phantasms and associate them freely, can be observed in the composition of a song, a poem, a book, etc. In the present connection, however, we are concerned only with *involuntary* association.

Laws of Association

There are primary and secondary Laws of Association. The primary are: the law of contiguity, of similarity, of contrast. The secondary are: vividness of impression, frequency of repetition, recentness.

The Primary Laws of Association

The Law of Contiguity. By this we mean the tendency of the imagination, in the presence of objects or events or in the presence of the phantasms of such objects or events, to recall other objects or events *connected* with them *in time or in space.* 'Contiguity' is really a spatial concept, but here it is used in the sense of 'closeness' in time as well as in space. This law is the formulation of a fact of common experience.

If I see or imagine my childhood home, there immediately arise before me objects and events connected with that place and period of my life: neighboring houses, streets, companions, relatives, events of school life, games, adventures, etc. If I imagine World War II, this recalls the attack on Pearl Harbor on December 7, 1941, the Japanese campaign against the Philippines, Malaya, Java, Burma, etc., or it may recall the succession of events and places connected with the Axis campaign in Europe and North Africa, etc. The techniques of art and skill all involve associations in time and space; whenever I practise or merely imagine a certain technique, a succession of temporal and spatial phantasms referring to its performance passes through my imagination. All *learning* depends on associations of objects or events contiguous in time or in space. As a rule, such associations contain elements in *both* time and space.

The Law of Similarity. This law states that present phantasms of objects, events, perceptions, and so forth, tend to reproduce in our imagination *similar* experiences of the past. We read, for example, an account of the French Revolution and are immediately reminded of the American Revolution. We see a scene on the Rhine and our imagination pictures a similar scene on the Hudson. We look at the photograph of our mother, and we recall her person. The law also applies to perceptions of taste, smell, pain, touch, temperature, etc. The *esthetic pleasure* derived from the arts of painting, poetry, sculpture, drama, opera, and so forth, is based to a great extent on imitation and the suggestion of similarly experienced or imagined things and events.

The Law of Contrast. This law states that present phantasms of objects, events, perceptions, and so forth, tend to reproduce in our imagination *contrasted* experiences of the past. It is a well-known fact that if one member of a pair of contraries is mentioned or imagined, the other member of the pair readily suggests itself: hot-cold, black-white, rich-poor, health-sickness, young-old, up-down, north-south, quiet-loud, pleasure-pain, full-empty, and so on. Viewed superficially, this linking of contraries is one of the oddest facts of our mental life, because there seems to be no associative bond between such opposites. Upon closer inspection, however, it will be seen that the Law of Contrast is really a combination of the Laws of Similarity and Contiguity. These opposites are the extremes, the beginning and the end, of a common series; and the beginning and the end of a series are similar in this that they are terminal points. For this reason, too, it is customary to mention the extremes of a series in the same sentence, because thereby, in a way, we cover the entire series; we thus have the association of contiguity in thought and language.

Obviously, the lines of associations as expressed in these laws frequently converge and combine, so as to strengthen the bond between imaginal phantasms. We then speak of *compound, complex,* or *co-operative* associations. To many a soldier the word 'New Guinea' will recall the countryside, the din of battle, the death of a comrade, wounds, destruction, pride in victory, patriotism, and many other things. Reversely, there are *conflicting* or *obstructive* associations which impede the recall of a desired image by diverting the mind through counter-associations. We may wish, for example, to recall a certain melody; but a somewhat similar melody forces itself upon our imagination, and we are unable to rid ourselves of it, thus blocking the path for the recall of the melody desired.

The Secondary Laws of Association

Vividness of Impression. When an impression is very vivid, either in its very nature or because of its accompanying circumstances, such an impression is more readily reproduced by the imagination. No picture or description can impress us so deeply as the actual participation in a stirring event. No king will forget his coronation, no president his election, no mother the birth of her child, no author his first book, no soldier his baptism of fire.

Frequency. The more frequently an impression is repeated, the easier it is to recall. Hearing a person's name once, listening to a melody once, reading a poem once, viewing a scene once, etc., does not create a strong associative bond as a general rule. Frequent repetition, however, has a tendency to reinforce an impression, and through this repetition its reproduction is facilitated. Frequency is usually the basis of learning.

Recentness. When an impression has occurred recently, its trace is still fresh, and the reproduction of the impression by the imagination encounters little difficulty. When, however, many other impressions intervene between occurrence and recall, the traces of the older impressions are weakened and perhaps even obliterated. It may be comparatively easy, for example, to reproduce through our imagination the main events of the last week, but well-nigh impossible to recall those during the same week a year ago.

It is unquestionable that association plays a very prominent and important part in our mental life. A knowledge of the laws which govern association should enable us to apply these laws intelligently for the practical purposes of everyday existence, particularly in mastering the techniques of our profession or occupation. A genius may be born, but even a genius must develop his native abilities.

The Constructive Imagination

The *constructive imagination* is the imagination in so far as it has the power to unite phantasms which, in *this* particular combination, have *never been experienced* by the subject. We observe its free workings in dreams and fancies, its controlled workings in the products of art and science. In all these activities combinations of phantasms occur which, prior to the imaginative function, represent things never perceived by the individual in question. The result of the function of the constructive imagination may be the phantasm of a single object, such as a winged horse or a castle in the clouds, or it may be the phantasms of a series of events, like the Iliad of Homer or a trip to Mars.

Except perhaps in dreams and free fancies, the workings of the productive imagination are strongly influenced, and often almost completely controlled, by the *intellect* and *will*. The arts and sciences are proof of the influence of intellect and will in the products of the imagination.

The Arts. We speak of the 'creations' of art. Strictly speaking, the artistic imagination does not create; it merely unites images taken from the various sensory impressions with ideas of the intellect and combines them into beautiful forms which are an idealization of the real and a realization of the ideal. The total effect is an esthetic whole which is a work of art, a supreme achievement of the constructive imagination. The Hamlet of Shakespeare, the Divina Commedia of Dante, the Pietà of Michelangelo, the Sistine Madonna of Raphael, the Parsifal of Wagner, the Cathedral of Rheims — these show the productive imagination of human genius at its best, because they are an expression of culture in its highest form. Needless to say, imaginative art may assume humbler forms, as we observe it in a mother's lullaby, a child's play-acting, a boy's fancy diving, a girl's crocheting, a man's sales talk, and so forth. Even the appliances of the household are embellished by the artistic touch of man, so that a utilitarian article becomes a thing of beauty.

Science and Invention. Many discoveries and inventions of a scientific character were the result of fortunate accidents. As a rule, though, they were the outcome of laborious research. Research means the formulation of hypotheses, and hypotheses are the imaginative construction of probable assumptions concerning causes and effects. Research means the imaginative application of general principles to problematical particular instances and the imaginative synthesis of isolated facts into problematical universal laws. Research means the imaginative devising of instruments, ranging from Geiger counters for trapping individual electrons to giant telescopes for studying immeasurable galaxies of stars. Research means the imaginative development of experiments for the verification or disproof of scientific theories which may affect the welfare of entire nations and change the course of history. Modern civilization, in a great measure, has been profoundly influenced by epoch-making inventions, such as the telephone, the locomotive, the steamship, the automobile, the airplane, the radio, and such inventions are the products of man's imagination applying the principles of science to the needs of life. There has not been a single instrument, from a wheel and a knife to a turbine generator and a rotary press, which does not show the impress of the constructive imagination of an inventive genius. Nor has there been a single science, starting from a few disconnected facts and ending in a grandiose synthesis of all relevant facts and laws, which could have developed into a system of knowledge without the aid of the imagination of a host of scientific workers.

It is true, of course, that the constructive imagination, operating with sensory phantasms only, could never achieve these results; it must be controlled and directed by the intellect and will. But it is equally true, that the intellect and will derive their data concerning the outside world from the perceptions of the external senses and the phantasms of the imagination; without this assistance, as we are at present constituted, intellect and will would be helpless powers of the organism as a whole. It would be more accurate to speak of the 'constructive imagination' as being the imagination and the intellect in collaboration.

The *development* of the constructive imagination is interesting, for it follows closely the biological development of man himself.

In *children* we observe the first stage of development. One of the outstanding activities of the constructive imagination of the child is its tendency to interpret inanimate things as living. To the little girl the doll is always a real baby, and to the little boy the teddy bear is always a real animal. Not that they actually believe it; their imaginative fancy is at work. The child also shows its constructive imagination in its play. Girls can spend an entire afternoon playing house, and a boy will build house after house with blocks. Another feature of childhood imagination is the love of fairy tales and narratives. Children will listen with rapt attention to the stories of Little Red Riding Hood and of Jack and the Beanstalk. In our day father and mother must read to them the adventures of the comic strip.

In *youth* the constructive imagination finds its outlet in games and competitive sports. In the early part of youth the games are still very imaginative, but a considerable amount of bodily activity is required. This period helps to develop muscular co-ordination and mental ingenuity. In the latter part of youth, the games become more and more strenuous, and the competitive spirit is strongly emphasized. Sport, for sport's sake, predominates. Games and sports serve the purpose of preparing the girl and boy for the serious duties which lie before them in afteryears. At the end of youth, the element of sex enters strongly into the workings of the imagination. Sex interest is revealed in the type of books the young folks read and in the social events which they enjoy.

In *adulthood* a further radical change occurs. The constructive imagination is now employed in the serious problems of life, the foundation of future social security, the rearing of a family, the complete development of all bodily and mental faculties. What was begun in childhood as a matter of sheer fancy has grown into mighty forces for good or evil in the battle of individuals and of nations. The boy and girl have become the man and woman, upon whose shoulders rests the burden of civilization.

Some Phenomena

In our normal waking state the activities of the imagination are checked by the constant impact of stimuli impinging on the external senses and by the control of intellect and will. A completely uncontrolled imagination in our waking states is a comparatively rare occurrence. It is in *dreams* that the imagination has free play.

Dreams possess a number of characteristic features. In sleep the activity of the cortical centers is in abeyance, so that outside impressions lose a great amount of their correcting influence. As a result, dreams have a decided *appearance of reality*. There is also a *lack of coherence*. Since intellectual criticism and voluntary control are missing, the scenes and events pictured in dreams shift about in kaleidoscopic fashion, frequently ending in something entirely different from the beginning, because the imagination seizes upon an accompanying association and promptly veers off in that direction. Nevertheless, there is, as a rule, a certain *degree of consistency* in dreams, probably due to sets or configurations of associative bonds present in the imaginal material. Since striking images stand out among the vague mass of fleeting phantasms, they acquire disproportionate value for the moment, and that probably accounts for the *exaggeration* so noticeable in dreams.

As for the *stimulus* of dream states, it is safe to assume that some dreams originate from auditory, pressure, temperature, and visceral sensations dimly experienced during sleep. Other dreams undoubtedly have their start in worries, problems, fears, unsatisfied desires, etc. Many dreams have the definite character of *wish-fulfillment*. *Freud* made wish-fulfillment the basis of his technique of *psychoanalysis,* but he gave it a one-sided development by insisting that the wish-fulfillment of dreams is based almost exclusively on inhibited sex desires. It is true, of course, that sex desires may and do play a prominent part in dreams, due to the repression of sex impulses in normal waking states; during sleep such impulses are practically out of control and rise to the surface, thereby producing dreams of wish-fulfillment with a sexual content. It is unwarrantable, however, and a distortion of fact, to interpret all dreams in terms of ultimate libido, as Freud and the regular psychoanalysts do. *Fear,* with its corresponding emotions, is also a dominant factor provocative of dreams, and such dreams should be interpreted as simple expressions of fear, without having recourse to a very obscure and doubtful symbolism of hidden sexuality. Thus, the horror dreams of soldiers, who have gone through the ordeal of a terrifying battle, should be laid to the fear for personal safety and not to suppressed libidinous desires. Similarly, many dreams are the play of *indifferent* images which happen to cluster around some impressive event which occurred in a recent experience; to interpret them in any other way is to do violence to simple facts. There is no absolutely uniform pattern of dreams originating from a single type of stimulus.

An interesting phenomenon of imagination activity is *eidetic imagery*. An eidetic or eidetiker is an individual who can form images of unusual clarity and vividness, so that these images are faithful reproductions of the original sensory experiences. The power of forming eidetic images is found in some children and is lost at about the age of puberty; in very exceptional cases it persists into adulthood. If a picture is placed against a gray background, and the child scans it for 10 to 15 seconds, then, upon removal of the picture, the child apparently still sees the original picture as if projected against the neutral background; this image of the original picture is the eidetic image. The child will not only describe, but point out, the details of the picture as if the picture were still there. If the gray background is turned around, the eidetic image travels with it (apparently), and the child sees it upside down. The accurate description of the details shows that it is not a question of memorizing the contents of the picture, because the time of exposure is too brief for memorizing so many details; the eidetiker simply 'sees' the picture. Experiments have been made with 'double' pictures which represent one face when placed erect, and another face when placed upside down. The eidetiker, of course, is left in ignorance of this peculiarity of the picture; when the background is turned upside down, the eidetiker is surprised to see a new face before him. It would be erroneous, however, to think that eidetikers 'see' the entire picture just as presented originally; the picture seems to take on detail as they visualize it by going from one part to another. Eidetic images are usually of the visual type, but experiments with other types have also been successful. Most eidetikers are able to recall their eidetic images after the lapse of some time. It is probable that the individuals termed 'lightning calculators' are really eidetikers, because eidetic children have been known to still 'see' the figures of a problem on the blackboard even after the figures were erased. In as much as the power to form eidetic images is nearly always lost at about the advent of puberty, it seems to be based on biological factors; just what these factors might be, is still unknown. Even a change in diet, in some cases, alters the eidetic imagery. E. R. Jaensch and his collaborators have done good work in this field.

It is a well-known phenomenon of imaginal phantasms that they have a certain *motor character* and *motor effect*. Actual perceptions are usually accompanied by muscular contractions of some sort. The phantasms, since they are representations of perceptions, naturally include such motor images, and as a result incipient movements of the musculature accompany phantasms. There is always the tendency present to carry out the motor part of the phantasm through appropriate muscular action. When we make an intensive task of memorizing an address, we unconsciously form soundless words with our tongue and mouth. Imagining that we are playing a musical instrument produces in us a faint impulse of performing the action itself. The vivid imagination of a fine meal stimulates the salivary gland and induces salivation. The passenger in an automobile, sitting alongside the driver as he wends his way through congested traffic, feels the impulse to step on the brake and finds that he has pressed his foot firmly against the floor boards. Watch the crowd at a tense moment in a sports event, such as a football game, tennis match, horse race, bowling, baseball, basketball, etc., and note that practically all execute some movements reflecting the action of the players.

This motor character of phantasms explains a number of curious phenomena in human behavior. There is the fact of unconscious *imitation*. Someone yawns, and soon everyone present is yawning. Someone has a hearty, infectuous laugh, and, before we realize it, we are smiling or even laughing, without knowing what it is all about. The passion-charged actions of the actors in the 'big moment' of a drama electrify the audience on the other side of the footlights, and the audience lives the scene with the players to such a degree that it laughs, weeps, and becomes almost hysterical. Mob psychology is based on this fact. *Sleepwalking* is another instance of the power of the motor character of phantasms. In the waking state we check the motor impulse of phantasms and stop the resultant actions before they become pronounced. In sleep some persons are incapable of checking the impulse, and it then happens that motor dreams are carried out through a train of completed bodily actions. The actions performed in *hypnotism* undoubtedly admit of a similar explanation. The hypnotized persons in a deep trance resemble sleepwalkers in so far as they are unconscious of their surroundings and cannot check the motor impulse produced by the phantasm; they differ from sleepwalkers in this, that their imagination is open to the suggestions of the operator, to whom alone they pay attention. When given a suggestion involving certain actions, the suggestion awakens the motor phantasm in their imagination, and the command of the operator is automatically carried out.

Other important, though abnormal, phenomena pertaining to the activity of the imagination are hallucinations and delusions. Some persons have subjective perceptual experiences which lack obvious sensory stimuli; although the senses receive *no relevant stimulation,* such persons erroneously perceive facts as present to the senses which are not actually there. These erroneous perceptual experiences are termed *hallucinations.* Sensations, as a rule, play their part in hallucinations, but the imaginal content plays the dominant part in the total experience; in some instances, actual sensations are a negligible factor or may be, so far as can be discovered, entirely missing. Some hallucinations involve a single sense only, others involve a combination of senses; one subject, for example, may have merely a visual or auditory or tactual hallucination, while another may experience a complex hallucination combining visual, auditory, and tactual imagery. The causes may be organic (toxic conditions, injuries, etc.) or psychic (fears, anxieties, etc.). In *delusion,* on the other hand, the subject suffers from a mental disorder which manifests itself in a misinterpretation of the general state of affairs; delusion is due to an error of judgment rather than to an error regarding the facts immediately present to the senses. A delusion is characterized by a false belief of judgment regarding the self; such is the delusion of grandeur or of persecution, found in some forms of insanity or mental disease.

The activities in the imagination show plainly that, over and above the functions of the neural mechanism itself, some *unifying principle* is demanded, in order to account for the conservation, reproduction, and construction of phantasms. Since these phantasms combine the general qualities of the various sense objects into unified wholes, the separate cerebral centers, individually and collectively, are incapable of effecting the unification. Here again, man is seen to be an *integral organism,* in which the biological functions and the psychic functions are co-ordinated into a vital unit.

Summary of Chapter VIII

In order that we may have an abiding knowledge of objects in their absence, we must retain the contents of perceptions in the form of images. The *imagination* performs this function.

1. *The Concept of Imagination.* It is the *power to form mental images or phantasms of perceived objects, together with the ability to reproduce these images or phantasms even in the absence of the perceived objects.* Its functions are: the formation and conservation of images; their reproduction; the construction of images into new combinations.

2. *The Conservatory Imagination.* Ultra-spiritualist philosophers place the conservation of phantasms in the soul or mind alone; materialistic philosophers place it on a purely neurological basis. The former are wrong, because bodily factors facilitate and impede conservation; the latter are wrong, because psychical factors are involved, in as much as phantasms contain the mental element of conscious cognition. Imaginal phantasms have a *psycho-physiological* character. We do not know the exact nature of the 'trace' which underlies the phantasm, nor do we know how it is conserved.

3. *The Reproductive Imagination.* It is the power of forming phantasms of objects and events which have been previously perceived. The reproductions of related phantasms is called 'association.'

4. *Laws of Association.* The primary Laws of Association are: contiguity in time and space; similarity; contrast. The secondary Laws are: vividness of impression; frequency; recentness.

5. *The Constructive Imagination.* It is the power to unite phantasms which, in this particular combination, have never been experienced by the subject. Constructive imagination plays a prominent part in the arts and sciences. It passes through various stages of development in childhood, youth, and adulthood.

6. *Some Phenomena. Dreams* are the products of free imagination. Psychoanalysis makes use of dreams. *Eidetic* images are images of unusual vividness and clarity, so that they are faithful reproductions of the original sensory experiences. These images seem as if projected externally. Phantasms have a certain *motor character;* incipient movements of the muscula-

ture accompany phantasms. The motor character of phantasms results at times in imitation, sleepwalking, and in hypnotic actions. *Hallucinations* and *delusions* are abnormal phenomena in connection with the imagination.

Like the central sense, the imagination ultimately demands a vital principle as the principle of unification.

Readings

Harmon, F. L., *Principles of Psychology,* Ch. 8. — Maher, M., *Psychology,* Ch. VIII, IX. — Brennan, R. E., *General Psychology,* pp. 211–223. — Gaffney, M. A., *The Psychology of the Interior Senses,* Ch. III.

Chapter IX

MEMORY

IN REVIEWING the progressive stages of our sensory knowledge discussed so far, we find that this knowledge proceeds along the following lines. The exteroceptive, interoceptive, and proprioceptive senses respond to stimuli from objects and send nerve impulses to the brain; the response is a definite sensation of color, sound, flavor, pain, etc. The central or synthetic sense then consciously compares, distinguishes, and combines these various sense qualities and refers them to their respective objects, thereby forming perceptual wholes. The imagination thereupon accepts the data of the central sense and fashions a phantasm or image of the perceived object; this phantasm leaves a trace or disposition in the imagination, so that the phantasm is revivable, either voluntarily or involuntarily, in the absence of the object and its stimuli.

The objects of sense do not remain in our presence. If the knowledge of these objects is to be true knowledge, we must be able to refer the information contained in the phantasms to the definite objects for which they stand. We must, therefore, be able to *recognize* (re-cognize, i.e., cognize or know again) the objects and the experiences represented (re-present, i.e., make present again) by the imaginal phantasm. Recognition is the function of *memory*.

The Concept of Memory

By *sensory memory* we understand the *power to recall past objects and states of consciousness and recognize them as having been present in former experiences.* The characteristic feature of memory is the *concrete recognition* of something as having been present before.

Many psychologists and philosophers refer the entire process of the retention and reproduction of past images or phantasms to memory. The expressions 'memory trace' and 'memory image' are common phrases. Many also bring the Laws of Association into connection with memory. This is permissible, but it must be borne in mind that the retention and reproduction of the images of objects and events does not necessarily involve memory. Oftentimes objects and events, which were actually a part of past experiences, are reproduced by us in phantasmal form at a later date, but we do not recognize and remember them as having been previously experienced; when confronted by such objects or events, or when someone calls our attention to them, we confess that we "do not remember them." We thus have retention and reproduction, but not memory. Hence, retention and reproduction are more properly functions of imagination than of memory. The *distinctive element* of memory is the *recognition of past objects and events,* not their phantasmal retention and reproduction.

Maher gives the following concise description of the *difference* between imagination and memory. "The chief features in which remembrance differs from mere revival of images are: (1) The freedom of the imagination as to the number and variety of its acts, the limited character of our recollections; (2) the casual and variable order of the former states, the serial fixity and regularity of the latter; (3) the isolated nature of imaginary events, the solidarity or relatedness of remembered occurrences, which are inextricably interwoven with multitudes of other representations; (4) finally, the peculiar reference to my own actual experience involved in the act of identification or recognition, which forms part of the recollection but is absent from the creations of fancy."[1]

The reproductive imagination and memory are closely connected. The imagination supplies the phantasm of a former

---

[1] *Psychology,* 9th ed. (Longmans, Green, 1930), p. 165.

experience, and memory recognizes the phantasm as the representation of an experience had before. Without this recognition, we have the activity of the imagination, but not that of memory. However, for the sake of convenience, it may not always be necessary to make too close a distinction between the reproductive activity of the imagination and the recognitive activity of memory.

There are *two main features* to memorial activity: the recognition of the past, and the estimation and measurement of the past.

Recognition or Remembrance. By this is meant the apprehension of the sameness of two representations or perceptions, one present and one past. I am aware that my present representation or perception is identical with a representation or perception which I have had on a former occasion.

It may be a question of two perceptions, as when I see a traffic policeman on a corner and remember that I had seen him there yesterday. Or, of two representations (phantasms), as when I imagine Times Square in New York and then remember that I also imagined it last week. Or, of a perception and a representation, as when I see a friend and then remember that I had thought of him (imagined him) only an hour ago. Or, of a representation and a perception, as when I imagine the Old Faithful geyser and remember that I had seen it a number of years ago. These are instances of recognition or remembrance, and the past and present are always linked together.

Mere knowledge of the sameness between one thing and its representation is not sufficient to classify this knowledge as 'remembrance.' For example, I visit a man in his home and I see, let us say, his photograph on the mantlepiece while he is conversing with me. Although I perceive the sameness between this man and the man on the photograph, this is an instance of mere knowledge without memory, because both perceptions occur simultaneously. On the other hand, if I see the man now and recall that I have seen him formerly, it is a case of memory and not of mere knowledge.

The objects of memory are always accompanied by a feeling of *familiarity,* of *acquaintanceship.* Oftentimes we see an object or person, or we hear a melody, or we feel a pain; almost immediately the object, person, melody, pain, etc., seems familiar to us, as if we had had the experience before. A little effort may recall the exact occasion of the former experience, and then the act of memory is complete. It may happen, though, that no amount of effort enables us to recall the occasion; while it is possible that we may be mistaken concerning the fact of a former experience, this 'familiarity' probably indicates a confused and vague remembrance.

Estimation and Measurement of the Past. It is a fact of everyday occurrence that we *date* and *localize* our experiences in memory by placing them at a definite point in the chain of events reaching into the past; and it is a further fact that we concretely *measure* the time when the past experience took place. How is this estimation and measurement accomplished?

The *psychological process* is as follows. The stimulations of the external senses and the perceptions of the central sense occur successively, so that we have a series of internal conscious states following one after the other. We can gauge the slowness or rapidity of the flow of our internal acts by the rhythmic movements of the breathing of the lungs or of the beating of the heart. We thereby possess a means of estimating and measuring *subjective time* in a concrete manner. By using this standard of subjective time we can now estimate and measure the *objective time* involved in the sensations and perceptions of objects. The succession of events as we perceived them is fixed according to a 'before' and 'after' in the very series itself. If we now represent to ourselves this internal series of perceptual events, from the present backwards, we not only apprehend 'time' and the 'duration' of time concretely, but we are able to 'date' and 'localize' a particular event by placing it at a definite point in the series of past events. Certain external events in this series, such as night and day and the annual seasons, stand out in strong relief and become fixed points for dating other events. In this manner we become accustomed to using subjective and objective time for dating and localizing events in memory.

Brutes, too, possess memory. A dog remembers the location of his kennel, recognizes his master, and knows what to do or not to do at a certain command. A delivery-wagon horse remembers all the stops on his regular route. Pigeons remember the cote to which they belong. Bees roam far afield, but they return unerringly to their own hive. Robins discover a cherry tree or a strawberry patch and always find their way back. The training of animals is based on the fact of their being able to remember a certain sequence of actions. Many of the conditioned reflexes induced in the animal experiments of Pavlov and others would be impossible, if the animals had no memory.

Animals have also a concrete estimation of time. The cattle on the farm wend their way to the barn when milking time arrives. Some dogs will stand at the gate every evening at the same time, awaiting the master's return from work. Pigeons remember their regular feeding time and congregate accordingly. In the salivary conditioned-reflex experiments, if the routine calls for food to be given one minute after the signal, the animal remembers the time interval, and salivation does not start until toward the end of the interval. Such instances and experiments prove that animals have memory and estimation of time.

In all that has been said here about time and its estimation, it should be noted that it is the sensory memory that is involved. The abstract concept of time is an object of intellectual insight and is treated in cosmology.[2]

Learning

In as much as retention and recall play such a predominant role in remembering and forgetting, psychologists have conducted numerous experiments in memorizing, hoping thereby

---

[2] See the author's *From Aether to Cosmos* (Bruce, 1941), pp. 194 ff.

to obtain a better understanding of the inner workings of memory. Many interesting facts have been brought to light by the various methods employed. It would serve no useful purpose to give a detailed description of these methods and their results, but a few of the outstanding facts will be recorded. Unfortunately, most experimenters fail to make a distinction between sensory and intellectual memory, and in consequence materials of both the sensory and intellectual type are used rather indiscriminately, so that it is practically impossible to restrict ourselves here to the data of sensory memory.

In order to test the ability of memory experimentally, something must be 'learned.' Then it is possible to examine how much of the material is remembered and in what manner it is retained, and a statistical score of successes and failures can be established. A number of variable factors enter into the problem of learning: the quantity and quality of the material, the time of learning and other circumstances. These items should make a difference, and they do.

One thing discovered very early in all experiments is the fact of *individual differences*. Memory is not a mechanical device, and not everyone reacts to the same learning methods in the same way. Some persons have a better memory than others. It is in the last analysis a native endowment, dependent on the individual's psycho-physiological organism. To offset these individual differences, psychologists use groups of approximately the same age, educational background, etc., in order to strike a fair average in their experiments. In this connection it is worthy to note that the power of memory shows no marked difference in the two *sexes*. With respect to *age*, young persons in childhood and adolescence are more adept in word and rote learning, but less adept in learning material according to its intellectual content; the reverse is true of adults. In youth the imagination develops rapidly, while the intellect develops more slowly, due to the fact that the intellect must obtain its data from the central sense and imagination. Adults, therefore, neglect the practice of word and rote learning in favor of memorizing facts and their intelligible relations. Memory is at its best in the years from twenty to thirty, and from then on the curve of learning declines steadily but slightly until far into middle age. Continuous practice will keep the learning curve at a fairly even level until almost into old age. Memory becomes poor in old age because of the general deterioration of the organism as a whole.

In experiments with the *quantity* of material to be learned, the usual procedure is to have the subject read a list of numbers or nonsense syllables and then observe how many items he can repeat after one presentation. The amount of material remembered after a single presentation is an index of the 'memory span.' No matter what methods or materials are used, there is a *natural limitation* in the amount that can be absorbed by the memory at a given time. This limitation is in all probability due to the fact that after a while the refractory phase of neural activity begins to show its effect.

The *quality* of the material used makes a great difference in learning. Meaningful material is more easily learned than meaningless material. It is possible to connect meaningful words mentally through associative bonds, so that one word will recall the other. It is much more difficult to memorize a list of nonsense syllables like 'zut,' 'koq,' 'gif,' etc., than it is to memorize meaningful words like 'rose,' 'foot,' 'here,' etc., because nonsense syllables must be learned by a sheer act of memory without aid from natural or artificial associations. Due to this fact, memory, as memory, can be tested much better in its power of retention and recall by means of nonsense syllables and numbers.

The *time* element also makes a difference. Given the same quantity and quality of material to be learned, it makes a difference whether five minutes or thirty minutes are given to memorize a lesson. A longer period, with the possibility of repeating the learning process, gives the memory trace a better chance to become set and fixed in its character. Similarly, if the material is allowed to be 'relearned' after an idle period of retention, memory can be tested by noting the 'time saved' in rehearsing as compared to the time required for the first learning. The memory trace is strengthened considerably by relearning, and recall is facilitated. This *spaced practice,* as it is termed, is of considerable importance in learning extensive material. The periods between relearning should be filled out with a totally different occupation, in order to obtain best results. 'Cramming' is a poor method of learning. The neural mechanism, after a period of protracted activity, always needs time for rest and recuperation; it cannot be active without the expenditure of nerve energy, and this energy is limited in amount. The refractory phase sets in, and the nerves demand a period of relative inactivity. To continue the memorizing of the same material during the refractory phase of nerve activity is not only harmful to the nerves themselves, but does not help the task of memorizing. After a certain span of time, which naturally differs with different individuals, a point is reached where the memory is saturated and can absorb no more.

The period of rest consists in some form of relaxation for the particular set of cortical centers used in the previous task of memorizing. Just what the form of relaxation happens to be, is of minor importance. Experiments, however, show that the best method is to apply one's self to the memorizing of a task just before retiring at night, provided one is not too fatigued, and then relearn it in the morning. The traces of the phantasms impressed upon the nervous elements thus have a better chance to become strengthened. This strengthening of the traces is probably due to the *perseveration* tendency of images, namely, the tendency of images to reappear soon again in consciousness. We are confronted with a curious phenomenon of the retention of images, reminiscence.

Reminiscence

By *reminiscence* is meant the spontaneous and gradual improvement of memory with a subsequent higher score in recall, without a relearning or rehearsal of the memorized material.

If true, we face a paradoxical situation. It is a known fact, of course, that we usually do not retain and remember all we attempt to learn. It is also a known fact that memory images fade rapidly after learning, so that the ability to revive them deteriorates as time progresses unless reinforced by relearning and rehearsal. Reminiscence would be the opposite. It implies that the memory traces, if left to themselves during a period of mental incubation, are not inactive, but pass through a stage of latent organization and of gradual development in the subconscious recesses of the mind.

Certain *experiences* apparently indicate that there is a rhythmic character to the memory curve, a waxing and waning of the memory trace. According to this view, spaced learning and perseveration would receive a neat explanation. Perseveration is a fact. Images have a tendency to crowd up to the level of consciousness not long after the original experience. We hear a striking melody; and the melody continues to haunt us for hours, periodically running through our mind. Things we have heard or seen float in and out of consciousness in a sort of rhythmic succession, at least for a time. In spaced learning, as we know, we can memorize more material and are able to recall this material more effectively than if we used the same amount of time in a single span of learning. It would seem that the curve of retention is like a wave, with crests and troughs; when the period of relearning coincides with the crest of subconscious memory activity, the traces are reinforced and thereby strengthened.

The 'inspiration' of genius lends color to this theory of reminiscence. The biographies of great artists narrate many instances where an artistic theme, left dormant for a while, suddenly flashed through their mind with the perfection of a completed product. It was as if the imaginative power or, if we wish, memory worked subconsciously on the theme and, without interference or aid from any conscious course, brought it to fruition. A stubborn problem is often best solved by laying it aside for a period of time and then taking it up again. Oftentimes, too, when a name or word eludes all efforts at recall, we brush the whole matter aside and occupy our mind with something else; sometime later, and quite suddenly, the desired name or word will probably burst upon consciousness. Do such experiences prove the fact of 'reminiscence,' so that a spontaneous and gradual consolidation of memory traces actually occurs in the workshop of the subconscious mind? The professional psychologists have taken up the problem.

Experiments have been made in an effort to prove or disprove the alleged phenomenon of reminiscence. The method used was to have subjects learn a memory task. Tests consisted in comparing the results of immediate recall and delayed recalls, the subjects being kept in ignorance of the fact that delayed recalls were to be made. Philip Ballard (1913) undertook a large number of experiments with school children. Taking the score of the immediate recall as 100, he found their average score after one day to be 111, after two days to be 117, after three days to be 113, after four days to be 112; and from there on the score dropped gradually. Nicolai (1922), exposing a box of assorted toys to children, also found that their average score of recall had risen from 5.4 objects to 6.3 in one hour, and to 7.8 in twenty-four hours; even after four weeks their average score was 7.4. Nicolai was certain that no rehearsal had been possible at least for the first hour, because their time during this hour had been filled out with school work. Welborn and Killiam (1934) made tests with college students. In the tests the memorized material was presented to the students in two forms; some sentences were presented verbatim, while other sentences were presented according to the substance of the subject matter. Tests of verbatim items after 10 minutes and after 30 days showed a score of 37.7 and 33.5 respectively; tests of substance items for the same intervals were 19.1 and 26.9 respectively.

On the other hand, experiments made by Williams (1926), Warner Brown (1923), Raffel (1934), and others, show no latent consolidation and improvement. Woodworth[3] is convinced that the facts can be explained by chance recall and by

[3] *Experimental Psychology* (H. Holt, 1937), pp. 64–68.

the 'condition of readiness,' and there is no need to have recourse to 'reminiscence.'

The problem is admittedly a thorny one. Since the process of recall itself is not open to inspection, the only available method is that of the recall score. This method would be good, if it were possible to exclude all rehearsal on the part of the subjects. It is not a question of deliberate rehearsal on their part, but of sporadic, intermittent rehearsal of a casual sort; the subjects may just 'think about it' off and on between tests, without even realizing that this amounts actually to rehearsing. A control over this kind of indirect review of the memorized material is next to impossible. Following this line of thought, G. O. McGeoch (1935) made experiments with school children. After the tests, upon her inquiry, it was discovered that approximately 77 per cent admitted some rehearsal; oddly enough, though, the recall score of those who did not review the material also showed improvement.

And so opinions differ. The controversy is not settled. Experiments are still being conducted, to determine, if possible, the exact nature of the phenomenon.

Retroactive Inhibition

Psychologists understand by *retroactive inhibition* the tendency of mental activity to impair the recall of memorized material, if this activity is placed between the time of learning and the time of recall. The term 'retroactive inhibition' is open to misinterpretation. The expression might be understood to mean that such an activity is 'retroactive' in the sense that the effect of its influence reaches back into the past beyond the point of time when the activity itself, as the cause, actually occurred. Such a view would be equivalent to the statement that the effect is prior to its producing cause — a patent impossibility. Psychologists, of course, do not attach such a meaning to the term. What they intend to imply is, that mental activity, interpolated between learning and recall, *interferes* in some manner with the recall of previously memorized material; in other words, such an interpolated activity has the tendency to make us *forget* what has been learned immediately before.

The *fact* itself is certain. Common experience shows that best results in memorizing are obtained, if a period of rest follows the period of learning; the results are not so good, if the period of learning is followed by strenuous mental activity of the same or of a similar kind. Psychologists observed the same fact in their psychological research work on memory.

Since the turn of the century, many *experiments* have been made to determine the character of retroactive inhibition. Müller and Pilzecker (1900) had observed that recall after a period of idleness was more than 50 per cent better than when learning was immediately followed by intense mental activity. Müller and Pilzecker were the first to call attention to the phenomenon of 'perseveration,' and they interpreted this perseveration as a consolidation of the memory traces, so that the traces have the natural tendency to re-occur in consciousness for a time. Retroactive inhibition, then, would hinder this consolidation of the memory traces, in as much as intense mental activity, following a period of learning, would hinder the original traces from going through their normal phase of consolidation. Viewed this way, retroactive inhibition is a form of *anti-consolidation.*

While not all psychologists agree with the Müller and Pilzecker theory of anti-consolidation, their experiments confirm the fact of retroactive inhibition in general. It was found, however, that the retroactive inhibition of interpolated mental activity depends on the *type of activity* to a great extent. Retroactive inhibition is strongest when the interpolated *material* is rather *similar in form,* though of a *different content,* to the original material memorized. When the interpolated material is of a markedly different character, inhibition is not so pronounced; but any type of strenuous mental activity exerts an inhibitory effect in some degree. The same situation prevails when the mental *operations* are similar or dissimilar in type. Quite naturally, retroactive inhibition will be strongest when both material and operation are similar to, and weakest when material and operation are dissimilar to, the material and operation found in the original task of learning. Experiments were made along these lines by Robinson (1920), Skaggs (1925), McGeoch and McDonald (1931), Nagge (1935), and others. All revealed the fact that retroactive inhibition occurs, but they do not seem to confirm the theory of anti-consolidation as propounded by Müller and Pilzecker. Müller and Pilzecker maintained that the factor in retroactive inhibition which hindered the consolidation of the memory traces was the *strenuousness* of the interpolated mental activity. Were the 'strenuousness' the factor, the similarity or dissimilarity of the interpolated material or operation, with respect to the material and operation of the original task, should not influence the recall one way or the other; so long as the interpolated activity is not strenuous, consolidation of the traces and subsequent recall should proceed normally. These more recent experiments, however, show plainly that *similarity of form* in the material and operation is the disturbing factor in retroactive inhibition, even though perhaps not exclusively.

There is a further point to consider. In the anti-consolidation theory of Müller and Pilzecker the *time element* seems essential. In order that the traces can consolidate properly, a period of relative rest should follow immediately after the period of original learning. Given this period of rest for consolidation, retroactive inhibition should not occur. But it does occur. Müller and Pilzecker found that even a brief pause after learning eliminated the effect of retroactive inhibition to a large extent. On the other hand, Robinson (1920) and McGeoch (1933) found that any activity interpolated between learning and recall, whether at the beginning or middle or end of the interval, brought on retroactive inhibition. Whitely (1927) and von Restorff (1933) maintain that inhibition will take place and diminish recall, if the mental activity immediately *precedes* the original memory task instead of being interpolated between learning and recall; such an inhibition would be proactive, not retroactive.

In view of these findings, some psychologists prefer the *transfer* or *interference* theory of DeCamp (1915) and Webb (1917) to the anti-consolidation theory of Müller and Pilzecker. According to the transfer theory, the original and interpolated activities intermingle, so that the two sets of traces become a single mixed set with subsequent confusion of recall results, or the traces of the original material are used with the traces of the interpolated material and become modified thereby.

It is questionable whether the anti-consolidation and the transfer theories are strictly antagonistic and exclusive. The facts seem compatible with both theories. Müller and Pilzecker may have been mistaken in ascribing restrictively the effect of retroactive inhibition to the 'strenuousness' of the activity interpolated immediately after the period of original learning; however, the facts brought to light in the experiments of recent years do not necessarily rule out the possibility of a consolidation of the traces. Both the transfer theory and the anti-consolidation theory are plausible interpretations of the facts discovered, but each may possibly be only a partial interpretation of all the facts involved. Further investigation is still needed.

If we now turn our attention to the familiar phenomenon of *forgetting,* we find that normal forgetting is accounted for by two main factors. The first is the *natural fading* of the memory trace. Unless an experience is recalled from time to time, so that the trace is strengthened and made ready for further recall by associative bonds of some sort, the lapse of time makes the trace weaker and less capable of recall. It is a question, however, whether the trace is ever completely obliterated, because sometimes past events, long forgotten, are recalled with a startling vividness of detail. The second factor is the effect of proactive and retroactive *inhibition* on the part of interfering mental activity. The present discussion brings out this point. Proper methods of memorizing will retard the negative process of forgetting by furnishing aids toward the consolidation and strengthening of the traces.

Recall and Recognition

Recall is the mental reproduction of a former stimulus or experience. Recall, of course, is dependent on the trace left by the former stimulus or experience. If this trace should have become obliterated for some reason, recall is impossible; if the trace is still present, no matter in how strong or weak a condition, recall is, theoretically at least, always possible.

Recognition is the consciousness that the stimulus or experience now present has been present formerly. It also is dependent on the trace left by the former stimulus or experience. If this trace were obliterated, recognition would be impossible; the present stimulus or experience would indeed be the repetition of a former stimulus or experience, but it would not be 'recognized' or 'remembered' as such and would simply be considered as being present for the first time. The same trace, therefore, is active in both recall and recognition.

It would be erroneous, however, to judge from their mutual dependence on the memory trace that the functions of recall and recognition are identical and to state, as Stevenson Smith (1927) does, that there is no definite difference between them. Mutual dependence on something does not necessarily mean identity.

The facts show that recall and recognition are *distinct functions.* We can have recall without recognition, and we can have recognition without recall. Consider the following experiment. A subject is made to memorize a list of 50 meaningful words. After two days he is told to write a list of 50 words, including in this list all the words of the original list which he remembers; he is then requested to make a check mark back of the words which he recognizes as having been on the original list. On comparing the two lists, we find the following (here, of course, hypothetical) results: 20 correctly checked words, recalled and recognized; 30 unchecked words, supposedly not on the original list. Upon examination, however, we find 20 entirely new words among the unchecked words and 10 of the original list; these 10 were, therefore, recalled but not recognized. The score: recall, 60 per cent; recognition, 40 per cent. In actual experiments the results will, in all probability, be somewhat different; but something of the sort usually happens, showing that more items are recalled than are recognized. And if the remaining 20 unrecalled and unrecognized words of the original list are now mixed with 30 new words, so that a new list of 50 words is presented to the subject, he will, in all probability, be able to pick out a fair number of words which he now recognizes as having been on the original list, though they were not recalled in his test list. Here, then, we have recognition without recall, while in the test we had recall without recognition and also recall with recognition.

Everyday experience confirms these findings. We sometimes have recall without recognition. In an idle moment of relaxation we may hum what we think is a spontaneous melody of our own composition. Later on, we hear an orchestra on the radio play a piece which contains the main features of this melody. We had most probably heard the melody on a former occasion and recalled parts of it, though we had not recognized it as a previous experience. It happens, too, that authors are guilty of what may be called 'unconscious plagiarism.' They read something striking, and it makes an impression; but they soon 'forget' all about it. At a future date, they have occasion to write on this particular subject. Among the matter written may be found a few sentences which, as a matter of fact, are practically verbatim repetitions of what they had read formerly, although they are unaware of this fact; it is an instance of recall, but not of recognition. The reverse is also true. Somebody speaks to me of a person who is supposed to be a mutual acquaintance; he may relate place, date, incident, conversation, etc., but to no avail. Upon showing me a snapshot of the person, I now recognize him, though up to that moment recall was impossible. It often happens, too, that we cannot recall a certain song or orchestral composition; but we have immediate recognition of it, when we hear it again.

Recognition without recall is a very frequent occurrence in memorizing, let us say, a lengthy poem or an address. After having read it over a few times, we will be able to recall some parts of the poem or address, but most of it we cannot recall. When, however, we glance over the poem or address for re-learning, we experience no difficulty in recognizing it in its entirety. The trace is present, but too weak to be activated into full recall; the item itself, though, when presented, is readily recognized as having been presented before.

We thus come to the conclusion that recall and recognition are distinct functions. Were they identical operations, the presence of the one would of necessity involve the presence of the other. When the one can be present and the other absent, they must be diverse operations.

There are a number of *characteristic differences* which mark off recognition from recall. They show that recognition and recall are not identical functions. T. V. Moore[4] enumerates the main ones.

Complexity of detail in the original stimulus creates a greater difficulty for recall than it does for recognition. The details of a poem, for example, may be incapable of recall after a single reading, but their recognition should be an easy matter. A musician may not be able to recall the details of a musical score after hearing it for the first time, but he probably would have little difficulty in recognizing the piece when hearing it again. Increasing the number of words in a test makes recall more difficult, but the recognition of the list itself is made scarcely more difficult on that account. A mechanic may find considerable difficulty in recalling all the parts of a complicated machine, but he recognizes each part when he sees it. Children are often unable to recall the exact spelling of lengthy words, but they recognize the words when reading.

Recall is affected more adversely by *retroactive inhibition* than is recognition. Strenuous mental activity, following immediately after a memory task, interferes with the recall of

[4] *Cognitive Psychology* (Lippincott, 1939), pp. 448–451.

the contents of this task but it does not interfere with recognition. The memorizing of two poems in succession, similar to each other, brings on retroactive inhibition, and recall is thereby impaired; but it does not impair the recognition of the poems. A lesson in Italian, succeeding a lesson in Latin, induces retroactive inhibition, because of the similarity of form existing in the two lessons; recall is impeded, but recognition remains relatively intact.

Primacy and *recency* influence recall more than they do recognition. When memorizing a series of items, such as a list of words, syllables, or numbers, it has been found that the first and last items of the series, all things being equal, are retained better and can be recalled easier than the middle items of the same series. The earliest (first, primary) and the most recent efforts in learning have an advantage, so far as retention and recall are concerned, over the efforts which occur in between. The fact itself is beyond dispute. Psychologists offer the following explanation. The beginning of a series receives full attention, because nothing precedes it; hence, the impression of the memory trace is deeper and stronger. The memory trace of the middle of the series is interfered with by the proactive inhibition of the first part of the series and by the retroactive inhibition of the last part of the series. The last part of the series is not interfered with by retroactive inhibition, because nothing follows it. The middle part of the series, no doubt, produces a retroactive inhibition upon the first part and a proactive inhibition upon the last part. But the first and last part of the series thus suffer from only one factor of inhibition, while the middle part suffers from two factors. Whatever may be the true explanation of the fact, primacy and recency are advantageous for recall. As for recognition of the items of a series, the first and last parts have no advantage over the middle part; all are recognized with equal facility.

A *single rehearsal* makes recall difficult, but not recognition. As a rule, the material, if somewhat extensive, must be rehearsed a number of times before it can be effectively recalled. The recognition of this material, however, is much easier after a single rehearsal than its recall. After a single rehearsal, a subject may recall but a few items from a list of words; when presented with the words, however, the subject will readily recognize many more words as present in the list than those which he was able to recall.

Meaningful material facilitates both recall and recognition, but recognition is affected more than recall. Nonsense syllables are much harder to recall and to recognize than meaningful words. Similarly, memorization, with subsequent recall and recognition, of material in one's native language is far easier than that in an alien language. Obviously, too, the recognition of meaningful material is not as difficult as the recognition of material without meaning.

The *will to remember* is an important factor for recall and recognition, but more important for recall than for recognition. Since recall is a more difficult operation than recognition, the will to remember naturally benefits recall more than recognition.

These facts prove that recall and recognition are distinct functions. In ordinary conversation we seldom make the distinction, using both terms indiscriminately, but the distinction is there and should not be overlooked.

Pathology and Memory

Pathological disturbances of memory throw the functions of retention and recall into high relief. The causes of such disturbance may be either organic or psychogenic. The *organic* causes involve a destruction or impairment of cerebral nerve tissue, due to injuries (a fall, a head wound, etc.), disease (syphilis, etc.), poisoning (alcohol, carbon monoxide, etc.), and similar agencies. The *psychogenic* or mental causes involve a functional impairment, due to excessive mental strain, emotional shock, hysteria, and so forth. The resultant amnesia differs in the two types of cases. In the cases where organic factors are the cause, amnesia takes the form of inability to store new impressions, while the power to recall impressions stored prior to the onset of the cause remains relatively intact. In the cases where psychogenic factors are the cause, amnesia takes the form of inability to recall impressions of the past, but the power to store new impressions following the onset of the cause remains relatively intact. At times, of course, both organic and psychogenic causes are involved, and in such cases the impairment of memory is more pronounced and general in character. Psychogenic amnesia usually clears up rapidly of its own account. Organic amnesia is not so amenable to treatment and cure, especially where cerebral lesions have occurred; where poisoning is the cause, the elimination of the poison frequently leads to partial or complete restoration of memory. Psychogenic amnesia is more in the nature of retroactive inhibition, while organic amnesia is more in the nature of a partial or total inability of the memory traces to register, due to the partial or total destruction of a section of nerve tissue itself.

It is thus clear that retention, recall, and recognition are distinct functions. It is also clear that the imagination cannot function in the absence of an object without retention and recall. Either, then, imagination and memory are parallel powers, both utilizing the same material through retention and recall; or retention and recall should be assigned to imagination, leaving recognition and the estimation of time as the proper functions of memory. The latter view seems preferable.

Summary of Chapter IX

Memory is one of the internal senses.

1. *The Concept of Memory. By sensory memory we understand the power to recall past objects and states of consciousness and recognize them as having been present in former experiences.* The distinctive element of memory is the recognition of past objects and events, not their retention and reproduction. The two main features of memorial activity are the recognition of the past and the estimation or measurement of the past.

Recognition or *remembrance* is the apprehension of the sameness of two representations or perceptions, one present and one past. By the *estimation* and *measurement* of the past we mean that we date and localize our experiences in memory by placing them at a definite point in the chain of events reaching into the past and concretely measure the time when the past experience took place. *Brutes* also possess memory in these two features.

2. *Learning.* Experiments in learning reveal how much of the memorized material is remembered and in what manner it is retained. There are a number of variable factors which enter into the problem of learning: the quantity and quality of the material, the time of learning, and other circumstances. Generally speaking, 'spaced learning' is the best method of memorizing; this fact is probably due to the perseveration tendency of images.

3. *Reminiscence.* By this is meant the spontaneous and gradual improvement of memory with a subsequent higher score in recall, without a relearning or rehearsal of the memorized material. It implies that the memory traces, if left to themselves during a period of mental incubation, are not inactive, but pass through a stage of latent organization and of gradual development in the subconscious recesses of the mind. Opinions differ with regard to the existence of reminiscence.

4. *Retroactive Inhibition.* By this term psychologists understand the tendency of mental activity to impair the recall of memorized material, if this activity is placed between the time of learning and the time of recall. The fact itself is certain, as proved by common experience and by psychological experiments. Retroactive inhibition is strongest, when the interpolated material is similar in form, though of different content, to the original material memorized; it also occurs when the mental operations of the interpolated activity are similar to those of the original task.

Müller and Pilzecker have advanced the theory that the strenuousness of interpolated activity hinders the consolidation of the memory trace. Their theory is the *anti-consolidation theory* of retroactive inhibition. Many psychologists prefer the *transfer* or *interference theory* of DeCamp and Webb. According to this theory, the interpolated and original traces become a single mixed set, or the traces of the original material are used with the traces of the interpolated material and become modified thereby.

Forgetting is due either to the natural fading of the memory trace or to proactive and retroactive inhibition.

5. *Recall and Recognition.* They are distinct functions. We can have recall without recognition, and recognition without recall. If they were identical, the presence of the one would involve the presence of the other. There are a number of *characteristic differences* between recall and recognition.

6. *Pathology and Memory.* The causes of the pathological disturbances of memory are either *organic* or *psychogenic.* The former involve a destruction or impairment of cerebral nerve tissue, due to injuries, disease, poisoning, and similar agencies. The latter involve a functional impairment, due to excessive mental strain, emotional shock, hysteria, and so forth. *Organic amnesia* takes the form of inability to store new impressions, while the power to recall impressions stored prior to the onset of the cause remains relatively intact. *Psychogenic amnesia* takes the form of inability to recall impressions of the past, but the power to store new impressions following the onset of the cause remains relatively intact.

Retention, recall, and recognition are distinct functions. It seems preferable to assign retention and recall to imagination and consider recognition and the estimation of time as the proper functions of memory.

Readings

Gaffney, M. A., *The Psychology of the Interior Senses,* Ch. IV. — Woodworth, R. S., *Experimental Psychology,* Ch. II, III, IV. — Gruender, H., *Experimental Psychology,* Ch. X. — Moore, T. V., *Cognitive Psychology,* Part VI, Ch. I–IX. — Harmon, F. L., *Principles of Psychology,* Ch. 12, 13, 14.

Chapter X

INSTINCT

SO FAR we have examined the external senses and three of the four internal senses.

The purpose of the entire process of sensory knowledge is to make us acquainted with ourselves and with the objects of the external world, so that we may be able to adjust ourselves to our environment in accordance with the needs of our *well-being* as individuals and as members of a species. The individual must live, and the race must survive; that is the law of nature. In brutes and men the knowledge acquired by the senses must serve the ultimate demands of the well-being of the individual and of the species.

Knowledge thus acquired, however, is insufficient to achieve the realization of the well-being of the animal organism in all its necessary phases. This realization is achieved to a great extent through the activity of the fourth and last of the internal senses — *instinct.*

The Concept of Instinct

The term *instinct* (Lat., *instinguere,* to incite, to goad) connotes a drive, an urge, an *impulse to action,* analogous to the prodding of an animal by a goad or spur, urging it to move forward toward a goal. The term designates the impulsive tendency toward actions which are conducive to the *well-being* of the individual or of the species, either by attaining what is good and useful or by avoiding what is evil and harmful. The term also implies that the impulse to such actions is a *native endowment* of the organism, independent of whether or not the individual has a 'logical understanding' of the purposiveness of such actions or of the good to be attained and of the evil to be avoided. Finally, the term is usually employed to designate the impulse to a definite set of actions serving the well-being of the individual or the species *prior to any learning by experience* on the part of the individual performing the actions.

Besides this dynamic element in instinct, there is also the *cognitive element.* Even though the term 'instinct,' as commonly used, is viewed primarily as referring to action, instinct does not exclude knowledge. As a rule, and perhaps always, men and animals acting instinctively are aware of their actions, even if they are not aware of the 'why and wherefore' of such actions; they know what they are doing when they do it, though the 'reasons' for their action may be little understood or not understood at all.

Such is the general concept of 'instinct' in popular parlance. This concept is sufficient as an approach to the internal sense under discussion. How far this concept is justified, will become clearer at the end of our investigation.

The Existence of Instinct

In order to determine whether such a thing as instinct exists, the behavior either of men or of animals can serve us as a guide in our investigation. In the case of human behavior we have the advantage of introspection; but we also have the disadvantage that intellectual activity controls our actions to such a degree that it is difficult to discern where instinct ends and intellect begins or how far they intermingle. In the case of animal behavior we have the advantage that we know that intellect plays no part in the action; but we also have the disadvantage that we can arrive at a knowledge of the mentality of the animal only by inference and not by direct observation. Instinct, if it exists, will certainly appear in a purer and clearer form in animals than in men, because of the fact, as we will see later, that they are not influenced by an intellect and will. For this reason it is customary to base the study of instinct more on the actions of animals than of men.

Animal behavior manifests instinct.

A few typical cases will show conclusively that animals possess an *innate impulse, antecedent to all individual experience,* determining them to certain *uniform, purposive actions, useful for the individual and the species.*

Animals perform some actions in virtue of an *innate impulse,* prior to experience. Flourens narrates the incident of a beaver that was captured soon after birth and placed in the Jardin des Plants in Paris, where it was reared in a cage. When the beaver was fully grown, an experiment was tried with the animal. Soil, twigs, and water were placed at its disposal. The beaver, although in no need of a hut, went to work without any hesitation and built the typical hut of its species. This beaver had never seen a beaver hut and could not have learned the plan and principles of construction from its parents nor from individual experience. What is the explanation? Only one explanation is possible: upon sight of the building material it had the impulse, fixed in its nature, to build a hut in a definite way according to a definite plan, and the typical beaver hut was the result.

Another example. W. S. Ritter placed a number of trap-door spiders, as soon as they were hatched, in a dish containing moist earth. Though still immature, each spider began its nest according to the standard pattern of the nest made by the mature spiders, only smaller in size so as to fit the size of its immature body. The lid or trap door of such a nest is a most ingenious contrivance, and the little spiders fashioned the lids with utmost nicety and skill, although they had never seen a nest and could not have learned the procedure from any other spider. Here again we observe a sequence of actions which manifest an innate impulse, independent of any prior experience.

Birds, even when reared in a cage from the time they are hatched, will always, when liberated, build a nest of the same material and pattern as the other birds of the same kind, although they have never seen a nest built. Spiders, too, will spin the typical web of their species, without ever having seen a web or the spinning of a web. Ducklings will take to water and swim, immediately after they have been hatched. The leaf-roller insect will construct its nest in a leaf, thereby solving incidentally a most intricate problem of geometry, under circumstances which preclude the possibility of learning by experience or in any other manner. The life history of animals is replete with instinctive actions which manifest innate impulses.

That such actions are the result of an *impulse,* and not of a rational understanding of their purposiveness, should be equally clear. If they were due to intellectual insight or a process of reasoning, one would be constrained to place animals on a higher mental plane than man, because some of these actions, always performed unerringly and unfalteringly, are eminently purposive in character and highly ingenious in pattern. Man could not solve some of the problems involved in such actions without considerable study and preliminary education. Notwithstanding the ingenuity displayed in instinctive behavior, animals reveal no signs of genuine intellectual insight. On the contrary, the behavior of animals shows that they have an almost irresistible 'drive' to perform a determined set of actions, but have no 'understanding' of the intrinsic reasonableness of their actions.

The action of the beaver mentioned above manifests an impulse, but no understanding, because it had not use for a hut under the circumstances. H. Fabre, the eminent French naturalist, narrates many incidents of animal behavior which reveal phenomenal mental obtuseness in what is otherwise an apparently highly intelligent performance. On one occasion he experimented with a sphex, a type of solitary wasp. This particular type stored grasshoppers in an excavated nest as food for its young. The routine is as follows: the sphex brings the grasshopper to the rim of the nest, enters the nest to explore its condition, returns to the top, and then drags the grasshopper into the nest. While the wasp was exploring the interior of the nest, Fabre removed the grasshopper a short distance; the wasp, returning to the top, saw the grasshopper, brought it back to the rim of the nest, and went to explore the interior once more, although it had done so only a moment before. Fabre repeated the experiment over and over, always with the same results. This behavior on the part of the wasp shows an impulse to perform a certain set of actions according to a definite plan, but it also shows a complete lack of understanding of the purpose of the plan. On another occasion, Fabre made an experiment with a honey bee. The bee is to all appearances a very intellectual insect, since it solves a logarithmic problem in the construction of its cell. Fabre wished to test the mental insight of the bee. A bee had already partially filled a cell with honey. He pierced the bottom of the cell, so that the honey flowed away. The bee continued to put honey into the cell and add wax material to the walls. The bee made thirty-two trips, collecting honey and building material, but not once did it occur to the bee to investigate why the cell was always empty of honey. Impulse was present, but no reason or intellectual insight.

Instinctive actions are eminently purposive in themselves, but the animal performing them evidently carries them out because of an impulsive drive and not because of any understanding of their aptness. Whenever unusual circumstances break the routine of the sequence or frustrate its purpose, the impulse still persists, and the animal attempts to carry the action through to its normal conclusion, although the continuance of the action can serve no useful purpose.

While animals possess a certain amount of individuality and adaptability in instinctive actions, as will be pointed out a little later, their actions always follow a definite *uniformity* of pattern. Each kind of bird builds its nest in the same fashion and of the same general materials as the rest of its kind; this characteristic can be observed in the swallow, the sparrow, the canary, the woodpecker, the wren, the ostrich, the eagle, etc. Bees build their cells alike the world over. Rabbits, woodchucks, gophers, chipmunks, moles, foxes, etc., make their burrows in the same way as their fellows. The wolf, the cat, the dog, the lion, the tiger, the otter, etc.—all hunt according to the method of their type and that uniformly. There is no tendency on the part of the animal to improve on the method of its action or to use other means to accomplish the same end; the course of the action is set, and the animal runs faithfully through the course.

Instinctive actions are not random performances, but purposive. Some involve a marvelous complexity of co-ordinated movements, occupying a considerable length of time. When it is stated that instinct drives to 'purposive' actions, this simply means that these actions are, as a matter of observable fact, *purposive in themselves,* adapted as means toward the realization of a definite end or goal.

If we seek this purpose, we find that it consists in the *well-being* of the individual and of the species.

As for the well-being of the *individual,* all the instincts governing the search for food and self-defense belong to this category. Animals know instinctively what foods are good or harmful for them, and they know just how to go about acquiring the food they need. This instinct is more specialized in some animals than in others. Some types of birds will starve to death, if their particular kind of food has been destroyed through a wide area, even though the food of other birds or animals be present in abundance. As for self-defense, each class of animals has its own method of defense in time of danger, and the members of each species react to danger in the same general way. To quote Muckermann: "For what other reason but to seek protection from danger do worms contract the segments of their body, hedgehogs roll themselves into balls bristling with spikes, snails retire into their shells, turtles withdraw their heads and legs and hide themselves in the sand, young snakes jump into the mouth of their parent, chickens seek protection under the wings of the hen?" The fact of general uniformity in the actions of the members of the same species shows that such behavior is instinctive.

The technique required for the well-being and *preservation of the species* is never learned by the individual animal. Whatever may be the process of reproduction, sexual or asexual, the perpetuation of the species is maintained by a sequence of wonderfully co-ordinated actions directed toward this end in virtue of an instinct rooted in the inmost nature of the animal, and this instinct cannot be denied. To quote Muckermann again: "Nor can any other explanation than 'purpose' be given for those actions by which animals preserve their species. Or why do they always deposit their eggs in places which offer the most suitable food for their offspring? Why do mosquitoes drop their eggs into water, the only place where the young can develop, cabbage-butterflies deposit them on the under side of the cabbage leaf, sitaris in the nest-entrance of Antophoras? Why does the fly Gastrus equi paste them on the breast of a horse, where they are licked up by the horse's tongue and forwarded into the stomach, the only place where the maggots find their specific and necessary nourishment? Why do several species of solitary wasps fasten their eggs on the bodies of living but paralyzed spiders, caterpillars, and grasshoppers? Why does the great water-scavenger, Hydrophilus piceus build a little boat for its eggs, and Lochemusa, Xenodusa, Atemeles . . . bring them into the nest of ants; why in short, does every species find those places and conditions which are best adapted to secure the welfare of its offspring? There can be no question of chance where such a universal experience confronts us with such wonderful facts, and it is consequently evident that a 'purpose' in finding suitable nourishment, in protecting the individual and propagating the species, is an essential constituent of all instinctive actions of animals."[1]

Such are some of the facts, taken from among millions, which show the operations of instinct and thereby reveal its nature. Summing up the essential features of instinctive actions, we can now define *instinct,* with William McDougall, as *"an innate disposition which determines the organism to perceive (to pay attention to) any object of a certain class, and to experience in its presence a certain emotional excitement and an im-*

[1] Muckermann, *The Humanizing of the Brute* (Herder, 1906), pp. 28–29.

pulse to action which find expression in a specific mode of behavior in relation to that object."[2]

Instinct and Experience

In considering instinct, as expressed in the definition just given, one is liable to draw the conclusion that instinctive activities are so stereotype in character as to be beyond the modifying influence of experience. Such a conclusion would be erroneous. Instincts can be *modified* to a certain extent by the *experience* of the animal.

Some birds use pieces of string, cord, paper, cloth, and similar objects in the construction of their nest. In the beginning these birds could not have been prompted by their instinct to use such artificial products, for the simple reason that the birds made nests before man made such articles. Barn swallows now frequently attach their mud nests to the inside of barns, and chimney swallows to the inside of chimneys. This method of nest-building is a modification of their original instinct, because they certainly built nests long before barns and chimneys existed. Canadian partridges construct a little roof over themselves in Canada, for the purpose of shelter; in a warmer climate they omit the shelter roof. Wrens, sparrows, martins, etc., use birdhouses made by man for nesting purposes. The mud-dauber wasp makes its mud nests in hollow trees and overhanging rocks; but it will also make them in structures built by man.

We thus notice that instinct is not a rigid and uncontrollable automatism, but an innate disposition which possesses a certain amount of plasticity and flexibility, capable of being modified and adapted to the requirements of existing circumstances.

Experience and Intelligence

Animals act by instinct. But not always. They also act by *learning through experience*. Experiential actions often re-

[2] *Outline of Psychology* (Charles Scribner's Sons, 1923), p. 110.

semble instinctive actions, in so far as they are purposive in themselves and tend toward a definite goal; they are, however, not the result of an innate disposition or drive, present in the animals antecedent to experience. The sense of well-being prompts animals to act, and so they seek to attain what is good for them and to avoid what is evil; and experience teaches them what is good and what is evil. Experiential actions possess a spontaneity and individuality of expression which is lacking in typically instinctive actions.

Pleasure is a good and pain an evil which animals associate with experiential actions, and thereby they learn to perform or avoid certain kinds of activities. The *training* of animals is based on this general principle. Punishment is meted out to them, if they do something undesired by the trainer or refuse to do something desired by him; a reward is given to them, if they do what the trainer desires or omit to do what he wants them to omit.

Animals, however, can also learn by experience *of their own accord*. A cat which burns her paw at a hot stove will refrain from going near it. A dog, once scratched by a cat, will be wary of the cat the next time. Animals and birds in isolated regions or in refuge areas show at first no fear of man; but it does not take them long to learn to distinguish between those who are kind to them and those who wish to do them harm. In Yellowstone Park the bear, the bison, the elk, and the mountain goat are relatively tame, because they experience no harsh treatment.

While it is true that the general pattern of the instinctive actions of a species is predetermined and uniform, it is equally true that the details are subject to modification and change. The animal, in many cases at least, adapts its method of searching for food, of defense, of escape, of mating, of parental care, to the changing circumstances of the environment.

Have animals *intelligence?*

The question has agitated the minds of psychologists and philosophers for a long time, and a considerable controversy has grown up around the problem. Consider the following facts.

William McDougall relates how his son, K. D. McDougall, experimented with a dauber wasp making a nest of mud cells for her eggs. Oddly enough, the wasp proceeded to attach the cells to a suspended wire. While the wasp was away collecting material to finish a nearly completed cell, McDougall made a hole through the blind-end wall of the cell. The wasp returned with a pellet of clay to build the wall, but saw the hole, fussed around in an agitated manner, and finally began to repair the damage with the pellet that should have been used to build the upper wall. She brought two more pellets, plugged the hole completely, and then continued to build the rest of the wall where she had left off. A number of experiments of this type, but with variations, were made. The result was the same: the damage was always repaired, but the procedure of repair was different in the different instances. This repair work was certainly not included in the instinctive building schedule of the wasp; yet the wasp rose to the occasion and finished the task, notwithstanding outside interference.

Many laboratory experiments have been conducted with animals. Thorndike's experiments are famous. White rats, for example, were allowed to become very hungry, so as to stimulate their food-seeking instinct. Food was then placed in a box, and the rat had to find its way into the box. The box was so constructed that the rat had to push a lever, pull a string, or perform some other operation, in order to be able to enter. The rat invariably proceeded according to a trial-and-error method. When at last the rat succeeded accidentally in tripping the opening mechanism a few times, it remembered the procedure and from there on went through the proper sequence without fail. In this manner a rat can train itself to operate a number of latches before being able to obtain its food. McDougall made a puzzle food box with fourteen interlocking latches, and a white rat finally learned to master the device. Once such an animal memorizes the sequence, it experiences little trouble in opening the box.

Animals, it will be observed, possess a certain spontaneity and initiative in their actions, so that they are capable of learning by experience; they can also modify the sequence of instinctive actions in a measure, so as to suit them to existing conditions. And so we are back to the question: Do animals possess *intelligence?*

We can answer this by posing another question: Just what is meant here by 'intelligence'? There is nothing in such animal behavior which manifests true signs of *intellect* and *reason,* if that is what is meant by 'intelligence,' because there is no need to postulate the power of *abstract thinking* and the mental process of *reasoning* for the performance of their actions. If we examine the behavior of animals carefully, we notice nothing more than the *concrete connecting of concrete acts to concrete ends.* Perceptual insight and memory suffice to explain their behavior. Everything takes place on a *sensory level.*

If, however, we mean by 'intelligence' the 'capacity to improve upon native tendency in the light of past experience,' as William McDougall[3] does, then we can admit that animals possess 'intelligence.' The name is of little importance, and a name should be given to the animal's capacity for learning by experience. The term is used quite extensively in modern psychology, and so we may as well adopt it. In that case, however, we should draw a sharp line of distinction between human intellect and animal intelligence, the former being the power of abstract thinking and the latter the power of sensory insight based on experience.

Animals, therefore, perform *two distinct types of actions:* actions which result from 'instinct,' instinctive actions, and actions which result from 'intelligence,' experiential actions. Both types involve a *sensory appreciation or estimation of the concrete usefulness or harmfulness of a perceived object with reference to the animal's organism or to the species.* The origin-principle underlying both types is the *well-being* of the organism or the species, and all actions conspire toward the realization of this well-being as the means toward the end.

Moderns use the term 'intelligence' in diverse meanings. As

---

[3] *Op. cit.,* p. 71.

applied to brute animals, 'intelligence' is nothing more than the general cognitive power of the animal, and this power is one of the factors present in instinctive behavior. 'Instinct' is a complex pattern involving several capacities, cognitive, appetitive, and motor. There is no real distinction between the cognitive power manifested in the stereotyped instinctive behavior and the 'intelligence' as a general cognitive power capable of spontaneous learning; it is the same power which is active in every type of cognition. In both types of action, instinctive and experiential, the animal organism is stimulated to action by the perception of an object or situation presented by the central sense as something useful or harmful for its well-being.

St. Thomas Aquinas calls this cognitive power the *vis aestimativa* (the *estimative power*). In as much as man perceives the useful or harmful character of particular things not merely in a purely sensory fashion, but also by means of a collation of ideas, he calls this sense in man the *vis cogitativa* (the *cogitative power*) or *particular reason,* thereby distinguishing it from intellectual reason. D. Card. Mercier calls it 'the sense of well-being' (le sens du bien-être). T. V. Moore combines the estimative power with the 'common sense' into what he calls the 'synthetic sense.'

Human Instincts

Man, too, is an animal organism. As such he has instincts and acts according to their impulses. Instincts are noticeable particularly in infants and children, because they live more on a sensory level. The adult's actions are so influenced by intellect and will, that he is seldom aware of the force the instincts exert on his conduct. On the other hand, some instincts never come into play until man enters into adolescence and adulthood.

If we attempt a *classification* of the instincts, we discover two fundamental divisions: those which serve the well-being of the *individual* and those which serve the well-being of the *species.* The preservation of the individual and the propagation of the species are the two great purposes which determine instinctive actions. No enumeration of the single instincts is altogether satisfactory, because it is difficult to isolate them out of the mass of intermingling activities.

Instincts of *self-preservation.* Most fundamental is the *food-seeking* instinct. Infants instinctively seek their mother's breast and know, prior to learning by experience, how to extract the milk through the complicated motor mechanism of sucking and swallowing. The food-seeking instinct perseveres through life; man must always seek food to sustain life. Akin to this instinct, but really its reverse, is the natural *aversion* man experiences toward many substances which might be taken for food but are obnoxious to his well-being. Man also has the instinct of *curiosity,* the insatiable drive to investigate objects and learn what they are; he thereby discovers what objects are useful or harmful for his well-being. Then there is the instinct of *appeal,* expressed by sobbing, weeping, and whining, seeking aid and comfort in personal distress which cannot be relieved by personal effort. Man also has the instinct of *acquiring* and keeping or *hoarding* things, from toys to junk to homes and earthly wealth. The *constructive* instinct is strongly active in children, manifesting itself in games, play-acting, etc. Man also possesses the important *communal* instinct, the impulse to associate with others and form social groups; this instinct is the foundation of human society and government. In connection with the communal instinct we notice the instinct of *self-assertion,* which seeks to dominate the group, and the instinct of *submission* to the recognized superiority of others. In the face of threatening danger the instincts of *escape* or *combat* are unmistakably present.

Instincts of *race-preservation.* These instincts are too well-known to require more than cursory mention, for we observe them displayed at every turn. The *mating* instinct begins to manifest itself around the age of puberty. From that time on youth becomes sex conscious. Courting and the choice of a mate follow. If the union of husband and wife issues in offspring, the *parental* instinct induces the parent to give utmost care and protection to the children, even at the sacrifice of many personal comforts. There is, without doubt, no nobler instinct in all nature than the self-immolation of parental love, because it is the most unselfish.

This enumeration of the human instincts, given for the sake of convenience, follows the well-known thirteen instincts given by William McDougall. William James enumerates a larger number; J. Lindworsky accepts but a single instinct (the striving after pleasure and happiness); others give other lists. The list mentioned in our text may not be complete or entirely accurate, but it should serve the purpose of enabling us to understand and appreciate human conduct better.

Nature of Instinct

Following the lines of certain philosophical systems, there are a number of *theories* which must be considered as an attempt to explain the nature of instinct.

Pure Mechanism

René Descartes (1596–1650) defended the purely mechanical concept of an organic body. The essence of every body is extension. To him, every organic body, including that of man, was no more than a machine. "I suppose that the body," he wrote, "is merely a statue or earthen machine made by God on purpose to resemble us as much as possible." Speaking of the functions of vegetancy and sentiency, "I want you, I say, to consider that these functions quite naturally follow in this machine from the mere arrangement of the organs, neither more nor less than the movements of a clock or other automaton, from its weights and works."[4]

Like all other vital functions, the instinctive actions of animals, according to Descartes, are the mechanical actions of a robot, without psychical content. This theory represents mechanism pure and simple, with no place in the system even for

[4] *Oeuvres de Descartes,* ed. Cousin, iv, pp. 336, 347–349, *apud* Mercier, *The Origins of Contemporary Psychology* (Kenedy and Sons, 1918), pp. 22–25.

a nervous reflex action. Today, extreme mechanism is rejected by all serious thinkers.

The Theory of Tropism

By 'tropism' biologists understand the involuntary movement of an organism or any of its parts, involving turning or curvature and axial orientation, and induced either automatically or in response to one or more stimulating influences. Such influences may be light, heat, electricity, a chemical substance, etc. Plants in a cellar, for example, send shoots toward the direction of the incoming light; seed shoots turn upward, while the roots turn downward, no matter how the seed may be placed in the soil; the amoeba, the paramoecium, the earthworm, and, in fact, most animals with a primitive nervous system are subject to tropisms of various kinds. When the organism moves in a direction toward the stimulus, the tropism is 'positive'; when in a direction away from the stimulus, the tropism is 'negative.' The influencing agencies being some form of physical or chemical energy, tropisms are conceived by biologists to be purely physical or chemical reactions, excluding all sensation and consciousness; hence, sensory cognition and appetency play no part in tropisms.

A few biologists and psychologists, among them A. Bethe (1898) and Jacques Loeb (1912), have attempted to explain all vital activity, including 'instinctive' action, in terms of *tropism*. The theory has not met with much success; it is doubtful whether any biologist of note today subscribes to it.

That tropisms exist in the lower forms of animal life can be accepted without dispute. That, however, is a far cry from the assumption that all animal behavior, and especially the highly complex trains of action observed in the instinctive performances of insects, fishes, birds, and mammals, are the result of tropisms. H. Jennings[5] and S. Holmes, who have made extensive studies of the life histories of protozoa, are convinced that the principle of tropism is inadequate as the total explanation

[5] *The Behavior of Lower Organisms* (Columbia University Press, 1906).

of the actions of even such simple beings as amoebae and paramoecia. The tactics of these animalcules manifest real behavior, not tropism, because their actions show individuality and spontaneity, without any observable change having occurred in the environmental medium.

When we apply the theory to the higher animals, it breaks down completely. Only the most deep-seated prejudice of mechanistic materialism could prompt a scientist to consider tropisms as an explanation, for example, of the spawning journeys of the eel and the salmon, of the seasonal migrations of the various species of game fowl, of the nuptial flight of bees and ants, of the nest building of birds, of the courting and mating of animals, of the parental care of mammals for their offspring, and so on. These types of activity may be mysterious and difficult to explain, but it certainly is erroneous to degrade them to the level of a tropistic mechanism. *Cognition* and *experiential adaptation to circumstances* are too evident to be denied, and these are *psychical* elements far removed from the mechanical character of tropisms.

The Theory of Reflex Action

The *behaviorists* and *reflexologists* contend that all human and animal activities eventuate either visibly in muscular movement or invisibly in glandular secretion as a reflex action in response to physical stimuli. Reflexes may be either unconditioned (unlearned) or conditioned (learned). According to this theory, there is no need to appeal to 'consciousness,' 'sensations,' 'perceptions,' 'intelligence,' 'purposive action,' 'experience,' 'innate propensity,' and similar unobservable and unpredictable factors as an explanation for so-called 'instinctive' actions; all one need assume is a *chain of reflexes* released through response to external stimuli, the only difference between a simple reflex, such as the pupillary reflex, and instinctive action being one of degree in complexity. 'Psychic factors' must be eliminated and 'reflexes' substituted as the ultimate explanation of all animal behavior, including the behavior usually described as 'instinctive.' As a matter of fact, there is no such thing as an 'instinct,' as something which is an innate drive or urge to perform actions which are conducive toward the welfare of the individual and the species. An 'instinct,' conceived in this manner, is a superfluous concept of psychology. The concept of 'reflexes' is sufficient to account for all actions usually ascribed to 'instinct.' Such is the attitude and theory of the thorough-going behaviorist and reflexologist, e.g., J. B. Watson.

Unfortunately, however, like the theory of tropism, to which it bears a close resemblance, the reflex theory is an *over-simplified explanation* of the type of animal actions which are grouped together as 'instinctive.' That some of these actions, or portions of the entire train of actions, are reflex in character, is undoubtedly true; but the fallacy of the reflex theory of instinct consists in arguing from the truth of the part to the truth of the whole, from the truth of the particular to the truth of the universal, from 'some' to 'all.'

Instinctive actions involve much more than reflexes, namely, *psychic factors.*

We know that reflexes are responses of the neuro-muscular mechanism to physical stimuli, and these responses, to be genuine reflexes, must be effected through a reflex arc *independent of a determining or modifying conscious process.* Whenever an action is determined or modified by an antecedent or concomitant conscious process or perception or appetency of any kind, it is no longer a 'reflex action' in the meaning of the term as universally accepted in psychology. A reflex action may, or may not, enter consciousness, but the entire action must be carried out on a purely neuro-muscular level without conscious control. Reflex action, we claim, is insufficient as an adequate explanation of instinctive action.

For one thing, the response of an organism to a stimulus (heat, light, pressure, etc.) in a reflex is *direct, automatic, stereotype.* Given the stimulus, the response must follow. Instinctive actions, however, follow a different course. Preparation for the care of the prospective offspring (building a nest, constructing a cell, etc.) occurs only when the offspring is on the way. Birds are uninfluenced by the sight of twigs, grasses, etc., until the necessity arises to construct a proper abode for the eggs that are to be laid. Mud wasps are not interested in caterpillars, spiders, or grasshoppers, until the time arrives for them to lay eggs. The stimuli are thus present, and the reflex actions should take place, if instinctive actions were nothing more than a chain of reflexes; since they do not take place, it is evident that instinctive actions are not mere reflexes.

Again, reflexes are responses to *stimuli,* while instinctive actions are responses to *objects* and *situations.* Most instinctive performances represent a complex series of many types of actions quite different from the reflex responses to a stimulus such as light, heat, touch, and so forth; they may cover considerable territory and consume considerable time, but they always form a unitary activity, a planned whole, and they always center around definite objects or situations. Watch a bird build a nest, a squirrel collect nuts, a dog chase a rabbit, a mud wasp sting a caterpillar, a bee construct a honey cell, a colony of ants wage war on a neighboring colony, a beaver cut down a sapling, a hawk swoop upon a hen — these and similar typically instinctive actions reveal the operations of a number of senses in *concerted perceptual responses,* not merely reflexes in response to isolated individual stimuli.

Furthermore, notwithstanding the typical character of the instinctive action, there is a degree of *spontaneity, initiative,* and *adaptability* in the chains of actions as a whole which is altogether foreign to the concept of a reflex. No two robins, for example, build their nests of absolutely the same material on the same kind of branch in the same kind of tree with the same kind of routine. Yet the final result is peculiarly similar for the purpose in hand, showing that, whatever may be the robins' response to the individual twigs, straws, branches, etc., 'the nest as a whole' is the guiding principle of the series of actions, permitting considerable latitude in the details of construction, so long as the nest as a whole is built. Or, consider a cat stalking a bird among some shrubs. The cat slinks along the ground, stops, crouches, moves forward again, now faster and now slower, taking advantage of every point of concealment, closing in on the unsuspecting victim, and then makes its climactic lunge, sinking its claws into the body of the bird and devouring it. The technique of hunting is typically similar in all cases, but the details change according to locale and circumstances; the instinctive principle is the same, but the execution is adapted to the prevailing conditions. There is very little in common between this type of perceptual action and the stereotype, automatic character of a reflex.

Finally, typically instinctive actions, seemingly so fixed in routine as to resemble the directness and inflexibility of reflexes, are at times *modified* to meet artificially introduced conditions at variance with the routine of the instinctive actions. One need but recall the amazing performance of the dauber wasp repairing the damage done to its mud cells by K. D. McDougall (p. 221). The wasp recognized the incompleteness of the cells and promptly went about to set things right by deviating from the routine procedure of its work. Henri Fabre (p. 215) narrates how he interfered with the usual routine of the sphex by moving the grasshopper a short distance away from the rim of the excavated nest, while the sphex was exploring the interior. He repeated the experiment dozens of times, until he grew tired and desisted, convinced that the unintelligent behavior of the sphex would result in an endless repetition of the same performance. Fabre was not patient enough. The Peckhams, husband and wife, also made the experiment of Fabre, but with a totally different result. After many repetitions of the procedure, as in the experiment of Fabre, the sphex dragged her prey, without depositing it at the rim as it had done heretofore, directly into the nest and finished her job. This action of the sphex manifests a perceptual appreciation of the task to be accomplished and a corresponding modification of the routine procedure usual under the circumstances.

These few incidents of animal behavior are sufficient to show that animals are not mere 'reflex machines,' but are organisms which are actuated in their instinctive actions by impulses set in motion by sensory data synthesized into perceptual wholes.

The Theory of Innatism

While the inner constitutional elements of the animal organism, as expressed in instinctive action, will always remain very much of a mystery, we are now in a position to outline the *true nature of instinct.*

The facts presented demand that the animal, during the course of instinctive actions, have the *ability to perceive* the various objects and their concrete relations, the immediate task to be performed in connection with these objects, and the present actions required as the task unfolds step by step toward the attainment of the goal as the end-result of the action series. Besides this perceptive ability, the animal must have the *executive ability* to begin, to develop, and to complete the task before it. That they possess this executive ability is obvious from the actual performance of the task. However, neither the ability of perception nor the ability of execution would be of any value, if the animal did not have the *propensity* or inherent impulse to undertake and execute the task under the proper conjunction of the circumstances of time and place. Animals do not perform instinctive actions except in definite circumstances of time and place; but when these circumstances are present, they show that they are driven by an irresistible impulse to begin and to continue the act until the goal is reached.

The intrinsic factors of instinct are *inherited* and therefore *innate;* they are not learned, at least not fundamentally and ultimately, by experience. Many instinctive actions are done but once, have never been observed before in operation, are performed practically at birth, and are always carried through with unhesitating dispatch and with unfailing accuracy. Animals simply never have the opportunity to learn the sequence of some of these actions by experience. Hence, these intrinsic factors must be innate and inherited.

Two causes seem to unite to produce instinctive action. Certain objects excite the animals's imagination into activity; they are the *objective* cause. Due to a natural disposition present in the animal, the images aroused in the imagination excite the appetency, impelling it to perform certain actions in connection with the object perceived; these images are the *subjective* cause. Instinct, then, would seem to consist in the native power of associating certain images, which has as its object the immediate actions necessary for the task before it. These actions are subservient to the well-being of the individual and of the species and as such are *naturally* and *inherently purposive.*

The Origin of Instinct

In as much as instincts are inherited and innate, and not the result of experiential learning on the part of the individual animal, the question is unavoidable: *What is the origin of instinct?* Instinct emerges from the past into the present; its origin, therefore, must lie in the past, not in the present. Observation and historical record demonstrate that the same kind of animal, everywhere and always, performs its instinctive actions according to a pattern typically the same for all. How, then, was the instinct acquired by the species?

The crux of the problem is this: Since purposive action is the realization of a goal set in the future, with the selection of proper means to attain the goal, it definitely implies the *prevision of the goal and the means* required to attain the goal. Since instinctive actions are purposive, tending to realize the well-being of the individual and the species as a goal set in the future, instinctive actions should also require the prevision of this goal and the selection of its means of attainment. Such a prevision, though, apparently demands *intellectual foresight.* Someone, then, had to set the goal and determine the means for all the instinctive actions of the entire animal kingdom from the very beginning of animal life, provided these instincts have operated in the same fashion throughout the past eras of animal history. If these instincts did not operate in the same fashion throughout the past, but *originated in the course of time,* then how did they originate? They must be accounted for.

The Theory of Direct Creation

The defenders of this theory claim that the Creator, the Supreme Intellect, created the animals, endowing their constitution with all powers necessary for the survival of the individuals and of the species. Since the animals themselves are devoid of intellect and cannot, therefore, set a goal and select the proper means to attain this goal (the well-being of the individuals and of the species), the Creator implanted in their nature the instincts necessary for their preservation. Only the Creator has control over the entire animal kingdom, so that He alone, in their very creation, could give them these native endowments manifested in instinctive behavior. The prevision of the goal and of the means required to attain the goal resides in the Creator, not in the individual animal; the Creator imposed the law of instinct upon the animal's nature, and the animal carries out the law without knowledge of its intrinsic purposiveness. This theory obviates the preposterous necessity of ascribing a superhuman intellect to subhuman animals, and gives an adequate explanation for the existence of purposive instincts present in all the individuals and species of animals throughout time and space. Since the animals themselves cannot be the cause of the origin of their own instincts, being completely dominated by these instincts, the cause of the origin of their instincts must be referred to the intelligent cause of their very nature, namely, to the Creator.

According to this view, the instincts, complete and perfect, came into existence in the animal nature by virtue of direct creation. These native endowments, then, were handed down from generation to generation to the present time through heredity.

There are *three particularly strong points* in favor of the theory of direct creation. It gives an adequate explanation of the exquisitely *purposive* character of instinct in all its manifestations, without the necessity of ascribing to the animal an intellectual insight into the purposiveness itself; it gives an adequate account of the *uniformity* of instinct in all the individuals of a species; and it also gives an adequate account of the *universal distribution* of instinct in the animal kingdom with respect to time and space.

The Theory of Evolution

The theory of evolution appears in a *variety of forms,* chief among which are the following.

According to *Charles Darwin's* theory of evolution by *natural selection,* the offspring of organisms differ in minor variations from the parents; and if these variations give an individual an advantage over its fellows in the struggle for existence, then by a natural process, called 'natural selection,' those best adjusted to their environment will survive ('the survival of the fittest'), while the others will perish. These small fortuitous individual variations are transmitted by generation and preserved by heredity, and in this manner the gradual accumulation of such variations gives rise to new species. The instincts originated in like manner, beginning with isolated, casual acts and gradually developing in the course of long periods of time into complicated, marvelously 'purposive' sets of instinctive actions. All is, of course, the work of chance, operating through the blind mechanism of natural selection. Most evolutionistic biologists now relegate 'natural selection' to a minor position among the factors operating in evolution.

Herbert Spencer, though an evolutionist, rejected natural selection. According to his view, all actions which are now instinctive were performed in the past *consciously* and *intelligently* for the satisfaction of some need or for the attainment of a definite goal. In the course of time these actions, through constant repetition, became hereditary habits, so that instincts are, so to say, the result of a 'lapsed intelligence.'

Henri Bergson's concept of evolution is unique. All organisms have evolved through the agency of an original life force, an *élan vital,* present throughout nature. Mind in its evolution developed along two different lines, along the line of 'intelligence' and along the line of 'instinct.' Intelligence developed in increasing perfection among the vertebrates and mammals, reaching its peak in man, while instinct developed to its fullest extent in the insects.

Emergent evolution, advocated by *Lloyd Morgan* and many moderns, has as its basic idea the principle that nature is the product of evolution in such a manner that entirely new and unpredictable properties originate through synthesis and thereby form new and higher levels of reality. These new properties are not mere resultants obtained by addition or subtraction from among previously existing properties; rather, these new properties have no counterpart in the lower levels and simply 'emerge' with specific characters not discoverable in the former (lower) levels. It is thus that mind, and with it instinct also, originated.

In all these variations of evolutionary theory, *no intrinsic goal* is assumed to exist for the process of evolution. It is a blind process produced by blind forces; everything just *happens* to work out this way. Instinct is merely one of these evolutionary products.

It is our contention that evolution, conceived in this fashion, *cannot account for the origin of instinct.*

First, these evolutionary theories are based on the idea of the transmission of properties by generation through heredity. Now, very many instincts are of such a nature that the very existence of the individual and the generation of its offspring depend on the instinct being *perfect,* both as to ability and execution, *from the start.* Such are the food-seeking and mating instincts. Imperfection here would doom the individual and the species to extinction, because no second generation could arise to which anything could be transmitted. Unless, therefore, the first animal of a species were natively endowed with the complete instinct, there would be no future generations in which this instinct could 'evolve.' That being so, how did the instinct originate in this first individual? Certainly not through evolution.

Second, we must bear in mind that certain animals exercise a certain instinct *only once in their life*. The nuptial flight of the queen bee occurs only once. The cabbage butterfly lays its eggs only once and puts them under a cabbage leaf, never seeing its offspring. This larva becomes a butterfly, lays eggs in the beginning of summer on the leaves of a tree (contrary to the action of its parent); these larvae spin a cocoon for themselves on a tree, become butterflies in August, and then they spin their cocoon around the entire leaf with stem and twig, so that the eggs are properly protected for the winter. Thus the butterflies of spring act in an entirely different manner from those of autumn, and this only once in their life. Since they do not see their offspring, they cannot know the purposiveness of their action; but the purposiveness is there. It cannot be a question of hereditary habits or of a gradually acquired variation or insight, because the butterflies perform the action but once and never know its result. And yet, if the action were not perfect from the start, there would be no second generation.

There are many such instances of instincts. How is it possible for the parent to acquire such an instinct and transmit it to the young, since they have never seen it exercised and have not themselves exercised it before? The parent certainly cannot transmit the instinct to the young present in the eggs, because these young exist already, and the parent first begins to exercise its care for the eggs after the young exist; and not to subsequent young, because it lays eggs only once. The parent does not even know that there is such a thing as an offspring. Yet the omission of a single step in this instinctive operation would be fatal to the offspring.

Third, the *care of the young,* as manifested in many instinctive actions, could never have been learned by the parent nor could it have been the chance result of blind forces of nature. The mud wasp, for example, paralyzes spiders, grasshoppers, and caterpillars by puncturing their motor centers with its stinger. It puts the paralyzed insect in the mud nest, pastes an egg onto the insect's body, and seals the nest, never to return to observe the results. The wasp itself does not eat flesh meat, but its young cannot exist on anything else in the beginning. If the insect were not paralyzed, the egg would be crushed through the squirming of the insect against the walls of the mud nest. But how should the wasp know this, since it never sees the results of its operation? And how should it know that its offspring needs flesh meat? And how should it know that stinging the insect will stop its movements through paralysis? And how should it know where to sting and how many times to sting? If the very first wasp did not succeed in its amazingly purposive chain of actions, the species would not have survived the first generation. Experience could not have taught the wasp how to proceed, because it knows nothing of the result of its actions; insight is out of the question, for the same reason; a fortunate chance action could never be transmitted through heredity. Hence, again, if this entire set of actions would not be perfect from the start, the species would have become extinct with the first wasp. This example is just one among thousands.

Last, it is difficult to understand, on the principles of these evolutionary theories, how certain animals can transmit through heredity *an instinct they do not possess,* and how certain instincts can survive when their *possessors do not propagate their kind*. We refer to *neuter* insects, such as working bees, etc. "Neuter insects which do nothing to propagate their race can do nothing to transmit instinct or anything else. Yet these neuters do all the work of the community and require the most complicated instincts to do it. To fit them for their object, even their bodily form has often to be entirely different from that of the males and females; and in some species the neuters destined for different branches of work differ entirely from one another. Thus in one kind of ant there are working neuters and soldier neuters, with jaws and instincts extraordinarily different. Yet these neuters are the offspring of males and females, none of whom, and none of whose ancestors, ever did a stroke of work in their lives."[6]

[6] J. Gerard, *Science and Scientists* (Catholic Truth Society), p. 118.

No matter what type of the above-mentioned evolutionary theories one may choose to accept, their explanation of the origin of instinct leads to the almost inevitable conclusion that the *effect is greater than the cause*. While the instinctive actions are eminently purposive and intelligent in themselves, neither the animals nor the forces of evolution possess the requisite intelligence to give an adequate account of the rise, development, and survival of the instincts. Evolutionists usually appeal to the unknown 'conditions of the past' to gloss over any difficulties they may encounter in their explanation; but such an argument is a plain *appeal to ignorance* which explains nothing at all. So long as there is no intelligence working in or through nature, no adequate explanation for the intelligence manifested by the instincts will ever be forthcoming.

The Theory of Purposive Evolution

Do the arguments just adduced prove that evolution never took place? Not necessarily. Evolution itself, obviously, is not impossible, but it must be a *purposive evolution*. Since, however, purposiveness implies an intelligent foresight into the future, and since this intelligent foresight cannot be ascribed either to the forces of nature or to the animals themselves, the only possible alternative is the assumption that the *Supreme Intelligence endowed nature with a purpose* and with the necessary principles of action to realize this purpose *through evolution*. The required intelligence would reside not in nature itself but in the Author of nature. It would then make little difference whether evolution were gradual or emergent in character. Animal species would arise, and their instincts with them, whenever the laws of evolution, imposed on nature by the Creator, would produce the conditions necessary for their origin. Hence, if the instincts derived their origin through evolution, this evolution must have been a purposive evolution imposed on nature by the Creator. Such a type of evolution would indeed render an adequate account of the origin of instincts and is acceptable.

Our *answer,* then, to the question of the origin of instincts must be that the instincts originated either through direct creation or through purposive evolution. Whether evolution has actually occurred, is a problem all by itself; and with that we are not at present concerned.

We have now studied the external senses—the somesthetic senses, taste, smell, hearing, and sight; and also the internal senses—the central sense, imagination, memory, and instinct. These are the *cognitive sensory powers* of man and, more or less, of all animals. Man is indeed an organism endowed with many wonderful powers. But one great fact stands out in bold relief: Man is an *integral organism* manifesting a marvelous unity of nature amid all the complexity of parts and powers.

Summary of Chapter X

The fourth internal sense is *instinct.* It occupies itself with the well-being of the organism.

1. *The Concept of Instinct.* Instinct connotes an impulsive tendency toward actions which are conducive to the well-being of the individual or of the species. This impulse is a native endowment, present in the animal prior to any learning by experience. Instinct also implies a cognitive element.

2. *The Existence of Instinct.* Their behavior shows conclusively that animals possess an innate impulse, antecedent to all individual experience, determining them to certain uniform, purposive actions, useful for the individual and the species.

We may define instinct as an innate disposition which determines the organism to perceive (to pay attention to) an object of a certain class, and to experience in its presence a certain emotional excitement and an impulse to action which find expression in a specific mode of behavior in relation to that object.

3. *Instinct and Experience.* Instinct is not a rigid and uncontrollable automatism, but an innate disposition which possesses a certain amount of plasticity and flexibility, capable of

being modified and adapted to the requirements of existing circumstances.

4. *Experience and Intelligence.* Besides acting by instinct, animals also learn through experience, seeking what is good for them and avoiding what is harmful. Both types of action involve a sensory appreciation or estimation of the concrete usefulness or harmfulness of a perceived object with reference to the individual or to the species. The animal's capacity to improve upon native tendency in the light of past experiences is often called *intelligence*. This power to estimate what is a concrete good or evil for well-being St. Thomas calls the *estimative power.*

5. *Human Instincts.* The instincts of *self-preservation* include food-seeking, aversion, curiosity, appeal, acquisition and hoarding, the constructive instinct, the communal instinct, self-assertion, submission, escape, and combat. The instincts of *race-preservation* include mating and parental care.

6. *Nature of Instinct.* There are a number of theories. *Pure mechanism* considers the body as a mere machine without psychical content. *The theory of tropism* explains all animal actions, including instinct, as tropisms. The theory is erroneous, because cognition and experiential adaptation to circumstances are too evident to be denied. *The theory of reflex actions* interprets all instinctive actions in terms of a chain of reflexes. The theory is erroneous, because all evidence points to the fact that animal actions are determined or modified by antecedent or concomitant conscious processes of perception and appetency. *The theory of innatism* holds that the true nature of instinct involves the *ability to perceive* objects and their concrete relations, the immediate task, and the actions required to perform the task. It also involves the *executive ability* to carry out the task and the *propensity* to execute the task imposed by instinct. These factors are inherited and *innate,* not the result of experiential learning. The stimulating object is the 'objective' cause; the natural propensity to carry out the action is the 'subjective' cause; these actions are then naturally and inherently *purposive.*

7. *The Origin of Instinct.* There are a number of theories which attempt to explain the origin of instinct.

The Theory of Direct Creation. According to this theory, the instincts, complete and perfect, came into existence in the animal nature by virtue of a direct creation.

The Theory of Evolution. The theory appears in a variety of forms: Darwin's theory of evolution through natural selection, Spencer's theory of lapsed intelligence, Bergson's theory of a life force, and Morgan's theory of emergent evolution. These theories, as proposed, are inadequate. Many instincts must be perfect from the start. Many are exercised only once in the life of the individual. The instinct of parental care could not have been learned, nor could it be the chance result of blind forces of nature. No logical account can be given of neuter insects and their instincts. Considering the purposive and intelligent character of instinctive actions, the origin of instinct, according to these theories, would mean that the effect is greater than the cause.

The Theory of Purposive Evolution. If instincts originated through evolution, this must be a *purposive evolution,* in the sense that the Creator endowed nature with a purpose and with the necessary principles of action to realize this purpose through evolution.

Hence, instincts originated either through direct creation or through purposive evolution.

Readings

McDougall, William, *Outline of Psychology,* Ch. II, III, IV, V; *The Energies of Man,* Ch. III, IV, V, VI, VII. — Gaffney, M. A., *The Psychology of the Interior Senses,* Ch. V. — Harmon, F. L., *Principles of Psychology,* pp. 418–424, 429–433, 459. — Maher, M., *Psychology,* pp. 587–592. — Gruender, H., *Experimental Psychology,* Ch. XII, XIII. — Brennan, R. E., *General Psychology,* pp. 224–239.

CHAPTER XI

SENSUOUS APPETENCY

THE external and internal senses and their functions have now passed in review. Physical objects act upon the external senses, and these senses, in conjunction with the brain, react with sensations. Bits of information concerning these objects are thus conveyed to the sentient subject, are arranged into perceptual wholes, and then referred back to the stimulating objects. Thereby the properties of these objects, and through these properties the objects themselves, become known in a concrete sensory manner. This mental process is perception, and by its means external objects receive a *cognitional existence within the sentient subject.*

Sense knowledge is one phase of the life of the brute and of man. There is another phase, and it is equally important: it is *sensuous appetency.* Through perception the object is brought into contact with the subject; through appetency the subject is brought into contact with the object.

Concept of Appetency

In a very general way, *appetency,* or appetite, is the *tendency of one thing toward another.* This is clear from the etymology of the term, for 'appetency' is a Latin derivative (*ad* and *petere*) meaning 'to strive for,' 'to seek for,' 'to tend toward,' something. This tendency of one thing toward another is different in different types of objects.

The appetency present in the animal organism is a *conscious* appetency. It is termed 'conscious,' because the animal is aware of the object for which it strives, and this conscious apprehension of the object is a deciding factor in its striving. A double influence is present in conscious appetency: the 'objective' influence of the object attracting the apprehending subject; and the 'subjective' influence of the apprehending subject responding to this attraction by inclining toward the object with a conscious act of striving.

The appetency of animals is the result of a *spontaneous inclination* following conscious apprehension. Conscious apprehension and spontaneous inclination are *psychic* factors which are essential to the concept of appetency in animals.

Depending upon whether the knowledge preceding appetition is sensuous or rational, the distinction is made between *sensuous* and *rational appetency*. The latter is exclusively a human characteristic; the former is common to brute and man. Rational appetency is called the 'will.' In the present discussion we are concerned solely with sensuous appetency; rational appetency will receive a separate consideration in a later chapter.

Whatever may be the type of appetency, that which moves it to action is the *good,* and the 'good' is what is *suitable* in some manner for the striving subject. The *well-being* of the organism itself is the all-embracing goal of its appetitive activities, because nothing is so basically good and suitable for an individual as its own being, its own nature.

An animal strives for an object because it satisfies some need, some demand, some exigency, some natural aptitude; it helps the animal in some way, or completes it in some fashion, or gives it pleasure in some form, or actualizes some potentiality of its nature, or has the capacity to realize some end and purpose in it. In a word, the animal strives for something because it is 'suitable' and in so far 'good' for the organism.

The very fact, though, that animals strive for anything at all, makes it clear that they cannot have their *complete actuality* from the beginning. If they had all their entity, if they possessed all the reality they are capable of receiving, they would no longer tend toward, or strive for, anything. To strive for something means that there is still some potentiality in their being which needs and demands realization. And in so far as something is suitable for this fuller realization and actualization of the animal, it will be 'good' for it. What, in particular, is suitable to a being, will naturally depend upon what the animal *needs* and what some other being has to *offer* for the satisfaction of this need.

Now, all animals have a nature or essence peculiar to themselves as members of a species and as individuals. And each such nature has a very real and definite *purpose or end within itself* which it tends at all times to protect and to bring to full completion and *perfection.* A thing is 'perfect' when it has everything that it is supposed to have according to the exigencies of its nature. Perfection may be taken absolutely or relatively. Absolute individual perfection is the complete and final actualization of a being in its totality; relative individual perfection is the actualization of a being at a particular stage of its development as demanded by it at this point. In either case it possesses at the moment as much reality as its nature demands. Not everything will suit every type of animal nature, and the same thing will not suit every animal in all the periods of its life. What is suitable for a lion, need not be suitable for man; and what is suitable in infancy, need not be suitable in adulthood.

Each animal nature—and this, of course, includes the nature of man, because man is an animal organism—thus possesses a *specific natural tendency* within itself for its well-being, and things will be 'good' for it in so far as they promote its well-being. Nothing, however, will suit the nature of a being more than the very *entity of this nature;* its entity is an 'intrinsic' good for it. Consequently, all natures or essences are good for the individuals which possess them, and for this reason animals always strive to preserve and protect their existence. On the other hand, any *other beings* which help to develop or actualize the animal's nature will be suitable and therefore good for them; they are an 'extrinsic' good for the animal, and the appetency of the animal is directed toward them as means toward an end.

Reversely, no animal seeks what is harmful to itself. The animal *avoids what is harmful* to its nature, because it is unsuitable for the satisfaction of its needs. If something harmful confronts the animal, the animal either avoids it or fights it; it never consciously seeks it and strives for it.

Sensuous appetency, then, has *two phases:* the *positive* phase, in which it consciously and actively seeks to attain what is suitable to its being; and the *negative* phase, in which it consciously and actively seeks to avoid what is harmful to its being. In both phases, appetency becomes active after something is consciously *apprehended* as being concretely good or harmful for the animal's being.

From the above it should be clear that sensuous appetency in the brute is closely linked to the *estimative power*. The estimative power enables the brute to recognize what is useful or harmful, good or evil, for its well-being. This knowledge may be acquired through experience, as when a cat or dog learns that certain cooked foods are good or harmful; or it may be instinctive, as when the hen knows that the hawk flying overhead is an enemy and the ducklings know that water is not harmful. The appetency of the brute is, of course, more conspicuous in instinctive actions, because these actions are dynamical in character and represent definite drives and impulses. On the other hand, the appetency manifested in experiential actions are more spontaneous in character and show more clearly that sensuous appetency depends upon the conscious apprehension of objects and situations as useful or harmful. In either case, however, the animal first perceives something to be useful or harmful, and then its appetitive power becomes active, urging the animal to tend toward what is apprehended as good and to avoid what is apprehended as evil.

There is no necessity to *prove the existence* of appetency in the animal's constitution. The fact is too obvious to be denied. The foregoing chapter can very well be taken as containing the evidence of the appetitive striving of animals. Even a superficial study of animal behavior should suffice to convince the observer that animals possess appetency based on sensuous knowledge.

We can, therefore, define sensuous appetency as *a power in virtue of which a sentient being tends toward a consciously apprehended sensuous good and away from a consciously apprehended sensuous evil.*

Kinds of Appetency

Scholastic philosophers distinguish between two kinds of sensuous appetency: the *concupiscible* and the *irascible.* D. Card. Mercier suggests the more modern terms of 'propensity to enjoy' (propension à la pouissance) and 'propensity to fight' (propension à la lutte). Mercier's terms, at any rate, explain what the scholastics mean by the more formidable terms of 'concupiscible' and 'irascible' appetencies.

The *reason* for the division lies in the *object* which arouses the appentency. This object may be something which is good and useful simply as such, something enjoyable in itself; no difficulties beset the attainment and enjoyment of such a good, and the animal strives for it *directly.* Or, this object may be something harmful and disagreeable in itself; here, too, no difficulties beset the avoidance of the evil, and the animal avoids it by merely leaving it alone. An example or two will illustrate the point. A dog finds a bone and enjoys the appetizing morsel as he gnaws it to pieces; on seeing a boy approach whom he has learned to mistrust, he takes the bone between his teeth and leisurely trots off to a more secluded spot to finish his meal. A cat feels the warmth of the stove and curls up comfortably at its side, but it sedulously avoids coming too close, because on a former occasion it touched the stove and was burned. In these cases the attainment of the good and the avoidance of the evil were achieved directly and without any difficulty. Matters, however, are not always so simple. Sometimes obstacles stand in the way of obtaining or keeping a good and of avoiding or removing an evil. Then the animal must fight, and the direct object of appetency is the *removal of the obstacle.* If Fido, the dog, has a bone, and Spitz, another dog, sees this, a fight ensues: Fido fights to retain possession of the bone, and Spitz fights to obtain possession of it, and both fight to remove an obstacle which threatens to hinder them from enjoying the good they seek. A boy with a stick chases a cat, and the cat runs into a shed to escape its pursuer; but when cornered in the shed, the cat turns and fights furiously with naked claws in an attempt to drive its tormentor away. The life history of practically every species of animal will show similar types of behavior, disclosing these two fundamental tendencies.

The concupiscible appetency, therefore, strives directly for what is sensuously pleasant and useful and shuns directly what is sensuously unpleasant and harmful; the object acts directly on the appetency as agreeable or repugnant *in itself.* The irascible appetency strives to obtain and retain an *arduous good* and seeks to avoid or remove an *arduous evil;* the object presents considerable difficulties and dangers which hinder the animal from obtaining and retaining what is a good or from avoiding and removing what is an evil, and these difficulties and dangers the animal seeks to overcome. It is thus seen that the concupiscible appetency is a more 'receptive' disposition, while the irascible appetency is a more 'active' disposition. The former is grounded on simple concupiscence, the latter on anger.

Aristotelian-scholastic philosophers differ in their opinion as to the *nature of the distinction* between concupiscible and irascible appetency. St. Thomas[1] and many others defend the view that a *real* distinction exists between the two, so that they are two different powers. Suarez[2] and others reject this view and claim that it is a single appetency expressing itself in two tendencies; the distinction is a *virtual* one, the foundation for the distinction being the two kinds of tendencies.

---

[1] *Summa theol.,* 1, q. 81, a. 2; 1a 2ae, q. 23, a. 2, ad 3; *Quaest. disp.,* q. 25, de verit., a 2.

[2] *De an.,* l. 5, c. 4, n. 3.

Feelings

Feelings and *emotions* are important factors in behavior. Feelings and emotions are mental reactions associated with cognitive and appetitive activity, and are usually grouped together under the common term *affective states*. Feelings are relatively simple states, while emotions are considerably complex in character.

Feelings and emotions are conscious *subjective* states and they differ according to the attitude of the experiencing subject. I look out of the window, let us say, and notice that it is raining. That is an act of knowledge, not a feeling. If I had intended to go on an outing, and the outing must now be called off, I experience displeasure; that is a feeling. Or, if I had intended to sprinkle the lawn and now am relieved of the chore, I experience pleasure; that is a feeling. The same fact and observation, therefore, is accompanied by different feelings, depending on the subjective condition of the observer.

In ordinary conversations the terms 'feeling' and 'emotion' have a rather vague and confused meaning. Psychologists, however, attach a specific meaning to these terms. 'Feelings,' to them, mean the more *elementary* affective states which are ultimate in character and cannot be analyzed or resolved into anything simpler as component states.

All psychologists agree that *pleasantness* and *unpleasantness* are elementary feelings. Formerly, it was customary to speak of 'pleasure' and 'pain.' At present, however, the term 'pain' is restricted to the sensation resulting from the stimulation of the sensory receptors for pain; in its stead they use the term 'unpleasure' or 'displeasure.'

Pleasant and unpleasant feelings may accompany *every type of conscious activity,* all the way from the sensations of the somesthetic senses to the highest operations of intellect and will. Mild pressure is pleasant; excessive pressure, unpleasant. Moderate temperatures of warmth and cold are pleasant; extreme warmth and cold, unpleasant. Visceral sensations, when the functions are normal, are pleasant; when abnormal, unpleasant. Equilibrium, reported by the static or vestibular sense, is pleasant; disturbances of equilibrium, unpleasant. Proper exercise of the muscles and proper disposition of the bodily members produce kinesthetic sensations which are pleasant; otherwise, unpleasant. Many tastes and odors are pleasant; and many are unpleasant. Some color combinations impress us as pleasant; others, as unpleasant. Tones, harmonies, and melodies are pleasant; discordant noises are unpleasant. We find the same condition with respect to the operations of the internal senses. Depending upon the kinds of sensations presented to the central sense, the perceptions of objects and situations affect us pleasantly or unpleasantly. The recall of such objects and situations through imagination and memory affects us the same way; when we imagine or remember an act of kindness, we have a pleasant feeling, but if we imagine or remember a humiliating insult, we have an unpleasant feeling. Instinctive reactions to something agreeable are pleasant, while those referring to something disagreeable are unpleasant. The same is true of the strivings of sensuous appetency when not instinctive; seeking a sensuous good is pleasant, while fighting off a sensuous evil is unpleasant. Even intellectual and volitional processes are toned with pleasantness and unpleasantness. We experience pleasure, when we succeed in solving a difficult intellectual problem; we experience displeasure, when we are unable to solve it. Many decisions of the will are pleasant, especially when they follow our inclinations and habits; when in opposition to these, they are decidedly unpleasant.

Pleasant and unpleasant feelings are thus seen to accompany all types of activity.

Kinds of Feelings

The question of how many *kinds* of elementary feelings there are, is a controversial issue. Many psychologists hold the view that pleasure and unpleasure (pleasant and unpleasant reactions) are the only genuinely elementary feelings. Others are not so sure. Those who maintain a larger number are not in agreement as to the number.

W. Wundt proposed an interesting *tridimensional theory* of simple feelings. There are, he says, three distinct pairs of feelings. The first pair are pleasantness and unpleasantness; some tastes are pleasant, others unpleasant. The second pair are excitement and restfulness (depression); the sensation of seeing a red color, Wundt says, causes excitement, while the sensation of seeing a blue color causes restfulness. The third pair are tension and relief (relaxation); waiting for the striking of a clock causes tension, and then the actual striking causes relief or relaxation from the tension. Wundt conceived these three classes of feeling to be like the three dimensions of space, so that any feeling could be accurately analyzed by placing it somewhere in these dimensions. Some feelings would be described as pleasant, exciting, and tense; some as pleasant, restful, and tense; others as unpleasant, exciting, and tense; others as unpleasant, depressed, and relaxed; and so forth. Consider the following action in the closing seconds of a football game. The score is six to six, one team having just made a touchdown. The try for the point after touchdown is under way. The ball is snapped, placed, booted. The ball is in the air. This is the critical moment. One half of the crowd is pleasantly affected; the other half is unpleasantly affected. Everybody is tense, excited. It is good! The score is seven to six. The tension is over; relief takes its place. There are shouts of joy and moans of displeasure, surging excitement and numb depression. This incident is an illustration of Wundt's theory.

It is questionable whether excitement and restfulness, tension and relief are elementary feelings. Most psychologists are doubtful. T. V. Moore[3] inclines to the view that these six feelings mentioned by Wundt are elementary. He thinks that there may be more, perhaps even as many elementary feelings as the number of emotions, each emotion being built upon the

---

[3] *Dynamic Psychology* (Lippincott, 1926), p. 106.

basis of a particular elementary feeling. Other authors suggest various feelings as possibly elementary, but there is no uniformity of opinion on the subject. All agree, however, that pleasant and unpleasant feelings are really elementary.

Pleasant and unpleasant feelings can be divided into *sensory* and *rational.* Aristotle[4] calls attention to the fact that things and activities differing in kind are completed by things differing in kind. The activities of thought differ in kind from the activities of sense, and so, therefore, also do the pleasures which are their complement. The same line of reasoning applies to unpleasant feelings. His conclusion is sound. They are fundamentally different, as anyone will recognize who compares the pleasant feeling attending the smell of a fragrant rose with that attending the acquisition of scientific knowledge, or who compares the unpleasant feeling of a gnawing hunger with that of one's failure to master a dominant habit. Because sensory and rational processes are of an entirely different order, the feelings of pleasure and unpleasure accompanying them must also be of a different order.

Aristotle[5] also points out another division. Feelings of pleasure and unpleasure differ according to the *animal species.* Since each species has its proper function and nature, it will also have its proper pleasure and unpleasure. Horse, dog, and man differ in their pleasures, and Aristotle quotes the saying of Heraclitus that 'asses would prefer sweepings to gold.' Species differing in kind, therefore, also have pleasures differing in kind.

The Nature of Feeling

The question of the *nature of feeling* is also a controversial issue. Many opinions have been voiced on the subject.

Plato was of the opinion that pleasure is replenishment, the satisfaction of a want or need, just as pain or unpleasure is the lack of something which the being requires or needs.

---

[4] *Nicomachean Ethics,* Bk. X, Ch. 5.
[5] *Ibid.*

Pleasure, then, is a *transition from pain.* Spinoza and Kant held similar views. Aristotle[6] has already refuted this contention. Not all pleasures are satisfactions of organic cravings like hunger and thirst. Some pleasures do not follow pain or unpleasure. Aristotle mentions the pleasures of smell, sound, and sight, the pleasures of learning, the pleasures of memories and hopes; these do not presuppose the lack of anything, as if these pleasures would supply an organic deficiency of some sort.

Pleasure, according to Descartes and Leibnitz, is the *consciousness of possessed perfection.* There is some truth in this contention; the consciousness of perfection possessed does give pleasure. There are, however, many kinds of pleasure of which this is not true. The consciousness of perfection and its possession, for instance, does not enter into such pleasures as are experienced in odors, sounds, and color combinations.

Passing on to the era of *modern psychology,* we encounter a variety of views.

Materialists and sensationalists identify feelings with *sensations.* Feelings and sensations, however, are not identical. First, when sensations are placed in the focus of attention, they become more vivid and can readily be observed and studied; but feelings become diffuse and, so to speak, evaporate when we pay close attention to them and seek to analyze them. Second, sensations proceed from sense organs and are localized in them; there are no organs for pleasure and unpleasure. Third, the senses are activated by specific stimuli; the eye responds to light, the ear to sound, and so on. The feelings of pleasure and unpleasure, however, are experienced with the activation of any and all the senses. Fourth, sensations are the direct result of external stimuli and are referred to external objects; they have the character of a representation of objects. Feelings have no such representative, cognitive character, but are rather the conscious reaction to such sensations. Lastly, the pleasure derived from intellectual pursuits, such as is experienced in the solution of a philosophical or mathematical problem, has no meaning when interpreted in terms of sensations.

[6] *Ibid.,* Ch. 3.

The theory that feeling is an *attribute of sensation,* is favorably accepted by some psychologists. This view is also erroneous. It is true, of course, that pleasant and unpleasant feelings have intensity, quality, and duration, like sensations; it is wrong, however, to say on that account that they are nothing more than attributes of sensations. For one thing, if their theory were correct, then these feelings should cease when the sensations cease. However, pleasant or unpleasant feelings which have accompanied sensations may persist a long time after the sensations themselves have ceased to be present. Again, the attributes of sensation (intensity, quality, duration) correspond in general to the attributes of the stimuli. The attributes of feelings, however, are strongly subjective in their very nature and do not parallel the sensations. Finally, the feelings which accompany the rational processes are not based on sensation at all; hence, they cannot be attributes of sensation.

Perhaps the most satisfactory theory is the one advanced by *Aristotle* and held by the majority of scholastic philosophers. St. Thomas Aquinas subscribed to the views of Aristotle on this question.

According to Aristotle, activities, whether sensory or rational, are pleasant in so far as these activities are normal and natural for the active subject. Pleasure is a concomitant quality of every vital function, the result of a free and normal release of vital energy. The proportionate exercise of every vital power is accompanied by an appropriate pleasure. The healthy function of the vegetative organs, muscular exercise, seeing, hearing, tasting, imagination, intellection, volition — all are productive of a certain measure of agreeable feeling.

"Since every sense," says Aristotle, "is active in relation to its object, and a sense which is in good condition acts perfectly in relation to the most beautiful of its objects . . . , it follows that in the case of each sense the best activity is that of the best-conditioned organ in relation to the finest of its objects. And the activity will be the most complete and pleasant. For, while there is pleasure in respect of any sense, and in respect of thought and contemplation no less, the most complete is pleasantest, and that of a well-conditioned organ in relation to the worthiest of its objects is the most complete; and the pleasure completes the activity. But the pleasure does not complete it in the same way as the combination of object and sense, both good, just as health and the doctor are not in the some way the cause of a man's being healthy. (That pleasure is produced in respect to each sense is plain; for we speak of sights and sounds as pleasant. It is also plain that it arises most of all when both the sense is at its best and it is active in reference to an object which corresponds; when both object and perceiver are of the best there will always be pleasure, since the requisite agent and patient are both present.) Pleasure completes the activity not as the corresponding permanent state does, by its immanence, but as an end which supervenes as the bloom of youth does on those in the flower of their age. So long, then, as both the intelligible or sensible object and the discriminating or contemplative faculty are as they should be, the pleasure will be involved in the activity; for when both the passive and the active factor are unchanged and are related to each other in the same way, the same result naturally follows."[7]

These acute observations of Aristotle furnish a neat explanation of the diversified character of pleasure, of its essential subjectivity, and of its spread over the entire mental field from sensory cognition and appetition to intellection and volition; for pleasure is the complement of every type of normal and healthy activity.

Aristotle's theory also explains the nature of *unpleasure* or *displeasure*. Displeasure is the result of an excess or defect in the activity of a power or faculty. There is a minimum and a maximum limit to the exercise of every vital power; to exercise a power below the minimum or beyond the maximum will be disproportionate and therefore disagreeable or even

[7] *Ethica Nicomachea,* tr. by W. D. Ross, from *The Works of Aristotle,* vol. 9, ed. by W. D. Ross (Oxford: Clarendon Press, 1925), Bk. X, Ch. 4, 1174 b.

painful. For the same reason continuous pleasure is impossible; the power being limited, its activity is also limited, and so is the pleasure which accompanies it. When the limit is exceeded, the activity is no longer pleasant; it begins to dull and finally turns to displeasure. Change is necessary.

Emotion

Emotions, like feelings, are affective mental states; but unlike feelings, which are simple and elementary, emotions are a complex of constitutive factors. In emotions the individual is deeply stirred, agitated, excited, both in mind and body.

Elements both of *cognition* and *appetency* are dominant factors in emotion; in fact, they are essential to the concept of emotion. The animal nature reacts consciously to the presence of some good or evil, recognizes the good or evil present, and the entire organism grows excited and agitated in its effort to possess the good or avoid the evil. Consider the behavior of an affectionate dog greeting his master upon the latter's return after an absence of a few days. The dog grows tense with excitement, barks joyously, wags his tail, jumps up and down, frisks about, and in every way displays delight on again seeing his friend. And then consider the dog's behavior when another dog attempts to steal his bone. Every muscle is tensed with the readiness to fight, he crouches for the spring, snarls, bares his teeth, barks furiously, lunges at his enemy, bites viciously; he exhibits anger in his entire attitude and in every movement. These are instances of emotion, showing how the elements of conscious cognition and appetency are blended together into a complex affective state involving both mind and body.

Emotion always begins with the *perception* of some object or situation as an alluring good or a threatening evil. Perception is followed by an act of *appetency,* due to the aroused impulse to seek the apprehended good or avoid the apprehended evil. *Changes* in bodily function then result leading to *behavioral reactions.* In this sequence, perception or cognition is the cause of the emotion, the behavioral reactions are the effect of the emotion, while the act of appetency, together with the concomitant bodily changes, form the agitated experience of emotion itself. This agitated experience, consisting of the appetitive act and the bodily changes, is the very *essence of emotion;* there can be no emotion without either the appetitive impulse or the agitated bodily condition. It should be borne in mind, however, that the cognitive, appetitive, and organic factors are irrevocably linked together in the integral emotional pattern.

That emotions can and do occur on a purely *sensory* plane, is evident from the facts that *brute animals* exhibit many types of emotional behavior. They show joy, fear, anger, lust, courage, aversion, and so on. In this respect brute and man are alike. Man, however, being also rational, frequently displays emotional behavior which is touched off by *intellectual* apprehension and *volitional* appetency. Entire nations can be aroused to intense emotion through the enthusiastic support of an ideal, such as the defense of their liberty. An individual may rise up in anger when a derisive epithet is spoken to him or when his honesty is questioned; he may be filled with exaltation when hearing a stirring piece of oratory or when contemplating a beautiful work or art. The cry 'God wills it!' sent hundreds of thousands of crusaders off to a long and bitter religious war. No matter what the particular cause happens to be, the emotional pattern is always more or less alike.

Bodily resonances are the *expression* of emotion. By 'bodily resonances' we understand the organic, physiological changes which occur in the body as a part of the emotional experience. Extensive experimental studies of these changes have been made, some of which are worthy of note.

The *face* of man has always been recognized as an index of emotion. The emotions play upon the facial muscles as upon an instrument. These muscles are very numerous and mobile, and the changes in emotion are reflected in the changes of facial expression.

Cardiovascular changes, due to emotional excitement, also occur. These changes manifest themselves in the rise or fall of the blood pressure and in the rate and frequency of the heartbeat. Variations of this type are observed and measured.

Respiration also undergoes changes during emotion. There may be a decrease or increase in the frequency of breathing, or the breathing may become deeper or shallower. These variations are measured by the pneumograph.

In general, it may be stated, that in pleasant emotions the pulse is strengthened and retarded, and the breathing accelerated, while in unpleasant emotions the pulse is weakened and accelerated, and the breathing retarded.

Visceral changes also occur through the excitement of the emotional state. No matter what the type of emotion may be, if the excitement is intense, the adrenal glands pour out more of their secretion of adrenalin into the blood stream. This adrenalin in turn produces an increase of blood sugar. Adrenalin stimulates muscular contraction. Increased muscular contraction consumes energy, and bodily energy is supplied by blood sugar. The purpose of this metabolic mechanism is apparent. Intense emotional excitement occurs when the animal faces a difficult situation which can be overcome only through a struggle involving considerable muscular exertion. If the animal is not to succumb to fatigue, muscular efficiency must be sustained, and it is sustained by the quick production of sugar through the action of the adrenalin.

If we now attempt a *definition* of emotion, we may describe emotion as an *affective mental state of the animal organism, following the cognition of an object or situation, characterized by strong feeling, by an impulse to action, and by physiological changes in bodily function.*

Kinds of Emotions

The *classification* of emotions is a difficult matter. The objects and situations occasioning them on the 'objective' side, the cognitive and appetitive factors, both sensory and rational, and the bodily resonances accompanying them on the 'subjective' side, are so manifold and variable in kind, quality, and degree, that it is extremely difficult to classify the emotions according to clear-cut types. Some attempts at a comprehensive classification will be enumerated.

The traditional *aristotelian-scholastic classification,* in vogue for centuries, is based on the concupiscible and irascible character of appetency. According to this classification, there are *concupiscible* and *irascible* emotions or, as these philosophers preferred to call them, 'passions.' Since the concupiscible appetency strives for the good and flees the evil, there are two fundamental emotions: (1) *love* of a good simply as such, and (2) *hatred* of an evil simply as such. This love and hatred may be referred to absent or present objects. We thus arrive at the corresponding emotions: (3) *desire* for an absent good, (4) *aversion* or abhorrence of an absent evil; (5) *joy* or delight in the possession of a present good, (6) *sadness* on account of a present evil. These six emotions refer to good and evil uncomplicated by a supervening difficulty. When the good is difficult to attain and the evil is difficult to avoid, the irascible appetency is aroused, giving rise to irascible emotions. From this standpoint, we arrive at five emotions: (7) *hope,* which considers the good as absent and difficult, but possible of attainment; (8) *despair,* which considers the good as absent and difficult and impossible of attainment; (9) *courage,* which sets itself against a threatening evil considered as conquerable; (10) *fear,* which considers the threatening evil as unavoidable; (11) *anger,* which is an emotion aroused in the presence of an evil that has actually befallen the organism. Anger has no opposite emotion. The present good calls forth the emotion of joy; the present evil, if it does not provoke anger, calls forth sadness; anger thus has no paired member.

It will be noticed, that the concupiscible and irascible emotions correspond to what modern psychologists often refer to as 'normal situations' and 'emergency situations.' There can be no question that this classification rests on a solid logical and psychological foundation. The objection is made that the classification is incomplete and rudimentary, many emotions being omitted; no place is found in the list for emotions like pity, surprise, awe, regret, anxiety, and many others. Many emotions, it is true, are omitted. The list, however, contains only the *primary* and *fundamental* emotions; all others would be blends of some sort, and no classification can enumerate all these.

Maher[8] gives a classification which is more in accord with the trends of modern schools of psychology. He classifies the emotions as follows: (1) *Self-regarding* emotions, which include self-esteem, self-complacency, self-commiseration, pride, vanity; remorse, self-condemnation, shame; fear, anger, sense of power. (2) *Altruistic* emotions, among them primarily sympathy; its opposite would be antipathy. (3) *Feelings* attached to *intellectual* activity, among which should be enumerated novelty, surprise, wonder. (4) *Aesthetic* emotions, which are aroused by a contemplation of the beautiful, the sublime, and the ludicrous. (5) *Moral* sentiments, which embrace feelings of obligation, responsibility, approbation, disapproval, remorse, self-commendation, reverential fear, guilt, and so on. With regard to this classification, Maher himself observes that the categories are not mutually exclusive. The question can also be raised whether all of these enumerated items contain the element of excitement and agitation universally associated with emotion; there need not be anything exciting, for example, about self-esteem or disapproval or the sense of responsibility, etc. Generally speaking, however, the classification is serviceable.

W. McDougall's[9] classification meets with approval in many quarters. He bases his division on the *instincts*. First, there are fourteen *primary* emotions, corresponding to the fourteen instincts which he enumerates (the instincts are enclosed in parentheses): fear (instinct of escape), anger (combat), disgust (repulsion), love or tenderness (parental), distress

[8] *Psychology*, 9th ed. (Longmans, Green, 1930), Ch. XX.

[9] *Outline of Psychology* (Charles Scribner's Sons, 1929), Ch. XI, XII.

(appeal), lust (mating), curiosity or wonder (curiosity), subjection (submission), elation (assertion), loneliness (gregarious), gusto (food-seeking), feeling of possession (acquisition), feeling of creativeness (construction), and amusement (laughter). Second, there are the *blended* or *secondary* emotions. McDougall gives a number of instances of the blending of primary emotions, such as scorn (anger and disgust), awe (admiration and fear), gratitude (love and the sense of inferiority), and so forth. Third, *derived* emotions. Among these he enumerates confidence, hope, anxiety, despondency, despair, regret, remorse, sorrow, joy, surprise. While this classification is in many respects a good one, one must object to the fundamental point of division. It seems rather arbitrary to base the primary emotions on the instincts alone. What is 'primary' should be relatively simple and elementary in character; but some of these so-called 'primary' emotions are anything but simple and elementary. Joy and sorrow, for example, seem more simple and elementary than a sense of inferiority or a feeling of creativeness.

An interesting and promising attempt at a *natural classification* of the fundamental emotions has been made by G. J. Schramm,[10] in view of the results obtained from experiments conducted in late years on animals and children. Prominent in these researches were M. Bentley, K. M. Bridges, C. Bühler, W. B. Cannon, H. Carr, J. F. Dashiell, P. Furfey, A. Gesell, F. Goodenough, H. S. Jennings, W. Kuo, C. P. Richter, G. J. Schramm, M. and I. C. Sherman, E. L. Thorndike, E. C. Tolman, L. S. Tsai, J. Watson, R. S. Woodworth, T. P. Young, and many others.

Schramm distinguishes *three main factors* as responsible for emotional behavior: the nature of the stimulus acting on the animal organism; the nature of the organism reacting to the stimulus; the conditions separating the organism from the stimulus. All three factors have an important bearing

[10] *The Journal of Abnormal and Social Psychology,* Vol. XXXI, No. 1, April–June, 1936.

on the classification of the emotions, because they give rise to fundamental types of emotional states.

Stimuli, which arouse the emotions by acting on the organism, are objects or situations that affect the perceiving organism as something good or evil, agreeable or disagreeable, for its maintenance. Schramm terms this quality of a stimulus the factor of its 'favorableness' or 'unfavorableness.' For example, the sight of food is a favorable stimulus for an animal, while the sight of an enemy is an unfavorable stimulus.

Much depends, too, on the *nature of the organism,* namely, on its age, health, maturity, native and acquired bodily equipment, etc. In the presence of a favorable or unfavorable stimulus, the organism may have a constitution with marked superiority, or with marked inferiority, or with general competence (superiority-inferiority), making it very easy, or very difficult, or moderately easy (difficult) to obtain the good and avoid the evil. Anatomically, animals possess distinct structures and powers which enable them to obtain a good and avoid an evil: senses for perceiving an object or situation at a distance (sight, hearing, etc.); bodily members designed for moving toward, or away from, an object (wings, legs, fins, etc.); structures for apprehending and holding an attractive good or fending off and destroying a threatening evil (claws, teeth, stings, etc.); receptors and functions of deep sensibility for intimate contact and possession (organs of nutrition, reproduction, etc.). Schramm groups all this under the factor of the 'superiority,' 'superiority-inferiority,' or 'inferiority' of the organism; for brevity's sake, he speaks simply of the factor of 'superiority.'

The factor of *separating conditions* comprises the elements of time, space, obstructions, etc., which intervene between the stimulating object or situation and the reacting organism. Such conditions obviously evoke different emotions. Depending on the anatomical sub-factors just mentioned, one must distinguish four critical loci or zones in the time and space extension of an emotional behavior period. These are: the point where the organism becomes aware of the stimulus ('point of distant fixation'); the point where the organism seeks to overcome the separating conditions or obstructions ('point of locomotion to obstruction'); the point where the organism makes external contact with the stimulus object by seizure or combat ('point of external contact'); the point where the organism makes intimate contact with, or takes possession of, the objects ('point of intimate fixation'). Schramm calls this temporal period and situational area of emotional behavior the factor of 'space relation.'

It is on the *interplay of these three basic factors* that Schramm builds up his natural classification of emotional phases, as can be seen in the accompanying table.

A PERIODIC TABLE OF EMOTIONAL PHASES

Factor of Organism's	Factor of Space-Relation				Factor of Stimulus's
	Point of Distant Fixation	*Point of Locomotion to Obstruction*	*Point of External Contact*	*Point of Intimate Fixation*	
Superiority	Orientation *Desire*	Approach *Hope*	Success *Dominance*	Adjustment *Elation*	Favorableness
Superiority-Inferiority	Orientation *Desire*	Approach *Hope*	Failure *Submission*	Adjustment *Delight*	Favorableness
Inferiority	Orientation *Jealousy*	Withdrawal *Despair*	None *None*	None *None*	Favorableness
Inferiority	Orientation *Anxiety*	Withdrawal *Fear*	None *None*	None *None*	Unfavorableness
Superiority-Inferiority	Orientation *Repugnance*	Approach *Courage*	Failure *Inhibition*	Adjustment *Depression*	Unfavorableness
Superiority	Orientation *Repugnance*	Approach *Courage*	Success *Vengeance*	Adjustment *Disgust*	Unfavorableness

Explanation of Table: "In the above table it will be seen that the superior organism reacts in an approaching or attacking manner, and the ensuing conflict with an obstruction or resistant stimulus object ends in a success for the organism. The activity of the partially superior organism ends in a partial victory, compromise or submission with dependent maintenance. The completely inferior organism neither surmounts the obstruction nor attains the desired stimulus object. It continues suspended in a vicious circle of desire and despair, or anxiety and fear. The favorable stimulus has an attracting influence in all its factorial situations and yields satisfaction when attained in whole or in part. The unfavorable objective has the opposite effect.

"Among the listed phases, the outer columns are mild reaction phases, since they are essentially fixation states. The inner columns are of emergency behaviors and involve large muscle activities in overcoming obstructions and resisting stimuli objects. The three upper lines of phases yield satisfying experiences, the lower three are dissatisfying. The top and botton lines of phases have dominance resemblances, the inner lines list the submissive behaviors, the innermost have no contacts with the stimuli nor permanent adjustments, they are deficiency reactions."[11]

Many other classifications have been attempted. None, however, seem entirely satisfactory.

The Nature of Emotion

Emotions are elusive reactions. Though powerful in their expressions when unrestrained and left to run their natural course, they subside rapidly when studied by the subject experiencing them.

Three decisive factors stand out prominently in all emotional reactions. First, emotional reactions follow the *perception* of some object or situation which is recognized as being good or evil for the percipient subject. Second, this perception is followed by an *impulse* to acquire the good or to avoid the evil. Third, there ensues the stage of *mental excitement* and the actual *release of energy* (bodily resonance) in the effort to acquire the good or to avoid the evil. Cognition (perception), appetency (conation), and organic agitation (bodily resonance) are inextricably bound together as factors in all emotional reactions; if one of the factors is missing, there is no genuine emotion.

[11] Schramm, *op. cit.*, p. 96.

Some authors incline to the view that emotions are the acts of a *third power* or faculty, radically distinct from the powers of cognition and appetency. It is unnecessary to postulate a third power of this sort. No sufficient evidence has ever been produced to show the existence of this third distinctive power or aptitude. An analysis of emotional states shows that they are nothing more than complex products of *appetency* or *conation* (striving) in the presence of a perceived good or evil affecting the well-being of the organism. Emotions are essentially a protective mechanism, insuring the well-being of the individual by arousing it to action in procuring what is good and in shunning what is harmful.

One must distinguish between *impulse* and *emotion;* they are often confused. An impulse is always a conscious tendency toward or away from something, a 'wanting to act,' and it need not be accompanied at all by any sort of excitement or agitation. I may, for example, want to eat a piece of candy or take a stroll; that is an impulse, and I may, or may not, carry out the impulse. Ordinarily speaking, however, I do not have a 'strong feeling' about the matter. But if someone were to snatch the piece of candy from my hand, just as I am about to put it into my mouth, I might resent this strongly and 'feel very angry' about it; that would be an emotion. One must, therefore, make a distinction between the 'agitated conscious state' which is an emotion and the mere 'tendency to do something' which is an impulse.

It is also well to distinguish between *instinct* and *emotion.* Instincts are always native impulses of some kind or other, and, since emotions are distinct from impulses, there must also be a distinction between emotions and instincts. Instincts involve actions directed toward external objects, while emotions are more in the nature of internal responses. Instincts are often active over a long period of time, while emotions are as a rule ephemeral in character. Emotion and instinct frequently go together, but not always. A person, for example, may follow the instinct of escape by keeping well away from the edge of a precipice without experiencing the mental agitation of fear on that account. Reversely, a person watching an angry lion in a cage may feel the emotion of fear, but the instinctive impulse to combat or escape may be absent because there is no danger. Again, we may experience the emotion of joy in watching the graceful flight of a bird or the playful gambol of a lamb; it would hardly be appropriate, however, to say that some instinct of ours toward the bird or the lamb were thereby called into action. On the other hand, there are also similarities between emotion and instinct. Both are complex patterns involving cognitive, appetitive, and motor factors; both seem to tug at the autonomic nervous system. Emotion has an essentially appetitive core; instinct, an essentially cognitive core.

There is also a distinction between *emotion* and *feeling*. Feelings are simple, emotions are complex. The feeling of pleasantness or unpleasantness often accompanies sensations directly, as in taste or smell. Sensations, as such, never arouse emotions. Objects and situations, to be capable of arousing emotions, must have a *meaningful* significance for the subject, must be recognized as something beneficial or harmful; experience and knowledge, therefore, are prerequisite conditions for emotion. A slap in the face, for example, may be painful or disagreeable, no matter whether it be given in a playful or in a vindictive mood. My personal reaction, from an emotional standpoint, will be very different in the one case and in the other. If I realize that the action was playful, I may laugh at it; but if I realize that the action was intended as an insult, my resentment and anger may be very keen and intense. Why the different emotional reaction? The difference cannot lie in the slapping itself, because that action is a single action. It can lie only in the insight into the meaning of the action taken as a whole in the context of the entire situation. In man, at any rate, emotion has its source in intellectual thought.

In the *traditional* view, *bodily resonance* is the 'effect' of emotion. Because consciousness is in an excited, 'stirred-up' condition, it affects the body, giving rise to a number of physiological changes which are the expression of emotion. In other words, the emotions are the cause of bodily resonance as an effect. The sequence would then be as follows: the perception produces the emotion in the perceiving subject, and the emotion then produces the bodily changes; because a man feels fear, he trembles, and because he feels anger, he clenches his fist and strikes. The *James-Lange theory* of emotion reverses this sequence.

According to this theory, propounded by William James (1884)[12] and C. Lange (1885), the "bodily changes follow directly the perception of the exciting fact, and our feeling of the same changes as they occur *is* the emotion." As James puts it in his usual graphic style, "the more rational statement is that we feel sorry because we cry, angry because we strike, afraid because we tremble, and not that we cry, strike, or tremble, because we are sorry, angry, or fearful, as the case may be." According to this view, perceptions cause bodily resonance, and bodily resonance causes emotion.

James appeals to *three sets of facts* as proof of his theory. He shows that objects excite body changes, and every change of consciousness registers in the organism as in a sounding board. He points out that every bodily change is felt the moment it occurs. Finally, he appeals to the introspective fact that if we imagine a strong emotion and then abstract from this emotion all the feelings of bodily symptoms, there is nothing left of the emotion itself.

The theory is untenable. The facts he adduces are admitted. These facts, however, merely prove that *bodily changes are an integral part of emotional experience.* No one denies that. But his argument is beside the point. What James should prove is that the emotion is the effect, and not the cause, of bodily changes. He does not prove this point; he shows that bodily changes are always present in emotional reactions, but he does not show that these changes *precede* the emotional excitement.

[12] *Principles of Psychology* (Holt, 1931), Vol. II, Ch. XXV, pp. 449 ff.

If James' theory were correct, then *genuine emotions* should be aroused in a subject whenever the proper physiological conditions are present. Consider the following case. In thalamic lesion, hyperactivity in the thalamus follows, and as a result the patients often break out into spasms of uncontrollable laughing or crying. According to the James-Lange theory, this laughing and crying should be true emotion. The patients themselves, however, confess only to a feeling of shame, because they feel ridiculous for laughing or crying without reason; they felt no gladness in their laughter and no grief in their tears, both laughter and crying occurring against their will and better judgment.

Again, if the James-Lange theory is correct, the recordings of the *plethysmograph* and the *pneumograph,* made during experiments on emotional reactions, should precede the emotional state itself. The facts, however, are against the theory. These instruments register a perceptible interval of time between emotion and bodily change, the mental state always preceding the bodily symptoms. Practical application of this principle occurs in the so-called 'lie-detector' experiments, where the mental excitement of telling a lie in the face of damaging admissions is always followed by changes in pulse, respiration, etc., which subsequently show up on the graph. Bodily resonance, therefore, follows emotions as the effect follows the cause. This result is also observed in *hypnotic* experiments. Certain emotions, if suggested, produce bodily changes which, when recorded by the plethysmograph and pneumograph, follow the same sequence as in the case of real emotions: first the mental state, and then, after an interval, the bodily changes.

Furthermore, the work of W. Cannon on the *secretion of adrenalin* during emotional excitement does not favor the James-Lange theory. The perception of danger arouses the emotion of fear, but it takes some time before the secretion of adrenalin produces the physiological changes in the organism; these changes occur too late to be the real cause of the emotion. When adrenalin is injected into the system of a person, this person feels the sensations of muscular tension, etc., usually experienced under the stress of emotion, but the emotion itself, as a strong affective state of consciousness, is not experienced on that account.

Finally, the visceral changes are *common to all emotional* states. The same bodily changes, for example, occur in deep anger and in deep fear. No reason can be assigned why, according to the principles of the James-Lange theory, the same bodily resonance should produce such radically different emotions. Since anger and fear are specifically distinct emotions, they should be caused by specifically distinct, not common, bodily changes. The cause, therefore, must lie elsewhere.

For these and other reasons, the James-Lange theory must be rejected as an inadequate explanation of the nature of emotion.

Walter B. Cannon[13] has advanced what he terms the *thalamic* or *emergency* theory of the emotions. The thalamus, as we know, is a part of the brain stem. On the basis of experiments with animals, Cannon showed that animals will manifest all the bodily changes and expressions of emotion, even when the cortex is removed, provided the thalamus is left intact; but when the thalamus is severed from the rest of the central nervous system, the bodily resonances disappear. According to Cannon's conclusions, then, the stimuli for emotional reactions first travel to the thalamus. A double neural action now takes place. A part of the neural activity passes upward to the cortex, arousing conscious emotional experience; a part passes downward into the motor channels controlling the viscera and the skeletal muscles, thereby producing the bodily changes so noticeable in emotional excitement. The cortex itself, in consequence of the conscious experience, may, and usually does, send nerve impulses back to the thalamus, reinforcing or inhibiting the neural impulses sent to the viscera and musculature. The thalamus, therefore, is a center of coordination for emotional behavior.

[13] *American Journal of Psychology* (1927), Vol. 39, pp. 106–124; *Psychological Review* (1931), Vol. 38, pp. 281–295.

In general, the role of the thalamus in emotional responses seems pretty well established; but this role is a subordinate one in the whole context of emotional responses. It does not explain everything. Experience shows, for example, that anger, fear, and very many other emotions are aroused through conscious concentration on *imagined* or *remembered* objects and situations. Here no neural impulse passes through the thalamus in the first place; everything begins with images in the cortex, and from the cortex the neural impulses are probably sent to the thalamus. It will thus be seen that the thalamic theory does not give enough prominence to the *cognitive* element of emotion.

The findings of experimental psychology in the field of emotion bear out the explanation of *St. Thomas Aquinas,*[14] in which he insists that emotion involves the *psychic* factors of cognition and appetition, and also the *organic* factor of bodily change. Cannon's experiments show that 'emotional expressions' may be present without true emotion; but true emotions, in a normal individual, always imply bodily resonance as an integral part of emotional experience, something which Aquinas had recognized long ago.

In looking back over the present discussion, we are again struck by the fact that the conative processes of sensuous appetency, together with their accompanying feelings and emotions, are intimately linked with the cognitive processes of the various senses. All are subservient to the welfare of the animal as a whole. Sensuous appetency is another phase of man's mental life which highlights the fact that man is in all truth an *integral organism.*

Summary of Chapter XI

Sense knowledge is one phase of mental activity; *sensuous appetency* is another phase.

1. *Concept of Appetency.* In general, appetency is the

[14] *Summa theol.,* Part I–II, q. 22, a. 2; q. 23, a. 1–4; q. 25, a. 1–4.

tendency of one thing toward another. In animal nature it is 'conscious' appetency, the result of a spontaneous inclination following apprehension. That which moves the appetency to action is the good, the suitable. The animal organism thus seeks what is good or useful for itself and avoids what is evil or harmful for itself. Sensuous appetency is defined as *a power in virtue of which a sentient being tends toward a consciously apprehended sensuous good and away from a consciously apprehended sensuous evil.*

2. *Kinds of Appetency.* Sensuous appetency is either *concupiscible* or *irascible.* The former strives directly for what is good in itself; the latter strives to obtain and retain an arduous good and to avoid or remove an arduous evil. Some scholastic philosophers look upon the distinction between concupiscible and irascible appetency as a real distinction; others, as a virtual distinction.

3. *Feelings.* They are affective mental states and as such subjective in character. By feelings, as distinct from emotions, psychologists understand *elementary* feelings. All agree that *pleasant* and *unpleasant* feelings are elementary. They may accompany every type of conscious activity.

4. *Kinds of Feelings.* Many psychologists recognize only pleasantness and unpleasantness as elementary; others enumerate a larger number, but there is no uniformity of opinion. Wundt proposed a *tridimensional* theory of simple feelings: pleasantness and unpleasantness; excitement and restfulness; tension and relief.

Pleasant and unpleasant feelings can be divided into 'sensory' and 'rational.' Aristotle contends that pleasure and displeasure differ in the different species of animals.

5. *The Nature of Feeling.* Plato thought that pleasure is the satisfaction of a want, a transition from pain. Descartes and Leibnitz thought that pleasure is the consciousness of possessed perfection. Materialists and sensationalists identify feeling with sensation. Others consider feeling to be an attribute of sensation. According to Aristotle and most scholastics, pleasure is a concomitant quality of every vital function,

the result of a free and normal release of vital energy; displeasure is the result of an excess or defect in the activity of a power or faculty.

6. *Emotion.* Emotions begin with the *perception* of some object or situation as an alluring good or a threatening evil; perception is followed by an act of *appetency,* seeking the good and avoiding the evil; *bodily changes* then result, leading to behavioral reactions. Emotion is an affective mental state of the animal organism, characterized by strong feeling, by an impulse to action, and by physiological changes in bodily function.

7. *Kinds of Emotions.* The aristotelian-scholastic classification enumerates eleven primary emotions. There are six concupiscible emotions: love and hatred, desire and aversion, joy and sadness. There are five irascible emotions: hope and despair, courage and fear, and anger. Maher classifies them as follows: self-regarding emotions, altruistic emotions, feelings attached to intellectual activity, esthetic emotions, and moral sentiments. McDougall divides emotions into 'primary,' based on the various instincts, 'blended' or 'secondary' emotions, and 'derived' emotions. G. J. Schramm classifies the fundamental emotions by distinguishing three main factors as responsible for emotional behavior: the nature of the stimulus acting on the organism; the nature of the reacting organism; and the conditions separating the organism from the stimulus.

8. *The Nature of Emotions.* Three factors are involved in emotions: perception; impulse; mental excitement and bodily resonance. No third power is necessary, in order to account for emotions; they are complex products of appetency or conation in the presence of a perceived good or evil affecting the well-being of the organism.

One must distinguish between emotion and impulse, emotion and instinct, emotion and feeling.

In the traditional view, bodily resonance is the effect of emotion. In the *James-Lange theory,* emotion is the effect of bodily resonance. The arguments of James are beside the point, because they merely show that bodily changes are an integral part of emotional experience, something no one denies. Many facts speak against the theory.

W. B. Cannon advanced the *thalamic* or *emergency theory* of emotion. The thalamus is the center of co-ordination for emotional behavior. The theory does not account for emotion arising from imagined or remembered objects and situations.

St. Thomas Aquinas explains emotion on the basis of the psychic factors of cognition and appetition and of the organic factor of bodily change. Trends in modern psychology confirm his view.

Readings

Maher, M., *Psychology,* Ch. X, XI, XX. — Moore, T. V., *Dynamic Psychology,* Part III. — Woodworth, R. S., *Experimental Psychology,* Ch. X, XI, XII. — James, William, *Principles of Psychology,* Vol. II, Ch. XXV. — Harmon, F. L., *Principles of Psychology,* Ch. 18.

Chapter XII

INTELLECTION

IN THE foregoing chapters we considered man on the sensory level of his being, treating those processes which he has in common with brute animals. These processes include sensory cognition, as acquired through the mediation of the various external and internal senses, and sensuous appetency. Though different types of function, they are interrelated and interdependent in many ways, so that they are activities of one and the same integral organism.

Intellectual and volitional activities were also mentioned now and then, but more or less incidentally. Due to the complexity of man's nature, intellection and volition frequently intermingle with sensory function, so that we do not find it easy to exclude them, even when endeavoring to give a description of sensory function as such. The reverse is also true; though we will now discuss the *rational processes* in man, it will not be possible to exclude the sensory processes completely, because the rational processes presuppose the sensory processes as an antecedent requisite condition.

The rational processes are characteristically human functions. These are *intellection,* or rational cognition, and *volition,* or rational appetition. Just as in the sensory field sensory cognition precedes sensuous appetition, so too in the rational field intellection precedes volition. We will, therefore, first discuss the function of intellection and then that of volition.

Intellection

Viewed from the standpoint of psychological experience, it is universally recognized that intellection comprises *three distinct processes:* the formation of ideas or concepts, the formation of judgments, and the formation of inferences.

The *concept* or *idea* is the intellectual representation of a thing. It is expressed in the definition of a thing. When we say that 'Man is a rational animal,' we give the definition of 'man,' and that is the concept or idea we have of 'man.' It is not the words of the definition that is of importance, but the *meaning* behind the words; it is what we 'have in mind' in the use of these words that expresses the concept or idea. The words will change from one language to another and even in the same language, but the meaning, and therefore also the concept or idea, is always the same. We could, for example, also define 'man' as 'a material, living, sentient, rational substance'; the words are different, but the idea is identical.

The *judgment* is the pronouncement of agreement or disagreement between two ideas. It is expressed in the declaratory sentence, as when we state that 'Oaks are trees' and 'Birds are not mammals.' We have the concepts 'oaks,' 'tree,' 'birds,' and 'mammals,' and then express their agreement or disagreement among themselves as they appear to our mind. Here also it is not so much a question of the words used in the sentence as of the knowledge present in our mind.

An *inference* is the reasoning process in which, from truths known, we conclude to a truth previously unknown. Somebody asks: 'Fred weighs more than Jack, and Al weighs less than Jack; does Fred weigh more or less than Al?' We conclude that 'Fred weighs more than Al' and 'Al weighs less than Fred.' From the data given we drew our conclusion; that is an inference.

Concepts, judgments, and inferences are grouped under the heading of 'intellection,' and psychology is interested in the process of their formation. If we have a clear knowledge of this process, we can venture a conclusion as to the nature of intellection.

Attention and *abstraction* play an all-important role in the formation of concepts. They throw considerable light on the inner working of the mind in this connection, and it is imperative to understand their operation.

Attention

By *attention* we understand the direction of the cognitive process toward an object, an activity, or a thought. Attention brings something within the focus of conscious activity, so that the mind becomes aware of its presence. The object upon which we concentrate our attention may be of the sensory order, as when we pay attention to the flight of a bird or the color of a flower, or it may be of the intellectual order, as when we pay attention to the products of our thinking processes.

Attention is analogous to vision. The objects which are focused upon the center of the retina are clear and distinct, while those whose image falls upon the peripheral portions of the retina are vague and diffused. At most, we are able to see only a few objects clearly at one time — about half a dozen beans among a scattered group or about half a dozen words on a printed page. Similarly, the range of attention is rather narrow. We are unable to concentrate our attention at one time upon more than a very few items; the others remain vaguely within the outer fringe of consciousness. In order to bring many items into the clear field of attention, we must shift our attention, just as we shift the focal point of the retina, from point to point in successive mental movements.

Attention may be *volitional,* as when we deliberately concentrate our attention away from the book we are reading to the street noises outside. Oftentimes, though, it is *involuntary,* as when a clap of thunder or the shrill wail of a fire engine's siren forces our attention momentarily away from reading. At times, too, attention may be more or less *habitual,* due to a mental set or attitude, as when we are confronted by a definite task which engrosses our attention to the exclusion of everything irrelevant.

Some psychologists claim that attention is based entirely on the *strength of the stimuli* demanding attention; the strongest stimulus, they say, receives attention. While true enough in very many instances, it is not universally true. It happens on some occasions that we deliberately turn our attention away from sights or sounds or thoughts which clamor insistently that we give heed to them; we may close our eyes or stop our ears to shut out an unwelcome sight or sound, or inflict discomfort upon ourselves to banish a certain train of thoughts.

There is more truth to the contention of some psychologists that attention is fundamentally a question of *interest.* That interest facilitates attention is natural. Interest, however, is only one factor which normally arouses attention; it is not the total explanation of attention. We may be intensely interested in a certain activity; if we realize, however, that our interest is misplaced or excessive, we can center our attention on something entirely different.

Some psychologists, especially those of a sensationalistic and associationistic trend of mind, advance the *drainage theory* of attention. According to this theory, only a limited amount of nerve energy can be utilized at any one time in perception. For example, when we listen attentively to the song of a robin, this limited amount of available energy in the brain is conducted into the auditory set of nerves and thereby drained away from the nerve paths of the other senses. This is an interesting theory, but it is highly speculative. Some such physiological arrangement may be present, but it would hardly account for those cases where we focus our attention on purely intellectual and voluntary operations or upon our own Ego. Just why the range of attention is so narrow in extent is very much of a mystery.

Behaviorists explain attention by *bodily attitudes.* Because the apparatus of a certain sense is definitely adjusted or 'attuned' to some stimuli, these stimuli produce sensations which force themselves into the focus of our attention. There is, of course, some truth to this claim, but it is only a part of the truth. It does happen at times that we hear certain faint sounds, because our hearing is 'keyed up' for some reason or other. But it is equally true that sometimes we deliberately induce bodily attitudes through antecedent attention, as when we purposely strain our ears to hear the faint ticking of the watch lying before us on the desk.

Whatever may be the ultimate explanation of the basic nature of attention, it is an obvious fact of experience that through attention we direct our cognitive processes, voluntarily or involuntarily, upon an object or set of objects and thereby become aware of their presence before the mind. *Without attention we cannot cognize an object.* To form an idea or concept of an object, therefore, we must focus our attention upon this object.

Abstraction

Attention is the first stage in the formation of an idea or concept. The next stage is that of *abstraction.*

Broadly speaking, abstraction is the *intellectual process in which,* through an act of selective attention, *we leave out of consideration one or more aspects of a complex total object so as to attend to some other aspect or aspects of this object.* An example will clarify the meaning of this definition. In looking at the leaves of a chestnut tree, I concentrate my attention, let us say, upon their characteristic 'shape,' leaving out of consideration their color, chemical composition, biologic function, relation to the branches, etc. In separating mentally the 'shape' of the leaves from these other aspects of the complex total object of the 'leaves,' I have performed the mental process of abstraction. By applying this selective attention upon the 'shape,' I draw this 'shape' away (Lat., *abstrahere, ab* and *trahere,* to draw away from or out of) from the other aspects or items present; I do not deny the presence of these other items in the leaves, but I ignore them in my consideration and put them mentally aside. Again, I may direct my attention upon the 'color' of the leaves, or their 'chemical composition,' omitting the other items from consideration; this, too, is abstraction in the meaning defined.

Every act of abstraction involves an act of attention, but every act of attention does not involve an act of abstraction. In abstraction we select one item in a *total object* for special consideration ignoring the rest but without denying their presence in the total object. Abstraction thus involves an act of attention focused on the one item to the exclusion of other items. Of all the items present in the total object 'chestnut leaf,' I focused my attention solely on the 'shape.' We may, on the other hand, have attention without abstraction. We may, for example, concentrate our attention on a chestnut tree, and then turn our attention to an oak or an elm standing nearby. Chestnut, oak, and elm trees are distinct entities and do not form a 'total object' among themselves; each has a separate existence of its own in nature, so that they are different 'total objects.' In abstraction, however, the various items exist together in the same 'total object' as a unit, and it is only *ideally* or *mentally* that the act of selective attention separates one item from the others and gives it special consideration. Attention and abstraction, therefore, are not identical processes in all respects. Abstraction is a species of attention, a particular type of attention.

Because of this mental separation of items through selective attention, we speak of *positive* and *negative* abstraction. The item selected for special consideration moves into the focus of attention, and we become aware of its presence in a clear and vivid manner. This act of attention is a positive act or process. The abstraction resulting from this act of selective attention is, therefore, a 'positive abstraction,' and the item thus mentally abstracted from the other items present in the total object is said to be 'positively abstracted.' The other items, not selected by the act of attention, thereby automatically move into the outer fringe of attention and are automatically separated or mentally dissociated from the selected item. By the very fact, for example, that we positively abstract the 'shape' of the chestnut leaf from the other items present, we also abstract these other items from the 'shape'; the separation of the one involves the separation of the others. Since the abstraction of the 'shape' is the result of a positive act of attention, the abstraction of the other items is a 'negative abstraction,' and they are said to be 'negatively abstracted.'

There are two forms of abstraction: *generalizing* and *isolating* abstraction. The formation of concepts cannot be understood without a thorough grasp of these two forms of abstraction.

Generalizing Abstraction

Generalizing abstraction is that form of abstraction in which we separate mentally, through an act of selective attention, *items which are common to a number of individual objects* from those items in which these objects differ and then *arrange the objects having the common items into a class as a unit.*

There are, for example, many kinds of trees — chestnut trees, oak trees, elm trees, apple trees, pear trees, maple trees, pine trees, etc. They differ in many items, but they also have certain items in common. If we concentrate our attention on the items they have in common, we find that all are 'woody perennial plants having a single main stem or trunk arising from the soil, their tops consisting of branches and foliage.' By leaving aside all the items in which they differ and considering only the items in which they are alike, we arrange them all into a single class and designate them as 'trees.' This is an instance of 'generalizing abstraction,' and by its means we have arrived at the *concept* or *idea* of 'trees.' The items contained in this concept of 'tree' are such that they can be applied to any single tree taken *individually,* such as the elm tree growing on the lawn in front of my house or the solitary apple tree growing in my back yard, and also to all trees taken *collectively* as a class, no matter what their kind or number. The content of the idea 'tree,' as expressed in the definition given above, is an *identical* and *permanent content,* applicable to the whole class and to every member of the class. The content of the idea is thus universal in application, and such an idea is therefore said to be a *universal idea,* i.e., an idea which represents some common nature or attribute which can be applied to a *class as a whole* and to *each individual* of that class. The product of generalizing abstraction, therefore, is the universal idea.

The fact, whether there exists in the intellect anything like the process of generalizing abstraction, has long been a matter of dispute among English-speaking philosophers. John Locke

(1690), in his *Essay Concerning Human Understanding*[1] claimed that he had a general (universal) idea of a 'triangle.' George Berkeley (1710) was convinced that he possessed no such wonderful faculty of abstracting ideas. "For myself," he says, "I find indeed I have a faculty of imagining or representing to myself the ideas of those particular things I have perceived and of variously compounding and dividing them. . . . The idea of man that I frame to myself must be either of a white, or a black, or a tawny, a straight, or a crooked, a tall, or a low, or a middle-sized man. I cannot by any effort of thought conceive the abstract idea above described."[2] He is convinced that there are no such things as abstract (general or universal) ideas.

Berkeley's contention is easily tested. Consider the idea of 'man' as advanced by Berkeley in the quotation just given. It is, of course, entirely concrete and particularized, not abstract and universal. And now consider the following analysis of the idea 'man' as subjected to a process of selective attention and abstraction.

Human beings are individuals, and no two are altogether alike. They possess differences in color, weight, size, bodily formation, mental and emotional peculiarities, etc., which distinguish one human being from another. Some are, as Berkeley points out, white, some black, some tawny; some are straight, some crooked; some tall, some short, some middle-sized. Some are male, others female; some are vicious, others virtuous; some are healthy, others diseased; in age they range from infants to centenarians. Individual men are perceived in this manner and imagined in sense-images; perceiving and imaging in this manner is an everyday occurrence. So far, our selective attention has been directed toward the features in which individual men *differ*. But the mind does not stop with contemplating these individual differences; it can, and does, also focus its attention on the features in which the individual men *agree* and which they have *in common*. Focusing our attention on

[1] Bk. IV, Ch. 7, § 9.
[2] *A Treatise Concerning the Principles of Human Knowledge,* Introd. 10, 14.

the features common to all men, we find that all men, no matter what their individual differences may be, possess a body which exists for itself, independent of all others; man is, therefore, a 'bodily substance.' Like the plants, men take in food, assimilate it, grow; man, therefore, lives and is a 'living bodily substance.' Like the brutes, man has external and internal senses which enable him to obtain sensory knowledge; man, therefore, is a 'sentient living bodily substance.' Unlike chemicals, plants, and brutes, men think, reason; *man,* therefore, *is a rational, sentient, living, bodily substance.* These features are not sensed or imagined, but they are true features of man, and they are the features which all men have *in common* and which are *essential* to man *as man,* irrespective of all individual differences. Now, a 'sentient, living, bodily substance' is termed an 'animal,' and man is thus defined as a *rational animal.* The individualizing features have been left aside, and the common, essential features have been grouped together. By means of this process of selective attention we have 'abstracted' the common, essential features, ignoring, though not denying, the differentiating qualities, such as 'white,' 'black,' 'tawny,' 'straight,' 'crooked,' etc. The result was obtained by a process of *abstraction.* This definition of 'man' as a 'rational animal' can now be applied in all truth to every single man, because this thought-content is present in each individual; we are thus able to say 'George Berkeley is a rational animal.' But it can also be extended in its application to all men taken collectively as a group, as when we state that 'Man is a rational animal.' Now we have *generalized* the features common to all men, applying the thought-content 'rational animal' to all men as a class and to each individual of that class. We have performed the mental operation of a *generalizing abstraction,* and through it we have arrived at an idea of 'man' quite different from that of Berkeley. Berkeley's so-called 'idea' of man is no idea of all, but a sense-image. Ours is a true *idea* or *concept,* namely, the *intellectual representation* of 'man.'

The Chinaman and the Zulu, the Mohawk and the Inca, the Egyptian and the Greek, the Roman and the Englishman, the

European and the American—all, individually and collectively, possess the same (not identical, but *like*) common human nature or essence. The idea (concept) of this common nature or essence then also applies to all, individually and collectively, and is therefore a truly *general* or *universal idea.*

There is really nothing mysterious or wonderful about this mental power of abstraction. It is a commonplace thing, used every day in the week. Even children use it constantly. They soon learn to 'abstract' the features common to dogs, cats, horses, men, dolls, dresses, houses, etc. If they did not possess the power of abstraction, it would be impossible for them to point to an object or picture and designate it as a 'dog,' a 'cat,' a 'doll,' a 'house,' and so on; they recognize the individual thing as belonging to a definite class because of some common feature or features present in all members of that class.

We thus see that the process of generalizing abstraction is nothing more than a particular form of selective attention, and the product of this abstraction is the universal idea.

After having described the process of generalizing abstraction which results in the formation of universal ideas or concepts, it is easy to find *evidence of its presence.*

We find this evidence in the *common vocables* or words existing in every language. Nouns and adjectives, in their usual forms, are all universal ideas. They represent items common to a class as a whole and to every member of that class. Among nouns we may mention at random ideas such as 'house,' 'watch,' 'pencil,' 'dog,' 'bird,' 'fly,' 'book,' 'orange,' 'cloud,' and so on. Among adjectives, 'red,' 'soft,' 'small,' 'metallic,' 'bright,' 'transparent,' 'fluid,' and so forth.

Every general *definition* represents a universal idea. The dictionary is a collection of universal ideas defined. Take the definition, for example, of a 'triangle' as 'a figure formed by three lines intersecting by twos in three points, and so forming three angles.' It makes no difference whether the individual triangles be equilateral, isosceles, right-angled, obtuse-angled, or scalene;

the definition or idea fits each one individually and all of them as a class.

Scientific *nomenclature* and *classification* consist of universal ideas obtained through generalizing abstraction. The only reason why scientists are able to group the objects of their science into varieties, species, genera, families, etc., is due to the fact that they recognize the features common to many, so that they can be arranged into definite classes and subclasses. Without generalizing abstraction they could describe nothing but individuals.

Generalizing abstraction, therefore, is an ordinary fact of mental experiences found in young and old, in the illiterate and in the educated.

Generalizing abstraction appears in three degrees or grades: *physical, mathematical,* and *metaphysical.*

Consider again the instance of the 'tree.' My sense image of a 'tree' places before me, either in perception or in imagination, a single object clothed with all the individualizing circumstances of color, shape, size, time, and place. It is either *this* chestnut tree, or *this* oak tree, or *this* apple tree, and so forth. By comparing the various kinds of tree, I abstract those items *common to all 'trees,'* omitting all the items peculiar to the single kinds of trees and to all individual trees. This degree of abstraction is *physical* abstraction.

It may be a question of leaving all sensible matter out of consideration and concentrating one's attention solely on the *magnitude, extension,* and *quantity* present in bodies. We then have abstract ideas of a 'point,' a 'line,' a 'plane,' a 'square,' a 'triangle,' a 'circle,' a 'square root,' etc. Our concept of a 'triangle,' for example, is not only divested of color, shape, size, and so on, but also of all materiality. This degree of abstraction is *mathematical* abstraction.

The highest degree of abstraction consists in this, that we divest things of all that distinguishes one kind of thing from another kind of thing (matter and spirit, sensible and suprasensible, creature and God) and select only those items in which *all things* agree and which they have in common. Such abstract ideas will then apply to all things. Among these ideas are, for example, 'being,' 'substance,' 'good,' 'true,' 'cause,' 'actuality,' and so forth. This degree of abstraction is *metaphysical* abstraction.

Scholastics group these three degrees of abstraction under the common term of *formal abstraction*. They also speak of *total abstraction*. By the latter they understand the abstraction of the universal whole in progressive stages. For example, we abstract or extract the concept of 'man' from Joe and Jane, then that of 'animal' or 'sentient being,' then that of 'living being,' then that of 'substance.'

Isolating Abstraction

The second form of abstraction is *isolating abstraction*. It is the mental process by which, through selective attention, we mentally separate a particular feature from the *subject* in which it exists. The separation is mental, not physical. We concentrate our attention upon this feature, to the exclusion of others, and consider it in our mind as if it existed independently of a subject. The product of the isolating abstraction is the *abstract* idea.

Language is replete with abstract ideas. Such are ideas like 'whiteness,' 'brightness,' 'softness,' 'transparency,' 'humanity,' 'triangularity,' 'animality,' 'rationality,' etc. The difference between a concrete and an abstract idea should be fairly obvious. 'White' is concrete; 'whiteness,' abstract. 'Transparent' is concrete; 'transparency,' abstract. 'Man' is concrete; 'humanity,' abstract. 'Triangle' is concrete; 'triangularity,' abstract. Concrete ideas always imply a *subject* with an attribute. 'White,' for example, always means 'something white.' Abstract ideas consider the item mentioned *as if* it had *no subject*. The use of concrete and abstract ideas as predicates in sentences reveals their difference. We say that 'The rose *is* (something) white,' but we say that 'The rose *has* whiteness.' Or, 'Peter *is* a man,' but 'Peter *possesses* humanity (meaning 'human nature').' Again, 'The sun *is* bright,' but 'The sun *has* brightness.'

When we turn our attention upon a *quality, attribute,* or

activity existing in some thing and make a noun or substantive of it, thereby lifting it mentally out of the subject in which it is found and exists, we use isolating abstraction. By isolating such a quality, attribute, or activity from its subject, we treat the quality, attribute, or activity as if it existed independently, as if it were a substance, and no longer a mere quality, attribute, or activity belonging to a subject; in other words, we *substantivize* or *personify* the quality, attribute, or activity.

This type of abstraction is very common in our mental operations. We perform the operation so frequently, that we even fail to notice the performance. Read the preceding and the present paragraphs carefully, and note the abstract ideas contained therein. Among them are 'attention,' 'quality,' 'attribute,' 'activity,' 'abstraction,' 'operation,' 'performance.' In nature, as actually existing, we have indeed an 'attending, active, abstracting mind or human being,' but there exists no such thing as 'attention,' 'activity,' or 'abstraction' by itself. We treat these realities as if they existed outside a subject, due to the substantivization of the process of isolating abstraction.

Scientific treatises swarm with abstract ideas of all kinds. Rather than mention the subject-plus-quality on all occasions, scientists simply substantivize the quality, when they desire to speak of the quality in which they are interested. Such a procedure is, of course, perfectly legitimate, so long as we remember that in actual existence the underlying subject is also present, even though not mentioned. Biologists thus speak of 'life,' 'growth,' 'nutrition.' Physicists speak of 'motion,' 'velocity,' 'vibration,' 'sound.' Mathematicians speak of 'magnitude,' 'extension,' 'triangularity,' 'number.' Psychologists speak of 'sensation,' 'appetency,' 'emotion,' 'thought,' 'perception,' 'abstraction,' 'intellection,' 'volition,' 'attention,' and so forth.

It is important to bear this fact about isolating abstraction in mind. Though the underlying subject of the isolated items is not mentioned, *the underlying subject is not denied but implied.*

We thus see that generalizing and isolating abstraction are two very important functions of the mind. They are the instruments which the mind uses to penetrate beneath the appearance of sense into the inner, hidden *nature* of things. They reveal, as Aristotle expressed it pithily, 'what a thing is.' The senses merely perceive 'how a thing appears,' but the intellect understands 'what a thing is.' A 'man,' viewed from the standpoint of the senses, is 'white or black or tawny, straight or crooked, tall or low or middle-sized'; viewed from the standpoint of the intellect, a 'man' is a 'rational animal.' The senses elaborate an image of 'man'; the intellect elaborates an idea of 'man.' Both the image and the idea are representations of one and the same object, 'man'; but the image is a sensory representation, while the idea or concept is an intellectual representation, and both representations are entirely different in character and content. The sensory image is the product of sensation and perception, the idea or concept is the product of abstraction and intellection.

The Idea or Concept

Intellection consists in the formation of ideas, judgments, and inferences. We must now turn our attention specifically to these mental items.

The *concept* or *idea,* as was stated before, is the intellectual representation of a thing; that is to say, it represents 'what a thing is.' How many *kinds* of things do concepts cover? How far do concepts extend in the range of objects?

For one thing, we have ideas of the objects of sense and of their attributes. I perceive, let us say, a 'white man,' a 'moving automobile,' a 'red flower,' a 'glowing sun.' Through the process of abstraction I evolve the ideas of 'whiteness,' 'man,' 'motion,' 'automobile,' 'redness,' 'flower,' 'glow,' 'sun.' Anything and everything, which affects the senses and is perceived can become the object of an idea or concept by means of generalizing and isolating abstraction. But we also have ideas of objects and attributes which are spiritual and immaterial and which are not perceived by the senses. Such are, for example, our ideas of 'soul,' 'God,' 'good,' 'evil,' 'truth,' 'error,' 'intellect,' 'thought,' 'infinite,' 'law,' and a host of others. It makes no difference in this connection whether such things actually exist or do not exist; the fact is simply that we have ideas of them. The sum of all the objects and attributes included within the range of our concepts is termed the *material object* of the intellect.

The common, *formal object* of the human intellect is that particular aspect of things in virtue of which they are the object just of the intellect, and not, for example, of the senses; it is that which is 'intelligible' in all things. There must be some intelligible content in all things, material and immaterial, finite and infinite, which represents a *common element* present in everything of which we can form ideas. The common, formal object of the intellect is *being*. The only intelligible element in which all things (God and creature, material and immaterial, object and attribute) agree is that they are 'things,' 'beings.' *Being, thingness, whatness,* therefore, is the common, formal object of the intellect.

Philosophers make a distinction between the *primary* and the *secondary* formal object of the intellect. The 'primary' formal object is the proper, proportionate, direct, natural, and immediate object to which the intellect turns its attention and of which it forms its ideas; it is, one might say, that particular type of object which the human intellect, by its very nature and constitution, is 'made to know.' Anything else would be a 'secondary' formal object. Now, what precisely is the primary and what is the secondary formal object of the human intellect?

The primary formal object is the 'sensible,' but as abstract and universal.

In saying that the primary formal object of the human intellect is the 'sensible,' we mean to state that the intellect is so constituted, that it derives its ideas directly and naturally from the *sense objects* presented in sensory experience. And now for the proofs.

First, normal and abnormal psychology reveal the fact that a very close connection exists between *nerve action* and intellectual activity. A normal functioning of the nervous system facilitates rational knowledge, while pathological disturbances interfere with the orderly processes of thinking. One need but remind one's self of the influence of drugs and of cerebral injuries upon thinking, in order to realize the close connection between nerve action and intellectual activity. Persons blind or deaf from birth can form no adequate idea of color or sound; this fact is definite indication that the human intellect obtains its ideas by turning to the data presented by the external and internal senses.

Second, *consciousness* is witness to the same general fact. It is a common practice in the elucidation of difficult and abstruse problems to have recourse to images and analogies taken from sensible objects. Images and analogies can make abstract ideas clear only on the supposition that the intellect derives its concepts first and primarily from sensible objects. The primitive words of every language are concrete and sensible in character. Anglo-Saxon words, for example, are seldom abstract, but rather concrete, in form. Highly abstract technical terminology, such as is used in scientific and philosophical discussions, is the product of advanced culture and mental development extending over a period of centuries. Even technical terms show their sensible origin in their etymology. Mainly, however, our concept of immaterial and spiritual realities shows that our intellect derives its ideas naturally and originally from material and sensible objects since the terms are negative or analogical in their ultimate meaning. 'Immaterial,' for example, means 'not-material' and 'spiritual' means 'breath-like' (*spiritus,* breath). The only way in which we can express supra-sensible things is to use a sensible term and deny the limitations inherent therein, as when we say that 'the soul is immortal (not mortal)' and 'God is infinite (not-finite).' This method of using images and analogies makes it plain that the primary formal object of the human intellect is the *sensible,* not the spiritual.

Third, our thinking has the tendency to be accompanied by *images* of some sort. Whether there is such a thing as 'imageless thought,' will be taken up later. The fact remains that images seem to run along with our concepts. If we think of a 'triangle,' we will probably find a faint image of a triangle present at the same time. If we think of a 'tree,' a 'fish,' a 'house,' a 'street,' a 'man,' etc., some sort of image of these things will in all probability accompany their ideas. It would take a distinct effort on our part to exclude these images, which would hardly be the case if they were foreign elements intruding themselves upon our consciousness. We must, then, conclude that the materials for the formation of ideas are presented to the intellect by the senses. The sensible, therefore, is the primary formal object of the intellect.

The primary formal object of the human intellect is the sensible, but the sensible as *abstract and universal.*

That we conceive the sensible as abstract and universal, should be clear from what has been said above concerning generalizing and isolating *abstraction.* Sensible objects are individual objects, no two of which are perfectly alike in all respects. If our ideas of sensible objects were concrete and individualized like these objects themselves, they would fit a single object only and could not be applied to a class as a whole and to each individual of that class. What I perceive in nature is 'this elm,' 'this oak,' 'this birch,' 'this pine,' etc. They are single things perceived singly. There is no such thing in nature like a 'universal elm' or a 'universal tree.' By abstracting the features common to all elms and to all trees and expressing them in a single concept, I obtain the abstract idea of 'elm' and 'tree,' which designates 'what an elm is' and 'what a tree is.' I then extend the idea 'elm' to all elms and the idea 'tree' to all trees, so that these ideas have a universal application. Ideas thus express the *class-nature,* applicable to each and all; they are abstract and universal.

It is because of this character of abstractness and universality, that *words* and *language* are an *intelligible vehicle of ideas.* Words stand for ideas, and ideas stand for the class-nature of things. Because ideas are abstract and universal, the words symbolizing them convey knowledge from one intellect to another which is permanent, unchangeable, and essential, independent of the changing individual things from which these ideas were originally derived. Scientific works would have no lasting value, if the scientists had not abstracted the common and essential features of objects and activities, universalized the information contained in their ideas, and then expressed them in words which are also abstract and universal. Words partake of the nature of the ideas which they represent.

We thus see the truth of the statement that the primary formal object of the human intellect is the sensible, but abstract and universal.

It follows as a necessary consequence that whatever is *suprasensible,* spiritual, and extra-mundane is not the primary but the *secondary formal object* of the human intellect. Among such objects must be included 'soul,' 'spirit,' 'God,' and all that pertains to them.

Consider our thinking *experience.* We experience far greater difficulties in forming concepts of these types of being than we do of sensible objects. It is, for example, more difficult to arrive at a comprehensive and clear idea of the 'soul' than of a 'tree' or a 'triangle.' Ideas of spiritual realities never enter the mind spontaneously, but by indirection and inference; we draw conclusions concerning them from the objects and facts of sense presented in sensory experience. Again, our ideas of spiritual realities reveal their ultimate *sensory origin* by the fact that their basic meaning is derived from concepts having sensible significance. We have an example, mentioned before, in the word 'spirit' which originally meant 'breath.' In thinking of God and His attributes we start with the perfections of creatures (material, finite, powerful, knowing, etc.), deny the imperfections (im-material, in-finite), and then ascribe to Him these creatural perfections in a boundless manner (all-powerful, all-knowing). Our ideas of purely spiritual beings and realities thus being acquired by a direction of the mind to the ideas abstracted from sensible objects and realities, it is evident that the supra-sensible is not the proper, direct, immediate, and natural object of the intellect of man, but its secondary object.

The present discussion proves the truth of Aristotle's famous pronouncement: *There is nothing in the intellect which was not first in the senses.* Our knowledge begins with sensory experience and ends up in intellectual ideas.

Idea and Image

Berkeley, it will be remembered, confused his 'image' of man with the abstract and universal 'idea' of man. The same confusion occurs frequently among modern psychologists. It is advisable, therefore, to point out the *main difference between ideas (concepts) and images (phantasms).*

In speaking of 'image' and 'phantasm,' we include both the 'percept' of the central sense, as synthesized from the sensations aroused by stimuli in the presence of a sense object, and the 'image' of an object which is revived in the imagination in the absence of the original sense object. For the sake of convenience, the terms 'idea' and 'image' will be used.

For one thing, the image is always *concrete* and *individualized,* fitting at the most only a few objects at one and the same time; and if the image is very clear and detailed, it can fit but a single object. The reason is obvious. An image is taken from a sensible object and represents this object; an object, however, is always concrete and individual. We indeed have what are called 'general images,' such as the general image of a cat, a fish, a house, a boat, and so forth; we retain in such a general image only the most striking features of a particular set of objects, so that our image is more or less schematic. It is impossible, however, to form an image which would resemble all the members of even a single class. We cannot, for example, form the image of a 'man' which would adequately fit at the same time a baby, a girl of eighteen, Napoleon, George Washington, a negro woman, and an Indian. Much less would the single image of an 'animal' fit such heterogeneous types of animals as a spider, a snake, an ostrich, a shark, an elephant, and an amoeba.

We experience no such difficulty in applying an idea to the

different kinds of individuals and classes, because the idea is *universal*. Our idea of 'man' as a 'rational animal' fits all individual human beings without exception, no matter what their age, sex, race, color, or personal characteristics. Similarly, our idea of 'animal' as a 'sentient living bodily substance' fits all the heterogeneous types of animals mentioned above.

Another difference is this, that an image becomes very *vague and indistinct with complexity and minuteness of detail,* while the idea remains clear and distinct. It is not difficult to form an image of 5 trees in a row; but it is utterly impossible for me to form an image of 50 (not 49 or 51) trees in a row. Yet my idea of 50 or of 5,000,000 trees is just as clear to me as my idea of 5 trees. Again, I cannot form an image of a geometrical 'line' which has only length and no depth or width; but my idea of such a 'line' contains no depth or width, as my definition of a line shows.

Finally, in many instances we have very clear *ideas* of things, but we are incapable of forming any *reasonable image* of them. Since we speak of such things as 'economics,' 'law,' 'virtue,' 'soul,' 'life,' 'God,' 'will,' 'knowledge,' 'ignorance,' 'death,' 'inference,' 'abstraction,' 'psychology,' etc., and even define them, we certainly have ideas of them. If we search our mind, however, we find no proper image of such ideas. Or, can we invest 'abstraction' with anything like shape, weight, size, color, sound, and similar qualities, so prominently present in our images? To put this question is to answer it.

Experimental psychology also has supplied evidence which shows that ideas are different from images. If ideas are images, then it must be impossible for ideas and images to become *separated in experience*. But they do occur separately in temporal sequence. Laboratory experiments, made to determine the time required for a meaning (idea) and for visual or kinesthetic images to appear relative to the same object, definitely show that ideas and images do not appear simultaneously. The images appear later than the meanings or ideas.[3] This time difference proves that ideas and images are different as entities.

[3] See T. V. Moore, *Cognitive Psychology* (Lippincott, 1939), pp. 334 ff.

Pathology also furnishes evidence along these lines. In the chapter on the central of synthetic sense, instances were cited where damage to the cerebrum caused serious interference with the operations of this sense. Persons so afflicted did not recognize an object or a picture or a drawing placed before them; the image was present, but it had no meaning for them, so that they could not state what the image represented. They had, however, clear ideas of these things; because, when asked about them, they talked intelligently and understandingly concerning these things, thereby showing that they knew 'what the thing is,' even though the image itself conveyed no meaning to their mind. Ideas, therefore, must be distinct from images.

From the evidence adduced it should be apparent how utterly erroneous is the view of James Mill, as expressed in the following passage: "If I say I have the idea of a horse, I can explain distinctly what I mean. I have the ideas of the sensation of sight, of touch, of hearing, of something with which the body and actions of a horse have impressed me. These ideas combined, and so closely, that their existence appears simultaneous and one. This is my idea of a horse."[4] On the contrary, this is not an idea, but an image.

The Judgment

Ideas lead to judgments. A *judgment* is *an act of the mind pronouncing the agreement or disagreement of ideas among themselves;* or, to express the same meaning in different words, it is *an act of the intellect affirming or denying one idea of another.*

The judgment always appears in one of two ways: it will either *affirm* or *deny*. In stating that 'The rose is a flower,' I affirm the agreement between the two ideas 'rose 'and 'flower.' And in stating that 'The whale is not a fish,' I deny the agreement (or, affirm the disagreement) between the two ideas 'whale' and 'fish.'

[4] *Analysis of the Phenomena of the Human Mind* (London, 1869), Vol. I, Ch. 6.

Psychologically, the following stages occur in the intellect in the formation of a judgment: two ideas are presented by the intellect to itself for consideration; the meanings of the two ideas are grasped and understood separately; these meanings are compared with each other; the intellect perceives their mutual agreement or disagreement; then follows the mental expression or pronouncement of their mutual agreement or disagreement, and this pronouncement is the judgment proper. Here is an example. The two ideas 'man' and 'animal' are presented to my intellect. A 'man,' I understand, is a 'rational, sentient, living, bodily substance,' and an 'animal' is a 'sentient, living, bodily substance.' I now compare these two meanings with each other. I perceive that the thought-content of 'animal' as a 'sentient, living, bodily substance' is included in the thought-content of 'man' as a 'rational, sentient, living, bodily substance,' and in so far both thought-contents are in agreement with each other. I now express or pronounce this agreement in the mental judgment that 'Man is an animal.' If I were to compare the two ideas 'whale' and 'fish,' I would go through the same procedure, but I would perceive that the thought-contents of 'fish' does not agree with that of 'whale' (for the whale is a mammal, not a fish), and I would pronounce their disagreement by the judgment that 'The whale is not a fish.' Depending upon the ideas compared, my judgment will contain an affirmation or a denial.

Three elements, then, enter into the *composition* of a judgment: two ideas, and the mental act pronouncing their agreement or disagreement. One idea, the subject-idea, is the one 'about which' something is said; and the other idea, the predicate idea, is the one 'which is said about' the other. The two compared ideas are the *matter* of the judgment, because they are the materials which enter into composition in the judgment. The act pronouncing their agreement or disagreement is the *form* of the judgment, because this pronouncement constitutes the very essence of the judgment as a judgment, distinguishing it from the concept and the inference. From the standpoint of its 'matter,' the judgment is a composition of two distinct elements, the ideas; from the standpoint of its 'form,' the pronouncement, it is a single intellectual act fusing the two ideas into one or separating them from each other. Such is the nature of the judgment.

The *foundation* of the judgment consists in the *intellectual insight into the logical relations* which exist between the subject-idea and the predicate-idea. The mind perceives that the subject-idea is contained (or not contained) within the class-extension of the predicate-idea, and that the thought-content or comprehension of the predicate-idea is contained (or not contained) within the thought-content or comprehension of the subject-idea. Correspondingly, the intellect pronounces its judgment of agreement or disagreement.[5] These relations, it will be observed, are of a *logical* nature and entirely different from the sensible relations which exist in the associative bonds present between images, due to contiguity in space or time, similarity, or contrast. The judgment is not a connection between images, but a composition of ideas.

Judgments are not just private exercises of the intellect combining and separating ideas. Ideas being representations of things, they convey to us the meaning of the things for which they stand, and in so far the judgment is a *representation of reality*. Every judgment presupposes and implies the existence of reality, and this is known as the 'existential import' of the judgment.

Judgments thus contain within themselves the *claim of truth,* although the fact is also acknowledged that at times they may be false. *Truth* and *error* lie in the judgment. When the intellect compares two ideas with each other and pronounces an agreement or disagreement between them, it actually compares two things with each other and judges about their agreement or disagreement among themselves as they are in reality. Hence, if a judgment coincides with reality, it is true; if not, it is false. In consequence of this relation between ideas and things, we are not at liberty to judge as we please. Because in

[5] For an elucidation of the 'extension' and 'comprehension' of ideas, see the author's *The Science of Correct Thinking* (Bruce, 1935), pp. 28 ff.

reality things are (or are not) so and so, the mind has no choice but to represent reality as it actually is or, at least, as it judges it (perhaps erroneously) to be. The mind *accepts* the truth, it does not make it; and it accepts the truth, because it is determined by the objective evidence furnished by reality itself.

The judgment, therefore, is the product of an intellectual insight, and *not of the will* and its deliberate choice, as Descartes and Malebranche claimed. Nor are some fundamental judgments dictated by blind *instinct,* as Thomas Reid maintained. Emmanuel Kant also is wrong, when he asserted that we judge as we do because of *innate mental categories* which have no bearing on reality as it actually exists. These theories are contrary to all the evidence of experience. It is only in the case of *doubt* that the will, for practical reasons, may demand the assent of the intellect to a judgment.

The Inference

The intellect forms concepts; it forms judgments. It has also a third type of operation: it forms *inferences* or *ratiocinations.* Inferences are the products of the reasoning power of the intellect. Inference, in general, is defined as the *process by which, from certain truths already known, the mind passes to another truth distinct from these but necessarily following from them.*[6]

We find that the basic *construction* of an inference contains the premises, the truth of which is already known, and the conclusion which follows from the premises with necessary consequence. Because the premises are true, the conclusion must also be true. The conclusion is contained implicitly in the premises; in drawing the conclusion, we merely state explicitly what the premises stated implicitly. The intellectual *insight* into the logical *relations* existing between the premises on the

---

[6] The various types of inferences are treated extensively in Logic. In psychology we presuppose that the student is familiar with these types. See the author's *The Science of Correct Thinking,* Parts 3 and 4.

one hand and between the conclusion and the premises on the other constitutes the psychological factor which compels the intellect to draw the conclusion and to acknowledge its truth and validity.

As a typical illustration of an inference, we give the following example of a categorical syllogism:

All residents of the sixth ward vote in the sixth-ward school;
John S. Jones is a resident of the sixth ward;
Hence, John S. Jones votes in the sixth-ward schoolhouse.

The logical relations between the premises and between the conclusion and the premises are clear. *If* (or, *since*) all residents of the sixth ward vote as directed; and *if* (or, *since*) John S. Jones, upon inquiry, is found to be a resident of the sixth ward; *therefore* it follows with logical necessity that he must vote in the sixth-ward schoolhouse. No other conclusion can be drawn from these premises, because this conclusion is implicitly contained in the premises.

Psychologically, the knowledge of the premises must *precede* the knowledge of the conclusion, with a priority in the order of *nature* and in the order of *time*. The conclusion depends for its truth and validity on the truth and validity of the premises; without the premises the conclusion cannot be drawn. That, however, which depends on another for its existence must, in its very nature, succeed and not precede this other upon which it depends. Hence, since an inference is a question of knowing, the knowledge of the premises must precede the knowledge of the conclusion, so far as the elements of the inference are concerned. And since it takes a certain amount of time to cognize each premise and the conclusion individually and the logical relations existing between them, the knowledge of the conclusion must be temporally later than the knowledge of the premises, even though the final insight into their mutual relationship is an instantaneous act of the intellect.

The premises are the foundation of the conclusion; they contain the conclusion implicitly. It is only because this necessary relationship between the premises and the conclusion is understood by the intellect, that we are entitled and compelled to draw the conclusion. Premises and conclusion form a *constructional* and *logical unit*. In order, then, that the intellect be able to make the inference, the intellect must embrace in a *single psychological act* the premises and their mutual relationship; otherwise the intellect would not have the insight that the conclusion follows with necessary force from the logical relation of the combined premises.

Some modern psychologists have attempted to explain the reasoning process as a *fusion of images*. Applied to the example of the categorical syllogism given above, the process might be conceived to go along the following lines: an image of a section of the city, containing a school building; the image of a man (John S. Jones), included in the general image of the first image; the image of the man fusing with the image of the schoolhouse, as the man enters the building. It takes but a moment's reflection to see how utterly inadequate such an explanation really is when compared with the actual process of an inference. The intellectual *insight* into the *logical relations* between the judgments is the basis of the inference, not the mere juxtaposition and fusion of images. It is on the basis of the *abstract principle* that 'What is true of the logical whole must also be true of every part of that logical whole,' that I draw the conclusion that John S. Jones must cast his vote at the designated place. All residents of the sixth ward form a class, a logical unit or whole, and what is true of this whole class must be true of every one belonging to this class; John S. Jones belongs to this class, is a member of this class as a logical unit or whole; and so he must vote in the place assigned to the class. We have here a general principle applied to an individual instance, not a mere fusion of imaginal elements.

Intellectual activity, or intellection, is of a *totally different order* than sensory activity, because sensations and images alone cannot account for the formation of ideas, judgments, and inferences. Nevertheless, intellection would be impossible without antecedent sensory knowledge, because the senses furnish the raw materials from which the intellect abstracts ideas and then proceeds to utilize ideas in the formation of judgments and inferences. Sense and intellect are not foreign to each other. Man is a sensory-intellectual being, a rational animal, an *integral organism.*

Summary of Chapter XII

The rational processes of man's mental life consist of *intellection* and volition.

1. *Intellection.* It comprises three distinct processes: the formation of ideas or concepts, the formation of judgments, and the formation of inferences.

2. *Attention.* It is the direction of the cognitive process toward an object, activity, or thought. Some psychologists base attention on the 'strength of the stimuli'; others, on 'interest.' Some favor the 'drainage theory' as an explanation of attention. Behaviorists attempt to explain attention by 'bodily attitudes.' Without attention we cannot cognize an object.

3. *Abstraction.* It is the mental process in which, through an act of selective attention, we leave out of consideration one or more aspects of a complex total object so as to attend to some other aspect or aspects of this object. Abstraction is either *positive or negative.*

4. *Generalizing Abstraction.* It is that form of abstraction in which we separate mentally, through an act of selective attention, items which are common to a number of individual objects from those items in which these objects differ, and then arrange the objects having the common items into a class as a unit. The product is a *universal idea,* applicable to the class as a whole and to each individual member of that class. Evidence for the existence of universal ideas is found in the common vocables of language, in definitions, and in scientific nomenclature and classifications. There are three degrees or grades of abstraction: physical, mathematical, and metaphysical. Abstraction may be either *formal* or *total.*

5. *Isolating Abstraction.* It is that form of abstraction in which, through an act of selective attention, we mentally

separate a particular feature from the subject in which it exists and consider it as if it existed independently of a subject. The product of this abstraction is the *abstract idea.*

6. *The Idea or Concept.* An idea is the intellectual representation of a thing. The *material* object of the human intellect is the sum of all the objects and attributes included within the range of our concepts. The common, *formal* object is that particular aspect of things in virtue of which they are the object just of the intellect, and not, for example, of the senses. The formal object of the intellect is 'being' in general. The *primary* formal object of the intellect is the proper, proportionate, direct, natural, immediate object to which the intellect turns its attention and of which it forms its ideas; anything else would be a *secondary* object.

The primary formal object is the *sensible,* but *abstract* and *universal.* The secondary formal object of the intellect is the *supra-sensible,* spiritual.

7. *Idea and Image.* Images are concrete and individualized; ideas are universal. Images become vague and indistinct with complexity and minuteness of detail, while ideas remain clear and distinct. We have clear ideas of many things of which we are incapable of forming any reasonable image.

8. *The Judgment.* It is an act of the mind pronouncing the agreement or disagreement of ideas among themselves. It appears as an affirmation or denial. It contains three elements: two ideas, and the mental pronouncement of their agreement or disagreement; the ideas are the 'matter,' and the act of pronouncement is the 'form,' of the judgment. The foundation of the judgment consists in the *intellectual insight into the logical relations* of the *subject* and *predicate.*

9. *The Inference.* Inference is the process by which, from certain truths already known, the mind passes to another truth distinct from these but necessarily following from them. Inference is based on the *intellectual insight* into the *logical relations* existing between the premises and conclusion. Psychologically, the knowledge of the premises must precede the knowledge of the conclusion, with a priority in the order of nature and in the

order of time. The intellect must embrace in a single psychological act the premises and their mutual relationship.

Readings

Moore, T. V., *Cognitive Psychology,* Part V. — Maher, M., *Psychology,* Ch. XII, XIV, XV. — Harmon, F. L., *Principles of Psychology,* Ch. 11, 15. — Brennan, R. E., *General Psychology,* pp. 321–352. — Woodworth, R. S., *Experimental Psychology,* Ch. XXVII, XXIX, XXX. — Gruender, H., *Experimental Psychology,* Ch. XIV, XV, XVI.

Chapter XIII

THE ORIGIN OF IDEAS

MAN has always considered himself superior to the brute. Evidence for this superiority was found in man's power to think. When philosophy came into existence in ancient Greece, the problem of the nature and origin of ideas in the human mind was bound to arise sooner or later. The problem received a sharp impetus under Socrates. Plato, Socrates' disciple, made it the very heart of his philosophic system. And from that time on up to the present day, the problem has engrossed the attention of the greatest thinkers. The problem can be formulated briefly as follows: If ideas are essentially different from sensations and images, *how do ideas originate?*

In the preceding chapter it was shown that ideas are fundamentally distinct from sensations and images because of the *abstract, universal* character of ideas. Nevertheless, ideas are derived somehow from the sensible and are rooted in the sensible. This truth will receive confirmation from a study of the various systems of philosophic thought which have been advanced in the course of the centuries as an explanation of the origin of ideas.

Roughly, all theories on the subject can be grouped into three main classes: the theory of *innate ideas;* the *empiricist* or *sensationalist* theory; and the *peripatetic* or *aristotelian-scholastic* theory. The first group overemphasizes the function of the rational mind in the formation of ideas; the second overemphasizes the function of the senses; the third seeks to emphasize the function of both the rational mind and the senses in proper proportion. The problem will be treated along the lines indicated by these groups of theories.

Plato's Ultra-Realism

Plato (427–347 B.C.) was aware that the world of sense and sense objects is in a state of continuous change. From the fact of continuous change he concluded that there is nothing real and stable in the sense world. The universal ideas, however, have a content which is stable, real, unchangeable, eternal; the knowledge acquired through universal ideas is truly 'science.' Unless we are willing to admit that the scientific knowledge acquired through universal ideas is an illusion and a fiction, these ideas must be the representation of objective reality; and since the reality of the sense world is always changing and not eternal, it cannot be the reality of the sense world which is represented in the universal ideas. Hence, the existence of universal ideas in the human minds demands the existence of a supra-mundane world of *pure essences,* which are stable, real, unchangeable, and eternal and of which the universal ideas of man are a true representation. These pure essences Plato called *Ideas.*

The Ideas alone have reality in the strict sense; they exist as real entities (noumena) apart from the world of sense (phenomena). The objects of the sense world are but faint, changing replicas or imitations of the eternal, unchanging Ideas; the Ideas are the eternal prototypes or exemplars of the objects of the sense world. The universal ideas of the human mind are true representations of these noumenal Ideas and cannot have their origin in the changeable and changing objects of this visible universe. It follows, according to Plato, that men's souls must have had a *pre-existence* in a former life in the noumenal world, where they contemplated the Ideas as these Ideas existed in themselves. On being united to the body in its present earthly existence, the soul forgot the knowledge of the Ideas, but the universal ideas thus acquired slumber in the soul until awakened; they lie *innate* in the recesses of the mind. For every object existing in the universe (tree, dog, sky, house, rose, etc.) there exists a corresponding Idea in the noumenal world. On seeing such an object in the present life (some individual tree, dog, etc.), we *remember* what we have known before and have forgotten: the innate slumbering universal idea is awakened and brought to consciousness. Hence, Plato's theory of innate ideas is also called the *theory of reminiscence.*

Criticism. For one thing, Plato supposes that the connection between body and soul in man's earthly life is *forced* and *unnatural;* the relationship between the two is *extrinsic,* similar to the relationship between a horse (body) and its rider (soul). In this view, death should be a welcome event, a release for the soul from the imprisonment in the body. We know, however, that man dreads death. Man is by nature, as all evidence proves, a *psycho-physiological integral organism.* The dread of death shows clearly that the union of body and soul is natural. If their union were merely extrinsic, it is inexplicable how the union of the body with the soul could blot out the knowledge of the Ideas formerly contemplated, because the body could not possibly influence the *inner* activities of the soul.

Aristotle opposed Plato's theory on the grounds that it is poetic and fantastic and contrary to the *testimony of consciousness.* If we actually had a former existence, the awakening of the innate universal ideas should also revive the memory of this previous existence itself. But we have no such memory. The theory is pure assumption on the part of Plato.

Finally, in the foregoing chapter it was pointed out how we acquire our universal ideas from sensible objects through a process of *abstraction.* There is no need to have recourse to a noumenal world of Ideas and a previous existence in order to explain a process of knowledge which is as natural to man as sensation and perception.

Descartes' Ultra-Spiritualism

R. Descartes (1596–1650) taught that man's body and soul, though united, are two intrinsically independent substances. The essence of the soul is *thought* or 'thinking,' and the essence of the body is *extension,* and the two have nothing in common. There can be no cognitional communication between body and mind, because the disparity between them is too great. The body is merely a machine (Chap. X, p. 225). 'Corporeal movements' reach the brain, and at the *occasion* of their presence the mind produces the ideas or representations of external and extended objects entirely in itself and by itself. Descartes denied the necessity of innate ideas which would be something distinct from the intellect itself. Because the intellect is innate to man, the ideas of the intellect are also innate, in the sense that a disease is innate to the man who is born with the disposition for this disease. The intellect, according to Descartes' theory, is the exclusive *cause* of all knowledge. Descartes thus considered ideas to be present in the mind from the beginning as 'dispositions,' and these dispositions are not derived from sense objects; ideas are *potentially* existing and subsequently become actual. His theory amounts to innatism.

Most of Descartes' followers assert that at least some fundamental ideas are innate, such as the ideas of 'God,' our own 'existence,' 'good,' 'evil,' 'free will,' and others. We have a 'habitual' knowledge of these, and this knowledge becomes 'actual' when the intellect turns its attention to these innate 'forms' of knowledge.

Criticism. Descartes placed an *ultra-spiritualistic* interpretation on the mind and an *ultra-mechanistic* interpretation on the body; the result was an ultra-dualism in the concept of 'man' which made it impossible to explain human intellectual knowledge in a natural manner. Descartes had no right to restrict the essence of the mind to 'thought.' If the activities of man are such that the triple functions of *vegetancy, sentiency,* and *'thinking'* are integrated operations of one and the same psycho-physiological *organism,* then Descartes committed an unpardonable error in limiting the essence of mind to 'thought' alone. That man is an integral organism is amply proved in the preceding chapters. Descartes' ultra-dualism is thereby disproved and with it the necessity of trying to explain the origin of our ideas through innatism.

All bodily and sensory functions are accompanied by *coenesthetic* (common general organic) sensations of some sort, making us aware of the body and bodily conditions as our own. Such sensations always involve an obscure feeling of the existence of the 'Ego'; the origin of the idea of the 'Ego' is thus explained, so that there is no need to consider it as innate. As for the ideas of 'God' and other supra-sensible objects, we have already seen that they are analogous ideas developed from ideas derived from sensible objects by heightening their perfections and denying their imperfections.

From all that has gone before, it should be clear that the *sense organs* are not mere mechanical structures and contrivances. They are *vital instruments* of knowledge which contribute actively their own part to the production of knowledge. Since they are extended organs, sensible objects can affect them through stimuli; since they are vital organs, they can respond vitally to the stimuli and furnish a cognitional representation of the objects in perception. Through abstraction from these sense representations the intellect, organically united to the body and its senses, can *form ideas*. Nothing more is needed.

The Monadism of Leibnitz

G. Leibnitz (1646–1716) tried to overcome the ultra-dualism of Descartes in a unique way. All beings consist ultimately of *monads*. A monad is an elementary individual being, psychical or spiritual in nature. God is a monad; spirits are monads; the human soul is a monad. Even physical being consists ultimately of monads; thus, the body of man is a system of monads. There is *no interaction* between the single monads. All possess the 'power of representation,' and each monad in its representation mirrors within itself whatever takes place in all other monads throughout the universe; some do it consciously, like the mind-monads, others unconsciously, like the body-monads. Monads are 'windowless,' so that no knowledge is acquired from without but is developed from within. All ideas, therefore, are *innate,* present from the beginning as dispositions or 'natural virtualities' (*virtualités naturelles*) until evoked into actuality in the consciousness.

Criticism. Monadism is a *gratuitous* theory, artificial in the extreme, without any foundation in fact. The existence of such a universe of monads is a pure assumption. It disrupts the human organism into an aggregate of independent individual monads. It is disproved by the existence of the *nervous system* in man, which centers in the cerebral cortex as the evident center of sensory knowledge in response to stimuli reaching it from the peripheral *organs.* Monadism leads to *solipsism,* that extreme form of subjective idealism which maintains that man can know nothing but his own subjective internal mental states, without the possibility of ever knowing whether anything objective corresponds to his ideas.

Ontologism

Ontologists, chief among whom are Malebranche (1638–1715), Rosmini (1797–1855), and Gioberti (1801–1852), assert that *God* and the *divine Ideas* are the primary objects of the intellect, and the *first act* of the intellect is the *intuition of God.* They base their view on the grounds that material objects can make no impression on an unextended intellect; the intellect, therefore, can derive no ideas from them. The intellect is also too imperfect to derive ideas out of its own nature as such. It beholds them in another spirit, the Infinite Being, whose Ideas are the types and exemplars of all created things. The intellect intuits the Ideas of God and in them acquires a knowledge of creatures. This intuition is possible because God is united to the souls of men in such a manner that one can say that He is in truth 'the place of spirits.'

Criticism. If God and the divine Ideas were really the primary object of our intellect and the object first known by it, so that we behold the objects of the sense world in Him and in His Ideas, we should be *conscious* of this tremendous fact of experience. Needless to say, we are not. Again, if this supposition of the ontologists were true, the existence of God would be indubitably *certain* to man; doubt would be as impossible in this respect as the doubt about our own existence. Experience, however, shows that we must prove God's existence to our own satisfaction from the facts discovered through a study of the universe. Finally, while ontologists assert that we do not intuit the substance of God, but God and His Ideas only in so far as they are in relation to creatures, this distinction is invalid. In God everything is one and the same infinite reality. To behold the Ideas of God means to behold God's *infinite essence* and substance. In that case, however, our ideas of God should be direct and positive, not indirect, analogous, and by negation.

Kant's Transcendental Criticism

Immanuel Kant (1724–1804), alarmed at the trend of thought manifested by the sensationalism of English philosophy, attempted to revindicate the validity of human knowledge and free it from the bane of skepticism prevalent since David Hume. He accepted without question the ultra-realism of Descartes and took as his starting point the principle that the mind of man can know only its own internal states and cannot go outside and beyond the limits of consciousness. He considered it to be the essential error of all previous philosophic systems that they endeavored to make the mind conform to the objects; he would reverse the principle and make the objects conform to the mind. His critique or criticism, therefore, intended to find out whether there existed *a knowledge independent of experience. Empirical* knowledge has its sources in experience (*a posteriori*), while knowledge independent of experience has its sources in the mind (*a priori*). Correspondingly, our ideas will originate either in the mind and be innate or will originate in experience and not be innate. Have we an *a priori knowledge?* Kant is convinced we have.

According to Kant, experience can reveal nothing to us except what is *individual* and *contingent;* it never reveals anything that is strictly universal and necessary. If, then, our judgment at any time is thought with *strict necessity* and *universality,* such knowledge cannot have been acquired through experience but must be *a priori* and must proceed directly *from the mind itself.*

Kant admits the existence of *noumena* or things-in-themselves in the external world, and they affect the senses. The sense faculty responds with an 'intuition' or perception. These impressions are unarranged, chaotic. The chaotic 'manifold' of sense impressions must be arranged in a certain order by means of *two innate sense-forms,* namely, *space* and *time.* These forms are present in the mind antecedent to all experience. 'Space' and 'time' are in no way attributes of the things-in-themselves, but are *mental forms* which condition the perception of the things-in-themselves, so that they *appear* as arranged in the order of 'space' or in the order of 'time.' Since all things appear in this double order, 'space' and 'time' are universal and necessary conditions of sense-perception and as such must exist *a priori* (innately) in the mind. The physical objects themselves, the noumena or things-in-themselves, are, so far as we know, spaceless and timeless. We can know nothing at all about the noumena, because we never perceive them directly. What we 'perceive' and know, therefore, is nothing more than the *appearances* or *phenomena* of things, and these are subjective in character, possibly without any resemblance to the things-in-themselves. The external, physical world remains forever an unknown *X.*

Passing from sense-intuition to *intellection* proper, Kant also finds a number of *a priori forms* of the pure understanding, and these he terms the *categories.* According to Kant, to think is to judge. When, therefore, we find judgments that are contingent and particular (e.g., 'This table is square'), they result from experience and are *a posteriori;* but when we find judgments which are necessary and universal (e.g., 'The sides of a square are equal to one another'), they must be the result of an *a priori* element or 'form,' namely, the 'category.' These categories express the necessary and universal relation which exists between the subject and predicate of a necessary and universal judgment or proposition. There are twelve such relations, and for each relation there exists a corresponding innate *a priori* category. They are: unity, plurality, totality; reality, negation, limitation; subsistence and inherence, causality and dependence, reciprocity (active and passive); possibility and impossibility, existence and non-existence, necessity and contingency.

These categories are *empty forms* of intellectual knowledge. The contents of intellectual knowledge must come from experience. After the 'manifold' of sense impressions is molded and arranged by the forms of 'space' and 'time,' the categories are applied to these sense intuitions; the result is universal and necessary intellectual knowledge. One must remember, however, that this intellectual knowledge never penetrates to the noumena or things-in-themselves, but only to the *phenomena* or appearances. Noumenal knowledge is simply impossible. What the physical, noumenal world is like in itself, is forever excluded from the ken of the human mind.

Reason, in its inferences, leads us to *three fundamental ideas:* the idea of the *soul,* the idea of *matter* or the totality of phenomena, and the idea *God.* As such, these ideas are mere *a priori forms* of the mind and pertain solely to *phenomena,* having a regulative function only. They are indeed the highest 'forms' of the mind, but they are nothing more than 'forms,' on a level with the forms of 'space,' 'time,' and the 'categories.' Reason, therefore, cannot prove the existence of the soul, of the world, and of God as entities independent of the mind. It is only from the *moral law* that we know that the soul, matter, and God actually exist; *intellectual* knowledge reaches only as far as the phenomena.

Summing up Kant's doctrine, we find that man is *incapable of transcendent knowledge;* his knowledge cannot contact the noumenal but only the phenomenal. Man's knowledge is governed completely by *transcendental* (*i.e., a priori, mental*) *forms.* Kant's theory is a *transcendental idealism.*

Criticism. Entire books have been written on Kant's theory of knowledge. Kant's views led to the great systems of idealism which flourished in the 19th century. They have had their day. As a criticism of his theory, we wish to stress the following points.

First, Kant's final conclusion was that our intellectual knowledge is *intrinsically illusory.* The intellect can know nothing of the things-in-themselves as they exist in the world around us; it can judge only of *phenomena,* and the phenomena reveal only the appearances, *not the reality,* of things as they impress the senses. But the intellect and its operations do not belong to the world of phenomena, because they do not affect the senses; they are an integral part of the mind itself. Since they cannot be phenomena, they must be noumena, things-in-themselves. Kant presumes to give us a thorough description of the intellect and its operations. Either, then, Kant actually did acquire a valid knowledge of noumena, notwithstanding the fact that he claimed we can never know the noumena; or, since all noumenal knowledge is impossible and illusory, his entire theory of the intellect and its operations is illusory and therefore false. In either case his theory breaks down.

Second, Kant maintained that a *physical world* of things-in-themselves, even though we can know nothing about it, actually *exists.* He assumes its existence on the grounds that the impressions made on the senses must be *caused* by external objects. Later on, however, he asserts that the concepts of 'causality' and 'causal dependence' are mere categories, and categories are but 'empty forms' contributed by the mind and without objective validity. Either, then, the category of 'cause' and 'effect' applies validly to noumena and is not an *a priori* mental form at all; or, if it is an *a priori* form, Kant is inconsistent in concluding from the existence of sensations to the existence of a noumenal world. Besides, Kant assures us that the noumenal world of things-in-themselves is a *chaotic manifold.* In giving us this important information, he claims to know something about the *objective reality* of the world distinct from phenomena. And here again he is inconsistent.

Third, Kant's theory is *contrary to the science of psychology.* He maintains that 'space' and 'time' are subjective 'forms' of the mind, given prior to all experience. The findings of psychology are definitely opposed to this claim. Sensory experience contributes its share to our perception of 'space' and 'time,' as experimental psychology has definitely established. We acquire our knowledge of space and time from a perception of objects which are larger or smaller and which are at rest or in motion. Persons suffering from a congenital cataract have no antecedent knowledge of visual space; after a successful operation, they must acquire knowledge of space through *experience* and *perception.* If the subjective mental form of 'space' were, as Kant claims, a necessary condition for perception, making the perception of phenomena possible, then there seems to be no valid reason why the mind cannot impose the form of 'visual space' upon the incoming impressions, even though a person be congenitally blind. The evidence, however, points clearly to the fact that the knowledge of space on the part of the mind is conditioned by the perception of the objects, and not that the perception of space is conditioned by some *a priori* form present in the mind antecedent to experience. But if 'space' is an attribute of bodies, then so is 'time,' because both are on a par in this respect.

Fourth, Kant's theory is contrary to the fundamental principles of the *physical sciences.* Kant evolved his theory for the expressed purpose of revindicating scientific knowledge and freeing it from the bane of Hume's skepticism. He failed. Science treats of the *physical objects* of the extra-mental world and not of mental constructions; Kant's world, however, is a world of *phenomena,* and these phenomena are mental constructions which give us no insight whatever into the nature and reality of things as they are *in themselves.* According to Kant's conclusions, the physical, noumenal world is unknown and unknowable. Science is convinced that it contacts and knows *real things* outside the mind. Science is based on the *objective validity* of the Principle of Cause and Effect operating between physical objects and physical agencies; according to

Kant, this principle is an empty *a priori* form merely regulating our judgments and applying only to phenomena. The *laws* which science establishes are considered by scientists to be real laws operating in physical bodies independent of our thinking; according to Kant, these laws merely relate to phenomena within the mind and not to nature at all. Kant states: "It sounds no doubt very strange and absurd that nature should have to conform to our subjective ground of apperception, nay, be dependent on it, with respect to her laws. But if we consider that what we call nature is nothing but a whole ['Inbegriff'] of phenomena, not a thing by itself, we shall no longer be surprised."[1] We are indeed surprised that Kant would accept this conclusion of this theory rather than see therein the utter fallaciousness of the theory itself which could consistently lead to such a 'very strange and absurd' conclusion. That such a conclusion destroys the validity of science in its very foundations, must be obvious.

Fifth, Kant's theory destroys the foundations of *all intellectual knowledge.* Ideas and judgments are supposed to reflect and represent reality; they are supposed to tell us 'what things are.' Truth and error reside in the judgment. We have shown that in forming judgments we first understand the contents of ideas and then have an *intellectual insight* into the relation existing between the subject-idea and the predicate-idea. According to Kant, we do not make judgments because we perceive the objective relation of the subject-idea and the predicate-idea, but because a *blind, subjectively necessitating law* of our mental constitution draws certain sense-intuitions under certain intellectually empty categories *prior* to our thinking, and we do not know *why* these particular categories, rather than others, were imposed by the mind on these sense-intuitions. Our 'knowledge' is as blind as the law that produces it. Intellectual knowledge is thus utterly valueless, because it gives us no insight into the nature of the reality our ideas and judgments are supposed to represent.

---

[1] *Critique of Pure Reason,* tr. by Max Müller, 2nd ed. (Macmillan, 1900), p. 94.

Kant, in accepting Descartes' ultra-dualistic separation of body and mind, was forced to consider the mind as the sole contributing factor in the formation of universal and necessary ideas, judgments, and inferences. Everything is purely subjective. Subjectivism is the inevitable conclusion of any theory which overlooks the facts that man is an *integral psycho-physical organism.*

The theories of innate ideas or mental forms are thus seen to be false, based on false assumptions.

Locke's Empiricism

Descartes' ultra-dualism of body and mind proved to be a fateful legacy for philosophic thought. His interpretation of the mind or soul, being ultra-spiritualistic, led to extreme idealism. His interpretation of the body, being ultra-mechanistic, led to empiricism, sensationalism, associationism, and materialism.

John Locke (1632–1704) followed in the footsteps of Hobbes (1588–1679), who was a sensationalist. Locke strenuously opposed Descartes' doctrine of innate ideas. In the beginning, he says, the mind is devoid of ideas, a 'blank sheet.' All knowledge has its origin in *experience,* in sense-perception. Experience is twofold, *sensation* (perception of external phenomena) and *reflection* (perception of the operations of the mind itself). From both sources we obtain 'ideas.'

Locke's philosophy centers in his theory of the ideas. Here is his understanding of an *idea:* "It being that term which, I think, serves best to stand for whatever is the *object* of the understanding when a man thinks, I have used it to express whatever is meant by *phantasm, notion, species, or whatever it is which the mind can be employed about in thinking.*"[2] In this superficial definition Locke unfortunately lumps together as 'ideas' things which might conceivably be radically different in nature, namely, "phantasm, notion, species, or whatever it

[2] *An Essay Concerning Human Understanding,* Introd., ed. by A. C. Fraser (Oxford, 1894), p. 32.

is which the mind can be employed about in thinking." By thus arbitrarily blurring the nature of the 'idea' so as to include the images of sense-perception ('phantasm, species'), he laid the foundation for *sensism,* in which all 'thinking' is nothing but a form of 'sensation.' Descartes placed all sense-perception in the spiritual mind, thus identifying sense-perception with spiritual activity; Locke here does the reverse, by reducing ideas, at least in part, to the level of sense-perception.

This confusion of ideas and images is present in all his philosophy. He does not hesitate to assert that the Creator can make *matter think*: "I see no contradiction in it that the first eternal thinking Being should, if he pleased, give to certain systems of created senseless matter, put together, as he thinks fit, some degrees of sense, perception and thought."[3]

Criticism. For one thing, Locke simply assumes without proof that 'ideas' and 'images' are identical. This identification of ideas and images wipes out the distinction between sensory and intellectual knowledge simply by *definition.* Again, according to his definition of the 'idea' the *idea* is the *object* of our understanding, instead of the *reality of things* being the object of our intellectual knowledge. All we can know, then, are 'ideas,' internal states of the mind; in that case, however, we can acquire no knowledge of the material world as it is in itself. If carried out to its logical conclusion, such a theory must inevitably end in subjective idealism. Furthermore, his confusion of 'ideas' and 'images' led him to the curious conclusion that God can make *matter think*. The empiricism of Locke made him reduce 'thinking' to a property of matter, because he could not bridge the ultra-dualism of Descartes. But God, as T. V. Moore rightly observes, can no more make nonliving matter think than He can make a square circle. Only on the supposition that man is an *integral organism,* consisting of body and mind, is it possible to explain how sensations can give rise to images, and images to ideas through the process of abstraction. Finally, since all ideas originate either from sensation or from reflection on mental activities, Locke

[3] *Ibid.,* Bk. IV, Ch. 3, § 6.

can give no proper explanation of ideas such as 'God,' 'soul,' 'good,' 'evil,' 'spirituality,' and a host of similar important ideas. We simply do not *experience* such realities in any form. Such ideas, then, should not be present in the intellect at all; they are, however, present and must be accounted for, though not according to the principles of Locke's empiricism.

Locke's empiricism was developed into a complete system of *sensism* by Condillac (1715–1780) who reduced the entire contents of the mind to 'transformed sensations.' Another offshoot of the empiricism of Locke is the *positivism* of Comte (1798–1857) who maintained that all knowledge is illusory except the 'positive' science of phenomena derived from sensation.

Sensationalism and Associationism

David Hume (1711–1776), accepting the fundamental tenets of Locke's empiricism, was more consistent than Locke and developed a thoroughgoing system of *sensationalism.*

According to Hume, the total content of the mind consists of *perceptions.* Perceptions are of two kinds: 'impressions' and 'ideas' or 'thoughts.' *Impressions* are those perceptions which are more lively and forceful, and they include sensations and emotions. The faint images of these impressions Hume terms *ideas* or *thoughts.* Impressions (sensations and emotions) are experienced; ideas or thoughts (faint images of sensations and emotions) are revived in imagination and memory. 'Perceptions' thus form the total contents of our mental states, and they are *all we can know.* We can know nothing of objects or the qualities of objects. Even when we think we perceive our own body and its members, we perceive nothing but "certain impressions which enter by the senses." There is no such thing as a 'substance.' The mind is nothing but "a heap or collection of different perceptions united together by certain relations, and supposed, though falsely, to be endowed with simplicity and identity."[4] Nothing is left, then, for knowledge but *phenomena,*

[4] *Works,* ed. Green and Grosse (1890), I, 534.

subjective mental states, perceptions. As for the *cause* of the impressions which arise from the senses, Hume professes complete ignorance.

Relative to *universal ideas,* Hume maintains that we find a resemblance between objects and apply the same *name* to them; then, after a 'custom' of this kind has been established, the name revives the 'idea,' and the imagination conceives the object represented by the 'idea.'

A prominent part of Hume's philosophy is his theory of *associationism.* We speak, for example, of the Principle of Causality, and consider it to be a universally and necessarily valid axiom that 'Every effect must have a cause.' Hume claims that this axiom is derived from *experience.* What we perceive is an *invariable sequence of events:* one thing invariably follows an antecedent event, and from this sequence we conclude that the antecedent event 'causes' the one that follows as an 'effect.' We do not perceive anything like the 'production' of one thing by another. From his phenomenalistic, sensationalistic standpoint, Hume could not admit real 'causation.' Whenever we observe one event to occur, we feel the mental compulsion to assert that the other will follow. But whence the mental compulsion to conjoin just these two events as 'cause' and 'effect'? Hume gives as the reason that "the mind is *carried by habit,* upon the appearance of one event, to expect its usual attendant and to believe that it will exist."[5] In other words, it is the *association of ideas* which compels us to formulate necessary and universal judgments, axioms, and principles. Such judgments, axioms, and principles have *no objective value,* but are mere associations of impressions derived from the succession of phenomena. As for the mental mechanism of association, it finds its explanation in the Laws of Association.

Criticism. First, Hume's explanation of *ideas* as *faint images* of sense-impressions is totally inadequate. Since both are of a sensory character, they are concrete and individualized. Our ideas, however, are abstract and universal. There is, as we have shown, a radical difference between 'sensations' and 'images'

[5] *Ibid.,* IV, 62.

on the one hand and 'intellectual ideas' on the other. To ignore or deny these differences is a serious error.

Second, Hume's explanation of *universal ideas* is totally inadequate. The process of forming universal ideas is not at all the way Hume pictures it. We acquire them by a process of *abstraction,* taking the objective features common to a number of individuals and then generalizing the resultant idea so that it applies to the whole class and to every member of the class. It is not a question of merely labeling objects with a common *name.* Intellectual insight into the nature of these objective features, not 'custom' or habit, enables us to group them together into a class.

Third, Hume's explanation of the origin and nature of the necessarily and universally true *axioms* and *principles,* such as the Principle of Causality and the Principle of Contradiction, is totally inadequate. He explains their necessity and universality through *association.* Now, the laws of association are purely subjective laws with a purely subjective result. Consequently, the 'necessity' which we experience relative to the logical connection between subject and predicate in these principles would not be due to anything coming from the reality represented in these judgments, but solely to the *associative force* existing in the mind. It is a subjective and *psychological,* not an objective and *ontological,* necessity. The mind does not judge these principles to be true because it *sees* they cannot be otherwise; it *cannot see* them to be otherwise because the mind in its present constitution must judge them to be true. So far as objective reality is concerned, $2 + 2$ might equal 3 or 5 or any other number; and there might be a cause without an effect, or an effect without a cause. If Hume's contention were correct, that our observation of 'invariable sequence' is the reason for assuming an antecedent event to be the 'cause' of the subsequent event, then we should perforce experience the same psychological necessity of judgment *in all cases* where we notice an invariable sequence in successive events. Experience, however, contradicts this view. For instance, day follows night in an invariable sequence; but nobody would dream of asserting that the night is the 'cause' of the day. In an automobile factory one car follows the other on the belt line in invariable sequence; but this association does not compel us to think that the preceding car is the 'cause' of the one following. Reversely, when an explosion occurs but once in our experience, we search for the 'cause' of this 'effect' and are convinced there must be a cause present; here, however, there can be no question of an 'invariable sequence' of events.

Fourth, Hume's theory, if accepted as true, must *destroy all scientific knowledge.* The very foundation of science lies in the Principles of Contradiction, Sufficient Reason, and Causality. If these principles are valid only for our mind and do not apply with inviolable necessity to physical objects in nature, the scientist has no means of knowing whether his conclusions are objectively valid. His knowledge is nothing but a *purely mental construction* which may or may not agree with extra-mental reality. But science treats of physical systems and their operations, not of mental constructions. Since, according to Hume, we can know nothing but our internal states of consciousness, we could never discover whether the external world and other minds exist at all; driven to its logical conclusions, such a theory can end only in *solipsism* or in *skepticism.*

Fifth, Hume's *Laws of Association* are valid, of course, in themselves; they were known and accepted, long before his time, by Aristotle and the Schoolmen. Hume, however, makes an illogical and illegitimate use of them, viewed from the standpoint of his own theory. According to Hume, the *total content* of the mind consists of *perceptions* (impressions and 'ideas' or images). Now, the Laws of Association, considered in themselves, are *not perceptions,* whether impressions or their images ('ideas'). The Laws of Association control, *regulate,* and link together these ideas; they are, therefore, over and above the ideas and *distinct* from them. According to Hume's own principles, then, they do not, and in fact cannot, belong to the content of the mind at all. Yet they are there.

Sixth, according to Hume, *the mind is its content.* In this view, there is no abiding mind or Ego in which impressions and ideas reside; all we have are perceptions (impressions and ideas) in a continuous flow; there is *no mind or Ego* distinct from these perceptions. Hume is very emphatic on this point. Theoretically, he denies the existence of 'mind' or 'Ego'; practically, he cannot, and actually does not, get along without a 'mind' or 'Ego.' He speaks continually of 'the mind,' 'we' and 'I,' and such terminology is inconsistent, to say the least. As a matter of fact, a 'mind' or 'Ego' is indispensable and *necessary to his theory,* notwithstanding his denial of their existence. The reason is plain. The Laws of Association, so basic to his theory, are merely the laws *according to which* ideas are conjoined; they themselves do not do the conjoining. Something, then, must be present which *applies* the Laws of Association to the ideas and *associates* them; without this 'something' these laws would be inoperative. Hume cannot explain the operation of these laws without a 'mind' or 'Ego' to operate them. Thinking demands a thinker, just as motion demands a moving object.

Seventh, Hume's theory is *atomistic.* It cannot be otherwise. Every sensation, emotion, and idea is a single item of consciousness, similar to an atom in nature. Each, as Hume expressed it, is a 'distinct existence.' Each is a solitary reality, having only an instantaneous existence; it comes, abides for a moment, and is irrevocably gone. No two items exist simultaneously; one succeeds the other in the flow of conscious events. And the important point is this: there is no 'mind' or 'Ego,' distinct in being from these experiences, which would be an abiding reality behind them, capable of experiencing them. Since each item of experience has but a momentary, isolated, and solitary existence, there is nothing present which could hold them together, *compare* them, and *synthesize* them. All we can have is an unrelated, kaleidoscopic succession of items. The formation of *general ideas, judgments,* and *inferences* should thus be utterly impossible, since there is no 'mind' or 'Ego' present to observe whatever *relations* might exist between ideas or things. But we have such general ideas, judgments, and inferences. Hume's theory, therefore, is utterly false.

Hume himself gave expression to the *dilemma* of the position in which he had placed himself. He said: "There are two principles which I cannot render consistent; nor is it in my power to renounce either of them, viz., *that all our distinct perceptions are distinct existences,* and *that the mind never perceives any real connection among distinct existences.* Did our perceptions either inhere in something simple and individual, or did the mind perceive some real connection among them, there would be no difficulty in the case."[6] This statement is a frank confession that a 'thinking mind or Ego' is necessary to explain our thought processes. But Hume would not accept this conclusion and thereby pronounced the complete failure of his theory of knowledge. He became a skeptic.

Hume exerted a tremendous influence on English and American philosophy, an influence which is felt even to this day.

Imageless Thought

Sensationalism and associationism dominated psychology for a long time. Each philosopher treating of psychological subjects introspected his own personal mind and its operations and then proceeded to make dogmatic pronouncements concerning them. Such was the method employed by Locke, Berkeley, Hume, J. Mill, Bain, Spencer, and other prominent English writers. Experimental methods were not used, for the simple reason that experimental psychology was not as yet in existence. The application of experimental methods to psychology did much to remove personal speculation and place psychology on a sounder factual basis. The first consistent experimental investigations into the nature of the thought processes began around the turn of this century.

A. Binet (1903) tested the sensationalist theory, to which he subscribed, through experiments on his two young daughters, expecting to find that thoughts were nothing but images. He came to the definite, and to him amazing, conclusion that

---

[6] *Ibid.,* Append., Vol. I, p. 559.

'naked thoughts' existed in the mind and that 'images' are extraneous to real 'thinking.'

More extended and systematic investigations along these lines were made by the psychologists of the *Würzburg School,* prominent among whom were *Oswald Külpe* (1862–1915), *K. Marbe,* and *K. Bühler.* Using the method of proposing questions and problems to their observers, they attempted to find out just what takes place in the mind in the formation of ideas, judgments, and inferences. In this manner they hoped to settle the question whether *ideas are identical with images* or whether *thinking transcends imaging.*

Sifting the evidence obtained from the subjects concerning their experiences, it was found that images of various types usually were present in the thought processes. The evidence, however, revealed a clear distinction between *knowing* and *sensing* or *imaging.* 'Understanding' and 'insight' were something totally different from the images. 'Meaning' was something over and above the images flitting through the mind during the process of thinking. In many instances, the subjects claimed, ideas were present, but no perceptible image; they experienced *imageless thought.* In any case, whenever images were present together with ideas, the images were recognized as merely accompanying the ideas, as adventitious to thoughts, and not as constitutive of, or essential to, the meanings. Usually, too, the images were soon forgotten, while the meanings, the ideas, the knowledge remained and were remembered. The psychologists of the Würzburg School soon learned that a distinction had to be made between the 'picturable and unpicturable contents of conscious processes' (*anschauliche und unanschauliche Bewusstseinsinhalte*). They mean that some contents of our mind can be 'pictured' or 'imaged,' such as a 'house' or 'horse,' while other contents cannot be 'pictured' or 'imaged,' such as a 'negation' or the 'will.' The latter are ideas. Ideas, therefore, are not images, even when images accompany ideas. From these and similar facts brought to light in the psychological laboratories of the Würzburg School, Bühler drew the general conclusion: "What enters into consciousness so sporadically, so very accidentally as our images, cannot be looked upon as the well-knitted, continuous content of our thinking."[7]

The main point about all these experiments is not whether thoughts can occur without images, but whether thoughts are identical with images. These psychologists have adduced considerable evidence in favor of *imageless thought;* but the evidence is not conclusive, and further experiments will have to be made. They have, however, definitely established the fact that *ideas are not images.* Sensationalism has thus been disproved on experimental grounds.

Later experiments, made by R. S. Woodworth, G. H. Betts, T. V. Moore, R. Clark, A. Willwoll, J. Lindworsky, and others, have confirmed the findings of the Würzburg School.

In general, the Würzburg School agrees with the teachings and principles of the traditional aristotelian-scholastic philosophy concerning abstraction, universal ideas, judgments and inferences, as expounded in the foregoing chapter. Experimental methods thus furnish positive proof that intellection is a supra-sensuous process.

E. B. Titchener (1867–1927), the noted head of the department of psychology at Cornell University, disputed the findings of the Würzburg School. On the strength of the experimental studies conducted under his guidance, he claimed that his observers always thought in images. Titchener, a sensationalist himself, contended that all thought processes can be reduced to 'sensations,' so that the 'sensation' is the 'structural unit or element' of everything occurring in consciousness; his theory is therefore sometimes referred to as *structuralism,* but it is really nothing more than a form of sensationalism.

Titchener denies that there are 'unpicturable meanings' of ideas. He himself, he says, always imaged meanings, even 'meaning' itself. Here is his description of 'meaning' as he images it: "I see meaning as the blue-grey tip of a kind of scoop, which has a bit of yellow above it (probably a part of

---

[7] *Tatsachen und Probleme zu einer Psychologie der Denkvorgänge.* Arch. f. d. ges. Psychol., 9, 1907, p. 317.

the handle), and which is just digging into a dark mass of what appears to be plastic material." One of his subjects saw 'meaning' as the "unrolling of a white scroll"; another saw it as "a horizontal line, with two short verticals at a little distance from the two ends."[8] Here we have, if images are really ideas, three distinct individual meanings of 'meaning'! These irrelevant images are not what we *understand* by 'meaning'; 'meaning,' as any dictionary will disclose, is that which is signified by an idea or word and which is expressed in a definition, the comprehension or intention of a word or idea, and that is something very different from the images mentioned above.

The egregious fallacy of the Cornell method consisted in the presupposition that ideas and images are identical; the subjects were instructed to *look for images* in their thought processes. They neglected 'ideas' in the search for 'images.' Thus, Dr. Geissler was told to look for the meaning of the sentence 'Did you see him kill the man?' He reported that he had "No meaning all the way through."[9] By 'meaning' he meant 'image.' He had no 'image,' but he certainly *understood the sense* of the sentence; any child would understand that. In other words, he had an 'idea' but no 'image.' If anything, such a report bears out the main contention of the Würzburg School that *images are only accessory products* of the thinking process.

It was the abuse of the introspective experimental method of the Cornell School that called forth a denunciation from Watson and prepared the way for behaviorism.

Gestaltism

Besides the Würzburg School of experimental psychology, the psychology of *Gestalt* or *configuration* has risen in opposition to sensationalism. There are really two Schools of Gestalt. The *Old School* originated with *F. Brentano,* in 1874. He had

---

[8] *Lectures on the Experimental Psychology of the Thought-Processes* (Macmillan, 1909), p. 19.

[9] Quoted by T. V. Moore, *Cognitive Psychology* (Lippincott, 1939), p. 197.

been trained in scholastic philosophy, and he stressed the supra-sensuous character of thought. But it was the work of two of his students, *A. Meinong* and *C. von Ehrenfels,* who developed the ideas of Brentano into what is now known as the Psychology of Gestalt. In particular, it was von Ehrenfels (1890) who showed that 'configurational qualities' exist in many types of perceptions, so that we apprehend these complex perceptions as 'wholes' rather than as mere 'aggregates' of sensory impressions. Meinong came to the conclusion that in Gestalt, in many instances, *meanings* are involved which are more than the resultants of sensations and cannot be explained on the basis of sensation, because they are altogether *objects of a higher order,* namely, conceptual or intellectual. This view was, of course, diametrically opposed to the 'atomistic' sensationalism prevalent in psychology at the time and practically amounted to a return to scholastic psychology, because over and above the sensory data of perception there must be the interpretative thought process as the configuring principle. Since Meinong taught at Gratz, the Old School of Gestalt psychology is often referred to as the *School of Gratz.*

The *New School* is called the *School of Berlin,* because *M. Wertheimer* and *W. Koehler,* who, together with *K. Koffka,* were mainly responsible for the new development of configurational psychology, taught at Berlin. These authors extended and deepened the researches begun by their predecessors of the Old School, especially by applying the experimental methods of modern psychology to the problem of configuration in perception. The New School began with an essay by Wertheimer on the perception of movement, written in 1912. Today Gestaltism is receiving considerable attention and has a large following.

The final conclusion of the studies of the Gestaltists can be condensed into the statement: Perception is not the mere sum of individual 'atomistic' sensations, but the resultant of the total sensory impression.

Unfortunately, the School of Berlin opposed the intellectualism of the parent School of Gratz and attempts to explain all configuration on the basis of sensory perception, ignoring entirely the *intellectual interpretation* of the cognitive processes. The pathology of perception, as noted in cases of cortical blindness and in persons operated on for cataract (see above, Chap. VII, p. 156 ff.), reveals the fact that configurations may be 'apprehended' and yet not 'understood.' Over and above perception, therefore, we have supra-sensuous thought processes dealing with intellectual meanings. The School of Berlin is still caught in the web of *sensationalism,* although it stands in opposition to the old-style sensationalism of Hume and his followers. Nevertheless, it is a step in the right direction.

For three centuries the ill-fated ultra-dualism of Descartes has played havoc in the minds of philosophers. System after system has been devised, only to be found in the end to be inadequate. Slowly but steadily experimental psychology is forcing philosophers and psychologists into recognizing that man is not pure spirit nor pure matter, but a unitary being composed of a material body and of a sentient, intellectual mind, an *integral organism.* We will next consider the peripatetic theory.

Summary of Chapter XIII

There are three main classes of theories which attempt to explain the *origin of ideas:* the theory of innate ideas; the empiricist or sensationalist theory; and the peripatetic theory.

1. *Plato's Ultra-Realism.* In order to account for the unchangeable and universal character of universal ideas and scientific knowledge, Plato postulated the existence of a supramundane *world of Ideas* or pure essences. Man must have lived in this world in a former existence, contemplating the Ideas, and he recalls them in the present existence. Universal ideas are thus innate.

Plato's theory presupposes that the relation between body and soul is *unnatural* and *extrinsic;* this relation however is natural and essential. We should be able to *remember* our former existence; but we do not.

2. *Descartes' Ultra-Spiritualism.* Descartes taught that body and soul are two intrinsically independent substances. The body is a mere machine; the intellect is the exclusive *cause* of all knowledge. Ideas are *potentially* innate and subsequently become actual.

Descartes overlooked the fact that man is a psycho-physiological *organism.* Sense organs are *vital instruments* of knowledge, and ideas can thus be formed through a process of abstraction from sense images.

3. *The Monadism of Leibnitz.* Every being consists of *monads,* all of which are without contact with other monads but have 'power of representation.' All ideas are innate as 'natural virtualities.'

Monadism is a gratuitous theory. If the theory were correct, there would be no need of sense organs and a *nervous system.* The theory leads to *solipsism.*

4. *Ontologism.* The theory claims that man intuits *God* and the *divine Ideas* in their relation to creatures and knows the objects of the world thereby.

This theory is contradicted by consciousness. If we beheld the divine Ideas, we would behold God's essence; but our knowledge of God is *indirect, analogous,* and by *negation.*

5. *Kant's Transcendental Criticism.* There is a noumenal world of things-in-themselves; of this world we can know nothing. The noumena affect the senses. Sense impressions are cast into the molds of two *innate a priori* mental *forms,* 'space' and 'time,' giving us phenomena. In the intellectual field there are twelve *innate a priori* judgment forms, the 'categories.' Reasoning is government by three *innate a priori* forms, the ideas of 'soul,' 'matter,' and 'God.' None of these 'forms' have objective value, but they are the conditions which make knowledge possible; they are present in the mind antecedent to all experience and therefore innate. The necessity and universality of ideas, judgments, and inferences are derived from these innate forms.

The theory is false. It makes knowledge *illusory*. We can know nothing of the external noumenal world; yet Kant knows that it is a 'chaotic manifold.' The theory is contrary to the science of *psychology* which shows that sensory experience contributes to the perception of 'space' and 'time.' It is contrary to *physical science* which treats of a real, not a merely phenomenal, world. It destroys *intellectual knowledge,* since it bases knowledge on the blind compulsion of mental 'forms' instead of 'insight.'

6. *Locke's Empiricism.* Locke considers the *object* of the intellect to be the *idea;* and he confuses the idea with the phantasm or image. He contends that *matter can think.*

The object of the intellect is *reality,* not the idea. By confusing 'idea' and 'image,' he wipes out the distinction between intellectual and sensory knowledge. 'Thinking matter' is as impossible as a 'square circle.' Locke cannot explain the origin of supra-sensuous objects, such as 'God,' 'good,' etc., because we do not experience them.

7. *Sensationalism and Associationism.* According to Hume, the total content of the mind consists of *perceptions,* namely, 'impressions' and 'ideas'; the latter are faint images of impressions. All we can know are phenomena. The universality and necessity of judgments rest on *association:* because we observe an invariable sequence of events, we judge the antecedent events to be the 'cause' of the subsequent events.

'Ideas' are not 'faint images' of sense-impressions: ideas are abstract and *universal.* Universal ideas are the result of abstraction. Axioms and principles are the result of intellectual *insight,* not of association. His sensationalism destroys all *scientific knowledge,* because all knowledge would be but a mental construction. The Laws of Association are *not perceptions;* they control and regulate perceptions. He eliminates the 'mind' or 'Ego,' but the Laws of Association demand something that *applies* them. Hume's theory is *atomistic* and therefore excludes the possibility of *synthesis.*

8. *Imageless Thought.* The experimental methods of the Würzburg School disproved the identity of 'images' and 'ideas.'

Images usually accompany ideas; but they are *accidental* and *accessory,* not essential to ideas. Many thoughts, some of these psychologists insist, are 'imageless.'

Titchener defends sensationalism. His method was faulty, because his subjects were instructed to look only for images in their processes.

9. *Gestaltism.* The School of Gratz arrived at the conclusion that 'meanings' cannot be explained by sensation, but are objects of a *higher order.* The School of Berlin explains configuration or Gestalt on the basis of sensory perception, ignoring the *intellectual interpretation* of the cognitive processes. The School of Berlin, although it disproves the 'atomism' of Hume, is sensationalistic.

What most of these systems overlook is the fact that man is an *integral organism* consisting of body and mind; hence their errors in explaining the origin of ideas.

Readings

Turner, William, *History of Philosophy.* — Moore, T. V., *Cognitive Psychology,* Part II. — Gruender, H., *Experimental Psychology,* Ch. XIV, XV, XVI. — Maher, M., *Psychology,* Ch. XIV. — Walker, L. J., *Theories of Knowledge.*

Chapter XIV

ARISTOTELIAN IDEOGENY

THE formation or genesis of ideas is termed *ideogeny.* There is one theory which offers a far better explanation than any of the theories discussed in the preceding chapter. It is in fundamental agreement with all the data brought to light by modern experimental methods, though this theory itself was not developed and formulated on the basis of experimental method but on the basis of wide observation, acute introspection, and logical deduction.

The theory dates back to *Aristotle* (384–322 B.C.), perhaps the greatest philosophical genius of all times. Because of his custom of strolling about while discussing problems with his pupils, the followers of Aristotle were named 'peripatetics,' and his teachings 'peripateticism.' His theory of the origin or genesis of ideas in the human intellect is therefore often referred to as *aristotelian* or *peripatetic ideogeny.*

Aristotle's philosophy was adopted by the Schoolmen or scholastics of the Middle Ages, and they developed his doctrines along many lines. The combination is usually styled *aristotelian-scholastic philosophy.* To *St. Thomas Aquinas* (1225–1274), the pre-eminent medieval philosopher, must go the credit of having introduced Aristotle's complete philosophy to the Western World and then developing it into a grand Christian world-synthesis. Due to his epoch-making work, history has linked his name to that of Aristotle and characterizes this rejuvenated peripateticism as *aristotelian-thomistic philosophy.*

It is the aristotelian-scholastic theory of ideogeny which will be outlined in this chapter.

Intellect and Thing

That man's ideas contain a true knowledge of the external world, is the conviction of all mankind; it is also the conviction of scientists and psychologists who are not prejudiced by philosophical theories. The epistemologist[1] has the duty to prove that this conviction is rationally justified. The problem before us consists in giving a satisfactory account of the various stages which intervene between the things of the world as they are in themselves and the ideas representing them as formed by the intellect.

Now, it is an axiom of aristotelian-scholastic psychology that *nothing is in the intellect which was not first* (*in some manner*) *in the senses* (*Nihil est in intellectu quod non fuerit prius in sensu*). The axiom is in perfect accord with everyday experience and with experimental psychology.

We have no innate ideas. That was shown in the discussion of the various theories of innatism. As far back as our memory reaches, we are conscious of *three successive states of mind* concerning knowledge. At first we are in ignorance relative to a subject matter (for example, history, geometry, language, etc.), so that we are in a state of 'potential' knowledge only. Then, we acquire a knowledge of a subject matter by learning, so that at the time we possess 'actual' knowledge of it. Finally, this actual knowledge recedes into the storehouse of memory, remaining there in a latent condition but capable of being recalled; this latent knowledge is called 'habitual.' The study of the knowledge process of infants and children confirms this view; they show no signs of ready-made innate ideas, but acquire their ideas and knowledge as just indicated. By a process of legitimate induction, therefore, we must conclude that the intellect of man is *originally devoid of ideas,* a *tabula rasa* or 'blank slate,' and it must acquire its knowledge 'from without.' Our ideas, therefore, have their *source outside the intellect;* they are acquired and formed, not innate and given.

[1] See the author's *Reality and the Mind* (Bruce, 1936), Ch. X–XII.

Knowledge implies three things: the thing that becomes known; the subject or intellect that knows the thing; and the process whereby the thing becomes known to the intellect. There must be a *union* between the knowing subject and the known thing, so that the thing is made present to the subject.

The intellect alone is not sufficient for cognition. Of itself, the intellect is indifferent as to what sorts of things it knows; it is not determined by its own constitution to know just this and that definite thing or this thing rather than that thing. A person blind or deaf from birth through physical disability has no knowledge of color or sound. Somehow, then, the *physical things* must be brought before the intellect. And this union between thing and intellect must be such that the knowledge thus acquired corresponds to reality; otherwise this knowledge would be false and useless.

The union between intellect and thing can conceivably take place in one of two ways. It might be a *physical union;* in that case the thing itself in its concrete entity would be taken into the entity of the intellect. Or, it might be a *union by representation* or *resemblance;* in that case the physical thing itself would remain outside the intellect, but some sort of representation, resembling the physical thing and thereby making it known, would be produced in the intellect. It is obvious, that things do not enter or contact the intellect in their physical entity and existence. When I acquire knowledge of a person or house, that person or house does not travel to me, enter physically into my intellect, and thereby become known to me; nor does my intellect travel to the person or house, envelop it, and thereby come to know it. Intellect and thing remain physically apart and retain their separate existence. Hence, the union between mind and object must be by representation or resemblance.

This representation or resemblance of the thing must be one either *of nature or of image.* The representation or resemblance in the intellect is one of 'nature,' if the thing and its representation in the intellect would exist in the same natural conditions. For example, in such a supposition a windowpane as existing in the world and its representation in the intellect would both be made of glass; if the thing is made of gold or brass or wood, its representation in the intellect would also have to be made of gold or brass or wood. The representation or resemblance in the intellect is one of 'image,' if it is a likeness of the thing, but differs from the thing in its natural conditions or materials. For example, a photograph or painting of a person is a representation, resemblance, or likeness, but it does not consist of the same materials nor does it exist in the same natural conditions as the person represented. It is obvious, of course, that our representation of a brick wall is not made of brick, and our representation of a widowpane is not made of glass. Nor is such an identical representation required. A photographic image can give us accurate knowledge of the appearance of a person, although the material or nature of the represented person and the representing likeness or image is totally different. A motion picture resembles the persons and scenes it depicts, and we acquire thereby considerable knowledge of them, even though the picture is devoid of the conditions and materials present in the original things. Hence, the representation, resemblance, or likeness present in the knowledge process of the intellect must be one of image. A *cognitional image* suffices and is necessary, in order to make the thing known to the intellect.

The external thing, then, becomes known to the intellect by means of a cognitional image. In as much, however, as the intellect, at first, is in a state of potential knowledge, this cognitional image must in some manner be derived *from the thing*. By what process is this cognitional image made?

Role of the External Senses

We know the answer from the sciences of physics and physiology. Things do not produce cognitional images in the intellect directly. *Forms of energy* (light-waves, air waves, heat, electricity, etc.) issue from the things and impinge on certain nerve terminals situated in certain structures of the human body; these structures and their nerves (sense organs) are specifically designed to act as receptors for these energy influences. The physical stimuli, proceeding from the things, activate the external senses by arousing a nerve impulse which travels along the afferent nerve fibers to receptive centers of the cortex of the brain. The response of this neurological mechanism is a *sensation* of color, sound, flavor, odor, pain, warmth, etc.

The response of sensation to the energy stimuli is not purely passive; it is an active vital process on the part of the sentient subject. The stimuli themselves are not vital and are not sensations; they are physical causes which stimulate the sentient subject to *actively produce within itself the vital response of sensation.* Just what kind of sensation is produced by the sensing subject within itself depends on the type of stimuli proceeding from the object. Sensation, therefore, is not a purely subjective product of the sensing subject. The sensing subject is determined in its sensory response partly by its own vital nature and partly by the character of the incoming stimuli. Sensation is thus seen to be the product of a double factor: one *objective,* the physical stimuli issuing from the external thing; and one *subjective,* the vital power of the sensing subject to respond to the particular stimuli with particular kinds of sensations.

That such a process actually occurs, should be clear from what has been said about the sensations in previous chapters. There it was shown that sensation is not a mechanical process in which the sensing subject participates in a purely passive fashion. On the contrary, the sensing subject responds actively by producing within itself a *vital modification.* This vital modification, the sensation, corresponds to the nature of the stimuli activating the senses, but it also differs from them in many respects. Since the stimuli reveal the thing to the sensing subject, this vital modification or sensation is a *cognitional image* of the object, but only an 'image' in its rudimentary stage; it is the first step in making the thing known to the intellect.

Even in this rudimentary stage, it will be noted, the cognitional image is not physical, but *psychical.* It does not consist of material stuff, such as exists in the thing which it represents.

The image is of the nature of the sensing subject rather than of the sensed thing; it is a mental image, not a physical copy. As the seal leaves upon the wax a likeness of itself without giving to it any of its material, so the material things are instrumental in impressing upon the senses their image without the gross conditions of matter.

In order to understand the nature of this cognitional image, even in its rudimentary stage, the body of man must be considered, not as an aggregate of inanimate chemical elements and compounds, but as a *vitalized organism.* Sensations are 'vital' mental products, different from the physical stimuli to which they are a response. The sensation of 'color,' for example, is something very different from the pattern of ether waves spread over the retina, and the sensation of 'sweet' is very different from the reaction of sugar with the chemical substances of the tongue. If sensations were the exclusive product of the sensing subject, we would have sensations, but no 'representation' or 'image' of the thing; and if the response were the product of a nonvital sense mechanism, we would have chemical and physical reactions, but no 'sensation.' But if man is an *integral organism,* we can understand how physical and chemical stimuli can affect the vitalized physical and chemical constituents of the senses and arouse in them a vital sensory response. And we can also understand how the sensing organism can respond to the causal action of the stimuli with sensations which are a rudimentary cognitional image capable of being elaborated eventually into a completed image of the thing.

Role of the Internal Senses

The rudimentary cognitional image of the thing, given in the sensations experienced by the sensing subject in response to the various types of stimuli issuing from the thing, is made into a completed cognitional image through the operation of the *internal senses.*

Sensations are in the nature of irreducible and isolated items of mental experience. They are like the single pieces of a jigsaw puzzle. Viewed separately and individually, the pieces are fragments of a picture; put together in their proper order and position, they form a unified and complete picture (representation, image, likeness, similitude) of a thing or scene. If there were no *central* or *synthetic sense,* the sensations would remain in their isolated and fragmentary condition. But the central or synthetic sense makes the sensing subject aware of the various sense qualities (a color, a tone, an odor, a flavor, etc.) as occurring simultaneously, combines them, and refers them to some definite thing as a *perceptual whole.* It synthesizes the jigsaw pieces of sensations into a unified *phantasm* of the sensed thing. This phantasm is the total sensory impression or completed cognitional image of the thing furnishing the stimuli which arouse the sensations. The phantasm is the unitive bond between the sensing subject and the thing, making the thing known in a sensory manner.

An example. Before me there is an orange which I proceed to peel and eat. My sight has a sensation of yellowish color on a surface which has a spherical contour; my fingers have a sensation of the texture of the orange, partly rough and partly smooth, together with a sensation of spatial dimensions; my nostrils have the sensation of a fruity odor; as I munch the segments, my tongue has the sensation of sweetness; my mouth has the sensation of pressure and temperature. Each sensation is a separate item mediated by a separate sense; each single sense knows nothing of the sensation mediated by the other senses. If this were the entire story of our experiencing, we would have only a confused and confusing mass of isolated sensations. All these isolated sensations, however, are experienced simultaneously (or nearly simultaneously) by the one sensing subject; they are combined into a *total sensory impression* or *phantasm* by the synthetic sense and referred as a 'perceptual whole' to the same thing, the 'orange.' This phantasm is the *completed cognitional image* presenting the thing to the sensing subject though the mediation of the synthetic sense in co-operation with the external senses.

In the terminology of aristotelian-scholastic psychology, the sensations are the *received* or *impressed sensible image* (*species sensibilis impressa*), which arouses the synthetic sense into action by its presence. The synthetic sense responds to this 'sensory determinant,' as D. Card. Mercier styles the impressed sensible image, by forming the phantasm or completed sensory cognitional image of the object. The phantasm or completed sensory cognitional image, elaborated into a perceptual whole from the sensations by the synthetic sense, is the *formal* or *expressed sensible image* (*species sensibilis expressa*). For brevity's sake, this completed sensory cognitional image representing the sensed thing is called *phantasm*. The phantasm, therefore, is formed by the synthetic sense while the thing is *present to the senses* and activates them through its stimuli. This phantasm truly *represents* the thing, because it manifests the qualities and attributes of the thing to the subject by means of the stimuli and of the sensations resulting therefrom.

It must be stressed again, that the phantasm (cognitional image) is a representation of the external thing, but it is a *psychical* or mental, not a physical or purely material, likeness. The senses perceive color, sound, bitterness, hardness, etc., but the phantasm itself is not colored, sonorous, bitter, hard, etc. The phantasm is a vital modification of the knowing subject and as such partakes of the nature of the knowing subject. This fact is expressed in the axiom: *The known object is in the knower according to the nature of the knower* (*cognitum est in cognoscente secundum modum cognoscentis*).

Once the phantasm ('expressed sensible image') is formed by the synthetic sense, it is taken over by the *imagination* and stored away. The phantasm does not remain in the imagination precisely as a 'phantasm,' such as it was when formed by the synthetic sense, but as a 'trace,' or 'disposition.' Later on, this 'trace' or 'disposition' can be activated, so that the 'phantasm' or 'image' will be revived. In the absence of the original thing, therefore, the phantasm or image can be reproduced and contemplated; for cognitional purposes, the phantasm or image *takes the place of the original thing,* and the thing can be studied in its cognitional image as if the thing itself were again present. The thing itself may have been sensed for only a brief period of time, never to be actually sensed again, as when we travel once and only once through a city or country. The recalled image of the thing can be studied at leisure in a sort of vicarious sensory experience; the intellect thereby has a greater opportunity to form ideas of the thing.

Memory also plays its part in this psychological process. It is memory which dates and localizes past experiences and identifies a certain phantasm or image as representing some particular thing *sensed before* at a definite time and place. It recognizes the object in its cognitional image, so that the intellectual ideas derived from this image are equivalent to ideas derived from the thing itself as represented in the phantasm of the synthetic sense made in the thing's own presence.

These, then, are the two preliminary stages in the total process of the formation of ideas: the genesis of the *rudimentary cognitional image* ('impressed sensible image') of the sensations, produced by the external senses and the cerebrum in response to physical stimuli proceeding from the thing; and the completed or *formal cognitional image* ('expressed sensible image') of the *phantasm,* made by the synthetic sense from the sensations and conserved by the imagination.

Agent Intellect

From the sensory field we pass to the intellectual field. Intellection begins where sensory experience ends.

Ideas are of a higher order than images; ideas are abstract and universal, while images are concrete and individualized. It follows that images cannot be the efficient cause of ideas, because there would be a disproportion between cause and effect. Just as the phantasm had to be formed by the synthetic sense through a sensory process in response to the stimuli in the sense organs, so the formation of ideas must proceed from the *intellect* through an *active intellectual process* in response to the phantasm or image. There are no innate ideas in the intellect, and there is nothing in the intellect which was not first somehow in the senses; the intellect, therefore, must derive its ideas in some manner *from the senses.* How does the intellect do this?

According to the aristotelian-scholastic theory, the intellect forms its ideas by *turning its attention upon the content of the phantasm* (*se convertendo ad phantasmata*). Most scholastics interpret the term 'phantasm,' used by Aristotle and St. Thomas in this connection, as meaning the revived phantasm or image of the *imagination.* Taken in this sense, ideas are not derived from the phantasm made by the synthetic sense in the presence of the stimulating thing. This view is probably erroneous. T. V. Moore,[2] after an analysis of pertinent passages of Aristotle and St. Thomas, arrives at the conclusion that both understood the term 'phantasm' in a *generic* sense, including the phantasm formed by the synthetic sense in the *presence* of the object and the revived image of the imagination in the *absence* of the object. Both types of images are 'phantasms,' and the intellect can form ideas by turning its attention to either one. After all, the *cognitional content* of both is *identical.* The image of the imagination is fashioned from the phantasm of the synthetic sense and is a replica of it. No valid reason can be assigned why the intellect should not be able to turn its attention to the original phantasm of the synthetic sense as well as to the derived image of the imagination; if the intellect can turn its attention to the latter, it must be able to turn its attention also to the former. After all, experience shows that we form ideas of objects *while we actually perceive them,* i.e., while we have a percept of them in the synthetic sense.

Ideas are formed, then, by the intellect in one of two ways: by turning its attention *either* to the phantasm of the *synthetic sense* in the actual perception of the thing *or* to the phantasm (image) of the *imagination* in the recalled impression of the absent thing. The result is, in general, the same, because the cognitional content of both types of phantasms is the

---

[2] "The Scholastic Theory of Perception," in *The New Scholasticism,* Vol. VII (1933), pp. 222 ff. In opposition to Moore's interpretation, see the article, "Phantasm and Phantasy," by F. A. Walsh, in *The New Scholasticism,* Vol. IX, 1935, pp. 116–133.

same: both are a psychical likeness of the perceived thing.

The *superiority* of the idea, relative to the phantasm, consists in this that the content of the idea represents the thing as *divested* of the *material conditions* proper to material things. The senses represent things in the concrete conditions of their individualizing material determinations (shape, size, color, etc.); the intellect, however, represents things as divested of these concrete conditions, by leaving the individualizing material determinations aside and concentrating its attention on the *essence* or *'whatness'* of the thing ('what they are,' instead of 'how they appear'). The intellect divests the representation of its concrete conditions, by the now familiar process of *abstraction;* thereby the 'sensible' becomes *'intelligible'* to the intellect. The 'essence,' or 'nature,' or 'whatness,' is said to be 'abstracted' from the phantasm by the intellect.

When it is said that the 'whatness' or the 'quiddity' (Lat., *quid,* what; *quidditas,* whatness) is 'abstracted' from the phantasm, we must guard ourselves against placing too literal an interpretation on the term 'abstraction.' It does not mean that the intellect actually 'draws out' the phantasm from the synthetic sense or imagination, immaterializes the phantasm itself, and then takes it over as an 'idea,' thereby converting the sensible image into an intelligible image. The phantasm remains in the synthetic sense or in the imagination as a sensory representation of the thing, unchanged and intact. The intellect, however, while contemplating the phantasm present in the synthetic sense or imagination, *actively generates within itself* an intellectual representation of the thing according to its essence or 'whatness (quiddity),' thereby making the thing *actually intelligible* or understandable for the intellect. Aristotelian-scholastic psychology speaks of this process as 'illuminating the phantasm' and 'abstracting the essence or nature from the phantasm.'

Since the idea is a supra-sensible (because 'abstract') representation of the thing, the abstractive process whereby the idea is formed must be a *supra-sensible process,* and the abstracting intellect must be a *supra-sensible power.* The phantasm, therefore, since it is but a sensory product, cannot make an impression on the supra-sensible intellect by being, as it were, projected on the intellect; for the same reason, the phantasm can neither be converted into an idea nor reside in the intellect. The intellect forms its idea of the thing during the contemplation of the phantasm by means of an *active interpretation* of the content of the phantasm.

This interpretation of the content of the phantasm is possible, because the same knowing subject is consciously active in sensation and intellection and is consciously aware of the phantasm and its content as a sensory representation of the thing. Since the one who senses and the one who thinks is the same perceiving individual man, man is not only aware of the phantasm but also is aware of what the phantasm represents and *means;* he *interprets* the phantasm as a representation of the thing and thereby knows *what the thing really is in itself.*

Now, this power or capability which actively *modifies itself so as to represent within itself in an abstract manner what is concretely represented in the phantasm,* is termed the *agent intellect.* Some call it the 'active intellect.' St. Thomas and the Schoolmen termed it *intellectus agens;* so the term 'agent intellect' seems preferable.

The agent intellect is a certain instinctive supra-sensory energy or power which acts spontaneously on the phantasm present in the synthetic sense or imagination and generates within itself an *intelligible cognitional image of the thing* represented by the phantasm.

The agent intellect is the principal efficient cause in the formation of this intelligible cognitional image. The phantasm presents the quiddity or essence of the thing, but this quiddity is concretized in material conditions and determinations. I behold, for example, a human being and make a phantasm of him in all his individualized concreteness of shape, color, size, sex, etc. The agent intellect unites its activity with that of the perceiving synthetic sense, drops all the concrete particulars, and abstracts from the phantasm those features which are essential to man as 'man.'

Without the sensory cognitional image of the phantasm the agent intellect can do nothing. When, however, the phantasm is present, the agent intellect naturally and instinctively goes over into its abstractive activity. The product of this abstractive activity is the *vital determination of the intellect* to the act of understanding, to the *intellectual perception* of the quiddity of the thing represented in the phantasm. This 'vital determination' of the intellect is termed the *received* or *impressed intelligible cognitional image* (*species intelligibilis impressa*) or the 'impressed intelligible species.' The impressed intelligible species is still not the full and complete 'idea' of the thing, but the immediate preparation for the 'idea'; its relation to the full and complete 'idea' is the same as that of the 'sensations' to the full and complete 'phantasm' of the synthetic sense.

M. Maher characterizes the agent intellect as follows: "The intellectus agens [agent intellect] must be conceived as instinctive or blind; its 'abstractive' action is *productive* of intelligence, not formally intelligent itself. Its function is to *effect* the modification by which the act of intellectual consciousness is immediately awakened. It may be here asked if the action of the intellectus agens be *instinctive,* why does it issue into the precisely appropriate activity? Why does it *effect exactly the right modification* to represent the object of sensory impression when the latter cannot directly act upon it? The answer lies in the fact that *both senses and intellect have their source in the same individual soul,* which is so constituted that on the *stimulation of the former* the *latter sympathetically responds* by a higher reaction of its *own* — somewhat as the appetitive faculty, which conceived as such is blind, tends towards an object apprehended by a cognitive faculty as good. In both cases it is the soul itself which acts through the faculty."[3]

The Potential Intellect

The phantasm, then, is 'potentially intelligible,' because it contains the essential elements of the thing in a concrete

---

[3] *Psychology,* 9th ed. (Longmans, Green, 1930), p. 308.

form; it becomes 'actually intelligible' when the agent intellect grasps the essential elements through its abstractive activity. These essential elements must now be fashioned from a rudimentary cognitional image (impressed intelligible species) of the agent intellect into the *completed or formal cognitional image,* namely, into an 'idea.'

The *power* or *capacity* of the intellect to *express the essence of the represented thing in an 'idea' or 'concept'* is termed the *potential intellect* (*intellectus possibilis*). The term 'potential' does not mean 'inactive.' It merely signifies that the intellect is 'receptive' of the vital determinant or modification (impressed intelligible species) received by it from the agent intellect, before it proceeds to its own activity of generating the idea proper.

This vital determinant having been received into the potential intellect, the potential intellect expresses *in conceptual terms* the nature of the thing represented concretely in the phantasm. In other words, the essential elements of the thing, abstracted from the phantasm by the agent intellect, are gathered together by the potential intellect into a *definition* or *abstract intellectual representation* of the thing. This conceptual definition is the completed or *formal intellectual cognitional image* of the object, the 'expressed intelligible species (*species intelligibilis expressa*)' or *idea.* The formation of the 'idea' as an intellectual expression or representation of the thing is now complete. The intellect's abstract idea of man is 'rational animal,' and this idea is obviously something very different from the phantasm of 'man' in the synthetic sense or in the imagination; the phantasm is always concrete and material, while the idea is always abstract and conceptual.

The idea, immediately upon its formation, is a *potential universal.* The idea expresses the nature or essence of the thing, stripped of all individualizing conditions. As such, it represents what this thing has in common with all individuals of the same class. Before the intellect, however, is aware of this, it must compare this thing with things of the same type; it recognizes the fact that this nature is the same in all individuals of the class and then applies the idea to the whole class as a class and to every individual belonging to the class. The idea is now a *formal universal*. Universality is another feature of the idea which distinguishes it from the phantasm, because the phantasm, being derived from an individual thing, is always individualized and never universal.

Aristotelian-scholastic psychologists disagree among themselves as to whether the agent intellect and the potential intellect are two really distinct powers or two phases of one and the same fundamental power. Similarly, they disagree as to whether the phantasm is an (instrumental) efficient 'cause' in the production of an idea or merely a necessarily required 'condition.' Furthermore, they disagree as to whether the 'impressed intelligible species' and the 'expressed intelligible species' are really distinct from each other or merely two aspects of one and the same reality. These are abstruse problems which need not detain us.

The aristotelian-scholastic ideogeny, as here described, is an *ideological theory* which attempts to explain the process of the formation of ideas in the human mind, and as such it must be judged.

Understanding and Reason

We understand some things directly, because they are self-evident to the mind. Among these are the *ideas* we acquire through the direct perception of things, as when we interpret the things immediately presented to us by the phantasm in sensory experience; we need no 'reasoning' process to understand them. In a similar manner, we understand the meaning of *first principles* and perceive their truth and validity, without the necessity of proving them; they are immediately evident. Such principles are, for example, the Principle of Identity, the Principle of Contradiction, the Principle of Excluded Middle. The power of the mind which perceives the truth and validity of ideas and principles on the basis of direct and immediate evidence is termed *understanding*.

Some ideas, principles, and judgments, however, are not

self-evident. They are *derived ideas, principles,* and *judgments,* the result of a process of elaboration and demonstration from previously acquired ideas, principles, and judgments, and are known through 'mediate inference' on the basis of definite reasons and proofs. This process is termed 'reasoning,' and the power of the mind which perceives the truth and validity of derived ideas, principles, and judgments on the basis of indirect and mediate evidence is termed *reason.*

The question then arises: *Are understanding and reason two distinct powers of the intellect, or are they merely two aspects of one and the same intellect?*

There have been some *differences of view* on the nature of understanding and reason. According to *Kant,* it is the function of the understanding to cognize the phenomena of experience and to arrange the material of experience by means of the innate forms of the categories; and it is the function of reason to conclude from the conditioned to the unconditioned by means of the innate forms of the ideas of 'soul,' 'world,' and 'God.' He seems to view the two as distinct powers. According to *Jacobi,* the understanding is the capacity to know the sensory world, while reason is the capacity to know the suprasensory realities (God, soul, essence, etc.) by means of a sort of faith without intellectual insight. According to *Hermes,* we know the data of experience by means of the ideas of the understanding, while the ideas of reason enable us to apprehend that which is known in its grounds and causes. A view, similar to that of Hermes, was held by *Günther.*

We hold that understanding and reason are *really identical with the intellect* and merely designate two aspects of one and the same cognitive power.

Understanding and reason both have the same proper, connatural, immediate *object,* namely, the sensible in an abstract form. They differ only in this that cognition through understanding is immediate, based on the self-evidence of fundamental ideas and principles, while the cognition through reason is mediate, based ultimately on the self-evidence of the fundamental ideas and principles from which this cognition is derived. The 'mode' of knowledge is different, but the 'kind' of knowledge is the same. The formal object of understanding and reason being the same, there is no need to consider them as really distinct powers. Again, reason is to understanding as the *imperfect to the perfect.* The essence of all cognition is that things become evident to the knowing subject. Cognition is perfect, when the intellect 'knows' things directly and immediately; it is imperfect, when the intellect must seek reasons and grounds to make them known. Now, the cognition of the understanding is of the first type, while the cognition of reason is of the second type. It is only because of the weakness and limitation of the human intellect that it cannot acquire a full knowledge of all things through direct intellectual perception, but must 'conclude' to their existence by a process of reasoning. Imperfection of cognition, however, does not necessitate a distinct power.

Intellectual Memory

While treating of the sensory memory, it was pointed out that modern psychologists, as a rule, bulk together sensory and intellectual material without distinction in their investigation of human memory. They seem to take it for granted that memory is a single power. This concept of memory is erroneous. Besides sensory memory, man possesses an *intellectual memory.*

We not only recall and recognize past items of sensory experience, but also items of experience and knowledge which are definitely *supra-sensory* in character.

Since *ideas* are *abstract* and *universal,* they cannot be the product of a sensory process and they cannot be stored in a sensory memory. Everything in the sensory memory is concrete and particular, affected by the material conditions of the sensations and of the phantasms of the synthetic sense, just as the latter are affected by the material conditions of the physical things from which they are derived. The *judgments, principles, and laws* which constitute intellectual knowledge and science, even when they pertain to the physical world, are meaningful interpretations, not sensory representations, of reality, and as such far exceed the capacity of the senses and of sensory memory. For example, the definitions, rules, and methods of logic cannot be perceived by the senses, because they are mental realities which emit no physical stimuli and therefore cannot affect the senses; no sensory image of their 'meaning' can be made by the synthetic sense, stored, recalled, and then be recognized by the sensory memory. The *truth* of judgments and inferences possesses no sensory qualities which could possibly be imaged, but is a matter of intellectual insight into the suprasensory relations exiting between ideas and judgments. We are forced, therefore, to conclude that intellectual memory exists and that it is a power really distinct from sensory memory.

This conclusion is confirmed by *experimental psychology,* although little experimental work has been done to separate the sensory and intellectual factors of memory. Certain facts point definitely to the existence of two kinds of memory, one based on sensory experience and the other on intellectual apprehension.

The *learning of meaningful material* is achieved far more easily then that of nonsense syllables, words, and mere numbers. Ebbinghaus (1885) discovered that we expend only one-tenth as much energy in learning meaningful material as we do for the same amount of meaningless material. His findings were verified by Binet, Henri, Neumann, Reed, and many other investigators. If memory involved nothing more than the recall and recognition of certain printed letters and numbers, it should make no difference whether their combinations contained a meaning or not, because the sensory image would be equivalently the same in all instances. The presence or absence of meaning, however, makes a decided difference. Since the difference cannot be accounted for by the senses and the sensory memory, the difference must be due to the intellect and the intellectual memory.

Similarly, the *curve of forgetting* is much more rapid and much more steadily downward for nonsense material than it is for meaningful material. Intellectual insight makes a great difference in this respect, as studies by S. Austin, A. G. Dietze, G. E. Jones, R. A. Davis, C. C. Moore, and others, conclusively show.

L. V. Zankov, in tests made on morons, discovered that they experienced a sudden development of intellectual or 'logical' memory when about ten or eleven years of age, due to an awakening of intellectual insight at that period, while no change occurred in their rote memory.

Facts of this kind and of a similar nature point to two types of memory. One is sensory, where learning depends on the repetition of sensory impressions; the other is intellectual, where learning depends on the understanding of non-sensory logical relations.

Sensory and intellectual memory, however, are not totally independent. On the contrary, the intellectual memory, to a great extent, is *dependent on the sensory memory*. Intellectual knowledge has its origin in sensory experience, and ideas are derived from phantasms through abstraction. Due to this intimate relationship between sensory and intellectual processes, their mutual influence is bound to be deep and lasting. Any pathological disturbance of the sensory memory will naturally also effect intellectual memory. Word-blindness, for example, brought on by disease or injury of the brain, interferes with recall and recognition of words and their meaning; but it does not interfere with the understanding and recognition of logical relations, ideas, and principles as such.

According to the principle that 'entities should not be multiplied without good reason,' we accept the view that *intellectual memory is identical with the intellect itself,* and not a power distinct from the intellect. The *knowledge* retained by the memory and then revived at a later period is identical with that originally acquired by the intellect, and we are *conscious* that this knowledge is the same. There seems to be no valid reason for assuming that intellectual knowledge is 'acquired' by one power and 'retained' by another. On the other hand, it is logical to assume that the knowledge, which at first was actual, simply becomes 'habitual' by being reduced to the condition of a *trace* or *disposition* in the intellect, capable of being activated anew and recognized as having been present before. Nothing more seems to be required.

If we now summarize the salient facts pertaining to the origin and nature of ideas, we note the following *stages in the developmental process:*

First, the external things send forth certain forms of energy which impinge on the sense organs. The vital subject responds through its sense mechanism with sensations, and these sensations are a rudimentary cognitional image of the external thing. This cognitional image is 'rudimentary,' because the sensations, as such, are only isolated items of experience.

Second, in the presence of these sensations, the synthetic sense combines them into a perceptual whole by forming them into a unified phantasm and referring them to the external thing which they represent. The phantasm is the completed or formal cognitional image which makes the thing known to the knower in a sensory manner. The imagination conserves the content of the phantasm as a dispositional image which can be revived and recognized by the sensory memory.

Third, when presented with the phantasm or image, the agent intellect abstracts the essential elements of the thing from the concrete conditions in which they are found in the phantasm or image, thereby making the phantasm or image intelligible. These abstracted essential elements are the rudimentary intelligible cognitional image of the object.

Fourth, the agent intellect presents these abstracted essential elements to the potential intellect, which now goes into action and mentally expresses this intelligible content in conceptual terms, thereby forming the idea of the thing in an abstract and universal manner. The 'idea' is the completed or formal cognitional image of the external thing in the intellect and is stored away in the intellectual memory for future recall and identification.

While much of this is speculation, the theory gives a rather neat explanation of the deep problem of bridging the sensory and intellectual processes involved in the origin and development of ideas.

Summary of Chapter XIV

This is an account of *ideogeny* according to Aristotle and the scholastics.

1. *Intellect and Thing.* There is nothing in the intellect which was not first (in some manner) in the senses. There are no innate ideas; they have their source outside the intellect; the intellect must derive them from the things. Hence a union between intellect and thing by means of a *cognitional image* is demanded.

2. *Role of the External Senses.* In the presence of the stimuli proceeding from the thing, the sentient subject actively produces within itself the vital response of *sensations.* These sensations represent the thing and are the *rudimentary cognitional image* of the thing, the 'impressed sensible image.'

3. *Role of the Internal Senses.* The central or synthetic sense combines the isolated sense qualities into a perceptual whole and refers them to the same definite thing. The result is the *phantasm,* the completed or *formal cognitional image* or 'expressed sensible image' of the thing. The phantasm completes the knowledge of the thing on the sensory level. The phantasm is taken over by the imagination as an image which can be recalled and can be identified by the sensory memory.

4. *Agent Intellect.* The intellect forms its ideas by turning its attention upon the content of the phantasm either of the synthetic sense or of the imagination. By means of abstraction, the intellect grasps the *essential elements* of the thing represented in the phantasm, leaving aside the individualizing material determinations, thereby making the phantasm 'intelligible.' This power or capacity of the intellect, whereby it actively modifies itself so as to represent within itself in an abstract manner what is concretely represented in the phantasm, is termed the *active* or *agent intellect.* The result of this abstractive process is the *impressed intelligible cognitional* image, the 'idea' in a rudimentary form.

5. *The Potential Intellect.* The power or capacity of the mind to express the essence of the represented thing in an 'idea' or 'concept' is termed the *potential intellect.* The essential elements, after being abstracted from the phantasm, are presented by the agent intellect to the potential intellect; the latter expresses the elements in conceptual terms by gathering them together into a *definition* or *abstract intellectual representation* of the thing. This 'idea' is the completed or *formal intellectual cognitional image* of the thing ('expressed intelligible species').

6. *Understanding and Reason.* The power of the intellect which perceives the truth and validity of ideas and principles on the basis of direct and immediate evidence is termed *understanding.* The power of the intellect which perceives the truth and validity of ideas and principles on the basis of indirect and mediate evidence is termed *reason.* They are not distinct powers, but merely two aspects of one and the same intellect.

7. *Intellectual Memory.* Ideas are abstract and universal and as such supra-sensory. The judgments, principles, and laws which constitute intellectual knowledge and science are meaningful interpretations, not sensory representations, of reality. Such mental items, therefore, exceed the capacity of the senses and of sensory memory. Hence, *intellectual memory* must be really distinct from sensory memory. Intellectual memory is identical with the intellect itself and not a power distinct from the intellect.

Readings

Moore, T. V., *Cognitive Psychology,* pp. 462–472. — Maher, M., *Psychology,* pp. 305–313. — Brennan, R. E., *General Psychology,* pp. 327–334.

CHAPTER XV

VOLITION

SO FAR we have discussed the mental life of man as it appears in sense-perception, in sensuous appetency, and in intellection. Sense-perception makes us acquainted with the objects of the universe and with our own bodily states and conditions. Sensuous appetency seeks to bring us into union with objects which are recognized as sensuously good for us and to remove us from objects which are recognized as sensuously evil. The intellect penetrates the concrete appearances of things and cognizes the sensible in an abstract and universal manner, thereby arriving at a knowledge of 'what things are.'

There is still another phase of man's mental life which must be added to these. It is *volition,* the activity of the *will.* Just as sensuous appetency is the counterpart of sense-perception, so volition is the counterpart of intellection. There are two kinds of cognition, and there are two kinds of appetition.

The Concept of the Will

The best approach toward an understanding of the will is an examination of those types of experiences which reveal the acts of the will in everyday life. During the course of a day we set our will in action hundreds of times. Here are a few characteristic samples.

The alarm clock rings in the morning, and the father of the family becomes awake. The bed is comfortable, he is drowsy, and he feels a strong urge to snatch a little more sleep; however, he *resists* the impulse and gets up. He goes over to the wardrobe and, after a few moments' hesitation, *selects* his brown suit. At the breakfast table he makes a number of *decisions* as to quantity and quality of food; although he had *resolved* long ago to take only light breakfasts and *usually kept his resolution,* this morning, being rather hungry, he *changes his resolution* and eats a large portion of ham and eggs instead of the customary cereal and toast. Being of considerable corpulence, he *detests* walking and *prefers* to use the car to go to business; nevertheless, *desiring* to reduce his weight by some form of exercise and *consenting* to his wife's advice, he strolls to his office. Upon entering the office, he notices that his secretary is wearing a canary-yellow ensemble. He *disapproves* of this type of garb during business hours and *feels tempted* to make a caustic remark; on second thought, however, he *refrains* and, *forcing himself* to be pleasant, extends the usual greeting. Opening his mail, he reads the letter of a customer who makes a number of very unreasonable demands. He *hates* the tone of the letter and, momentarily *yielding* to his emotions, utters a few explosive epithets; on seeing the startled expression on the face of the secretary, he expresses his *regret* over his *impulsive action,* admitting that he *should have had better control* over himself. The letter annoys him greatly. He *feels inclined* to give a point-blank *refusal* to the demands and to answer in a revengeful spirit of pique; but he also realizes that he *ought* to overlook the truculent tone of the letter from a *motive* of Christian charity and patience; finally, he needs the profits to be derived from this business for rearing his growing family which he *loves* very devotedly. What shall he do? It is a momentous decision for him to make, and he knows he *should not* act hastily in the matter. He deliberates for some time about the course he should pursue and then *decides,* for the sake of the welfare of his family, to *accede* to the demands. Having made his *choice,* he thinks he deserves a *reward* for his virtuous act, *selects* one of three cigars he carries in his pocket, lights it, and smokes contentedly in the realization that he has exercised great *will power.* And so the day passes, similar incidents occurring continuously.

In this brief description we notice a number of attitudes and acts of the will. Emotions and sensory impulses are present, and so are considerations of an intellectual, social, and moral character. The person in question makes decisions to act and not to act, to perform one kind of act rather than another; he makes a selection between various objects of equivalent value, and he chooses between moral good and moral evil. He is conscious of influencing motives, but also of freedom of choice and responsibility of action; he acts on impulse, but he also acts after serious deliberation. His intellect proposes different motives and methods of procedure, but he himself determines the issue by making whatever decision and choice he prefers.

'Resisting,' 'selecting,' 'deciding,' 'resolving,' 'detesting,' 'preferring,' 'desiring,' 'consenting,' 'approving,' 'disapproving,' 'feeling tempted,' 'refraining,' 'forcing oneself,' 'hating,' 'yielding,' 'regretting,' 'losing control,' 'feeling inclined,' 'refusing,' 'loving,' 'acceding,' 'choosing' — all these mental states and experiences involve attitudes or acts of the will with reference to objects, persons, and situations. The feature common to all such states and experiences is a conscious inclination toward an intellectually perceived good and a conscious aversion from an intellectually perceived evil.

Whatever may be our ultimate judgment concerning the will and its nature, the *will* is conceived and defined as *rational appetency* or *the power to strive for an intellectually perceived good and to shun an intellectually perceived evil.* The exercise of willing is termed 'volition.'

The Object of the Will

Experience shows that we strive for *material,* concrete, particular objects which seem good to us, such as food, sleep, money, exercise, health, and so forth. Over and above the sensible good, we strive also for the things of a supra-sensible and *spiritual* character, such as scientific knowledge, virtue, fame, esteem, and the like. Since our intellect abstracts the universal concept of 'good in general' from the single good objects, we strive for *good in general,* without a view toward any particular kind or class of objects.

When we perceive that this universal concept of good is realized in any 'particular' good, we can strive for this particular good, because it partakes of the general good which we have come to know and toward which the will inclines. Since we find the concept of the 'good in general' exemplified in material and immaterial things, the will is capable of striving for both classes of objects.

To have a universal concept of the 'good in general,' is an *intellectual* acquisition. Man abstracts that which is 'good' in all types of objects classified as 'good' and expresses the content of the 'good' in conceptual terms, formulating an intellectual definition of the 'good.' Something is 'good,' if it is suitable to a thing; abstractly speaking, *goodness* is the *suitability of a thing to a natural tendency or appetency.*

The general concept of the 'good' leads us to a consideration of what is the 'adequate' and the 'formal' object of the will.

The *adequate object* of the human will is *everything that is good.*

Every conscious *appetitive* power or appetency extends as far as its corresponding *cognitive* power. Sensory appetency can strive only for something that is a sensible good; it is limited to the concrete, material, particular, because the senses are restricted in their knowing capacity to the concrete, material, particular. The human will, however, has no such limitations. The intellect, absolutely speaking, is capable of knowing whatever is (ontologically) true. And since everything that is (ontologically) true is also (ontologically) good,[1] the intellect can apprehend all things under the aspect of 'goodness,' and the will, in consequence of this, can embrace with its striving power anything and everything that contains reality of whatever kind. *Everything,* therefore, that possesses 'being' and *is a being* (God and creature, the material and

[1] 'Goodness' and 'truth' are transcendental attributes of 'being,' so that every being, in so far as it is a being, is also 'good' and 'true.' These attributes are essentially identical. See the author's *Domain of Being* (Bruce, 1939), Ch. XIV.

immaterial) *belongs to the adequate object of the will* as a rational appetency, because every being is a 'good' in some form or other.

The *formal object* of the human will is *the good as good* (*bonum qua tale*), provided it be *suitable to the willing subject* in some manner.

By this assertion we claim that the will cannot desire a good object in so far as it is an evil in any way, but only *in so far as it is a good strictly as such.* Nor can the will ever desire an evil precisely as an evil. Whatever the will desires it must desire under the aspect of a 'good.'

The will is an appetitive power, and it is the essence of an appetitive power to strive for things, so as to bring about a union between the striving subject and the desired thing. Now, if it were possible for an appetitive power to strive for the evil as such and shun the good as such, it would by its very nature seek the *destruction* of the subject. An appetitive power of this kind, however, would be a perverse and contradictory reality, a useless and destructive tendency, existing in man as an integral part of his constitution; the creation of such a being, however, would be contrary to the wisdom of the Creator.

Again, the will is given to man as the rational complement of his intellect, in order that he may strive in a better manner than the sentiently cognitive brute for that which is conducive to his rational nature. Now, the natural tendencies of the brute are directed exclusively toward the good. Consequently, the human will also has as its natural object the good exclusively, otherwise it would be *less perfect* than the sensory appetency of the *brute;* in fact, it would be much *worse,* because the will dominates the sensory appetency in man and can hinder it from executing its natural tendencies. It follows, then, that the proper and formal object of the will is the 'good as such.'

In order, however, that the will be able to strive actually and effectively for a thing, this thing must be a *good for the subject* using the will; it must be *suitable* in some manner to the subject and must be intellectually perceived as such by the subject. Only the good is desirable, and it is desirable only because it assists in some manner toward perfecting the individual person who strives for it. After all, the will is a personal power, given for the benefit of the person possessing it; otherwise there would be no relation between will and object for this particular person.

The will itself is said to be *blind*, because it is not a cognitive power; it is an appetency or appetitive power. The intellect must furnish the necessary judgment as to whether a particular thing is a good or evil for the person; the will then strives for the good and shuns the evil. Ultimately, of course, it is the *human person who thinks and wills;* the human person perceives the goodness in a thing with his intellect and strives for it with his will, perceives the evil in a thing with his intellect and shuns it with his will.

Types of the Good

In as much as the adequate object of the will is everything that is good, it is well to know the different classes of the good. The main divisions of classification are as follows:

Ontological, Physical, Moral Good. A thing is an *ontological* good, when it is a good in its very *entity* or *reality*. Every being, since it possesses a certain amount of entity or reality, is an ontological good, because its entity or reality is suitable for the tendency of its own nature to be what it is and to perfect itself and to retain its perfection.

A thing is a *physical* good, when it satisfies the demand of the *nature of a being*. Each being has its own specific and individual nature, and as such it has a very definite end and purpose. What suits one nature does not necessarily suit another. The physical exigencies of man, for instance, differ from those of a horse, a cow, a bird, a fish, or a tree. Whatever suits such a specific or individual nature, perfecting it in some way, is a physical good. Thus, for man sight, hearing, well-functioning organs of digestion, etc., are physical goods.

A thing is a *moral* good, when it has everything demanded of it by the *moral law*. An action, for example, may be physically perfect, but it may contravene the moral law; in that case, it would be physically good but morally evil.

Absolute and Relative Good. An *absolute* good is anything suitable *to a being itself,* irrespective of other beings. Any reality which a being possesses, whether substantial or accidental, is an absolute good for that being; in man, for example, all bodily structures, organs, powers, and functions are absolute goods. A *relative* good is anything which is suitable *to another being;* food, drink, clothes, shelter, etc., are relative goods for man.

Objective and Subjective Good. An *objective* good is anything that is a good *in itself.* Any absolute or relative good, as just defined, is an objective good in this sense. By *subjective* good we mean the actual *possession* of an objective good. An artistic painting, for instance, is an objective good in itself; it becomes a subjective good for me, if I acquire it as my own.

Real and Apparent Good. A good is *real,* when it is judged to be good for a being, and it *actually is* good for that particular being. The nature, bodily limbs, senses, intellect, will, etc., are real goods for man. Something is an *apparent* good, when it is judged to be good for a being, but it is *actually not good* for it. A certain kind of food many seem a 'real' good for a critically ill patient, but it may be very harmful; under the circumstances it is an 'apparent' good, even though it is something which, in itself and for itself, is ontologically good. Similarly, pleasure is a physical good; but if its enjoyment is in opposition to the moral law, it is an 'apparent' rather than a 'real' good, because the moral law must stand higher in man's estimation than pleasure.

Disinterested, Delectable, and Useful Good. A *disinterested* good (*bonum honestum*) is any good considered merely as *giving perfection,* irrespectively of any pleasure derived through its acquisition or from its possession; health, knowledge, virtue are such. A *delectable* good (*bonum delectabile*) is a relative good which gives *pleasure* and enjoyment. What is really desirable here is the thing itself which gives pleasure; oftentimes, however, the pleasure itself becomes the object of desire. Food, drink, companionship, the use of sex, etc., belong to this class. A *useful* good (*bonum utile*) is a relative good which is desired as a *means* to acquire perfection or pleasure; there is always an ulterior end in view when a good of this kind is desired. A game of golf, for example, is a useful good, desired as a means to promote one's health, to gain fame, to obtain the pleasure of companionship, and so on.

Every good is a *value*. Value is that which is 'perfect' or 'perfective.' Value, considered as something which is perfect, coincides with the absolute good, because it is identical with the reality, substantial and accidental, which a being possesses. Considered as something perfective, it coincides with the relative good, because its perfection is a good for another being. Everything, therefore, has 'value' in so far as it is a good for itself or for another. 'Goodness' and 'value' are thus seen to be synonymous terms, when viewed in their ultimate, metaphysical implications.

Evil and the Will

Evil is the antithesis of 'good.' *Evil* is the *unsuitability of something for a natural tendency or appetency.* It is not a being, but it is not a mere absence of being. It is the absence of a reality which ought to be present, of a reality due to a thing; it is a defect, a privation of reality — the *privation of a required good.*

In view of what has been said about the good as the formal object of the will, it should be fairly obvious that the will cannot desire the *evil as such.* If a being could desire an evil as such, it would strive for its own harm; however, according to all laws of nature, every being tends to preserve its own entity and perfection. The will naturally shuns the evil, just as it naturally desires the good; by the very fact that it is intrinsically necessitated to strive for the good, it is also intrinsically necessitated to shun the evil.

An objection is frequently advanced against this view. The opponents point out that people desire things that are *physically harmful* and *morally evil*. People eat and drink to excess, even though they realize that they are inflicting serious injury upon their system; they desire the amputation of a diseased member of their body; they seek illicit sex pleasure, well knowing that they are committing an immoral act. These and similar facts cannot be disputed.

The answer to this is simple. All creatural things are finite, limited in entity and consequently limited in their goodness. Because of this natural limitation of goodness, they are *not suitable* to the specific and individual nature of every other being; and in this respect they are an evil for some beings. In other words, creatural beings are ontologically good; but they are a 'relative evil' to a great many other beings, because they are unsuitable to them. When, therefore, a creatural being is desired, it is desired *because of the goodness* present in it, and not because it is a relative evil. In all such cases, the evil is the 'material' and 'indirect' object of the will, while the good is the 'formal' and 'direct' object of the will. We must remember that the will is blind and relies on the judgment of the intellect as to whether something is good or evil. The intellect, however, is fallible and often erroneously considers some things as altogether good and desirable which are only partially so or only so in certain circumstances and under certain conditions. Hence, whenever the will strives for something that is evil, it does so solely *under the aspect of a good.*

Experience proves this fact. We may know, for instance, that excess in drink will eventually ruin our health; if we nevertheless drink to excess, we do so because the pleasure derived from drinking is a present physical good which, as such, is desirable. Where the attainment of a physical good contravenes the moral law, we simply choose the minor (physical) good in preference to the greater (moral) good. Similarly, we choose a minor evil in preference to a greater evil, as when we decide to undergo a painful operation rather than die; the operation, however, is not chosen because it is an evil in itself, but because it is, compared with prolonged pain or death, a relative good which will lead to health and well-being for the organism as a whole. Even a person committing suicide does not strive for death because it is an evil, nor does he seek to take his life because he desires to rid himself of a good; he commits suicide because he considers the freedom from shame or sickness or poverty a greater good than living in shame, sickness, or poverty. 'Freedom from misery' is the good for which he is really striving; death is considered to be a useful good to bring about this freedom, a means toward a beneficial end, and under this aspect the suicide strives for a good and not for an evil. He is mistaken, of course, in his judgment; but that is beside the point.

In all instances where persons seem to strive for an evil, a close examination will show that they desire a 'real' good or, at the very least, an 'apparent' good in the object of their choice. The extreme case may happen that someone deliberately chooses what he knows is an evil for himself; he seems to make his choice out of sheer perverseness of will, entirely against his better judgment. Even in such a case, however, he does not seek an outright evil recognized as such. He chooses an evil through *pride in his ability to choose it;* the exercise of his pride and of his will is the motive of his action, and that appears to be a good for him worthy of choice.

Motive and Motivation

The activity of the will is closely linked to *desire*. Desire is a longing aroused by the conscious representation of an absent good. Some object or experience is represented to the subject and is recognized as a possible physical, intellectual, or moral 'good.' The object or experience thus represented produces in the subject an attraction toward this object or experience, with the result that the will has a natural tendency to seek its attainment; the will is 'moved' toward the attractive object or experience and is said to be influenced by a 'motive.'

A *motive,* then, is anything which prompts or excites the will to action. The object or experience must contain some sort of objective goodness in itself, in order to become a motive for the will, because only the good is desirable. But the mere presence of objective goodness alone does not suffice to make it a motive. The object or experience must be *apprehended* by the intellect as something good and therefore desirable, for nothing is willed except it be known (*nihil volitum nisi cognitum*). A double factor is thus involved in a motive: the objective factor of the goodness of the object or experience, and the subjective factor of the intellectual knowledge of this goodness on the part of the willing subject. Unless the object or experience be a good in itself, it cannot be desired; and unless the subject knows of its goodness, the subject cannot desire it. The good desired is thus a 'value.' And we can define a *motive* as *an appreciated value realizable through an act of volition.*

Since the will is entirely dependent on the intellect for the recognition of value (goodness), it is evident that the attractiveness of the motive lies more in the manner in which it is presented by the intellect than in the objective goodness. The objective goodness of one kind of object or experience may be far greater than that of another; yet, if the greater objective value is not recognized as such or not recognized at all, the minor value will have greater force. Similarly, a person may concentrate his attention upon one value, refusing to consider any other; under the circumstances the one value alone will act as a motive. Much, therefore, depends upon the actual knowledge, the intellectual and moral training, and the general temperament of the individual person, whether an object or experience will be a strong or weak motive or even a motive at all. Value is relative to the person desiring it, and for this reason the *intellectual presentation* of value as a motive is a most important factor in willing.

Motives may be *physical, intellectual,* or *moral.* Material objects and sensory experiences are physical goods, and as such they are 'physical' motives for volition; examples are food, shelter, wealth, the pleasures of sense. Intellectual attainments also influence the will to action and are 'intellectual' motives; knowledge and science are such values. Objects and experiences, which are commanded by the moral law or are in conformity with it, possess moral value and are 'moral' motives; the virtues belong to this class. We also differentiate between *inner* and *outer* motives. 'Inner' motives regard the self and its perfection, as when we strive for knowledge for the development of our mind; 'outer' motives regard other beings, as when a father strives for wealth in order to support his family. In general, there are as many kinds of motives as there are *kinds of goods.*

By *motivation* is meant the arousal of the will from a state of inaction into a state of action. Modern psychology includes under the heading of motivation various kinds of obscure psycho-somatic conditions, as feelings, organic movements, unconscious and subconscious drives, etc. Such conditions are more in the nature of general sets or attitudes than motives properly so-called. As explained above, a value, in order to be a genuine motive for the will to act, must be appreciated as a value, and hence must *enter consciousness* and be perceived as something desirable. Conscious apprehension is the first condition for motivation. The second condition is that a motive have *sufficient strength* to produce volition. We often hesitate to make a decision; it is then necessary to strengthen the motive, so as to help the will overcome its hesitancy. We may give more attention to the good under consideration, examining it from various viewpoints, and thereby convince ourselves that the value is really greater than was at first supposed. Or, we may compare a good with related evils, enhancing the value by contrast. Or, we may induce the will to strive for a certain good by adding some other motives, so that the weak motive receives strength from participation with stronger motives. Finally, we recall past experiences or resolutions, thus influencing the will to act, even though the present motive appears weak and insufficient of itself.

The more powerful the motives, the easier it is for the will to pass from indecision to decision. It must be remembered, however, that motives are only preliminary *conditions* of volition; they 'appeal' to the person to exercise his will. Motives reside in the intellect; the intellect makes the *practical judgment* that this or that thing is desirable and thereby elicits the act of the will. Motives thus set a goal for the striving of the will, and the practical judgment brings the goal into relation with the will. When conflicting motives are present, the relative objective strength of the motives does not, strictly speaking, decide the issue and compel the will to act; it is the person who decides which motive shall have the greatest weight.

Natural and Deliberate Volition

The internal acts of the will are by no means all alike. Volition appears in different modes, giving rise to distinct *types*. The two main types are *natural* and *deliberate* volition.

It lies in the very essence of the will as an appetency to incline toward the good and, as a consequence, to shun the evil. Its ultimate end and purpose is to strive for *happiness* or *beatitude*. By happiness or beatitude is meant a perfect state acquired through the possession of all that is good for a being. Such a state excludes any and every kind of evil; conversely, it embraces every kind of good required for the complete satisfaction and perfection of the nature of the respective being.

The will cannot be indifferent toward happiness. If the intellect proposes happiness to the will as an object for its volition, the will must approve of it and consent to it; if the will acts at all, it must incline toward it with love and desire. It is *not free* in this respect. Man seeks his happiness with necessity, not through choice. Since the good is the formal object of the will, and since happiness or beatitude is fullness of good, the will, by its very nature, *must* strive for it. Because of this fact, this type of volition is termed *natural* volition. The only choice in this matter within the power of the will is to divert the attention of the intellect away from the thought of happiness and force it to think of something else. Under no circumstances, however, can the will be really indifferent toward happiness; much less can the will's attitude toward it be one of displeasure or aversion, because that would contradict the inmost nature of the will as a rational appetitive power of man.

Generally speaking, we experience the possibility of preference and choice in volition, when values are presented to the will for acceptance. As stated before, creatural beings possess only limited goodness and they are not suitable for every kind of being to the same degree; they may be desirable from one viewpoint and undesirable from another. Particular objects and experiences satisfy our wants only partially. When such values confront the intellect and the will, none of them are so attractive as to compel acceptance to the exclusion of the rest. The situation demands an examination of values, a weighing of motives, a consideration of alternatives. After some *deliberation* over the respective merits of the particular values proposed, a preferential choice is made among these conflicting values, and the will goes into action. This type of volition, which results in consequence of a deliberation, is termed *deliberate* volition.

When a preference is given to a value after careful deliberation, so that we are conscious of the reasons for choosing as we do, our choice is said to be *reasonable*. When we have not the time for careful deliberation, or are not inclined to give much thought to reasons for preference, and resolve our hesitancy by making an impulsive and offhand decision, our choice is said to be *impetuous*. When we make a decision through force of habit, by following the line of least resistance, by submissively giving way to other people's suggestions, and so forth, our choice is said to be *acquiescent*. When we decide on a course of action which is important, beset with difficulties, and which involves serious and prolonged effort, our choice is said to be *grave*. And when our choice runs counter to cherished interests and demands a painful renunciation and struggle, all for the sake of a duty to be performed, our choice is said to be *conscientious.*[2]

Voluntary Control

By *voluntary control* we understand the control which the will exercises over the powers and actions of the human organism. This control, as it is commonly conceived, is exercised by the will by means of a 'command': the will issues a command to a power to go into action, and the action follows.

Everyday *experience* convinces us that we have voluntary control over powers and actions of our own person. Through an act of the will we direct the course of our thoughts in solving a problem; we set the associative mechanism of the imagination going, consciously combining and dissociating images according to a definite plan; we control the movements of our eyes and of its focusing apparatus, forcing them to look at the objects we desire to inspect; we command our tongue and lips to speak, our legs to walk or run, our hands to write or type or manipulate a machine, our body to stand erect or lie down or bend forward; and so on, with a hundred and one different kinds of actions.

Voluntary control, however, is not universal, nor is it uniform in effectiveness. Some activities of the human body are *not subject* to voluntary control. We need but mention the activity which takes place in the *cells.* The functions of the *vegetative organs* can be controlled only *indirectly* by the will. The metabolic processes go forward day and night without interruption. The will cannot stop the beat of the heart, the digestion of the stomach, or the secretion of the kidneys by any direct command. Indirectly it can influence their action; for example, through the withholding or selection of food materials, the injection of drugs, the arousal of emotional states, overexercise, dissipation, etc. We have also indirect control

---

[2] See William James, *Principles of Psychology* (H. Holt, 1931), Vol. II, Ch. XXVI, pp. 531 ff.

over the functions of the *external senses,* mainly by control of the stimuli which activate the senses. Once the stimuli have impinged upon the sense organs, we cannot hinder them from carrying out their proper functions; but it is possible for us to control, at least in many instances and to a considerable extent, the chemical and physical agencies which influence these organs and thereby also their functions.

We have *direct,* though not absolute, control over *bodily movements* through the striped muscles, over the activities of the *internal senses,* and over the *intellect.* That we normally control the movements of our bodily members in walking, writing, etc., by a direct act of volition, is evident from experience. Though much of the activity of the synthetic sense, the imagination, and sensory memory is spontaneous, their activity is also to a great extent subject to the direct control of the will. Regarding the intellect, the will cannot, of course, compel it to deny an obvious fact or principle, nor can the will force it to accept a contradiction. It can and does, however, direct the attention of the intellect to this or that fact or principle, and thereby it directly controls its activity along certain lines of thought. Similarly, when the evidence is conflicting and certitude is impossible, the will can influence the intellect to resolve its doubts by forming a definite opinion. It happens quite frequently that the intellect passes a judgment on a matter, not so much according to objective evidence, but according to the inclinations and desires of the will. Shakespeare expressed this fact saying that "The wish is father to the thought." Many erroneous opinions, snap judgments, hasty generalizations, and prejudices can be traced to the direct control of the will over the activity of the intellect.

Concerning *voluntary movements,* one phenomenon deserves particular consideration; it is the *gradual mechanization* of such movements under the influence of volition. Many movements involve the co-ordinated activity of a large number of nerves and muscles in an intricate series of part movements. Psychologists speak of such a neuro-muscular co-ordination as a *kinetic unit.* Kinetic units are present in movements of everyday life, as walking, lifting, grasping articles with the hands, etc., and in skilled actions, as typewriting, playing a musical instrument, pole-vaulting, etc. One need but watch an expect musician play a piece on a piano, in order to observe the marvelous co-ordination of nerves and muscles required for this performance. The remarkable thing about these movements is the fact that the will merely intends the *series in general,* and then the movements follow almost unconsciously and mechanically; oftentimes, as we know, the performance is actually carried out unconsciously. How are kinetic units established?

Some kinetic units are not acquired and learned; they are *hereditary.* John B. Watson and M. G. Blanton, through observations made on infants, have established the fact that children possess some kinetic units from birth as a native endowment. Examples are: the neuro-muscular co-ordination required to fixate and follow a moving light or object with the eyes, grasping an object with the whole hand, kicking, and so forth. In most cases, however, the component parts of a complicated movement must be pieced together by *direct volition.* Repetition fuses the component parts into a kinetic unit, so that less and less attention and voluntary control need be given to the component parts. Frequent repetition then makes a *habit* of the entire movement. As a consequence, all that is needed in order to carry out the entire movement, without any conscious attention to the details, is to make an initial act of the will intending the movement as a whole, and the neuro-muscular system takes care of the rest. Voluntary movement has thus become gradually 'mechanized.' We intend, for instance, to walk to a friend's house; having willed the action, we automatically walk along the street, our attention being engrossed by the things we see. Similarly, a pianist, after deciding to play, let us say, the 'Humoresque,' renders the composition with flawless accuracy, practically unconscious of the movements of his arms and fingers while he imagines the melody.

Bodily movements, therefore, may be actually, virtually, or habitually voluntary. A movement is *actually* voluntary, when it is willed directly here and now, as when I decide at this moment to write these words. It is *virtually* voluntary, when a particular movement is a component part of a kinetic unit and I will the entire unit; by deciding to perform the entire movement as a whole, I virtually will the component parts of the entire movement. When, for example, the entire movement of an extended stroll is actually willed, the single steps are virtually included in this general act of volition. A movement is *habitually* voluntary, when at present it is mechanized through a neuro-muscular co-ordination which, though built up on a former occasion through repetition by means of distinct voluntary acts, now carries out the movement automatically without attention and without conscious voluntary control. A stenographer, for example, acquires 'word-habits' which enable her to type entire words, even when conversing with someone.

Kinetic units, except for the limited number which are inherited as native endowments, must be acquired through direct voluntary control. Once acquired, however, we need but will the *end-result* of the entire action; association and habit complete the action. Directing one's attention or volition to the component parts of the action nearly always exerts a disturbing and inhibiting influence upon its smooth performance. Kinetic units are but another illustration of the fact that man is an integral organism in which everything conspires toward his general well-being.

What N. Ach (1905, 1910) called *determining tendencies,* is of a similar character. In his experiments on volition, Ach discovered that the subjects, after making an act of the will or resolution to perform a certain task, carried out this task even when they no longer adverted to the resolution formerly made. Having accepted the task of multiplying the numbers which would be flashed on a screen or of making a rhyme to a nonsense syllable when given, they performed the task, notwithstanding the fact that their mind was diverted at the time by other thoughts and they had forgotten about their former resolution. Ach rightly concluded that such results were intelligent operations and could not be accounted for by the mere association of images. Accordingly, he postulated the existence of some sort of psychic force which, acting subconsciously, proceeded from the resolution and carried out the task to a correct conclusion. This force he called a 'determining tendency.'

There seems, however, to be no need of postulating such a psychic force distinct from the will and other powers of the mind. J. Lindworsky[3] (1922), an eminent authority on the will, opposed Ach's concept of the determining tendency as a new force. He pointed out that 'voluntary attention,' when applied to an image complex, is sufficient to explain the facts. Whenever we will something and include it in a specific resolution, we must turn the intellect toward the task intended, thereby giving attention to the objective of our willing. The image complex involved in the performance of the task is thus singled out and strengthened in preference to others. Kinetic units accompany such an image complex to a great extent. Since a particular image complex is thus favored, it will lead to the desired operation in consequence of the initial resolution, even when the resolution itself is not immediately present in consciousness. In this respect the execution of the task resembles virtual or habitual voluntary actions.

The Existence of Volition

The question before us now is not the question of the freedom of the will; rather, it is the question whether *volition* exists as an operation distinct from previously considered and acknowledged mental states. It is also the question whether man possesses a *will* distinct from other mental powers. If volition is not a distinct type of operation, then the will does not exist as a distinct power or man; on the other hand, if volition is a distinct type of operation, then its

[3] *Training of the Will,* 4th ed. (Bruce, 1929), pp. 28 ff.

existence also demands the will as the power from which it proceeds.

The existence of the will and of volition is denied or ignored by many modern psychologists. If they do speak of 'voluntary control' or 'voluntary action,' it is done in deference to popular views and expressions; their explanations show that they identify volition with some other elements of mental life which are decidedly not 'voluntary' in the philosophic sense of the term, namely, sensations, images, feelings, or sensory appetitions.

T. V. Moore[4] sums up the evidence for the existence of volition as a distinct mental operation under the following comprehensive headings:

Facts of Attention. Practically all books on modern experimental psychology, when treating of the mental process of attention in man, distinguish between *involuntary* and *voluntary attention.* The facts themselves are plain. If someone shrieks into our ear, or if a fire engine's siren wails past us on the street, or if we fall and hurt ourselves painfully, or if someone pushes us forcefully, or if a bright light is turned on when we are in a dark room, or if we inadvertently take a pinch of quinine into our mouth — our attention is drawn to the circumstances, no matter how occupied our mind may be. We simply cannot avoid noticing these things; we involuntarily give our attention to them, because they *force* themselves upon our attention. In many instances, however, our attention is *deliberately decided* by ourselves, *directed* toward something which is in no way conspicuous, and *personally controlled* throughout the duration of its existence. We can, for example, direct our attention upon a particular blade of grass, a particular page in a book, a particular spot on the wall, a particular person in a crowd, etc., and then deliberately direct it to a different blade, page, spot, person; and this is done simply because we decide to do so, without there being anything in these things to attract our attention in a special manner.

---

[4] *Dynamic Psychology,* pp. 312 ff.

Resolving on a Task. When a task is proposed to us by somebody, or when we propose a task to ourselves, we are conscious that it rests with us to accept or refuse it. When we resolve to accept the task, we experience a certain *determination* on our part to carry out the task, and this determination is something very different from the accompanying sensations, images, feelings, and motives. These latter may drop out of consciousness after a while, but the determination of the resolution may persevere for hours, days, and even years, influencing the very course of our life. Sensations, images, feelings, and intellectual acts of insight are fleeting realities, while the resolution is a persistent fact of mental life extending over and beyond these passing states.

Reaction-time Experiments. Psychologists have made experiments with subjects relative to the time required to make a choice to do something or not to do it, and to make a choice to do one thing or another thing. In all experiments of this kind, it was found that the subjects arrived first at a stage of readiness or preparedness to go into action, but the action itself would not follow until a distinct choice had been made and the *command* or *fiat* had been issued to proceed with the action. This 'command' or 'fiat' was distinct from an understanding of the various actions contemplated and the particular action chosen. The command was a distinct element in the total process.

Control of Emotions. While it is not possible to control our emotions directly, it is possible to control them indirectly, namely, by a direction of our attention. Bringing the *causes* of the emotion into the focus of our attention, intensifies the emotion, as when we think of the insult which causes our anger. However, when we concentrate our attention on the emotion itself and analyze it, our emotion evaporates rapidly. It is precisely the *effort to divert our attention* away from the cause of emotion toward the emotion itself that manifests voluntary control, because under these circumstances we work in opposition to the natural stimulus of the emotion.

Inhibition of Impulses and Desires. Impulses and desires are the springs of action, and normally they lead to the execution of the actions prompted by them. We observe this fact plainly in the brutes; they actively strive for the sensory good and actively shun the sensory evil. In so far as man has a sensory nature, he is on a par with the brutes and in many respects acts accordingly. Not always, however. Many times he curbs and *inhibits* his natural impulses and desires, often under conditions which entail great effort and sacrifice. Although the natural impulses and desires drive to action, the action fails to result. Man thus acts or desists from acting from a sense of duty or because of an ideal of conduct which he has set for himself to follow. Now, a sense of duty and an ideal of conduct, placed in opposition to impulses and desires in this manner, is something rational and supra-sensory, and demands the activity of an appetency which is also rational and supra-sensory.

Readjustment of the Mode of Life. It happens occasionally, through illness, financial reverses, death in the family, the collapse of a business, etc., that a person is forced to adopt an entirely new plan of life. The readjustment required is both difficult and painful. By shirking this responsibility, one could follow the line of least resistance and avoid much unpleasantness; by changing one's mode of life completely, one must follow the line of greatest resistance and make many sacrifices. Natural inclination prompts persons to adopt the former course. Yet it occurs not infrequently that persons adopt the latter; but in doing so, they are conscious of a great effort, a momentous decision, and a strong determination, in opposition to their inmost natural wishes and inclinations. The existence of volition as a unique mental state, as an internal act of a distinct mental power, is most evident in experiences of this kind.

Moore is right, when he concludes that no kinesthetic sensations, no feelings of being happy or sad, and no complex of images can account for these facts. The facts demand 'volition' and a 'will.'

The same conclusion must be drawn from the *experiments*

on volition made by Ach. In the course of the experiments, his subjects experienced various kinds of sensations, feelings, emotions, images, and intellectual judgments. What distinguished volition from these mental states was the fact that they clearly perceived the *Ego-in-action* in every deliberate decision as the *originator* of the act of willing, and not merely as the subject in which volition occurred. It was precisely this *active interposition of the Ego* in deciding an issue and in making a deliberate choice which manifested the act of the will to them as an experience distinct from all other conscious processes. The experimental work of A. Michotte, Prüm, and of H. M. Wells on the psychology of choosing confirmed the data of Ach. The voluntary action of choice was effected by a definite decision made through an active interposition of the Ego.

Volition, then, is an operation *differing in kind* from other operations and elements of our mental life. As such, it must be the activity of a *specific power,* the will; and the will is in truth, as previously defined, a 'rational appetency.'

Summary of Chapter XV

Besides sense-perception, sensuous appetency, and intellection, man experiences *volition,* the activity of the *will,* as a phase of his mental life.

1. *The Concept of the Will.* Man's everyday life manifests many attitudes and acts which reveal the activity of the will. The will is conceived and defined as *rational appetency* or the power to strive for an intellectually perceived good and to shun an intellectually perceived evil.

2. *The Object of the Will.* We strive for material and spiritual things which seem good to us. From the individual things which are good the intellect abstracts the universal concept of the 'good in general.' 'Goodness' is the suitability of a thing to a natural tendency or appetency.

The *adequate object* of the human will is *everything that is good.*

The *formal object* of the human will is *the good as good,* provided it be *suitable to the willing subject.* Whatever is an object of the will, is striven for under the aspect of a 'good.'

3. *Types of the Good.* We distinguish between the ontological, the physical, and the moral good; between the absolute and the relative good; between the objective and the subjective good; between the real and the apparent good; between the disinterested, the delectable, and the useful good. Every good is a 'value,' recognized and appreciated as something perfect or perfective.

4. *Evil and the Will.* Evil is the privation of a required good. By the fact that the will is necessitated by its very nature to strive for the good it is also necessitated to shun evil. When people desire things that are physically harmful or morally evil, they do so because they consider such things to be a 'good' for them.

5. *Motive and Motivation.* A *motive* is an appreciated value realizable through an act of volition. A *double factor* is involved in a motive: the objective factor of the goodness of the object or experience, and the subjective factor of the intellectual knowledge of this goodness on the part of the willing subject.

Motives may be of a physical, intellectual, or moral character; there are also inner and outer motives.

By *motivation* is meant the arousal of the will from a state of inaction into a state of action. Motives reside in the intellect; the intellect makes the *practical judgment* that this or that thing is desirable and thereby elicits the act of the will.

6. *Natural and Deliberate Volition.* Since the good is the formal object of the will, and since *happiness* is the fulness of good, the will, by its very nature, must strive for happiness; this kind of striving is *natural volition.* Volition is said to be deliberate when, after a consideration of the respective merits of particular values, a preferential choice is made.

7. *Voluntary Control.* By voluntary control we understand the control which the will exercises over the powers and actions of the human organism. Experience proves that we

exercise voluntary control, though this control is neither universal nor uniform. We have *no control* over the functions of the cells. The functions of the vegetative organs and of the external senses are subject to *indirect* control. We have *direct* control in some measure over bodily movements, over the activities of the internal senses, and over the intellect. Voluntary movements have a tendency to become gradually 'mechanized.' Some kinetic units are hereditary; most of them, however, are acquired by direct volition through repetition of acts. Movements may be *actually, virtually* or *habitually* voluntary. *Determining tendencies* resemble virtual or habitual voluntary actions.

8. *The Existence of Volition.* That volition, as a distinct type of mental experience, actually exists, is proved from the facts of *attention,* from *resolving* on a task, from *reaction-time* experiments, from the *control of emotions,* from the *inhibition* of impulses and desires, and from *readjustments* of the mode of life.

Experiments on volition reveal the Ego-in-action in every deliberate decision as the *originator* of the act of willing, so that the active interposition of the Ego manifests the act of the will as an experience distinct from all other conscious processes. The act of willing, therefore, demands a *specific power,* the will.

Readings

Moore, T. V., *Dynamic Psychology,* Part VI, Ch. I–V. — Maher, M., *Psychology,* Ch. XVIII. — Brennan, R. E., *General Psychology,* pp. 347–364. — Gruender, H., *Experimental Psychology,* Ch. XVII. — Lindworsky, Johannes, *Der Wille; The Training of the Will,* Ch. I. — James, W., *The Principles of Psychology,* Vol. II, Ch. XXVI.

Chapter XVI

FREEDOM OF WILL

MAN has a will—a specific power with a distinctive activity. It reacts to the motives presented to it by the intellect. Motives are values which prompt the will to conative action; and usually the will seeks to attain the value which is perceived to possess the greatest amount of realizable good under the prevailing circumstances.

The influence of motives brings up the problem of the *freedom of the will.* It would seem that the predominant motive must always prevail over the will and force it to act. If this were so, freedom of the will could hardly exist. Yet it is the universal conviction of mankind that man has a free will. On what grounds is this conviction based? Is it a rationally justified conviction? Or is it merely an illusion?

The question is of paramount importance, because the entire structure of man's individual and social life rests upon the concept of the freedom of his will. If the human will is free, man is indeed the most privileged creature in the universe; but if it is not free, our entire educational, social, and moral system must be discarded or revised.

Statement of the Problem

The term 'freedom' is used in different meanings. In order to avoid confusion of thought, it is imperative to clarify the concept of freedom as it applies to the will.

In the *widest* sense, freedom is the *absence of external coercion* or restraint which hinders an appetency from expressing itself in external action. A man locked in a room or held by physical force, so that he cannot do as he pleases or is forced to do what he does not want to do, lacks external freedom; when the restraining force is removed, he has 'freedom from coercion.' This type of freedom applies to bodily movements and has nothing to do with the will.

In the *strict* sense, *freedom* means *the absence of intrinsic necessity or determination in the performance of an act.* Something is 'intrinsically necessary,' when it is determined by its very nature to be what it is and to act as it does. This type of 'freedom' applies to the will when we speak of 'free will,' and we mean that the will is free from intrinsic necessity or determination in *at least some* of its acts. Hence, when it is said that the will is 'free,' it is implied that the will is not necessitated by its nature to act in a determined manner, but is *capable of choice even when all the conditions for acting are present.*

The advocates of free will do not claim that the will is free in every respect. They admit that it is governed by intrinsic necessity or determination in seeking happiness, as was pointed out in the foregoing chapter. They also admit that the will in many circumstances acts impulsively and indeliberately. They admit further that certain mental states and conditions make it impossible for the will to exercise its freedom or impair its freedom to such an extent that responsibility is wholely or partially lacking. Such states are sleep, profound absent-mindedness, delirium, pronounced narcosis, hypnosis, marked emotional unbalance, insanity, and in general all disturbances of attention which hinder the intellect from giving proper consideration to a motive. These factors, however, are extrinsic to the will itself.

The *conditions* required for the exercise of free will are: a normal state of attention; an objectively indifferent judgment of the intellect; and a conflict of motives resulting from such an objectively indifferent judgment.

A normal state of *attention* is required. The will can desire only what the intellect proposes to it as good. Obviously, then, anything that interferes with the normal state of attention interferes with the proper judgment of the intellect and thereby with the proper act of the will. An *objectively indifferent judgment* of the intellect is required. In order that a free choice of the will be possible, the intellect must judge that a certain object or act or situation is good under one aspect but evil under another; if the object or act or situation were judged to be altogether good and therefore essential for happiness, the will would of necessity strive for it, and freedom of choice would be impossible. Given this objectively indifferent judgment, a *conflict of motives* arises, and that is a condition which is also required for the exercise of free will. The will cannot desire an evil as such; it can desire only a good. In order, then, that the will be able to exercise its freedom, it must choose between two or more goods which act as motives; in other words, there must be a conflict of motives, before there can be a choice between them. The freedom of the will consists precisely in this that it has the power of self-determination in arbitrarily choosing between conflicting motives. The intellectual judgment which presents an object or act or situation to the will as 'objectively indifferent,' that is to say, as being something which is neither altogether good nor altogether evil, is termed the *root of freedom*. Since the will itself is 'subjectively indifferent' toward the presented motives, the freedom of the will is sometimes termed the *freedom of indifference*. And since this subjective indifference enables the will to make an arbitrary choice between motives, the freedom of the will is also designated the *freedom of choice*.

The will exercises its free choice in three distinct ways, and correspondingly we distinguish between *three types of freedom* in the acts of the will.

First, there is the *freedom of exercise* or *contradiction*. The will can choose freely between willing and not willing, between acting and not acting. Since it is a question here of the will exercising or not exercising its power of choice, it is called 'freedom of exercise'; and since exercising and not exercising are contradictory opposites, it is also called 'freedom of contradiction.' A person, for example, can freely choose between studying and not studying, between eating a piece of candy or not eating a piece of candy.

Second, there is the *freedom of specification.* From this point of view, the will can choose freely between one object and another object and therefore also between one act of the will and another act of the will; it specifies which kind of object or act shall be the goal of its choice. A person, for example, decides freely whether he shall study or take a stroll, whether he shall eat a piece of chocolate or a caramel.

Third, there is the *freedom of contrariety.* The will possesses the freedom of choosing freely between a moral good and a moral evil. Good and evil are contrary opposites. A person, for example, can choose freely between telling the truth and telling a lie, between acting chastely and acting impurely. The freedom of contrariety can be reduced to one of the first two, since it is a choice either between acting or not acting or between one object and another object.

From the above it should be clear that the freedom of the will does *not consist* in *motiveless* volition. The will cannot act without a motive of some kind, because it can desire an object or an experience only in so far as it is intellectually apprehended as 'good.' Nor does it consist in *causeless* volition. The self or person possessing the will is the cause of the free act of the will. The will is not a thing apart, existing and acting independent of the person or self who is the abiding subject of the will. The motive is the moral cause, and the person or self is the efficient cause. It is permissible to say that the will is the cause of its own act, provided it be understood that the will and its act must ultimately be referred to the person or self as the agent operating through the will.

Free will is *defined* as *the ability of the will, all conditions for action being present, to decide whether to act or not to act and whether to act in this manner or in that manner.* From a psychological standpoint, free will is the ability to choose arbitrarily between conflicting motives through the active interposition of the Ego. Many authors define it briefly as 'the power of self-determination.'

The *essence* of the freedom of the will, as just defined, consists in indetermination, so that the will, no matter what the strength of the conflicting motives or the nature of the antecedent external and internal conditions for action may be, is *not determined to act by necessity*. This doctrine is therefore designated as *indeterminism* or *libertarianism*. This indeterminism, however, is not absolute, because in the pursuit of 'happiness' the will is, as stated before, determined. We advocate, then, a *relative* or *moderate indeterminism*.

Determinism

The doctrine opposed to free will is styled *determinism* or *necessitarianism*. Modern psychology has adopted the former term. According to this doctrine, the will is not intrinsically free, but is determined by the antecedent psychical and physical conditions and causes to act as it does; it is necessitated in its volition. Determinism appears in a variety of forms.

Among the ancients, many held the view that the entire course of man's life is predetermined by an inexorable *fate* or *destiny*. Astrology is akin to this. Some Christian sects denied the existence of free will; the activity of creatures is only apparent, because *God alone* is active. In modern times, we find free will denied by *materialists* and *pantheists*. The materialists admit the existence of nothing but matter and material activities. Since matter is governed completely by the necessary laws controlling chemical, physical, and mechanical agencies, there is no place for a free-acting cause like free will. The will is determined in its volition by physical factors, such as the hereditary constitution of man and the environment in which he lives, and by psychical factors, such as images, feelings, emotions, and the preponderance of motives. If 'psychical' factors are mentioned, they are usually considered to be mere refinements and complexes of material factors. The pantheists maintain that all reality is ultimately one, God or the Absolute. The world, man included, is but a phase in the eternal evolution of the Absolute, and this evolution takes place according to laws which operate with inevitable necessity. There is no freedom of action anywhere. Among the materialistic theories denying free will we must place the philosophical systems of associationism, positivism, and behaviorism; the systems of Spinoza, Fichte, Schelling, Hegel, and their offshoots are representative of pantheism in one form or other. All are deterministic.

Some modern philosophers and psychologists speak of the will as if they admitted its freedom of action. Analysis of their ideas and explanations, however, reveals that they interpret 'free will' in a fashion which is either a perversion of the true concept of freedom or which makes the will so dependent on the conditioning factors as to preclude genuine indeterminacy. It is a case of what William James has described as "soft determinism."

Relative Indeterminism

What, then, is the *true problem* of free will?

It is this: All the conditions and circumstances required for volition being given, is the will, when confronted by *conflicting motives* presented by the intellect in a normal state of attention and deliberation, *compelled and determined to decide for one of the motives* to the exclusion of the others? Or, on the contrary, everything given as just stated, is it within the ability of the will, through the *active interposition of the Ego,* to make an *arbitrary choice* between these conflicting motives, *irrespective of their relative attraction,* by simply *determining itself to choose* any one of the motives and thereby conferring a *subjective preference* on this one over the others? If the former alternative is verified, there is no freedom of the will; if the latter, then the will is truly free in at least some of its acts.

We claim that the will is truly free, as specified, in *some* of its acts; that is all that is needed to disprove the universal determinism advocated by the determinists. The proofs for the truth of the freedom of the will are of three kinds: psychological, based on the evidence of our conscious experience; ethical, based on the concepts of right and wrong; and metaphysical, based on the philosophical concept of the will as a rational appetency. These proofs will now be treated individually.

Psychological Proof

As a preliminary observation, it must be stressed that the court of last appeal in matters of knowledge is consciousness; the testimony of our consciousness is the ultimate criterion of natural truth for man. If this criterion is rejected by a philosopher or psychologist, all knowledge must end in universal skepticism.[1]

Our consciousness gives indubitable testimony to the fact that our *will is free in many of its acts.*

By means of an *introspective analysis* of the *will in action,* I am conscious that the will is not only capable of arbitrary choice between motives, but actually makes such an arbitrary choice. True, motives are present, and these motives attract the will to action; at the same time, however, I am conscious that these motives do not force the will to action, but leave it *within the power* of the will, notwithstanding the attractiveness of the motives, to act or not to act, to act this way or that way. The will settles the issue through an active interposition of the Ego, by deciding simply *as it pleases.*

Everyday experience proves this contention conclusively. The idea presents itself to me to take a stroll; but I am also inclined to continue with the reading of this interesting book. Both are pleasant to me. What shall I do? I realize that it is entirely up to me 'to make up my mind.' Neither motive is compelling. I decide to take a stroll. Shall I go to the left or to the right? I have no particular preference; there is certainly no necessity to go in one direction rather than in the other. But which shall it be? Let it be to the right; "it makes no difference anyhow." And to the right I stroll. During this entire procedure I am conscious that in the final analysis everything I do depends upon my *free decision;* my will is not determined, except in so far as it *determines itself* to act.

The fact of free decision is brought out very clearly in so-

[1] See the author's *Reality and the Mind* (Bruce, 1936), Ch. VI.

called *indifferent acts.* I lift my hand, for instance, about six inches above the table, palm upward. I can now deflect it one inch (or shall it be two inches? or three?) to the right or the left; I can also leave it as it is. I can crook my index finger (or shall it be the little finger? or the thumb?); I can also leave the hand as it is. What motive have I for doing any of these things? There is no motive in the actions themselves which prompts or necessitates me. The only motive I can discover is this: I merely *want to;* it is *my will* to do so; I can *do as I like.* The will acts simply because it *decides* to act rather than not act in the described manner, and there is nothing that compels it. The particular actions, taken for themselves, are indifferent; the decision lies completely and freely in the power of the will. Many actions are performed in this way.

In particular, a number of mental processes reveal the free will in action.

Attention. Attention, besides manifesting the existence of volition as a distinctive mental operation, also manifests the 'freedom' of the will. Attention is often *selective* and *preferential,* due to a free decision on our part. In working out a problem, in preparing an address, in pursuing a discussion on some topic, etc., we are conscious of the fact that *we ourselves* direct the marshaling of our ideas, force some of them to dwell in our consciousness longer than others, divert the entire train of ideas into other channels, recall them for further consideration, dismiss them at our pleasure, and so forth. We can restrict our attention exclusively to motives of less agreeableness, if we so desire, and give these the preponderance. In fact, it lies in our power of the will to be or not to be attentive, and just how long and how intensively to be attentive. In all phases of voluntary attention we are conscious that we are the *free cause* of the operation.

Deliberation. It is a fact of experience that we often deliberate on the merits of conflicting motives, ask counsel from others as to what course we should pursue, and so on. We are conscious that it lies in our power to deliberate or not to deliberate. If we decide to deliberate at all, it is in our power to carry on the deliberation for hours or days or months or only for minutes. We can interrupt and resume our deliberations as we please. No matter what the motives and their strength may be at the moment, we can withhold our decision and look for counter-motives. All the while we are conscious that this process of deliberation is freely inaugurated, freely continued, and freely terminated by the active interposition of the Ego; and this process is perceived to be totally different from the familiar impulsive character of many actions which occur in our life more or less against our will. Motives are present, certainly, but our consciousness is witness to the fact that they do not compel our consent.

Decision in Matters of Conduct. In the course of a temptation, we are irresistibly convinced that consent lies in our free power, to give or to withhold. We are very much attracted by the allurement of the temptation; to consent means to follow the line of least resistance, while to resist means to follow the line of greatest resistance. We resist, though the effort is very painful, and we know that thereby we are struggling against the preponderant motive, the motive of greatest attraction. It amounts to what William James has called "deliberately thrusting a thorn in one's flesh." The main point here, too, is the consciousness that it would be easy to yield and that the yielding would be a free decision of our will, just as resisting is a difficult matter and is the laborious result of a hard-fought volitional battle freely undertaken. No quibbling can shake our conviction that in such circumstances our will is truly free.

Laboratory experiments confirm the evidence of everyday experience.

A. Michotte and H. M. Wells devised a number of experiments to test the *act of choice.* There is no need to describe the details of the procedure. In Michotte's experiments the subjects had to choose between the addition or subtraction, the division or multiplication, of numbers presented to them. In Well's experiments the subjects were asked to choose between known liquids and to drink them; the choice was between liquids which were equally pleasant, equally unpleasant, or equally indifferent as to taste. There was nothing difficult about any of the tests. The motives of attractiveness or unattractiveness were, so far as the subjects were aware, balanced so evenly that they experienced no preponderance of motive which induced them to choose one alternative in preference to the other. Here was, to all appearances, the predicament of Buridan's ass that starved to death — so the story claims — between two equally attractive bundles of hay. Prior to the act of choice itself, there was *neither an objective nor a subjective difference between the alternatives* for the subjects. Yet they made their choice. The subjects were aware of the fact that they *simply decided on one alternative* by an act of *self-determination,* thereby giving added strength to one motive, although both motives were of equal objective strength and value. It was not the motive which determined the choice; it was the choice of the *Ego-in-action* that determined which of the equal motives shall prevail. By concentration on one course of action, to the exclusion of the other, the *Ego itself* (concretely, the 'person' or 'will') cut short all deliberation and *decided to act,* without regard to the objective equality of the motive, in favor of one of the alternatives. Deciding to act is but another way of saying that the human will is *free in its choice,* when confronted by conflicting motives. Scientific psychology thus also confirms the freedom of the will.

Ethical Proof

Nothing, perhaps, makes us more convinced of the freedom of our will than our *experiences about right and wrong.*

We experience *joy* and *satisfaction* in many of our actions, because we are conscious that we have done something 'morally good' and have 'performed a duty.' On the other hand we experience *remorse* and *repentance,* because we have done something 'morally wrong' and have 'neglected our duty.' We feel in ourselves the presence of a sense of *obligation* and of *responsibility.* We know that we *ought* to do something and that it is within the *power* of our will to do it or not to do it. If we do it, we have the experience of joy and satisfaction; if we do not do it, we have the experience of remorse and repentance. We know, beyond cavil and dispute, that we are *bound by the law* in our conduct; but we also know that we are *not forced* by this moral law. We can, but we need not, obey the moral law.

Conduct of such a sort, however, involves free will. Without the existence of the freedom of choice in such matters, such an attitude toward our own conduct would be both ridiculous and irrational. If the acts of our will are as necessarily determined as the falling of a stone or as the course of an electric current, then there should be *no experience of a difference between right and wrong acts;* all acts are *equally necessary.* We have, however, the definite experience of blameworthiness and praiseworthiness with reference to many of our acts, and we make a clear-cut distinction in this regard.

If we unknowingly and unintentionally injure someone in his person or property, we naturally deplore the fact and express our regret; but we do not feel guilty of any wrong, because we did not will the harm done. If we break a leg in an unavoidable accident, we are sorry; but we do not really reproach ourselves. But if, contrary to our better judgment, we are reckless, fall, and thereby suffer a serious hurt, we feel remorse for our rash action, clearly perceiving that we *ought* not to have done it and *could have* avoided it. Such an attitude, however, has sense only under the supposition that our will is free in its decisions and not intrinsically determined in its acts.

The *universal conviction of mankind* is in accord with our personal experience in this respect.

All nations and individuals speak of their freedom, of their immunity from necessity. All languages express ideas of right and wrong, virtue and vice, command and permission, merit and demerit, natural defects and culpable delinquencies, praise and blame, reward and punishment, appeal and threat, etc. All men thereby give expression to the conviction that we possess freedom of the will.

Before action, men deliberate, seek and give counsel, exhort and induce others to follow a certain course of action by promises of reward or threats of retribution. All nations have *courts* which punish the criminal for his misdeeds and a police force which protects the law-abiding citizen and curbs the nefarious activities of the lawbreaker. All nations have *laws* governing traffic, business transactions, and public morals. All nations enter into *treaties* with one another, regulating rights and duties, so as to safeguard international peace and promote the welfare of peoples.

Such actions and laws would be foolish and useless, if man has no free will and cannot help acting as he does. This universal conviction of mankind cannot be explained except by the fact that the evidence for free will is inescapable and irrefutable.

The *practical life of the determinist* is also proof for the freedom of the will.

Like idealism, determinism is an *unlived* and *unlivable doctrine*. In their dealings with other people and in their personal conduct, determinists behave, not on the supposition that man in all his decisions and actions is controlled by an inexorable determinism, but in a manner which is patterned on the conviction that man is indeed the lord and master of his conduct. The structure of society is based on the principle of free will and responsibility, and the determinists not only expect others to live according to this principle but do so themselves. They make a contract and carry out its stipulations, and they demand that the other party do the same; they also seek redress before the courts for violations of the contract. They respect the person and property of other citizens, and demand the same consideration for themselves. They believe in the 'rights' and 'duties' of their citizenship, although rights and duties can have no legitimate meaning in a deterministic doctrine. They observe the regulations and laws of their community and country like the ordinary man of the street. They praise and blame people for their actions, forgetting their doctrine of determinism for the time being. Determinists are determinists on *theoretical* grounds; in actual life they are libertarians like the rest of men.

Since all men, including the determinists themselves, behave according to the principle of free will, what could possibly be assigned as the *cause* for this *universal conviction* and *behavior?* Not passion, because freedom, involving ideas of responsibility and punishment, is opposed to passion in this case. Not ignorance, because all humanity cannot remain ignorant for long in a matter of such vital moment. The cause can only be *rational insight,* and this must be based on *truth,* because human nature cannot lead man into an irresistible error in something which affects his essential well-being and happiness.

Metaphysical Proof

We have a further proof of the freedom of the will in the very *nature of the will itself.*

The will is a *rational appetency.* Its proper and connatural object is the *good as such;* to this it cannot be indifferent. Since happiness is the fullness of good, the will must desire it and strive for it; in this regard it is not free. Similarly, whatever is perceived by the intellect as a good in every respect, as an essential means to happiness, irresistibly draws the will in its direction.

The reverse is also true. The will cannot desire the evil, provided it is apprehended by the intellect as an evil and proposed as such to the will. Whatever is perceived to be an *evil in every respect,* must be rejected by the will; here, too, the will is not free. The will, by its very nature as a rational appetency, must strive for the good as such.

So far, then, as the intellect perceives *something good* in an object, it is *desirable;* and the will can desire it and strive for it. So far as the intellect perceives *something disagreeable* in an object, it is *undesirable;* and the will can turn away from it and reject it. Now, there is no creatural object which is an absolute good in every respect; all objects have limitations and deficiencies of some sort which make them more or less undesirable. In as much as every object contains some good, the will can desire it; and in as much as it contains some deficiency, the will can reject it. Since a creatural object is neither absolutely good nor absolutely evil, the will can desire or reject it, depending upon whether attention is centered on it as a good or as an evil. All creatural objects, whether material or spiritual, being partially good and partially not good, the will can strive for them under the aspect of their desirability or reject them under the aspect of their undesirability; the will is not constrained in either direction. In fact, because of this dual aspect of all creatural things, the will is not compelled to act at all. Even the *act of volition itself* can be apprehended by the intellect as something partially good and partially not good, so that it lies within the power of the will to exercise volition or not to exercise it.

The only object to which the will is irresistibly drawn is the absolute good. Concretely, this is the *Infinite Good,* namely, God Himself. However, the will can desire only what the intellect perceives and proposes. If our intellect, while we sojourn here on earth, could perceive God as He really is in all His infinite perfection and goodness, we would be conscious that He constitutes our ultimate and essential happiness in an infinite measure. Unfortunately, we have no adequate concept of God. As Maher rightly observes: "The inadequate and obscure notion of God possessed in this life, the difficulty of duty, the conflict of man's pride and sensuality with virtue, all make the pursuit of our true good disagreeable in many respects to human nature, so that we can only too easily and freely abandon it."[2] It thus happens that the will is able to love God or not to love Him, to seek Him or not to seek Him, to desire Him or to reject Him.

Hence, the *freedom of the will is the result of man's rational nature,* which enables him to have the notion of a *universal good* that is desirable in every respect and also the notion of *particular goods* that are partly desirable and partly undesirable. Because of this dual character of particular goods he can decide to exercise or not exercise his power of choice with regard to them, and that is *freedom of exercise;* he can prefer one particular good to another particular good, and that is

[2] *Psychology,* 9th ed. (Longmans, Green, 1930), p. 414.

freedom of specification; he can choose between the morally right and the morally wrong, and that is *freedom of contrariety.*

Objections Against Freedom of Will

Our modern era has become so impressed with the progress made by the physical sciences that it is hardly capable of interpreting anything except in physical and mechanical concepts. The spiritual and immaterial is alien to the minds of many modern philosophers and psychologists. In consequence of their materialistic, mechanistic training, the freedom of the will is something 'unintelligible' and 'inconceivable.' Causes, as they come to know them in physical nature, act necessarily, and so it happens that the concept of 'cause' is synonymous in their reasoning with 'necessarily acting cause.' The will as a 'freely acting cause' is to them a contradiction in terms: they see no place for it in a mechanically operating universe.

The *facts* in favor of the freedom of the will are very clear, so far as everyday experience goes; they cannot very well be denied by these determinists. Yet the freedom of the will is diametrically opposed to the *theoretical assumptions* of their materialistic, mechanical system of philosophy. Loath to admit the error of these assumptions and of their philosophic convictions, they have advanced many objections against the freedom of the will. The point of the attack varies considerably. Some objections are psychological in nature, some are metaphysical, and some are based on the physical, physiological, and sociological sciences.

While many of the arguments against free will are specious and amount to nothing more than sheer quibbling, some of them deserve serious consideration. The more important objections will now be stated and answered.

Unconsciousness of Freedom

J. Stuart Mill (1806–1873) voices an objection against the freedom of the will on psychological grounds. He contends that we *cannot be conscious* of this freedom. To be conscious that we are free in our volition, it would be required, before we act, that we be conscious of the fact that we could really act otherwise than we do. Consciousness, however, Mill claims, merely tells us what we actually do or feel; it never tells us what we are *capable of doing*. In other words, we are conscious of the *act* of willing, but not of the *power* of willing; hence, it is impossible to know whether the power is free or determined.

We admit that the power of the will as such is not an object of direct consciousness. Mill, however, failed to note that every act of volition involves the actuation of the power of the will, the *fieri* or *developmental process* of the volitional act itself.

In the developmental process of many volitional acts, I am conscious that they are *elicited* by motives, but the motives do *not determine* and necessitate the acts; *I myself* determine the acts. I clearly perceive that I have here a motive plus something else which makes the impulse of the motive effective; the act of the will is thus eventually determined, not by the motive, but by the will itself. An analysis of the act of volition shows that two factors are required: an *impulse* flowing from a motive which elicits, but does not compel, me to act; and a *positive consent of my will,* supplementing the deficiency of the objective motive. At times, therefore, I observe that I consent to the impulse originating from the motive, and at other times I observe that I withhold my consent to the impulse originating from the motive; whether the act of volition is set or not set, thus depends on the *active interposition of my Ego* and not merely on the presentation of the motive. So long as the process and *fieri* of volition is protracted and not completed, the final decision to act or not to act, to act this way or that way, rests in my power of determination. The will, therefore, is the master of its own determinations; and as such it is free, because the *consent,* as I know from my internal experience, is a freely exercised act of the will. The experiments of Ach and others, mentioned in the preceding chapter, have definitely revealed the Ego-in-Action in every deliberate decision.

Illusion

Determinists frequently assert that our conviction of the freedom of the will is but an *illusion* based upon an *ignorance of the causes* which produce the acts of the will. Since we are not conscious of the underlying causes which determine the will to act, we have the *feeling* of freedom in our acts; in reality, however, all acts of the will are determined.

In answer to this objection, we assert, first of all, that an appeal to ignorance is the worst sort of argument anyone can advance. Determinists labor under this ignorance as well as the libertarians. The determinists have no more right to suppose that the unknown causes of our voluntary acts are necessary in their operation than that they are free; we simply could not know whether the will is free or determined under any circumstances.

Secondly, this assertion of the determinists *contradicts the experience of consciousness,* and consciousness is the ultimate source of knowledge in this matter. Our experience tells us that the ignorance of the cause of actions occurring within us does not necessarily induce in us the conviction that this cause is free. On the contrary, when we act on a momentary impulse and without reflection, not knowing why we act, then we are convinced that our act was *involuntary, unfree,* and *irresponsible.* On the other hand, when we reflect upon a project with careful deliberation, consider all its advantages and disadvantages, investigate the various means at our disposal, lay out a plan in all its details, weigh all the motives for and against a course of action — in a word, when our knowledge is at its best — then it is that the conviction of the *freedom* of the will and of its choice is greatest. It is, therefore, the incontrovertible testimony of our consciousness that our conviction of freedom is not based on the illusion of ignorance but on the certainty of *knowledge.*

It is true, of course, that *subconscious motives* often influence the will. A *mental act* or attitude frequently brings about the performance of an external act contrary to our resolutions. If we bear in mind, however, the conditions required for the free exercise of the will, as stated in the first section of this chapter, it will readily be observed that one or the other of these conditions has not been verified. No libertarian claims that *all* acts of the will under *all* circumstances are free, but borderline cases do not invalidate the instances where the requisite conditions are clearly perceived by consciousness to have been verified for the free exercise of the will. While many cases will always remain doubtful, many cases of the free exercise of the will must be allowed by an unbiased observer.

It is the verdict of our consciousness that the will is free in many of its acts. This verdict must be accepted as true; otherwise the truth-value of our consciousness is destroyed, and skepticism is the inevitable result.

The Strongest Motive

It is a stock argument of determinists that the *strongest motive* always does and always must prevail, so that the will is intrinsically determined to yield to the strongest motive; the will, therefore, is not free in its choice.

The objection is invalid. Since the will is an appetency and as such can strive only for what is perceived to be good, it is obvious that the motives draw the will in proportion to the amount of value they contain. Slight values influence the will slightly, great values influence it greatly. It is but natural, therefore, that the will, under ordinary and normal circumstances, should and does strive for the greatest value contained in the proposed motives. It would indeed be most unusual, if this were not the case.

The argument of the opponents, however, to be valid, must prove that man, *under all conditions,* is *necessitated* to choose what is intellectually apprehended as possessing the *greatest objective attractiveness* for the will.

It will not do to assert, as the British philosopher Bain apparently asserts, that the strongest motive is the one which actually prevails. He is guilty of a begging of the question. Certainly, the motive which is willed is the one which prevails, and in a sense this motive is the strongest. This only means that the motive which prevails actually prevails, but does not settle the question whether the will is *determined or free* in making a particular motive prevail.

The only legitimate meaning which can be attached to the statement that 'the strongest motive always prevails and must prevail' is the deterministic meaning that the *objectively strongest* motive must prevail; the will must necessarily follow the motive containing, among other motives present, the *more preferable good* considered by the intellect as such.

J. Stuart Mill interprets the 'strongest' motive as the one which is *most pleasurable,* because that is the more preferable good. He contends that the will is constrained to accept this motive and yield to it. We claim that personal *experience* disproves this contention. It is not true that we always choose the course of action which is most pleasurable. Every decent person not infrequently resists temptations, recognized to be most pleasurable, for the sake of an ideal or from a sense of duty, conscious of the fact that yielding to the temptation would be easy and offering resistance to it is most difficult. Soldiers and martyrs prefer death to the violation of their duty, even when excruciating agony accompanies the performance of their duty. To uphold an ideal and to fulfill one's duty under such conditions is indeed the stronger motive, but only because *the will makes it so;* it is not more pleasurable in itself.

Most determinists interpret the 'strongest' motive as the one which, among others present before the mind, represents the *greatest good or value,* without specifying whether or not it be the most pleasurable; such an object or experience, presented as a motive, is the more preferable and as such forces the will into acceptance. The *point at issue* is this: Is the will compelled to choose the motive which the intellect proposes to it as possessing the greatest value or attractiveness among conflicting motives, so that this particular motive has *objective preference,* considered independently of any action of the will? Or, on the contrary, can the will (the Ego) confer *subjective preference* on any of the motives presented, *irrespective of their objective merits,* thereby making an objectively weaker motive the strongest? In the former alternative the objectively 'strongest' motive prevails under all conditions, and the will is determined in its volition; in the second alternative the will itself determines which motive shall prevail, and it cannot be said to be determined in its volition by the (objectively) 'strongest' motive.

Of course, the will in choosing always *prefers* one motive to another and thereby shows that this one pleases it more than the others; but *does this preference of the will correspond to the preceding judgment of the intellect as to preferableness?* If man can act in opposition to this judgment of the intellect and can prefer the weaker motive, then he *determines himself* and is independent of the strength or weakness of the motives proposed by the intellect. Herein lies the crux of the problem of free will.

Ordinarily, the will accepts the side proposed as the better or best; but *not always.* If it were really true that the will always and necessarily prefers that which the intellect perceives to be better or best, how then can it happen that we frequently *deplore* after our decision that we have 'acted against our better judgment,' that we have 'acted foolishly,' having carelessly or obstinately disregarded what we knew to be the better or best course of action? In many instances we act contrary to our own interests, *simply because we so desire,* knowing full well that we are harming ourselves by acting according to the whim of our will rather than according to the objective merits of the motives as recognized by the intellect.

It is not the objectively strongest motive which prevails against the will and determines it to act; it is the act of the will which determines which motive shall be strongest and shall actually prevail.

Influence of Character

Some determinists, among them Schopenhauer, Wundt, Sidgwick, and others, impugn the freedom of the will on the grounds that *every act* of man is determined by his *character* and by the motives which influence the will at any particular moment. Oddly enough, some of these philosophers and psychologists are reluctant to discard the concept of man's responsibility for his actions; they attempt to reconcile responsibility and the determinacy of character by pointing out that 'character' is to a very great extent the result of man's own actions and habits.

Character, we admit, undoubtedly exerts a great influence on the decisions of our will. Knowing the character of a person often enables us to predict with probability how such a person will act in a given set of circumstances. However, we are not determined entirely in our will acts by the inherited and acquired dispositions of character.

Here again we must appeal to *personal experience*. We are conscious of the weakness and faultiness of character, of the pressure of long-standing acquired habits, of the frequency of yielding to urgent passions; but we are also conscious that we can, though no doubt with difficulty, resist the impulses which storm the citadel of the will. Many a drunkard and drug addict has succeeded, perhaps after frequent relapses, in conquering his reigning passion by a persisent struggle of his will.

It is futile for the opponents to speak of 'responsibility' by stating that a person's character is the result of his own actions and habits. If the will is not free but determined, then all the actions and habits which contribute to the formation of character are also determined. Man cannot be held responsible for something he is incapable of doing or avoiding. Responsibility presupposes the freedom of the will.

The Principle of Causality

Many determinists find the freedom of the will 'inconceivable' and 'unintelligible' because, in their opinion, a free act of the will would be *an effect without a cause*. They contend that a free act would violate the *Principle of Causality*.

In *answer* to this argument, we deny emphatically the supposition that an act of the will, merely because it is a free act, is an effect without a cause. The Principle of Causality is a metaphysical principle, and it is immediately evident. It states that where there is an effect there must of necessity be a cause which produces this effect; that is to say, everything which receives being and existence must receive this being and existence from something or somebody, because a nonexistent being cannot give being and existence to itself.

We admit the validity of the Principle of Causality in the case of the free act of the will as an effect. A *double cause* is active in its production: a *moral* cause, namely, the motive; and an *efficient* cause, namely, the Ego using the will as power. Hence, the opponents are wrong when they assert that a free act of the will violates the Principle of Causality.

The Principle of Causality demands that every effect must necessarily have a cause; but whether this cause acts in a free or in a determined manner, lies outside the purview of the principle. So long as there is an efficient cause for the effect produced, the principle is satisfied. In order that their objection be valid, determinists would have to prove that the Principle of Causality demands that every effect must be produced by a *necessary* and *not by a free cause*. They arbitrarily change the meaning of the axiom that 'Every effect must necessarily have a cause' into the axiom that 'Every effect must have a necessarily acting cause.' The latter axiom, however, involves an unwarranted assumption which amounts to a begging of the question, because the postulate of a necessarily acting cause is the very point at issue.

Physiological Determinism

Materialistic philosophers and psychologists reduce all mental events, including volition, to the level of *physiological* and *neurological processes*. The older materialists, such as Moleschott, Büchner, Haeckel, and others, held the crass view that all psychical processes are nothing more than *glandular* in character. The more refined modern materialists identify volitions with *cerebral functions, motor impulses,* or *kinesthetic sensations* of some sort. Representatives of this general view are Maudsley, G. H. Lewes, M. Luys, E. B. Titchener, R. H. Wheeler, J. Watson, and many modern psychologists. There is obviously no place in such doctrines for a will capable of free acts.

Physiological and neurological processes play an important part in a man's mental life, because the operations of the senses furnish the materials from which the intellect abstracts its ideas. Any serious disturbance of the physiological and neurological processes is bound to hamper the intellect in its proper functions. Distortions of intellectual judgments, on their part, influence the will adversely, because the will is dependent on the intellect for the proper presentation of motives.

Nevertheless, determinists need more than this dependence of the will on physiological and neurological conditions in order to prove that the will is determined and necessitated by these conditions in its acts. They must *prove* that it is an *intrinsic dependence;* only then would the will be determined. An *extrinsic* dependence of the will on these conditions would leave the inner nature of the will intact and free. The *facts* we have adduced are proof that the will can and does determine itself. At any rate, the burden of proof rests on the shoulders of our opponents, and they fail to prove that the will is 'intrinsically' dependent on physiological and neurological conditions.

The will is to the human organism what the pilot is to a ship. The ship does not control the pilot; the pilot controls the ship. He directs the course of the ship by means of the steering gear. If the steering gear is defective, the pilot has difficulty in keeping a proper course; and if the steering gear breaks down completely, his control of the ship is lost. The pilot's dependence on the steering gear is very real, yet it does not determine the pilot's decisions. Under normal conditions the ship obeys the pilot's directions and follows the course he decrees. Similarly, the organism normally obeys the commands of the free will; but when serious disorders hamper or destroy the proper functioning of the organism, the will, notwithstanding its intrinsic freedom of action, suffers from the refractory medium through which it must control the organism.

Just *how* the will controls the organism, so far as it can do so at all, is a *mystery*. Every vital action is at bottom a profoundly mysterious reality which no scientific experiment or analysis is able to explain completely. A thousand difficulties, however, cannot disprove a fact. And it is a fact, as we have seen, that the human will is a power which *determines itself* to act or not to act, to act this way or that way, *as it desires*. It is *free* in its decisions, no matter whether or not we understand fully how the will operates.

The Conservation of Energy

Determinists also raise the objection that the freedom of the will would nullify the *Principle of the Conservation of Energy*. The principle states that the sum-total of energy in a closed system, such as the universe, is always constant. They argue that the will, in causing bodily movements, introduces new energy into the organism, thereby increasing the sum-total of energy in the universe and overthrowing the principle mentioned.

Now, the Principle of the Conservation of Energy is an *empirical law*, the result of a partial scientific induction, generalized and applied to the universe at large. As applied to the universe, the principle is incapable of proof, because no one can measure the energy of the universe; it may not be true, as scientists generally admit. In fact, present-day physicists defend the view that energy can be converted into mass and mass into energy.[3] Hence, even if the action of the will did actually increase the sum-total of energy by a small amount, that would be no reason to deny the free action of the will.

It does *not seem necessary* to admit that the will, in causing bodily movements, introduces any *new energy* into the organism. D. Card. Mercier explains the action of the will as follows:

[3] See the author's *From Aether to Cosmos* (Bruce, 1941), p. 80 ff.

"The will is not an efficient cause producing mechanical effects. All that the will does is to direct the power of local movement possessed by the organism to some action. This effect does not require the expenditure of any active force, for the action of the will is not transitive, having an external effect, but is immanent. All the energy that is put forth externally comes from the sensitive appetite and the locomotive faculty, which are material faculties subject to the law of the conservation of energy."[4]

Moral Statistics

Determinists frequently quote *moral statistics* as a proof against the freedom of the will. If the acts of the will are really free, they argue, there should be *no uniformity* in human actions. Yet the records show that the number of marriages, illegitimate births, murders, burglaries, divorces, suicides, etc., vary but little in a country year after year. From these statistics they draw the conclusion that moral acts, which are supposedly free, are *subject to laws* and must be determined in their very nature.

We deny the validity of the argument. All men possess a *similar nature*. They are presumably influenced by the same general factors of natural inclinations, heredity, environment, education, and so forth. It is but natural, therefore, that human beings of a certain social level will act in a somewhat uniform manner. To a very great extent, the lives of men are governed by routine and habit, not by serious deliberation and decision. The impulses of self-preservation, of propagation, of parental and filial attachment, of love and hate, of greed and self-interest, are strong and urgent and universal; and men, as a general rule, are more inclined to yield to these influences than to resist. The regularity of these influences explains the regularity of human conduct.

It must be remembered, however, that this regularity is a *regularity of averages*. It is possible to predict the average num-

[4] *Psychology* (in *A Manual of Modern Scholastic Philosophy*, Kegan Paul, Trench, Trübner and Co., 1916), p. 277.

ber of events which will occur, but it is impossible to predict which *individuals* will be responsible for the events. Therein lies the difference between a *moral law* and a *physical law*. Given all the conditioning antecedents in a specific instance in physical nature, we can predict the effect with absolute certainty, because such an effect is determined by physical law. In the case of a human being, however, we can predict his action only with moral probability, because he is not forced by the conditioning antecedents to act in a definite manner; he probably will act as expected, but he may, being free, act otherwise.

The will exists, and it is free. The objections raised against the freedom of the will fail to prove the determinacy of volitional acts.

Summary of Chapter XVI

It is a universal conviction of mankind that the *will is free*. Is this conviction rationally justified?

1. *Statement of the Problem. Freedom* means the absence of intrinsic necessity or determination in the performance of an act. The *conditions* required for the exercise of free will are: a normal state of attention; an objectively indifferent judgment of the intellect; and a conflict of motives.

There are *three types of freedom* in the acts of the will: the freedom of exercise or contradiction; the freedom of specification; and the freedom of contrariety.

Free will is *defined* as the ability of the will, all conditions for action being present, to decide whether to act or not to act and whether to act in this manner or in that manner. The doctrine of freedom of the will is called *indeterminism* or *libertarianism*. We advocate a *relative* or *moderate indeterminism*.

2. *Determinism*. The doctrine opposed to free will is styled *determinism* or *necessitarianism*. Among the ancients we find the doctrine of 'fate' or 'destiny.' In modern times, the doctrine of free will is denied by materialists and pantheists.

The *true problem* is this: All the conditions and circumstances for volition being given, is it within the ability of the will, through the active interposition of the Ego, to make an arbitrary choice between conflicting motives, irrespective of their relative attraction, by simply determining itself to choose any one of the motives and thereby conferring a subjective preference on it over the others?

3. *Psychological Proof.* Introspection shows that the will, in many of its acts, decides the issue between conflicting motives through an active interposition of the Ego, by choosing *as it pleases.* The freedom of choice is particularly clear in *indifferent acts.* Free will can be observed in a number of *mental processes,* such as voluntary attention, deliberation, decision in matters of conduct. The laboratory *experiments* of Michotte and Wells confirm our experience.

4. *Ethical Proof.* Our experiences of *joy* and *satisfaction* or of *remorse* and *repentance,* and our sense of *obligation* and *responsibility* are meaningless without free will. This view is confirmed by the universal conviction of mankind and by the lives of the determinists themselves.

5. *Metaphysical Proof.* The nature of the will as a *rational appetency* is proof that it possesses freedom of choice. A creatural object or experience is neither altogether desirable nor altogether undesirable. Hence, the will can strive for it or reject it.

6. *Objections.* Determinists oppose the freedom of the will on *theoretical* grounds, not because the *facts* are not plain.

7. *Unconsciousness of Freedom.* We are, they say, conscious only of what we do, not of what we *can* do.

Answer. In the *developmental process* of many volitional acts, we are conscious of the impulse of the motive, eliciting but not compelling consent, and also of the positive consent supplementing the deficiency of the motive.

8. *Illusion.* The feeling of freedom is an *illusion* based on the *ignorance of the causes* determining the will.

Answer. Experience shows that the more we deliberate and understand the motives, weighing all conditions, the more we are conscious of freedom.

9. *The Strongest Motive.* The strongest motive, determinists assert, must prevail.

Answer. Usually it does, but not always. The 'strongest' motive, from a deterministic point of view, must mean the one having *objective preference* as proposed by the intellect. Experience proves, however, that the will gives *subjective preference* to a motive in its choice, irrespective of the objective merits of the motives as proposed by the intellect.

10. *Character.* Others claim that *character,* whether natural or acquired, determines the will.

Answer. Their contention disagrees with *personal experience.*

11. *The Principle of Causality.* Determinists say that a free act would be an *effect without a cause.*

Answer. Every act of the will, even when free, has a moral cause, the motive, and an *efficient* cause, the will or, rather, the Ego using the will as power. The Principle of Causality demands that every effect have a cause, but it does not demand that it have a necessarily acting cause.

12. *Physiological Determinism.* Materialists identify volition with glandular or cerebral functions, with motor impulses, or with kinesthetic sensations.

Answer. Determinists cannot prove that the dependence of the will on these factors is an *intrinsic* dependence; we claim it is *extrinsic.* The facts proving the freedom of the will are plain.

13. *The Conservation of Energy.* The opponents maintain that a free act would introduce *new energy* into the organism, thereby increasing the sum-total of energy in the universe.

Answer. The law is an *empirical* law and not proved for the universe at large. Besides, the will would, in all probability, merely *direct the use* of the energy present in the organism.

14. *Moral Statistics.* Statistics prove that moral acts follow laws, making it possible to predict their frequency. Hence, the opponents conclude, the will cannot be free.

Answer. The general factors found in all men explain the *similarity* and *regularity* of moral acts. But, unlike physical laws, this is only a law of averages. It is impossible to predict which *individuals* will perform the acts and thus fall under the statistical law.

Readings

Moore, T. V., *Dynamic Psychology,* Part VI, Ch. VII. — Maher, M., *Psychology,* Ch. XIX. — Gruender, H., *Experimental Psychology,* Ch. XVII; *Problems of Psychology,* Ch. III.

Chapter XVII

CONSCIOUSNESS

ONE of the foremost phenomena of human mental life is *consciousness.* The term 'consciousness' is used frequently in the ordinary affairs of human beings. It is a very general term; nevertheless, the concept underlying the use of the term is fundamentally the same. In psychology, we must attempt a more exact description of the characteristics of consciousness.

Consciousness is an all-pervasive mental experience, since it is found to be present as an accompaniment of all mental operations ranging from sense-perception to intellection and volition. As such, one would think that every psychologist should recognize consciousness as a most important factor in the study of the human mind and person. *Behaviorists,* however, ignore consciousness, if they do not deny its existence altogether. Man, according to their principles of psychology, must be studied in his external behavior exclusively. This position is extreme and is now, fortunately for psychology, practically abandoned.

Concept of Consciousness

Consciousness, being an ultimate datum of experience, admits of *no strict definition,* because it lies at the very root of all mental activity. It can, however, be pointed out and described. Consciousness is that state of the mind in which we find ourselves when we are *awake,* as contrasted with the state of our mind in dreamless sleep or in a coma or when under complete anesthesia. A simpler term for consciousness is *aware-*

ness. We are 'conscious' of something when we are 'aware' of it, no matter how dimly or fleetingly. Again, we may say that we are 'conscious' of a thing or of a mental state when we *notice* its presence to mind. If we are 'unaware' of something and do 'not notice' its presence in any manner whatever, we are then said to be 'unconscious' of it. Consciousness is not a special cognitive power; it is simply the 'awareness' inherent in every act of sensory and intellectual cognition.

Consciousness has a *content*. In order to be conscious, we must be conscious *of something*. When we see or hear or taste or smell or feel something and 'know' or 'are aware' that we sense it here and now, then we are conscious. When we have a mental image of an object or experience and 'know' or 'are aware' of this image present within us, then we are conscious. When we think about something intellectually in the form of ideas, judgments, or argumentations and 'know' or 'are aware' of our thinking about it, then we are conscious. When we have feelings, emotions, or volitions and 'know' or 'are aware' that we have them, then we are conscious. The content of consciousness thus includes all the *mental acts* which are present in our normal waking state and of whose presence we are aware — sense-perceptions, mental images, acts of the intellect, acts of the will, feelings, and emotions. It also includes the various *objects* toward which these acts are directed, as when we are aware not only of the act of seeing but also of the house that we see, not only of the anger we experience but also of the person with whom we are angry. Whatever attracts our *attention* in some way, whether it be an external object or an internal state of the mind, thereby enters our consciousness and belongs to the content of consciousness.

Field of Consciousness

Psychologists often speak of the *field of consciousness* and mean thereby the sum-total of all items present in the consciousness of an individual at any given moment. It expresses the range or area over which consciousness extends at a particular point of time, measured by the number of objects or mental states of which the mind is aware and by the degree of attention given to them.

Viewed in this manner, the total field of consciousness is divided into the *focus* of consciousness and the *margin, fringe,* or *periphery* of consciousness. The expressions are taken from the field of vision, because vision and consciousness are very similar in this respect.

Objects or experiences are said to be in the *focus* of consciousness when they are accorded the *maximal* amount of attention among all the objects or experiences present here and now in consciousness. It is a common fact, noticeable every hour of the day, that our attention shifts to a considerable extent from one thing to another and appears in varying degrees of concentration. At any particular moment, some object or experience occupies our attention in a primary manner, so that it stands out before our conscious observance with exceptional distinctness and vividness; everything else is pushed into the dim background of attention for the time being. While watching, for instance, a long forward pass in a football game, our attention is directed primarily to the flight of the ball and to the pass receiver; we are only dimly aware of the actions of the majority of the other players at the moment. Similarly, when we are suffering from a sharp toothache, this intense pain forces itself upon our attention to such a degree that we are hardly capable of thinking of anything else. Such an object or experience occupies the 'focus' of the field of consciousness.

Objects or experiences which are not in the focus of consciousness but which are still *noticed to some degree,* along with the primary object of conscious attention, are said to belong to the *margin* or *fringe* or *periphery* of consciousness. Such objects or experiences occupy a place in the field of conscious attention similar to that of objects in the field of vision which throw their image on the peripheral regions of the retina. They are observed, but in a vague and blurred fashion;

they lack the distinctness and vividness of an object or experience in the focal position of awareness. Taking the examples mentioned in the preceding paragraph, while we are watching the flight of the football through the air, we are also aware of the roaring shout of the spectators, but only in a secondary and coincidental manner; and while the sharp pang of the aching tooth is our main conscious concern, we still listen to the conversation carried on by those around us, even though only in a desultory and half-attentive manner.

As in vision, consciousness shades off from the maximal concentration of attention at the focus imperceptibly in diminishing degrees through the peripheral region, until it reaches a point where objects and experiences no longer make an impression and are lost to consciousness altogether. There is no fixed and clear line of demarkation in conscious attention. Sometimes an individual object or experience is so strongly placed in the focus of consciousness that we are practically unaware of anything else; at other times, especially when drowsy or very fatigued, the entire field of consciousness seems rather confused and chaotic. In any case, the states of consciousness occupying a position intermediate between maximal and zero attention is designated as the 'margin' or 'fringe' or 'periphery' of the field of consciousness.

Unconsciousness

Unconsciousness, as the term indicates, is the *absence of consciousness.*

The term 'unconscious' may be taken in an *objective* or *subjective* sense. Taken 'objectively,' something would be termed 'unconscious' in the sense that, by its very nature, it is devoid of the attribute of consciousness altogether and thus never becomes an object of awareness in our mental life. Many processes occurring in the human organism are objectively unconscious. Chemical and purely physiological and neurological processes are of this type; they never enter consciousness, though we may become aware of their results.

Through the stimulation, for example, of the retina, of the optic nerve, and of the visual center of the cerebral cortex, we become conscious of the act and of the object of vision, but we are totally unconscious of the chemical, physiological, and neurological processes which precede and accompany vision. Similarly, we are totally unconscious of the many processes which take place in the metabolism of the body, in many reflex actions of the nervous system, in the storage and recall of memory images, etc. Without doubt, such processes influence our consciousness in diverse and profound ways; but the processes themselves never enter the field of consciousness directly. They are, by their very nature, objectively unconscious processes.

Taken 'subjectively,' something is 'unconscious' in the sense that it *actually,* as a mere matter of fact, does not enter our consciousness, though of itself it could. The human subject is simply not aware of the object or action under the existing conditions; but the nature of the object or action is such that, under other conditions, the mind could make it an object of its focal or peripheral attention. While I am writing, for instance, I may be unaware of the pressure of my forearm on the desk; it would be, however, a simple matter to direct my attention to this pressure and thereby bring it within the field of consciousness. Again, while in profound sleep, I am unconscious of the sensory stimuli which affect my bodily organs; but when awake, these same stimuli give rise to conscious sense impressions. When, therefore, the mind is unconscious of objects or actions which could be consciously perceived, it is said to be in a state of 'subjective unconsciousness.'

Periods of unconsciousness, placed between periods of consciousness in our normal waking states, are facts beyond dispute and no psychologist denies them. Ordinary deep sleep is a period of unconsciousness. Many authors, however, are loath to admit that total and *absolute* unconsciousness of the mind ever occurs. The evidence, they say, is at best only negative, resting on the fact that in our normal waking state we cannot recall what has taken place in the mind during the period of so-called unconsciousness. The inability of recall is no convincing proof of absolute unconsciousness, because we know from experience that we are often unable to recall objects and experiences which were consciously perceived on a former occasion. More happens in the deep recesses of the mind than can be remembered while awake. There always remains, then, the possibility of some sort of conscious experience in dreamless sleep, coma, and other states of apparent unconsciousness, which never rises to the surface of conscious memory when we are awake. This argument, of course, is also negative. From the very nature of the case, positive proof for or against the fact of absolute unconsciousness is excluded.

Subconsciousness

A proof that unconsciousness is not so complete as is commonly supposed is found in what modern psychology calls *subconsciousness* or *subliminal consciousness.*

The term *subconscious* is used to designate certain mental items and processes which are apparently of the same nature as the normally conscious items and processes, yet of which the subject is not aware in the waking state. These items and processes are conceived as occurring 'beneath' or 'underneath' the ordinary waking consciousness; hence the terms *sub*conscious' and '*sub*consciousness.' It is as if, figuratively speaking, a 'threshold' (Lat., *limen,* threshold) divided and partitioned off the items and processes of the ordinary waking consciousness, of which we are aware when awake, from those other items and processes belonging also to the cognitive order, but of which we are unaware in the waking consciousness. For this reason, the subconsciousness is also termed the *subliminal* consciousness, while the ordinary waking consciousness is also termed the *supraliminal* consciousness.

In order to understand these terms properly, we must advert to a number of pertinent facts.

Consciousness, in general, means to have knowledge (to be aware) of what occurs within us. Since man's knowledge is of a double nature, he possesses a *double consciousness:* sensuous and intellectual.

Man's *sensuous* consciousness embraces everything of a sensory character, and this type of consciousness man has in common with the brutes. To the field of this sensuous consciousness belong the acts of sense-perception (sight, hearing, taste, etc.), the images of the imagination and sense-memory, sensuous feelings, emotions, and appetitions. Man's *intellectual* consciousness is of a higher order. It comprises the rational acts of intellection and volition and the affective states based upon intellectual and volition; and it also comprises the sensory acts and states, in so far as these are reflexly cognized and made the objects of thought and will.

Both types of consciousness have a focus and a periphery in their field in the ordinary waking state. Whatever is perceived by this double consciousness in the ordinary waking state, whether focally or peripherally, belongs to the 'supraliminal' consciousness. Specifically, everything is included which has attracted our attention is some measure while awake and whatever can be recalled arbitrarily from memory.

There are, however, many items of experience which do not belong to the category just mentioned, but which, nevertheless, cannot be excluded from consciousness altogether. When in the ordinary waking state our attention is deeply engrossed by some object or experience, very many *faint impressions* are made on the mind; they go unnoticed at the time and do not enter our waking consciousness, but they are somehow registered and recorded. There can hardly be a doubt that practically every action of our bodily limbs and organs arouses nerve impulses of some kind which reach the brain along obscure and circuitous paths; they must leave impressions, no matter how weak, and these impressions, though unperceived by the waking consciousness, cannot be ruled out entirely from the field of mental experience.

Again, due to the shifting and the natural limitation of attention, the periphery of our waking consciousness is filled with numberless fluctuating ideas, sensations, feelings, and so forth, which are but very dimly perceived for a moment and then pass into oblivion, never capable of being arbitrarily recalled in the future. It even happens that objects and experiences were distinctly perceived and reflexly cognized in our waking consciousness on a particular occasion; but they were objectively unimportant and too loosely connected with the vital facts of our existence to make a strong impression on our memory, and so they faded out and after a while joined the host of forgotten things. Yet they were present and left a record of their presence in our mind.

Such impressions are not lost entirely. Their *vestiges* remain and leave their *collective mark* on our mind and character, influencing us in diverse ways; at times they appear again in consciousness, unrecognized and unremembered.

This body of processes and experiences, *'split-off'* and *dissociated* from the content of the waking consciousness, belongs to the field of the *subliminal* consciousness (subconsciousness). It should be noted that much of what has been designated as 'subjectively unconscious' is classed here as 'subconscious.' Specifically, subconsciousness comprises the processes and experiences which were not reflexly cognized and which were not perceived by the ordinary waking consciousness as having been present, though they possess the general nature of mental items belonging to the field of consciousness; the faint, fleeting processes and experiences, noticed dimly in the marginal region of the waking consciousness for a moment and then forgotten, so that they are incapable of arbitrary recall; the processes and experiences which were reflexly and attentively cognized by the waking consciousness at some time or other, but faded from active memory in such a manner that they are beyond voluntary recall.

It is a peculiarity of our mental life that the mind in its subliminal (subconscious) states can and does perform *connected and consistent functions,* unknown to the ordinary waking consciousness. These 'split-off' and dissociated processes at times form a definite stream of consciousness, isolated from, and running parallel to, the stream of consciousness prevalent in our waking state, so that they may even seem to issue from a different mind or personality.

Here are some of the facts which, to all appearances, indicate the existence of a separate, subliminal stream of consciousness beneath the threshold of the ordinary waking consciousness.

While carrying on a conversation in an intelligent manner, a *second train of thought,* on an entirely different subject, may run through our mind and be brought to its logical conclusion. Or, while reading a paper or book, our attention is diverted to some other subject or occurrence; yet we find that we have continued to read. Our supraliminal consciousness cannot recall what we have read in this period of mental distraction, but the content of our reading may suddenly come back to us later with clarity and precision.

Oftentimes we do our utmost to *recall* a certain name, person, fact, or mental operation; but all our efforts are to no avail. In despair, we turn our mind to something else, confident that the items cannot be recalled. Later, the forgotten items rise into our waking consciousness with startling abruptness. Upon investigation, we are unable to discover any association of ideas which can account for their appearance. The recall was made, not through any process known to our waking consciousness, but by some kind of subconscious process.

The *execution of problems,* unfinished in the waking state, is often carried out by the subconscious mind. Not infrequently a problem presents itself to us, and we experience considerable difficulty in marshaling our ideas to find the proper solution. The solution escapes us, and we put the problem aside. To our astonishment, the solution, ready-made and complete in detail, suddenly flashes into our consciousness at a time when we are thinking of something totally different. The secondary, subliminal consciousness has worked out the problem for the primary, supraliminal consciousness. In all probability, the inspirations of genius can be accounted for in this manner.

Far more striking and convincing are the experiments made in *automatic writing.* By 'automatic writing' psychologists understand script produced by a subject unknowingly and involuntarily. The phenomenon can be evoked quite readily in hypnotic trance, but in exceptional instances it also occurs in the ordinary waking state. The procedure is somewhat as follows. The subject is made to read aloud a fascinating book or article, so as to engross his attention completely. A pen or pencil is placed in the hand of the subject, and the hand is screened off from the subject's view. The experimenter then asks a question to which the subject should write the answer at some length. While reading aloud, the subject's hand writes a fluent, intelligent, and consistent account. The subject's waking consciousness, totally occupied with reading, is unaware of the contents written by the hand. 'Automatic writing' is thus seen to result from the activity of the secondary or subliminal consciousness.

Hypnotism offers further evidence for the existence of subconscious processes unknown to the ordinary waking consciousness. What happens in deep hypnosis remains, as a rule, unavailable for recall when the hypnotized person returns to the normal state; in a subsequent hypnotic trance, however, the experiences of the former trance can be recalled. Furthermore, many items of mental experience, mysterious and unexplainable to the ordinary waking consciousness, can be traced in their origin and development by the subconsciousness during hypnosis. Hypnosis seems to open a hidden door to the secret workshop of the mind.

Coconsciousness

In recent years the term *coconsciousness* has come to the fore. Morton Prince[1] is mainly responsible for the rise and spread of the term and its meaning.

Prince divides the 'subconscious' into two distinct sections, namely, the 'coconscious' and the 'unconscious.'

The *coconscious,* according to his view, is any actual subconscious *idea* or *thought process* present in the human sub-

[1] *The Unconscious* (Macmillan, 1924).

ject but unknown to him in his ordinary waking state. It is only when the term 'subconscious' is used to qualify 'ideas' or 'thought processes' actively present beneath the threshold of the supraliminal or waking consciousness that the term 'subconscious' is equivalent to the term 'coconscious.'

The *unconscious* comprises two types of items. The one type consists of *inactive neural dispositions* (conserved dormant 'neurograms'), which are the vestiges of former sensations, etc., conserved in the nervous system, particularly the brain, after the sensations, etc., have ceased to be active and have left their traces as dormant 'neurograms.' The other type consists of *neural processes* (active functioning 'neurograms'), which come into existence when the dormant 'neurograms,' for some reason or other, are stimulated into becoming again an active process.[2] Both types of items, the inactive neural dispositions and the neural processes, are devoid of any quality of consciousness; hence the term 'unconscious.' The 'coconscious' and 'unconscious' have their place beneath the level of the waking consciousness and as such belong to the 'subconscious' as two species under a common genus.

According to Prince, then, the term 'unconscious' has a rather restricted meaning, quite at variance with the meaning commonly attached to the term. It applies exclusively to inactive and active neurograms, i.e., to inactive neural dispositions and to neural processes. It does not, in itself, apply to metabolic and other dispositions and processes which are also devoid of consciousness. This restriction of the meaning, if intended, is unjustified. Furthermore, the inclusion of the 'unconscious' under the 'subconscious' as a species under its genus, seems a strange and unwarranted procedure. After all, the term 'subconscious,' as usually employed by psychologists, designates a certain form of *consciousness,* while the 'unconscious' is acknowledged to be devoid of any quality of consciousness. The use of accustomed terminology in such an unusual fashion can only lead to confusion.

As for the term 'coconscious,' it is appropriate enough. How-

[2] *Ibid.*, pp. 14, footnote, and 253.

ever, if we omit the 'unconscious' from the 'subconscious,' there appears to be little reason for making a distinction between 'coconscious' and 'subconscious.' Distinctions and terms should not be multiplied without necessity.

All things considered, it seems advisable to make only the following distinctions and divisions among the states and conditions affecting the human organism:

1. *Unconscious* (items not qualified by any attribute of consciousness, such as metabolic and purely neural items).
2. *Conscious:*
    a) *Normal waking consciousness* (primary, supraliminal),
    b) *Subconsciousness* (secondary, subliminal).

Self-Consciousness

Self-consciousness is characteristic of man. It is the consciousness of his *self* or *Ego* as the subject and bearer of all the conditions and states affecting his being, particularly of consciousness itself.

Just as consciousness has a content, so it also has a subject or bearer, namely, the 'self' or 'Ego.' Whatever we may think of the ultimate nature of the 'self' or 'Ego,' introspection reveals the indisputable fact that it is the 'self' or 'Ego' to which all conscious phenomena are, in the last analysis, referred. To doubt this means to doubt the validity of the very foundations of all knowledge.

Consciousness is not a mere 'stream' of conscious states succeeding one another like flashes of light or like motion pictures on a screen. This analogy is convenient, but it is not the whole truth. Beneath these fleeting states of consciousness is the conscious self as the subject and bearer in which they exist and subsist; they are not independent items floating in some sort of mental vacuum.

'Self-consciousness' means that the mind (self, Ego) recognizes all mental states and activities as *its own*. Not only are these states and activities present, but *I myself,* by an act of reflex cognition, know that they are present and know that they belong to me as *modifications of myself.* Common speech is proof of this. We seldom say: 'Sight, hearing, pleasure, thought, volition, etc., are present.' We invariably say: '*I* see, *I* hear, *I* experience pleasure, *I* think, *I* will, etc.' The subject and bearer is always mentioned together with the conscious state. We thus make a clear distinction between the conscious state and the self underlying it as the conscious agent. It is precisely this feature of our mental life which makes *introspection* possible and invests it with value as an instrument of knowledge in psychology. If there were no conscious self or Ego, we could not report on the presence or absence of a mental state.

I therefore not only know, but I know that I know; I not only have knowledge, but I have a knowledge of my knowledge; I not only am conscious, but I am conscious of my consciousness. By means of the reflex act of self-consciousness I become aware that I, the thinking and conscious subject, *apprehend myself concretely* in my mental acts and states. It is my *self-same Ego* which is active and passive, whether in the domain of sense or in the domain of intellect, and my Ego is *one, single individual;* there is no duality or multiplicity here, notwithstanding the radical difference between the acts and states themselves, between sensuous and intellectual consciousness. Even my consciousness is only a modification of my self or Ego, because I am conscious of *myself as conscious* in the same way that I am conscious of myself as seeing, hearing, thinking, and willing; I express both facts in an identical manner, namely, '*I* hear a sound' and '*I* am conscious of myself.'

The Ego is not consciousness; it is the *possessor* of consciousness. The Ego is not experience; it is the *experient.* And so, too, the Ego is not memory; it is the *bearer* of memory. The act of remembering is a present act, but it always has a reference to past persons and events. I perceive with evidence that I, the Ego, who am conscious at this very moment, am the *self-identical* Ego who have had the 'past' experience recorded by my memory. I am writing at this moment; but I am also conscious that I was writing ten minutes ago, that I took a walk an hour ago, that I attended a meeting yesterday. Notwithstanding the fact that I was in a state of unconsciousness during my sleep last night, I am aware that 'I' am the self-identical 'Ego' who existed, worked, ate, wrote, perceived, and reasoned yesterday, a week before, a month ago, and through all the years down to my youth and childhood. The events belonged to me before, in the past; and my Ego preserved its self-identity, while they came and passed on. How could I remember them as 'mine,' as having happened in 'me,' if my Ego were not a *permanently abiding reality in whom* they occurred? My Ego is clearly perceived to be the *abiding subject* of these transitory states. Whatever may be the nature of the Ego, the data of my conscious states show plainly that my Ego is distinct from the conscious states themselves; the latter are only modifications of the permanent Ego, existing *in* and *by* and *through* my Ego as their agent-patient subject. So much is clear to me from an analysis of the data of memory and consciousness.

John Stuart Mill considered the mind to be nothing more than a *series* of conscious states which is aware of itself as a series. Such a view is in flat contradiction to the facts, as just pointed out. We make a clear distinction between the states and the self or Ego as the self-conscious bearer of the states of consciousness. Besides, the series of conscious states of today, having begun after a period of unconsciousness during sleep, is totally different from the series of yesterday and of a year ago; how then could the Ego of today be conscious of the identity of itself with the Ego of yesterday and of a year ago, if the Ego were nothing more than a series conscious of itself as a series? It would definitely have to be conscious of itself as a different Ego entirely, because the series themselves are numerically and entitatively different.

The same objection applies to William James' concept of the Ego as a *stream* of consciousness in which each passing thought is itself the 'thinker' or 'Ego.' We may, of course, speak of the aggregate of successive conscious states as a 'stream.' This figure of speech is misleading. A 'stream' suggests unbroken continuity. The 'stream of consciousness,' however, possesses no unbroken continuity. On the contrary, the continuity is broken by every period of unconsciousness to which the human mind is subject, such as sleep, coma, anesthesia, etc. It should, then, be utterly impossible for memory to identify the Ego of one series or stream with that of a former series or stream. In fact, since the present passing thought is not identical with the immediately preceding thought, much less with the thought of yesterday or of a year or ten years ago, we should be conscious of as many 'thinkers' and 'Egos' as there are passing thoughts, not of an *abiding Ego* present as the bearer of the present and past thoughts through the years. Yet the identity of the Ego in the past and present is precisely what our consciousness reveals to us with unmistakable clearness: the Ego which thinks today is the self-identical Ego which thought yesterday and all the days before. This fact is inexplicable, if the theory of James were correct. Finally, why should there be any reference of our conscious states to a single, permanently abiding Ego at all, if there were no such underlying Ego present? If only conscious states were present and a permanently abiding Ego as their subject were nonexistent, why should consciousness give testimony of the supposed existence of a nonexistent reality? There should, in that case, be merely a consciousness of *passing states,* but never of a *permanent Ego* as the bearer in which they exist and which they modify. We must, therefore, reject the theory of James and his followers.

Consciousness, then, reveals to us the existence of our self or Ego as the single, permanent, self-identical subject and bearer of all our states and experiences.

The Seat of Consciousness

Ever since F. J. Gall, G. Spurzheim, P. Flourens, P. Flechsig, and others, made their investigations into the problem of cerebral localization of sensory and motor activities, the problem of the *seat of consciousness* also received attention. It was evident that certain conditions affecting the nervous system also affected consciousness, at least the consciousness of the normal waking state. Some neurologists, therefore, concluded that the seat of consciousness must be located in the *brain,* the central organ of co-ordination for sensory and motor activities. Even the ordinary man of the street feels that consciousness resides somehow "in the head."

The particular problem which confronted neurologists and psychologists was to decide whether the *entire brain* or a *definite portion* of the brain could be designated as the seat of consciousness. Opinions differed. In the course of time, however, certain facts began to throw some light on this complicated and perplexing question.

Some scientists believed that consciousness depended on the left cerebral hemisphere in right-handed persons and on the right cerebral hemisphere in left-handed persons. We now know that this view is erroneous. A number of cases are on record where the corresponding cerebral hemisphere had been extirpated, and no marked changes in consciousness of personality took place. Such cases have been reported by Dandy, Gardner, Rowe, Zollinger, and Kocher. The seat of consciousness, then, does not lie in any one of the two hemispheres as such.

Others identified mental life with the *frontal lobes* of the brain, either the right or the left or both. This view also proved to be false. Operations for the removal of one or the other frontal lobe have been performed, without serious impairment of the mental faculties. Ackerly reports the cases of the removal of both prefrontal lobes, and the patient retained normal intelligence.

Nor is the seat of consciousness in the *thalamus* or *hypothalamus.* Even extensive destruction of these important subcortical regions leaves consciousness essentially intact. Most remarkable, in this respect, is the *Mittelhirnwesen* ('mid-brain creature') studied by Gamper and reported by him in 1926. The child lacked a cerebrum, possessing only the mid-brain and the fragment of a thalamus. One would suppose that this unfortunate child must be devoid of all consciousness. However, it had alternating periods of sleeping and waking, and occasionally it smiled. The child, obviously, could not indicate whether or not it possessed consciousness in the accepted meaning of the term. But if sleeping and waking are, respectively, states of unconsciousness and of consciousness, then the conclusion is justified that the child did actually experience consciousness in some form. It would be erroneous to conclude from this case that the seat of consciousness is in the *mid-brain,* because the history of medicine records instances of considerable damage in this anatomical region without complete loss of mental activity.

Nor is the *medulla oblongata* the seat of consciousness. True, pressure in this region produces unconsciousness; but unconsciousness can be produced in many ways, independent of the medulla. To produce unconsciousness in a certain region is one thing, and to say that this particular region is the point center of consciousness is quite another thing. The very fact that the visual, olfactory, and auditory nerves do not terminate in the medulla but in the cerebrum, is reason enough to eliminate this anatomical structure from being the seat of consciousness, because visual, olfactory, and auditory perceptions most certainly are part and parcel of our conscious life.

There is, of course, a dependence of consciousness on the *nervous system,* because the nervous system is a system of channels which furnish the necessary materials for sensory and intellectual activity. No definite portion of this system, however, can be singled out as the point center of consciousness. All we can say is that it is the *individual* who is conscious, with a dependence on the nervous system; but it is neither the brain nor the nervous system which, as such, is conscious.

The Function of Consciousness

Man is a unit being, an integral organism. All mental states, including consciousness, are states of the self or Ego. Man is not an isolated being in a world of isolated beings. The world is a co-ordinated whole, a true 'universe,' and man is a part of this co-ordinated whole.

As a part belonging to the world as a co-ordinated whole, man must be capable of making an *intelligent adjustment* to the world in which he lives. To achieve this adjustment, he possesses the equipment of his bodily limbs, his vegetative organs, his external and internal senses, his feelings and emotions, his intellect, and his will. He must be able to safeguard himself against harmful agencies and to perfect his own being, and it is through the proper use of these powers that he is able to do this. These powers are the necessary instrumentalities by means of which he can *perceive* and *interpret* the surrounding world. These perceptions and interpretations are recorded in the sensuous and intellectual memory, so that not only present impressions but also past experiences can be utilized to best advantage for the purpose of adjusting his conduct in accordance with the needs of his being.

Without *consciousness* man could not make this adjustment of his conduct. It is precisely because his perceptions and interpretations are 'conscious' that he is able to meet the conditions prevalent from moment to moment and turn them to his advantage. One need but think of what would happen to man, if he were in a continuous state of sleep or in a continuous coma, in order to understand the necessity of a normal waking consciousness. Even though we admit the importance of the influence of subconscious states on man's conduct, it is primarily through his waking consciousness that he has contact with the world at large and makes his adjustments to it.

It is, therefore, not difficult to state the *function* or *purpose* of consciousness in the economy of man's life. T. V. Moore has expressed its function and purpose, when he describes "normal consciousness as a state of the human mind, in which it can perceive and interpret its surroundings, and in which the past experience of the individual is fully available for the adjustment of the individual to the needs of the present moment."[3] He goes on to explain that the phrase "fully available"

[3] *Cognitive Psychology* (Lippincott, 1939), p. 3.

must be taken in a relative sense, excluding pathological and abnormal conditions.

This description applies with equal force to the function and purpose of the *subconsciousness* or *coconsciousness.* Because of the natural limitations existing in the power of attention during ordinary waking consciousness, many impressions, too faint to attract attention, will be recorded and stored in the lower levels of the mind, forming a secondary stream of consciousness and partly dissociated from the activity of the waking consciousness. These items are also subservient to the general welfare of the individual and assist in the shaping of his conduct.

Because of the tremendous importance of consciousness as a determining factor in human life, it is obvious that disorders of consciousness are particularly harmful to man in their effects.

Disorders of Consciousness

Disorders of consciousness arise either from *organic* causes, as epilepsy, or from *psychogenic* causes, as hysteria; in many instances both types of causes are present. When disorders are organic in character, the cause is always found to be an impairment or destruction of important nerve tissue due to lesions, internal hemorrhage, diseases, etc. When they are psychogenic in character, the cause is inevitably of a psychic nature, such as fears, anxieties, mental conflict, maladjustment to social conditions, and the like. Some people, for example, become blind through injury to the eyes, the optic nerve, or the visual center in the brain; others become functionally blind after passing through a severe emotional crisis.

Total loss of consciousness may result from poisons, and then we speak of 'coma'; or from head injuries, and this is 'concussion'; or from an improper distribution of blood in the brain, and then we have the condition known as 'swooning' or 'fainting.'

Partial loss of consciousness occurs in varying stages of depth and degrees of intensity. 'Stupor' is an intensive clouding of consciousness, characterized by a condition of marked unresponsiveness and usually accompanied by torpidity of perception, thought, and emotion. 'Confusion,' milder than stupor, is a mental state of clouded consciousness, in which the symptoms are an unstable attention, a poor perception of reality, a disorientation concerning time or place or person, and a more or less marked inability to act coherently. When accompanied by conditions of excitement and hallucination, confusion is termed 'delirium.' Some authors use the phrase 'twilight state' to designate 'confusion.'

Other disorders, involving partial loss of consciousness, are derealization, depersonalization, and amnestic fugues. In 'derealization' persons suffer from a disturbance of perception, so that the objects of the world have a sensory appearance quite different from that in their normal experience. Since interpretation, as a rule, remains unimpaired, derealization appears to be the result of some organic factor affecting the sensory nervous system. In 'depersonalization' patients are afflicted by a mental condition in which they experience a profound change in their own personality, so that their own actions, thoughts, and emotions appear to be those of an automaton or to belong to a totally different person. In some instances there is 'somatic doubling,' so that the person seems to possess two distinct bodies, to one of which he transfers whatever is disagreeable or painful in his experiences. In an 'amnestic fugue' or, as it is less properly called, 'ambulatory automatism' the disorder of consciousness consists in a somewhat protracted condition characterized by wandering and other abnormal actions, followed by considerable loss of memory concerning this particular period. In these three states of partial loss of consciousness there is no 'splitting' of the personality of the subject.

In the following disorders of partial loss of consciousness, there occurs the phenomenon of so-called *split personality*. In this connection the word 'personality' is taken in the sense of 'character,' as the integrated group of acquired habits, emotional trends, behavior tendencies, temperament, etc., distinguishing one individual from another. It is a question, therefore, of the empirical personality, in so far as the self or Ego manifests itself in its mental states. By 'split personality' is meant an abnormal condition of mental dissociation in which the same human mind manifests alternatingly two or more very different characters or personalities.

This condition appears in a variety of forms. When it is a case of 'alternating personality,' there are two memory chains, one for each personality. As the personality changes, the respective memory chain comes to the foreground. In one type of alternating personality, one memory chain is continuous, while the other is interrupted; in another type, both chains are interrupted. Not only are there cases of double personality, but also cases of 'multiple personalities,' running in number from three to half a dozen and more. During these alternations only one personality is present at any particular time. If one memory chain is continuous and the other interrupted, the first personality remembers everything done by the second, but the second does not remember what was done by the first; if both are interrupted, neither personality remembers what was done by the other. Ever since Morton Prince (1908, 1925) presented the case of Miss Beauchamp, psychologists also speak of 'coconscious personalities,' in which two personalities are co-existent, the primary personality knowing at all times what the secondary personality is doing, but the secondary knowing nothing about the primary.

At times the changes in split personality are rather profound; at other times, more in the nature of changes of mood. When split personality has its origin in hysteria, a defense mechanism of the individual is always at work. Subconscious desires bring about a dissociation of memory items and form them into separate groups. In epileptic conditions, the dissociation is due to an organic cause, but the result is practically the same.

A number of psychologists and philosophers have built up a *metaphysical theory* on the facts of split personality. They claim there must be as many *minds* (selves, or Egos) in the individual as there are 'personalities.' This conclusion is unwarranted. The facts merely reveal a *dissociation* of memory material. While much of the memory material is available for voluntary recall to the normal consciousness, much of it is not. Under special conditions, the submerged, subconscious memory material may become dissociated into groups which, when utilized separately, give the appearance of a different personality. "After all," as Miss Beauchamp once remarked, "it is always myself."[4]

Psychoanalysis

Psychoanalysis is a method devised and developed by Sigmund Freud for the examination of the contents and mechanisms of an individual's mind, for the purpose of treating and curing mental disorders. He began his psychoanalytic therapy shortly before the turn of the century. C. G. Jung, A. Adler, A. Meyer, C. Baudouin, Franz Alexander, and others developed the principles and methods of psychoanalysis along divergent lines.

Freud bases his views on *three aspects* of mental life: the dynamic, the economical, and the topographical.

From the *dynamic* point of view, he considers all mental processes, except the reception of stimuli in sensation, to be the result of the interplay of *instincts*. There are two groups of instincts: the 'ego-instincts,' which aim at self-preservation; and the 'object-instincts,' which are directed toward external objects. Two fundamental latent instincts underlie these two groups: 'Eros' and the 'instinct for destruction.' The 'Eros' instinct drives toward ever closer union, and the manifestation of it is called by Freud *libido* or *sexuality*. The 'instinct for destruction,' as the name indicates, strives for the destruction of what is living. Instincts are always dynamic. Relative to one another, they sometimes co-operate, sometimes antagonize, sometimes compromise.

From the *economic* point of view, Freud contends that all

[4] Morton Prince, *The Dissociation of a Personality* (Longmans, Green, 1925), p. 525.

ideas or images representing the instinctual forces have an 'affective charge,' measurable in definite quanta of energy. The discharge of this energy is regulated by the *pleasure-pain principle,* so as to bring about a smooth functioning. Later, as the individual develops to adolescence and adulthood, the 'pleasure principle' is replaced to a great extent by the *reality-principle;* as a result of the operation of the 'reality-principle' pleasures of satisfaction are postponed and temporary feelings of pain are tolerated.

From the *topographical* or structural point of view, Freud distinguishes *three layers* or levels in the mental apparatus. The deepest and most primitive is the *id.* The 'id' is unconscious; it is also the storehouse of the instinctive impulses and of all memories which are inaccessible to normal consciousness. The next layer is the *ego,* the subsconscious. The external world influences and modifies the 'ego,' and it is also developed through the activity of preformed instincts. The uppermost layer is the *super-ego.* The 'super-ego' exercises a dominating influence on the 'ego'; it contains the ideals, the moral notions, the conscious aims, the principles of art, science, and religion, the precepts of social convention, etc., which are the result of education and inhibit the instincts in their natural activities.

There is a *theoretical basis* to psychoanalysis. According to Freud, in order to understand the nature of neuroses, three things must be borne in mind: the condition of 'repression' and 'censorship'; the importance of the 'sexual instincts'; and the practical fact of 'transference' in the technique of psychoanalytic procedure.

Instincts are the mainsprings of action. They cannot be suppressed. The desires and tendencies emanating from them may be temporarily frustrated, through considerations of moral ideals, social conventions, and the like. Frustration, however, induces tension, and, since gratification cannot be postponed indefinitely, mental and emotional conflicts arise which lead to substitutive gratifications replacing the natural gratifications of these instinctual desires and tendencies. The result is a neurosis.

The patient naturally tries to remove the disagreeable experiences of the mental conflict. He does this by endeavoring to *forget* them. The painful memories are pushed out of sight, so far as the waking consciousness is concerned, and thus these memories become buried in the dark recesses of the unconscious. They are, however, not dead, but always active; consequently, the conflict and the neurosis persists, working havoc in the patient's life.

To effect a cure, these destructive memories must again be brought to consciousness, analyzed, and finally resolved by the analyst. But here the mechanism of the mental apparatus presents an obstacle very difficult to overcome. At the threshold of consciousness is the 'ego,' which acts as a *censor* and seeks to hinder all tendencies which displease it from entering consciousness and influencing conduct. Such tendencies, submerged in the unconscious, are said to be 'repressed.' Hence the phenomenon of *repression,* found in all cases of neurosis. When the physician, in the course of his examination, comes close to these hidden memories and attempts to bring them to the surface of the patient's consciousness, he produces a mental *resistance* in the patient, because the patient does not want to remember them as the 'censor' seeks to block their entrance into consciousness. The 'censor' is unceasingly vigilant; but not so vigilant that the submerged memories cannot give indications of their presence and character in devious ways. *Hypnotism* often discloses them. *Free association,* in the form of a detailed description of the patient's life history, frequently uncovers helpful clues. Mainly, however, indications of the conflict in past experiences come through *dreams,* because dreams are based on wish-fulfillment. The 'censor' permits these memories to pass in the form of dreams, but disguised and masked in *symbols* which need interpretation by an expert in order to be recognized for the memories which they represent.

The *sexual instincts* are the most potent and most important. For reasons of morality and social convention, however, their natural tendencies are the ones which are repressed the most.

It is in the field of repressed sexuality (*libido*) that substitutive gratification occurs; hence, neurotic symptoms are symptoms of *repressed sexuality* and are always libidinous in character. Since sexual life begins in earliest childhood, long before puberty, the psychoanalyst must look for the roots of neurosis far back in the earliest days of childhood.

Hypnosis, Freud soon discovered, is not necessary for the uncovering of former mental conflicts and their hidden memories. Free association in conversation and the expert interpretation of dreams suffice. Therein consists the technique of the Freudian psychoanalytic method.

In the course of this procedure the physician encounters what Freud calls *transference*. Patients, it seems, enter into an emotional relationship, both affective and hostile, with the psychoanalyst himself. There is really nothing strictly personal about it. They merely 'transfer' their childhood relations to their parents, which is the basis for the original conflict, over to the physician, making him the substitute. Once the memories of the hidden conflict are revealed to the consciousness of the patient and are relived in the present, the irrationality of the grounds for the conflict are pointed out and explained by the analyst. When the patient perceives the explanation of the past conflict, the painful memories lose their effectiveness as psychogenic agencies of mental disorders, the mind is at rest, the transference ceases, and the cure is complete.

As a *therapeutic method* of curing psychogenic mental disorders, Freud's psychoanalysis can boast of remarkable success. As a *psychology,* it is based on theoretical assumptions of very questionable validity. Freud overemphasizes sexuality. He underestimates the importance of intellect and will in human conduct. His theory of the instincts and of the censorship of the 'ego' finds little support in experimental psychology. His underlying philosophy is materialistic and hedonistic, making religion, morality, and social life the natural causes of neurosis.[5]

---

[5] See Rudolf Allers' *The Successful Error* (Sheed and Ward, 1940), for a thorough critique of Freud's psychoanalytic principles. See also T. V. Moore's *The Nature and Treatment of Mental Disorders* (Grune and Stratton, 1943), Ch. II.

On the other hand, psychoanalysis has demonstrated the influence of mind over body and body over mind, has stimulated a greater interest in the early educational care of the child, and has forcibly brought to the attention of a biologistic psychology that mental treatment can cure a large group of bodily ailments.

The workings of the normal consciousness and of the subconscious are still very obscure. Little by little, however, the veil is being lifted, enabling us to cast more penetrating glances into the depths of the human mind.

Summary of Chapter XVII

One of the foremost phenomena of mental life is *consciousness.*

1. *Concept of Consciousness.* A strict definition of consciousness cannot be made, because it is an ultimate datum of mental experience. It is the state of our mind in which we find ourselves when we are *awake.* It is the same as *awareness.*

Consciousness has a *content.* The content includes all mental acts of whose presence we are aware in our waking state and the objects toward which these acts are directed.

2. *Field of Consciousness.* It is the sum-total of all items present in the consciousness of an individual at any given moment. The field is divided into the *focus,* in which objects or experiences receive maximal attention, and the *margin, fringe,* or *periphery,* in which objects or experiences are still noticed to some degree.

3. *Unconsciousness.* It is the absence of consciousness. We distinguish between *objective* and *subjective* unconsciousness. Something is 'objectively' unconscious, when it is devoid of the attribute of consciousness altogether; it is 'subjectively' unconscious, when it actually does not enter consciousness, though of itself it could.

4. *Subconsciousness.* Those mental items and processes are 'subconscious,' which are apparently of the same nature as the normally conscious items and processes, but of which the sub-

ject is not aware in the waking state. This mental state is termed *subconsciousness* or *subliminal consciousness*. The waking consciousness is also called *supraliminal* consciousness. Man has a sensuous and an intellectual consciousness.

Many items of experience, too faint to be noticed by the waking consciousness, are recorded in the subconsciousness; they are 'split off' and dissociated from the supraliminal consciousness.

Indications of the existence of subconsciousness are: double trains of thought; sudden recall of forgotten memories; the execution of unfinished problems; automatic writing; hypnotic phenomena.

5. *Coconsciousness.* By this is meant any actual subconscious *idea* or *thought process,* unknown to the human subject when awake.

6. *Self-consciousness.* It is man's consciousness of his *self* or *Ego* as the subject and bearer of all the conditions and states affecting his being, particularly of consciousness itself. Not only are mental states and activities present in consciousness, but I myself, by an act of reflex cognition, know that they are present and know that they belong to me as *modifications of myself*. Through memory I am aware that the Ego is a single, permanent reality, distinct from the mental states themselves; existing through the years, the Ego is perceived to be *self-identical* at all times.

7. *The Seat of Consciousness.* Neither the cerebral hemispheres, nor the frontal lobes, nor the thalamus, nor the hypothalamus, nor the medulla can be considered to be the seat of consciousness. It is the *individual* who is conscious, with a dependence on the nervous system.

8. *The Function of Consciousness.* The function and purpose of consciousness is to enable man to perceive and interpret his surroundings, to make his past experience available for adjustment to the needs of the present moment.

9. *Disorders of Consciousness.* Disorders arise from organic or psychogenic causes. They are of various kinds:

Total loss: coma, concussion, swooning.

Partial loss: stupor, confusion, derealization, depersonalization, amnestic fugue; these occur without 'splitting' of the personality. In the cases of 'split personality' we have an abnormal condition of dissociation in which the same human mind manifests alternatingly two or more very different characters or 'personalities.'

10. *Psychoanalysis.* It is a method devised for the examination of the contents and mechanisms of an individual's mind, for the purpose of treating and curing mental disorders.

Readings

Moore, T. V., *Cognitive Psychology,* Part I; *Dynamic Psychology,* Part I. — Prince, Morton, *The Unconscious.* — Jastrow, Joseph, *The Subconscious.* — Freud, Sigmund, *New Introductory Lectures on Psychoanalysis.* — Allers, Rudolf, *The Successful Error.* — Adler, Mortimer J., *What Man Has Made of Man.*

CHAPTER XVIII

EXTRANORMAL MENTAL STATES

FROM the dawn of recorded history up to the present day, the claim has been persistently made that some persons are gifted with mysterious powers, outside and beyond the range of the normal capabilities. Instances of 'premonition,' 'clairvoyance,' 'telepathy,' 'trance,' 'hypnotism,' and the like, are cited in support of this claim.

These phenomena are termed *extranormal,* because they do not occur with everybody or at all times. They are *not abnormal,* in the sense that there is anything, so far as is known, strictly pathological about them. Some of them are definitely *supernormal,* such as clairvoyance and telepathy; or so at least it would seem. Other phenomena, such as the mysterious workings of the hypnotic state, do not appear to be 'supernormal,' but they certainly do not belong to the 'normal' experiences of everyday life; they are, therefore, at least 'extranormal.' The word 'extranormal' can thus be used as a convenient term under which to group these exceptional experiences.

These extranormal phenomena will be discussed under two main headings: *hypnotism* and *extra-sensory perception.*

Hypnotism

We can describe *hypnotism* or *hypnosis* as a trance-like nervous condition resembling sleep, induced by the suggestions and (or) manipulations of the operator ('hypnotist'), the hypnotized subject remaining in mental communication ('rapport') with the operator and responsive to his suggestions.

The hypnotic state is usually characterized by alterations of the character or 'personality' of the subject, together with changes of the functions of memory and of perception.

Hypnotism, except for the name, is nothing new. The trance state, so noticeable in the hypnotic condition, was known in antiquity. Pliny, Galen, and Aretaeus discussed the subject. Paracelsus attributed it to a force or fluid emanating from the stars, comparing it to the magnet and calling it *magnale*.

It remained for *Anton Mesmer* (1733–1815), a Viennese physician, to bring the phenomena into the focus of scientific inquiry. He supposed the cause to be a universally diffused fluid, set in motion by the will. He gave it the name *animal magnetism,* because he considered it to be analogous to that of mineral magnetism but peculiar to organisms or animal bodies. Different kinds of inanimate bodies, such as metals, crystals, and magnets, according to his view, also possessed this force or fluid, so that they could be used to induce and terminate the phenomena. In 1778 Mesmer came to Paris and publicized his views. The sick flocked to him in large numbers, and he effected numerous cures with his novel method. The French Academy investigated the matter through a commission and attributed the phenomena to imagination or imitation. 'Magnetism' or *mesmerism,* as it came to be called, soon had a number of adherents, among them the Marquis de Puységur, who discovered the phenomena of somnambulism. Mesmerism dropped out of vogue during the French Revolution.

Abbé Faria, about 1814, revived hypnotism. A true pioneer of science, he discarded the theory of a 'magnetic fluid,' showing that the phenomena were attributable to the power of *suggestion*. Nothing, he maintained, comes from the operator, everything from the subject; at bottom, the magnetic trance is nothing more than a form of sleep, the condition often being induced by fixedness of look and cerebral fatigue; the phenomena are produced through the action of the subject's imagination in response to the suggestions of the operator. These acute observations aroused considerable interest among scientists for a time.

James Braid (1795–1860), of Manchester, took up the matter (1841). He became convinced that the phenomena were a result of a *mental concentration on a single idea.* Fixed gazing, the concentration on a real or imaginary object, and so on, produced what he called *mono-ideism,* while in the normal waking state man's attention is divided among a number of things. The fixed gaze, he contended, brought on a paralysis of the frontal brain, thereby producing trance and somnambulism; in this manner the subject lost the power of neutralizing the dominant idea and fell under the power of suggestion. Later on, Braid realized that the theory of mono-ideism was too narrow in scope, because he noticed that several phenomena (psychic deafness and blindness, rigidity, anesthesia, etc.) could be present simultaneously. He called this trance condition 'neur-hypnotism' (nerve-sleep), and from his designation the modern term *hypnotism* derives its origin.

From this point on, hypnotism became an object of intense scientific study. Two schools of thought in France did much to bring hypnotism to the foreground through a heated controversy on the fundamental nature of hypnotism. These were the *Salpêtrière School of Paris,* headed by Charcot, and the *Nancy School,* represented by Liébeault, Beaunis, Bernheim, and Liegois.

Charcot (1825–1893) and the *Salpêtrière* (*Paris*) *School* explained hypnotism in terms of *nerve physiology.* Charcot made his experiments with patients afflicted with hysteria. To induce hypnosis, he made use of a bright light or a sudden sound; he also made the patient stare fixedly at some object. Correspondingly, he considered the inducing cause to be *physical,* not mental, and hypnosis itself due to a nervous or cerebral modification of the subject. Hypnosis, therefore, Charcot and his followers claimed, is a pathological condition, a *neurosis,* a form of *hysteria;* consequently, there is a profound difference between normal sleep and hypnotic trance. Since hypnosis is a condition induced by purely physical means, Charcot contended that a person might be hypnotized, as it were, unknown to himself.

Bernheim and the *Nancy School* took a diametrically opposite view. Hypnosis, according to this view, has but a single cause, and it is a *psychical* cause, namely, *suggestion;* suggestion is the only essential factor. Everybody is suggestible; to suggest to a person to be more suggestible, that is neither more nor less than hypnotism. Consequently, no fundamental difference exists between normal and hypnotic sleep. The state of normal suggestibility is simply increased by the action of suggestion itself, because every idea has the tendency to actuate itself. Hypnotic phenomena are very similar in character to many normal acts; even under normal conditions we perform acts which are *automatic, involuntary,* and *unconscious.*

The controversy between these two schools attracted the attention of the entire scientific world. It gave a tremendous impetus to the experimental research into the phenomena in question and into the methods of inducing and controlling them. Many interesting facts were brought to light, so that our present knowledge of hypnotism is quite extensive.

The Phenomena of Hypnotism

The phenomena which occur in the hypnotic state are many and varied. Some are psychological, others physiological.

Psychological Phenomena

Consciousness. The hypnotic condition may be light or deep. Light hypnosis is, at times, hardly distinguishable from the normal waking state. There are many degrees and stages in hypnosis, shading imperceptibly from the nearly normal waking state to deep hypnosis. In deep hypnosis, the subject is in a trance and apparently, though not actually, asleep. Generally speaking, the subject is, to a lesser or greater degree, *always conscious* in hypnosis. Even in deep hypnosis the subject hears the voice of the hypnotist and carries out suggestions. Hypnosis, therefore, can be said to be a mental state which lies between ordinary sleep and normal waking. The hypnotized person is more conscious than in sleep, but less conscious than in the waking state.

Suggestibility. Everybody is suggestible in some measure. We see someone yawn, and we also yawn; we hear an orchestra play a tune, and our feet tap the rhythm; we observe a person staring at a certain spot, and we involuntarily do the same: such and similar actions are the result of 'suggestion.' The inclination or tendency to carry out a suggestion is termed 'suggestibility.' In hypnosis this suggestibility is increased and heightened, so that the hypnotized person carries out the suggestions of the operator with greater facility and readiness than in the normal waking state.

Rapport. A mental alertness exists in the subject toward the suggestions given by the operator. When the subject is in a state of deep hypnosis, he will respond to the operator's suggestion, no matter how slight, whether it be expressed by word or sign. As a rule, the suggestion is carried out without opposition. At the same time, the subject is, to all appearance, totally oblivious of his surroundings, paying no attention to the presence or suggestions of other persons, unless ordered to do so by the operator. Provided rapport has been established through definite suggestion, the subject will remain in mental contact with the operator, responsive to his voice, even after an interruption of hours or days. If, for any reason, this rapport is broken during deep hypnosis, the subject passes over into a state of normal sleep, to awaken later of his own accord, just as he would in ordinary sleep.

Memory. Memory is affected by hypnosis, but the change, if there is a change, depends on a number of factors — the personality of the subject, the kind of suggestion given by the operator, and the depth of the hypnotic state.

Sometimes memory remains *unchanged,* particularly in light hypnosis. The subject then remembers in hypnosis everything that has occurred in the waking state and also remembers everything in the waking state that has occurred in hypnosis. Furthermore, the operator can suggest that the subject shall remember in the waking state what has occurred in hypnosis.

During deep hypnosis, however, there ordinarily occurs a *change of memory.* In deep hypnosis the subject is able to recall the events of his normal waking life and also the events of former hypnoses; on waking, however, the events occurring in the hypnotic condition are forgotten, especially if post-hypnotic amnesia has been suggested. It is a controverted point whether a subject in the waking state can recall, either by reflection or chance association, something which has occurred in deep hypnosis, if the operator has suggested complete amnesia. The trance of deep hypnosis, characterized by complete post-hypnotic amnesia, is called 'somnambulism.'

Upon suggestion, the subject can be made to forget selected events of the normal waking life and also events of a former hypnotic state. This amnesia can again be abolished through counter-suggestion. For example, it may be suggested to a person who knows German that he be unable to speak it on awakening; he will not be able to use the language on returning to the normal waking state. In all probability, however, this condition will not be permanent, unless reinforced periodically by renewed suggestions. One must bear in mind, too, that the willingness of the subject is presupposed and required; a subject can always resist things disagreeable to himself and refuse to have items blotted out from memory.

Increased memory is a common phenomena associated with hypnosis. Many items can be recalled in the hypnotic state which are unavailable for memory in normal life. While the earliest remembered incidents of an individual's life history ordinarily date from about the sixth or fifth year, the subject, when hypnotized, is often able to remember events pertaining to the fourth and third year. All events are remembered with greater fullness of detail than is possible under normal circumstances. It was this fact which led the way to psychoanalysis. *Memorizing* is much easier in hypnosis than in the waking state. After a single reading, difficult prose passages or verses can be retained and, upon suggestion, be repeated later when out of hypnosis.

Post-hypnotic Suggestion. By 'post-hypnotic suggestion' is meant a suggestion given during hypnosis, but to be carried out by the subject after hypnosis has been terminated. The operator, for example, may suggest to the subject an abhorrence for liquor or tobacco after awakening and, if the subject uses either, an attack of vomiting; after hypnosis is terminated, the suggestion will be carried out. Again, during hypnosis, a point of time may be specified in the normal waking state for a certain phenomenon to manifest itself; at the appointed time it will occur. The suggestion, for instance, may be given to the hypnotized subject that, one hour after being awakened, his leg will feel lame and he will walk with a limp for ten minutes; the lameness will appear at the specified time, and the subject, due to post-hypnotic amnesia, will be unable to account for the fact. Not all persons are post-hypnotically suggestible, but practically all subjects in deep hypnosis are capable of carrying out this type of suggestion.

Another very interesting and mysterious phenomena of hypnotism is that of *post-hypnotic appreciation of time.* In order that a certain act be performed at a specified future moment, it seems evident that some sort of time calculation must be made by the subject. Many experiments have been made involving time appreciation and time calculation. The subject was told, for example, to perform a simple act after 300, 450, 700, 1500, etc., minutes; post-hypnotic amnesia was suggested, and the subject awakened immediately. No clock or watch was allowed to be seen by the subject, so that the subject had no starting point for the calculation of time. The operator himself did not know at what time of the day or night the act would be due. In most cases the suggestion would be carried out correctly, though there was a deviation of a few minutes in some instances. Sometimes the subject resisted the impulse, because the act seemed senseless and ridiculous; but the impulse itself was present at the appointed time. J. Milne Bramwell[1] made a series of 55 experiments with one subject, telling her to make a cross on a piece of paper with a pencil and write down the time of the writing without consulting a watch or clock. The time element varied, of course, in the different experiments. On one occasion, the subject was ordered

[1] *Hypnotism, Its History, Practice, and Theory,* pp. 122 ff.

to make the cross and write the time after 21,434 minutes. Forty-five experiments of the series were carried out successfully; in one experiment the performance occurred five minutes too soon; in the remainder, one to two minutes too soon. On being re-hypnotized and questioned as to the method of calculation employed, she informed him that at the time of the suggestion she made no calculation and did not remember the suggestion in the waking state, but that at a specified moment she felt an impulse to take paper and pencil and experienced the idea of making a cross and writing certain figures, without looking at a clock or watch while doing so. Other experimenters have encountered the same situation. The subjects do not seem to know just how they estimate and calculate the time.

Change of Personality. By means of suggestion, the hypnotist can modify the personality of the subject to a great extent. He can make the subject relive the developmental stages of his past life, so that the subject will think, speak, write, and act like a person of 5, of 10, of 15, of 20 years, and so on. Similarly, at the command of the hypnotist, he will assume the character of a general, a lawyer, a salesman, a preacher, a woman, a dog, a lion, etc., and do his utmost to play the role assigned to him. These hypnotic 'personalities' may become so distinct and pronounced, that the one has apparently no knowledge of the other.

Automatic Writing. As a result of post-hypnotic suggestion, the subject in the waking state can be made to read aloud from a previously unknown book and simultaneously write out a discourse of some kind at the same time. The subject knows and remembers what was read, but has no waking knowledge of what was written. When re-hypnotized, the subject recalls the mental processes involved in the writing.

Physiological and Sensory Phenomena

The Muscular System. The *voluntary* muscles are affected by suggestion. The operator, through suggestion, can produce a marked increase in muscular power and activity. The subject can lift weights much heavier than he is capable of lifting under ordinary conditions. The operator can also suggest functional paralysis of the muscles. The entire body may be made rigid as a board, and this rigidity can be maintained for hours without apparent fatigue.

Even the *involuntary* muscles and the *vasomotor* system are affected by suggestion. The rate of respiration and of the pulse can be increased or decreased. Nose-bleeding has been obtained. Defecation, urination, perspiration, the shedding of tears, and other secretory functions, have been successfully suggested. It is claimed that blistering of the skin can at times be suggested.

Normal *sensibility* can be *increased* to a remarkable degree in hypnosis. One subject could read print reflected in the operator's eye. Attendants in mental hospitals have been hypnotized and their hearing sharpened, so that the slightest sound coming from the patients would be perceived, even though the attendants were asleep. Very minute differences in weight or temperature can be clearly distinguished. After a meal, hunger and thirst can be suggested, so that the subject will eat a second meal with relish.

Just as sensibility can be increased in hypnosis, so it can also be effectually *decreased, inhibited,* and *changed.* Blindness, color blindness, double vision, deafness, change or loss of taste and smell, can be produced temporarily. Hunger and thirst can be alleviated and even removed. If the operator suggests anesthesia, the subject loses the sensation of touch; if he suggests analgesia, the subject no longer experiences pain. In such cases, the subject will not notice the thrust of a needle or of a knife through his flesh. Surgeons have performed operations on hypnotized subjects; Esdaile excised a very large tumor from a man and amputated a woman's leg below the knee.

The production of *sensory hallucinations* in hypnotized persons is a common phenomenon. They can be made to see, hear, taste, smell, and feel practically anything the operator desires. The imagination produces images so vivid that to the subject they appear as real objects actually perceived. These hallucinations may be either positive or negative. If, for instance, the subject sees an article, and if the operator then suggests that a second article is placed in front of the former, hiding it from view, the subject will see the imaginary article and will not see the real article; this effect is a case of 'positive' hallucination. Or, if the subject sees an article and sees a second article being placed behind the former, and if the operator then suggests the first article way, then the first article will (apparently) vanish, so that the subject sees the article hidden behind it; this effect is a case of 'negative' hallucination. Hallucinations can also be post-hypnotically suggested, so that the subject, upon awakening, will see an imaginary cow or hear an imaginary orchestra, etc.

When suggested by the operator, a subject will temporarily experience *feelings* (pleasure, displeasure) and *emotions* (fear, piety, anger, joy, disgust, etc.). Some types of *mental disorders* have been successfully treated by suggestion, particularly phobias; where complete cures have not been effected, improvement has often been obtained.

Criminal Acts and Hypnotism

Are hypnotized persons mere automatons, completely under the control of the hypnotist, so that they are irresistibly compelled to carry out his commands? If the hypnotist suggests a criminal act, such as theft, murder, arson, adultery, etc., *must the subject obey,* or *can the subject resist?* Liébault, Bernheim, and Beaunis, of the Nancy School, were convinced that subjects, while in the hypnotized condition, could be induced to commit crimes. Delbeouf, Bramwell, and most experimenters deny it.

In the course of time, extensive experiments have been made along these lines, and a number of facts have been established which have an important bearing on this problem.

Hypnotized persons are not mere automatons. The hypnotic

state does not place them under the absolute control of the hypnotist. They do not lose the essential use of reason and will. They can and do resist suggestions; they can and do refuse to carry out orders. They act in this manner not only when the suggestions are morally offensive, but also when they are innocuous and indifferent. Many instances are on record where subjects have refused to obey out of sheer *whim* and *caprice*. Oftentimes subjects will not co-operate, although they are aware, as they themselves admit, that it is only an experiment, a 'laboratory crime'; it offends their *moral sense* to do something which they know is nothing more than an 'imaginary crime.'

It is true, of course, that subjects have been induced to perform 'laboratory crimes,' such as stabbing someone with a rubber or cardboard knife, putting poison (sugar, suggested as arsenic) in another's coffee, and so forth. These instances, however, prove nothing, because the experimenters were reputable men, and the subjects placed their trust in them, confident that a real crime would never be suggested.

Are we to conclude that no *real crimes* have ever been committed by subjects under the hypnotic influence of unscrupulous operators? It would indeed be rash to deny either the possibility or the fact of the commission of genuine 'hypnotic' crimes. Forel, after an examination of the pertinent material, comes to the conclusion that normal persons can always resist criminal suggestions, but that the childish, the psychopathically inferior, and the ethically weak and defective person, lacking moral balance and resistance, can be induced to commit real crimes through suggestion. Schrenk-Notzing and others agree with him. Forel's opinion is, in all probability, the correct answer to the question. Virtuous persons cannot be compelled to commit, or to consent to, suggested crimes. It is not quite clear whether the operator, because he possesses their confidence, could break down their resistance by persuasion or false information. If, however, the criminal suggestion agrees with the principles, dispositions, and habits of the subject, it will probably be carried out.

Theories of Hypnotism

Leaving out of consideration the obscure opinions of the ancients and beginning with the views of Anton Mesmer, a number of theories have been advanced as an explanation of the *nature of hypnotism.*

Magnetism. Mesmer and his followers considered the cause of hypnotic phenomena to be *physical,* namely, 'animal magnetism,' 'magnetic or vital fluid,' 'od or odylic force.' Scientists have been unable to discover any such force or fluid. The theory is crude and primitive, and it is totally discredited.

Suggestion. Abbé Faria looked for the cause in *suggestion,* maintaining that everything comes from the hypnotized subject, not from the operator. So far he was correct. The operator merely directs the course of events; the phenomena originate in and by the subject at all times. Whatever happens has its cause in the subject's own nature. Suggestion, however, is not really the 'cause' of hypnotic phenomena; it is merely the 'signal' which sets the cause in action.

Mono-Ideism. Braid's theory of mono-ideism points out the fact that there exists a considerable narrowing of consciousness in the hypnotized subject, and subsequent experiments have verified his contention. He was wrong, however, in restricting the concentration of consciousness to one single idea. He realized his error and later rejected mono-ideism, because it is possible to have more than a single hypnotic effect present at any given time. He advanced the understanding of hypnotism by stressing it *psychic character.*

The Salpêtrière School. According to Charcot and his followers, hypnosis is an artificially induced *neurosis,* and it can be produced only in persons suffering from *hysteria.* Since about eighty to ninety per cent of adults can be hypnotized, the vast majority of persons should be hysterical, which is not true. Soldiers, sailors, and students can readily be hypnotized, because of their habitual attitude of accepting commands (suggestions), and they are not hysterical. Charcot was also mistaken when he claimed that persons could be hypnotized by *purely physical means* and unknown to themselves. Hypnosis demands the co-operation of the subject, because hypnosis is primarily a psychical affair and the subject is the principal agent in the production of all phenomena.

The Nancy School. Bernheim and his associates saw no real difference between *natural sleep* and the *artificial sleep* of hypnosis. A considerable difference, however, exists between the two states. Consciousness is responsive to the suggestions of the operator in hypnosis, but is not alert in natural sleep. Hypnosis lacks the haphazard character of dream states. Hypnosis tends to act out the suggestions of the operator externally, something rarely found in natural sleep. Bernheim also maintained that the hypnotized person is a mere *automaton,* without self-determination. The actions of the hypnotized subjects are, to a certain extent, automatic; but the subject is not thereby deprived of the power of self-determination, if he desires to use it. Hypnosis, the Nancy School asserts, is essentially *increased suggestibility,* and the increase is produced by suggestion itself. Increased suggestibility, however, is merely a symptom of hypnosis, not its essence. Suggestion and increased suggestibility do not explain the profound *physiological and psychical changes* which occur in hypnosis. Increased suggestibility seems to be rather the result than the cause of these changes. The real nature of hypnosis must lie deep down in the nervous and mental constitution of the subject.

The Subliminal Mind. F. W. Myers, William James, and many others sought the explanation of the mystery of hypnosis in the 'subliminal mind.' Most of these authors look upon the subliminal mind as a mind *distinct* from, and *independent* of, the normal, supraliminal mind, having vastly more complex and accurate processes of mental activity than are found in the mind of the waking state. The subliminal mind is a fully developed 'self,' superior to the supraliminal self.

This theory is *inadequate,* because it fails to account for all facts.

Granting, for the sake of argument, the existence of such a

secondary or subliminal mind as the agent of hypnotic phenomena, the *appreciation and calculation of time* in certain post-hypnotic experiments receives no proper explanation. As a rule, the subject, even when re-hypnotized, has *no memory* of the calculation and has *no knowledge* of how the calculation was made. In other words, the subliminal mind itself is unaware of how the phenomenon was produced. Hence, a third or fourth mind must be postulated. In as much as psychologists have distinguished as many as a dozen and more 'personalities' in one individual in various phases of hypnotic experience, consistency demands that we postulate the same number of subliminal minds or selves; but such a postulate seems unreasonable.

The distinction between these 'minds' or 'selves' is based on the distinction between *alternating consciousnesses* and *alternating memories*. The one consciousness is supposed to be altogether different from the other or others, and the one memory altogether different from the other or others. This difference, however, is not as great as is usually assumed. These consciousnesses and memories are not mutually exclusive, but overlap. As a matter of fact, a definite *bond of unity* runs through all the hypnotic phenomena of an individual. The knowledge and use, for example, of *language* is preserved and remembered in all states and stages of hypnotic experience, particularly if the subject knows and uses but a single language. As a rule, too, the subject retains his general knowledge of persons, objects, localities, etc. Such facts are evidence for the *essential identity of memory and consciousness* in every individual. It takes more than changes of moods and alternating groups of memory items to constitute distinct minds and selves in a person.

Dissociation. Most modern psychologists find the cause of hypnotic phenomena in 'mental dissociation.' Joseph Jastrow[2] is representative of this group. Here is his line of thought.

Man's normal waking consciousness is characterized by the

[2] *The Subconscious* (Houghton, 1906), pp. 464–529.

close and full association of his various faculties (senses, imagination, memory, intellect, will, etc.) and their activities. Normal experience is the result of three particular activities or 'privileges,' namely, incorporation, orientation, and initiative.

When we have a sense impression of an object and are aware of it, we give it a place among our conscious perceptions; this process is termed *incorporation*. We are conscious at the same time of the relative position of this object among the other objects of the physical world. Thereby we adjust ourselves consciously to the outside world; the resulting adjustment is *orientation*. Ordinarily, our mental experience is such that we control and direct our ideas, perceptions, imaginings, etc.; in other words, we have *initiative*. The joint, associated, normal functioning of incorporation, orientation, and initiative constitutes our normal waking state. When any of these activities are interfered with, impaired, or absent, we speak of a *dissociation*. The effect of dissociation is a subnormal or abnormal mental state. Instances of subnormal states are sleep, profound distraction, dreams, etc.; instances of abnormal states are hysteria, somnambulism, intoxication, insanity, etc.

Impairment of the 'incorporative' activity makes us partially or totally unaware of our surroundings—*psychic anesthesia*. We observe this state in hypnosis. The subject actually sees, hears, and feels things; but due to suggestion, he excludes the visual, auditory, and tactual images from his conscious experience and treats them as if they did not exist. Double personality arises, when the mind abnormally concentrates its attention on one group of experiences, thereby failing to incorporate this group of experiences into the normal stream of consciousness.

Impairment of 'orientation' brings on a partial or total inability to distinguish between imagined and objective reality. A person so afflicted lacks the corrective influence of external impressions on the workings of the imagination and accepts the images of the imagination as objectively real, as it happens in dreams. *Hallucinations* result from impaired orientation.

Thus, in hypnosis, the suggestions of the operator, due to a restricted and narrowed consciousness, are not offset by corrective judgments based on external perception and consequently are taken for objective reality. When this impairment is profound, so that one group of memory images is split off from the rest, there may arise the hallucination of distinct empirical 'selves' in the same individual, and then we speak of 'double personality.'

Impaired initiative, since it involves partial or total lack of personal control and direction, leads to *imperative impulse* and *enforced action.* A person with impaired initiative readily responds to an impulse imposed on the will by an outside agent. We observe this condition in hypnosis, where the operator's suggestions control and direct the actions of the subject. A marked impairment of initiative, together with an impairment of incorporation and orientation, is generally present in 'double personality.'

The impairment of one or the other or all of these human 'privileges' is present in all cases of mentally subnormal and abnormal conditions, ranging all the way from absentmindedness to permanent insanity.

The theory of dissociation has the advantage that it preserves the essential *unity and identity of the mind and self* and avoids the improbabilities of the subliminal mind theory mentioned above. It does not, however, give a complete explanation of the mystery of hypnosis. What happens in the nervous system, particularly in the cortical centers of the brain, when there is an impairment or disturbance of incorporation, orientation, and initiative? And how can the willingness of the subject and the suggestion of the operator produce such a profound impairment or disturbance? Therein lies precisely the mystery of hypnosis, and a mystery, it seems, it will always remain.

Among the various theories advanced in the course of the history of hypnotism, that of *mental dissociation* is the most promising. It agrees best with the findings of psychology in other fields of research.

The state of mind with the closest resemblance to hypnosis is the state of mind operative in *sleepwalking*. In sleepwalking (ordinary somnambulism), the mental images arouse the motor centers of the brain into carrying out bodily actions according to a fixed plan or idea (auto-suggestion). In hypnotic somnambulism, the images producing bodily action come from the suggestion of the operator (hetero-suggestion). The underlying mental mechanism is undoubtedly the same in both cases.

Extra-Sensory Perception

The problem of *extra-sensory perception* is a much-discussed question. 'Extra-sensory perception' is defined as a perception obtained through channels other than those of the known senses. Psychologists speak of the extra-sensory perception of *objective* events, i.e., knowledge of objects or occurrences not obtained from another mind, and of *subjective events,* i.e., knowledge of objects or occurrences obtained from another mind. The extra-sensory perception of objective events is termed *clairvoyance,* while the extra-sensory perception of subjective events is termed *telepathy*.

The distinction between clairvoyance and telepathy can be clarified by a simple illustration. A playing card, picked at random from a shuffled deck and no one having seen its face, is placed in an opaque envelope or box; the clairvoyant person has the ability to name the card correctly, because he perceives the card as it is, although it is impossible to perceive it with the ordinary senses. A person thinks of a certain verse, without pronouncing a single syllable; the telepathic person, perhaps miles away, perceives what is going on in the other person's mind and mentions or writes down the verse correctly. In the first instance there is an extra-sensory perception of an external or 'objective' event (clairvoyance), and in the second instance an extra-sensory perception of a mental or 'subjective' event (telepathy).

Extra-sensory perception is such an extraordinary phenomenon that scientists, who as a matter of principle refuse to accept anything as a fact which cannot be verified by the senses in some form or other, derided its possibility. In the course of time, however, so many cases were recorded by reliable witnesses that the accumulated evidence could no longer be ignored. A number of eminent scientists thereupon founded the Society of Psychical Research in England in 1882. Prominent names are found on the roster of its membership; among them are Henry Sedgwick, the first president, A. J. Balfour, W. F. Barrett, Balfour Stewart, Edmund Gurney, Frederic W. H. Myers, Oliver Lodge, William Crookes, Lord Rayleigh, and Alfred Russell Wallace. Similar societies were established in America (1884) and other countries. These societies did heroic service in checking available material. The result of the investigation was a residue of fact which seemed to prove definitely the existence of clairvoyance and telepathy. After some time, the investigation was placed on an experimental basis. Here, too, the result was positive. Some scientists became convinced, but very many were still skeptical.

The Duke Experiments

In 1930 a group of psychologists of *Duke University,* inspired by William McDougall, head of the psychology department there, began a systematic experimental investigation of extra-sensory perception. These men were Helge Lundholm, Karl E. Zener, and Joseph B. Rhine. Their aim was to discover whether parapsychological ('unconventional,' extranormal) phenomena actually occur and to find an explanation for their occurrence. The laboratory experiments were to be conducted with strictly scientific precautions, so as to exclude both fraud and unconscious sensory perception.

The method selected was 'card calling.' Zehner devised a set of cards with symbols — a circle, a cross or plus sign, a rectangle, a star, and three wavy lines. A pack consisted of twenty-five such cards, each symbol appearing five times in the deck. These are the famous 'Zener' or 'ESP' ('extra-sensory perception') cards. Since each symbol appears five times in the deck of twenty-five cards, the average chance of the symbols being called correctly must be one in five or one fifth of the total. A score considerably beyond this average, especially when the experiments run into hundreds and thousands, must be adjudged 'significant'; persistent high scores would furnish scientific proof for the existence of extra-sensory perception.

The experiments begun in the Duke Parapsychology Laboratory are now being conducted in at least a score of other universities. The methods vary. The technique, however, is similar. Neither the subject nor the experimenter knows the order of the cards. The subject must call the top card; his call is recorded, the card is placed aside, and the next card is called and recorded. After all have been called, the cards are checked with the record, to see how many 'hits' have been made. Or, a sample card of each of the five suits is placed before the subject, and he must match them by placing the cards of the deck in front of the five key cards in such a manner that the suits agree; none of the cards of the deck are allowed to be turned face up until the entire deck has been called. Only then are the hits and misses checked. Or, the five key cards, one of each suit, are placed face down, no one knowing their order; the entire deck is placed face down before the subject and he must match the unknown key cards with the corresponding cards of the deck. Or, a screen having been set up between the subject and the experimenter, the subject is required to call the cards of the deck hidden from him by the screen or he must match them with the key cards placed in front of himself; in no case does either the subject or the experimenter know the sequence of the cards until the experiment is finished. Or, the entire deck, face down, is set before the subject and, without disturbing or touching the deck in any way, the subject must call each card down through the deck; after all the cards have been called, the hits and misses are checked. Such are some of the standard types of experiments made to determine the presence of extra-sensory perception. Mechanical shuffling devices are sometimes used, so that no personal idiosyncrasy in shuffling can give the subject any sensory cues.

Naturally, only those persons are used for experiments who show signs of extra-sensory perceptivity. Once they are chosen, however, they are made to go through hundreds and even thousands of trials. The results of these trials, whether favorable or unfavorable, are recorded in detail, checked and double-checked, and filed away for reference. Utmost precautions are taken to prevent error, loss, or tampering. In this way scientific accuracy is obtained. The very simplicity of the method reduces the number of extraneous factors, which might vitiate the result, to a negligible quantity and makes mathematical evaluation a relatively easy matter.

Clairvoyance and Telepathy

Ever since the parapsychological laboratory of Duke University began its research in 1930, the number of tests made there and in other places amounts to far more than 2,000,000. What are the conclusions to be drawn from these experiments in extra-sensory perception?

The card-calling experiments just described are tests for *clairvoyance,* provided no one knows the actual sequence of the cards beforehand. If somebody knows the sequence beforehand, the possibility cannot be eliminated that the subject was able to 'read the mind' of the person possessing this knowledge and discovered the sequence in this fashion; that would be telepathy, not clairvoyance. But if no one knows the sequence, it is evident that the subject must 'read the cards themselves,' in order to know their sequence; and this would be clairvoyance.

At present there can hardly be a reasonable doubt that *clairvoyance is a scientifically demonstrated fact.* According to all the mathematical laws and calculations concerning probability, the results are significantly above the level of chance. In some instances the odds against the results having been obtained by chance run into the billions and even much higher.

Averages of 10 or more hits out of a possible 25 are not uncommon; a score of this kind is far beyond the expected chance results, particularly when one considers the fact that these averages cover perhaps hundreds of tests for the same subject. Scores for individual tests sometimes run as high as 15, 20, and more. In more than one case the subject performed the astounding feat of calling all 25 cards correctly; on one occasion a child 12 years of age called all cards correctly.

While most card-calling tests were made in a manner which would either prove or disprove the existence of clairvoyance, a certain amount of tests were made by Rhine and his associates to discover instances of *pure telepathy*. In the very nature of the matter, such tests are far more difficult to control scientifically than those of clairvoyance. In telepathy the subject must be able to read the mind or thought of the experimenter; hence, nothing can be used that exists in printed, written, or spoken form, otherwise clairvoyance would not be positively and definitely excluded from the test.

While the number of tests made concerning pure telepathy are relatively meager, those made gave *positive results*. The experimenter would arrange in his thoughts a sequence of symbols to his own liking, and the subject would be asked to name the sequence. In order to insure scientific accuracy, the experimenter and the subject would be placed in different rooms or buildings. The procedure was regulated by a stop-watch arrangement. At the appointed time, the subject had to call the sequence, and his calls were recorded. After the time for the test had elapsed, the experimenter wrote down the sequence he had in mind during the test. Thereupon the subject's calls were checked against this list for hits and misses. In one series of tests, with Miss Ownbey (a staff member of Duke) as 'sender' and Miss Bailey as 'receiver,' Miss Bailey made an average of 9.7 out of 25 in 450 trials, both being in separate rooms; she also made an average of 12.0 in 150 trials, both being in separate rooms, a distance of something like 30 feet away. On one occasion tests were made by Miss Ownbey as sender and Miss Turner as receiver over a distance of 250 miles. The daily tests called for a run of 25 calls, to be made at a specified time, with five-minute intervals between each call. Miss Turner made an average of over 17 correct calls out of a possible 25 during the three-day period of the tests. More tests were made. While she did not achieve the phenomenal success of the first tests, her over-all average was 10.1 for the entire series. Tests made by other psychological laboratories have substantiated the findings of the Duke experiments.

The Nature of Extra-Sensory Perception

Accepting clairvoyance and telepathy as factual occurrences demonstrated by scientific methods, what is their *nature?* The first question which must be answered is: Are they fundamentally *sensory* or *extra-sensory?*

For some reason or other, many critics simply cannot conceive of extra-sensory perception as possible and insist that *sensory cues,* imperceptible to ordinary persons or under normal circumstances convey the necessary information to the clairvoyant and telepathic subjects. They are supposed to be gifted with 'hyperesthesia,' or in plain words, with extreme sensitivity to minute visual, auditory, or tactual stimuli.

This theory, however, does not seem to cover the facts. So far as *visual cues* are concerned, they are, to all appearances, definitely excluded. No doubt, each card has peculiarities which, if known, might serve as a visual cue for the symbol printed upon it. The circumstances of the tests, however, make such cues useless. All decks are changed frequently; new decks are introduced continuously. The decks, in most tests, are screened, so that the subject cannot see them. Many subjects have their backs turned toward the cards; some walk back and forth in the room during the tests; others close their eyes; others lie on a couch at some distance from the cards, etc. Considering the properties of light, since light is essential for vision, it should be physically impossible for subjects to obtain visual cues, when they are separated from the cards by rooms, walls, and buildings, or when the cards are placed in sealed opaque containers. Blind-from-birth subjects have made significant scores, even when the cards were placed in opaque envelopes behind screens. In the 'down-through' tests, where the subject must call all cards down through the entire screened deck before the check is made, the cards beneath the top card are invisible to the eye, so that visual cues are excluded. Under the conditions surrounding the tests in modern psychological laboratories, the precautions taken against the use of visual cues are so stringent, that the sense of sight cannot explain the phenomena of clairvoyance and telepathy in an adequate manner.

It has been suggested that unconscious whispering on the part of the experimenter might give the subject *auditory cues,* so that clairvoyance and telepathy are nothing more than cases of supersensitive hearing. This theory supposes that the experimenter possesses the information in advance of the test. In many modern card-calling experiments, however, no one, not even the experimenter, knows the actual sequence of the cards until each card of the entire deck has been called by the subject. Auditory cues are simply impossible under such test conditions. Hence, clairvoyance and telepathy cannot be explained by the sense of hearing.

Tactual cues are also excluded in many of the methods employed in the tests. The subject, as a rule, is not allowed to handle or even touch the cards. Oftentimes, new decks are used in successive tests, so that the subject cannot associate any peculiarities of individual cards with the respective symbols. In the 'down-through' test, the subject cannot touch, even if permitted to do so, any card but the one on top of the deck. In distance tests tactual cues are entirely absent, because the subject is nowhere near the cards.

Olfactory or *gustatory* cues can hardly come into consideration at all, and no one advances a theory based on them.

Some critics speak of a 'sixth sense,' but no such sense has ever been discovered. It is possible, even probable, that clairvoyance and telepathy have a sensory basis of some sort. The real question, however, is: Can these phenomena be explained as the results of sensory stimuli affecting the *known, recognized senses,* such as sight, hearing, feeling, tasting, smelling, etc? The evidence is against such an explanation. All indications point to the 'extra-sensory' character of clairvoyance and telepathy.

That clairvoyance and telepathy are *extra-sensory* in the meaning defined, is borne out by a comparison of this type of perception with that experienced through the channels of the ordinary senses. *Organic structures* act as organs of sensation in ordinary perception. Perception thus involves a definite *localization* of the respective stimuli and their effects in the nervous system of the body. Nothing resembling organs and definite localization has been observed in extra-sensory perception. The subjects are unable to specify any particular organ of the body as the reception center of their extra-sensory impressions. They simply know or do not know what the symbols on the cards happen to be.

Another important difference is the *angle* or *position of the objects* for the two types of perception. It seems to make no difference in clairvoyance and telepathy whether the cards be held edgewise or broadside to the person of the subject, whether they be flat or folded, whether they be near or far away, whether they be placed openly in the presence of the subject or screened by walls, whether the symbols be large or minute, etc. Such factors, however, influence ordinary sense perception to a large degree.

Furthermore, none of the recognized senses are capable of perceiving directly what *thoughts* or *images* are present in another person's mind; visual or auditory signs are required. No such signs are required in telepathy. Distance, too, seems to be no effective barrier between mind and mind in telepathic communication.

Finally, science enumerates the various kinds of *energy* which are the stimuli for the ordinary senses: light energy for vision, sound energy for hearing, chemical energy for smell and taste, mechanical energy for pressure, etc. But science, so far at least, has been unable to point out what kind of energy, if any, is the causal agency involved in extra-sensory perception. No known energy seems to fit the facts of clairvoyance and telepathy. Radiant energy appears to be the necessary stimulus. X-rays, radio waves, gamma rays, etc., have been advanced as a possible cause for the phenomena in question. However, all these types of energy lose efficiency through distance and are affected by intervening objects, conditions which seems to have no appreciable influence on extra-sensory perception. Besides, no wave theory seems adequate as an explanation of how a 'thought' can be transferred from one mind to another, as occurs in telepathic messages. Then, too, if waves or rays are the efficient cause, how does it happen that the waves or rays emanating from the mind or brain of the sender, located perhaps a hundred miles away, are received by the subject, while those emanating from other persons much nearer are not received? To say that these minds are 'attuned' to each other, is a facile phrase, but it is merely an analogy and explains nothing. We may as well face the fact that the science of physics can contribute little to our understanding of the nature of extra-sensory preception.

Is then extra-sensory perception a *purely intellectual operation?* It does not seem so.

There is, without question, a close relationship between the higher mental operations and extra-sensory perception. Judgment, volition, attention, and mental concentration are required for good results in both types of activity. And yet it would seem that clairvoyance and telepathy belong essentially to the *sensory order of cognition.*

Practically all experiments in clairvoyance and telepathy have *objects* and *images* as the materials which form the basis of the tests. Both types of perception seem to meet with the greatest success, when the experimenter attempts to 'send' geometrical figures, words, melodies, etc. Apparently then, the imagination plays the dominant role in clairvoyant and telepathic perception.

Again, whatever lowers the efficiency of the higher centers

of the *sensory nervous system,* interferes with extra-sensory perception. Illness and fatigue bring about a decrease in the scoring averages. A dissociating drug, like alcohol or sodium amytal, does the same. On the other hand, a stimulant, like caffeine, increases perceptiveness, when applied to a subject affected by drowsiness or fatigue. These facts are indications that a good state of nervous integration is required for successful work in extra-sensory perception.

Experiments in *psychometry* corroborate the view that clairvoyance and telepathy are of the sensory order. In experiments of this kind, an object is placed in the hand of the subject. Sometimes the subject is blindfolded; sometimes the object is in an opaque container; sometimes the subject is allowed to see and handle the object. In any case, the psychometrizing subject gives the past history of this particular object. The interesting feature about the whole matter is the fact that this history comes to the subject in pictorial scenes of the *imagination.* These scenes, perhaps indistinct at first, become clear, and then fade out, other pertinent scenes following in succession. Psychometry is a variant of clairvoyance, but a clairvoyance that reaches into the past. R. Tischner has conducted a number of such experiments and claims that they are genuine. Others have made similar experiments with the same results. If genuine, they bear out the hypothesis that clairvoyance is sensory in nature. And since modern experimenters are convinced that both clairvoyance and telepathy derive their origin from the same fundamental faculty, the conclusion is logical that all extra-sensory perception is essentially sensory in nature and not purely intellectual. According to all indications, it is the *imagination* which is directly involved in extra-sensory perception. The images present in another mind seem to rise up spontaneously in the imagination of the subject.

In that case, though, what sort of energy acts as the stimulus for extra-sensory perception? We do not know. Like the states of hypnosis, extra-sensory perception is a mystery of the human mind. The facts are there, but no theory so far has been able to give us anything like a fair understanding of the phenomena of these extranormal mental states.

Summary of Chapter XVIII

Hypnotism and extra-sensory perception are *extranormal mental states.*

1. *Hypnotism.* Hypnotism or *hypnosis* is a trance-like nervous condition resembling sleep, induced by the suggestions and (or) manipulations of the operator ('hypnotist'), the hypnotized subject remaining in mental communication ('rapport') with the operator and responsive to his suggestions.

The phenomena of hypnotism have been explored by Mesmer, Faria, Braid, the Salpêtrière School of Paris, the Nancy School, and by many other scientists.

2. *The Phenomena.* Some are psychological, others physiological.

Psychological Phenomena. Consciousness is narrowed, but always present. *Suggestibility* is increased. The subject is always in *rapport* with the operator. *Memory* undergoes a change, especially in deep hypnosis. Most subjects are able to carry out *post-hypnotic suggestions* involving the mysterious power of time appreciation. Hypnotism is often accompanied by a *change of 'personality.' Automatic writing* is a common phenomenon.

Physiological and Sensory Phenomena. The *muscular system* can be affected by suggestion. *Normal* sensibility can be increased, decreased, inhibited, and changed. *Hallucinations* can be produced.

Criminal Acts. Hypnotized persons are not automatons; they do not lose the essential use of reason and will. They can and do resist suggestions. If, however, the criminal suggestion agrees with the principles, dispositions, and habits of the subject, a crime may, in all probability, be successfully suggested.

3. *Theories of Hypnotism.* A number of theories have been advanced in explanation of the *nature* of hypnotism.

Magnetism. Mesmer's theory of 'animal magnetism' as a physical force is crude; no such force has ever been discovered.

Suggestion. Faria maintained that the cause of hypnosis is suggestion. It is not so much the 'cause' which produces the phenomena as the 'signal' which sets the cause in action.

Mono-Ideism. This theory of Braid cannot account for the fact that a number of hypnotic effects can be present at the same time.

The Salpêtrière School. The theory is erroneous because the majority of adults are hypnotizable, but are not hysterical.

The Nancy School. Hypnosis is essentially *increased suggestibility* produced by suggestion. This theory does not explain the profound physiological and psychical changes which occur in hypnosis.

The Subliminal Mind. The advocates of this theory postulate a duality of minds in man. The subliminal mind is supposed to be the source of hypnotic phenomena. Since cases are known in which a dozen or more 'personalities' have occurred in hypnotic subjects, one must logically conclude that there are the same number of 'minds' present; such a view, however, seems preposterous.

Dissociation. Most modern psychologists find the cause of hypnotic phenomena in *mental dissociation.* Impairment or absence of incorporation, orientation, or initiative produce dissociation; its effect is a subnormal or abnormal mental state. This theory seems to give the best explanation.

No theory explains the profound changes which occur in the nervous system, particularly in the cortical centers, during hypnosis.

4. *Extra-Sensory Perception.* We understand by this term a perception obtained through channels other than those of the known and recognized senses. *Clairvoyance* is the extra-sensory perception of 'objective' events; *telepathy,* of 'subjective' events.

5. *The Duke Experiments.* Since 1930, the Department of Psychology of Duke University has made a systematic and

scientific attack on the problem of extra-sensory perception. The method selected was *card-calling.*

6. *Clairvoyance and Telepathy.* In clairvoyance the subject has an extra-sensory perception of *objects;* in telepathy, of *thoughts* or *images* present in another person's mind. The results obtained for both clairvoyance and telepathy were definitely positive.

7. *Nature of Extra-Sensory Perception.* Sensory *cues,* of whatever kind, seem ruled out as an explanation, due to the precautions taken in the tests. Extra-sensory perception *differs from normal sensory perception* in a number of important points: it has no recognizable organ of reception; the angle or position of the objects has no appreciable influence; no conventional signs are required to perceive the thoughts or images of another mind; no energy known to science seems to be the causal agency.

Extra-sensory perception, to all appearances, belongs to the *sensory order of cognition.* Tests in clairvoyance and telepathy succeed best when objects or images are the materials used in the experiments. Whatever lowers or heightens the efficiency of the higher centers of the nervous system also lowers or heightens the scoring average in extra-sensory perception. Experiments in psychometry corroborate this view, because the subject sees the past history of the object in pictorial scenes of the imagination. The *imagination,* it seems, is the internal sense directly involved in extra-sensory perception.

As in the case of hypnosis, extra-sensory perception is an obscure process, a mystery of the human mind.

Readings

Bramwell, J. Milne, *Hypnotism, Its History, Practice, and Theory.* — Forel, A., *Der Hypnotismus.* — Maher, M., *Psychology,* Supplement B, pp. 594–601. — Rhine, J. B., *New Frontiers of the Mind.* — Pratt, Joseph G. and associates, *ESP After Sixty Years.* — Tischner, Rudolph, *Telepathy and Clairvoyance.* — Sinclair, Upton, *Mental Radio.*

CHAPTER XIX

THE VITAL PRINCIPLE

The scientific psychologist is satisfied when he has obtained and has given a scientific description and explanation of the psychical process. The philosophic psychologist feels the necessity of delving into the implications of human processes and arriving thereby at an understanding of the *nature* of man.

Agere sequitur esse, 'action follows the being (nature),' is a sound axiom. As a being *is,* so it *does.* The nature of a being determines what kind of action a being can and will perform. In accordance with this principle, the *action* of a being is *a manifestation of its nature.* Hence, from the type of action performed by a being, we can legitimately conclude to the underlying nature which is the root of its action. If the actions of various beings are specifically the same, the natures of these beings must be specifically the same; if they are specifically diverse, the natures must be specifically diverse. No other conclusion is logical.

Man, as we have seen, combines within himself the vegetative processes of the plant, the sensory cognition and appetition of the brute animal, and the intellectual and volitional activities peculiar to himself. These types of action assuredly reveal man's nature. In order, however, to arrive at a real understanding of man's nature, it will be necessary to understand organic life in general.

Nature of Organic Beings

In attempting to explain the ultimate nature of organisms, a number of fundamental theories have found approval in scientific and philosophic circles in the course of time. The modern theories date from the time of René Descartes who is mainly responsible for the mechanistic explanation of organic bodies.

In general, *biological mechanism* is the application of atomism to biology. *Extreme mechanism* teaches that *'matter and force'* suffice to explain all bodies and activities. According to this theory, bodies are masses of 'matter' consisting of indivisible, inert, and immutable atoms. 'Force' is nothing more than incessant local motion pushing the masses of matter around. All bodies are mere aggregates of atomic particles passively affected by motion; as such, they are incapable of efficient causality, because they possess no powers of physical activity in virtue of their own intrinsic constitution. There can be, therefore, no real distinction between animate and inanimate, organic and inorganic, bodies.

In the field of biology, atomism is called *micromerism* or *merism* (Gr., μέρος, a part; μίκρος, small). The organic body is conceived as an aggregate resulting from the *additive summation* of cells, chromosomes, and genes; these particles, in turn, are mere aggregates of molecules, atoms, electrons, protons, neutrons, etc. Extreme mechanistic merism, then, seeks to explain the organism by 'breaking down' the organic body into its smallest parts and by reducing all its activities to simple mechanical motion. In consequence, the organic body is not an 'integrated unitary being' but an 'aggregate' or 'colony' of individually autonomous particles; its unity is more apparent than real. All that is required to obtain a complete organic body, is to put the single parts together; the sum of all the parts adds up to an 'organism.'

Few biologists and philosophers in our day defend this extreme mechanical merism. Though they adhere to the additive concept of merism as a basic theory, they admit the existence of mechanical, physical, and chemical 'forces' in material particles, together with efficient causality resulting from these forces. They advocate, therefore, a *mitigated biological mechanism.*

In opposition to merism (or micromerism), we find the

theory of *holism* (Gr., ὅλος, total, whole). This 'totality-theory' considers the organic body to be primarily an 'organized unit,' an 'integrated whole,' and this unit or whole is more than the mere addition and summation of its constituent parts. Over and above the activities of the individual parts, the organism performs activities which characterize it as a 'unit' or 'totality' and which cannot be reduced to the activities of the individual atomic and subatomic particles which make up the general structure of the organic body. In other words, the living body is not a 'machine' but an 'organism.' A machine can be taken apart and put together again, because a machine is nothing more than the sum of all its parts. An organism can also be broken down into its respective parts, but then it dies; the reconstruction of the parts into the whole, if that were possible, will never produce a living organism, because the organism is more than the sum of all its parts. Hence, the theory of holism is also called *organicism*.

Many biologists and philosophers demand *something distinctly vital* in the organism to account for the structural and functional unity of the organism as a whole. The mere forces of inanimate nature and the mere organization of material particles, taken alone by themselves, do not give an adequate explanation of the nature of the organism. This theory is called *vitalism*. Some vitalists find this 'vital' element in a special kind of qualitative force or energy which is immaterial; others consider it to be material, but different from the ordinary mechanical, physical, and chemical forces.

Vitalism is often holistic, combining the structural and functional unity of holism with some kind of vital factor. Some vitalists, however, are at the same time merists; they accept the fundamental tenet of merism that the organism is ultimately the sum of its constituent parts, but add a vital element or factor or principle to the atomic or subatomic particles. Similarly, a holist need not be a vitalist; the non-vitalistic holist accepts the structural and functional unity of the totality-theory, but he admits nothing 'vital' as distinct from the ordinary inanimate forces.

Finally, according to the general teaching of *scholastic philosophy,* which is both vitalistic and holistic in the general meaning of these terms, that which gives life to an organism and distinguishes animate from inanimate beings is a *vital substantial principle.* Matter and the vital principle are incomplete part-substances which, in their intimate and compenetrating union, constitute the *unitary living substance.*

We observe that these main general theories of life criss-cross and overlap due to the fact that the starting-point for nearly all of them is biological mechanism. The *main theses of biological mechanism* are, *first,* that the organism is but the sum of its parts, i.e., it is essentially meristic, and, *second,* only mechanical forces are present in the organism, and living and nonliving matter are essentially identical. Holists and vitalists oppose either the first or the second thesis or both; some vitalists oppose only the second thesis or only that part of the second thesis which denies the difference between animate and inanimate bodies. Hence, the confusion and overlapping of theories.

Meristic Biological Theories

In general, we may divide the modern biological theories into *two main groups,* those advocating a form of *merism* and those advocating a form of *holism.* Each of these will be either *vitalistic* or *anti-vitalistic.*

Merism has its roots in the doctrine of atomism, materialism, and mechanism. These doctrines were in vogue among a number of Latin and Greek philosophers in ancient times and exerted their influence on modern biological theories.

Anti-vitalistic (Mechanistic) Merism

The first modern mechanist of importance was *Descartes* (1596–1650). His theory was a mixture of divergent views. The essence of all bodies, including organic bodies, is pure extension; this concept is mechanistic. Plant and animal bodies are not living; they are body-machines pure and simple.

External physical stimuli travel through these bodies by means of certain *spiritus animales* (animal humors or vapors), and the body movements result therefrom. Man's body is also a machine; but the spiritual soul is attached to it in the pineal gland at the base of the brain, and the body moves through stimuli or impulses received from the soul. The body itself has no life, nor is it an organized, integral whole vitalized by the soul; the soul alone really lives, is conscious, and has knowledge. Descartes, therefore, is a dualist, but also an anti-vitalistic, anti-holistic mechanist. P. Gassendi (1592–1655), J. A. Borelli (1608–1679), H. Boerhave (1668–1738), and F. Hoffman (1660–1742) held similar views.

The *French empiricists* of the eighteenth century were entirely atomistic, materialistic, and mechanistic in their interpretation of life and living beings. Representatives of this group are J. de la Mettrie (1709–1755), P. H. d'Holbach (1723–1789), and P. J. Cabanis (1757–1808).

Toward the end of the eighteenth and in the beginning of the nineteenth century, vitalism came to the foreground. It seemed evident to many biologists that a radical difference existed between inorganic and organic bodies. On the other hand, *chemistry* was placed on a sound scientific basis about the same time, and the mechanistic theory of life received a new impetus. Many biologists opposed the concept of 'vital force' and 'vital energy' and maintained that the general *physico-chemical forces* suffice as an explanation of the phenomena of life, even though a complete account of all organic processes cannot as yet be given. Among the group of scientists who upheld this general mechanistic view are J. C. Reil (1759–1813), J. Berzelius (1779–1848), F. Magendie (1785–1855), and C. Bernard (1794–1867).

The next period is that of *materialistic evolutionism,* brought on by Darwin's theory of general evolution. Extreme mechanism of a thoroughgoing materialistic type were propounded by T. H. Huxley (1825–1895), F. Büchner (1824–1899), J. Moleschott (1822–1893), K. Vogt (1817–1895), E. Haeckel (1834–1919), and many others.

Present-day biologists are more conservative in their views on the nature of organic life. Many of them, however, when given to theoretical discussions, advocate a *physico-chemical* interpretation of vital processes. They may admit that physical and chemical forces are inherent in matter and that some sort of 'efficient causality' exists in nature, but the general explanation advanced is that of a summative mechanistic merism.

Many biologists of our time recognize the fact that the *unity of the organism* is something unique and cannot be adequately accounted for by ordinary physico-chemical forces. They postulate the existence of certain *chemical units* which direct the organization of matter into an organic whole and control its activities. The machine-concept, however, still prevails. Various names have been given to such hypothetical units as producers of 'life.' Among them we find the 'biogens' of Verworn, the 'idioblasts' of Hertwig, the 'biophorids' of Weismann, the 'pangenes' of de Vries, the 'organogenetic substances' of Wilson and Rable, and 'bioblasts' of Altmann, and the 'mitochondria' of Benda. At present, the tendency among such biologists is to identify these chemical life-producing units with the genes as the active agents of heredity.

C. Lloyd Morgan's theory of emergent evolution finds favor with a large number of modern philosophers. In the course of evolutionary progress, the theory states, some types of forces or beings arise or 'emerge' which are not the mere resultants of pre-existing forces; they are something new and unpredictable. Among these unpredictable 'emergents' are life and mind. 'Life' is thus conceived as a novel quality emerging from a special arrangement of nonliving matter, when the latter has arrived at a certain level of organization. The active forces, however, are still the ordinary physico-chemical forces operating in a fortuitous and mechanistic fashion, so that there is no essential difference between organic and inorganic bodies. Morgan's theory, therefore is a *moderate mechanism,* because it accepts no principle of vital activity distinct from material forces.

Vitalistic Merism

Vitalists all admit that organisms contain a *certain vital plus-something* which distinguishes organisms radically from inorganic bodies. Consequently, they attack the mechanistic position, maintained in the anti-vitalistic theories given above, which sees the difference between living and nonliving bodies to be a difference only of degree and not of kind. Meristic vitalists postulate some *special kind* of 'vital force,' 'vital energy,' or animate matter, to account for this difference; but they still cling to the concept that organisms are *meristic* in their constitution, i.e., they are the result of a mere additive summation of very small parts.

Old Vitalism assumed the existence of *vital energies* in the organism which do not belong to the order of mechanical, physical, and chemical forces of inorganic nature. 'Vital energy' or 'biotic force' is responsible for the phenomena of irritability, sensibility, co-ordination and co-adaptability of living function and structure. It regulates and controls the physico-chemical forces active in the organic body; in many instances it opposes the action of these forces, whenever the latter tend to work against the welfare of the organism. The first to stress this vitalistic viewpoint in consistent fashion was A. Haller (1707-1777), although W. Harvey (1578-1657) had already postulated 'vital spirits' as operating in the medium of the blood.

Best known is the *School of Montpellier* as representative of Old Vitalism. According to M. Bichat (1771-1802), this vital or biotic force is immaterial and therefore not subject to physical laws. It acts in opposition to material force. The material forces active in the physical world tend to disrupt and destroy the organism; the vital forces active in the organism oppose the destructive tendency of these material forces and tend to keep the organism alive. The theory is crystallized in the definition of life given by Bichat as 'the sum total of the forces that resist death.' This type of vitalism is ultra-spiritualistic.

Others have different views about the nature of this vital energy or force. J. B. van Helmont (1577–1644) calls it *archaeus;* C. F. Wolff (1733–1794), *vis essentialis,* 'essential force'; J. F. Blumenbach (1752–1840), *Bildungstrieb,* 'formative power.'

Neovitalism, which arose in the latter half of the nineteenth century, differs from Old Vitalism mainly in this, that it considers vital energies to be subject to the general law of the conservation of energy.

J. Reinke, for example, maintains the difference between the organism and the machine and attempts to account for this difference by the presence of certain 'dominant forces' or 'life dominants' which are immanent in living matter. Nevertheless, the meristic concept prevails. D. E. Cope and O. Lodge held similar views.

Some biologists claim that the vital forces existing in every type of organism are *conscious,* psychic factors; these conscious factors are present in every living cell. This theory is called *psycho-vitalism;* it is also meristic in character. Among the defenders of this theory or of a similar theory we find A. Pauly, R. H. Francé, G. Bunge, R. Neumeister, P. Jean, A. Wagner, E. Rignano, S. Butler, J. Ward, S. Eldridge, and others.

All these views, whether anti-vitalistic or vitalistic, are fundamentally meristic; that is to say, they consider the organism to be the result of nothing more than a *morphological aggregate* of cells, atoms, and subatomic particles and a *physiological summation* of partial processes. At most, the defenders of the meristic concept of organic life admit that efficient causality is at work, denying altogether the existence of anything like intrinsic purposiveness (finality, teleology) in the structure and function of organisms.

Holistic Biological Theories

Holists oppose the atomistic, meristic concept of organisms. Observation and experiment, they say, force us to admit that the organism is primarily and fundamentally a *whole,* a *unit,* a *totality.* The various parts of an organism are interdependent, and the organism as a whole dominates and directs the parts both structurally and functionally.

Most modern biologists are content to accept the wholeness of the organism as a scientific empirical fact and leave the matter rest at that. The philosopher has no quarrel with these scientists for restricting their discussions to empirical data. Many biologists, however, attempt an explanation of the unity manifested by the organism and thereby essay a solution of the *nature of the unitary organism;* they then leave the field of empirical science and become philosophers.

Philosophic holism, like philosophic merism, appears in two types, anti-vitalistic and vitalistic.

Anti-vitalistic Holism

Foremost among the advocates of anti-vitalistic holism stand the present-day *Gestaltists,* as represented by W. Köhler. Köhler and his followers look upon the organism as a Gestalt, a unitary being, which is dominated as a whole or totality by the pattern or configuration producing a harmonious interrelation of parts and functions, so that the whole is more than the mere sum of all of the structures and functions. In this contention the Gestaltists are undoubtedly correct. Nevertheless, according to these authors, there is no essential difference between a physical Gestalt, such as a system of electrical condensors with its resulting electrical field, and an organic Gestalt, such as is found in a plant, an animal, or a man. The same forces being operative in physical and organic unitary systems, inorganic and organic matter is essentially the same. Hence, this theory is mechanistic and anti-vitalistic; intrinsic finality is excluded from the organism. Somewhat similar views are held by M. Heidenhain, T. Haering, B. Fischer, H. Pxribam, and others. They are mechanistic holists.

Some holists, while rejecting the meristic concept of organic beings, find the explanation for the unity, individuality, and totality of the organism in the *subjective attitude* of our reason. Strictly speaking, our reason is constrained by its own subjective laws to view the organism as a purposive whole, but in reality the organism is devoid of all immanent finality; in its ultimate objective nature, the organism is conceived in mechanistic fashion. Advocates of this view, though with individual differences, are M. Hartmann, H. J. Jordan, A. Meyer, and others.

It is an odd fact that these philosophic scientists recognize, on empirical grounds, the necessity of a holistic interpretation of the organism and yet refuse to accept some sort of principle or intrinsic factor to account for the 'whole-making tendency' observed in every organic being. They fail to see that a mechanistic explanation must inevitably end in merism.

Vitalistic Holism

Vitalistic holism, as a general theory, stands in opposition to the mechanistic and meristic concept of organic life. It maintains the *specific difference between inorganic and organic beings* and seeks to explain the unity and wholeness of the organism by means of a *unifying vital factor or principle* distinct from the physico-chemical forces operating in the organic body. However, authors differ among themselves as to the nature of this vital factor or principle, and this difference gives rise to divergent theories.

J. S. Haldane must be classed among the vitalistic holists, but he seems to place the difference between the natural wholes, as found in inorganic and organic bodies, more in the attitude of the reasoning subject than in the bodies themselves.

Far more important is the theory of *Hans Driesch.* He was forced to relinquish the mechanistic viewpoint through his experimental studies on embryonic development. He observed, when a newly-segmented egg of a sea urchin was halved, that each half developed into a complete individual half the size of a normal sea urchin. Reversely, when eggs were fused together, a single individual resulted from the fusion. Normally, of course, each half of the egg would develop into one half of the body; and each single egg would develop into a complete individual. The half-egg, however, and the fused egg possess the 'prospective potentiality' of forming the complete individual. Prospective potentiality is totally at variance with the machine-theory of the organism, because no machine, when halved, and no two machines, when united, ever show the least tendency to develop into a *single* machine. There exists a *purposive tendency* in the organism which far exceeds the inherent powers of inorganic matter and physico-chemical forces. No meristic summation of parts and processes can explain this fact. A distinct *vital principle* is required as a 'whole-making causal factor.'

Driesch calls this principle the *entelechy,* a term taken over by him from Aristotle; he uses the term, however, in an entirely new (and unwarranted) meaning. This entelechy, according to Driesch, has a reference to space, but does not exist in space; it is non-spatial, non-mechanical, and non-physical. Matter, in his view, is in no sense whatever the foundation of life. Life comes into the organism through the entelechy; the entelechy is non-material and supra-material in character. This Drieschian entelechy, then, does not combine with matter to constitute a unitary substance and nature, but is a non-spatial and supra-material something which controls the physico-chemical forces of inanimate matter in the organism; organic matter is itself not 'living.' We have here a view which closely resembles Plato's horse and rider and Descartes' body-machine and soul.

In Driesch's theory, the entelechy is the formative agent which is responsible for the structural organization of matter. It is an operational principle; with Aristotle, it is primarily an entitative principle, the 'substantial form' or 'soul.' Besides the entelechy, Driesch accepted a directive principle, the *psychoid,* an organic factor which directs all vital processes according to specific needs of the particular organism and utilizes the physico-chemical energies of nature for the purposes inherent in the organism. Because of this *excessive dualism* in Driesch's theory, his entelechian vitalism fails to account for the evident unity and the individuality observed in organisms.

R. Woltereck calls the principle of unity the 'reaction-norm.' Similar to the entelechy of Driesch, it is an immaterial principle, and it possesses, even in the case of plants, fundamental psychic powers of knowing and willing.

According to J. von Uexküll, each cell is autonomous, a distinct unit for itself, a 'nerve-person.' Since the purposiveness of the organism is 'immaterial' and each cell is autonomous, the organism consists of matter and a number of vital immaterial principles.

A number of modern biologists call the principle of unity *hormé* (urge, drive), postulating its existence because of the purposive developmental evolution found in organisms. P. T. Nunn, W. McDougall, and C. von Monakov, among others, propounded the hormic theory of organic life.

The *élan vital* or 'life force' of H. Bergson is of a similar nature. It passes in creative evolution from one generation of living beings to another. This life force creates all species of living beings in the process of its evolution. All matter is thus endowed with an impetus of life.

These vitalistic theories represent a *functional* concept of organic life and as such fall short of a complete and adequate interpretation of organisms as unitary natures.

A number of biologists in the course of the history of biological science have demanded a vital principle which is an *objective immanent principle* as the factor responsible for the immanent purposiveness (finality, teleology) present in the structure and function of organic bodies. They are holistic vitalists who approach the hylomorphic theory of Aristotle and the scholastics in many points. Among the older biologists belonging to this class are J. Stahl (1660 – 1734), C. Bonnet (1720 – 1793), and J. P. Müller (1801 – 1859). In our day, the 'immanence theory' is proposed by von Bertalanffy, A. von Gurwitch, P. Weiss, J. Schaxel, A. Pütter, and K. Sapper.

Aristotelian-scholastic hylomorphism (Gr. ὕλη, matter, and μορφή, form), as a general theory of organic bodies, is vitalistic and holistic. It envisions the organism as follows. Every organism is a *unitary material substance.* This substance is composed ultimately of two incomplete substances or substantial part-principles, namely, *primordial matter* and the *vital principle.* The vital principle is also termed the *substantial form* or *soul.* Both part-principles are complementary to each other; together they constitute the *complete substance* of the plant or animal or man. Primordial or prime matter is the *passive, determinable* factor, capable of being made into any type of specific body; it is the universal stuff of which all bodies, inorganic and organic, are made. The vital principle (substantial form, soul) is the *active, determining* factor in the organic body; it is the life-giving, organizing principle which 'informs' matter and builds it into the living body of a *specific type* of organism, for example, into an oak or a rose, into a dog or a snail, or into a man. Hence, all vital phenomena, present in any species of organism, proceed primarily from the vital principle. The real, fundamental *subject,* however, of all vital phenomena is neither the matter alone nor the vital principle alone, but the *substantial composite* of matter and vital principle. Both are united together in the most intimate union, thereby forming a single substance or *nature* which is the ultimate constitution of the organism and from which all structural developments and vital operations proceed. This 'nature' of the organism possesses an *immanent tendency* or *purposiveness,* typical of each species and particular for each individual, and it utilizes the physico-chemical forces present in the elements of the organic body to realize the inherent goal toward which it tends in virtue of its constitution. In as much as this theory is animistic (Lat., *anima,* soul), it is properly termed *vitalistic animism.*

Facts and Conclusions

In evaluating the facts of organic life, as revealed in biological research, we must not be swayed by any preconceived scientific or philosophic theory. The facts must speak for themselves, and our conclusions must be based on these facts.

Perhaps the best way to arrive at a solution of the nature of organic life will be to examine the main theses of biological mechanism in the light of the discovered facts. There are, it will be remembered, two main theses; *first,* the organism is meristic, i.e., it is but the sum of its constituent parts; *second,* only mechanical (or physico-chemical) forces are present in the organism, and living and nonliving matter are essentially identical. The second thesis, it should be noted, consists of two parts.

Is the organism meristic?

Merism advocates the *machine theory* of the organic body. The summation of all the parts (subatomic particles, atoms, molecules, tissues, organs, etc.) accounts for all the structural and functional phenomena of what we call 'life.' There is nothing more to an organism than an aggregation of these parts and processes. This concept of the organism is *erroneous.*

The organism is *holistic* in its nature. A mere summation and aggregation would be similar to a heap of sand or a pile of bricks. Even a machine cannot be explained on the meristic basis of a summation of different pieces of metal. Consider the facts.

One of the most remarkable phenomena of the organism is its all-pervasive *unity of being,* manifested by the marvelous *co-adaptation of structure and activity.* Each single cell possesses an intricately complicated structure. Some features of this structure are common to all cells, namely, the cytoplasm and the nucleus. So, too, every cell has functions which are the same as those of every other cell, namely, assimilation and dissimilation, growth and division. And yet, cells also possess individual and specific peculiarities, so that cells differ greatly among themselves. In multicellular organisms the cells group themselves into various kinds of *tissues* and *organs;* and these tissues and organs perform activities distinctively their own, over and above the general functions of their cells as the biological units of life. Again, cells, tissues, and organs group themselves into the higher unity of the *organism as an individual being functioning as a whole.*

The single cells, tissues, and organs are endowed with a certain *autonomy* and *individuality.* Each cell, as we know, has its own cycle of proper functions, the result of the activities of its various structural parts. In plants, the roots, trunk, bark, leaves, and blossoms have separate functions, so that each part is a unit in its own right. In animals, the bones, muscles, skin, glands, afferent and efferent nerves, sensory organs, and the brain manifest autonomy and individuality of structure and function; the stomach, for example, digests, the muscle contracts, the salivary gland secretes, the eye sees, the tongue tastes, etc. Yet all these types of apparatuses, notwithstanding their distinctive structures and functions, are not isolated and independent, but *interconnected* and *interdependent* as parts of the organism as a whole; and this interrelationship of whole and part constitutes the 'organization' of the organism. Everything in the organism conspires toward the co-adaptation of all parts in the construction of the organism as a supreme unit. The autonomy and individuality of the cells, tissues, and organs is only *relative,* both in structure and in function.

The supreme law which governs the structure and functions of cells, tissues, and organs is the *need,* the *exigency,* of the type of organism of which they are the subsidiary parts. What kind of food material shall be digested and assimilated, depends entirely on the nature of the organism; the same kind of grass will be transformed into the flesh of a cow, a horse, a sheep, or an elephant, according to the needs of the animal that eats it. How far the reciprocal relationship of all parts of an organism reaches, can be seen from the fact that an expert zoologist can deduce, with a fair degree of certainty, the complete organism from a single typical organ or part. As an illustration, Milne-Edwards deduces the characteristics of a carnivorous mammal from its teeth. The teeth are such that the animal can eat flesh meat. The entire digestive apparatus must be of such a character and arrangement that flesh meat can be digested and assimilated; it will, therefore, deviate considerably from the structure of the digestive apparatus found in herbivorous mammals. In order to obtain flesh meat, the carnivorous animal must be able to capture its prey; hence, its muscular apparatus must be powerful and capable of a rapid expenditure of energy, so that the animal can be swift and sure in its movements. To fulfill this requirement, it must possess a skeletal arrangement with appropriate leverage in the limbs. Swift movement demands a quick combustion of energy-providing substances in the body; quick combustion is possible only with a large supply of oxygen; a large supply of oxygen, in turn, presupposes deep inhalation of air and large areas of lung surface. In order that the oxygen can reach the muscles in ample quantity for quick combustion, the circulatory apparatus must permit the blood to travel rapidly through the entire system; the arteries, veins, and heart must be constructed accordingly. Then, too, a carnivorous mammal must be able to locate its prey at a distance; this requires acute senses of sight, hearing, and smell. Once the animal overtakes its prey, it must kill it; hence, it will have either strong legs with sharp claws, or strong jaws with sharp teeth, or both. The entire body, therefore, is built according to the requirements of the animal's being, all parts being *mutually dependent* and *harmoniously interrelated.*

The organism thus manifests an unmistakable morphological and physiological *unity, individuality, and totality*. The organism is primary; the structures and functions are secondary. The organism exists *for itself;* the structures and functions exist *for the organism.* The organism acts *as a whole;* the structures and functions are *subservient* parts of the whole. It follows, therefore, that merism is a false theory.

Are only mechanical or physico-chemical forces present?

We will leave out of consideration the theory that *purely* mechanical forces alone are present in the organism; no one seriously defends this theory any more.

Some exponents of vitalism, both meristic and holistic, postulate the existence of *biotic* or *vital forces,* distinct from the physico-chemical forces of inanimate bodies, as present and operative in organisms. This vital force is assumed to be non-material in nature and operation, and it is through this 'vital force' that organisms are truly 'living.' The assumption of these ultra-spiritualistic vitalists is *unwarranted* and *erroneous.*

It is one of the triumphs of the biological research methods to have proved that the chemical reactions occurring in the cells, organs, and tissues of organisms are of the same *material kind* as those occurring outside the organisms in inorganic bodies. The heat generated in organic bodies is the result of an oxidation process which is the same as that occurring in any test tube or furnace. The electricity present in nerve action is plain electricity and can be measured by a galvanometer. All forces operating in the organism are material forces. In no instances has science been able to discover any kind of biotic energy or force distinct from the ordinary material physico-chemical forces and energies.

It is true, of course, that organic compounds are made in and by the organism, which the inorganic elements, of their own accord, never make. But this fact does not prove that 'vital forces' are at work; it merely proves that a totally different principle operates in the organism, utilizing the ordinary forces for its own purposes and in its own way. Laboratory technicians have succeeded in forcing the elements to unite in the formation of compounds which are identical with organic compounds. We need but mention synthetic rubber, synthetic alcohol, synthetic perfume, synthetic urea, vitamins, hormones, etc.; the number of such synthetic organic compounds runs into the thousands, and the number is increasing day by day. These technicians use the ordinary inorganic forces to bring about such compounds. It is, then, a logical conclusion to assume that the same material forces, and not 'vital forces,' are at work in organisms.

We must agree, therefore, with the biological mechanists

that only physico-chemical forces are operative in organisms. We do not agree, however, that biological mechanism is the true interpretation of the nature of the organism. Mechanism depends on the truth of its argument that physico-chemical forces *alone* account for *all* the phenomena of organic life. If so, then, of course, there is no essential distinction between living and nonliving bodies.

Are living and nonliving matter essentially identical?

Again, we must consider the facts. According to the tenets of biological mechanism, the ordinary physico-chemical forces, operating as *material efficient causes,* suffice to produce all 'vital' activities; there is *no purposiveness* (finality, teleology) present in the structures and functions of any organism. We contend that the biological facts contradict this basic assumption.

While it is true that the forces operative in organisms are the same as the material forces operative in inorganic beings, their *manner of operation* is radically different in living and nonliving matter. Among inorganic substances, action is always *transient* (or *transitive*) in character. Transient action is the action in virtue of which one being influences and changes another being. The energies of light, heat, electricity, magnetism, physical impact, gravity, etc., are such that the goal of their influence is *outside* their efficient causality; they tend to change *other* bodies. A heated body tends to raise the temperature of a colder body; an electrified body tends to charge a neutral body; a body in motion tends to impart motion to the body with which it comes in contact; sodium and chlorine tend to change each other and form a salt; and so forth. Such action is always 'transient.'

On the other hand, the inherent tendency of all *vital* activity within an organism is *the organism's own development and perfection*. All vital activity originates in the organism, remains in the organism, is carried out by the organism, and has as its natural goal the well-being of the organism itself. Hence, vital organic action is rightly termed *immanent.* (Lat., *manere in,* to remain, reside in.) No matter how much the vegetative, sensory, and rational processes may differ, they are characterized by 'immanence.' Immanence or spontaneity of vital action proceeds from the *inner constitution* of the organism which reacts *as a whole* to outside agencies. Life is essentially self-perfection through self-development.

Why this radical difference between the actions of living and nonliving bodies? Immanence of action demands an adequate explanation. The only explanation the mechanists can logically offer is the constitution of the atoms and molecules which form the organic body. These atoms and molecules, however, are forever the same, and so, too, are their physico-chemical forces. Consequently, the manner of operation of these forces should also remain forever the same, whether they are operative in organic or inorganic bodies. Hence, the manner of operation of material forces should always be 'transient' and never 'immanent.' But vital action *is* 'immanent.' Biological mechanism, therefore, cannot explain the immanence of vital action. There must be, then, something 'vital' in the organism which makes the physico-chemical forces perform immanent actions.

Besides, *organic compounds* are the result of the *natural tendencies* operating within the organism. The inorganic elements have no natural tendency to produce such compounds. Outside the organism, the elements combine according to the general laws of affinity. Under these conditions, the elements tend to form rigid combinations with a stable equilibrium; the proteins and other organic compounds, however, are extremely complex and in an unstable *colloidal* state. That the principle operating in the formation of organic compounds is different from that operating in the formation of inorganic compounds, can be seen after the *death* of plants, animals, and men. The organisms decay, and the organic compounds dissolve, reverting again to the status of ordinary inorganic compounds and elements. If organisms and organic compounds were the effects of elements and their physico-chemical forces alone, and not of some higher principle utilizing them, no sufficient reason can be assigned why such organic compounds should not continue indefinitely in existence, even after 'death,' somewhat after the manner of a crystal. The fact of synthetic compounds is no argument in favor of the mechanistic theory. Synthetic compounds are *forced products,* made by technicians under laboratory conditions; we might stress the parallel by saying that the organisms, too, must have a technician in their laboratory, namely, a vital principle which forces the elements to enter into organic combinations against their normal tendencies.

One of the fundamental tenets of mechanism is the *denial of final causes* and purposiveness in organisms; *only efficient causes* are at work. This contention is easily disproved. Man is an organism. Our own consciousness is witness to the fact that *we act for a purpose* and do many things in order to *realize a future goal.* Practically all our social, commercial, educational, and industrial acts are done 'for a definite purpose.' We set a goal, realizable in the future, and then go about selecting and applying the means to make the goal an actuality. The goal is 'that for the sake of which' something is done, and to strive toward the realization of a goal is 'finality' or 'purposiveness.' Animals also display purposiveness, as when a cat pounces on a mouse, when a dog pursues a rabbit, when a bird builds its nest, when a bee builds its honeycomb, and so on.

Every organism is characterized by an *inherent natural purposiveness.* 'Ends' and 'purposes' permeate the structures and activities present in the organism. This inherent natural purposiveness follows a double course: the realization of the well-being of the individual and the preservation of the species.

That the realization of the *well-being of the individual* dominates the entire life history of an organism, should be evident to any unprejudiced observer. It manifests itself from the first to the last moment of the organism's existence. Consider the organism's *embryonic development.* The ovum and the sperm cell prepare themselves for fertilization by ejecting one half of the normal number of chromosomes, so that the normal number will again be restored through the fusion of the ovum and the sperm cell. If this halving were not done, each succeeding generation would have double the number of chromosomes found in the cells of the organisms of the foregoing generation; after a series of reproductions, the number of chromosomes would be so large, that the organism could no longer survive. Hence, the purposiveness of the maturation division. Once the parent cells have fused, the fertilized ovum begins to develop itself, *by its own innate power,* into a full-grown organism. This development, however, is not the result of a fortuitous concurrence of chance factors; it is the result of a definite and precise *plan,* carried out in a definite and precise *manner.* The fertilized ovum develops into a *specific type* of being. The original embryonic cell of an oak develops only into an oak; that of a cat, only into a cat; that of a man, only into a man. The various tissues and organs are formed, long before they can be of any possible use to the organism — legs, wings, nerves, stomach, eyes, heart, etc.; they are built for the *future.* And if it should happen, as it occasionally does, that the first two embryonic cells are split apart, the two cells do not develop into two half-organisms, but each cell develops into a complete individual of that particular type; the entire structural plan of the organism is simply doubled and carried separately to completion. This prospective potentiality of the germ cell is one of the most remarkable features of embryonic life. It is as if one were to cut a machine in half, and each half-machine would then proceed to shape itself into an exact duplicate of the original machine. The purposiveness of the entire process of embryonic development is as apparent as that of an architect in planning and erecting a house, but with this difference: the house of the organism is built *by itself* from a single 'magic brick,' as Alexis Carrel so aptly puts it, which gradually fashions itself into kitchen, plumbing, windows, walls, rooms, telephone, and a million other items.

That the well-being of the individual also controls the *mature life* of the organism as an 'end' and 'goal' to be achieved, can be seen in the fact that it tends to *preserve its identity of being* under all circumstances. It adapts itself to its surroundings, fights off injurious agencies, repairs the damage done to its tissues, assimilates proper food and rejects unsuitable material, seeks pleasure and avoids pain. To perform these functions, the organism has the necessary equipment in its own body, furnished by itself.

The *preservation of the species* is another fundamental natural end or goal inherent in the organism. Whatever may be the type of plant or animal, the organism eventually arrives at a stage in its existence when it tends to reproduce itself by bringing forth an individual similar to itself. The method of reproduction varies, but reproduction itself is universal and is eminently purposive. Whether the method of generation be asexual or sexual, there is perhaps no greater marvel in the world, viewed from a purely organic standpoint, than the wonderful arrangement of structure and function for the purpose in view. In *bisexual* generation the individuals of the species are grouped into two sexes, male and female. The generative organs of each sex, taken singly as male and female organs, have no meaning and significance for the individual possessing them. It is only in relation to each other, though in different individuals, that they have meaning and significance. Their inherent natural purpose, however, is unmistakable. The organs are made to complement each other, and so are the individuals possessing them. Each type of generative organ is insufficient of itself for reproduction; in conjunction with each other they achieve their obvious purpose — the generation of a new individual and the preservation of the species. Mating, gestation, care of the young, and so forth, are all subservient to this supreme purpose of organic life. A more patent and universal illustration of inherent natural purposiveness could hardly be found.

Action flows from a principle of action. Since the action of organisms is beyond the natural capabilities of ordinary atoms and their physico-chemical forces, vital action must flow from a *vital principle*. Vitalism, therefore, is the correct theory of organic life, and it must be a *holistic vitalism*.

There are various theories of holistic vitalism. Which one should be adopted? We claim that the theory of vitalistic animism is the one which gives the best explanation of all the facts.

Vitalistic Animism

The *cardinal points* of vitalistic animism (Lat., *anima,* soul) are these: Every organism consists of two ultimate constitutive substantial principles, matter and the vital principle, which are united together into a complete substance and nature. These points must now be established.

One of the ultimate constitutive principles of every organism, including man, is *matter*. 'Matter' is the basic stuff of which all bodies are composed.

Whatever we may think about the ultimate nature of 'matter,'[1] it should be obvious that *every organism consists of matter* and that matter is an ultimate constituent of the organic body. All organisms — plants, animals, and men — are 'spatial,' both as to the structures and their functions; the forces active in organisms are 'material' forces and as such are rooted in matter. Every biologist, whether mechanistic, meristic, holistic, or vitalistic, concedes this. Hence, matter is an ultimate constitutive principle in the nature of the organism.

Vitalistic animism, however, contends that we must also accept a second, equally important, constitutive principle in organisms, distinct from matter, namely, the *vital principle*. Without a distinct vital principle, co-equal with matter, the phenomena of life cannot receive an adequate explanation.

No effect can be greater than its cause, otherwise something would exist without a sufficient reason for its existence. Now, the activities and phenomena of organic life *exceed the*

[1] See the author's *From Aether to Cosmos* (Bruce, 1941), pp. 288–290, for an explanation of 'primary' and 'secondary' matter, and Chap. XII and XIII for an elucidation of hylomorphism and the hylomorphic theory. In the present context we are not concerned so much with the existence of 'matter' as with the nature of a 'vital principle' distinct from matter.

inherent causality of inorganic substances. One cannot, by the wildest flight of fancy, conceive of sensory and intellectual knowledge, consciousness, and appetitive behavior, as phenomena directly resulting from the actions and reactions of atom complexes considered as such. Even the colloidal state of protoplasmic material and the formation of organic compounds cannot be adequately accounted for on the basis of ordinary chemical affinity between elements; much less the processes of nutrition and reproduction. The inherent natural purposiveness of organisms, in virtue of which they plan and build for future use, is a qualitative factor far beyond the capabilities of mere atoms and their aggregates. Above all, the dynamic unity of the organism as a whole, with complete subordination and co-adaptation of all structures and activities for the well-being of the individual and the preservation of the species, is something so unique, that it cannot receive its ultimate explanation in the grouping of billions of inanimate atoms fortuitously thrown together by the ordinary chemical, physical, and mechanical forces into an accidental chance product. Such an explanation would do violence to all the laws of reason.

Nor can the explanation be found in the *environment.* The circumstances of the environment are frequently very diverse, but the organisms preserve the identity of the individual and of the species intact. And where the environment is the same, we observe a great diversity of organic species living side by side. Hence, the conditions of organization are not the result of environment.

Since inanimate matter is incompetent to produce the marvelous effects observed in organic life, we must reduce these effects to a causality distinct from the causality of matter and its forces. Organisms, it is true, consist of matter; and that is why matter must be considered as a constitutive principle of organic life. The matter present in organic bodies, however, is *organized* and *living,* and matter as such is incapable of producing this effect; hence, besides matter, we must postulate a distinct *vital principle,* from which the phenomena peculiar to living matter proceed, as a second constitutive principle of organic life.

Both constituent principles are *mutually irreducible.* There can be no question of this so far as concerns matter. The matter or basic stuff present in the atoms and elements exists in them prior to their entrance into the organism; matter, therefore, cannot be reduced to the vital principle. On its part, the vital principle cannot be reduced to the matter present in the atoms and elements. If it were reducible to matter, the vital phenomena themselves would be nothing more than manifestations of atoms and elements and their natural inanimate forces; mere atoms and elements, however, cannot adequately account for vital phenomena. Hence, the vital principle must be a reality distinct from matter and as such not reducible to it. It follows, then, that both matter and the vital principle are *ultimates in their own line* as constituents of the organism.

Matter and the vital principle must be *substantial* principles. They are the constituent principles of the organism, and each organism is a substance. A substance is a being existing in and for itself and does not exist in another as in a subject. Such being the type of existence which the organism possesses, its ultimate constituent principles must also be substantial, because every being is what it is through its ultimate constituent principles. If matter and the vital principle were not 'substantial' principles, the organism resulting from them could not be a 'substance.'

While matter and the vital principle are substantial and mutually irreducible, they cannot be said to be complete substances; on the contrary, they are *incomplete substances.* A substantial principle is said to be an 'incomplete' substance, when it must be united with a second substantial principle in order to constitute a complete individual being. Neither principle suffices of its own accord to constitute the complete individual being; but each principle is an intrinsic coprinciple complementing the other, so that in their union they constitute the complete individual being. Every plant and animal and man is a complete individual being and as such a 'complete substance,' because it exists in itself and for itself and needs no other being or principle to complete it as a substance. If both matter and the vital principle were 'complete substances,' the organism would be a double-substance, a being consisting of two 'complete substances.' Under such circumstances, the two 'complete substances' would merely be allocated in juxtaposition along parallel lines without ever coalescing to form a single individual being or substance. Now, every organism, whether a plant, animal, or man, is a *unitary substance functioning as a whole;* it is not a double being consisting of a material substance and of a vital substance conjoined in some sort of harmonious relationship, but a *single substance* which is at one and the same time *both material and vital.* No other view will account for the fact that the organism is a dynamic unit of vital action. Hence, matter and the vital principle, though substantial, cannot be 'complete substances,' but must be 'incomplete substances' or 'substantial co-principles' which, through a most intimate union, coalesce to constitute the organism as a single, individual, 'complete substance.' In consequence of this union, matter ceases to be inanimate and becomes truly vitalized; the result is *living matter* capable of the functions of life.

The organism is thus seen to be a *composite substance,* and the component ultimate realities are matter and the vital principle. Matter is the determinable, vivifiable reality, while the vital principle is the determining, vivifying reality. Matter is compenetrated by the vital principle and is transformed into living matter. When the vital principle vanishes from the organism, death supervenes, and the atoms and elements again return to the lifeless condition of inanimate substances through decay and decomposition. In its *ultimate constitution,* therefore, every organism is a single but *composite substance consisting of matter and a vital principle.*

This exposition of the cardinal points of vitalistic animism enables us to understand the characteristic phenomena of organic life. That an organism is a 'material' being, is due to the fact that *matter* is an essential constituent, because matter exists in the atoms and elements as the ultimate basic stuff of which they are made and which they carry into the structure of the organism when they become an integral part of it. Because matter enters into the organic composite, the forces operative in the organism are the ordinary chemical, physical, and mechanical forces present everywhere in the world. The processes of vegetative, sensory, and intellectual 'life,' however, considered precisely as such, are superior to the forces and activities normally present in matter and must be attributed to a principle fundamentally and essentially distinct from matter, namely, to the *vital principle.* It is because of the presence of a vital principle in organisms that matter and its material forces are capable of forming organic compounds in a colloidal state and of being the bearers of vital activities far beyond their natural capacities. And it is because of the essential differences in vital principles that plants, animals, and men represent different *levels of life* and that there are so many *distinct species* among the plants and animals. As regards 'matter,' they are all alike; but as regards their 'vital principles,' they are specifically different types of organisms, because the vital principles differ specifically among themselves. Without matter, there would be no 'organisms,' but spiritual beings. Without the vital principle, there would be no 'living matter,' but inanimate chemical substances. Without the specific differences between vital principles, there would be no 'specific types' of organisms, but only a single species.

We therefore define the *organism* as a *substance* consisting of *matter animated by a vital principle.*

The Plant Soul

In common parlance, the vital principle is referred to as the *soul.* In accordance with this usage, it is customary to speak of a 'plant soul,' an 'animal soul,' and a 'human soul,'

One of the essential attributes of the plant soul is its *unicity*. By the unicity of the plant soul we mean that each plant has but a *single* soul as the animating principle of the entire organism. Unicity follows as a logical consequence from the nature of the plant as a unitary substance. All structures and activities of the plant serve to promote the well-being of the organism as a whole. The plant acts as a dynamic unit throughout its life. Hence, the soul, the principle of all vital phenomena in the plant, must be one, not two or many.

Since the soul of the plant is singular, it is actually undivided. It is not, however, indivisible like a spiritual entity. On the contrary, the plant soul is *indirectly divisible* and therefore *potentially multiple*. There is ample evidence for this statement in facts. A cell can be cut into pieces, and each piece, provided it contain a portion of the nucleus, will rebuild itself into a complete cell and continue to live. The slips of many plants, for example, of the geranium, the willow, etc., will grow roots and develop into normal plants. The explanation seems simple enough. The plant soul, though one and undivided, is potentially divisible and multiple. Once the division of the plant body is made, the soul is also divided with it and accompanies the divided parts; each animated part then continues to function as a whole plant. There is no need for assuming that a new soul is generated in the separated parts. When a shoot from an apple tree is grafted onto a pear tree, the shoot of the apple tree becomes one with the pear tree, but it lives as a parasite, merely using the sap furnished by the roots and stem of the pear tree; two souls are present in the same tree, one an apple-tree soul and the other a pear-tree soul, each functioning in its respective part of the tree as a whole.

The plant soul is *material,* in the sense that it is *totally immersed in matter* and *intrinsically dependent on matter.* We cannot, of course, perceive the plant soul itself. In passing a judgment on the inner nature of the plant soul, we must conclude from its activities to its essence. Now, there is nothing in the activities of the plant to indicate immateriality.

Everything about the plant is on a material plane, both as regards structure and activity. If the plant soul were immaterial, a mere division of the matter (body) of the plant should not result in two living plants; one part might remain living, but the other part should be dead. It is true that one cannot make a division of the more highly organized plants, so that both parts remain living after the division. Nevertheless, plants are plants, essentially alike in nature, no matter to what particular species they belong. Hence, the fact that such a division, with both parts remaining alive after the division, cannot be made on all plants, is no valid objection against the argument. We must conclude, therefore, that the plant soul is essentially material.

The Animal Soul

When we speak here of the 'animal soul,' we restrict our remarks to the soul of the *brute animal,* not to man.

Like the plant soul, the animal soul is a *single soul* animating each individual animal. Each insect, bird, fish, mammal, etc., is an individual being acting as a unit of structure and activity. There cannot be two souls in the animal, one controlling the vegetative structures and activities as a vegetative soul and the other controlling the sensory structures and activities as a sentient soul.

While it is true that some organs and functions of the animal are characteristically vegetative and others characteristically sensory, there is no absolute line of demarkation separating the one type from the other, so that two distinct souls, one vegetative and the other sentient, would be demanded. All tissues and organs, whether they belong to the vegetative or sensory system, derive their origin from one and the same parent cell. From the very beginning of embryonic development, the plan of a *vegetative-sensory* organism prevails. Both types of organs and tissues, vegetative and sensory, are fashioned from the same cells and in the same process. Throughout the life history of the animal the formation, growth, and repair of the sensory system is carried out by the vegetative processes of the animal; *vice versa,* the requirements of the vegetative system, such as the procurement of proper food, etc., are taken care of by the sensory activities and instinctive actions of the animal. In this manner, all structures and activities collaborate conjointly and harmoniously toward the realization of the vegetative and sensory life of the animal as a unitary organism. This *complete unity of being* demands a single vital principle or soul.

It should be obvious that the *animal is specifically superior* to the plant. Cognition and appetition exceed in perfection anything found in the activities of the plant. Hence, the animal soul is superior to the plant soul. Since, then, there can be but a single soul in the animal, the conclusion is inevitable that the animal soul is a vital principle which, together with matter as a co-principle, is the active principle for both vegetative and sensory functions, so that the capacities of the lower vegetative soul are contained in the superior animal soul. All structures and activities, vegetative as well as sensory, have as their ultimate goal and purpose the well-being of the animal as a single, unitary organism. If it is difficult at times, especially among the lower forms of life, to distinguish accurately between animals and plants, that is due to the limitations of our knowledge; organisms capable of sensory perception are animals, not plants, no matter how primitive in organization they may happen to be, and as such must have a sentient soul.

Like the plant soul, the animal soul is one and undivided, but *indirectly divisible* and *potentially multiple.* Some animals, for instance, the hydra and others, can be divided into sections, each section then developing into a complete individual of the same species. By dividing the body of the animal, the soul is also divided, though indirectly, and multiplied. In technical phrasing, the soul is said to be indivisible *per se* (as such, directly, in so far as its own being is specifically concerned), but divisible *per accidens* (incidentally, indirectly, in so far as the body of which it is the animating principle is concerned); what is primarily and directly divided is the whole body, and the soul is incidentally and indirectly divided with it.

Furthermore, like the plant soul, the animal soul is *totally immersed in matter* and *intrinsically dependent on matter;* consequently, it must be said to be *material* in its essence. All sensory organs and functions are spatial and material in character; even the higher senses of imagination and memory deal only with images that are based on quantitative extension in some form. Not a single activity of the animal is in any manner free from matter and material conditions. We have no reason, therefore, to attribute immateriality to the animal soul. This will become clearer when we analyse the rational activities of man.

It is imperative to view the question of the plant and animal soul from the angle of their relationship to the organism as a whole. It cannot be stressed too much that it is the *complete organism,* the individual plant and individual animal, which is generated, lives, and dies, and not the matter and soul as such. Matter and soul (vital principle) exist solely for the organism of which they are the constitutive principles. When a new plant or animal is generated, the soul is evoked out of the potentiality of matter through the agency of the generating cause (the parent organism or organisms). When a plant or animal dies, its soul simply perishes and is reduced to the potentiality of matter. The plant and animal souls, therefore, do not survive the death of the organism; they are *not immortal.*

Philosophic Concept of Life

Though 'life' is a readily distinguishable natural phenomenon, it has always been found to be difficult to define. Many definitions have been offered by savants, but most of them are unsatisfactory in one respect or another. These definitions are usually restricted to organic life and as such fail to define *life in general.*

The true definition of 'life' must express that distinctive attribute which is essential to every type of vital activity, whether it be vegetative, sensory, rational, or divine. We must not overlook the fact that 'life' is also predicated of *God and His activities,* and that primarily and in an infinite manner. The definition of life, therefore, must exclude everything which would be inapplicable to the life of God and must include the distinctive attribute which characterizes essentially all 'life,' creatural and divine. Obviously, then, since God is not an organic being, the definition, in order to be adequate, cannot be based solely on the vital activities of organic beings, such as plants, animals, and men. And yet, organic beings possess true 'life,' so the definition must apply to them as well as to God. Similarly, since the life of organisms involves qualitative and quantitative 'change,' while the life of God involves no change at all, the definition of 'life' must neither include nor exchange change, but must express that mark of vital activity which is compatible with both the presence and absence of change.

Our analysis of organic life has shown that there is one distinctive attribute common to the activities of vegetant, sentient, and rational organisms, and that is *immanence.* 'Immanent action' distinguishes the vital activity of organic beings from the 'transitive action' of inorganic, nonliving beings. Now, the life of God is also characterized by 'immanence of action.' All the activities of God have their origin, permanence, and goal in the being of God, because they are identical with His divine substance. Hence, 'immanence of action' is the essential attribute common to the life of organic creatures and of God; and it is the *only essential attribute* common to every type of life.

Consequently, *life is immanent action.* And a living being is one endowed with immanence of action. Such is the definition of life and of living beings given by Aristotle and St. Thomas Aquinas centuries ago.

What has been said about organic life and the vital principle, should assist us in understanding man and his soul.

Summary of Chapter XIX

The philosophic psychologist endeavors to arrive at an understanding of *man's nature* through a study of vital activities.

1. *Nature of Organic Beings.* The theory of merism contends that the organic body is an aggregate resulting from the additive summation of its smallest parts. The theory of *holism* views the organic body as an integrated whole which in its totality is more than the sum of its parts. The theory of *vitalism* sees something distinctly vital in the organism and demands a vital element or factor or principle to account for the 'life' of the organism. Merism may be vitalistic or anti-vitalistic; holism may be vitalistic or anti-vitalistic.

2. *Meristic Biological Theories.* Merism occurs in two types, anti-vitalistic and vitalistic. *Anti-vitalistic merism* advocates the view that the organic body is a machine actuated solely by physico-chemical or mechanical forces. *Vitalistic merism* postulates some special kind of 'vital force,' 'vital energy,' or animate matter to account for the difference between organic and inorganic bodies.

3. *Holistic Biological Theories.* Holism opposes the atomistic, meristic concept of the organism. It is either anti-vitalistic or vitalistic. *Anti-vitalistic holism* admits that organisms are integrated wholes functioning as units, but does not see any essential difference between inorganic and organic bodies. *Vitalistic holism* maintains the specific difference between inorganic and organic bodies and seeks to explain the unity and wholeness of the organism by means of a unifying vital factor or principle distinct from the physico-chemical forces operating in the organic body.

4. *Facts and Conclusions.* Biological *mechanism* is based on *two main theses:* first, the organism is meristic; second, only mechanical or physico-chemical forces are present in the organism, and living and nonliving matter are essentially identical.

The *first thesis* is false. The facts show that there exists in the organism an all-pervasive unity of being; the structures and functions are interconnected and interdependent; the law governing structure and function is the need, the exigency, of the organism. The organism is a morphological and physiological unit and individual acting as a whole. *Holism,* not merism, is characteristic of the organism.

The *first* part of the *second thesis* is correct. Science has discovered no 'vital force' or 'biotic energy' distinct from the ordinary physico-chemical forces.

The *second* part of the *second thesis* is false. There exists an *essential difference* between inorganic and organic bodies. The action of inorganic bodies is always 'transient,' that of organic bodies is 'immanent.' Organic compounds are the result of the natural tendencies operating within the organism, while inorganic elements show no tendencies to form such compounds. Vital activity is characterized by an inherent natural purposiveness, as can be seen in the realization of the well-being of the individual and in the preservation of the species. Such conditions demand a *vital principle.*

Holistic vitalism, therefore, is the correct theory of organic life.

5. *Vitalistic Animism.* The theory of vitalistic animism gives the best account of the nature of the organism. Its *cardinal points* are these: Every organism consists of two ultimate constitutive principles, matter and the vital principle, which are united together into a complete substance and nature.

Matter is one of the ultimate constitutive principles of the organic body, because the organism consists of material atoms and utilizes material forces.

Besides matter, and distinct from it, the *vital principle* is an ultimate constitutive principle of the organic body, because the activities and phenomena of organic life exceed the inherent causality of inorganic substances. They must proceed from a principle different from matter and its forces.

Matter and the vital principle are *mutually irreducible.*

Both are *substantial* principles, because the result of their union is a substance. Both, however, are *incomplete substances;* neither suffices to constitute the complete individual being. If both were 'complete' substances, the organic body would be a double-substance and it could not be a *unitary* substance functioning as a whole.

In its ultimate constitution, therefore, every organism is a *composite substance consisting of matter and a vital principle or soul.*

6. *The Plant Soul.* It is singular and actually undivided, but it is indirectly divisible and potentially multiple. It is material, in the sense that it is totally immersed in matter and intrinsically dependent on matter.

7. *The Animal Soul.* It, too, is singular and actually undivided, but indirectly divisible and potentially multiple. Since cognition and appetition are functions superior to the vegetative functions of the plant, the animal is specifically superior to the plant. The animal soul is also material, because sensory organs and functions are spatial and material. Being material, neither the plant nor the animal soul can be said to be immortal; they perish with the death of the organism.

8. *The Philosophic Concept of Life.* The true definition of 'life' must express that distinctive attribute which is essential to every type of vital activity, creatural and divine. This attribute is 'immanence of action.' Hence, *life is immanent action.*

Readings

Bittle, Celestine N., *From Aether to Cosmos,* Ch. XII, XIII. — Aristotle, *On the Soul.* — St. Thomas Aquinas, *Contra Gentiles,* IV, c. 11. — McDougall, William, *Modern Materialism and Emergent Evolution.* — Driesch, Hans, "The Breakdown of Materialism," in *The Great Design,* ed. by F. Mason. — Brennan, R. E., *General Psychology,* pp. 50–71. — Nordenskiöld, E., *The History of Biology.* — Van der Veldt, J., "The Evolution and Classification of Philosophical Life Theories," in *Franciscan Studies,* June and September, 1943.

Chapter XX

THE SOUL OF MAN

FOR many biologists and psychologists the term 'soul' has a bad taste. They either deny the existence of a soul in man or ignore its presence. At best, they contend, the soul is an intangible reality which cannot be perceived by introspection or subjected to scientific investigation by means of laboratory experiments. Hence, in their opinion the soul, if it exists at all, is a negligible factor in psychological experience and can very well be left out of consideration.

The philosopher disagrees with this superficial attitude. It makes a tremendous difference in our concept and understanding of 'the whole man,' if he has or has not a soul. If he has no soul, our understanding of man is beset with a thousand difficulties and is made practically impossible. If he has a soul, the mystery concerning man's vegetative, sensory, and intellectual life, and also the mystery concerning his origin and destiny, can be cleared up, at least within the limits of human knowledge.

Man an Integral Organism

Descartes was mistaken, when he proposed the doctrine that an organic body, including that of man, was a 'machine' composed of atoms and acting solely with the movements of atoms. As we have already pointed out, the mechanistic view fails to explain the main phenomena of organic structure and function observed in every type of living being. The vegetant and sentient organisms are of an order differing essentially from inorganic substances. Organisms demand a vital principle or soul.

Man, too, is an organism, and he is *an integral organism.*

Like the plant, he has vegetative organs and functions; like the brute animal, he has sensory organs and functions; and, exclusively typical of himself, he has the rational activities of intellection and volition. Contrary to the theory of Descartes, however, man is not a double-substance, consisting of a material substance (the body) and a spiritual substance (the rational soul), but a single, unitary substance, an integral organism. As in the case of the brute animal, his vegetative and sensory structures and activities are not split apart, so that they must be referred to distinct vital principles; they co-operate in perfect harmony, and one set is dependent on the other in being and in operation, so that it is evident that both sets of structures and activities must be referred to *one and the same* vital principle. Man, therefore, so far as his vegetant and sentient life is concerned, has a *vital principle* or *soul* which is vegetant-sentient.

Then what about man's *rational* activities, intellection and volition? Are they reducible to sensory activities? They are not. They are of a higher order and as such must derive their origin from a higher principle. An ordinary vegetant or sentient soul cannot give issuance to the products of intellection and volition; otherwise it would be necessary to admit that a cause could produce something superior to its own capabilities. The rational activities of man demand a principle superior to the vegetant and sentient soul, a *rational vital principle.*

Apparently, rationality introduces an ultra-dualistic division in man, similar to that of Descartes. Such a division, however, would be contrary to the nature of man as an integral organism. Man is not a double-being, vegetant-sentient and rational, but a single *vegetant-sentient-rational being*. Our entire discussion of man's being throughout this book emphasized this important fact. There is no absolute cleavage between rational life and vegetant-sentient life in man; they are interrelated in many ways. Bodily health and illness affect intellection and volition. Emotions, as we know from personal experience, exert a profound influence on thinking and willing. Sensory perceptions and images are the necessary starting point for the formation of ideas by means of intellectual abstraction, according to the well-known axiom that 'nothing is in the intellect which was not first in the senses.' On their part, intellect and will to a very great extent guide and control the senses in their operations, especially imagination and memory. Ideas are clothed in the habiliments of sensory images and words. The intellect can think of material things and sense qualities, but not without a previous presentation by the senses; if a certain sense is missing from birth, as in a person born blind, the intellect is incapable of forming ideas of the things or qualities which are normally perceived by this sense. The will desires goods which pertain to the vegetative and sensory order as well as those which pertain to the rational order. The will controls the members of the body through the voluntary or striped muscles. This mutual influence of activities would be impossible, if there were an absolute cleavage between the vegetant-sentient principle and the rational principle in man. The vegetant-sentient part of man's being could not influence the rational part, nor could the rational part influence the vegetant-sentient part; each part would be restricted to its own specific sphere of action. As it is, there exists a most intimate relationship of mutual influence between the two parts, with the result that man is indeed an integral organism, a single, complete, unitary being.

Consciousness also bears witness to this fact. The pronoun *I* expresses the personal, rational part of man; that much is clear. Much more, however, is referred to the *I* or *Ego* than purely intellectual and volitional acts and states. Statements like the following are very frequently made: 'I have grown in height and increased in weight; I have a good digestion; I feel cold; I have a stomach-ache; I see a house across the street; I hear the radio playing a symphony; I am imagining the scenes of my home town; I remember the friend I met last week; I have an idea of a perfect circle; I desire to be virtuous; I love God.' Such statements are not made in a figurative sense; they are intended as expressions of literal facts. Factually, therefore, vegetative, sensory, and rational acts and conditions are referred to the self-same Ego without restriction or discrimination, as vital activities of *one identical organism.* The same organism digests, senses, and thinks. The reference of all functions to the Ego would be inexplicable, if man were not an integral organism; and man would not be an integral organism, if the vegetant-sentient activities proceed from a vegetant-sentient principle and the rational activities from a rational principle, both of which are fundamentally distinct realities.

The conclusion to be drawn is evident. There are not two vital principles or souls present in man, one vegetant-sentient and the other rational. Nor has man a body (matter) animated by a vegetant-sentient soul, like the brute animal, to which a rational principle is somehow attached. Man is a *rational animal,* and the rational principle with its intellect and will is an integral part of his nature. Being an integral organism, functioning throughout as a dynamic unit, man can have but a single soul. This soul is not only endowed with the powers of vegetancy and sentiency, but also with the powers of rationality. Hence, the soul of man is a *single rational soul* which includes the lower functional capabilities of the vegetant soul as found in the plant and of the sentient soul as found in the brute.

In scholastic terminology, the vital principle or soul is said to be the *substantial form* of the living body. The 'substantial form' is defined as 'the determining principle which, by uniting with the matter which it actuates, constitutes a complete substance of a definite species.' Man, of course, is a specific type of being, different from inanimate chemicals and from plants and brute animals. Matter, the material co-efficient of the organism, is not the principle which brings about the specific differences existing in these types of being, because matter, due to the metabolic processes going on in the organism, is subject to continuous change, while the organism preserves its *specific identity* throughout all material change. The vital principle, or soul, or substantial form, therefore, is the determinant responsible for the placing of an organism in a definite species. Hence, the *rational soul* is the 'substantial form' of the human organism, because it is precisely through his rationality that man belongs to the 'human species' as distinct from that of plants and brutes.

A number of terms have now been used to designate the specific determinant of organisms—'vital principle,' 'soul,' 'entelechy,' and 'substantial form.' Fundamentally, they all mean the same thing, because they represent the same essential determining reality. The rational soul is the *ultimate ground or source* of all vegetative, sensory, and rational life in the human organism, making man to be precisely 'man.'

If we wish to *define* the *human soul,* we can define it as *the vital principle of the human organism,* or as *the substantial form of the human body*. Aristotle defines the soul as "the first act [first grade of actuality, form—Author] of a natural body possessed potentially of life."[1] These are technical definitions, couched in philosophical language. In a descriptive manner, we can define the human soul as *the ultimate principle in man in virtue of which he lives, senses, thinks, and wills.*

The Spirituality of Man's Soul

Spirituality is the same as *immateriality*. Something is said to be 'material' for one of two reasons: it is either composed of matter as an ultimate constituent of its essence; or, though not composed of matter itself, it is intrinsically dependent on matter, so that it cannot exist and act except in conjunction with matter. Reversing the concept, a thing is 'immaterial' or 'spiritual,' if it is *neither composed of matter nor intrinsically dependent on matter.*

Every subatomic particle, every chemical element and compound, and every organism is material, because matter is an essential constituent of their being; they are composed ultimately of matter. Man, therefore, considered in his entirety as an integral organism, is a 'material being.' Plant and animal souls are not composed of matter itself, because they are co-principles *with* matter and are conjoined *with* matter to

[1] *On the Soul,* Bk. II, Ch. 2.

constitute the ultimate nature and substance of the organic body; but these souls, as we have seen, are totally immersed in matter and intrinsically dependent on matter, so that they cannot exist and act except in conjunction with matter. Hence, plant and animal souls are essentially 'material' realities.

Man's soul, however, is *essentially immaterial* and *spiritual.* Man's soul is *not composed of matter,* because, like the plant and animal soul, it is a co-principle *with* matter as an ultimate constituent of the human organism. It can, therefore, only be a question of whether or not the soul is 'intrinsically dependent' on matter in its essence and operation. If the human soul is material, that is to say, if it is intrinsically dependent on matter, then it must conform absolutely to the capabilities and conditions of material forces and energies. Its operations could never transcend these capabilities and conditions, *not even in a single instance,* because these forces and energies would be the immediate causes of the operations as effects, and no effect can transcend the level of its cause. Hence, if it can be shown that the operations of the human soul actually *transcend matter* and its capabilities and energies, then the essence of the human soul must be intrinsically independent of matter and as such immaterial and spiritual. This conclusion follows necessarily from the principle: As the essence, so the operation, and as the operation, so the essence. We claim that *some* operations of the human soul plainly transcend matter and the capabilities and conditions of material forces and energies.

Thinking and Energy. If the soul of man is material in nature, then thinking is a material operation. Thinking must then be some sort of sensory function, on a par with seeing, hearing, imagining, and so forth. Being material, there should be a consumption and transformation of material energy in every act of thinking, because such an act would involve metabolic changes in the nerve tissues which serve as the material substrate for sensory function. The evidence, however, is entirely against such a view. Thinking, so far as scientists have been able to discover, does *not increase metabolism nor consume energy.* In this regard, Alexis Carrel states: "Intellectual work, strange to say, does not increase metabolism. It seems to require no energy, or to consume a quantity of it too small to be detected by our present techniques. It is, indeed, an astonishing fact that human thought, which has transformed the surface of the earth, destroyed and built nations, discovered new universes in the immensity of the sidereal spaces, is elaborated without demanding a measurable amount of energy. The mightiest effort of our intelligence has incomparably less effect on metabolism than the contraction of the biceps when this muscle lifts a weight of a few grams. The ambition of Caesar, the meditation of Newton, the inspiration of Beethoven, the passionate contemplation of Pasteur, did not modify the chemical exchanges of these great men as much as a few bacteria or a slight stimulation of the thyroid gland would easily have done."[2] Provided these scientific findings are correct, they prove that thinking, precisely as such, is not a material process but an immaterial operation. Whatever minute metabolic changes might occur, could be attributed to the formation of images which normally accompany all acts of thinking.

Intellection and Sensation. It is a common experience that the senses, after strong stimulation, are incapable of registering the impressions of weaker stimuli for a certain period of time. A loud report makes the ear insensible to faint sounds; a glance into the sun blinds the eye for a while to ordinary rays; a strong odor affects the sense of smell to such a degree that a weak fragrance remains unperceived until a certain time has elapsed. All senses act in this manner. The reason is simple. Nerve action is subject to the law of assimilation and dissimilation, because energy is consumed in nerve action, and energy is produced by means of a chemical breakdown of the material of nerve tissue. The stronger the stimulus, the stronger the nerve action; the result is, that an amount of energy greater than usual is expended. Before the sense organ can respond to

[2] *Man, The Unknown,* 27th ed. (Harper and Bros., 1935), p. 81. See also T. V. Moore, *Cognitive Psychology* (Lippincott, 1939), pp. 540, 541.

weaker stimuli, this expended energy must be restored by a counter-process of assimilation, and it takes a certain amount of time for the metabolism of the nerve tissue to bring the organ up to its former level of efficiency.

The character of intellection is radically different. When the intellect is occupied with ideas and truths of great clarity, sublimity, and magnitude, its understanding of ideas and truths of inferior scope and importance is not impeded. On the contrary, the insight into major truths facilitates the simultaneous insight into minor truths; no lapse of time is required for the intellect to pass from the one type to the other. Yet, if intellection were a material process, intrinsically dependent on material nerve tissues and organic structures, metabolic changes would of necessity occur, and a certain amount of assimilation would have to take place, before the intellect would be capable of perceiving ideas and truths of lesser clarity, sublimity, and magnitude. The character of intellection thus plainly indicates that intellection is of an order different from sensation and is *exempt from the conditions of materiality*. Intellection is, therefore, an immaterial operation. Aristotle[3] already called attention to this fact and used it as evidence of the essential difference between intellect and sense.

Of course, man being an integral organism, the intellect and its operations are not completely isolated from concomitant sensory processes. 'Mental fatigue' results from muscular tension which is usually present when lively interest is aroused.

Universal Ideas. Man acquires his intellectual knowledge of the world and its objects through the mental process of 'abstraction' from sensory images, and these images are derived from impressions made on the sense organs and the brain. Sense objects are material objects, and sense organs are material organs; both are, therefore, affected by the conditions of materiality. Every material object in the world is a concrete individual object, determinately circumscribed and particularized as to quantity, quality, space, and time. What I perceive with a sense, for instance with sight, is always a 'this' and

[3] *On the Soul,* Bk. III, Ch. 4.

'that,' an individual object which is affected by a determinate quantity (a certain size, weight, age, etc.), which possesses definite qualities (a certain color, warmth, energy, etc.), and which exists in a determinate place (in the sky, on the ground, in New York, etc.) and at a determinate time (now, today, yesterday, etc.). For example, if I perceive a dog, it is always an individual dog; and this individual dog is particularized as to size, weight, age (quantity), as to breed, sex, color (quality), as to his whereabouts (place), and as to when he exists and is perceived (time). Sense impressions and images, therefore, are concerned solely with *individual objects in particularized material conditions.*

Intellectual knowledge consists of *universal ideas.* Universals are representations of *class natures,* and as such apply to the whole class as a class and to each individual belonging to the class. They are divested of all particularizing determinations of quantity, quality, space, and time. My idea of 'animal,' for example, is that of a 'sentient organism.' It is a *generic* idea, not the image of an individual animal; it applies to all animals as a class, because all are included in the idea 'sentient organism,' and also to each individual animal belonging to this class, because each one is a 'sentient organism.' It thus includes all individuals and types of dogs, cows, eagles, sharks, men, etc., without any consideration of the particularizing determinations found in them as individuals. Universal ideas, therefore, are *not material sensory images.* No material image of an 'animal' can include within itself at one and the same time the representations of a dog, cow, eagle shark, ant, snail, and man, as the idea of an 'animal' does. Only individual animals exist in nature, and our sense impressions and images can represent only individuals, not a genus. Universal ideas, since they represent class natures divested of material conditions, must be immaterial. As a consequence, the intellect which elaborates universal ideas through abstraction from sensory images must also be immaterial. If the intellect were intrinsically dependent on a material organ, it could not surmount the conditions of materiality inherent in sensations and images, and universal ideas would be impossible. The fact that we have universal ideas proves that the intellect is an immaterial power, intrinsically independent of matter.

Ideas With Supra-Sensuous Content. Images are sensory representations of material objects and qualities; as such they are material in nature. If ideas are not spiritual, they also are nothing more than sensory representations; and in that case, they cannot represent supra-sensuous realities, because the effect cannot be of a nature superior to its cause. We have, however, numerous ideas which represent supra-sensuous realities. Such are the ideas of 'justice,' 'law,' 'freedom,' 'truth,' 'possibility,' 'immortality,' 'spirituality,' 'soul,' 'God,' and a host of others. The contents of these and similar ideas are not representations of physical objects and qualities which can affect a sense organ with their stimuli. They cannot, therefore, be perceived in a sensory manner. But if ideas were essentially sensory and material in nature, then it would be impossible for us to have ideas of these supra-sensuous and spiritual realities. Our intellect could not think of such realities, because it would be a material power absolutely restricted to the representations of material things. We do, however, think of them, form ideas of them, speak and write of them. Whether the contents of such ideas are actualities or not, is beside the question. The important thing, though, is the fact that our intellect in its ideas is capable of *transcending matter and material realities;* and only a power which itself transcends matter and material realities is capable of such an act. Hence, the intellect must be intrinsically independent of matter, i.e., spiritual.

The Intellect and the Future. Sense organs are *here-and-now* instruments of sensory knowledge, dependent on the stimuli which proceed from objects at a specified time from a specified place. The composite image of the synthetic or central sense, elaborated from sensations, is similarly characterized. The imagination is less restricted, since it can combine various elements of present and past sense impressions and images into new images. The imagination, however, is dependent on the synthetic or central sense for its materials. In some form or other, therefore, all senses are restricted in their operations to materials furnished by objects existing in the present or which have existed in the past. The future is barred to the senses; the sensory powers cannot elaborate images of future events, because future events cannot send stimuli to the sense organs existing in the present, otherwise a non-existent cause would produce an effect.

If the intellect, like the senses, were essentially dependent on the material organism in its operations, it would also be a here-and-now instrument of knowledge and could neither have ideas of the future nor predict future events. The fact is plain, however, that we have ideas of the future and actually predict future events. Scientists, in their experiments, know beforehand what results will follow from the combination of conditions which they place. Astronomers predict eclipses of the sun and moon for hundreds and thousands of years in advance of their occurrence. The senses, being material powers dependent on present material stimuli, cannot have a knowledge of the future. The intellect, therefore, cannot be a material power, but must be intrinsically independent of matter and of material conditions in its operation; it is a supra-sensuous, immaterial, spiritual power.

G. T. Ladd does not hesitate to write: "With no mere figure of speech we are compelled to say, every mind thus *transcends* completely, not only the powers of the cerebral mechanism by springing into another order of phenomena, but also the very existence, as it were, of that mechanism by passing into regions of space, time, causality, and ideality, of various kinds, where the terms that apply to the existence and activity of the cerebral centers have absolutely no meaning whatever. For example, the human mind anticipates the future and predicts, on a basis of experience in the past, the occurrences which *will* be but are not now. Into this future, which is itself the product of its own imagining and thinking, it projects its own continued and yet characteristically altered existence, as well as the continued similar existence of things. But the existence of the brain, and of its particular forms of nerve commotion, is never other than a purely here-and-now existence. This physical existence is, therefore, transcended in an absolute way by every such activity of the mind."[4]

Volition. An appetitive power can only desire something proportionate to its own nature. An appetitive power, immersed in materiality and essentially dependent on a brain or organ, cannot be influenced by, or strive for, anything except a concrete physical good. The brute animal, for instance, seeks only that which is good for its physical well-being. Man, however, is often influenced in his volition by goods which are decidedly *supra-physical* and *supra-sensuous.* Food, drink, pleasure, physical well-being, etc., are sensuous goods which affect the sensuous appetency, because they are concrete realities which affect the senses. Immaterial goods, however, like justice, righteousness, altruism, patriotism, charity, duty, love of God, etc., at times contravene our sensual desires and demand the sacrifice of sensuous goods and even of life itself; yet they not only influence the will, but are goods for which the will actively strives. The soldier in war willingly goes without food and drink, sacrifices many natural pleasures, and even deliberately gives up his life, thus acting in opposition to every instinct and desire of his sensuous nature, for the sake of an *ideal*—the defense of his country's sacred honor and right. The martyr, too, undergoes horrible pain and suffering and gladly lays down his life, for the sake of his religious convictions and for the love of God. In doing these things, man's will *transcends all sensuous desires and sensuous goods.* Such attitudes are possible only on the supposition that the will is a supra-sensuous, immaterial appetency.

Furthermore, the will is *free in its choice.* Material realities are subject to physical determinism. When all the conditions required for an occurrence are present, the material cause must act, and the effect must follow. Material agencies are simply constituted that way; they have no choice in the matter. It is on the basis of this law that scientists are able to forecast the

[4] *Philosophy of Mind* (Charles Scribner's Sons, 1895), pp. 400, 401.

actions of material beings. Man's will, on the other hand, is intrinsically undetermined. Even when all the conditions required for action are posited, the will can *determine itself* to act or not to act, to act this way or that way. Such a power, contrary to all the properties of material agencies, cannot itself be material, but must be immaterial and spiritual.

So far as these arguments for the immateriality and spirituality of the human soul are concerned, it makes no difference whether we accept the soul as the direct and sole subject of thinking and willing, or whether we refer thinking to the intellect as a power and willing to the will as a power, with the soul as the ultimate subject of these two powers. In the first case, the acts of thinking and will *modify the soul directly;* and, since these acts are immaterial and spiritual, the acting subject, which is the soul, must also be immaterial and spiritual. The argument is based on the evident principle that the effect cannot be superior to the producing cause. In the second case, according to the same principle, the powers of the intellect and will must be immaterial and spiritual. These powers, however, are agencies of the soul, residing in the soul as in their *ultimate subject;* and, since the powers are immaterial and spiritual, the agent soul must also be immaterial and spiritual, because these powers receive their *being and existence* from the soul and cannot be superior in nature to it.

We do not, of course, perceive the soul and we do not perceive its spirituality. We can only *conclude* from the nature of the acts to the nature of the acting subject. According to all the laws of reason, this conclusion is legitimate. From the spirituality of the acts of intellection and volition, we are, therefore, necessitated to draw the logical conclusion that the *human soul is spiritual in its nature and substance.*

The Simplicity of the Soul

By *simplicity* we understand that positive property in virtue of which the essence of a being is not composed of distinct and distinguishable parts or principles. An extended body has unity of being, but it is composed of *integrant,* or *quantitative,* parts into which it can be divided. A yardstick can be sawed into inch-lengths; the limbs of the human body can be severed from the trunk. These parts are integrant, or quantitative. The original body is undivided, but divisible; since it is composed of internal parts, actual division separates one part from the other. Living bodies are also composed of *essential,* or *constitutive,* parts or principles, namely, matter and soul. In the living body, these parts or principles are united and undivided; however, being essentially distinct realities, a division separates them. Such a division occurs when the living body dies; matter and soul are then divided and separated. Every material being, therefore, whether organic or inorganic, is composed of quantitative or constitutive parts or of both and as such is capable of being divided into these component parts. On the other hand, a simple essence is composed neither of integrant, quantitative parts nor of essential, constitutive principles; due to the perfection of its being, extension and composition are absent. Hence, a simple essence is not only one and undivided, but one and indivisible. A being which is so perfect that it is not composed of integrant, quantitative parts, is said to possess *quantitative simplicity;* one that is not composed of essential, constitutive parts or principles, is said to possess *essential simplicity.* Our definition of 'simplicity' is thus seen to be negative in form but positive in content; 'simplicity' is a perfection, not a deficiency.

The human soul is simple in its essence, excluding both the composition of integrant, quantitative parts and the composition of essential, constitutive principles.

That the human soul has *essential simplicity,* follows from its spirituality. The composition in question involves the union of matter and soul as the two constitutive principles necessary to form the living body of man. Man, as an integral organism, consists of matter and the soul. The soul, however, considered for and by itself, does not consist of matter; it is immaterial and spiritual, and it is, together *with* matter, an ultimate constituent of the human body. Hence, it is not itself composed of matter and another vital principle, but is the vital principle alone. Consequently, the human soul possesses essential simplicity.

The human soul also possesses *quantitative simplicity*. Only a material being, a body, has integrant, quantitative parts, because it is matter which gives to a body extension and, with it, parts beside parts. An immaterial being, since it is devoid of matter, has no quantitative parts. The human soul, however, is immaterial and spiritual. Hence, it is not composed of integrant, quantitative parts and, therefore, possesses quantitative simplicity.

A consideration of the acts of the intellect and of self-reflection proves the same point.

Take the act of *judgment*. In the act of judgment the intellect compares two ideas and expresses their agreement or disagreement among themselves. In the statement 'The rose is red,' there are two distinct ideas, namely, 'rose' and 'red.' We compare the two ideas in our mind by analyzing the attributes contained in 'rose' and 'red'; we are consciously aware that quality 'red' is actually present in the object 'rose.' After perceiving the factual agreement between the two ideas, we make the mental assertion that 'The rose is red.' An indivisible intellect is required to perform this operation. If the intellect (or the soul, which amounts to the same thing, because the soul is the root-principle of the intellect) consisted of parts, then the idea 'rose' would be apprehended by one part and the idea 'red' by another part; or, both ideas 'rose' and 'red' would be apprehended by each part. In the first alternative, one part would know about the 'rose' and the other about 'red,' but there would be no single subject to make the comparison and form the judgment combining the two ideas into a statement of agreement. In the second alternative, each part would make the same comparison and form the same judgment; the result would be double ideas, a double judgment, and a double assertion of agreement, but no unitary judgment. Since the intellect makes the mental synthesis of a unitary judgment, it cannot consist of parts, but is simple in essence.

H. Lotze recognized the force of this argument and its consequences. "Any comparison of two ideas, which ends by our finding their contents like or unlike, presupposes the absolutely indivisible unity of that which compares them; it must be one and the same thing which first forms the idea of *a,* and then that of *b,* and which at the same time is conscious of the nature and extent of the difference between them. Then again the various acts of comparing ideas and referring them to one another are themselves in turn reciprocally related; and this relation brings a new activity of comparison to consciousness. And so our whole inner world of thoughts is built up, not as a mere collection of manifold ideas existing with or after one another, but as a work in which these individual members are held together and arranged by the relating activity of this single pervading principle. This is what we mean by the *Unity of Consciousness.* It is this we regard as sufficient ground for assuming an indivisible soul."[5]

The act of *self-reflection* is unique. Man's intellect is the soul of man in so far as it knows intellectually. Man's soul not only has intellectual acts, but it knows that it has intellectual acts and recognizes itself in its acts. The Ego or *I* is the *subject* of its intellectual acts and is conscious of itself in these acts; it thinks of itself, and thereby it makes itself the *object* of its own thinking. When judgment is made that 'I am I' or 'I am myself,' the Ego is both *subject and object* of its intellectual act, agent and patient, the being knowing and the being known, the thing thinking and the thing thought. In self-reflection, a complete reversal or return of a thing upon itself takes place, so that the agent makes itself the patient or recipient of its own cognitive activity. A being consisting of parts cannot perform such a feat. It is possible for one part to influence another part, and it is possible for one part to bend over another part; but it is impossible for the parts to make

---

[5] *Metaphysics,* § 241.

themselves the object of their own action, or for the single parts to turn completely upon themselves. The hand, for example, cannot grasp itself, nor can it grasp its own grasping; the eye cannot see itself, nor can it see its own seeing; the ear cannot hear itself, nor can it hear its own hearing. Only an indivisible entity can perform the remarkable feat of making itself the object of its own percipient act, as the intellect (soul) does in self-reflection. Hence the soul is a simple entity.

Extrinsic Dependence

Although it has been established that the human soul is spiritual and simple in its essence, neither consisting of matter nor intrinsically dependent on it, the soul is not entirely independent of matter in *all* its operations.

The intellect demands the *active co-operation of the sense organs* in the formation of ideas. Man is an integral organism, and the intellect derives the materials for its ideas from the senses, because ideas are formed through the process of abstraction from sensory images. Ideas, as we have seen, are not innate. Ideas are not mere refinements of images, as the sensationalists assert; nor do they arise solely out of the depths of the soul itself, as the ultra-spiritualists claim. Ideas are indeed the spiritual products of the spiritual intellect, but the intellect must dip into the reservoir of sense images and draw their 'intelligible content' out of them; only in this manner can man, so long as the soul is the vital principle of the body, fashion ideas. Hence, disturbances and distortions on the sensory level, as psychiatry proves, bring on disturbances and distortions on the intellectual level. Sensory images are more than 'conditions' of thought. They are, as D. Card. Mercier, points out, *instrumental causes;* or, as St. Thomas puts it, "images are to the intellect as color is to sight."[6] In other words, the intellect is dependent on the senses for the 'object' of its ideas. The intellect (and, therefore, the soul) is thus

---

[6] *Summa theol.*, 1a, q. 75, art. 2, ad 3.

subjectively and intrinsically independent of the organism in its existence, but *objectively* and *extrinsically* dependent on the organism for the exercise of its abstracting ability.

The activities of vegetancy and sentiency are of a different nature. Since they are 'vital' activities, they have their primary source in the soul as the vital principle of the human organism. They are, however, 'organic' functions, and their real subject is not the soul alone, but the *organic compound* of matter and soul. The soul, therefore, taken by and for itself, is not capable of performing vegetative and sensory activities; it can perform them only in conjunction with matter as a co-principle of operation. So far, then, as *these activities* are concerned, the soul is intrinsically dependent on matter.

The Locus of the Soul

By the *locus* of the soul we mean the 'place' or 'seat' where the soul resides in the human organism. Descartes, it will be recalled, considered the pineal gland to be the 'locus' of the soul. Others have placed it in the blood, the heart, or in some unspecified portion of the brain. Such views are uncritical and philosophically untenable.

The soul is in the entire organism and in every living part of it.

The ubiquitous presence of the soul in the body follows from the very nature of the soul as the *vital principle* of the organism. Life has its primary source, not in matter, but in the vital principle or soul. Unless matter is animated by the soul, it is lifeless matter, incapable of any vital activity whatsoever; only in conjunction with the animating soul does matter become a partner in vital activities. Since there can be no life without the soul, *wherever life is, there the soul must be present.* Life, however, manifests itself as vegetancy, sentiency, and rationality in man. Consequently in every part of the organism, where any of these activities occur, the soul must be present as the primary active principle of life.

The cell is the biological unit of life. It performs the essential functions of vegetative life, namely, nutrition and reproduction. Furthermore, the entire cell-body is an organic structure, which, throughout its entirety, is actively engaged in the process of metabolism and generation. Hence the soul, as the vital principle, must be present *in every cell throughout its entire structure.* And since the entire human organism consists of cells, the soul must be present *throughout the entire body.*

This fact reveals an interesting feature of the soul. The soul has no parts. Hence, it cannot exist in one part of the body according to one part of its being and in another part of the body according to another part of its being. As a spiritual, simple, indivisible reality, *it must be entire wherever it is.* Consequently, it is entire in the smallest living portion of the organism and also entire in the total living organism. We cannot, of course, imagine this sort of presence, because we are acquainted only with the extended presence of material bodies; but we must bear in mind that thought, not imagination, must be our guide in philosophical problems. A spiritual essence is not circumscribed by the limitations of tri-dimensional extension, because it has no quantity or mass, and it would be utterly inappropriate to conceive of the soul's presence in the organism after the manner of a quantified body. The presence of the spiritual soul in the human organism is technically termed a *definitive* or *non-quantitative presence,* in virtue of which the soul exercises its life-giving power ubiquitously in the whole body and in every living part of it.

The soul is present everywhere in the organism according to its entire essence, but it does *not exercise all its powers everywhere.* If a certain bodily structure or organ is designed exclusively for a particular vital function, then it is there that the soul exercises this function, and nowhere else. The soul, therefore, exercises its cognitive sensory powers only in the sense organs, afferent nerves, and brain, and exercises its motor powers only in the brain, efferent nerves, and muscles; in other words, the soul as the vital principle of sentiency exercises its sentient powers only in and through the *nervous system*. Intellectual and volitional operations, being spiritual and simple in nature, are exercised exclusively by the soul itself as the rational principle and therefore occur nowhere but *in the soul*. In as much, however, as these operations are objectively and extrinsically dependent on the functions of the brain for the supply of necessary images from which to abstract ideas, one may say that thinking and willing take place 'in the head' or 'in the brain,' so long as one does not understand these phrases too literally. Intellection and volition are not localized in any brain centers like sight, hearing, taste, and the other senses. Hence, it is only in a very broad meaning that one may use the phrase 'The brain is the organ of thought.' Philosophically speaking, thought is not directly connected with any bodily organ at all, not even with the brain.

An intriguing problem arises out of the relation of the spiritual soul to matter in the human body. Since the soul is one and indivisible, and since the organism is undoubtedly a unitary substance, does it follow that the body of man possesses an unbroken *continuity?* Discontinuity in the body seems to involve division in the simple, indivisible soul. There can, however, be no doubt that the body of man, in its entirety, is *not a continuous substance* in the strict sense of the term. The blood is an organic substance, and it is replete with hemoglobin corpuscles and leucocytes; their existence and activity must be ascribed primarily to the action of the vital principle, the soul. The blood, however, is a fluid coursing uninterruptedly through the arteries and veins, and as such it is at best only *contiguous* with the walls of the arteries, veins, heart, and the rest of the bodily substance; yet it must, together with all other parts of the body, be 'informed' and vivified by the soul. The soul, therefore, can be present in discontinuous parts without sacrificing its indivisibility. An analogy for this type of presence is found in the presence of God's spiritual substance throughout the discontinuous parts of the world. The 'how' of such a presence is a mystery, but the fact itself is beyond dispute.

Man and Brute

The difference between man and brute is fundamentally the *difference between their souls.* Is this difference relative or absolute, accidental or essential? In many quarters there has been a persistent endeavor to eliminate any essential difference between the two, either by humanizing the brute or by brutalizing man.

Our discussion so far has brought out the point that the soul of man is endowed with powers and activities which are rational and as such superior to the powers and activities of sentiency. If there is no essential difference between man and brute, then the soul of the brute must also be rational. Now, no soul can be perceived directly; we can know it only by drawing an inference from its activities to its nature. In our own case, we have the advantage of an introspective analysis of our own mental operations. This advantage is absent in the case of the brute. We cannot analyze the brute's mental operations by any direct method. We must draw our conclusions as to the brute's rationality or irrationality from its external behavior.

On the basis of its behavior, we claim that *the brute manifests no rationality.*

The Absence of Progress. If brutes, like men, had the rational power of an intellect, then we have the right to expect that they would have made use of it as men have. They would then possess essentially the same nature and live in the same general environment and the same causes and conditions should, by analogy, have produced the same results. Now man, because he has an intellect, perceives the *abstract relationship between end and means* and understands that the same end can be reached by a variety of means. Realizing this, man is not satisfied with producing a desired result in a single, uniformly constant manner, but invents various *devices* and *techniques* to use and save energy and to increase efficiency by improved methods. Therein lies the secret of human progress.

Nothing of the sort is ever observed in the brute's behavior. Even when the brute is in daily contact with the inventive genius of man, it manifests *no tendency to learn* to do things man does, although it exhibits native curiosity in many ways. The brute has never invented a single device, although the materials are ever present and within easy reach. When archeologists find a piece of clumsily carved stone and geologists discover a primitively chipped flint, they unhesitatingly ascribe it to man, not to the brute, convinced that the simplest of tools and manufactured articles are beyond the mental capacity of the brute, because the brute cannot comprehend the relation of means to end involved in the construction of any sort of implement. Brutes can and do learn in some measure by actual experience, and occasionally incidents occur which seemingly reflect intellectual insight; but, as M. Maher sagely remarks: "The few trivial instances cited here and there of some animal seizing a club or other rude implement that fell in its way, only establish the more clearly the enormous chasm which separates the brute from the rational being."[7]

Very many of the actions performed by brutes are marvelously complex and purposive, revealing an eminent adaptation of means to specific ends. Such actions, however, are *not learned and devised,* but are the result of an inborn instinct. They show the invariable, stereotyped routine of an almost machine-like perfection, *without variation and improvement* of procedure acquired in the course of time; and the brute makes no attempt at variation and improvement, except in such a minor degree that the change can easily be explained on the basis of immediate perception of sensory relations. So far back as the knowledge of man goes, each species of animal, with the sole exception of man, reacts to his environment in practically an identical manner. Bees and ants, for example, retain the same mode of living wherever

[7] *Psychology,* 9th ed. (Longmans, Green, 1930), p. 583.

they are. Each type of insect, fish, bird, reptile, and mammal constructs its home, seeks its food, cares for its young, and in general lives, as it has always done is the past. Not even the apes and monkeys, notwithstanding their morphological similarity to man and reputed intelligence, have been able to devise and make a simple cutting tool or a wooden shelter.

If the mind of the brutes were truly intellectual, like that of man, then why is their behavior so confined to the level of the senses and of the instincts? Why would the brutes not change their methods, modify their manner of living, invent mechanical contrivances, and show progress in every direction? Man does, and the brutes, if truly intellectual, should also do it. They would have the capability, and they should also exhibit its use. Many of their actions, if really the outcome of intellectual insight, reveal a mind superior to man's. Then why the lack of progress? No valid reason can be given for this lack of progress, if they are capable of progress. The only valid reason that can be found as an explanation for this universal fact is this: *Instinct takes the place of reason.* Brutes have no reasoning powers, and hence no genuine progress is possible. Yet the individual and the race must be protected and perpetuated; and so they are endowed with strong and ingenious instincts, innate and ineradicable, to supply the deficiency of intellectual insight in the purposiveness of their actions.

The Absence of Language. Language is a system of conventional signs expressive of ideas. Sounds, gestures, written and printed symbols are used by man as the media of language, in order to express the meaning of ideas present in one mind and to communicate them to another. Some signs or symbols are 'natural.' Laughter is a natural sign of exhilaration, weeping and sobbing a natural sign of pain or grief, romping a natural sign of general well-being, depressed lethargy a natural sign of ill health, singing a natural sign of joy, snarling lips and a fighting pose a natural sign of anger. Similar attitudes are observed among the brutes, because every emotion tends to express itself in bodily form.

Language, however, is a system of *conventional* signs. Sounds, gestures, written and printed symbols are arbitrarily chosen by mutual agreement ('convention') to express ideas. Languages are made; they are an artificial product. The natural signs of emotions are the result of a spontaneous outburst and are more or less the same at all times and with all persons; for this reason it is usually easy to interpret their general import. Languages, since they are the invention of a rational mind, differ from race to race and from nation to nation, with regard to grammar, pronunciation, writing, and printing. One need but glance at a polyglot dictionary or listen to the speech of diverse national or racial groups, in order to observe the conventional and artificial character of languages. The ideas are the same, but their expressions in languages are totally different. Languages, therefore, must be *learned* before they can be understood, both as to single words and as to grammatical construction. Even the learning of words will not suffice; one must know the ideas which the words are supposed to represent. Languages are really codes of nonsense syllables made to make sense by filling their otherwise empty forms with the intellectual content of ideas. It takes intellect to devise languages, and it takes intellect to understand and speak them.

Language is a *universal accomplishment* of man. Even the uneducated savage has a language, because he has a rational mind. As new ideas arise, new words are formed to express them. A living language is thus a fluid thing, constantly in a process of formation and modification. It changes with the progress and culture of the people who use it.

Brutes possess *no language.* They give vent to their feelings and emotions through the medium of natural cries and bodily attitudes; but they have, so far as we can judge from their behavior, no systems of conventional signs which serve as a means of communicating their experiences from one mind to another. If they were actually endowed with an intellect, no valid reason can be assigned why they should not have devised some sort of code, even if it were only a code of dots and dashes. It might not be easy for us to decipher the code, but it would be relatively easy for us to recognize the fact that a code is being used and that it has an intellectual meaning. Most species of animal are not devoid of the necessary physical apparatus required for using a system of conventional signs. The dog's bark, the cow's moo, the horse's whinny, the crow's caw, the woodpecker's tatoo, and similar natural accomplishments, lend themselves admirably for use as languages. The vocalization abilities of the parrot are outstanding, for the parrot can memorize and speak words and entire sentences with astonishing fidelity. Practically every animal could scratch symbols or picture-drawings on the ground, to represent ideas and communicate messages.

If brutes possessed a rational mind, why this astounding *absence of language in every form* in the entire animal kingdom? The advisability and the occasion for language are certainly present; the physical ability is not lacking for the required invention of the necessary conventional symbols. Yet not even the parrot attempts to use its ability of imitating speech for the purpose of expressing its own ideas. All we observe are natural signs expressive of natural feelings and emotions. It is inconceivable that intelligent animals would not use their intellectual powers to invent some form of language among themselves which would be recognizable as such. And it is also inconceivable that domestic pets would not, if they could, express their ideas and sentiments to their human masters. The reason why brutes have no language can only be: *They have no ideas to express.* Where ideas are lacking, there can be no language.

Some advocates of animal intellectuality put forth the claim that brutes speak a language of their own, so that they understand one another. They adduce as evidence the melodies of birds, warning cries, mating calls, the whining of the young clamoring for food, and so on. The facts are admitted, but the interpretation of the facts is of very doubtful validity. The conditions expressed by these sounds and bodily attitudes are of a purely sensory nature, and the expressions themselves are *natural signs,* not conventional and arbitrarily invented symbols. These expressions are on a level with the natural signs found among humans, especially infants. The human infant also cries out in pain and fright, gurgles and coos in pleasure and comfort, and otherwise gives expression to his emotional states; but there is nothing intellectual about such natural manifestations, because the infant does not use his latent intellectual powers at this stage of existence. An older child, when injured, will weep and cry out "That hurts!" Weeping is a natural sign; the cry "That hurts!" is language. Man expresses his mental condition with both types of signs; the brute, only in the form of natural signs which demand no intellect to apprehend their significance. The human infant, as it advances in age, learns to speak, because it has an intellect. The brute, however, never goes beyond the level of natural calls and attitudes. The reason must be that it simply *has no intellect* which would enable it to use language as a medium of expression.

The Absence of Intellectual Insight. To test the relative intelligence of man and brute, much experimental research has been made in recent decades. Many types of animals were used for the purpose, among them monkeys, orangutans, chimpanzees, cats, rats, dogs, raccoons, etc. Representative of the group of experimenters are E. L. Thorndike, J. A. Bierens de Haan, P. E. Fields, L. Verlaine, H. G. Wyatt, N. R. F. Maier, G. Révész, G. W. Hartmann, A. A. Campbell, R. M. Yerkes, H. W. Nissen, T. L. McCulloch, H. A. Fjeld, W. Köhler, W. N. Kellogg, L. A. Kellogg, J. B. Wolfe, S. D. Shirley Spragg, and others.

A study of the results of these experiments shows that animals possess a synthetic sense and are capable of sensory analysis and synthesis. They have the power of *sensory abstraction,* selecting a predominant sensory item to the exclusion of others. But they are *incapable of intellectual abstraction* based upon the formulation of a general principle applicable to a number of similar things. Children readily grasp the logical relationship of part and whole, genus and species, general law and particular instance, etc., and they solve problems accordingly with true intellectual insight. Animals, however, solve problems on a sensory basis, but not when intellectual insight into logical relation is required. Where *deduction* is demanded, even in its simplest form, animals invariably fail. Animals cannot grasp an abstract 'principle' and work out a problem in accordance with the principle. If, for example, eight boxes are placed in a row, and food is placed in the first one for the first experiment, then in the second one for the second experiment, in the third for the third experiment, and so on through the series, the principle to be deduced and learned is that one must always choose the box next in line to the box which contained the food in the preceding experiment. The principle is simple, but animals never make the deduction; they always choose by the trial-and-error method. *They cannot reason.*

From their behavior, therefore, we must conclude that animals do not possess a rational soul.

Man is an integral organism, consisting of matter and soul. His soul is spiritual and simple. It is entire in the entire body and entire in every living portion of the body. The brute soul is not rational. Hence, there is an *essential difference between man and brute.*

Summary of Chapter XX

To have a proper understanding of 'the whole man,' it is necessary to understand the nature of *man's soul.*

1. *Man an Integral Organism.* Man is a single, unitary substance, an integral organism. His vegetative and sensory structures and activities co-operate in perfect harmony, and one set is dependent on the other in being and operation; hence, both sets of structures and activities must be referred to *one and the same* vital principle or *soul.*

Man's rational activities, being of an order higher than vegetancy and sentiency, demand a *rational soul.* There exists a most intimate relationship of mutual influence between the vegetant-sentient part and the rational part of man's nature:

he is a 'vegetant-sentient-rational' being, a single, complete, integral organism. Hence, he has but a single soul.

Man's *consciousness* is also witness to the fact that vegetative, sensory, and rational acts and conditions are referred to the selfsame Ego, as vital activities of one identical organism. Man, therefore, is 'a rational animal.' His soul is a *single rational soul,* capable of performing vegetative, sensory, and rational activities.

The human soul can be defined as 'the vital principle of the human organism'; or, as 'the substantial form of the human body'; or as 'the first act of a rational body possessed potentially of life'; or, as 'the ultimate principle in man in virtue of which he lives, senses, thinks and wills.'

2. *The Spirituality of Man's Soul.* Spirituality or immateriality is that property in virtue of which a thing is neither composed of matter nor intrinsically dependent on matter. Man's soul is *spiritual and immaterial.*

It is not composed of matter, because it is a co-principle *with* matter as an ultimate constituent of the human organism. It is also *intrinsically independent* of matter, because its operations *transcend matter.*

Thinking and Energy. If the soul is material, then thinking is a material operation and must consume energy, involving metabolic changes. To all appearances, however, thinking does not consume energy.

Intellection and Sensation. In sensation, the stronger the stimulation and nerve action, the more time it takes for the senses to register the impressions of subsequent weaker stimuli. With the intellect, the insight into truths of great clarity, sublimity, and magnitude facilitates the simultaneous insight into minor truths. The reason must be that intellection is not dependent on material nerve tissues and organic structures subject to metabolic changes and loss of material energy. Intellection, therefore, is *exempt from the conditions of materiality.*

Universal Ideas. A material object is an 'individual' object, determinately circumscribed and particularized as to quantity, quality, space, and time. Sense impressions and images are characterized in the same manner. Man's intellect has universal ideas which represent *class-natures* divested of all particularizing determinations of quantity, quality, space, and time. Universal ideas, therefore, are not material, sensory images, but are *immaterial representations* of things.

Ideas with Supra-Sensuous Content. Man has ideas which represent supra-sensuous realities, such as 'justice,' 'law,' 'truth,' 'God,' etc. If the intellect were a material power, it would be absolutely restricted to the representation of material things, and such ideas would be impossible.

The Intellect and the Future. Future events, being as yet non-existent, cannot possibly influence a present material power; the senses, therefore, cannot image future events, because the stimuli are absent. We have, however, ideas of the future and predict future occurrences in advance. Hence, the intellect transcends all material conditions of knowledge.

Volition. A material appetitive power cannot be influenced by, or strive for, anything except a concrete physical good. The will, however, is often influenced by, and strives for, goods which are decidedly *supra-physical* and *supra-sensuous,* transcending all sensuous desires and sensuous goods for the sake of an ideal. The will is also *free* in its choice, determining itself in its action, while material realities are subject to a physical determinism.

We must conclude, then, that the soul, the ultimate subject of intellection and volition, is neither composed of matter nor intrinsically dependent on matter.

3. *The Simplicity of the Soul.* By 'simplicity' we understand that positive property in virtue of which the essence of a being is not composed of distinct and distinguishable parts or principles. An extended body is composed of *integrant,* or *quantitative,* parts into which it can be divided. Living bodies are composed of *essential,* or *constitutive,* principles, namely, matter and soul. The human soul is *simple in its essence,* possessing both 'essential' and 'quantitative' simplicity.

Essential Simplicity. Since the soul is spiritual and immaterial, matter is excluded from its essence.

Quantitative Simplicity. The soul possesses no quantitative parts, because only a material and extended body has such parts.

The act of *judgment* expresses the agreement or disagreement of two ideas among themselves. An *indivisible* intellect is required to make a judgment. If the intellect consisted of parts, then the one idea would be apprehended by one part and the other idea by another part, or both ideas would be apprehended by each part. In the first alternative, there would be no single subject to make the comparison and combine the two ideas into a statement of agreement or disagreement; in the second alternative, we would have double ideas and double judgments, but no unitary judgment. Since the intellect makes the mental synthesis of a unitary judgment, it cannot consist of parts.

In the act of *self-reflection,* the Ego knows itself; the intellect makes its own thinking the object of its own thought. The Ego is both *subject and object* of its intellectual act. Such an act is a complete reversal of a thing upon itself, something impossible to a being consisting of parts. Hence, the intellect, and the soul, is a simple and indivisible entity.

4. *Extrinsic Dependence.* The intellect derives the materials for its ideas from the senses, because ideas are formed through the process of abstraction from sensory images. Hence, though the intellect and its operations are spiritual, the intellect is *objectively* and *extrinsically* dependent on the organism for the exercise of its abstracting ability.

5. *The Locus of the Soul.* By the 'locus' we mean the 'place' where the soul is situated in the body. The soul is entire in the *entire organism* and in *every living part* of it.

The soul is the vital, or life-giving, principle of the human organism. Hence, wherever life is, there the soul must be present. Every cell and every structural part of the cell is vitally active in the functions of vegetative life; and the entire body consists of living cells. The soul, therefore, must be present in the entire organism as a whole and in every living part of it. Since the soul is a simple essence devoid of parts, it must be entire wherever it is; hence, it must be entire in the smallest living portion of the organism and also entire in the total living organism. This type of presence is termed *definitive* or *non-quantitative*.

6. *Man and Brute*. On the basis of its behavior, the brute manifests *no rationality*. Evidence is found in the absence of *progress, language,* and *intellectual insight* throughout brute behavior. Instinct takes the place of reason.

Man, therefore, differs from the brute not only in degree, but in *nature* and *essence*.

Readings

Maher, M., *Psychology,* Ch. XXI; Supplement A. — Aristotle, *On the Soul.* — Moore, T. V., *Cognitive Psychology,* Part VII. — Brennan, R. E., *General Psychology,* pp. 450–456, 474–476. — Adler, M. J., *What Man Has Made of Man.*

Chapter XXI

THE HUMAN PERSON

MAN is an organism. Like every other organism, there are numerous aspects to the nature of man, and each aspect gives rise to special problems. Some of these problems are comparatively simple, others are deep and perplexing. It was necessary to treat of these many phases of man's being in piecemeal fashion. Such a division of material, however, is merely methodological; in reality, man is not an aggregate of separate parts, like the various parts of a machine which a deft hand can take apart and piece together again. Eventually, the philosopher must reverse his methodological procedure and seek to synthesize into the integrated whole of the *human person* what he was compelled to treat separately for reasons of convenience and clarity.

The complete synthesis of the various aspects of man's being into the higher unity of the human person has proved to be a grave difficulty for modern psychologists.

Many aspects of man's being are 'physical' and belong to his 'body'; others are 'psychical' and belong to his 'mind.' Integrating these two large groups of items constitutes the *body-mind problem* so prominent in modern psychology. Then, too, man consists of matter and a vital principle or, according to the usage of common language, of 'body' and 'soul.' Their relationship constitutes the age-old *body-soul problem*. Again, everything in man, 'body and mind' and 'body and soul,' is referred to the 'Ego' or 'self.' Thereby the body-mind problem and the body-soul problem merge in the modern *Ego-problem*.

And since man is a 'person,' an attempt at a complete synthesis becomes the *problem of the human person.*

The Empirical Ego

When we speak of the *empirical Ego,* we mean the 'Ego' or 'self' as it is revealed to each individual in his own *internal experience* in the introspective act of self-consciousness (Chap. XVII). Usually the empirical Ego is observed by the individual in the performance of some *action.* It may be a bodily action, as when I pay attention to manipulating a tool, to humming a tune, to pronouncing words, etc.; or it may be a mental action, as when I consciously read a book, solve a problem in arithmetic, write an essay, etc. It is in this manner that I perceive my 'self' or 'Ego' concretely in action.

In a similar way, I become conscious of my 'self' or 'Ego' in certain *states* which affect me more or less passively. I am aware, for example, that something has struck me, that I feel the cold wind, that I have a pain or headache, etc. Here also it is through introspective self-reflection that I become conscious of my 'Ego' as the passive subject in which these states occur.

Mainly, I become aware of my 'self' or 'Ego' when I consciously *exert* myself, either physically or mentally, as when I push my physical powers to the limit of endurance or resist a pleasurable allurement for the sake of duty and conscience. This *concomitant awareness* of my 'self' or 'Ego' in a personal action or affecting state is *an immediate datum of my internal experience.*

I am not, however, aware of my 'self' or 'Ego' at all times, but only when my attention is focused inwardly. When my attention is focused outwardly, as when I witness a stage play or an exciting game, I may be so absorbed in what is taking place before me as to forget my 'self' or 'Ego' for the time being. Attention to external happenings is *inspection;* attention to internal happenings is *introspection.*

The 'empirical Ego,' therefore, is the 'self' or 'Ego' as observed at *any present moment* in a here-and-now experience.

The Historical Ego

The *historical Ego* is the 'Ego' or 'self' of an individual as he perceives it through *memory* of his life's experiences from the present down through the past. Every individual has a history of past experiences. The traces of these experiences are stored away in the mind and are, to a greater or lesser degree, capable of recall at the present moment. Since these experiences belonged to the 'self' or 'Ego' as to their subject, the part which the 'self' or 'Ego' played in these experiences is also capable of recall. Hence, the 'Ego' itself has a history, peculiar to each individual.

The knowledge of my 'historical Ego,' since it is based on my memory of my past experiences, is of necessity subject to all the vicissitudes and vagaries of my memory. While many events have been forgotten and are perhaps permanently beyond recall, I am usually able to remember the principal experiences of my childhood, youth, and adulthood. All such experiences pertain to my 'historical Ego.'

Viewed in retrospect, the 'historical Ego' may undergo a considerable *change* in the course of time, as the pattern of life changes. Success and failure, education and environment, influence a person in remarkable ways. We are sometimes compelled to confess: 'I have changed greatly since the days of my youth.' This change can also occur through a change in *memory itself*. Injury and illness may bring about a state of dissociation in the memory content (Chap. IX). We then observe the mental phenomenon of a 'changing personality.'

The 'historical Ego' in each individual has its beginning with the first instance of the knowledge of his own 'self' some time in *childhood*. The knowledge of the 'self' or 'Ego' is not innate; it is acquired. The prenatal life of the child is mainly vegetative. After birth, the child accumulates sense impressions and develops an acquaintance with his own body and with surrounding objects. After a few years, the child suddenly becomes aware of his own 'self' as a person set apart from other persons and things; he has reached selfhood. From that moment on he has a knowledge of his 'empirical Ego,' using the terms 'I' and 'me'; that moment is also the starting point of his 'historical Ego.' From the data obtained in this manner man forms his *abstract concept* of the 'self' or 'Ego.'

It should be evident that the 'empirical Ego' is very meager in content and the 'historical Ego' very rich in content.

The Metaphysical Ego

From the data of the empirical and historical Ego it must be possible to draw certain definite conclusions concerning the *constitution and nature of the human Ego.* The Ego, considered in its constitution and nature, is termed the *metaphysical Ego.* The philosopher is interested in this deeper problem of the Ego.

That such a problem exists and clamors for a solution, is beyond question. Just what is this 'Ego' or 'I' or 'self' of which man is forever speaking?

Does the Ego belong to the mind, or does the mind belong to the Ego? The *mind* is generally understood to be the ultimate principle or, as others prefer to view it, the sum-total of all the powers, processes, and states found in the sensory and rational life of man. That mind and Ego are inseparably connected, is conceded by all psychologists and philosophers. Man becomes conscious of his Ego or self through a cognitive act of the mind; man, however, performs 'mental' functions in childhood before he is conscious of his Ego or self. It would seem, then, that the mind is prior to the Ego, so that the Ego is only a phase or part or state of the mind. On the other hand, after man has learned to pay attention to the workings of his mind through introspection, he invariably refers the mind to his Ego or self, convinced that *the mind belongs to the Ego* as a part to the whole. We thus say: *'I have a mind.'* And we also say: 'My sight; my imagination; my memory; *my mind.'* Such phrases are universal, used by all persons and at all times. They plainly indicate that all mental states and the very mind itself belong to the Ego, so that the Ego or self is their *subject* and *possessor*. The Ego, therefore, is more basic and ultimate than the mind itself.

We observe a similar relationship between the 'soul' and the 'Ego.' We frequently say, for instance: 'I have a soul; *my soul.*' Here, too, the soul is referred to the Ego as something more basic and ultimate than the soul itself. *The soul,* like the mind, *belongs to the Ego,* and the Ego is considered as its subject and possessor. The Ego, therefore, is neither the mind nor the soul, but something deeper and more fundamental in man.

There is something still more puzzling about the Ego or self. The material, corporeal part of man's being is also referred to the Ego. We say, for instance: 'I have hands and feet and a torso, *I have a body;* my nerves, my bones, *my body.*' The body, therefore, and everything pertaining to it, *belongs to the Ego* as to its subject and possessor.

Thus the material and mental, the physical and the psychical, body and mind, in a word, *man's entire being,* is conceived by us as belonging to the Ego or self as to its subject and possessor.

Considered from another angle, to what is the Ego or self referred? Viewed introspectively, and judging from the expressions used by all men, *the Ego is never referred to any deeper reality* in man. Occasionally, when a person becomes very philosophical, he may say: 'I am myself.' Since 'I' and 'self' mean the same thing, such a statement is equivalent to saying that 'I am I' and expresses a reflexive judgment of identity between 'I' and 'self'; the Ego is simply the Ego. The Ego, I, or self is the *ultimate reality* in man to which everything in man belongs, while the Ego itself does not belong to some more fundamental reality. Everything is united and unified in the Ego, and the Ego unites and unifies everything in man.

Therein lies the profound *problem of the human Ego.* How can the Ego embrace within itself such disparate and, one is almost inclined to say, contradictory realities and attributes as are found in body and mind? What is the Ego in its final analysis? Is it the body, or is it the mind? If the body, then what about the mind? Man certainly has a mind. If the mind, then what about the body? He also has a body. Or, is the Ego both body and mind? But how can that be possible, since both are such totally different kinds of being? Contradictory attributes seem to exist in one and the same Ego.

Man is, in many respects, like a jigsaw puzzle. The physiologists have succeeded in putting a large number of pieces together, and the picture obtained is that of a 'body.' The psychologists have also succeeded in putting a large number of pieces together, and their picture is that of a 'mind.' Neither picture, however, is really complete, because both major portions are supposed to be fitted together into the *higher synthesis of the Ego,* so as to form the composite picture of 'the whole man.' Yet the two major portions of the complete picture, namely, body and mind synthesized in the Ego, do not seem to match. Philosophers, by and large, find it extremely difficult to effect the synthesis.

The problem is, without doubt, not an easy one to solve. Many solutions have been offered. The best way to arrive at the correct solution will be to view the problem in its historical setting.

The Problem in History

The ancient philosophers knew nothing of an 'Ego problem.' For them the 'body-mind problem' was mainly a 'body-soul problem.' However, since the modern problem of the human Ego has its roots in the age-old problem of body and soul, it will be necessary to go back as far as Grecian philosophy.

Plato, as we have seen (Chap. XIII), maintained an *ultra-dualism* of body and soul (mind). The body is a material substance, and the soul is a spiritual substance; the two substances form a dynamic unit, but not a substantial unit. The relationship between the human spirit and its body is that of a rider and his horse, of a helmsman and his ship. This theory has already been refuted.

Aristotle, the greatest scientist and philosopher among the ancients, rejected this ultra-dualism of Plato as contrary to all evidence. He synthesized body and mind (Chap. XIV, XIX) by assuming that the soul of man is the formal, organizing, animating principle of primal matter. Matter and soul are two incomplete substances or substantial co-principles, and their union results in a single, *unitary substance,* namely, the human organism. While safeguarding body and mind (soul) as distinct realities, he gives a neat explanation of their synthesis into one substance.

In *medieval times,* under the guidance of *St. Albert the Great, St. Thomas Aquinas,* and other great masters, aristotelianism developed into a new and powerful system of philosophy. It received the name of *scholasticism.* Aristotle's doctrine on the nature of man as a composite substance of body and soul became one of the principal teachings of aristotelian-scholastic philosophy.

Toward the end of the Middle Ages, a period of philosophic stagnation set in. Originality of thought gave way to vain subtleties and sterile commentaries on the books of the masters. Scholasticism fell into disrepute, especially after the advent of the Renaissance and the introduction of more precise scientific methods in the solution of the problems of physics. Eventually, the genuine doctrines of the great medieval philosophers were practically forgotten by the thinkers of the rising new era.

Modern philosophy has its origin in the teachings of *René Descartes* (1596–1650). He broke completely with the philosophy of Aristotle and St. Thomas and attempted to place philosophy upon an entirely new basis (Chap. XIII). He defended an *ultra-dualism* of body and soul in man. Regarding man's body, he advocated a *mechanistic atomism;* regarding man's soul, an *ultra-spiritualism.* Man's ideas are potentially innate, not derived from sense data through intellectual abstraction. Here were the seeds of the subsequent theories of *materialism* and *idealism.*[1] Since man's mind can know only its own internal states, his theory of knowledge terminated in *subjectivism,* the

[1] Concerning the historical development of the modern theory of knowledge, see the author's *Reality and the Mind* (Bruce, 1936).

theory which plagues practically all modern philosophy. Descartes placed a gap between body and mind; bodily events and mental events were closed systems without intercommunication. It has become the main endeavor of modern philosophy, outside neo-scholastic circles, to find a bridge to span this gap. The gravity of the problem was obvious. Granted the assumption that body and soul (mind) were two complete substances merely in conjunction, how could the body influence the mind, and how could the mind derive any knowledge of the world through the body?

Arnold Geulincx (1625–1669) went a step farther. He denied all activity to creatural beings, reserving all activity to God. It is God who produces every kind of activity in the universe. In order to explain the apparent influence existing between body and mind, he compared them to *two clocks* synchronized so perfectly that both indicate the same hours. The two clocks do not influence each other; both are constructed by the same Divine Workman and have His will imposed upon them to work with perfect timing. Thus, when we have the will to speak, the tongue is simultaneously set in motion, but the will has no influence over the movements of the tongue. The theory that God, on the occasion of certain conditions, produces all activity in his creatures, is called *occasionalism.* Geulincx thought that his theory overcame Descartes' ultra-dualistic difficulties by simply denying all activity to both body and mind. He failed to see that the theory is contradicted by the testimony of our *consciousness,* which is witness to the evident fact that we are the causal agents of our own acts. His theory denies *free will* and destroys the foundations of morality, making God solely responsible for every good and evil human act.

Nicholas Malebranche (1638–1715) also accepted Descartes' ultra-dualism. He was an *ontologist,* defending a modified occasionalism. According to his theory, man acquires his knowledge from the contemplation of the divine Ideas of God. Similar views were held by *Rosmini* and *Gioberti.* The theory has been refuted elsewhere (Chap. XIII).

Gottfried W. Leibnitz (1646–1716) proposed the curious doctrine of *monadism* (Chap. XIII). He recognized no interaction between the mental and the material. Every material entity, however, has also a mental side; this doctrine is called *pan-psychism.* God has established a perfect harmony between the material and mental, so that, like the two clocks of Geulincx, material and mental activities follow parallel lines throughout. His theory of 'pre-established harmony,' therefore, is a form of *psycho-physical parallelism.*

Baruch Spinoza (1632–1677) sought a different solution for the cartesian dilemma. He defined 'substance' as something the concept of which needs no other thing from which it should be formed. Such a definition can apply only to God, because God alone is a substance the concept of which involves no other concept or thing. Spinoza accepted the implication of this definition: there is but *one substance,* and that substance is *God.* Hence, everything that exists is a modification of the divine substance, and that includes everything material and extended and everything spiritual and unextended. The divine nature, therefore, has *as essential attributes extension and thought.* As extension, the divine substance unfolds itself into the physical world; as thought, it unfolds itself into the human minds. The human mind is a mode or manifestation of the divine intellect. When, therefore, man's mind has an idea, it is really God who has this idea in the human mind, because He constitutes the essence of the human mind. And since the extended world and the unextended mind are one in the substance of God, it follows that the order and connection of ideas is identical with the order and connection of things. Viewed this way, the theory is a *psycho-physical parallelism* with its roots in a *pantheistic monism.* It is 'pantheism,' because everything is God, and God is everything. It is 'monism,' because there is only one kind of ultimate reality or substance in existence to which all things, physical and mental, are reduced; in Spinoza's system this reality is God.

There are a number of reasons which compel us to reject Spinoza's theory. God is, as Spinoza admitted, infinite. The objects in the universe and the human minds are finite;

finiteness, as we know, is an attribute at least of our own body and mind. God, then, must be both *infinite and finite* simultaneously — a contradiction in terms. Again, if our mind is a part of God's intellect and if God's substance constitutes the essence of our mind, we should be *conscious of our identity with God;* we are, however, not conscious of this identity. Furthermore, since man is an unfolding of God's substance, all human actions are really God's actions, and God is the responsible agent of all human *misdeeds and crimes;* but in that case God would not possess infinite perfection. Finally, the world consists of a *multiplicity* of objects and human beings. If we are certain of anything, we are certain that we are identical with ourselves and distinct from other things and other human beings; our consciousness does not include the consciousness of other minds, although speech assures us of the existence of other minds and physical contact assures us of the existence of other bodies. This testimony of our consciousness is either true or false. If true, then a multiplicity of things exists, and they do not form one ultimate substance, because something cannot be a single substance and a multiplicity of substances at the same time. If false, the foundation of all knowledge is destroyed, because knowledge rests ultimately on consciousness as the last court of appeal; the outcome is complete skepticism. The entire system of Spinoza is a deduction from his *definition of substance.* This definition is *arbitrary* in the extreme and rests solely on Spinoza's personal statements. It leads to contradictions and impossibilities which are a plain *reductio ad absurdum.* These contradictions and impossibilities should have warned Spinoza that his original definition must be *false,* because erroneous conclusions presuppose faulty premises.

In England the trend of philosophy was toward empiricism and sensationalism. *Empiricism* is the doctrine that all human knowledge is derived from the data of particular states of consciousness, so that experience is the exclusive source and criterion of all knowledge. *Sensationalism,* which is almost synonymous with empiricism, is the doctrine which assumes that all human knowledge originates solely in sensation and that all intellectual cognitions are ultimately nothing more than complex and elaborated products of sense impressions and their reproduced images. In both theories intellectual knowl- is only a refined form of sensory knowledge and not of a kind essentially superior to sensory knowledge. A *sentient* nature, therefore, suffices to explain all human knowledge, and a spiritual intellect or soul is a superfluous entity. The empiricist and sensationalist theory has its origin in the teachings of Locke.

John Locke (1632–1704) was an *empiricist*. He considered 'ideas' to be the sole object of thinking, and by 'ideas' he understood 'phantasms' (sense images) and 'notions' (concepts). By wiping out the distinction between sense images and concepts, he led the way directly to *sensationalism* and *materialism*. By asserting that our internal mental states ('ideas') are the sole *objects* of thought, he excluded from our knowledge all *things* of the physical world, as they are in themselves, except by a mediate inference from our ideas. His teaching leads to *subjectivism* and *idealism*.

Locke was unjustified in identifying sensory phantasms and intellectual concepts under the common term 'idea,' because ideas (Chap. XX) are abstract, universal, and spiritual in nature, while sense impressions and images are always concrete, particular, and material. Hence, although Locke rejected Descartes' theory of innate ideas, he did not succeed in overcoming the cartesian ultra-dualism of body and mind, because he could not explain how a knowledge of the material world could get into the mind.

George Berkeley (1685–1753) accepted Locke's dictum that the mind can perceive nothing but its own internal states. Locke maintained that a world of material substance actually exists, though its existence is a matter of inference only. Berkeley refused to follow Locke. Since we can know nothing but our internal states, to *be* is to be *perceived* (*esse est percipi*), and we have no right to conclude to the existence of an extramental world of inert corporeal substances. The only substances which exist are God and minds, i.e., spiritual substances; even the human body does not exist, except as a perception. Berkeley advocated *spiritualistic idealism* and *mentalism,* the theory that nothing exists but the spiritual mind.

Berkeley's theory solves the cartesian body-mind problem through the expedient of denying the existence of bodies and all material reality. The solution is entirely too simple. One cannot get rid of the human body and of the world by means of a mere denial. We are as certain of the existence of our body as we are of our own self, and the body is as much a part of our being as is the mind.

David Hume (1711–1776) adopted the empirical phenomenalism of Locke, maintaining that we can have knowledge only of our internal states. He agreed with Berkeley that we have no right to accept the existence of material substance. He even *denied the existence of all substance.* He formulated his argument in the oft-quoted passage: "I would fain ask those philosophers, who found so much of their reasonings on the distinction of substance and accident, and imagine we have clear ideas of each, whether the idea of *substance* be derived from the impressions of sensations or reflection? [These are the sole data of our knowledge, according to Hume.—Author. See Chap. XIII.] If it be conveyed to us by our senses, I ask, which of them; and after what manner? If it be perceived by the eyes, it must be a color; if by the ears, a sound; if by the palate, a taste; and so of the other senses. But I believe none will assert, that substance is either a color, sound, or taste. The idea of substance must therefore be derived from an impression of reflection, if it really exists. But the impressions of reflection resolve themselves into our passions and emotions; none of which can possibly represent a substance. We have therefore no idea of substance, distinct from that of a collection of particular qualities, nor have we any other meaning when we talk or reason concerning it."[2] And thus all substances are argued out of existence, leaving nothing but phenomena. Hume became the protagonist of *pan-phenomenalism,* the theory in which everything is reduced to mental states.

[2] *A Treatise on Human Nature,* Bk. I, Part I, Sect. 6.

Since there is no substantial reality underlying the transitory mental states, Hume contended that man is "but a bundle or collection of different perceptions, which succeed each other with an inconceivable rapidity, and are in perpetual flux and movement."[3] We have, then, *no personal mind and Ego* as the subject of mental phenomena. There are thoughts, but there is no thinker who thinks the thoughts. We should not say '*I* think,' but '*It* thinks.' Here we have the psychology of the *impersonal mind,* and the 'mind,' if we speak of it at all, is not distinct from the passing internal states. It is like movement without anything that is moving.

Locke and Hume had many followers. Chief among them are James Mill, J. S. Mill, A. Bain, J. Sully, H. Spencer, T. Ribot, H. Taine, E. Condillac, and the founder of positivism, A. Comte. They differ among themselves in many respects, but they all adhere to the general doctrine of empiricism and sensationalist phenomenalism.

Immanuel Kant (1724–1804), sought to offset Hume's skepticism and revindicate the validity of human knowledge (Chap. XIII). He arrived at the conclusion that we can know only *phenomena* (appearances), not *noumena* (things-in-themselves, as they are in reality). Among the items of phenomenal knowledge, acquired through introspection, is the *empirical Ego*. The 'idea' of the Ego, however, is an innate, *a priori* form of reason, pertaining solely to phenomena, and tells us nothing of what the 'Ego' is as a thing-in-itself. Similarly, 'substance' is an innate, *a priori* category, and all 'categories' have only a subjective, regulating function in ordering our thoughts, without any objective value in the world of things. Hence, when we think of the soul or Ego as a 'substance' possessing actual simplicity, unity, and spirituality, we harbor an illusion, because we then confuse the real order with the mental order. There is, of course, *a pure, noumenal Ego* beyond the phenomenal Ego of which we are aware in our consciousness, but we can never attain to a knowledge of its

---

[3] *Ibid.,* Part IV, Sect. 6.

reality; we can know only the phenomenal Ego, and such knowledge is a mere mental construction.

Kant's general theory has been subjected to a critical evaluation in connection with the origin of our ideas (Chap. XIII). Here we wish to stress the point that, if Kant's theory were correct, he could not even know of the existence of the 'pure Ego,' much less tell us anything about it. In psychology, we are interested in the 'Ego' as given *in our conscious experience* and not in some hypothetical 'pure Ego' conceived by Kant; otherwise *psychology is an illusory science* devoid of all value for life, because everything we can discover about our body, mind, soul, and Ego would tell us nothing of what these things are in themselves as objects of reality. Kant's theory is a form of *rationalistic idealism,* although he is a hypothetical dualist postulating the existence of an external world. He failed to overcome Descartes' antithesis between mind and matter; the mind remains imprisoned in its conscious states and can know nothing of the external world and non-Ego objects. His followers developed his ideas into a stark absolutism.

Johann Fichte (1762–1814) contended that thought cannot be derived from being, but being must be derived from thought; thought, therefore, is the ultimate and only reality, and the laws of thought are the laws of being. And since all thought is contained in consciousness, there is no other reality but conscious *Ego;* hence, all reality is unified in the Ego. The Ego, of course, does not mean merely human consciousness, but the universal consciousness of the Absolute or God. Fichte assumes the existence of an *Infinite Ego* which first posits itself, then posits a limited non-Ego (the world), and finally posits a limited Ego (the human mind or Ego) in opposition to the limited non-Ego. Fichte defends *pan-Egoism.*

Friedrich Schelling (1775–1854) viewed the universe as divided into two great actualities—nature and spirit (real and ideal, object and subject, matter and self, thing and mind). In reality, however, these opposites are originally and essentially identified in the *Absolute* or *Infinite,* so that they are but two phases in the evolution of the ultimate reality which is the Absolute. Hence, his doctrine is termed the *identity theory.*

Georg W. Hegel (1770–1831) also identified all things in the Absolute. But with him the Absolute is pure *Thought* or *Idea.* It evolves by means of a *purely rational and logical process of thought* into the ideal and real, into subject and object, into spirit and nature, into mind and matter. The Absolute is incessantly in a process of dialectic evolution, so that all being is thought realized. His system is *idealistic monism* driven to its highest peak; it is the one-ness of all things in the Absolute.

Idealistic monism, which seeks to eliminate the difference between the physical and the psychical by reducing them to the identity of one ultimate reality or Absolute, exerted a great influence on modern thinkers. Among those who followed this line of thought are A. Schopenhauer, E. von Hartmann, T. Green, F. Bradley, J. Caird, E. Caird, B. Croce, G. Gentile, and many others.

Disgusted with the brilliant obscurities of Kant and the idealists, others sought to bring the problem of man out of the clouds back to earth. Instead of following Descartes in the spiritualistic side of his ultra-dualism of human nature, they swung to the opposite extreme and chose the atomistic-mechanistic side pertaining to man's body. In opposition to the idealists who reduced the physical to the mental, they reversed the procedure and *reduced the mental completely to the physical.* The result was a *materialistic monism* which admits but a single ultimate reality, namely, matter.

Materialism, being a form of monism, is a metaphysical identity theory, because everything in man is identified with matter and material energy. What we call the 'psychical,' such as sensation, perception, memory, intellection, etc., is regarded by materialism as a *function* or *property* of organized matter, essentially of the same nature as any other physiological function of the human body. There is nothing in mental facts but movements of material particles; they are obscure manifestations of material energies and as such do not transcend matter and its conditions. *No interaction* exists between body and mind, for the simple reason that 'mind' is a mere abstraction; the only reality that exists is the body composed of atoms and molecules in organization. Mental life is identified with neural action. At best, some materialists admit that consciousness is an accompaniment or by-product of neural processes, determined by them but exerting no influence upon them, so that consciousness is but an 'epiphenomenon' of matter, matter being the real phenomenon. This doctrine is the theory of *epiphenomenalism*. By ignoring the specific character of psychical events and conditions, the materialists arrive at an easy solution of the problem of mind and body and of the human Ego.

Chief among these pseudo-philosophers were P. J. Cabanis, J. La Mettrie, L. Feuerbach, C. Vogt, L. Büchner, and E. Haeckel. Theirs was a very crude sort of materialism. Cabanis, for example, maintained that the brain secretes thought as the liver secretes bile.

Ever since experimental psychology has investigated mental phenomena with scientific thoroughness and precision, it has become increasingly clear to psychologists that the crude materialism of men like Moleschott, Büchner, and Haeckel is a failure. Nevertheless, many prominent experimentalists, due to the materialistic trend of the times in which they received their education and training, were loath to accept the idea of a spiritual soul informing the body as the principle of unification for body and mind. Generally speaking, they prefer some kind of *psycho-physical parallelism*.

Gustav J. Fechner (1801–1887) maintains that body and soul (physical and psychical) are not essentially different realities; at bottom, they are a single reality with *two aspects*. When I look at myself, I find that I am a conscious mental being; that is the 'psychical aspect' of myself as a man. When an outsider looks at me, I am a material being, because he cannot intuit my mental states; that is the 'physical aspect' of myself as a man. In so far as Fechner considers the physical and psychical to be merely two aspects of one and the same ultimate reality, his view is termed the *double-aspect theory;* and in so far as he postulates a single ultimate reality which is both physical and psychical, depending on the point of view one takes, his psycho-physical parallelism is an *identity theory.*

Wilhelm Wundt (1832–1920) was a psycho-physical parallelist. In his 'ideal-realism' he takes a stand midway between idealism and realism; as a scientist he leaned toward realism, and as a follower of Kant he could not free himself from idealism. Wundt denies the existence of all substance: "The contents of psychological experience should be regarded as an *interconnection of processes.* This concept of *process* excludes the attribution of an objective and more or less permanent character to the content of psychical experience. Psychical facts are *occurrences,* not objects."[4] Since the mind is conceived as a sum-total of psychical events, there is, in his view, no such thing as a permanent, substantial mind or Ego as the carrier of these mental states. The concept of 'mind-substance' has no value except to satisfy "a mythological and metaphysical need."[5] The mind is simply *act, actuality.* All we have is a manifold of interrelated occurrences, an inner (psychical) and an outer (physical) experience. Wundt's psycho-physical theory is, therefore, also termed the *theory of actuality.* Wundt considered the will to be the real Ego.

Many modern psychologists have adopted the theory of psycho-physical parallelism as best suited to the temper of the scientific investigator. Man is, as Huxley puts it, a 'conscious automaton.' Defenders of this *conscious automaton-theory* are, among others, Hodgson and Spalding. Many also, especially evolutionists, defend some sort of atomistic *mind-dust* or *mind-stuff theory,* as proposed by W. K. Clifford and H. Spencer, according to which an atom of consciousness or mind is attached to every atom of matter in the universe, both developing together in the evolution of beings, including man. As

[4] *Outlines of Psychology,* tr. by C. H. Judd (1897), Introd., § 2, n. 9, p. 14.
[5] *Ibid.,* § 22, n. 4, p. 312.

the material atoms, in the course of eons, massed themselves together to form the bodies of plants, animals, and men, so also the mind-atoms massed themselves together to form the more developed and refined minds of conscious animals and men. According to this view, all matter has the quality and potency of life and mind, and the 'mind' of man is a mere affair of psychic summation. The theory that all atoms of matter originally possess life is *atomistic hylozoism;* it is also a form of *pan-psychism,* since everything existing is conceived as fundamentally psychic or mental in nature.

William James (1842–1910), the eminent American psychologist, took a peculiar stand in this problem. He admitted frankly the reasonableness of the scholastic doctrine of the *soul.* "To posit a soul influenced in some mysterious way by the brain-states and responding to them by conscious affections of its own, seems to me the line of least logical resistance, so far as we yet have attained."[6] In order, however to remain "positivistic and non-metaphysical," he considered an *empirical parallelism* to be the wisest course.

We have already seen (Chap. XVII) that James viewed man's conscious life as a 'stream' of internal states *without a substantial Ego* as their subject. He followed in the footsteps of Hume and Wundt. For him, "the passing thought itself is the only *verifiable* thinker,"[7] and he can find no rational use for the concept of 'substance' or of a 'substantial soul.' James was fully aware of the consciousness of the 'identity of self' extending over gaps of unconsciousness, as evidenced by memory. How did he overcome the difficulty?

He compared the passing mental states to a herd of cattle, branded with the brand of the owner, who is the 'Ego' or 'self.' "How would it be," he writes, "if the Thought, the present judging Thought, instead of being in any way substantially or transcendentally identical with the former owner of the past self, merely inherited his 'title,' and thus stood as his legal representative now? . . . We can imagine a long succession of herdsmen coming rapidly into possession of the

[6] *The Principles of Psychology,* Vol. I (H. Holt, 1918), p. 181.
[7] *Ibid.,* p. 346.

same cattle by transmission of an original title by bequest. May not the 'title' of a collective self be passed from one Thought to another in some analogous way? . . . Each later Thought, knowing and including thus the Thoughts which went before, is the final receptacle — and appropriating them is the final owner — of all they contain and own. Each Thought is thus born an owner, and dies owned, transmitting whatever it realized as its Self to its own later proprietor."[8] In this manner, James believed, he could safeguard the identity of the self or Ego without having recourse to a 'substantial' Ego or soul.

James' analogy is ingenious. The only trouble with it is, that it does not fit the case; he places the cart before the horse. In our mental life, the internal states are transient, while the Ego or self is consciously observed to be permanent; the herd of cattle (which is supposed to represent our passing internal states) is permanent, while the herdsmen (who are supposed to represent the permanent Ego or self) are transient. The roles are actually the reverse of what they should be. In a succession of heirs to a particular piece of property (here, the herd), certainly *no heir feels himself to be identical with every other heir in the line of succession,* simply because he has succeeded to the title formerly held by the other proprietors. In the case of man, however, *the present Ego feels itself to be the one identical Ego throughout the years.* If James' analogy were correct, the present Thought or Ego could never feel itself identical with the preceding Thoughts or Egos, because they are in reality not the same any more than the succeeding heirs and owners are the same. It is always dangerous to build an important theory on an analogy. Facts should govern a theory; and the facts point very definitely to the *identity and permanence of the Ego* as the possessor of the transient mental states as they succeed one another. James did not prove his case; if anything, he proved that a *substantial Ego* is a necessary requirement for the proper explanation of our mental life.

---

[8] *Ibid.*, p. 339.

In our *present time* there are a number of distinctive movements and counter-movements in the psychological field. *Functionalism* considers the mental processes as the functions of the organism in its adaptation to, and control of, environment; it is the psychology of William James, J. Dewey, G. T. Ladd, and the pragmatic school of thought. *Structuralism* is an 'atomistic' psychology which analyzes mental states into component sensations, images, and feelings; E. B. Titchener and his followers are representative of this type of psychology. *Gestaltism* or *configurationalism* stresses the tendency of the mind to view things as formed 'wholes' rather than as isolated items of experience; among its advocates are W. Köhler, K. Koffka, and very many others. *Behaviorism* seeks to explain the mental in plain physiological terms of stimulus-response reactions, without taking consciousness and introspection into account; J. Watson, A. P. Weiss, and others defend this view. *Reflexological psychology* identifies mental life with neural reflexes; V. M. Bekhterev, K. N. Kornilov, A. L. Schniermann, and other Russian followers of Marxist materialism are expounders of this system. *Psychoanalysis,* as a psychology, explains mental life as the result of instinctive drives working in the lower levels of the mind. Then there is also the *hormic* psychology of W. McDougall which emphasizes the goal-seeking tendencies of organisms, and the *factor* psychology of C. Spearman, which seeks to determine the general and special abilities by means of correlation coefficients.

As a general policy, modern psychologists strive to remain within the limits of a 'scientific' treatment of their subject matter, disclaiming any sort of 'metaphysical' explanation of the nature of man and the relation of body and mind. The majority accept a *psycho-physical parallelism* of physical and mental events in man as a *methodological* convenience. As a rule, however, they make occasional commitments about the ultimate nature of man, because their basic ideas of body and mind are rooted in *metaphysical* concepts and theories; psychologists, therefore, often become, in unguarded moments, metaphysicians. Some individuals subscribe to panpsychism; others, to materialistic monism; others to idealistic monism; others to pantheistic monism; others, to strict parallelism, without attempting to define their position in any more definite manner. It is perhaps safe to say that the general trend of modern psychologists is toward some form of *materialism.*

The *reflexological* psychology of the Russian School is avowedly a materialistic monism. *Behaviorism* is materialistic. *Gestaltism,* though it contains elements of a sound psychology, does not rise above the fundamental tenets of materialism, because the chief exponents of the theory find the ultimate explanation of the whole-making tendency of the mind in the conditions of the brain. The *structuralism* of Titchener is materialistic. *Psychoanalysis,* as conceived by Freud, is also basically materialistic. *Functionalism* favors dualism and interactionism. The *hormic* psychology of McDougall is interactionistic and animistic, based upon a metaphysical dualism.

And thus we see how the ultra-dualism of Descartes, by destroying the essential unity of man's nature and placing body and mind in a position of antagonism toward each other, has brought on a deplorable confusion of psychological systems. He made a real *interaction* between body and mind impossible, and it has been the endeavor of subsequent thinkers to bridge the gap between these two realities in man.

Digest of Theories

After reviewing the historical development of the body-mind problem, which is also the problem of the human Ego and the human person, it is not difficult to summarize the various views and theories into a few *broad systems.* Starting with Descartes' ultra-dualism, which everybody seemed to accept without question, the following main solutions have been offered as a metaphysical explanation of man's nature.

Man has a *body;* man also has a *mind.* Whatever pertains to the body is physical; whatever pertains to the mind is psychical. The physical and the psychical, body and mind, have attributes and activities which are diametrically opposed to one another. The material and the mental are mutually irreducible, because the material is spatial while the mental is non-spatial; hence, they cannot reside in, nor be the product of, a single principle. Body and mind, therefore, since they have nothing in common, cannot interact upon each other; it is impossible for the mind causally to influence the body or for the body causally to influence the mind. Yet, such an interaction apparently occurs continuously. We must, then, accept a *double series of events,* one physical, belonging to the body, the other psychical, belonging to the mind. Each series is independent of the other, but running parallel to it, giving the impression of interaction. The result of this line of thought is the theory of rigid *psycho-physical parallelism* in a metaphysical sense.

Other thinkers were dissatisfied with this theory. It presupposes a *division* in man which is contrary to all experience. Man is not a double being, but a single being. If man were really a double being consisting of two irreducible parts, each part possessing an independent series of events without mutual interaction, one cannot explain the perfect synchronization or timing that exists between the physical and psychical series. Such a parallelism is inconceivable. The body-mind problem can only be solved by maintaining that body and mind are not distinct and separate entities, but fundamentally a single reality. In other words, there exists an *identity* of body and mind; their distinctness is merely apparent. These thinkers defend the *identity theory.*

Even when maintaining the identity of body and mind, the problem is not solved thereby. This disparity between body and mind still remains. One must either reduce the body to the mind, leaving the mind as the sole remaining reality; or, one must reduce the mind to the body, leaving the body as the sole remaining reality. The psychical must absorb the physical, or the physical must absorb the psychical.

To some philosophers it seemed evident that man is conscious, senses, thinks, and wills. The *mental,* therefore, is *real.* The existence of the mind must be maintained under all circumstances, because one cannot deny the existence of psychical experiences as a part of man's life. Consequently, the physical, the material, the body, must be identified with the mind. The mind, then, is the *only reality;* the physical, the material, the body, exist solely in the mind as a percept or idea. At the most, matter and the physical world can be nothing more than manifestations or modes of mind. This form of the identity theory is characterized as *idealistic monism.*

There is, however, also a reverse side to the identity theory. Other philosophers are convinced that man is a bodily being existing in time and space, with all the attributes and properties of matter. If we are certain of anything, we are certain that we are material organisms. The *material,* therefore, is *real.* Hence, the mental, the psychical, the mind, must be reduced to the reality of matter. Matter is, at bottom, the *only reality,* and the mental is fundamentally identical with the physical. The identity theory thus becomes *materialistic monism.*

Others take a metaphysical short-cut across all difficulties of explaining the union of body and mind by assuming that *all matter is living and endowed with mind;* or, as some prefer it, all bodies consist ultimately of some *neutral stuff* which is the substrate of both matter and mind. One need not wonder, then, that man possesses the attributes of a body and a mind in conjunction. These philosophers advocate *pan-psychism.*

It is seldom, however, that any of these basic systems are accepted in their pure form. Most psychologists and philosophers mix the principles of the one with that of another. They may be parallelists from one standpoint and idealistic or materialistic monists or pan-psychists from another; even a pantheistic monist may be a parallelist. Others adhere strictly to an idealistic or materialistic monism; the former admit nothing but mind and mental states, the latter nothing but matter and material states. Although psycho-physical parallelism really should exclude all interaction between psychical and physical events, yet some thinkers believe in interaction. Some believe that body and mind (soul) are distinct substances; others believe in one of the two as a substance; and others deny the substantiality of both body and mind. There is no unity of doctrine; everything is confusion.

Strictly speaking, every type of monism should be opposed to the dualistic concept of psycho-physical parallelism. Some monists, however, are parallelists, as our historical survey has shown. Under the heading of *parallelism* we find grouped together the most diversified theories—interactionism, preestablished harmony, occasionalism, sensationalism, the identity theory, the double-aspect theory, the actuality theory, automatism, the mind-dust and mind-stuff theory, epiphenomenalism, pan-psychism. Yet some of these theories are also fundamentally monistic.

Critique of Theories

Some individual theories and views have been submitted to criticism in previous chapters. Here, the *pure basic systems,* as outlined above, will be evaluated.

Psycho-physical Parallelism

The theory presupposes the ultra-dualistic opposition between matter and mind, between the physical and psychical, as propounded by those who deny the possibility of interaction between these supposedly antagonistic realities.

This denial is based mainly on the argument that such an interaction would be contrary to the *Law of the Conservation of Energy,* as H. Höffding contends, in as much as the total amount of energy in the physical universe would be decreased or increased by the causal action of the physical on the psychical or of the psychical on the physical. As was pointed out in connection with free-will activity (Chap. XVI), the validity of this argument is very doubtful. Furthermore, there is good evidence to show that intellectual (and volitional) activities do not consume physical energy (Chap. XX), so that there would be no infringement on the law. The main point, however, is that all evidence of our daily life definitely establishes the fact of a *mutual influence between the physical and psychical events* in man, irrespective of the postulates of any theory. The physical conditions of the body influence our sensations, imagination, memory, intellect, emotions, and will; there can be, for instance, no sensations without physical stimuli. Reversely, emotions have physical resonances in the body; and the will, as consciousness testifies, does control the movements of our bodily members throughout our waking state. The testimony of consciousness is so clear on this score and the mass of experiential evidence so overwhelming, that an unprejudiced observer cannot doubt the facts.

Parallelism rests on a *false assumption.* It places an *excessive division* between the body and mind of man, as if the two were completely separated entities. Such a division does not exist. Man is, as we have proved, a unitary, integral organism in which the physical, vegetative, sensory, and rational activities are fused into a single harmonious whole. The ultimate nature of man, therefore, must be a dynamic and entitative unit and not the extrinsic union of ultra-dualistic entities. It follows, that Descartes' and the parallelists' concept of the nature of man is an assumption which is erroneous in its foundation. The facts are true; the theory of parallelism is wrong.

Idealistic Monism

Every type of idealistic monism, whether it be spiritualistic (Berkeley), phenomenalistic (Hume, Bain, etc.), or absolutistic (Fichte, etc.), takes it for granted that, as Descartes proposed, we can know nothing but our own *internal mental states.* The body, the physical objects, the material universe — all have no existence except in so far as they are present in our perceptions and thoughts. At bottom, then, everything is mental; the mind alone exists, and matter is identified with mind. In this way, idealists claim to reduce ultra-dualism and parallelism to unity and the difficulty of the body-mind problem in man is overcome. The theory, however, is fallacious.

Idealism, for one thing, is contrary to the sound teachings and experimental findings of the *natural sciences.* Every natural science — physics, chemistry, geology, astronomy, biology, physiology, and all the rest — is based on the actual existence of *material bodies* endowed with spatial attributes and physical energy independent of the mind and its conscious contents. True, we cannot *know* that they exist unless we have a conscious percept or idea of them, but it does not follow that they have existence *only in knowledge.* Experimental psychology shows how our sensations are dependent on *external stimuli* for their origin and specificity; it also proves that *nerves* and a *brain,* which are material realities, are required for the transformation of the stimulus excitation into conscious perception. Without the body, there can be no reception of stimuli; without the mind, there can be no knowledge of the objects transmitting the stimuli.

If nothing exists but the nonspatial mind and its ideas, then our knowledge should absolutely be *restricted to the mind and its ideas.* But then it should be utterly impossible to have any perceptions and ideas of such nonexistent things as brains, nerves, bodily organs, houses, automobiles, cities, and countries. Yet we are as certain of these material things as we are of our mind and its conscious states. Our emotions and feelings are accompanied by definite bodily changes, as we know from the findings of experimental psychology; these facts are not the result of sheer imagination. When idealists speak as scientists and psychologists, they invariably speak of sensations and perceptions as if they possessed a *bodily character;* it is only when confronted with the difficulty of explaining the reciprocal action of body and mind that they seek to evade the difficulty by denying the existence of matter and material bodies. Man has both a body and a mind, and we are conscious of both; we have no more right to deny the existence of the one than of the other.

We are conscious of being *passively influenced* by extramental objects. When I close my eyes and imagine a parade, I know that I am the agent producing these images; but when

I watch a parade passing by, I am passive and do not myself determine what images I shall or shall not receive. Such a situation could not arise, if the production of sensations, perceptions, and ideas were solely dependent on the mind and its operation.

Idealism is inadequate, because it leaves out of account the *body,* which is just as much a part of man as his mind.

Materialistic Monism

Little need be said here in refutation of materialistic monism. If nothing exists but matter and material energy, then everything in man must be able to be interpreted strictly in *terms of matter and material energy*. However, not even the ordinary phenomena of *sensation* admit of such an interpretation. The sensation of 'blue,' for example, is something totally different from the physical stimulus of a definite frequency of light waves striking the retina; and the sensation of 'pain' has no similarity to the piercing of the skin by a needle point. *Cognition* and *consciousness* cannot be explained in terms of atomic oscillations of brain substance. *Ideas* (Chap. XII) are abstract and universal, while everything material is concrete and particular. *Intellection* (Chap. XX) is spiritual and intrinsically independent of material conditions; it cannot, therefore, be reduced to material activity.

Materialism accounts for the body, but it does not account for the mind. Yet the mind is as much a part of man as his body. The theory is inadequate, because it fails to give an explanation of the 'whole man.' Like idealism, it is an oversimplified system which evades the real issue by denying the existence of an essential part of man's nature.

Pan-psychism

Pan-psychism assumes, in one form or other, that everything material is also mental; in other words, every body is fundamentally endowed with life and mind. This assumption is gratuitously made and is contrary to the verdict of the *natural sciences*. The sciences make a clean-cut distinction between living and nonliving bodies, and they base this distinction on essential differences in *structure* and *operation*. Nonliving beings (Chap. XIX) are characterized by 'transitive' action, living beings by 'immanent' action. There is not a shred of evidence for maintaining that the electron, proton, and atom have life and mind. The metaphysical necessity of overcoming the cartesian ultra-dualism of mind and matter prompted the formation of the theory; the theory, however, is contrary to all known facts.

Scholastic Animism

The prodigious confusion of philosophical and psychological systems of the three preceding centuries stems logically from the *ultra-dualism of Descartes*. It is the clearest proof that Descartes' assumptions must be wrong, because this confusion furnishes a complete *reductio ad absurdum:* when the conclusion is so disastrous, the premises must inevitably be false. Wherein did Descartes err?

His error consisted in splitting man's nature into two antagonistic substances, body and spirit. He conceived the body as a mechanistic aggregate of atoms and the spirit as the sole seat of all mental states. A psycho-physical parallelism was unavoidable, and he thereby made a metaphysical explanation of man's unitary nature impossible. The result is seen in the fruitless attempt of most modern philosophers to restore the evident factual unity of man as an *integral organism* capable of both bodily and mental activities.

Descartes made his initial mistake in rejecting the traditional teaching of man's nature as embodied in scholastic anthropology. Here was the correct doctrine, but Descartes misunderstood it. In rejecting it, he led subsequent thinkers into a quagmire of errors. To remedy this desperate situation, we must return to the fundamental doctrine of the scholastics. We have shown the correctness of their views in a lengthy discussion (Chaps. XIX, XX) on vitalistic animism.

In vitalistic animism we find the *solution* of all the difficulties involved in the various systems mentioned above. Parallelism stresses the difference between the physical and the mental, but finds no means of combining them into the higher unity of the human Ego. Animism preserves the difference between the physical and the psychical, because the primary source of the physical is matter and the primary source of the psychical is the soul; but the real subject of both is neither matter nor the soul, but the Ego which is the composite unitary substance resulting from the substantial union of matter and soul. Idealism stresses the mental, but finds no place for the material side of man's nature; it reduces the physical to the psychical, thereby doing violence to man's physico-psychical nature. Animism does justice to the psychical side of man's nature, but it also safeguards the physical as an equally important part of man's being. Materialism emphasizes the physical, but it eliminates the psychical which is present in man's nature. Animism also accounts for the physical side of man's nature, but it safeguards the psychical as being equally essential to man. Pan-psychism is correct in maintaining that in man matter is living matter, but it goes contrary to all evidence when it asserts that all matter in the world is endowed with life and mind. Animism agrees with the sciences in distinguishing between living and nonliving matter, and it also agrees with biology and psychology in asserting that man's nature is both physical and psychical, material and mental. While Descartes' theory of man is an ultra-dualistic conception, based on the dissociation of man's nature into two distinct and separate complete substances, body and spirit, the theory of vitalistic animism is a *moderate dualism,* based upon the real distinction of matter and soul as part-substances, combined into the metaphysical unity of a single nature by means of a substantial integration.

Animism, therefore, contains whatever there is of truth in parallelism, idealism, materialism, and pan-psychism, while avoiding the errors of extremism found in each and all of them. The animism of aristotelian-scholastic philosophy alone accounts for all the facts and phases of man's complete nature.

The Human Person

What, then, is the human *Ego?* Whatever in man is bodily and mental, physical and psychical, material and spiritual, is referred by the Ego to itself: *I* weigh one hundred fifty pounds, *I* see a house, *I* think, *I* will. The physical and the psychical represent 'the whole man.' The *Ego,* therefore, is *the whole man*. Body and soul are integrated into one thing, the whole man, the Ego. The Ego, therefore, is not the body, not the soul, not the intellect, not the will, not consciousness, not life. All these things 'belong' to the Ego as constituting 'the whole man.'

The Ego is a *substance*. A 'substance' is an individual being whose nature it is to exist in itself and not in another as in a subject. A being whose nature it is to exist, not in itself, but in another as in a subject, is called, in philosophical terminology, an 'accident.' Accidents are modifications and modes of substance. Shape, color, motion, thought, feelings, etc., are modifications of some ultimate reality; they do not exist in and for themselves, but exist in the substance which they modify. Man, considered as a totality, is a self-contained being with a naturally independent existence of its own; man, therefore, is a 'substance.' And since the Ego is the whole man, the ultimate reality which possesses everything pertaining to man's being, it is evident that the Ego is substantial and not merely accidental.

The Ego (man) is a *person*. The term 'person' is never applied to a chemical being, to a plant, or to a brute animal; no one calls a piece of carbon, a tree, or a horse, a 'person.' Since man alone, among all material beings and organisms, is called a 'person,' what specifically constitutes man a 'person'? It is not 'materiality,' because chemicals, plants, and brutes are material. It is not 'life,' because plants and brutes are living. It is not 'sentiency,' because brutes are sentient. It must be that which distinguishes man from all these types of being, and that is 'rationality,' 'intellectuality.' Boëthius[9] has given us the following definition of a 'person': *naturae rationalis individua substantia*—an individual substance of a rational nature. A 'person' is, therefore, an *individual, complete, subsistent, rational (intellectual) substance.*[10] A moment's consideration will reveal the fact that the human Ego, or whole man, is indeed a substance which is individual and complete and subsistent and rational. Consequently, the human Ego, or man in his totality, is a 'person.'

We must make an exact distinction between 'personality' in this *metaphysical* sense and 'personality' in a *psychological* sense. Psychologists, when they use the term, mean the sum-total of human functions and capacities, traits and aptitudes, and this concept is akin to 'character.' The unity of 'personality' in this psychological meaning is a *functional* unity, and this functional unity may at times be impaired or destroyed, as we notice it in 'split personality,' 'dual personality,' and so on. 'Personality' in the philosophical or metaphysical sense is the essential mark of man's nature as a 'rational animal' and is never subject to change, because the essential constitution of man's being from the moment of conception to the moment of death remains the same. In other words, man is and remains at all times a 'person,' namely, an individual, complete, subsistent, rational substance, irrespective of what happens to the functional unity of his mental states and operations.

The human being, the human Ego, is a person. As a person, man is a substance consisting of two really distinct substantial co-principles, soul and matter. The soul is the animating principle and therefore the primary principle (in conjunction with matter) of the *vital* attributes and activities of vegetancy and sentiency. The soul, however, is spiritual in essence and as such the sole agent (though with an extrinsic dependence on matter) of the spiritual activities of intellect and will. Matter is the principle (in conjunction with the soul) which accounts

---

[9] *De persona et duabus naturis,* c. II.

[10] See the author's *Domain of Being* (Bruce, 1939), Ch. XVII, XVIII.

for all the *physical* attributes and activities in man's nature. Man is a unique being, the fusion of spirit and matter compounded into a single substance and organism. He is in all truth a *microcosm,* uniting within his person the essential realities of chemical elements, living plants, sentient animals, and spiritual intelligences.

How can spirit and matter be so intimately linked together that they constitute a single substance, nature, Ego, person? The *fact,* from all that has been said, is demonstrated beyond reasonable doubt; the *manner* of this union will never be clearly understood. We explain the union of spirit and matter in man by saying that the spirit is the *soul* of the body, the 'vital principle' or 'substantial form' or 'entelechy' of matter. Such terminology may not clarify the 'manner' of their union to any great extent, but it is a philosophical explanation which at least avoids the difficulties inherent in parallelism and monism and is in accord with all the material, sensory, and spiritual phenomena observed to be present in man. T. V. Moore's remarks are classic. "Since Infinite Power cannot make a square circle, neither can it make the essentially nonthinking and lifeless matter, while it remains nonthinking and lifeless, at the same time think and live. But it is possible for living matter to live by a principle of life inherent within it; it is possible for a sensory organism to have sensations by means of sense organs vitalized by a living soul; it is possible for man to be a living being with sense organs capable of being acted on by the energies of matter in the outside world, because these same sense organs are themselves material, but not lifeless matter, and live by the soul that vivifies the body. It is possible for this same living soul, which is a principle of life, vivifying the body and animating the sense organs, to be conscious of the way in which its sense organs are affected, and to think about those revelations of the world outside, which come to it through the sense organs, by powers which are in no way the activity of bodily organs, though they can interpret the data derived from bodily organs, and so understand and interpret the world outside by nonsensual and spiritual concepts."[11] No other theory can explain all the pertinent facts so clearly and completely.

Man is the *ultimate ground and agent* of everything that occurs within the realm of his being. Whatever pertains to his being in any manner whatsoever must, in its final analysis, be referred to his *person* and *Ego* and not to any particular part or power. Man is material and spatial. Man is composed of a matter and a spiritual soul, and is an organism. Man assimilates food and reproduces himself. Man has a nervous system and sense organs. Man sees, hears, tastes, smells, has the sense of touch, and feels pain. Man synthesizes the sense data, imagines, remembers, and performs instinctive actions. Man strives for sensuous good, avoids sensuous evil, and experiences various emotions. Man forms ideas, judgments, and processes of reasoning. Man exercises free will and desires spiritual values. Man is conceived, lives, and dies. The immediate principles of functions are powers or faculties, but the ultimate agent is *man,* the *person,* the *Ego.*

There are a thousand-and-one aspects to man's being, but they are all just so many phases of one ultimate substantial reality, the human person, expressing itself in multitudinous ways.

Summary of Chapter XXI

We must now synthesize the various aspects of man's being into the unity of 'the whole man.'

1. *The Empirical Ego.* It is the self or Ego as observed at any present moment in a here-and-now experience.

2. *The Historical Ego.* It is the self or Ego of an individual as he perceives it through memory of his life's experiences from the present down through the past.

3. *The Metaphysical Ego.* It is the self or Ego considered in its constitution and nature. Everything in man is referred ultimately to the Ego: mind, soul, body, and all bodily and mental states and activities. The Ego, however, is never

[11] *Cognitive Psychology* (Lippincott, 1939), p. 157.

referred to anything else in man; it is the *ultimate reality* in man. How can such diverse realities be referred to the same Ego, since 'body' and 'mind' seem to possess such antithetical attributes? The attempt to bridge the gap between 'body' and 'mind' has given rise to many theories.

4. *The Problem in History. Plato* maintained a theory of *ultra-dualism;* body and spirit are complete substances. *Aristotle* maintained that matter and soul are incomplete substances united together into a single substance. *Medieval* philosophers followed Aristotle.

Modern philosophy begins with *Descartes* who placed an antithetical *ultra-dualism* between body and spirit; he conceived both as complete substances. Man's mind can know only its internal states. *Geulincx* advocated occasionalism and *Malebranche* ontologism. *Leibnitz* proposed his monadology, a theory of pan-psychism and psycho-physical parallelism. *Spinoza* was a pantheistic monist. *Locke* was an empiricist who confused concepts and phantasms. *Berkeley* maintained a spiritualistic idealism. *Hume* denied the existence of all substances; his theory is pan-phenomenalism. *Kant* proposed a rationalistic idealism, which was developed by *Fichte, Schelling,* and *Hegel* into the idealistic monism of absolutism. Other philosophers went to the opposite extreme and defended a materialistic monism.

Fechner propounded the parallelistic view of the double-aspect theory. *Wundt* developed the actuality theory, *Huxley* the conscious automaton theory, *Clifford* the mind-dust theory. *W. James* advocated an empirical parallelism, denying the substantiality of the soul and making the passing thought the 'thinker' or Ego.

The present-day theories of psychology mostly advocate psycho-physical parallelism, and the general trend is still materialistic.

5. *Digest of Theories.* All views can be reduced to the following *general metaphysical* theories: psycho-physical parallelism, idealistic monism, materialistic monism, and pan-psychism.

6. *Critque of Theories. Psycho-physical parallelism* cannot explain the evident relationship and mutual influence of the psychical and physical in man. *Idealistic monism* is contrary to the natural sciences which maintain the existence of material bodies; it cannot explain the facts pertaining to the human body. *Materialistic monism* cannot explain man's mental life, as manifested in sensation, cognition, consciousness, ideas, and intellection. *Pan-psychism* runs counter to the findings of the natural sciences, which make a clean-cut distinction between living and nonliving bodies based on structure and operation.

7. *Scholastic Animism.* It is the doctrine that organisms consist of *matter* and *soul* as two incomplete substances united together into a single, composite substance. This unitary substance is the subject of all activities and states in man, physical as well as mental. It is the only theory which accounts for all the facts and phases of man's complete nature.

8. *The Human Person.* The human Ego is *the whole man.* The Ego, the whole man, is a 'substance' and a 'person.' The *soul* is the animating principle of matter and therefore the primary principle (in conjunction with matter) of the vital attributes and activities of vegetancy and sentiency; it is spiritual in essence and as such the sole agent of intellection and free will. Matter is the principle (in conjunction with the soul) which accounts for all the physical attributes and activities in man. The whole man is thus satisfactorily explained.

Readings

Brennan, R. E., *General Psychology,* pp. 418–427. — Gruender, H., *Problems of Psychology,* Ch. V, VI. — Mercier, D. Card., *The Origins of Contemporary Psychology.* — Maher, M., *Psychology,* Ch. XXI, XXII, XXIII, XXV. — Moore, T. V., *Cognitive Psychology,* pp. 131–190; 529–559. — Adler, M. J., *What Man Has Made of Man.*

Chapter XXII

THE ORIGIN OF MAN

OUR investigation into the nature of man has shown that he is a unitary but composite substance. Man consists of a material substance, taken from the ordinary elements, and a spiritual form or entelechy. The spirit of man is the animating principle of the material substrate, transforming the latter into organized, living matter; the human spirit, therefore, is the soul or psyche of the human organism, so that soul and matter are fused together into a single integral organism. Vegetative and sensory functions proceed from the organic compound as from a single principle of action or nature; they are intrinsically material vital functions. The rational activities of intellection and volition, being spiritual, proceed from the soul alone, but with an extrinsic dependence on the senses and the nervous system. Such is the constitution of 'the whole man.'

The next important philosophical question relative to man's being is the problem of *the origin of man.* The problem before us is the *ultimate origin of man.* And since man consists of a body and a spiritual soul, the question resolves itself into the double problem of the ultimate origin of man's *body* and man's *soul.*

The Origin of Life

Before going into the question of man's origin, it will be necessary to investigate the *origin of life in general.*

It is the unanimous verdict of the geologists that living

beings did not always exist on our globe. There were long ages in the history of the earth, in the early period of its development, when it was in a fiery-molten state. No organism, as we know it, could possibly have existed under such circumstances. Later, after considerable cooling, the upper mass of the earth solidified into a crust, forming a suitable habitat for organisms. Eventually, the organisms appeared on the earth; their fossil remains can be traced far down in the sedimentary deposits.

How did life originate on earth?

Did life originate through the extra-mundane causality of *God?* If so, there are two possibilities to consider. He could have made the entire organism, matter and soul, without using any pre-existing material whatsoever in its production. Such a total production out of nothing would be *direct creation.* Or, He could have used the matter already existing on the earth and transformed it into a living being; in doing so, He would be the primary cause in the production of life, while utilizing the agencies of creatural beings as secondary causes. This type of production is *mediate creation.*

On the other hand, many scientists and philosophers are reluctant about appealing to any extra-mundane, divine causality. Some take this position on the general principle that an appeal to divine agency must be avoided in all natural events, except as a final recourse; only when natural agencies are evidently incapable of accounting for the origin of life, would it be permissible to invoke the Creator as the cause of life on the earth. Materialistic monists, of course, approach the question from an entirely different angle. Since, in their view, there is no God and since matter and material forces are the sole agencies at work in the world, they must explain the origin of life as an emergence from matter alone. This theory, which defends the origination of life from nonliving matter, through forces which are indigenous to matter itself, is termed *abiogenesis.* In our day, the theory of abiogenesis is also called the *theory of absolute emergence.*

Abiogenesis

Biology informs us that living beings, under present conditions, originate from other living beings of the same type. Generation may be sexual or asexual, both among plants and animals, but some form of generative reproduction is necessary. Reproduction, however, does not settle the question of the origin of the first organism which appeared on our globe.

Formerly, the defenders of abiogenesis thought they had good evidence for the origination of life out of nonliving matter in the instances of so-called *spontaneous generation*. Up to the end of the seventeenth century even scientifically minded men believed that certain low types of animals were generated 'spontaneously,' i.e., abiogenetically. Worms were supposed to develop out of putrid flesh; frogs, it was thought, were produced from the mud of ponds through the action of the sun's rays; insects, and even rats and mice, were believed to originate without the generative action of living beings. Aristotle, St. Thomas Aquinas, and the medieval Schoolmen generally, taught spontaneous generation in such cases. Lack of scientific training and instruments were responsible for such views.

At present, no scientist would dare defend spontaneous generation on *scientific* grounds.

In 1668 Redi made a scientific experiment in the city of Florence. In midsummer, he placed two pieces of meat side by side, one covered with gauze, the other exposed to the free air. The latter alone developed maggots, because the flies could deposit their eggs on it.

Thereupon the defenders of spontaneous generation adduced other instances which seemed to exclude definitely any form of generation proper, since one never found eggs. Some organisms live in inaccessible places within animals, for example, in the peritoneum of rabbits, inside the muscles of pigs, in the brain of sheep, in the intestines of men and animals. Soon, however, it was proved that these organisms were reproduced through normal generation and then changed their habitation by entering into the system of other animals.

Driven back almost to surrender, the advocates of spontaneous generation received new courage when the high-powered microscope revealed organisms so minute that they seemed to be a transition stage between matter and organic life. Vegetable and animal infusions, when exposed to the air, were seen to contain innumerable little organisms for whose origin one found no generative cause. Hence, these 'infusoria' were considered to be the product of spontaneous generation. Tyndall, however, did much to disprove this contention.

The epoch-making experiments of *Louis Pasteur,* begun in 1860, exploded the theory of spontaneous generation beyond recovery. The genius of Pasteur, through a life-time period of experimentation, established beyond the shadow of a doubt that germs can originate only from germs. Against the claims of Pouchet, Musset, and Joly, Pasteur proved that putrifiable matter of any kind whatever, if sterile and properly protected against contamination from germs present in the surrounding media, such as the air, will never produce living beings. Although nothing was known at the time about such germs except their bare existence, the classic experiments of Pasteur convinced the scientific world that spontaneous generation never actually occurs.[1] Later, as microscopy became perfected, the lowly bacteria and protozoa were seen to reproduce their kind by means of division, a definite proof of Pasteur's original contention.

In 1905, John Butler Burke claimed to have discovered a case of abiogenesis. His experiments seemed to show that *radioactive substances* acting on gelatin media produced 'bacteria-like' cells, containing a nucleus, and that these cells grew and finally subdivided. But Sir William Ramsay, the famous investigator of radium, showed that the emanation of the radium decomposes the water in the bouillon into oxygen and hydrogen and coagulates the albumin. Hence, little bubbles of gas are formed, surrounded by a covering of coagulated

[1] For a brief summary of Pasteur's experiments, see the author's *Science of Correct Thinking* (Bruce, 1935), p. 313 ff.

albumin. As more gas is produced, the bubbles increase in size, so as to give the appearance of very small growing organisms. Burke had also noticed that the new-born organism melted away in the water. Ramsay supplied the explanation: the water gradually removed the gelatin from the 'cell walls,' the gases escaped, and the bubbles collapsed. The phenomenon was thus seen to be nothing more than an ordinary chemical, lifeless process.

In our own day, the discovery of *viruses* and *bacteriophages* has brought the question of abiogenesis again into the foreground. It is not known whether they are true organisms or chemical substances. Perhaps the electron microscope will determine their exact nature. If they turn out to be true organisms, the probabilities will not favor spontaneous generation.

Historically, the formula of the *Law of Biogenesis* has undergone the following development:

William Harvey (1651): *Omne vivum ex ovo;* every living being originates from an egg.

Francesco Redi (1698): *Omne vivum ex vivo;* every living being originates from a living being.

Rudolf Virchow (1855): *Omnis cellula ex cellula;* every cell originates from a cell.

Walter Flemming (1882): *Omnis nucleus ex nucleo;* every nucleus originates from a nucleus.

Theodor Boveri (1903): *Omne chromosoma ex chromosomate;* every chromosome originates from a chromosome.

All observations and experiments, therefore, have confirmed that organized substance originates only from organized substance. Hence, so far as science is concerned, *spontaneous generation (abiogenesis) never occurs.*

Helmholtz, Van Tiegham, Lord Kelvin, Arrhenius, and others have advanced the theory that life might have originated on earth through life-germs carried by *meteorites* from some other stellar body; or, the germs could possibly have *floated across* the intervening space and landed on the earth. This arbitrary assumption merely defers the question without solving it. How did life originate on these stars? They, too, were at one time in a fiery-molten state. Meteorites melt through friction on contact with the atmosphere of the earth, and the heat would kill all germs; the absence of heat and moisture in intersteller space would freeze the germs and desiccate them. Becquerel placed germs in a vacuum with a temperature of liquid air, thus approximately reproducing the conditions of interstellar space. The result, after exposing the germs to ultraviolet rays, which are so abundant in interstellar space, was the death of all germs. Hence, all life-germs would have died in transit. The theory is hardly worthy of serious consideration, but it reveals the desperate extremity in which the theory of abiogenesis has been placed.

When, therefore, certain scientists and philosophers maintain that abiogenesis *must* have occurred in the *bygone ages* of the earth's development, their assertion no longer rests on scientific proof. Abiogenesis is thus advanced as a *postulate* of science and philosophy. But a postulate is the assumption of something as true which is either so self-evident that it needs no proof or which must be accepted as true because it is the only rational and logical explanation of a fact which is obvious to us and of which we have certainty, although we cannot verify the assumption by direct demonstration.

From what has been discovered by science concerning the fact of abiogenesis, it is clear that abiogenesis is not a self-evident postulate; every bit of evidence is against its actual occurrence. Nor can it be said to be the only rational and logical explanation of the origin of life. Only on the supposition that a Supreme Being does not exist, would abiogenesis, or the absolute emergence of life in virtue of the forces inherent in matter, be a necessary postulate. Is the existence of a Supreme Being inconsistent with reason and logic? If not, then abiogenesis is not the *only* rational and logical explanation of the origin of life.

The Principle of Causality is the foundation of all science and philosophy. Reason and logic, according to this principle, demand that there be a *proper proportion between cause and effect.* The effect can never be actually greater than what is virtually contained in the cause, otherwise a part of the effect would be without an adequate cause and as such could never come into existence. It is true, that organisms consist of material elements in their structure and utilize material forces in their vital functions. But the *intrinsic purposiveness* of organic structure and function and the *spontaneity* and *immanence* of action, as manifested in metabolism and reproduction, far exceed the capabilities of matter and material forces taken by themselves. The simplest forms of plant and animal life, bacteria and protozoa, are so superior to inorganic elements and compounds, that even confirmed materialists are now forced to admit that they belong to different levels of being.

There is no need to restate the proofs that, besides matter and material forces, a *vital principle* or *soul* is required in plants and animals (Chap. XIX). Unless we wish to make the gratuitous assumption that all matter is living, the arrival of the organism on earth involves the arrival of something *totally new and superior,* namely, the vital principle or soul. The soul cannot be accounted for on the basis of mere matter and material force. Hence, it must be accounted for by some cause *outside of matter itself;* and, since the cause must be at least equal to the effect, this extra-material cause must itself be *endowed with life.* That the complicated structure and purposive function of even the lowest unicellular organism could be the result of haphazard chance-factors, *without intelligent planning,* would indeed be a greater miracle than creation. It is not sufficient for the first organic being to arise somehow through a fortuitous concurrence of atoms; this first organic being must have arisen completely endowed with cytoplasm, nucleus, chromosomes, and genes, and with the *perfect mechanism of the process of reproduction.* If this were not so, *no reproduction could occur,* and there would be no offspring, no second generation; life would become extinct with the very first organism, and there would be no life today. Yet there are no grounds for supposing that the first organism, arising from unintelligent matter and itself unintelligent, could have the power of reproducing future generations and transmit this power in perfect condition to its offspring. Reproductive power has a purpose for the future, but it is of no advantage for the reproducing individual organism. Such a purpose for the future implies intelligence, but this intelligence does not lie in the speck of living substance which we call 'organized matter.' Neither does the intelligence in question reside in the inorganic elements. Hence, there must have been an *Intelligent Cause,* distinct from matter and the material world, which produced life on our globe. Any other supposition is against logic and reason.

The statement of W. Branca, the well-known scientist, is as true today as when he uttered it in 1910: "Whoever accepts spontaneous generation [abiogenesis] here on earth, thereby believes that two diametrically opposed Laws of Nature have equal value. The first states: Life can originate only through Life. The second states: Life originates also or at least has originated in the past out of non-life. *The first law is proved by billions of facts,* and it is true without any doubt. The *second,* however, has until the present *never been proved by a single fact.* Both Laws of Nature contradict each other diametrically."[2]

Since, therefore, science cannot prove abiogenesis either by observation and experiment or by logical principle and deduction, abiogenesis is not a postulate of science but of *materialistic philosophy.* But a postulate which is based neither on reason and logic nor on the approved findings of science, is no real postulate at all; it is nothing more than a subterfuge designed to bolster a bankrupt philosophy of the origin of life.

Direct Creation

It is not within the province of psychology to prove the existence of an extra-mundane Supreme Being; the proof for

[2] *Der Stand unserer Kenntnisse vom fossilen Menschen* (1910), p. 91.

the existence of a personal God, all-intelligent and all-powerful, belongs to the philosophical department of theodicy. In this connection, we are entitled to accept His existence, particularly in view of the fact that the origin of life must be attributed to an intelligent cause distinct from all matter and material force. It will not be amiss, however, to quote the following statement of a modern scientist, C. C. Hurst: "At present it seems to be generally agreed that the material universe is finite and not infinite in space and time. If the material universe is finite in time, the matter of which it is composed must have had a beginning. In the strictest sense a beginning implies creation and creation involves a Creator. That is as far as modern science will take us."[3]

Granting, then, the existence of God, the question arises as to how He produced the first living being on earth. Was it by means of a direct creation? By *direct creation* we understand the production of a new reality *in its total being from nothingness,* so that no pre-existing entity contributes anything at all to the making of the new reality except the Creator and His creative power. Applying this concept to the origination of the first organism, it means that no material substance of any kind was used by the Creator in the production of the organism; the complete organism, both as to its matter and vital principle (soul), was produced directly by the creative act out of nothing and then placed readymade on earth.

It is obvious that a direct creation of this sort *could* have occurred. God in His omnipotence can create anything which does not involve a contradiction in terms. That no intrinsic contradiction exists in an organism, is evident from the very fact that organisms actually exist. Hence, a direct creation of the first organism is *possible.* It would, however, be a fallacy to conclude from possibility to actuality; because something 'can be,' does not prove that it 'actually is.'

In all probability, a direct creation, in the sense defined, did not take place. We must bear in mind that the body of all

---

[3] *Heredity and the Ascent of Man* (The University Press, Cambridge, England, 1935), pp. 105, 106.

organisms is composed of the ordinary elements found everywhere on earth and in the physical universe. Consequently, there was *no need* to create the bodily elements of the first organism out of nothing. As R. E. Brennan remarks: "No builder would go to the trouble and expense of bringing in a whole new array of materials if he already had all that was necessary for the construction of his building."[4] While the argument is not strictly cogent, it has enough force to make the theory of a direct creation of the total being of the first organism highly improbable.

Mediate Creation

How, then, did God produce the first organism? Life could not originate through an absolute emergence solely from matter and its indigenous forces. In some manner the creative causality of God was necessary for the production of the first organism, even though He used the pre-existing elements of the earth, because the *vital principle* or *soul* is by its very nature *superior to matter and material forces*. The vital principle or soul, therefore, demands the causality of God for its production, at least for the first organism.

Did the first vital principle or soul come into existence through direct creation on the part of God? Again, it *could* have; there can be no question of the *possibility*. On the other hand, the vital principle or soul of the plant and animal, as we have seen (Chap. XIX), is essentially *material* in nature, being intrinsically dependent on matter in its entity and existence; it is, in aristotelian-scholastic terminology, *educed* out of the potentiality of matter. Hence, a direct creation from nothingness is not required. All that would be required for the appearance of life and for the production of the first organism is the original *fiat* of God ordering and disposing matter and material agencies in a purposive fashion, so that at a given time and place the first organic vital principle or soul, the conditions being favorable, would *emerge* out of the

[4] *General Psychology* (Macmillan, 1937), p. 77.

hidden potentialities of matter. Life would thus emerge spontaneously, but in virtue of an *inherent tendency* placed in bodies from the beginning by the Creator. God would be the primary cause of the origination of life, with the agency of bodies as a secondary and instrumental cause.

If we wish to call this form of production a 'creation,' it could be called a *mediate* or *derivative creation*. The term *relative* or *restricted emergence* is perhaps a better designation.

According to the 'law of parsimony,' one should ordinarily accept a theory which provides the smallest amount of assumptions in reasoning and employs an economy of means for the realization of an end. The animation of pre-existing matter seems to conform to this law. Hence, mediate or derivative creation (relative or restricted emergence) appears to have been the method of production used by the Creator in the origination of organic life. The theory is, to say the least, very probable.

Organic Evolution

In a broad sense, *organic evolution* is understood to be the theory according to which the various species and types of animals and plants derive their origin, not through distinct and separate creative acts of God, but through development from other pre-existing species and types, all differences being accounted for by modifications acquired in successive generations according to purely natural laws. The theory maintains that the higher forms of animals and plants developed genetically from the lower, so that all species and types are the descendants of a very few simple organisms, perhaps even of a single one. The general trend of evolution has been from the simple and homogeneous to the complex and heterogeneous. Hence, the organic descent of all animals and plants should be viewed as representing a 'genealogical tree,' the various branches exhibiting manifold degrees and stages of divergence from the parent stock acquired in the course of time.

Most scientists advocate a *monophyletic* evolution, so that all organisms derive their descent from a single primitive organic cell; at least, they say, all plants evolved from an original plant and all animals from an original animal. Others advocate a *polyphyletic* evolution; according to this view, there are several independent pedigrees of plants and animals, representing distinct natural species, each of which has its own point of departure from which the evolutionary process started.

As for the *evidence* for evolution, the theory is based on a number of observations and deductions pertaining to various fields of science.

Paleontology, the science which treats of the life of past geological periods, shows the phylogeny and relationships of organisms and seeks to determine their age and chronology in the history of the earth. The story of life is contained in the fossils found in the superimposed strata of rock deposits of the earth's crust. The fossil remains are a record of the various species of animals and plants through the ages. From this record it is proved that animals (for example, trilobites) and plants (for example, algae) existed side by side in the earliest (Cambrian) formation. Some of the types are highly specialized forms of life. Generally speaking, the trend is from more primitive forms to more complex structures; the mammals, for instance, appear rather late. In some cases, there has been a deterioration of organic structure. Scientists find in this *progressive succession* a potent argument for organic evolution.

Scientists point to the *morphological* and *physiological similarity* of organic types as another general argument in favor of the evolutionary theory. There are certain structures which are fundamentally similar, though they belong to different species and genera. Thus, the hand of man, considered structurally, bears a remarkable resemblance to the paws of lions and mice, to the hoofs of cows and horses, to the wings of birds and bats, to the fins of fishes, and to the flippers of seals and whales, etc. The spinal column of vertebrates is, of course, similar in all these types of animals. The structure of plants is very much alike. The most important feature of morphological similarity, universal throughout the plant and animal kingdoms, is the cell, the basic unit of biological structure and function; it is fundamentally the same in every type of organism. Such similarity in structure, evolutionists claim, shows genetic descent and a common origin.

Ontogeny, the life history of the individual organism, is also adduced as evidence. Accepting E. Haeckel's 'biogenetic law,' evolutionists see in the ontogeny of the individual in its embryonic stage a recapitulation of the phylogeny of the race. As an example, they refer to the whalebone whale. As an adult, this whale has only dental plates, but in its foetal life it has teeth; in former ages, as paleontology reveals, it had teeth also in its adult life. The flounders, and similar fishes, have their two eyes on top of the head, because they swim in horizontal fashion, with one side of their body close to the ground; but when hatched, they have one eye on each side of the head, like ordinary fishes, and the one eye gradually moves over until it is near the other. Many such instances are known to science. Even man, they say, shows gill-pouches in his prenatal development, reminiscent of his phylogenetic relationship with the fishes. All that is required, in order to establish organic evolution on a sound scientific basis, is the extension of this biogenetic principle to all organisms.

There are other arguments, but these are broadest in scope and most fundamental in significance. It is the *cumulative force* of the various pieces of evidence upon which evolutionists rely to prove their case. While the outline just given is extremely brief, it indicates the line of thought which underlies the evolutionary theory.

Historically, the first serious attempt to explain the origin of the various species through genetic descent was made by *Jean de Lamarck* (1809) who accounted for all specific changes through the use and disuse of bodily organs. *Geoffroy Saint-Hilaire* (1828) sought the explanation more in the influence of the environment. *Herbert Spencer* (1852) stressed the 'survival of the fittest.'

The extraordinary work of *Charles Darwin* (1859), as expounded in his *Origin of Species,* made organic evolution acceptable to the scientific world. His famous 'principle of natural selection,' enabling the fittest to survive in the struggle for existence, seemed to supply the universal factor for changing one species into another in a practically mechanical way according to a purely natural law of development. All animals conform to a general type, but individuals possess slight variations. Such variations, gradually accumulated, are transmitted through heredity. Some of these variations are bound to give their possessors an advantage over their competitors in the struggle for existence, because the former are more fit. The result will be that the fit will survive, while the unfit and the less fit will perish. This preservation of advantageous variations and the rejection of injurious variations, is what Darwin meant by 'natural selection.' Through countless generations, succeeding one another over vast periods of time, the constant addition of small variations will eventually produce types so divergent from the original parent stock that *new species* arise. Such was Darwin's theory.

Hugo De Vries defended the theory of mutation, according to which important variations occurred suddenly, so that the offspring differed from the parent in well-marked characters. *August Weismann* (1893) opposed the view that acquired characters could be transmitted by heredity and based evolution on natural selection affecting the *germ plasm. Hans Driesch* (1894) invoked his quasi-intelligent *entelechy* to account for evolutionary development. *Lloyd Morgan* advocates an *emergent evolution,* in which unpredictable new levels of organic beings arise. Other theories have also been advanced.

According to the modern biological concepts of genetics, based on the laws of heredity discovered by the Augustinian Abbot *Gregor J. Mendel* (1822–1884) in 1866, the *genes* and *chromosomes* are the main factors in evolution. Four different vital processes contribute to the origin of new species: the mutation of genes, the transmutation of chromosomes, the mixing of genes and chromosomes through sex reproduction, and the progressive adaptation of their product to the manifold conditions of the environment.

The authors of these theories of evolution usually disclaim anything like *purposiveness* in the process of development. Modern biologists, however, in explaining evolution, use terms which savor strongly of 'purposiveness,' although they are very loath to admit it outright. The recent trend to teleological concepts, i.e., that there is a *tendency* in evolutionary processes to develop higher organisms, is represented by such scientists as L. J. Henderson, Jennings, Vialleton, Coghill, Agar, Goldschmidt, T. H. Morgan, Wheeler, and others.

In opposition to organic evolution is the *theory of permanence or fixity*. It maintains the stability of organic species, acknowledging only minor variations within the framework of the specific type. The theory presupposes that every single species received its existence through a creative act of God. The systematic arrangement and plan of organisms, based on their structural similarity, is merely an *ideal unity,* founded on the unity of the plan conceived and executed by the Creator of the universe. Up to the time of Darwin, this theory was the only one held by scientists and people in general. They observed no transformation of one species into another. The fact that hybrids of different species could not propagate, at least not indefinitely, seemed to preclude the possibility of all species having a common genetic origin.

Evolution or Permanence?

Strictly speaking, the problem of evolution or permanence is a *scientific problem*. If we grant the existence of God as the Author of nature and of life, either theory is tenable. It is evident that God could have created the various species of animals and plants directly. He could also have implanted in the first organism the tendency to develop into increasingly higher forms of life under the influence of internal and external developmental factors. There is nothing contradictory in either theory. Which plan was actually carried out, would be difficult to ascertain.

St. Thomas Aquinas and scholastics in general have always maintained the principle that, if something can be explained through the agencies of creatural causality, one should not have recourse to divine power. It has also been the consistent teaching of St. Thomas[5] that a planned hierarchy exists in nature, so that there is a *tendency* for elements to lead to compounds, for compounds to lead to vegetant beings, for vegetant beings to lead to sentient beings, and for sentient beings to lead to man, who is the end and the aim of all development. While St. Thomas was not an evolutionist in the modern sense of the term, because he was unacquainted with the data of the modern problem of evolution, his general metaphysical teaching about the world and about spontaneous generation could very well be harmonized with the theory of evolution, provided this evolution be conceived as being inaugurated by God according to a purposive plan. The rest would be left to the agency of natural causes.

The theory of evolution is not, in itself, irreligious and atheistic; but the scientists and philosophers are often irreligious and atheistic. The theory does not, in all probability, run counter to Christian principles and belief[6] or to the scriptural account in the Book of Genesis. A number of the early Christian philosophers maintained that creation was a single act of God set at the beginning of the world. All further developments occurred through natural agencies. If scientists can prove conclusively that evolution is a fact, then a fact it is.

Has science *proved the fact of evolution?*

The answer is definitely in the *negative,* as every reputable scientist admits. At best, is is a very plausible theory, but

[5] See *Contra Gentiles,* III, c. 22.

[6] See E. C. Messenger, *Evolution and Theology* (London: Burns, Oates and Washbourne, 1931); Canon Dorlodot, *Darwinism and Catholic Thought,* tr. by E. Messenger (Benziger, 1923).

nothing more than a 'theory', the dogmatic claims of certain pseudo-scientific magazine writers notwithstanding. Let us evaluate briefly the evidence.

Paleontology is a static, fossilized record; it must be interpreted to be understood, because it does not explain itself. It is a record of the *succession* of organic forms; succession, however, does not necessarily mean descent. *Post hoc, ergo propter hoc,* is a fallacious piece of reasoning. The white man came after the Indian in North America, but he did not on that account descend from the Indian. The succession of forms can be explained either by creation or evolution. Natural descent, therefore, would have to be established on other grounds than mere succession in time.

In *morphological* and *physiological similarity* the argument for evolution is based on *analogy,* and such an argument may easily be false, as every scientist and philosopher knows only too well. Similarity does not necessarily involve genetic descent. The camel and the llama are similar in many respects, but neither is the direct descendant of the other. Similarity *could,* without doubt, be due to phylogenesis and evolution; but is could just as well be the result of creation according to a plan of similarity.

The argument from *ontogeny* and *embryology* is a favorite with many evolutionists. This argument for general evolution, however, is not at all stringent. Articulate animals, such as insects, have their central nervous system on the ventral side of their body, while the vertebrates have theirs on the dorsal side. Now, the embryo of a vertebrate does not begin to develop its central nervous system on the ventral side and then gradually change it over to the dorsal side; the vertebrate's central nervous system is developed from the start on the dorsal side, contrary to the so-called 'biogenetic principle' that the embryonic development of the individual is a recapitulation of the history of the race. And it must be borne in mind that the invertebrates and the vertebrates are the two great divisions of the animal kingdom. Since the vertebrates are supposed to be the descendants of the invertebrates, no sound reason can be given why the former, if the biogenetic principle were correct, do not recapitulate the race history of the latter. That vertebrates and invertebrates start from a single cell and develop their embryonic body gradually is due to the fact that all embryonic body development proceeds from the 'general' to the 'special.'

It is necessary to stress a few *important facts* in connection with the theory of a general organic evolution. There is absolutely no evidence for the descent of *animals from plants,* or of plants from animals. Thousands of species and hundreds of genera appear *suddenly* and *without transition* in the geological record at various periods, and there is no evidence that they descended genetically from pre-existing types; all intermediate types are missing. Many types appear immediately as *highly specialized forms* of organisms; no pre-existing simple and primitive types exist from which they should have evolved, as might be expected. Of course, the geological record is, without question, fragmentary; but the burden of the proof for evolution rests upon the shoulders of the evolutionists.

These critical remarks *do not disprove evolution.* As a matter of fact, *partial evolution* seems a fairly established fact. *Eric Wasmann* has made out a good case for the Dinarda forms, a type of beetle. One might also cite the case of the horse, the whale, the elephant, and some others, as evolutionary in character. But such instances are a far cry from a proof for evolution in general. Nevertheless, the cumulative evidence makes the theory of general evolution a fascinatingly plausible and, perhaps, even a *probable theory* which cannot be lightly discarded. Man appeared so late on the globe and his span of historical knowledge is so short and piecemeal that a conclusive proof or disproof of the theory of evolution, whether general or partial, is practically impossible.

Much can be said for and against evolution. A mechanical evolution does not satisfy the philosopher. A purposive evolution, deriving its inherent tendencies from an Intelligent Creator, should be acceptable to all. Since the causal influence of God is necessary for the origin of life, as we have shown, it is reasonable to suppose that He would put the proper dispositions and tendencies in the original organisms, so that they would develop along definite lines into different species. This view is based, of course, on the supposition that He decided on an evolutionary development of species. The direct creation and permanence of all species is not required. Partial creation and partial evolution might be the answer, but it seems a half-hearted position. What method brought about the divergence of species among plants and animals, *facts* alone can determine, and the facts are obscured. The problem is still very debatable.

Origin of Man's Body

Not long ago it was almost a dogma among a large class of scientists that man is a direct *descendant of the apes.* All that seemed necessary for definite proof of this contention was the existence of fossil 'missing links' connecting man and ape. For a time the search for these links was carried on with feverish activity. At present, the view that man is a direct descendant of the ape has been relegated to the limbo of discarded theories. The theory now prevalent is that man and ape represent collateral lines of descent from a generalized common stock, known as the Dryopithecus, which is thought to have existed about ten million years ago.

Man is a newcomer on earth. Some of the fossil skeletal remains of ancient man date back to the *glacial epoch* of the Pleistocene Age, the geological age immedately preceding our own. It is customary to speak of four glacial epochs, though some geologists admit only two. There is no uniformity in the calculation of the lengths of these glacial epochs; depending on the methods of calculation, the time that man has existed on earth is variously estimated as being anywhere between twenty thousand and one million years. Even were no skeletal remains ever discovered, the presence of *flaked flint tools* is a sure indication that man existed in an early glacial period. Such tools of undoubtedly human manufacture are found in the deposits of the *Middle Pleistocene.* The eoliths (ancient chipped stones) of the Lower Pleistocene may have a natural and not human origin.

The *fossil remains* of prehistoric man are rather few. Leaving out of consideration the skull top of *Pithecanthropus erectus* of Trinil, Java, about whose simian or human nature scientists disagree, probably the oldest known human skull is that of the *Piltdown man,* found at Piltdown manor in Sussex, England, by William Dawson and Sir Arthur S. Woodward in 1912. The deposit of gravel, it appears, might possibly belong to an early Pleistocene period. Only parts of the fragmentary skull remain, and reconstruction was difficult. About a yard away from where the skull had been, the greater part of a jaw was found, but it is impossible to determine whether this jaw belonged to this particular skull. The jaw, it is claimed, is rather 'simian' in character, but the skull, oddly enough, except for the thickness of the bones, is essentially modern in type. The brain capacity of this individual is figured at approximately 1,350 cubic centimeters, practically the same as that of many living persons. Such a large brain capacity was rather disconcerting to evolutionists, who loved to picture primitive man as always having large supraorbital ridges, a low, receding forehead, a small cranial capacity, etc. It sounds almost like a complaint, when Alfred S. Romer, a confirmed believer in the evolution of man, writes: "To the type of skull . . . with the great brow ridges, retreating forehead, etc., the term paleoanthropic, 'ancient human,' may be usefully applied. At the end of the Pleistocene appears our own species, *Homo sapiens,* with 'new human' or neanthropic characteristics — the brow ridges reduced, the forehead high, the skull contours rounded. It is frequently assumed that neanthropic modern man has ascended through a long series of paleoanthropic ancestors. But in the Piltdown skull we have one of the oldest of human known fossils — a form probably considerably older than the paleoanthropic Java and Peking men — and yet the skull here is already of a typical modern neanthropic type!"[7]

The *Peking man,* or *Sinanthropus,* was discovered near

[7] *Man and the Vertebrates,* 3rd ed. (University of Chicago Press, 1941), p. 214.

Peking, China, in 1929. Various skull fragments, belonging to individuals of both sexes and to young and old, were found. All skulls are incomplete, but together they give a fairly accurate picture of the skull formation. The supraorbital ridges are pronounced, the forehead is low and receding, the skull is narrow and long. The jaw is chinless, as in all ancient men, but essentially human. The Peking man used tools and fire. The animal skeletons present indicate the period as *Middle Pleistocene*. The brain capacities reported are given as 915, 1,050, 1,100, and 1,200 cubic centimeters.

There are other fossil remains of ancient man—the *Solo* man, the *Rhodesian* man, the *Heidelberg* jaw, the *Swanscombe* skull fragment, the *Galley Hill* skeleton. They are, apparently, more recent than the Piltdown and Peking remains. In the earlier part of the last glaciation, there lived the *Neanderthal* race, of which a number of variants existed, distributed over Europe and western Asia. The men of this race had strong brow bridges, low foreheads, and prognathous jaws, similar to the Peking man. The *Cro-Magnon* race, of the Upper Pleistocene and last glacial period, was a type of tall, well-built individuals, with long heads and high foreheads, and a chinned jaw. They were an artistic race, as their implements and cave paintings reveal. The brain capacity of the skull sometimes exceeds that of modern individuals.

Modern man, of whom we are the descendants, seems to have migrated into Europe from Asia or Africa. Nothing is known as to how or where or when the human sub-races (white, negroid, mongoloid, etc.) originated. This much, however, is certain: All human beings, no matter what their color or structural differences may be, are true men. They intermarry, and their offspring is not sterile but fertile. We can, therefore, draw the conclusion that prehistoric man was also a true human being, like ourselves. Here and there we find living men whose skull structure resembles an ancient type, but they are not less 'human' on that account. What, then, are we to think of the question of the *evolution of man?*

Theoretically, viewed from a purely scientific and philosophic standpoint, the hypothesis of human evolution through brute ancestry, at least so far as man's body is concerned, could be maintained, *provided* the *general* evolution of all organic species from a primitive stock is established as a *fact*. After all, man is a mammal among mammals. His bodily structure and organs are patterned on the general plan of the vertebrate animals. *If* a universal evolution has actually occurred, it would be but natural to include man in the general scheme, because evolution, with its driving force of intrinsic purposiveness and direction, would then have been planned by God in the creation of the first organisms. We must, therefore, state that the evolution of man's body *could, per se,* have been included in the general scheme of the evolutionary process of all organisms. Evolution would be a fair *working hypothesis,* because it makes little difference whether God created man directly or used the indirect method of evolution. Man in either case, would be a creature of God.

Evaluating the *existing evidence,* we find it to be extremely meager. The lack of factual evidence, which makes the theory of general evolution so inconclusive, is even more pronounced in the past history of man. Millions of years, if the calculation is correct, in an enormous gap to span, and there is *no evidence* of the existence of *intermediate forms* linking man to the proposed and supposed ancestral stock. In no other field of scientific research would scientists dream of rearing so stupendous an edifice upon so precarious a foundation as they feel inclined to do in the case of the 'descent of man.' It is amusing and at times irritating, to read their statements on man's 'unquestionable descent' in the face of this absence of factual evidence.

Origin of Man's Soul

Whatever may be the ultimate verdict of science and philosophy concerning the origin of man's body, whether through organic evolution or through a special act of divine intervention, *man's soul is not the product of evolution.*

Materialistic evolutionists, since they deny the existence of a Creator, have no choice in the matter; they must maintain, at the expense of reason and logic, that life evolved out of lifeless matter, that consciousness evolved out of unconscious atoms, and that the total man evolved out of brute animals. We have demonstrated (Chap. XX) that man's soul is a *spiritual entity* endowed with the spiritual powers of intellect and will. As such, the soul transcends matter and material conditions. Matter is essentially quantitative, and so are its energies. Its causality is restricted to the material order. Unless we wish to see the entire edifice of science and philosophy crumble into dust, we must uphold the validity and inviolability of the Principle of Causality and maintain that no cause can produce an effect superior to itself. The effect, before being produced, must be contained virtually in the nature and power of its producing cause; this conclusion follows from the self-evident principle that a thing cannot give what it does not possess. Since matter and material energies do not possess spirituality, because that would be a contradiction in terms, they cannot produce a spiritual being. Man's soul, however, is a spiritual entity, devoid of quantitative parts. Hence, matter and material energies cannot produce the human soul. Plants and animals are organisms, material systems; even plant and animal souls are material in essence, completely immersed in matter and intrinsically dependent on matter in entity and operation. Consequently, neither the matter nor the soul of plants and animals could give rise to the existence of the human soul. Therefore, whether we view the human soul as originating by means of an *absolute emergence* from lifeless matter directly, or through a *generative process* on the part of plants and animals, or through the *transmutation* of a plant or animal soul into a human soul, the effect would exceed the capabilities of the cause. In no case can the spiritual and simple soul of man originate from material beings or through material agencies, whether inorganic or organic.

Pantheists identify the soul with God. The Stoics considered the human soul to be a *particle* of the divine substance. St. Augustine fought this view. He pointed out that, under this supposition, the substance of God would be subject to error and deception and would undergo many kinds of accidental changes; the substance of God, however, being infinitely perfect, is unchangeable in every respect. Other pantheists, especially in our era, look at the human soul as an *emanation* or *mode* of the divine substance passing through a process of development according to intrinsically necessary laws. The soul is considered a form or modification of God's substance. God's substance, however, as will be seen in theodicy, is an infinitely simple, unchangeable, spiritual, and perfect substance, without accidents or modes of any kind. Hence, the soul as an emanation or mode of the divine substance is a contradiction and therefore impossible.

The theory of *traducianism* or *generationism* sought to explain the origin of the individual human soul as the product of *parental generation. Corporeal* traducianism maintained that the material semen of the parents produced the entire child, body and soul; Tertullian and Apollinaris defended this view. *Spiritual* traducianism was the theory that a spiritual semen passed from the soul of the parents to the child in the moment of conception and thereby generated the spiritual soul of the child; St. Augustine upheld this opinion for a time. The former theory is erroneous, because a material generation of the spiritual soul would violate the Principle of Causality. The second theory is erroneous, because the soul of the parents, being spiritual and simple, cannot transmit a part of its substance to the child; besides, the soul of the child would consist of a part of the father's soul and a part of the mother's soul, and thus its essential unity, simplicity, and indivisibility would be destroyed.

The soul cannot be produced out of a pre-existing material or spiritual subject.

Since the human soul is spiritual in nature, it does not consist of matter nor is it intrinsically dependent on matter. Hence, it cannot be produced out of matter as out of a pre-existing subject. Nor can it be produced out of a spiritual substance, because a spiritual substance, since it is simple in essence and does not consist of parts, cannot give away a part which could be used for the production of the new soul. Hence, the human soul cannot be produced out of any spiritual substance as out of a pre-existing subject. Anything, however, which is brought from non-existence to existence without being derived from a pre-existing subject, is produced *completely out of nothing*. Such a production is termed *creation* in the strictest sense of the term. Creatures cannot 'create' things in this way; their total activity is restricted to influencing and changing existing beings. It follows that only an extra-creatural and extra-mundane cause can create the individual human soul, and that cause is God. Hence, every individual human soul is *created by God*. This doctrine is termed *creationism*.

The *objection* is made that, in the event of such a creation, parents are parents of their child in name only; they would not usher into this life a being of the same nature as themselves, but only a human body. The objection is valid only under the supposition that the soul and body form merely an accidental unit. Soul and matter, however, form a *single substance*, an *integral organism*. God, it is true, is the author of the soul through a creative act. But the formation of *the whole man* is also the work of the parents, because their generative act is the determining factor of the origin of the child; through their generative act it is brought about that God creates the soul and unites it substantially to matter, so that the *total effect* is a *human being* similar to their own nature.

Time of the Soul's Origin

At what particular time is the individual soul created? Were all souls created *in the beginning of time* and then united singly to their respective bodies? Or is the individual soul created at the moment of its *union with matter?*

Plato contended that the human spirits (souls) *pre-existed* in a noumenal world before being united with a body.

Origenes also believed in the pre-existence of souls. *No solid grounds* exist for such a belief. The soul must have been either active or inactive in its state of pre-existence. If *inactive,* there could have been no purpose to such an existence, and it is inconceivable that God would have created the soul for a purposeless existence. If *active,* the total lack of memory concerning events in our previous existence remains inexplicable. One might say that the union with the body brought on the loss of memory. But why should this happen? The soul being spiritual, its intellectual memory is spiritual and should not be affected by matter. Could the loss of memory be a punishment for some crime committed by the soul in its former state? Hardly, for how could the soul expiate its crime in this life, if it knows nothing of the crime? Furthermore, our present life would be a condition of deterioration for the soul. In that case, however, the union of body and soul would not be natural (though it is); and one cannot understand why the instinct of self-preservation should be so strong in us and why we should shrink from the separation of body and soul. If anything, we should naturally welcome death, so as to be relieved from the state of punishment; such, however, as we know only too well, is not our attitude toward death. Pre-existence, therefore, must be rejected.

There remains, then, the view that the human soul is created by God *at the moment of its union with matter.* This view alone is reasonable. The soul is a spiritual entity, but it is also the *vital* principle or substantial form of the body. Body and soul (matter and spirit) constitute a single nature and substance. The soul receives its entitative perfection in animating matter so as to form an integral organism; therein lies the natural purpose of its existence. When separated from the body, many of its natural operations, namely, vegetative and sensory functions, are impossible. Hence, since the soul has its *natural existence* only in conjunction with matter, thereby constituting the 'rational animal' which is the true 'human being,' it receives its existence when the human organism comes into existence.

Is the human soul created *at the moment of conception,* that is, at the moment when the male sperm cell unites with the female ovum? The question is controversial and highly speculative. *St. Thomas Aquinas*[8] held that the rational soul is not present in the earliest stages of the embryo's development. In his view, the paternal semen first disposes the maternal substance into organized matter; then a vegetative vital principle or soul is educed out of this organized matter, so that the human embryo at this stage is a vegetant organism; after the vegetative principle has developed and disposed this body for the reception of a sentient vital principle or soul, the sentient soul replaces the vegetative soul, so that the organized foetus is now capable of vegetative and sensory functions. When, under the progressive influence of the sentient soul, the foetal body is sufficiently organized and proximately disposed for the reception of the spiritual rational soul, the rational soul is created in the body, replacing the sentient soul and taking over all functions.

Duns Scotus differed with St. Thomas on this question. He would not admit a temporal succession of vital principles in the foetus. After the initial preparation of matter by the parents, and after the foetal body had developed sufficiently and was disposed to receive the vital principle, the rational soul is infused by God. In his view, no vegetative and sentient vital principles, distinct from the spiritual soul itself, are present in the human foetus before the creation of the spiritual soul. All vital functions, therefore, are performed by the rational soul, and not by any other.

Both St. Thomas and Duns Scotus have had a considerable following. D. Card. Mercier, one of the most prominent of modern scholastics, preferred the opinion of St. Thomas, although few accept his opinion in our day.

The *prevailing view* is that the soul is created and infused into the body at the moment of *conception*. Here is the argument. Since the rational soul contains within itself the capabilities of vegetative and sentient souls and performs the triple

[8] *Contra Gentiles,* II, c. 89.

functions of vegetancy, sentiency, and rationality in the human body at a later stage of its existence, no genuine reason can be adduced why the same spiritual soul should not be present from the very *beginning,* first performing vegetative functions, then sensory functions, and finally rational functions, depending on the developmental stage of the organism. In the prenatal life of the child, the vegetative development must prepare the organism for sentient life, and then the sensory development must prepare the organism for rational life. It is, therefore, only natural that sentiency should follow vegetancy, and rationality follow sentiency; but there is no need to postulate distinct vital principles in each of these successive stages of organic development. After all, it is the *same* body that is being developed, and it is a *human* body, not first a plant body and then a brute body. It is very difficult to grasp how a mere vegetative soul should fashion a 'sentient' body, and how a sentient soul should fashion a 'human' body; a development of this kind, since it tends toward a higher level of being, seems to exceed their intrinsic capabilities. But one can readily understand that a 'human' soul would be capable of fashioning the foetus into a 'human' body through the intermediate vegetative and sensory stages of organic development, because it is the purpose of the human soul to develop a 'human' body. Since, however, the development of the human body begins at the moment of conception, when the paternal sperm cell and the maternal ovum unite in fertilization, it is reasonable to suppose that the *organizing principle,* the spiritual vital principle or soul, be present at and from that very moment. That the human soul does not need to exercise its triple functions immediately and at all times, is proved by the fact that the rational activities of intellection and volition are in abeyance until some time after birth. Yet it is universally conceded that the human infant at birth possesses a rational soul, so that up to the point of the awakening of reason the soul exercises only vegetative and sensory functions. According to the 'law of parsimony,' therefore, no stringent reason can be assigned why the rational soul should not be present from the moment of conception, beginning its organization of the human body at that time. The position here taken, though not capable of direct proof, is undoubtedly logical.

Life thus originated in this world through the causative action of the Creator; abiogenesis, according to the evidence of science, never occurs. Organic evolution is a probable theory, but its factual occurrence has not been definitely proved. The descent of man from brute ancestry is, on purely scientific and philosophic grounds, a tenable but doubtful theory. The spiritual soul of man is created. The exact moment of the creation of the individual human soul is not known with certainty; it would seem, however, that it is created at the moment of conception. That is as far as philosophy can lead us.

Summary of Chapter XXII

The problem to be investigated is the *ultimate origin* of man's *body* and *soul.*

1. *The Origin of Life.* Life did not always exist on the earth. Theoretically, there are two possibilities to be considered. Life could have originated either through an act of creation or through abiogenesis (absolute emergence).

2. *Abiogenesis.* Abiogenesis, or spontaneous generation, is the origination of living beings from nonliving matter through forces which are indigenous to matter itself. A common opinion formerly, it has been definitely *disproved by science.* Living substances can originate only from living substance. The principle of causality precludes the possibility of a vital principle or soul originating from matter through material forces alone, because the effect would be greater than the cause.

3. *Direct Creation.* Life owes its existence to the action of the Creator. *Direct* creation, the production of a new reality in its total being from nothingness, could have been the cause of life; but there was *no need* of creating the elements of the first organic body, because these elements were already at hand.

4. *Mediate Creation.* Since the bodily elements are material,

and since the plant and animal souls are educed out of the potentiality of matter, a *mediate* or *derivative creation* (relative or restricted emergence) would suffice for the origination of the first living organism. This method of production seems to have been the one used by the Creator.

5. *Organic Evolution.* 'Organic evolution' is the theory that the various species and types of animals and plants derive their origin, not through distinct creative acts of God, but through *development* from other pre-existing species and types, all differences being accounted for by modifications acquired in successive generations according to purely natural laws. Evolution may be considered as monophyletic or polyphyletic.

The *evidence* for evolution is found mainly in the *fossil remains* present in the rock deposits of former geological periods, in the morphological and physiological *similarity* of organic types, and in the *ontogeny* and *embryology* of existing types. The various *factors* of evolution, as stressed by different authors, have given rise to a number of evolutionary theories.

The theory of *permanence* or *fixity* is in opposition to evolution and maintains that every species is fixed, having come into existence through a creative act of God.

6. *Evolution or Permanence?* Both evolution and special creation are acceptable theories. The *fact of evolution* has not been definitely proved by scientific research, but it is a *probable theory,* provided evolution be purposive. God, having created the first organisms, could have put the proper *dispositions* and *tendencies* in the first organisms, so that they would develop along definite lines into different species. From a scientific and philosophic standpoint, it is unnecessary to postulate special creation for the various species.

7. *Origin of Man's Body.* Man existed in the glacial epochs of the Pleistocene Age. A number of skeletal remains of ancient man have been found, chief among them being the Piltdown man, the Peking man, the Rhodesian man, the Neanderthal man, and the Cro-Magnon man. This evidence is very meager, if used as a proof that man descended from a stock which is common to ape and man. As a *working hypothesis,*

the descent of man through evolution, if we exempt man's soul, is tenable, but the *fact* itself has not been proved.

8. *Origin of Man's Soul.* Man's soul is *not the product of evolution.* Since it is a *spiritual* entity, the Principle of Causality precludes the possibility that it could have evolved out of the material body or the material soul of animals or plants. It cannot be a *particle* or *emanation* or *mode* of the substance of God, as *pantheism* asserts, because God's substance is infinitely perfect and unchangeable. Nor can it be the product of corporeal or spiritual generation, as *traducianism* (*generationism*) claims; the material semen could not produce a spiritual soul, and the souls of the parents, being simple and indivisible, could not emit a spiritual semen.

Since, therefore, there is no material or spiritual subject from which man's spiritual soul could have been made, the soul must be produced completely out of nothing. A total production is called *creation.*

9. *Time of the Soul's Origin.* The theory of the *pre-existence* of human souls must be rejected. We have no memory of a previous existence. The theory is a gratuitous assumption.

The soul is created *at the moment of its union with matter.* The soul, being the animating principle of the human organism, has its natural existence only in conjunction with matter; consequently, it receives its existence when the *human organism* comes into existence. In all probability the soul is created at the *moment of conception,* because it is a 'human' body that is fashioned from the beginning.

Readings

Brennan, R. E., *General Psychology,* pp. 72–82; 293–318. — Darwin, Charles, *The Origin of Species; The Descent of Man.* — Romer, Alfred S., *Man and the Vertebrates.* — Hurst, C. C., *Heredity and the Ascent of Man.* — Messenger, Ernest C., *Evolution and Theology.* — O'Toole, George B., *The Case Against Evolution.* — Wasmann, Eric, *Modern Biology and the Theory of Evolution.* — Kobel, Jerome, "The Evolution of Man," in *The Franciscan Educational Conference,* Vol. XV. — Hauber, U. A., "Evolution and Catholic Thought," in *The Ecclesiastical Review,* March, 1942.

CHAPTER XXIII

THE DESTINY OF MAN

ALL organisms — plant, animal, and man — owe their ultimate origin to God. Man is neither altogether animal, nor altogether rational. Animality and rationality are fused into a single substantial synthesis; man is in all truth a *rational animal.* So far as his physical being is concerned, he is akin to the mammalian vertebrates; so far as his spiritual soul is concerned, he is made in the image and likeness of God.

It is unthinkable that the all-wise Creator would make a purposeless being. In creating man's soul and giving man existence, God gave a purpose to man's being. The fulfillment of that purpose is *man's destiny.*

What is man's destiny? Can it be specified more exactly? To know his destiny is obviously an important matter for the individual and for mankind in general, since man's knowledge of his destiny will impart *meaning, value,* and *direction* to his life; without this knowledge, man will either live the life of a brute or wander about in a senseless maze of aimless endeavors. To be worthy of his dignity as a human person, man must discover his true place in the universe and then work diligently and conscientiously toward the fulfilment of whatever immediate and ultimate purpose God has set for his being.

The Rhythm of Growth

In a normal span of life, the individual human being passes, biologically and mentally, through a number of *natural periods.* There is a rhythm of growth for the whole man in the progress of his individual life. A. Willwoll very aptly likens these progressive periods to a symphony unfolding itself according to an inner law of art.

The *first phase* comprises *prenatal life* and *childhood.* Prenatal life builds the fundamental bodily structures and establishes the relationships of parts to parts and of all parts to the organism as a whole. It is in this stage that heredity is mostly at work. After birth the child receives and correlates the manifold impressions of sense. External and internal senses work together and develop harmoniously. The child learns to speak, becomes conscious of self, and after a number of years its reasoning powers are awakened. *Childhood* extends from birth to the age of puberty.

The *second phase* of man's growth begins with the completion of puberty. It is the period of *adolescence.* The body undergoes a profound biological change, preparing the boy and girl for fatherhood and motherhood. It is also the period in which the higher mental powers reach out to maturity. The individual becomes more serious-minded and strives to find his proper place in society by fitting himself for a definite vocation, so as to have an independent existence of his own.

The *third phase* sets in around the turn of the third decade. As a rule, the individual in these years of *middle age* attains the highest point of physical efficiency. The specific direction of his life's course is now set. Even though mental maturity does not follow bodily maturity as an effect upon a cause, there is a close relationship between the two, so that experience and achievement, in very many instances at least, reach their peak in these years.

The *fourth phase* begins with the changing years, when a person is about forty-five or fifty. Biologically, this is a period of gradual decline; the bodily mechanism has passed its zenith of maturity and slows down in efficiency. By contrast, due to the consolidation of the accumulated store of experience and knowledge, many persons, especially professional people, achieve their greatest mental vigor in this period.

The *fifth* and *last phase,* setting in with the sixth decade or thereabouts, is the period of final decline. Life obtains a leisurely aspect of rest and retrospect. Old age, with its retarded metabolism and with its infirmities, creeps over the bodily system. The sensory and mental faculties lose their keenness and alertness, and the mind turns more and more to events of the past. Occasionally, however, some individual seems to rise above the deterioration of the organic powers and attains the highest point of mental perfection in old age. Eventually, though, senility and general decrepitude mark the ruins of a once vigorous personality, until death steps in and ends the individual's earthly existence. The rhythm of growth has run through its cycle, and the symphony of life is ended in a whisper and a sigh.

Life is thus never at a standstill. Man is in a continuous stage of transition, from the moment of conception to the moment of death. Biologically, his development and decline proceed according to the inexorable laws of nature, even though the inevitable end be not hastened by unavoidable disease and avoidable neglect. Mentally and intellectually, his development and decline are governed far more by individual initiative and effort.

Man and the World

It would be a very grave mistake to consider man as an individual in isolation. According to the cartesian tradition, carried on by the empiricism of Locke and Hume and by the idealism of Kant and his followers, man's mind is forever chained within the prison of its own ideas and subjective states. Other things and objects either have no existence in their own right, or they cannot be effectively known as they exist in themselves. It is the fundamental error of all modern philosophy and psychology, that they attempt to derive the existence of the world from our subjective ideas, instead of deriving our ideas of the world from the objective things and objects existing in the world.

The world exists prior to man, and man is a part of the

world. The earth is man's *home* and *workshop*. The earth influences him, and he influences the earth.

There is no question that *geographical conditions* exert a profound influence on man's body and mind. It makes a difference whether he lives in the mountains or on the plains; in the tropical, or the temperate, or the arctic zone; in the steaming jungles or on the coast; in an arid or a fertile region; in an area of moderate or extreme changes in temperature. In the tropics, if food is abundant, the heat makes man indolent and sluggish; his culture, as a rule, does not reach a high level. In the arctic, climatic conditions are so severe and the battle for subsistence so hard, that man has no time for anything but the mere acquisition of food and shelter; he finds few opportunities for the things of the mind and of the spirit. It is in the temperate zone that man thrives best, both from a bodily and a mental point of view. The climate is stimulating, the seasonal changes tend to toughen the body, the labor involved in making a living is neither too hard nor too easy, and all conditions serve as an incentive to man to develop new methods of technique to conquer the earth, to establish an appropriate culture, and to give play to the higher mental powers in various forms of art and science.

The earth is not a paradise. Difficulties beset man at every step on his way through the lands. He can fulfill his destiny only through *work*. But man has an intellect and will, setting him apart from all other creatures of the universe, and with these superior powers he fashions the creative tools to master the earth wherever he chooses to roam and live. Nature thus becomes man's servant. The impress of his genius is seen everywhere.

Some authors, with a facetious turn of mind, speak of man as a worm crawling on a pebble, the earth, as a speck of life floating aimlessly through the immeasurable vastness of the universe. The idea is puerile. As if the greatness of a thing should be measured in terms of physical size and linear dimensions! Man's body stands at the half-way mark between the mass of the infinitesimal electron and the mass of the most ponderous star; he is the *pivotal point of the universe.* Comprising within his organic body subatomic particles, the chief elements, and all that is best in plants and animals, he is the *supreme representative of the universe.* His spiritual soul, with its penetrating intellect and conquering will enables him to pierce the veil of phenomena and uncover the hidden essences and laws, so that he is the natural *interpreter of the universe.* One single spiritual concept far outweighs the huge massiveness of an entire world of mere matter. One single spiritual soul has a greater value and a nobler destiny than a million solar systems and a billion galaxies of blindly whirling stars. In the spirituality of his soul, he is the *crown of the universe.* With his feet he is rooted in matter; but his soul reaches out beyond the uttermost boundaries of matter and space.

Man and Other Minds

Man is not a solitary, isolated being. There are other human beings in this world. The individual cannot fulfill his destiny by himself; he needs the assistance of *other minds.* How does he contact these other minds? How does he know what takes place in the minds of other persons?

The bridge which spans the gap between one mind and another must have a *sensory* component and an *intellectual* component. Man does not know directly what another mind is thinking about; hence, the indirect path of the senses must be used in communication between one mind and another. Sense knowledge alone, however, is not in itself sufficient. A system of sensory expressions must be devised, and these expressions must be symbols of ideas; only in this manner can the ideas present in one mind be communicated to another mind. *Language* fulfills these conditions.

The accumulated knowledge of millions of individuals and of thousands of generations is made available for everybody through the medium of spoken and written language. The wisdom of the ages becomes the property of individuals through language. It is not necessary for each individual to relearn everything through personal experience and observation. Whether transmitted by word of mouth or preserved in writing and print, the intellectual, emotional, religious, and moral experiences of other minds can be assimilated by each individual, according to his capacity and inclination, for his personal development.

Man and Society

Man, it is often stated, is a *social animal*. Though an individual human being, he must fulfill his destiny as an integral member of the *community of men*.

A *society* is a permanent union of a number of persons in fellowship and co-operation for a common purpose of benefit to all. There are two kinds of society, conventional and natural. A *conventional* society is one founded by a group of persons from free choice, for the attainment of some purpose specifically agreed upon. Examples of this type of society are political parties, labor unions, study clubs, commercial associations, athletic organizations, student fraternities. They satisfy the desires and needs of a certain class of individuals who band together for a common purpose by means of mutual agreement or 'convention.' A *natural* society is one which is established by men in general under a mandate of the 'natural law,' the law inherent in them as human beings. There is in man the *natural aptitude, inclination, and need* for a permanent union and companionship with his fellowmen, so that he cannot escape membership in this kind of society without doing violence to his human nature and running the serious risk of frustrating the purpose of his existence. Man is not born perfect; but he is born with a perfectible nature. It is his right and duty to perfect his nature; he cannot perfect his nature, however, except in a stable union with others throughout the course of his life. There are three natural societies among men, domestic society or the family, civil society or the state, and religious society or the church.

That man has the natural 'aptitude' for membership in such

societies, can be seen from the fact that he is gifted with speech. Speech enables men to communicate with one another, to exchange ideas, and to make known their needs and achievements; they can, therefore, give mutual assistance and work for the common good of all concerned. That he has the natural 'propensity' to combine his efforts with others, is also evident; he dislikes prolonged solitude and isolation, he seeks companionship, and he feels the necessity of consulting others for the solution of important problems. That he has the natural 'need' of association with his fellowmen, is all too obvious; he simply cannot receive life and grow to the full status of his bodily, mental, and spiritual maturity except in community with others within the framework of such natural societies. To be a member of these social organizations is, therefore, a requirement of his *nature* as a human being.

Membership in the community does not entail depersonalization of the individual. The individual possesses *inalienable rights,* flowing from his nature as a rational person, and these rights are never lost or forfeited by belonging to a society. Society respects and safeguards the rights of the individual, because its fundamental purpose is to work for the welfare of all members through mutual co-operation and the pooling of resources for the benefit of all in the fullest measure obtainable. The individual, however, also has *social duties* toward the other members of the community. If he is to receive the services of others for his own benefit, he must give his services for the benefit of the others. Society makes its contribution to his personal development, and he in turn must make his personal contribution toward the furtherance of the interests of society. Community life is thus grounded on the principle of *mutual benefit* and *mutual service,* because of the natural limitations and needs of man as an individual who must work out his destiny by developing all his powers, so far as possible, to their full capacity. Natural societies are, therefore, a mandate of the natural law. In its final analysis, of course, the binding force of the natural law is derived from the will of the Creator who made man to be what he is.

Man and Domestic Society

The *fountainhead* of social life lies in the union of man and woman in *marriage*. Biologically and mentally, the two sexes are complementary to each other. Perfect equality between the sexes never has existed and never will, due to their natural difference of position in the divinely ordained scheme of life. The man is the breadwinner, the worker, the explorer, the inventor, the scientist, the governor. Woman is essentially the homemaker and mother of the race who gives, nurtures, forms, and rears the new life. Masculinity and femininity are emotionally opposites and attract each other instinctively. Love and the sex urge prompt the man and the woman to enter into the most fundamental union of human society — marriage. Here the 'I' becomes the 'We' of society.

In marriage the purpose of their sex reaches its fulfillment in the procreation of a new human being similar to themselves — the child. The child is the concrete embodiment of their marital love. The parents now submerge their individual interests and their interests as husband and wife into the higher and more unselfish love of both for their child. The child and its interests enjoy a primacy. The presence of the child brings about an extension of the community life of husband and wife into that of father, mother and child. There now exists the *family*.

The *family* is the *basic unit of human society,* because the family is the source of life for all members of the human race and the primary institution for the bodily, mental, moral, and social development of man from birth to maturity. Man has the natural aptitude, propensity, and need to enter into the bond of marriage and establish a family; hence, the family is a natural society dictated by natural law. The single individual is not obligated to establish and rear a family; the obligation is incumbent upon mankind as a race, because the purpose of the law is the perpetuation of the race as such, and mankind as a whole does not fail to fulfill this obligation.

Authority in the family is divided between both parents, since both share in the giving of life and are responsible for the welfare of the children they beget. Due to their difference of position in the heart of the family, the father is the authoritative head of the family, while the mother is primarily concerned with the upbringing and education of the children. The relationship of parenthood confers upon father and mother certain rights, and involves specific duties, toward their children. On the other hand, children, both as individual human beings and as members of the family, enjoy the rights of proper sustenance and training; but they also have the duties of respect, obedience, and, when necessary, support of their parents. The family, in its very essence, is the fundamental form of human society.

Man and Civil Society

Just as man is by natural law a member of domestic society or the family, so he is also a member of *civil society* or the *state*. The state is an extension of the family. The family is prior to the state. The state results from the combination and organization of a number of families into a social union for the furtherance of their mutual welfare.

Man has the natural aptitude, propensity, and need to establish the broader social unit of the state, and hence the formation of the state is a mandate of the natural law. The state is a *natural society* and as such lies within the order ordained and willed by the Creator for the greater benefit of mankind. Neither the individuals nor the families are, as a rule, capable of acquiring and supplying everything needed for the maximal welfare of all. Resources are limited, and so are opportunities and capabilities. Dangers threaten from all sides, and the individuals and families are incapable of coping with them adequately. It is necessary, therefore, for individuals and families to form groups, communities, cities, tribal organizations, and national governments for mutual assistance and protection. Thus does the *state* or *commonwealth,* namely, a body of people occupying a definite territory and politically organized under a stable government, come into existence as a natural society. The particular form of government is of minor importance.

The state, since it is the outgrowth and extension of the family, must protect the inherent and inalienable rights of the family, because the family is the basic unit of society. The rights of the family have a primacy over the rights of the state. The rights of the family are not derived from the state, but existed before the state could even be established. Hence, the doctrine of the *absolutism* of the state is radically wrong. The intrinsic goal of all man's social activity is the satisfaction and completion of his natural powers, so as to insure *temporal happiness*. It is, therefore, the duty of the state to assist man in the realization of this supreme goal of earthly existence. It follows that the state does not possess arbitrary powers of government over its subjects, but must be guided by the essential purpose of all government in relation to its constituent groups, families, and individuals, namely, the *common weal* in accordance with the destiny of man. Hence, the state must establish and maintain *peace* and *order* throughout its domain, upholding all natural and legal rights and compelling the fulfillment of all civic duties on the part of its members. It must also, so far as possible and feasible, place within the hands of its members the opportunities and means of a full bodily, mental, and moral development. To achieve its mission, authority must be vested in an individual or representative body, together with the power necessary to enforce the laws for the benefit of all.

Man and Religious Society

Man is by nature not only a domestic and political, but also a *religious being*. Man is specifically what he is through his rational, spiritual soul. Whatever we may think of the origin of his body, his soul owes its total being and origin to the direct creative act of God. Everything man is and has, he is and has through the loving kindness of his Creator. The bond between man and God, therefore, is infinitely more intimate than the bond between child and parent.

Here we have the ultimate foundation of the *equality of all men* and the ultimate source of the inalienable rights of all men to *life, liberty,* and *the pursuit of happiness.* Man is a creature of God, made in His image and likeness, irrespective of sex, color, or race. The concept of a 'super-race' is an insult to man and God.

The very nature of man demands that he recognize his creatureship and dependence on the Creator. This relationship implies reverence, adoration, and homage; expressed externally, reverence, adoration, and homage assume the form of a religious rite. Man, therefore, has the natural obligation to *worship* his Creator, so that religious worship is incumbent on man as a dictate of the *natural law* of his being.

First and primarily, the *individual* has the obligation of worship. Since, however, he is by nature a social being, he has the aptitude, propensity, and need to fulfill the obligation of worship in his social union with others in a public manner. In other words, not only the individual but *society* must worship God. In accordance with this dictate of natural law, we find that all peoples have exercised their duty of worship through religious rites as a social group and even as a state. In virtue of his very being, then, man has the right and the duty to worship God as a member of a religious organization or society, either in conjunction with the state or apart from it.

Viewed from the standpoint of reason and philosophy, we must say that man is by nature impelled to be a member of domestic, civil, and religious society.

Man and Morality

Man is born not only into the physical and social order, but also into the *moral order*. Unlike brute behavior, human conduct is characterized by the quality of *right* and *wrong*. By 'human conduct' we understand those actions of the human persons which are controlled by the free will; these are qualified by the attribute of morality, in so far as they conform or do not conform to the norms and principles governing right living.

All men at all times have recognized the fact that free human actions are 'good' or 'bad,' 'right' or 'wrong.' It is not a question of whether certain actions are efficient or inefficient, expedient or inexpedient, pleasant or unpleasant, convenient or inconvenient; irrespective of such considerations, they are deemed to be good or bad *in themselves.* All agree that what is good 'ought to be,' while what is bad 'ought not to be.' The 'good' should be loved and striven for, the 'bad' should be abhorred and avoided. Who does what is 'right,' deserves praise; who does what is 'wrong,' deserves blame and punishment. This attitude is fundamental and universal.

Man feels under *obligation* to do what is good and avoid what is bad. He stands *under* the law of morality, not above it. There is an absolute and immutable element in morality which binds man's will in all deliberate, free acts and imposes itself upon him as an authoritative command. Kant terms this command the 'categorical imperative.' Whence the authoritativeness of this command?

Consider the *basic principles of morality.* They are general in character, but specific in intent. Such principles are: 'Do what is right, and avoid what is evil; reverence and worship the Supreme Being and do His will; do unto others as you would have others do unto you; respect your fellow man's person and property; you must not steal; you must not lie; esteem and obey your parents and lawful superiors and show them gratitude; murder and adultery are wrong and must be punished, etc.' It is obvious that such and similar moral precepts are not based on pleasure or external restraint or the limitation of physical capability. The moral principles just enumerated often run counter to natural inclination, impulse, and pleasure. Even when no restraining external force is present, man feels the obligation to carry out these precepts. The physical capability of performing a prohibited act may be unimpaired, but the sense of obligation still remains. The obligation to abide by the moral precepts, therefore, is not of man's own making, because man, of his own accord, would not impose such onerous duties upon himself.

We must conclude that morality is a *law* imposed on man by his own *rational nature*. Man is distinguished from the brute by the rationality of his intellect and the morality of his free will. Because man is a rational being, he is also a moral being. Man will lead a moral life, if his free actions are in harmony with his rational nature. Man's rational nature is thus the *proximate ground* of human morality. The *ultimate ground* lies in the will of the Creator who has endowed man with a rational nature. Brutes, not possessing rationality, have their behavior regulated by irresistible drives and impulses. Man, possessing intellect and will, must freely choose to regulate his conduct by practical principles and judgments, so that his conduct will be in conformity with his rational nature by free choice. Morality, therefore, is a *natural law* based upon an intellectually perceived obligation, not upon physical or physiological constraint. Man *can* violate the moral law, but he *should* obey it.

By the very fact that man is endowed by the Creator with the power and use of reason, he soon learns to make the necessary and practical judgments that some acts are in harmony with his rational nature, and therefore 'good' and 'right,' while other acts are in opposition to the fundamental character of his rational nature, and therefore 'bad' and 'wrong.' The practical judgment which applies the moral law to our own acts, informing us whether a particular act is in agreement or disagreement with the moral law, is called *conscience*. Conscience is an act of reason which interprets the moral law and demands obedience to the law. It is 'God's voice,' to use an apt figure of speech, telling man what to do and what not to do, if he would follow God's will. Conscience is the supreme arbiter in moral life, and its commands must be obeyed.

What is the *purpose* of conscience and morality? To make us live a life worthy of our dignity as rational beings and to make us like to God who created us. The *whole man,* not a mere part of his nature, must be taken as the norm and criterion of morality. Man is an individual being, with sensual and intellectual potentialities; he is also a social and a religious being. Whatever befits him in these various capacities and helps to develop them in their proper order, is morally good. Man's nature gives him a definite *scale of values* to guide him in right living. St. Thomas Aquinas marks off the scale of values in clear and concise terms: "There are certain activities naturally suited to man, and these activities are in themselves right and not merely by positive law. . . . It is natural to man to be a social being. Those things, therefore, naturally befit man without which the maintenance of human society would be impossible. . . . The use of lower creatures to meet the need of human life is a natural property of man. Now there is a certain measure in which the use of aforesaid creatures is helpful to human life. If this measure is transgressed, as in the disorderly taking of food, it results in harm to man and is inappropriate. In the natural order, man's body is for his soul, and the lower powers of the soul for reason. It is therefore naturally right for man so to manage his body and lower faculties of his soul so that the good of reason may be helped. . . . To every man those things are befitting, whereby he tends to his natural end; and the contraries are naturally unbefitting. But God is the end to which man is ordained by nature. Those things therefore are naturally right, whereby man is led to the knowledge and love of God."[1] It is, then, the purpose of conscience and morality to make man acquainted with what is befitting to his rational nature and to oblige him to seek the various values in their proper order; and man has the duty to follow the dictates of conscience and morality. Otherwise he cannot fulfill his destiny as a human being.

What is the *end* and *goal* of the moral order for the *individual?* It is the perfection of the 'whole man'; and this perfection entails *happiness.* The end and goal of all man's activities is his personal happiness. Whoever fulfills his moral

[1] *Contra Gentiles,* III, c. 129.

obligations faithfully, is bound to obtain happiness; and whoever refuses to submit to the moral order, must reach a state of final unhappiness. St. Thomas expounds this point with his usual clarity: "Wherever there exists a well-regulated order of ends, it is necessary that this established order lead to an end; anything which separates itself from that order, at the same time separates itself from its end. God has ordained a certain order for human acts in as far as their end is concerned, and this end is happiness. It follows, therefore, assuming this order to be solidly established, that those who follow its dictates will obtain their end, happiness; in other words, they will be rewarded; and those who disturb this order by the commission of sin will not obtain their end, happiness; in other words, they will be punished."[2]

Morality involves *sanctions*. A 'sanction' is a reward given for the observance of a law and a punishment meted out for the violation of a law. Sanctions are necessary to make the law effective. If there were no punishment for evil doers and no reward for the observers of the law, right order would end in chaos, the self-denial of the virtuous would be useless, and the wicked would be triumphant. Justice thus demands sanctions. Furthermore, the frailty of man needs a stimulus for the performance of duty and a deterrent which serves to curb his inclination and will to do wrong. The legal sanctions of the state are insufficient for the purpose, because the state has control only over external actions, and many violations of the moral law never become known. The sanctions of the moral law must come from the *author* of the moral law; since God is the Supreme Lawgiver, He must have attached the necessary sanctions Himself. God alone knows the secrets of the human will, and He alone can reward the just and punish the unjust in adequate measure. Now, happiness is the natural reward of the good, and misery the natural punishment of the evil. God, therefore, in His justice will see to it that the good receive their reward and the wicked their punishment.

Man *cannot escape the law* of morality. He may sidestep

[2] *Ibid.*, III, c. 140.

the duties of domestic and civil society by isolating himself from the rest of mankind, living by himself in some inaccessible place. But he cannot escape from himself and from God; he carries the moral law and his conscience with him wherever he goes. Hence, he cannot escape from the sanctions of the moral law.

And yet, is it true that the observance of the moral law brings happiness to the good and the violation of it brings unhappiness to the wicked? We are here face to face with a profound problem.

Survival After Death

Death is the cessation of life in an organism. When vital functions cease in an organism, without the possibility of the resuscitation of these functions, the organism is 'dead.' Since vital functions have their existence primarily from the vital principle or soul, death supervenes upon an organism when the soul of plant, animal, or man is no longer capable of animating the material substrate with which it is substantially conjoined as the vitalizing 'form.'

Death may occur in one of two ways: *dissolution* or *annihilation* of the organism. 'Dissolution' takes place, when matter and form are separated. The elements of the organic compounds then revert to the inanimate status of ordinary chemical elements and enter into new combinations according to the laws of chemical affinity. In 'annihilation' the total organism (matter and form, body and soul) is reduced to complete nothingness, so that no vestige of the organism remains in existence.

Man, of course, dies. His vital functions as an organism cease. Man, however, considered as an organism, is *not annihilated* in death. The material elements of his body remain in existence in the corpse, just as they do in the case of plants and animals. Man, therefore, dies by means of a *dissolution* of the substantial bond between body and soul (matter and form). The body disintegrates after death.

What happens to the *soul?* Does it also disintegrate? Does it cease to exist, when man, as an organism, ceases to exist? Or, does it survive the death of the organism as a whole and exist for itself? The answer to these questions is of surpassing importance for each individual human being. If the soul ceases to exist with the death of the organism, man's destiny is completed in his span of earthly life; if the soul survives the death of the organism, his destiny receives its fulfillment after death.

Survival after death is possible.

Whether the human soul can survive the death of the organism, depends on two factors: the intrinsic essence of the soul itself and its relation to the body with which it forms one nature.

Of itself and in virtue of its *essence,* the soul cannot be destroyed through death except on the supposition that it were composed of quantitative or entitative parts. A *composite* being can, by its very nature, be dissolved into its constituent parts and thus lose its identity through dissolution and disintegration, either through the power of an outside agent or through internal weakness. Reversely, what is not composed of quantitative or entitative parts, cannot be dissolved and so destroyed. Now, the soul is not composed of any parts whatsoever, because it is a *spiritual* and *simple essence.* Hence, in virtue of its essence, it cannot be destroyed. The death of the organism, therefore, does not entail the destruction of the soul.

In virtue of its *relation to the body,* the survival of the human soul would be naturally impossible, if the soul were completely immersed in matter and would thus be *intrinsically dependent* on matter for its existence and operations. It was, however, proved before (Chap. XX) that the human soul, unlike the plant and animal soul, is a subsistent spiritual entity, *intrinsically independent* of matter in its essence and only extrinsically dependent on the senses for the object of its intellectual knowledge. Vegetation and sensation are organic functions, but intellection and volition are spiritual activities essentially devoid of materiality. Hence, so far as its essence and rational activities are concerned, the dissolution of the organism does not necessarily involve the destruction of the soul. The human soul, therefore, being a spirit, can survive the death of the organism and carry on an independent existence of its own.

In such a disembodied existence after the death of the organism, the soul would not, of course, be capable of vegetative and sensory functions, because these require material structures and organs. The *rational activities* of intellection and volition, however, would remain intact in this after-death existence; they are not organic functions, but reside in the spiritual soul alone. The intellectual *memory* of past experiences would be carried over into the new life. Elaboration of previously acquired knowledge would also be possible, and no legitimate reason can be advanced against the acquisition of *new* knowledge, because the soul now has the mode of existence of a pure spirit and no longer needs the co-operation of the senses. The will, too, following the intellect, must be unhampered in its activities.

Survival after death is morally certain.

It has been the *universal conviction* of mankind that the human soul survives the death of the body. Ethnology has supplied a practically complete proof of this conviction. There is a considerable difference of belief as to the kind of life the soul will lead after death; but of the fact of survival itself there is a universal conviction throughout the world.

A universal fact of this sort demands a *universal cause* as an explanation. It is useless to assign ignorance, prejudice, or deception as the cause; these are not universal in character. The only adequate cause, co-extensive with man himself through all types of culture, is the *rational intellect* of man which finds itself constrained to accept the survival after death as a *necessary truth.*

But on what is this judgment based? On the *moral nature*

of man. Man is subject to the moral law. This law, to be effective, must be enforced by sanctions, reward or punishment. In this earthly life, however, reward and punishment are not of such a nature that they are adequate for the purpose intended. The good are by no means always rewarded in proportion to their virtues, nor the evil punished according to their misdeeds. Occasionally, virtue is a source of happiness, and vice a source of misery. In general, however, pleasure and pain, comfort and discomfort, wealth and poverty, honor and disgrace, enjoyment and self-denial, happiness and misery, are not meted out to the good and evil according to their just deserts, as the divine sanctions would demand.

The best proof for the inadequacy of the moral sanctions in this life is found in those instances where a person voluntarily *sacrifices his life* in supreme devotion to the moral law. Many maidens have died in defense of their chastity; many persons have been martyred for the sake of God and their conscience; many heroes have given their life in the charitable effort to save others; many soldiers have fought until death because of their sublime sense of duty. If the soul did not survive death, where is the sanction, the reward, for a magnificent moral deed magnificently done? Such actions, which we prize and praise so highly, would be utterly useless and foolish.

It is unthinkable that God, who is *infinitely just,* would permit such deeds of supreme devotion to the moral law to go unrewarded, particularly when man, out of love of God and His law, sacrifices his highest earthly possession, namely, his life. Since the sanctions of the moral law are of divine origin, and since the reward for good and the punishment for evil are not adequate in this life, we must conclude that the soul will survive the death of the organism and receive its just dues in the life to come. Without this balancing of the scales on the part of eternal justice in the soul's life after death, the entire moral order would be a delusion and a mockery, and man would be the most deplorable of all God's creatures. God is infinitely good and infinitely just; He will therefore, reward the virtuous and punish the wicked in adequate measure. Hence, the survival of the human soul after death is certain.

There is another point which must be considered. God does not create a thing without a purpose to its being; and the *purpose* of a being is revealed by the kind of *essence* which God has given it. Now, the essence of man's soul is spiritual, incorruptible, indestructible; by nature it can and should survive the death of the oganism. Creatural powers cannot touch the essence of the soul; they are as incapable of annihilating it as they are of creating it. Only God can create and annihilate the spiritual soul of man. The very fact, however, that God created the soul as a spiritual and naturally incorruptible essence, capable of surviving the dissolution of the body, shows that it was His *purpose* that the soul should live on after death. Since the purposes of God are infallible in their power of execution, He had the intention that the soul should not cease to exist with the cessation of life in the human organism. Of course, God *could* annihilate any of His creatures; He gives existence, and He can also take away existence. No creature has an indisputable and absolute right to existence. God, however, is not fickle and capricious. If He chose freely to create the soul of man as a spiritual and incorruptible essence, so that by its very nature it is capable of survival after death, we are justified in drawing the conclusion that it is His *will* that the soul survive. The spiritual essence of the soul, together with the necessity of adequate sanctions for the observance of the moral law, makes the *actual survival* after death not only a probability but a certainty.

Spiritism and Survival

Spiritism (or, as the adherents of the cult term it, *spiritualism*) makes the claim to have furnished empirical proof of the continued existence of the human soul after death. Many disembodied souls, spiritists maintain, not only can, but actually do, establish contact with the living in various ways. The chief manner in which the souls of the dead communicate with the living is through certain psychic persons. Such a specially gifted person is called a *medium* or *sensitive.*

Spirit communications are usually received in a seance, a meeting held in a more or less darkened room. The medium goes into a trance, and the spirit makes use of the bodily organs of the medium to produce 'manifestations.' Such manifestations are manifold in character; some are physical, others psychical.

Among the *physical phenomena* attributed to discarnate souls in mediumistic seances, the following are the most outstanding. Heavy bodies are moved with contact, but there is no mechanical exertion involved in the movement. Heavy bodies are moved without contact. Objects and human beings are lifted off the floor and remain suspended in mid-air without visible support. Articles move about from place to place without contact. Bodies change their weight, even when subjected to laboratory conditions. 'Raps' or percussive sounds are heard and are used as a means of intelligent communication. 'Spirit-lights,' resembling the luminosity of glow worms, appear and travel about the room. Phantom forms and faces 'materialize' and are visible to those present; these phantom shapes are said to be developed from ectoplasm, a psychic substance obtained from the body of the medium.

The *psychical phenomena* attributed to the spirit intelligences are equally remarkable. One is automatic writing concerning subjects with which the medium is totally unfamiliar. Then there is the writing done with the planchette or ouija-board, an instrument similar to a miniature table with three legs, one of which is a pencil or pen. Clairvoyance, telepathy, and psychometry also occur quite frequently. A medium of mediocre education and intellectuality may speak brilliantly on very abstruse and strange topics or in an archaic language. Detailed facts of historical events, long forgotten, are brought to light and verified through subsequent research.

The phenomena are startling. Numerous scientific bodies

have investigated the occurrences happening in the seance room. In many instances fraud has been detected. It would be rash, however, to ascribe everything to deception; some mediums are apparently above reproach. Eminent scientists and investigators have become convinced that many phenomena are genuine. Among them are Sir William Crookes, Alfred Russel Wallace, W. F. Barrett, Sir Oliver Lodge, Henry Sidgwick, F. W. H. Myers, Charles Richet, Fred. H. Van Eeden, R. Hodgson, J. H. Hyslop, William James, Gustav T. Fechner, Frederick Bligh Bond, Hans Driesch, and others. They have arrived at the conclusion that 'intelligences' are at work and manifest themselves to the living.

Are these extraneous intelligences the discarnate souls of persons who formerly lived on earth? The 'spirits' frequently make this claim in spiritistic seances and adduce evidence in support of their claim. That these intelligences are discarnate human souls is the central dogma of the religious cult of spiritism (spiritualism). In evaluating this main doctrine of spiritism as *empirical evidence for the survival of the human soul after death,* we must bear the following facts in mind.

First, the spiritistic practices of the ordinary seance room, as honest observers admit, are permeated by *fraud* and *trickery.* Since even the best of the famous mediums have occasionally been caught in the perpetration of fraud, the entire evidence of spiritism is of doubtful validity.

Second, the chief objection against the spiritistic hypothesis lies in the impossibility of establishing *spirit identity.* To be acceptable, spiritism must prove beyond reasonable doubt that the communicating intelligence is really identical with the soul of a former person. Though claims of identity are frequently made by the 'spirits,' and though investigators have done everything possible to establish identity, indubitable and conclusive evidence of spirit identity has never been proved in a single case even under most favorable conditions. Ignorance and deception on the part of the 'spirits' have frustrated every attempt to establish identity. The case of Stainton-Moses, one of the best mediums, is illuminating. His principal spirit controls gave their names as 'Imperator,' 'Rector,' and 'Doctor.' Before he died, Stainton-Moses obtained the supposedly real earth names of his controls and communicated these names to a single living person, F. W. H. Myers. After his death, a 'spirit' communicating through Mrs. Piper, another famous medium, claimed to be the soul of Stainton-Moses. It was suggested to the alleged spirit of Stainton-Moses that he reveal the three names given by him before his death to Myers, in order to establish an indubitable case of identity. After considerable delay and evasion, the control revealed three names. Not one of them had the least resemblance to the original names given by Stainton-Moses to Myers. Myers himself attempted to establish identity in his own case. Shortly before his death he gave a sealed message to Sir Oliver Lodge. Lodge placed the sealed letter in a bank vault. Soon after Myers' death, messages were received from all parts of the world, purporting to come from the spirit of Myers. After a few months, the message of Myers was taken from the vault and opened in the presence of official witnesses. None of the communications sent in bore the remotest resemblance to Myers' original message. The test ended in dismal failure, as did every other test ever made.

Whatever may be the nature of the intelligences operating in seances, we must conclude that spiritism does not furnish empirical proof of the survival of the human soul after death. The arguments for survival still rest, so far as philosophy is concerned, on the rational grounds adduced by speculative reason.

Immortality of the Soul

So far we have shown that man's soul will actually survive the death of the human organism and pass over to a new life after death. How long will this life of the soul last? Will it eventually come to an end? Will it last forever? Is the soul immortal?

By *immortality* is meant *endless duration of life.* The soul has a beginning to its existence, because it is created. Must it also have an end to its existence in the future life? If not, then it is immortal. Of itself, the human soul, since it is a spiritual and therefore a naturally incorruptible and indestructible essence, *can* live forever. Absolutely speaking, God *could* terminate its existence through annihilation. Consequently, the question resolves itself into this: *Will* God annihilate the soul at some point in the future or leave it exist forever? The philosopher must attempt to answer this question, not by an appeal to Christian revelation, but on the *grounds of reason.* On the grounds of reason alone, we must draw the following conclusion:

The soul will live without end; it is immortal.

Every individual living being seeks existence according to its nature. In beings endowed with knowledge, this seeking of existence and its preservation takes the form of a *natural desire* of the appetency, because knowledge precedes and produces desire. When something is known to be a 'good,' it is desired as such; and existence and its preservation is such a 'good.' The brutes apprehend existence and its preservation as a here-and-now 'good' and strive for it in that manner; their natural desire for existence and its preservation does not range beyond the present moment into the future. The intellect, however, apprehends *existence as such.* Existence conceived in this manner is simply *pure duration* extending endlessly into the future without limitations of time and space. The intellect, furthermore, apprehends this endless existence as a supremely valuable and desirable 'good.' The human will, then, following the lead of the intellect, naturally desires this endless existence, because it is the nature of the will to desire what the intellect proposes to it as a 'good' eminently suited to man's being and life. This desire for endless existence, therefore, flows from the very nature of man; it is a *natural desire,* the result of man's rational constitution. Such a natural desire cannot be futile, because God does not create a futile thing; but it would be futile, if it were incapable of realization.

Hence, this desire for endless existence is capable of realization and will be realized.

Another important point. Man has a *craving for perfect happiness.* This craving is universal and irresistible. It is *universal.* The craving for perfect happiness is the root of all man's striving; it underlies all the tendencies and urges of sensuous and rational appetency. It is at the bottom of the desire for power, for wealth, for honor, for pleasure, for comfort, for achievement, for sex love, for all the efforts expended in domestic and civil society. Art and science, industry and commerce, international rivalry and treaties, war and peace, morality and religion — all are inextricably tied up with man's insatiable craving for happiness. It begins with the infant's cry for food, endures through the years of youth and mature age, and flickers in the centenarian's feeble clutch at the thinning thread of life. Wherever man goes and whatever he does, everything in his being is an expression of this craving. And this craving for happiness is *irresistible.* It is not a matter of free choice on the part of man's free will. The will *must* desire what is proposed by the intellect as a perfect 'good,' and perfect happiness is such a 'good.' To strive for the realization of perfect happiness is simply the dictate of the *nature* of rational appetency. No human person can rid himself of this craving. It is only with a 'good' of limited value that man has freedom of choice; in its striving for perfect happiness the will is determined by the law of inexorable necessity. Deliberate violation of the moral law and blasphemous disrespect toward God may seem in opposition to this principle; nevertheless, a person exhibiting such conduct prizes his own will more than that of the Supreme Being and thinks he can find happiness in this kind of self-assertion and pride, notwithstanding the punishment which may follow. Even the act of suicide of a frustrated person is nothing else than an attempted escape from misery for the sake of a negative happiness in death and in possible extinction. The universality and irresistibility of man's craving for perfect happiness can only be explained on the supposition that it is a part of man's nature.

Such a *natural* craving, universal and irresistible in character, demands that the perfect happiness, toward which it is directed, *exist and be attainable;* and this happiness must be of *endless* duration. Why? For various reasons.

Contrary to the contentions of materialists and extreme mechanists, we live in a *rational teleological world.* This world is a world of *order,* not of irrational chance. Even the atom is a miniature world of orderly arrangement. The biological sciences, in particular, disclose more and more the marvelous reciprocal relationship which exists between organic structure and function and between the organism and its environment. When a biologist discovers an organ in a living being of any kind, it is a foregone conclusion that this organ has a definite function to perform in the cycle of the organism's life. He is so certain of this fact that he sets himself the task to find out the purpose and object of this function and the conditions under which it operates. If he discovers a 'rudimentary organ,' which now seems useless, he immediately draws the conclusion that this rudimentary organ either had a specific function in the past history of the organism or that it is in the evolutionary stage of becoming a useful organ in the future. He never judges such an organ to be an accidental, useless excrescence on the organic body. In fact, the existence of rudimentary organs is one of the main arguments used as proof for the theory of evolution.

Applying this principle of universal teleology or purposiveness to man's desire for endless existence and craving for perfect happiness, it is obvious that man must be *able to attain* endless existence and perfect happiness. Should man, the highest and noblest creature in the universe, alone be frustrated in his nature? If the digestive apparatus has the natural aptitude to assimilate food and actually does assimilate it, and if the nervous system has the natural aptitude to receive sense impressions and does actually receive them, then the human soul, since it has the natural aptitude for endless existence and perfect happiness, must be capable of actually attaining immortality and perfect happiness. Otherwise the constitution of his nature would be meaningless, and the natural tendencies of his innermost being would be purposeless. It is contrary to reason to suppose that the universal purposiveness of the world would reach its highest peak in man and then suddenly stop and end in a contradiction.

Again, God is the *Creator of all beings* through an act either of direct or derivative creation. He gave to each being its specific nature with all its powers and tendencies. Since God is infinitely *wise,* He would not have given man a soul which is naturally indestructible and therefore immortal, without making it also possible for his soul actually to be immortal. Nor would He have placed in the soul of man the irresistible craving for perfect happiness, if He never intended to place this perfect happiness within his grasp. God is also infinitely *just;* but it does not seem consonant with infinite justice to give man a rational nature which is filled with an unquenchable desire for endless existence which will never be fulfilled and with an irresistible craving for perfect happiness which can never be attained. God's wisdom and justice, therefore, demand immortality for the human soul.

Finally, the very *concept of perfect happiness,* which man craves with every fiber of his being, demands immortality. Perfect happiness involves the complete realization and satisfaction of the natural tendencies of man's spiritual soul after death. Now, if this happiness were not endless in duration, one of *three possibilities* would of necessity occur. Either the soul, while living its new life after death, would be aware of the eventual termination of its happiness; or it would be unaware of its termination, in such a manner that its ignorance is invincible; or, its ignorance would not be invincible, so that it could arrive at a knowledge of the actual or probable termination of its happiness. In the first case, there could be no perfect happiness; the mere fact of being aware of its termination would haunt the soul during every moment of its existence, and so its happiness would never be perfect, because it knows it will lose it some time. In the second case, this invincible ignorance would be an evil which precludes perfect happiness; besides, such an ignorance could only prevail under the unthinkable supposition that God would deliberately blind the soul to its real condition and permanently deceive it. In the third case, knowledge or doubt as to the actual or possible termination of its happiness would, as in the first case, destroy perfect happiness from the very beginning of its knowledge or doubt. Hence, the happiness of the soul in its life after death, in order to be perfect, would have to be endless in duration, or there is no possibility of perfect happiness at all. And yet, as we have shown, perfect happiness must not only be possible but actual. Consequently, this happiness must be endless in duration, and the soul must be able to enjoy it endlessly, knowing that it is endless. In other words, the soul is *immortal*.

The argument based on perfect happiness applies only to those who have followed the moral law and have died in the friendship and love of God, because they alone merit the eternal reward of perfect happiness. Whether those who have flouted the moral law and have died in wickedness should suffer an immortal life of punishment, is, viewed from a purely philosophical standpoint, not so clear. They certainly do not deserve eventual perfect happiness, because they have voluntarily separated themselves from the Author of perfect happiness. Since their death in wickedness is of their own choosing, it would be *reasonable* to conclude that God will leave them eternally in this state of wickedness and consequent punishment.

Some thinkers advance the doctrine of *metempsychosis*. Metempsychosis, or reincarnation, is the teaching that human souls at death transmigrate into another body or succession of bodies, whether of a brute or a man, for the purpose of purification or gradual perfection. If such were the truth, souls should remember the experiences of their former incarnation. The assertions of a few persons notwithstanding, man is not conscious that his soul has ever transmigrated from one body to another. Metempsychosis contains this grain of truth that the wicked must suffer punishment in the life to come; but the doctrine itself is without a shred of proof.

In as much as the soul of the wicked is naturally indestructible and immortal, the same as the soul of the just, reason is justified in assuming that it will also lead an immortal life, but in eternal separation from God. The thought is terrifying indeed. We must, however, bear in mind that God gives all men the same nature, with the same fundamental powers and tendencies, with the same calling for endless perfect happiness, and with the same opportunities to work out their destiny. The *destiny of all man,* as intended by the Creator, is *immortality with perfect happiness.* If the just fulfill this intended destiny, it is because, through free choice, they loved God and observed His moral law; if the unjust fail to fulfill this intended destiny, it is because, also through free choice, they ignored God and deliberately violated His moral law. Whatever befalls them in the life to come, the blame is theirs and theirs only. So much is certain: God cannot be ignored or offended with impunity. The sanctions of the moral law would become ineffective, if man could persistently disregard the moral law and yet attain perfect happiness or annihilation after a while.

We must, therefore, conclude that the soul after the death of the organism will enter upon an endless life. The soul of man, then, is truly immortal.

The Restoration of Man

What about the human body (matter)? Should not the *whole man* (body and soul, matter and form) be the bearer of immortal life in the world to come? Why should it be necessary for man to pass through the grim tragedy of death before entering upon immortal life? *Why death* at all? Is not the soul alone an incomplete substance in the new life, so that it is a sort of truncated being deprived of its natural counterpart, and would not this condition entail an *incomplete happiness,* at least on the part of the just who have fulfilled their natural destiny? These are pertinent questions.

We will consider the last question first. It is true that the soul alone is an incomplete substance and that the body is its natural counterpart. *Here on earth* the soul is destined to be the substantial form and animating principle of the body. The body, united substantially with the soul into one nature, has the natural purpose of being the *bridge of communication* between the spirit of man and the physical world; it supplies the sensory materials necessary for the formation of intellectual knowledge. As such, therefore, it acts very much in the nature of an 'instrument' for the spiritual soul. It could very well be that the body is no longer required in the new life of the soul's immortality. If this is the correct view, the soul would have *two forms of natural existence,* one with the body in its earthly life and the other without the body in its immortal life after death. In that case, the soul would not be a truncated being after death, nor would its happiness be incomplete. This solution, however, does not seem to be rationally satisfying. After all, man is by nature an *organism* of which the body is an integral substantial part. But then again, why death at all? Philosophy stands here before an apparent contradiction or at least before a mystery.

Christian faith gives a solution. Mankind in its present situation is a *fallen race.* It has sinned, and sin has tainted man's nature. Man's intellect is darkened, his will is weakened, and the flesh is in rebellion against the spirit; the result is ignorance in spiritual matters, difficulty in observing the moral law, and proclivity toward sensual excesses. And 'the wages of sin is death.' Even the just, in the vast majority of instances, shrink from death. There should have been no death; death and organic dissolution is a punishment for sin. The human organism, however, will eventually be restored, for there will be a *resurrection of the body,* and the body will again be *reunited to the soul.* The body had its share in the performance of virtue and in the practice of vice, so it also shall share in the happiness of the just and in the misery of the wicked in the life to come. Philosophy, basing its conclusion on the findings of reason alone, can neither prove nor disprove this doctrine. The doctrine, however, explains many things in the life of the individual and in the history of the human race which are very obscure and puzzling. As for the final restoration of the total man in the resurrection of the body some time after death, it is in eminent accord with the *logic of nature and reason.* Since the soul is by its very nature the substantial form or entelechy of the body, it has the natural exigency to be united to the matter of which it is intended to be the form. Hence, a final restoration of 'the whole man' is at least probable. We must, from the standpoint of philosophy and psychology, leave it rest at that.

And so we come to the end.

Psychology is the philosophical study of life of the whole man.

Man's body consists of physical elements, but these elements are compounded together into a living being, an *organism.* This organism consists of various types of structures. Some of these structures perform functions relating to nutrition and reproduction; man is a 'vegetant' being. Other structures perform functions relating to sensory perception; man is a 'sentient' being. Over and above these functions, man has the 'rational' activities of intellect and free will. Man is *a single vegetant-sentient-rational substance,* an integral organism, a unitary nature. Vital activity demands a vital principle, an animating substantial form, a soul. Man, therefore, is a single substance composed of matter and form, *body* and *soul.* This soul of man is spiritual and simple and comes into existence through an act of divine creation. The whole man belongs to the physical, the social, the religious, and the moral order — a veritable microcosm. Man must die, but his soul is created for immortality.

Man has a *glorious destiny.* God did not make man to live for a few years on this spinning planet and then doom him to death and extinction. The life on this earth is only a period of probation. Here man must become worthy of the perfect happiness which is intended for him in the endless existence of an immortal life. C. P. Bruehl has expressed this thought beautifully: "On account of the unlimited reach of his rational power, the object to give man perfect happiness must itself be limitless. It must be the fullness of truth, goodness, beauty, and every conceivable perfection. This is God, who is the plenitude of being. In Him unalloyed happiness can be found. It will be found in communion and fellowship with the Supreme Being, who is not impersonal but a personal Self and will be to us Father and Friend. With Him and all the good, man will live in a blessed community in which eternal harmony prevails and into which no disturbing shadow can fall, because it is centered on Him who is the source of all good, infinite, changeless, and everlasting. Perfect happiness will be ours when God, for whom we are made, becomes for us all in all."[3]

Summary of Chapter XXIII

God gave a purpose to man's being; the fulfillment of that purpose is *man's destiny.*

1. *The Rhythm of Growth.* Biologically and mentally, man passes through a number of *natural periods* in his development: prenatal life and childhood; adolescence; middle age; gradual decline after about forty-five or fifty years; the last phase, old age, after about sixty years until death. Mental maturity is slower than biological maturity.

2. *Man and the World.* The earth is man's home and workshop. Geographical conditions exert a profound influence on man's body and mind. Man is the pivotal point, the representative, the interpreter, and the crown of the universe.

3. *Man and Other Minds.* Man contacts other minds through the medium of language.

4. *Man and Society.* Man is an integral member of the community of men, of *society.* He has the natural *aptitude, propensity, and need* for a permanent union and companionship with his fellowmen in three great natural societies: domestic society, civil society, and religious society.

5. *Man and Domestic Society.* The fountainhead of social

[3] *This Way Happiness* (Bruce, 1941), p. 43.

life is marriage. Marriage develops into the *family* which is the basic unit of human society.

6. *Man and Civil Society.* The *state* is the extension of the family. The essential purpose of the state is the common weal of all individuals, families, and communities.

7. *Man and Religious Society.* Man is also by nature a *religious* being, because he owes everything he is and has to his Creator. As an individual and as a member of society, he has the obligation of worship.

8. *Man and Morality.* Human conduct is characterized by the quality of *right* and *wrong*. Man has the obligation to do what is good and avoid what is wrong. Morality is a *law* imposed on man by his own *rational nature* as its proximate ground and in the *will of God* as its ultimate ground. *Conscience* is an act of reason which interprets the moral law and demands obedience to the law. The end and goal of the moral law for the individual is the perfection of the 'whole man,' and this perfection entails *happiness*. In order that the moral law be effective, God must have attached *sanctions* to it, i.e., reward and punishment.

9. *Survival After Death.* Death may occur either through dissolution or annihilation. Man is not annihilated in death, because the corpse with its material elements remains after death. Does the *soul* survive the death of the human organism?

Survival is *possible*. In virtue of its essence, the soul is not subject to dissolution, because it is a *spiritual* and *simple* substance. It need not pass out of existence in virtue of its *relation to the body,* because it is intrinsically independent of matter.

Survival is *certain*. It has been a *universal conviction* of mankind that the soul survives the death of the body; such a conviction must be a necessary truth, the natural expression of man's rational intellect. This conviction is based on the *moral nature* of man. The *sanctions* of the moral law do not find their fulfillment in this life; hence, the moral sanctions must be applied in a life after death. Survival is necessary, particularly in the case where man gives his life in the performance of duty. God, who is infinitely just, would not permit such devotion to go unrewarded; there must, therefore, be a life for the soul after the death of the organism. Besides, the *essence* of a thing bespeaks its *purpose* of existence. Since the soul was made by God as naturally indestructible, it must live after death.

10. *Spiritism and Survival.* Spiritism makes the claim to have furnished empirical proof of the continued existence of the human soul after death. There are two main objections against this claim. For one thing, the *fraud* and *trickery* which permeates spiritistic practices makes the evidence doubtful. Furthermore, all attempts to establish *spirit identity* have ended in failure.

11. *Immortality of the Soul.* Man has the *natural desire* for an endless duration of life, because the intellect apprehends 'existence as such' which is *pure duration.* Such a natural desire cannot be futile. Man also has a *craving for perfect happiness,* and this craving is universal and irresistible; as such it is the dictate of the nature of rational appetency, and perfect happiness must therefore exist and be attainable. Perfect happiness, however, demands immortality.

The world is a rational, *teleological* world in which every natural power has its proper function. Man's natural desire for endless existence and perfect happiness must, therefore, be capable of fulfillment. God is infinitely *wise* and *just;* hence, He would not implant in man's nature such a desire and craving, if He did not intend that it should be fulfilled. The very *concept* of perfect happiness demands immortality, because it would not be 'perfect' if it were not endless in duration. Consequently, the soul of man is immortal.

12. *The Restoration of Man.* It is in eminent accord with the logic of nature and reason that there will be a *resurrection* of the body, so that the 'whole man' will eventually be restored.

Readings

Bruehl, Charles P., *This Way Happiness.* — Maher, M., *Psychology,* Ch. XXIV. — Brennan, R. E., *General Psychology,* pp. 483–485. — Fell, G., *The Immortality of the Human Soul.*

GLOSSARY

Note: In the case of qualified words, look for the word or noun qualified. For example: in looking for *Scientific Psychology,* see *Psychology, Scientific.*

Abiogenesis. The origination of life from nonliving matter, through forces which are indigenous to matter; spontaneous generation.

Abstraction. The intellectual process in which, through an act of selective attention, we leave out of consideration one or more aspects of a complex total object so as to attend to some other aspect or aspects of this object.

Abstraction, Generalizing. That form of abstraction in which we separate mentally, through an act of selective attention, items which are common to a number of individual objects from those items in which these objects differ and then arrange the objects having the common items into a class as a unit.

Abstraction, Isolating. That form of abstraction in which we mentally separate, through selective attention, a particular feature from the subject in which it exists.

Action, Reflex. An act performed automatically and involuntarily, as a response to a stimulus, by a partial mechanism of the nervous system.

Actuality, Theory of. The theory that the mind is the sum-total of psychical events, there being no permanent mind or Ego as the carrier of these mental states.

Afterimages. Sensations occurring after the stimuli causing them have ceased.

Anabolism. The synthesis of living protoplasm by which nutritive materials are absorbed and changed into the living substance of the cell.

Animism, Vitalistic. The vitalistic, holistic theory which maintains that every organism consists of two ultimate constitutive substantial principles, matter and the vital principle (soul), which are united into a complete substance and nature.

Annihilation. The reduction of the total being to complete nothingness.

ANTI-CONSOLIDATION. The theory of retroactive inhibition which maintains that intense mental activity of any kind, following a period of learning, hinders the original memory traces from going through their normal phase of consolidation.

APPETENCY. The tendency of one thing toward another.

APPETENCY, CONCUPISCIBLE. The propensity to enjoy a good.

APPETENCY, IRASCIBLE. The propensity to fight an evil.

APPETENCY, RATIONAL. The will.

APPETENCY, SENSUOUS. The power in virtue of which a sentient being tends toward a consciously apprehended sensuous good and away from a consciously apprehended sensuous evil.

ASSIMILATION. *See* Anabolism.

ASSOCIATION. The reproduction of related phantasms.

ASSOCIATION, LAWS OF. The principles which condition the reproduction of a related set of phantasms.

ASSOCIATIONISM. The theory that simple ideas are derived from the senses and that mental development proceeds entirely and exclusively through the combination of sensory elements according to the Laws of Association.

ATTENTION: The direction of the cognitive process toward an object, an activity, or a thought.

AUTOMATISM, AMBULATORY. *See* Fugue, Amnestic.

BEHAVIORISM. The doctrine that psychology should restrict itself exclusively to observations and concepts relating to behavior.

CEREBRUM. The large brain which is the final enlargement and amplification of the spinal cord and brain stem.

CLAIRVOYANCE. The extra-sensory perception of objective events.

COCONSCIOUS. Any actual subconscious idea or thought process unknown to the human subject in his ordinary waking state.

COCONSCIOUSNESS. That form of consciousness which is characterized by any actual subconscious idea or thought process unknown to the human subject in his ordinary waking state.

COLOR BLINDNESS. The partial or total inability to distinguish or recognize chromatic colors.

COLOR CONTRAST. The difference in the appearance of colors brought about by the stimulation of adjacent sets of rods and cones in the retina.

CONSCIOUSNESS. A state of the mind in which we are aware of our experiences.

CONSCIOUSNESS, SENSORY. The awareness of sensations and of the sense qualities present in the sensations.

Consciousness, Subliminal. *See* Subsconsciousness.

Consciousness, Supraliminal. Normal waking consciousness. *See* Consciousness.

Control, Voluntary. The control which the will exercises over the powers and actions of the human organism.

Creation, Derivative. *See* Creation, Mediate.

Creation, Direct. The production of a new reality in its total being from nothingness, so that no pre-existing entity contributes anything at all to the making of the new reality except the Creator and His creative power.

Creation, Mediate. The spontaneous emergence of life from non-living matter in virtue of an inherent tendency placed in matter from the beginning by the Creator.

Criticism, Transcendental. The theory of Kant and his followers that the universality and necessity of scientific knowledge is derived from certain a priori forms innate to the human mind.

Deduction. The legitimate inference from the more general to the less general, from a law or principle to a particular instance falling under the law or principle.

Delusion. A mental disorder which manifests itself in a misinterpretation of the general state of affairs, characterized by a false belief or judgment regarding the self.

Depersonalization. An abnormal state of consciousness in which a person experiences a profound change in his own personality, so that his own actions, thoughts, and emotions appear to be those of an automaton or to belong to a totally different person.

Derealization. An abnormal state of consciousness in which a person suffers from a disturbance of perception, so that the objects of the world have a sensory appearance quite different from that in his normal experience.

Desire. The longing aroused by the conscious representation of an absent good.

Determinism. In the problem of free will, the doctrine that the will is determined by the antecedent psychical and physical conditions and causes to act as it does.

Deuteranopia. Green blindness.

Dichromatism. Partial color blindness.

Disassimilation. *See* Katabolism.

Dissociation. The splitting of the consciousness into disunited parts.

Double-Aspect Theory. The theory that the physical and the psychical are merely two aspects of one and the same ultimate reality.

ECTOPLASM. A hypothetical psychic substance, derived from the body of the medium and supposedly used by spirits in the phenomena of materialization.

EGO, EMPIRICAL. The self or Ego as observed at any present moment in a here-and-now experience.

EGO, HISTORICAL. The self or Ego of an individual as he perceives it through memory of his life's experiences from the present down through the past.

EGO, METAPHYSICAL. The self or Ego considered in its constitution and nature.

EIDETIC. A person capable of producing eidetic imagery. *See* Imagery, Eidetic.

EIDETIKER. *See* Eidetic.

ELAN VITAL. Original life force.

EMERGENCE, ABSOLUTE. *See* Abiogenesis.

EMERGENCE, RELATIVE. *See* Creation, Mediate.

EMERGENCE, RESTRICTED. *See* Creation, Mediate.

EMOTION. An affective mental state of the animal organism, following the cognition of an object or situation, characterized by strong feeling, by an impulse to action, and by physiological changes in bodily function.

EMPIRICISM. In the problem of the perception of visual space, it is the theory which claims that our perceptions of space are entirely and exclusively a matter of experiential education; opposed to 'nativism.'

EMPIRICISM. The doctrine that all human knowledge is derived from the data of particular states of consciousness, so that experience is the exclusive source and criterion of all knowledge.

ENTELECHY. In Driesch's vitalistic holism, the formative agent, non-spatial and supra-material, which is responsible for the structural organization of matter in the organism; it is an operational principle. In Aristotle's vitalistic holism, it is the substantial form or soul which unites with primary matter to constitute the unitary substance of the organic body; it is primarily an entitative principle.

EPIPHENOMENALISM. The theory that consciousness is an accompaniment or by-product of neural processes, determined by them but exerting no influence upon them, so that it is but an 'epiphenomenon' of matter, matter being the real phenomenon.

EVIL. The unsuitability of something for a natural tendency or appetency; the privation of a required good.

EVOLUTION, EMERGENT. The theory that nature is the product of evolution in such a manner that entirely new and unpredictable properties originate through synthesis and thereby form new and higher levels of reality.

EVOLUTION, ORGANIC. The theory according to which the various species and types of animals and plants derive their origin, not through distinct and separate creative acts of God, but through development from other pre-existing species and types, all differences being accounted for by modifications acquired in successive generations according to purely natural laws.

EVOLUTION, PURPOSIVE. The doctrine that the Supreme Intelligence (God) endowed nature with a purpose and with the necessary principles of action to realize this purpose through evolution.

FEELING. An elementary affective state characterized by pleasantness or unpleasantness.

FIXITY. THEORY OF. *See* Permanence, Theory of.

FORM, SUBSTANTIAL. The determining principle which, by uniting with the matter which it actuates, constitutes a complete substance of a definite species.

FREE WILL. The ability of the will, all conditions for action being present, to decide whether to act or not act and whether to act in this manner or in that manner.

FREEDOM. In the widest sense, the absence of external coercion or restraint which hinders an appetency from expressing itself in external action; in the strict sense, the absence of intrinsic necessity or determination in the performance of an act.

FREEDOM OF CHOICE. *See* Freedom of Indifference.

FREEDOM OF CONTRADICTION. *See* Freedom of Exercise.

FREEDOM OF CONTRARIETY. The freedom of the will to choose between a moral good and a moral evil.

FREEDOM OF EXERCISE. The freedom of the will between acting and not acting; freedom of contradiction.

FREEDOM OF INDIFFERENCE. The freedom of the will in so far as it is subjectively indifferent in the presence of conflicting motives; freedom of choice.

FREEDOM OF SPECIFICATION. The freedom of the will to choose between one object and another object and therefore also between one act of the will and another act of the will.

FUGUE, AMNESTIC. An abnormal state of consciousness consisting in a somewhat protracted condition characterized by wandering and other abnormal actions, followed by considerable loss of memory concerning this particular period.

FUNCTIONALISM. The doctrine which considers the mental processes as the functions of the organism in its adaptation to, and control of, environment.

GAMETE. Sex or germ cell; spermatozoon and ovum.

GENERATION, SPONTANEOUS. *See* Abiogenesis.

GENERATIONISM. *See* Traducianism.

GESTALT. Form, shape, configuration; as used in psychology, it is the theory that there are wholes, the behavior of which is not determined by that of their individual elements, but where the part-processes are themselves determined by the intrinsic nature of the whole.

GESTALTISM. The psychological theory of Gestalt. *See* Gestalt.

GOOD. That which is suitable in some manner for the striving subject.

GOOD, ABSOLUTE. Anything suitable to a being itself, irrespective of other beings.

GOOD, APPARENT. Something which is judged to be good for a being, but which actually is not good for it.

GOOD, DELECTABLE. A relative good which gives pleasure and enjoyment to another.

GOOD, DISINTERESTED. Any good considered merely as giving perfection, irrespective of any pleasure derived through its acquisition or from its possession.

GOOD, MORAL. A thing or act which has everything demanded of it by the moral law.

GOOD, OBJECTIVE. Anything that is a good in itself.

GOOD, ONTOLOGICAL. What is good in its very entity or reality.

GOOD, PHYSICAL. A good that satisfies the demand of the nature of a being.

GOOD, REAL. Something which is judged to be a good for a being, and which actually is good for that particular being.

GOOD, RELATIVE. Anything suitable to another being.

GOOD, SUBJECTIVE. The actual possession of an objective good.

GOOD, USEFUL. A relative good which is desired as a means to acquire perfection or pleasure.

GOODNESS. The suitability of a thing to a natural tendency or appetency.

HALLUCINATION. An abnormal mental state in which a person has subjective perceptual experiences which lack relevant stimuli.

HEARING. The sense by which the vibrations of certain media acting upon the ear become known as sounds.

HOLISM. The 'totality-theory' which considers the organic body to be primarily an organized unit, an integrated whole, and this unit or whole is more than the mere addition and summation of its constituent parts.

HYLOMORPHISM, ARISTOTELIAN-SCHOLASTIC. The theory that the unitary substance of the organic body is composed ultimately of two incomplete substances or substantial part-principles, namely, primordial matter and the vital principle (substantial form, soul).

Hylozoism. The theory that all atoms of matter originally possess life.

Hypnosis. A trance-like nervous condition resembling sleep, induced by the suggestions and (or) manipulations of the operator ('hypnotist'), the hypnotized subject remaining in mental communication ('rapport') with the operator and responsive to his suggestions.

Hypnotism. *See* Hypnosis.

Idea. The intellectual representation of a thing.

Idealism. In general, the doctrine which holds that the being of things is conditioned by their being known; consciousness is constitutive of its objects; the being of sensible things is simply their being sensed, and their true characters are their sensed characters; the world we know is the world of our perceptual content; the mind cannot transcend its own internal, conscious states.

Identity-Theory. The theory that the physical and the psychical are at bottom identical realities.

Ideogeny. The formation or genesis of ideas.

Image, Expressed Intelligible. The essential elements of a thing, abstracted from the phantasm by the agent intellect, gathered together by the potential intellect into a definition or abstract representation; the 'idea' or 'concept' of a thing.

Image, Expressed Sensible. The completed sensory cognitional image representing the sensed thing in the sentient subject; phantasm, formed by the synthetic sense.

Image, Formal Intelligible. *See* Image, Expressed Intelligible.

Image, Formal Sensible. *See* Image, Expressed Sensible.

Image, Impressed Intelligible. The cognitional image of a thing, abstracted from the phantasm by the agent intellect, which is the vital determination of the intellect to the act of understanding, to the intellectual perception of the quiddity of the thing represented in the phantasm.

Image, Impressed Sensible. In the genesis of ideas, the sensation arousing the synthetic sense into action by its presence; the rudimentary cognitional image of the sensations.

Imagery, Eidetic. Images of unusual clarity and vividness which are faithful reproductions of the original sensory experiences.

Imagination. The power to form mental images or phantasms of perceived objects, together with the ability to reproduce these images or phantasms even in the absence of the perceived objects.

Imagination, Conservatory. The imagination in so far as it

conserves the images or phantasms of previous sensations and perceptions.

IMAGINATION, CONSTRUCTIVE. The imagination, in so far as it has the power to unite phantasms which, in this particular combination, have never been experienced by the subject.

IMAGINATION, REPRODUCTIVE. The imagination, in so far as it has the power of forming phantasms of objects and events which have been previously perceived.

IMMATERIALITY. *See* Spirituality.

IMMORTALITY. Endless duration of life.

INDETERMINISM. *See* Libertarianism.

INDUCTION. The legitimate inference of universal laws from individual cases.

INFERENCE. A reasoning process in which, from truths known, we conclude to a truth previously unknown.

INHIBITION, RETROACTIVE. The tendency of mental activity to impair the recall of memorized material, if this activity is placed between the time of learning and the time of recall.

INNATISM. As a theory of the nature of instinct, the doctrine that the intrinsic factors of instinct are inherited and therefore innate; not learned, at least not fundamentally and ultimately, by experience.

INSTINCT. An innate disposition which determines the organism to perceive (to pay attention to) any object of a certain class, and to experience in its presence a certain emotional excitement and an impulse to action which find expression in a specific mode of behavior in relation to that object.

INTELLECT, AGENT. The power or capability which actively modifies itself so as to represent within itself in an abstract manner what is concretely represented in the phantasm.

INTELLECT, POTENTIAL. The power or capacity to express the essence of the represented thing in an 'idea' or 'concept.'

INTELLECTION. Rational cognition.

INTELLIGENCE, ANIMAL. The capacity to improve upon native tendency in the light of past experience.

INTERFERENCE, OR TRANSFER. The theory of retroactive inhibition which maintains that the original and interpolated activities intermingle, so that the two sets of memory traces become a single mixed set with subsequent confusion of recall results, or that the traces of the original material are used with the traces of the interpolated material and become modified thereby.

INTROSPECTION. The method of studying mental phenomena by means of the internal observation of experience on the part of the individual person.

IRRITABILITY. The property of living matter of responding to changes in the environment (such changes are called 'stimuli') by change in shape, production or cessation of movement, or other activities of their organs or parts.

JUDGMENT. The pronouncement of agreement or disagreement between two ideas.

KARYOKINESIS. *See* Mitosis.

KATABOLISM. The destruction of protoplasmic material in the course of vital processes.

LIBERTARIANISM. In the problem of free will, the doctrine that the will, no matter what the strength of the conflicting motives or the nature of the antecedent external and internal conditions may be, is not determined to act by necessity.

LIBIDO. In psychoanalysis, the instinct of Eros or sexuality.

LIFE. Immanent action.

MAGNETISM, ANIMAL. An obsolete name for hypnosis. *See* Hypnosis.

MATERIALISM. In general, the doctrine which finds the ultimate solution of all phenomena, physical and psychical, in the nature and activity of universal matter or force.

MATTER, PRIMARY. An incomplete corporeal substance, undetermined but determinable, capable of receiving any kind of substantial form.

MATURATION DIVISION. The cell division characteristic of gametes, preparatory to fertilization.

MECHANISM, BIOLOGICAL. Mechanism, i.e., atomism, as applied to organic nature.

MEMORY. The power to recall past objects and states of consciousness and recognize them as having been present in former experiences.

MENTALISM. The theory that nothing exists but the spiritual mind.

MERISM. The doctrine that the organic body is nothing more than an aggregate resulting from the additive summation of cells, chromosomes, and genes; the latter, in turn, are mere aggregates of molecules, atoms, electrons, etc.

MESMERISM. *See* Hypnosis.

METABOLISM. The processes in plant and animal cells involved in the construction and destruction of living tissue during the course of the activities of life.

METEMPSYCHOSIS. The teaching that human souls at death transmigrate into another body or succession of bodies.

MICROMERISM. *See* Merism.

MIND. The conscious knowing subject or the conscious knowing part of the subject.

MIND-DUST THEORY. The theory that an atom of consciousness or mind is attached to every atom of matter in the universe, both developing together in the evolution of beings.

MITOSIS. The biological process of cell division.

MONADISM. The theory that all beings consist ultimately of monads.

MONISM. The doctrine which seeks to deduce all the varied phenomena of both the physical and spiritual worlds from a single principle which is in a continuous state of evolution; specifically, the metaphysical doctrine which holds that there is but one substance, either mind (idealism), or matter (materialism), or a neutral substance that is neither mind nor matter but is the substantial ground of both.

MONOCHROMATISM. Total color blindness.

MOTIVATION. The arousal of the will from a state of inaction into a state of action.

MOTIVE. An appreciated value realizable through an act of volition.

NATIVISM. In the problem of the perception of visual space, it is the theory which claims that our perceptions of space are the result of a native or constitutional property of vision itself, independent of learning and interpretation; opposed to 'empiricism.'

NECESSITARIANISM. *See* Determinism.

NEOVITALISM. The vitalistic theory of organic bodies which maintains that the vital energies are subject to the general law of the conservation of energy.

NERVE SYSTEM, AUTONOMIC. That part of the peripheral nervous system regulating responses not directly under voluntary control.

NERVES, AFFERENT. Sensory nerves.

NERVES, EFFERENT. Motor nerves.

NEURON. A nerve cell, with all its processes.

NEUROSIS. A functional mental disorder.

OCCASIONALISM. The theory that God, on the occasion of certain conditions, produces activity in His creatures, although the creatures, to all appearances, produce this activity themselves.

ONTOLOGISM. The theory that God and the divine Ideas are the primary object of the human intellect, and the first act of the intellect is the intuition of God.

ORGANICISM. The theory of holism. *See* Holism.

ORGANISM. Biologically, an individual constituted to carry on the activities of life by means of parts or organs more or less separate in function but mutually dependent. Considered philosophically, a substance consisting of matter animated by a vital principle.

Organization. Biologically, the characteristic of living bodies possessing organs or structural parts distinct from one another, each of which has a specific function to perform.

Pan-Egoism. The doctrine which identifies all reality with the universal consciousness or Ego.

Pan-Phenomenalism. The doctrine which holds that the human mind can know nothing but the phenomena or appearances of things.

Pan-Psychism. The theory that everything existing is fundamentally psychic or mental in nature.

Pantheism. The theory that God is everything that exists.

Parallelism, Psycho-physical. The doctrine which holds that the psychical and physical are but a manifold of interrelated occurrences, running parallel to one another without mutual influence.

Parapsychology. The psychology of extranormal phenomena, for instance, of extra-sensory perception.

Perception. The cognizing of the object which produces sensation.

Perception, Extra-sensory. A perception obtained through channels other than those of the known senses.

Permanence, Theory of. The theory which maintains the stability of organic species, acknowledging only minor variations within the framework of the specific type; opposed to organic evolution of species.

Person. An individual, complete, subsistent, rational (intellectual) substance.

Personality, Split. An abnormal condition of mental dissociation in which the same human mind manifests alternatingly two or more very different characters or personalities.

Phase, Refractory. The period of recuperation of an activated nerve during which it resists stimulation.

Presence, Definitive. As applied to the soul, it is the presence of the soul in the body in virtue of which the soul exercises its life-giving power ubiquitously in the whole body and in every living part of it.

Protanopia. Red blindness.

Psychiatry. That branch of medical science which treats of mental disorders.

Psychoanalysis. A method devised and developed by Sigmund Freud for the examination of the contents and mechanisms of an individual's mind, for the purpose of treating and curing mental disorders.

Psychology. Literally, the science of the soul. Some define it as the science of the mind; or, as the science of consciousness or of the conscious states; or, as the philosophy of organic life; or, as the philosophy of the nature of man.

PSYCHOLOGY, EMPIRICAL. *See* Psychology, Scientific.

PSYCHOLOGY, EXPERIMENTAL. *See* Psychology, Scientific.

PSYCHOLOGY, PHILOSOPHICAL. The philosophic science of the life of the human organism.

PSYCHOLOGY, RATIONAL. *See* Psychology, Philosophical.

PSYCHOLOGY, SCIENTIFIC. A department of knowledge which seeks to discover all facts pertinent to mental phenomena by means of observation and experiment, to describe these facts in their proper order, and to establish the general laws according to which these facts occur.

PSYCHOMETRY. Clairvoyant knowledge of facts concerning an object or its possessor through contact with, or proximity to, the object.

PSYCHO-PHYSICS. That branch of psychology which studies the relations between mental and physical processes by investigating the response to stimuli and the perception of physical magnitudes.

PSYCHO-VITALISM. The vitalistic theory of organic bodies which maintains that the vital forces existing in every type of organism are conscious, psychic factors.

RAPPORT. In hypnosis, a mental alertness in the hypnotized subject toward the suggestions given by the operator.

REASON. The power of the mind which perceives the truth and validity of derived ideas, judgments, and principles on the basis of indirect and mediate evidence.

REASON, PARTICULAR. *See* Sense, Cogitative.

RECALL. The mental reproduction of a former stimulus or experience.

RECEPTOR. A cell or group of cells which function in the reception of stimuli; a sense organ.

RECOGNITION. The apprehension of the sameness of two representations or perceptions, one present and one past. Remembrance.

REFLEX. *See* Action, Reflex.

REFLEX, CONDITIONED. The reflex response of a neural mechanism to a stimulus which has been substituted for the natural stimulus normally evoking this particular reflex action.

REFRACTORY PHASE. *See* Phase, Refractory.

REMEMBRANCE. *See* Recognition.

REMINISCENCE. The spontaneous and gradual improvement of memory with a subsequent higher score in recall, without a relearning or rehearsal of the memorized material.

REPRODUCTION. Biologically, the process by means of which cells produce new cells and plants and animals produce new plants and animals of the same kind.

Sanction. A reward given for the observance of a law and the punishment meted out for the violation of a law.

Self-consciousness. It is man's consciousness of his self or Ego as the subject and bearer of all the conditions and states affecting his being, particularly of consciousness itself.

Sensation. A conscious experience aroused by the stimulation of an organ of sense.

Sensationalism. The doctrine which assumes that all human knowledge originates solely in sensation and that all intellectual cognitions are ultimately nothing more than complex and elaborated products of sense impressions and their reproduced images.

Sense. A specialized mechanism or function by virtue of which an animal organism is receptive and responsive to a certain class of physical stimuli, resulting in knowledge of some sort.

Sense, Central. The mental power to consciously perceive, distinguish, and synthesize the objects and operations of the presently active external senses; synthetic sense.

Sense, Cogitative. Man's perception of the useful or harmful character of particular things not merely in a purely sensory fashion, but also by means of a collation of ideas. Particular reason.

Sense, Common. *See* Sense, Central.

Sense, Cutaneous. A sense located in the skin region. Pressure, pain, warmth, and cold are experienced by the cutaneous or skin senses. *See* Senses, Somethetic.

Sense, Equilibrium. *See* Sense, Static.

Sense, Estimative. The brute animal's sensory appreciation or estimation of the concrete usefulness or harmfulness of a perceived object with reference to the animal's organism or to the species.

Sense, Exteroceptive. A sense which is activated by stimuli originating outside the organism. The exteroceptive senses are sight, hearing, taste, smell, and the cutaneous senses of pain, pressure, cold, and warmth.

Sense, Interoceptive. A sense which is activated by stimuli originating within the viscera and within the vestibule of the internal ear. The interoceptive senses are the intraorganic visceral and static senses.

Sense, Kinesthetic. The sense which mediates sensations of the position and of the active and passive movements of the bodily members in relation to one another. *See* Senses, Somesthetic.

Sense, Labyrinthine. *See* Sense, Static.

Sense, Proprioceptive. A sense activated by stimuli originating within the organism by movement or tension in its own tissues; the kinesthetic sense.

Sense, Skin. *See* Sense, Cutaneous.

SENSE, STATIC. A sense, the end organs of which lie in the internal ear and are stimulated by the pull of gravity and by head movements. *See* Senses, Somesthetic.

SENSE, SYNTHETIC. *See* Sense, Central.

SENSE, TEMPERATURE. The sense or senses responding to stimuli with the sensation of warmth or cold. *See* Senses, Somesthetic.

SENSE, VESTIBULAR. *See* Sense, Static.

SENSE, VISCERAL. A sense which is activated by stimuli originating in the viscera. *See* Senses, Somesthetic.

SENSES, INTRAORGANIC. The somesthetic senses which are activated by stimuli originating within the organism. The kinesthetic, visceral, and static senses belong to this group. *See* Senses, Somesthetic.

SENSES, SOMESTHETIC. What is generally referred to as the sense of 'touch'; they comprise the intraorganic kinesthetic, visceral, and static senses, and also the cutaneous senses of pain, pressure, cold, and warmth.

SIGHT. The sense, whose end organ is the eye, which is responsive to the stimuli of radiant energy or light.

SIMPLICITY. That positive property in virtue of which the essence of a being is not composed of distinct and distinguishable parts or principles.

SMELL. The sense by which certain properties of bodies (called their smell, odor, or scent) become known through the stimulation of receptors responsive to chemical substances in a gaseous form or to minute particles which reach them normally from a distance and in low concentration.

SOCIETY. A permanent union of a number of persons in fellowship and co-operation for a common purpose of benefit to all.

SOMNAMBULISM. Sleepwalking; in hypnosis, the production of action on the part of the hypnotized subject through images derived from the suggestion of the operator.

SPECIES, EXPRESSED INTELLIGIBLE. *See* Image, Expressed Intelligible.

SPECIES, EXPRESSED SENSIBLE. *See* Image, Expressed Sensible.

SPECIES, IMPRESSED INTELLIGIBLE. *See* Image, Impressed Intelligible.

SPECIES, IMPRESSED SENSIBLE. *See* Image, Impressed Sensible.

SPIRITISM. The belief that departed spirits communicate with the living by means of physical and psychical phenomena, commonly manifested through a medium.

SPIRITUALITY. The property in virtue of which a being is neither composed of matter nor intrinsically dependent on matter; immateriality.

STRUCTURALISM. The theory that all thought processes can be reduced to sensations, so that the sensation is the 'structural unit or element' of everything occurring in consciousness.

Subconscious. Certain mental items and processes which are apparently of the same nature as the normally conscious items and processes, yet of which the subject is not aware in the waking state.

Subconsciousness. That part of consciousness which is, figuratively speaking, 'beneath the threshold' of the normal waking consciousness.

Suggestion, Post-hypnotic. A suggestion given during hypnosis, but to be carried out by the subject after hypnosis has been terminated.

Taste. The sense by which certain qualities (taste, savor, flavor) of soluble substances become known by contact with a particular set of epithelial end organs (taste buds) located mainly in the papillae of the tongue.

Telepathy. The extra-sensory perception of subjective events, i.e., the knowledge of objects or occurrences obtained from another mind in an extra-sensory manner.

Tendency, Determining. A postulated psychic force which, acting subconsciously, proceeds from a resolution and carries out the task to a correct conclusion, notwithstanding the fact that the former resolution is forgotten.

Thought, Imageless. The theory that an idea can occur without a perceptible image being present.

Touch, Sense of. *See* Senses, Somesthetic.

Traducianism. The theory which explains the origin of the individual human soul as the product of parental generation; generationism.

Transfer. A theory of retroactive inhibition. *See* Interference.

Trichromatism. The ability to perceive the three primary colors equally well.

Tritanopia. Blue-yellow blindness.

Tropism. The involuntary movement of an organism or any of its parts, involving turning or curvature and axial orientation, and induced either automatically or in response to one or more stimulating influences.

Unconsciousness. The absence of consciousness.

Understanding. The power of the mind which perceives the truth and validity of ideas and principles on the basis of direct and immediate evidence.

Unit, Kinetic. The neuro-muscular co-ordination of a number of nerves and muscles in an intricate series of part movements.

Value. That which is perfect or perfective.

Vision, Achromatic. Vision of neutral (achromatic) colors, namely, of white, black, and intermediate grays.

Vision, Chromatic. The vision of chromatic colors, namely, of the colors of the spectrum.

Vitalism. The theory which demands something distinctly vital in the organism, over and above the physico-chemical forces, in order to account for the structural and functional unity of the organism as a whole.

Vitalism, Old. The vitalistic theory of organic bodies which ascribes the phenomena of life to some kind of immaterial vital force.

Volition. Rational appetition.

Volition, Deliberate. Volition which results in consequence of a deliberation over the respective merits of particular values.

Volition, Natural. Volition which must follow the apprehension of a perfect good.

Will. The rational appetency or the power to strive for an intellectually perceived good and to shun an intellectually perceived evil.

BIBLIOGRAPHY

ACH, N., *Über den Willensakt und das Temperament* (Leipzig: Quelle und Meyer, 1910).

ADLER, ALFRED, *Problems of Neurosis* (Cosmopolitan Book Corp., 1930).

ADLER, MORTIMER JEROME, *Problems for Thomists: The Problem of Species* (New York: Sheed and Ward, 1940).

——— *What Man Has Made of Man* (New York: Longmans, Green, 1937).

ADRIAN, E. D., *The Basis of Sensation* (New York: Norton, 1928).

ALEXANDER, S., *Space, Time and Deity* (London: Macmillan, 1920).

ALLEN, A. H. BURLTON, *Pleasure and Instinct* (New York: Harcourt, Brace, 1930).

ALLERS, RUDOLF, *The New Psychologies* (London and New York: Sheed and Ward, 1933).

——— *The Psychology of Character*, tr. by E. B. Strauss (New York: Sheed and Ward, 1934).

——— *The Successful Error: A Critical Study of Freudian Psychoanalysis* (New York: Sheed and Ward, 1940).

ALLPORT, GORDON WILLARD, *Personality; A Psychological Interpretation* (New York: Holt, 1937).

ANGELL, JAMES ROWLAND, *An Introduction to Psychology* (New York: H. Holt, 1920).

APPEL, KENNETH E. and EDWARD A. STRECKER, *Practical Examination of Behavior Disorders, Adults and Children* (New York: Macmillan, 1936).

AQUINAS, ST. THOMAS, *Contra Gentiles*, tr. by the English Dominicans (London: Burns, Oates, and Washbourne, 1923).

——— *In Aristotelis Stagiritae Libros Nonnullos Commentaria*, De Anima.

——— *Opuscula Varia.*

——— *Quaestiones Disputatae.*

——— *Summa Theologica*, tr. by the English Dominicans, 2nd rev. ed. (London: Burns, Oates, and Washbourne, 1920).

ARISTOTLE, *The Basic Works of Aristotle*, ed. by Richard McKeon (New York: Random House, 1941).

AVELING, FRANCIS, *Psychology: The Changing Outlook* (London: Watts, 1937).

Bain, Alexander, *Mental Science* (New York: D. Appleton, 1870).
Baldwin, James Mark, *Handbook of Psychology*, 2 vols. (New York: H. Holt, 1890).
Barrett, E. Boyd, *The New Psychology* (New York: P. J. Kennedy and Sons, 1925).
Barrett, James Francis, *Elements of Psychology* (Milwaukee: Bruce, 1931).
——— *This Creature Man* (Milwaukee: Bruce, 1936).
Bateson, W., *Mendel's Principles of Heredity* (Cambridge, Eng.: University Press, 1930).
Bechterev, Vladimir M., *General Principles of Human Reflexology*, tr. by Emma and William Murphy from the Russian of the 4th (1928) edition (New York: International Publishers, no date).
Bentley, Isaac Madison, *Behavior, Knowledge, Fact* (Bloomington, Ind.: The Principia Press, 1935).
——— *The New Field of Psychology* (New York: D. Appleton, 1934).
Bergson, Henri, *Creative Evolution*, tr. by A. Mitchell (New York: H. Holt, 1911).
Berkeley, George, *Principles of Human Knowledge*, ed. by A. C. Fraser (Oxford: 1901).
Bernard, L. L., *An Introduction to Social Psychology* (New York: H. Holt, 1926).
Bills, A. G., *General Experimental Psychology* (New York: Longmans, Green, 1937).
Boring, Edwin Garrigues, *A History of Experimental Psychology* (New York: The Century Co., 1929).
Bowne, Borden Parker, *Introduction to Psychological Theory* (New York: Harper and Bros., 1887).
Bradley, John Hodgdon, *Parade of the Living* (New York: Coward-McCann, Inc., 1930).
Bramwell, J. Milne, *Hypnotism*, 3rd ed. (London: W. Rider and Sons, 1921).
Brennan, Robert Edward, *General Psychology* (New York: Macmillan, 1937).
——— *Thomistic Psychology* (New York: Macmillan, 1941).
Brentano, F., *Psychologie vom empirischen Standpunkte* (Leipzig: Meiner, 1925).
Bridges, James Winfred, *Psychology, Normal and Abnormal* (New York: D. Appleton, 1930).
Broad, Charlie Dunbar, *The Mind and Its Place in Nature* (New York: Harcourt, Brace, 1925).

CALKINS, MARY WHITON, *A First Book in Psychology* (New York: Macmillan, 1910).
CANNON, W. B., *Bodily Changes in Pain, Hunger, Fear, and Rage*, 2nd ed. (New York: D. Appleton, 1929).
——— *The Wisdom of the Body* (New York: Norton, 1932).
CARR, HARVEY A., *An Introduction to Space Perception* (New York: Longmans, Green, 1935).
CARREL, ALEXIS, *Man the Unknown* (New York: Harper and Bros., 1935).
CARRINGTON, HEREWARD, *The Problems of Psychical Research* (New York: Dodd, 1921).
——— *The Psychic World* (New York: G. P. Putnam's Sons, 1937).
Case For and Against Psychical Belief, The, ed. by Carl Murchison. Essays by Sir Oliver Lodge, Sir A. Conan Doyle, Frederick Bligh Bond, L. R. G. Crandon, Mary Austin, Margaret Deland, William McDougall, Hans Driesch, Walter Franklin Prince, F. C. S. Schiller, John E. Coover, Gardner Murphy, Joseph Jastrow, and Harry Houdini (Worcester, Mass.: Clark University, 1927).
CLARK, WILFRID EDWARD, *Early Forerunners of Man* (Baltimore: W. Wood, 1934).
COBB, S., *Foundations of Neuropsychiatry*, 2nd ed. (Baltimore: Williams and Wilkins, 1941).
COE, GEORGE ALBERT, *The Motives of Men* (New York: Chas. Scribner's Sons, 1928).
COGHILL, G. E., *Anatomy and the Problems of Behavior* (New York: Macmillan, 1929).
COLE, LAWRENCE EDWIN, *General Psychology* (New York: McGraw-Hill, 1939).
COLVIN, STEPHEN SHELDON, and WILLIAM CHANDLER BAGLEY, *Human Behavior* (New York: Macmillan, 1929).
CONGER, GEORGE PERRIGO, *New Views of Evolution* (New York: Macmillan, 1929).
CONKLIN, EDWIN GRANT, *Man, Real and Ideal* (New York: Chas. Scribner's Sons, 1943).
COURTNEY, ROBERT, *Beyond Behaviorism* (New York: Grant Publications, 1927).
CRAFTS, L. W., T. C. SCHNEIRLA, E. E. ROBINSON, and R. W. GILBERT, *Recent Experiments in Psychology* (New York: McGraw-Hill, 1938).

DALBIEZ, R., *Psychoanalytical Method and the Doctrine of Freud*, 2 vols. (New York: Longmans, Green, 1941).
DASHIELL, J. F., *Fundamentals of Objective Psychology* (Boston: Houghton, Mifflin, 1928).

DAVENPORT, CHARLES B., *How We Come by Our Bodies* (New York: H. Holt, 1936).
DE LA VAISSIÈRE, J., *Elements of Experimental Psychology,* tr. by S. A. Raemers, 5th ed. (St. Louis: Herder, 1926).
DENISON, JOHN HOPKINS, *The Enlargement of Personality* (New York: Chas. Scribner's Sons, 1930).
DESCARTES, RENÉ, *Discours de la Methode.*
——— *Méditations Touchant la Philosophie Première.*
——— *Principia Philosophiae,* tr. by John Veich, 13th ed. (Edinburgh and London: W. Blackwood and Sons, 1902).
DE VRIES, H., *The Mutation Theory,* tr. by J. B. Farmer and A. D. Darbishire, 2 vols. (Chicago: Open Court Publ. Co., 1909–10).
DEWAR, DOUGLAS, *Difficulties of the Evolution Theory* (London: E. Arnold, 1931).
DEWEY, JOHN, *Experience and Nature* (Chicago: Open Court Publ. Co., 1926).
——— *Psychology,* 3rd revised ed. (New York: Harper and Bros., 1891).
DEXTER, EMILY SMITH and K. T. OMWAKE, *An Introduction to the Fields of Psychology* (New York: Prentice Hall, 1942).
DONAT, J., *Psychologia,* 8th rev. and enlarged ed. (Innsbruck: F. Rauch, 1936).
DORLODOT, CANON, *Darwinism and Catholic Thought,* tr. by E. C. Messenger (New York: Benziger Bros., 1923).
DORSEY, JOHN MORRIS, *The Foundation of Human Nature* (New York: Longmans, Green, 1935).
DOYLE, SIR ARTHUR CONAN, *The New Revelation* (New York: Doran, 1918).
DRAKE, DURANT, *Mind and Its Place in Nature* (New York: Macmillan, 1925).
DREIKURS, RUDOLF, *An Introduction to Individual Psychology* (London: K. Paul, Trench, Trübner, 1935).
DRIESCH, HANS, *Alltagsrätsel des Seelenlebens* (Stuttgart: Deutsche Verlagsanstalt, 1938).
——— *Grundprobleme der Psychologie* (Leipzig: E. Reinicke, 1929).
——— *The Crisis in Psychology* (Princeton, N. J.: Princeton Univ. Press, 1925).
——— "The Breakdown of Materialism," in *The Great Design,* ed. by F. Mason (New York: Macmillan, 1934).
——— *The Science and Philosophy of the Organism,* 2nd ed. (London: Black, 1929).
DUBRAY, CHARLES ALBERT, *Introductory Philosophy* (New York: Longmans, Green, 1938).

——— *The Theory of Psychical Dispositions* (New York: Macmillan, 1905).

DUERK, H., *Psychology in Questions and Answers* (New York: P. J. Kennedy and Sons, 1936).

DUMAS, GEORGES, *Nouveau Traité de Psychologie* (Paris: Felix Alcan, 1930).

EBBINGHAUS, HERMANN, *Memory: a Contribution to Experimental Psychology,* tr. by H. A. Ruger and C. E. Bussenius (New York: Teachers College, Columbia University, 1913).

EHRENSTEIN, WALTER, *Einführung in die Ganzheitspsychologie* (Leipzig: J. A. Barth, 1934).

ELLIS, WILLIS D., *A Source Book of Gestalt Psychology* (New York: Harcourt, Brace, 1938).

ESSER, GERARD, *Psychologia* (Techny, Ill.: Techny Press, 1931).

ESTABROOKS, G. H., *Hypnotism* (New York: E. P. Dutton, 1943).

EUCKEN, RUDOLF, *Der Kampf um einen geistigen Lebensinhalt* (Leipzig: Veit, 1896).

Extra-Sensory Perception After Sixty Years, J. G. Pratt, J. B. Rhine, Burke M. Smith, Charles E. Stuart, and Joseph A. Greenwood (New York: H. Holt, 1940).

FABRE, H., *Bramble-Bees and Others,* tr. by A. T. de Mattos (New York: Dodd, Mead, 1915).

FEARON, ARTHUR DINELEIGH, *The Two Sciences of Psychology* (New York: Prentice-Hall, 1937).

FELL, G., *The Immortality of the Human Soul,* tr. by L. Villing (St. Louis: Herder, 1908).

FLUGEL, J. C., *A Hundred Years of Psychology* (New York: Macmillan, 1933).

FORD, E. B., *Mendelism and Evolution* (New York: L. MacVeagh, Dial Press Monographs on Biological Subjects, 1931).

FOREL, AUGUST, *Der Hypnotismus* (Stuttgart: F. Euke, 1911).

FOUILLÉE, ALFRED, *La Psychologie des Idées-Forces,* 2 vols. (Paris: F. Alcan, 1893).

FREEMAN, ELLIS, *Principles of General Psychology* (New York: H. Holt, 1939).

FREEMAN, G. L., *Introduction to Physiological Psychology* (New York: The Ronald Press, 1934).

FREUD, SIGMUND, *A General Introduction to Psychoanalysis,* tr. by G. S. Hall (New York: Boni and Liveright, 1920).

——— *Beyond the Pleasure Principle* (New York: Boni and Liveright, 1922).

——— *New Introductory Lectures on Psychoanalysis,* tr. by W. J. H. Sprott (New York: W. W. Norton, 1933).

——— *The Ego and the Id* (London: Hogarth Press, 1927).

——— *The Interpretation of Dreams,* tr. by A. A. Brill (London: Allen and Unwin; New York: Macmillan, 1915).

Fröbes, Joseph, *Lehrbuch der experimentellen Psychologie,* 2 vols., 3rd ed. (Freiburg im Breisgau: Herder, 1929).

——— *Psychologia Speculativa* (Freiburg im Breisgau: Herder, 1927).

Gaffney, Mark A., *The Psychology of the Interior Senses* (St. Louis: B. Herder Book Co., 1942).

Galton, F., *Inquiries Into Human Faculty and Its Development* (London: Macmillan, 1883).

Garland, Hamlin, *Forty Years of Psychic Research* (New York: Macmillan, 1936).

Garrett, Henry Edward, *Statistics in Psychology and Education* (New York: Longmans, Green, 1939).

Gates, Arthur Irving, *Elementary Psychology* (New York: Macmillan, 1936).

Gemelli, Agostino, *Über das Entstehen von Gestalten* (Leipzig: Akademische Verlagsgesellschaft, 1928).

Gilliland, Adam Raymond, *Genetic Psychology* (New York: Ronald Press, 1933).

Gilson, E., *The Philosophy of St. Thomas Aquinas,* tr. by E. Bullough (Cambridge, England: Heffer, 1929).

Goddard, Henry Herbert, *Psychology of the Normal and Subnormal* (New York: Dodd, Mead, 1924).

Goldschmidt, Richard, *The Material Basis of Evolution* (New Haven: Yale Univ. Press, 1940).

Goldstein, Kurt, *Aftereffects of Brain Injuries in War* (New York: Grune, 1942).

——— *Organism; A Holistic Approach to Biology Derived from Pathological Data in Man* (New York: American Book Co., 1939).

Goodenough, Florence Laura, *Developmental Psychology* (New York: D. Appleton, 1934).

Grabbe, Paul, *We Call It Human Nature* (New York: Harper and Bros., 1939).

Gray, H., *Anatomy of the Human Body,* 24th edition revised and re-edited by W. H. Lewis (Philadelphia and New York: Lea and Febiger, 1942).

Gregg, Fred Marion, *The Psychology of a Growing Personality* (Lincoln, Neb.: Personality Press, 1938).

GRIFFITHS, JOSEPH HARRY, *The Psychology of Human Behavior* (New York: Farrar and Rinehart, 1935).
GRUENDER, HUBERT, *Problems of Psychology* (Milwaukee: Bruce, 1937).
——— *Psychology Without a Soul* (St. Louis: Herder Book Co., 1912).
GUILFORD, JOY PAUL, editor, *Fields of Psychology* (New York: D. Van Nostrand, 1940).
GURNEY, EDMUND, *Phantasms of the Living* (London: K. Paul, Trench, and Trübner, 1918).

HALDANE, JOHN BURDON SANDERSON, *Adventures of a Biologist* (New York and London: Harper and Bros., 1940).
——— *New Paths in Genetics* (New York and London: Harper and Bros., 1942).
——— *The Causes of Evolution* (New York: Harper and Bros., 1932).
HAMILTON, SIR WILLIAM, *Lectures on Metaphysics*, ed. by H. Mansel and J. Veitch (1859).
HAMMOND, WILLIAM A., *Aristotle's Psychology* (*De Anima* and *Parva Naturalia*) (New York: Macmillan, 1902).
HARMON, FRANCIS LELANDE, *Principles of Psychology* (Milwaukee: Bruce, 1938).
HART, C. A., *The Thomistic Concept of Mental Faculty* (Washington, D. C.: Catholic University, 1930).
HARTMANN, GEORGE W., *Gestalt Psychology: A Survey of Facts and Principles* (New York: Ronald Press, 1935).
HARTSHORNE, C., *The Philosophy and Psychology of Sensation* (Chicago: Univ. of Chicago Press, 1934).
HAUBER, U. A., and M. ELLEN O'HANLON, *Biology* (New York: F. S. Crofts, 1937).
HAWES, MARION (EMSLEY), *What to Read in Psychology* (Chicago: American Library Association, 1942).
HEALY, W., AUGUSTA F. BRONNER, and A. B. BOWERS, *The Structure and Meaning of Psychoanalysis as Related to Personality and Behavior* (New York: A. A. Knopf, 1930).
HEATH, ARCHIE EDWARD, *How We Behave* (New York: Longmans, Green, 1927).
HEGEL, GEORG, *The Logic of Hegel*, tr. by William Wallace (Oxford: Clarendon Press, 1892).
HELMHOLTZ, H. L. F., *Treatise on Physiological Optics*, tr. from the 3rd ed. by J. P. C. Southall, 3 vols. (Ithaca, N. Y.: The Optical Society of America, 1924–25).
HENNING, H. K. F., *Der Geruch* (Leipzig: Barth, 1924).
HERBART, JOHANN FRIEDRICH, *A Text-Book in Psychology*, tr. by Margaret K. Smith (New York: D. Appleton, 1891).

Hickey, J. S., *Psychologia* (Dublin: M. H. Gill and Son, 1917).
Higginson, Glenn de Vere, *Fields of Psychology* (New York: H. Holt, 1931).
——— *Psychology* (New York: Macmillan, 1936).
Hobhouse, Leonard Trelawney, *Development and Purpose* (London: Macmillan, 1913).
Hoisington, Louis Benjamin, *Psychology* (New York: Macmillan, 1935).
Hollander, Bernard, *In Search of the Soul and the Mechanism of Thought, Emotion, and Conduct* (London: K. Paul, Trench, Trübner, 1920).
Hollingworth, Harry Levi, *Psychology: Its Facts and Principles* (New York: D. Appleton, 1928).
——— *The Psychology of Thought* (New York: D. Appleton, 1926).
Hooton, Ernest Albert, *Up from the Apes* (New York: Macmillan, 1931).
Howell, W. H., *A Text-Book of Physiology,* 12th ed. (Philadelphia: Saunders, 1933).
Hrdlicka, Alec, *The Evidence Bearing on Man's Evolution* (Smithsonian Institute. Annual Report, 1928, pp. 417–432).
Huet, F., *La Science de l'Esprit* (Paris: Chamerot, 1864).
Hume, David, *Treatise on Human Nature.*
Hunter, Walter Samuel, *General Psychology,* rev. ed. (Chicago: Univ. of Chicago Press, 1923).
——— *Human Behavior* (Chicago: Univ. of Chicago Press, 1928).
Hurst, C. C., *Heredity and the Ascent of Man* (Cambridge, England: The University Press, 1935).
Husband, Richard Wellington, *General Psychology* (New York: Farrar and Rinehart, 1940).
Huxley, Julian Sorell, *Evolution, the Modern Synthesis* (New York and London: Harper and Bros., 1942).
Hyslop, James Hervey, *Contact With the Other World* (New York: The Century Co., 1919).

Introduction to Psychology, Edwin Garrigues Boring and Others (New York: J. Wiley, 1939).

Jaensch, Erich, *Eidetik Imagery and Typological Methods of Investigation* (New York: Harcourt, Brace, 1930).
James, William, *The Principles of Psychology,* 2 vols. (New York: H. Holt, 1931).
Jastrow, Joseph, *The Subconscious* (Boston: Houghton, 1906).
——— *Wish and Wisdom* (New York: D. Appleton-Century, 1935).

Jennings, H. S., *Behavior of the Lower Organisms* (New York: Columbia Univ. Press, 1931).
Judd, Charles Hubbard, *Psychology* (Boston: Ginn, 1917).
Jung, C. G., *Contributions to Analytical Psychology,* tr. by H. G. and C. F. Baynes (New York: Harcourt, Brace, 1928).
——— *Psychology of the Unconscious,* tr. by B. M. Hinkle (New York: Moffat, Yard, 1921).
——— *Psychological Types,* tr. by H. G. Baynes (New York: Harcourt, Brace, 1923).

Kant, Immanuel, *Critique of Pure Reason,* 2nd ed., tr. by Max Müller (New York: Macmillan, 1927).
Keller, Fred Simmons, *The Definition of Psychology* (New York: Appleton-Century, 1937).
Keyser, Leander S., *The Problem of Origins* (New York: Macmillan, 1926).
Klein, David Ballin, *General Psychology* (New York: H. Holt, 1936).
Kobel, Jerome, "The Evolution of Man," in *The Franciscan Educational Conference,* Vol. XV, No. 15 (Washington, D. C., Brookland: Capuchin College).
Köhler, Wolfgang, *Gestalt Psychology* (New York: Boni and Liveright, 1929).
——— *The Mentality of Apes,* tr. by E. Winter (New York: Harcourt, Brace, 1925).
Koffka, Kurt, *The Growth of Mind* (New York: Harcourt, Brace, 1925).
Kraut, Maurice Haim, *Major Aspects of Personality* (Chicago: The College Press, 1933).
Külpe, Oswald, *Vorlesungen über Psychologie,* ed. by Karl Bühler (Leipzig: Hirzel, 1922).

Ladd, George Trumbull, *Outlines of Descriptive Psychology* (New York: Chas. Scribner's Sons, 1898).
——— *Philosophy of Mind* (New York: Chas. Scribner's Sons, 1895).
Ladd-Franklin, C., *Color and Color Theories* (New York: Harcourt, Brace, 1929).
Lashley, K. S., *Brain Mechanisms and Intelligence* (Univ. of Chicago Press, 1929).
——— *That Mind of Yours* (Philadelphia: J. B. Lippincott, 1927).
Leibnitz, Gottfried W., *The Monadology,* 2nd ed., tr. by Robert Latta (Oxford Univ. Press, 1925).
Levin, Albert Julius, *Current Psychologies* (Cambridge: Sci-Art Publishers, 1940).

Lewin, Kurt, *Principles of Topological Psychology,* tr. by Fritz and Grace M. Heider (New York: McGraw-Hill, 1936).

Lindworsky, Johannes, *Das Seelenleben des Menschen* (Bonn: P. Haustein, 1934).

——— *Der Wille,* 3rd ed. (Leipzig: 1923).

——— *Experimental Psychology,* tr. by H. R. De Silva (New York: Macmillan, 1931).

——— *Theoretical Psychology,* tr. by H. R. De Silva (St. Louis: Herder, 1932).

——— *The Training of the Will,* tr. from the 4th rev. ed. by A. Steiner and E. A. Fitzpatrick (Milwaukee: Bruce, 1929).

Locke, John, *An Essay Concerning Human Understanding,* ed. by A. C. Fraser (Oxford, 1894).

Lodge, Sir Oliver Joseph, *Evolution and Creation* (New York: G. H. Doran, 1926).

——— *Phantom Walls* (New York: G. P. Putnam's Sons, 1930).

Lorand, Sandor, ed., *Psychoanalysis Today: Its Scope and Function* (New York: Covici Friede, 1933).

Lotze, Rudolf Hermann, *Medizinische Psychologie oder Physiologie der Seele* (Leipzig: Weidmann, 1852).

——— *Metaphysic,* Eng. trans., ed. by Bernard Bosanquet (Oxford: Clarendon Press, 1884).

Louttit, Chauncey McKinley, *Handbook of Psychological Literature* (Bloomington, Ind.: The Principia Press, 1932).

Luckiesh, M., *Visual Illusions* (New York: D. Van Nostrand, 1922).

Lull, Richard Swann, *Organic Evolution,* rev. ed. (New York: Macmillan, 1929).

Lund, Frederick Hansen, *Psychology, an Empirical Study of Behavior* (New York: The Ronald Press, 1933).

Macmurray, John, *The Boundaries of Science* (London: Faber and Faber, 1939).

Maher, Michael, *Psychology: Empirical and Rational,* 9th ed. (New York: Longmans, Green, 1930).

Maritain, Jacques, *An Introduction to Philosophy,* tr. by E. I. Watkin (New York: Longmans, Green, 1930).

——— *The Degrees of Knowledge,* tr. from the 2nd rev. ed. by Bernard Wall (New York: Chas. Scribner's Sons, 1938).

Marston, W. M., *Emotions of Normal People* (New York: Harcourt, Brace, 1928).

Mason, F., ed., *The Great Design* (New York: Macmillan, 1934).

Mason, Phillipps, *The X of Psychology* (Cambridge: Harvard Univ. Press, 1940).

McCosh, James, *Psychology*, rev. ed. (New York: Chas. Scribner's Sons, 1909).
McDougall, William, *An Introduction to Social Psychology* (Boston: Luce, 1926).
——— *Outline of Psychology* (New York: Chas. Scribner's Sons, 1929).
——— *Psychology: The Study of Behavior* (New York: H. Holt, 1912).
——— *The Energies of Man* (New York: Chas. Scribner's Sons, 1933).
——— *The Frontiers of Psychology* (New York: Appleton-Century, 1935).
——— *Modern Materialism and Emergent Evolution* (New York: D. Van Nostrand, 1929).
McKerrow, James Clark, *Evolution Without Natural Selection* (New York: Longmans, Green, 1937).
Meinong, Alexius, *Abhandlungen zur Psychologie* (Leipzig: J. A. Barth, 1929).
Mercier, Card. D., *A Manual of Modern Scholastic Philosophy*, 8th ed., tr. by T. L. Parker and S. A. Parker (London: K. Paul, Trench, Trübner; St. Louis: B. Herder, 1916).
——— *Psychologie* (Paris: F. Alcan, 1923).
——— *The Origins of Contemporary Psychology*, tr. by W. H. Mitchell (New York: P. J. Kennedy and Sons, 1918).
Messenger, E. C., *Evolution and Theology* (London: Burns, Oates, and Washbourne, 1931).
——— *Psychology of the Other-One* (Columbia, Mo.: Missouri Book Co., 1921).
Miller, Leo Francis, *General Psychology* (New York: J. F. Wagner, 1928).
Monsarrat, Keith Waldegrave, *Human Powers and Their Relations* (London: Hodder and Stoughton, 1938).
Moore, Jared Sparks, and Herbert Gurnee, *The Foundations of Psychology*, 2nd rev. ed. (Princeton Univ. Press, 1933).
Moore, Thomas Verner, *Cognitive Psychology* (Philadelphia: J. B. Lippincott, 1939).
——— *Dynamic Psychology* (Philadelphia: J. B. Lippincott, 1926).
——— *The Nature and Treatment of Mental Disorders* (New York: Grune and Stratton, 1943).
Morgan, Conwy Lloyd, *Life, Mind, and Spirit* (London: Williams and Norgate, 1926).
——— *The Emergence of Novelty* (London: Williams and Norgate, 1933).

MORRIS, CHARLES WILLIAM, *Six Theories of Mind* (Chicago: Univ. of Chicago Press, 1932).

MOULTON, FOREST RAY, *The World and Man as Science Sees Them* (Chicago: Univ. of Chicago Press, 1937).

MUCKERMANN, H., *The Humanizing of the Brute* (St. Louis: B. Herder, 1906).

MULHOLLAND, JOHN, *Beware Familiar Spirits* (New York: Chas. Scribner's Sons, 1939).

MÜLLER-FREIENFELS, RICHARD, *The Evolution of Modern Psychology,* tr. by W. B. Wolfe (New York: Yale Univ. Press, 1935).

MURCHISON, CARL, ed., *A Handbook of Experimental Psychology* (Worcester, Mass.: Clark Univ. Press, 1934).

——— *A History of Psychology in Autobiography* (Worcester, Mass.: Clark Univ. Press, 1930).

——— *The Case For and Against Psychical Belief* (Worcester, Mass.: Clark Univ. Press, 1927).

MURPHY, GARDNER, *An Historical Introduction to Modern Psychology,* 4th rev. ed. (New York: Harcourt, Brace, 1938).

——— *General Psychology* (New York: Harper and Bros., 1933).

MUSE, MAUDE BLANCHE, *A Textbook of Psychology,* 4th ed., rev. (Philadelphia: W. B. Saunders, 1939).

NOBLE, EDMUND, *Purposive Evolution* (New York: H. Holt, 1926).

NORDENSKIÖLD, ERIK, *The History of Biology,* tr. by Leonard B. Eyre (London: Alfred A. Knopf, 1928).

OGDEN, CHARLES KAY, *The Meaning of Psychology* (New York: Harper and Bros., 1926).

O'TOOLE, GEORGE BARRY, *The Case Against Evolution* (New York: Macmillan, 1925).

PADMORE, FRANK, *Modern Spiritism* (London: Methuen, 1902).

PAINTER, GEORGE STEPHEN, *Fundamental Psychology* (New York: Liveright Publ. Corp., 1938).

PARSONS, LEONARD MILES, *The Universe of Our Experience* (London: Williams and Norgate, 1933).

PAVLOV, I. P., *Conditioned Reflexes,* tr. by G. V. Anrep (Oxford Univ. Press, 1927).

PESCH, TILMANN, *Institutiones Psychologicae,* 3 vols. (Fribourg: Herder, 1898).

PHILLIPS, R. P., *Modern Thomistic Philosophy* (London: Burns, Oates, and Washbourne, 1934).

PILLSBURY, WALTER BOWERS, *The Fundamentals of Psychology* (New York: Macmillan, 1937).

PLEYDELL-BOUVERIE, CHRISTOPHER, *Objective Evolution* (London: Williams and Norgate, 1936).

POTTER, CHARLES FRANCIS, *Beyond the Senses* (New York: Doubleday, Doran, 1939).

PRATT, CARROLL CORNELIUS, *The Logic of Modern Psychology* (New York: Macmillan, 1939).

PRINCE, MORTON, *The Dissociation of a Personality* (New York: Longmans, Green, 1908).

——— *The Unconscious* (New York: Macmillan, 1924).

Psychologies of 1925 (Clark Univ. Press, 1930).

Psychology: A Factual Textbook, ed. by E. G. Boring, H. S. Langfeld, and H. P. Weld (New York: J. Wiley, 1935).

PYNE, JOHN X., *The Mind* (New York: Benziger Bros., 1926).

REMER, VINCENT, 5th ed. rev. and enlarged by P. Geny, *Psychologia* (Rome: Apud Aedes Univ. Greg., 1925).

REXROAD, CARL NEWTON, *An Introduction to Psychology* (Columbia, Mo.: E. W. Stephens, 1938).

RHINE, J. B., *New Frontiers of the Mind* (New York: Farrar and Rinehart, 1937).

RICHET, CHARLES ROBERT, *L'Homme et l'Intelligence* (Paris: F. Alcan, 1884).

——— *Thirty Years of Psychical Research* (New York: Macmillan, 1923).

RIGNANO, E., *Man is Not a Machine* (London: K. Paul, 1926).

——— *The Nature of Life*, tr. by N. Mallinson (London: K. Paul; New York: Harcourt, Brace, 1930).

RITCHIE, ARTHUR DAVID, *The Natural History of Mind* (New York: Longmans, Green, 1936).

RIVERS, W. H. R., *Instinct and the Unconscious* (Cambridge Univ. Press, 1922).

ROBINSON, EDWARD STEVENS, *Man as Psychology Sees Him* (New York: Macmillan, 1932).

ROBINSON, E. S., and FLORENCE RICHARDSON-ROBINSON, *Readings in General Psychology* (Chicago: Univ. of Chicago Press, 1928).

ROMER, ALFRED S., *Man and the Vertebrates*, 3rd ed. (Chicago: Univ. of Chicago Press, 1941).

RUCH, FLOYD L., *Psychology and Life* (New York: Scott, Foresman, 1941).

RUCKMICK, C. A., *The Psychology of Feeling and Emotion* (New York: McGraw-Hill, 1936).

RUNES, DAGOBERT D., *Twentieth Century Philosophy* (New York: Philosophical Library, 1943).

RUSSELL, BERTRAND, *The Analysis of Mind* (New York: Macmillan, 1921).

SALISBURY, FRANK SEELY, *Human Development and Learning* (New York: McGraw-Hill, 1939).

SCHAFFER, LAURANCE FREDERIC, *The Psychology of Adjustment* (Ann Arbor, Mich.: Edwards Bros., 1933).

SCHMALHAUSEN, SAMUEL DANIEL, *Our Changing Human Nature* (New York: The Macauley Co., 1929).

SEABURY, DAVID, *Unmasking Our Minds* (New York: Boni and Liveright, 1924).

SEMON, RICHARD WOLFGANG, *The Mneme* (New York: Macmillan, 1921).

SEVERN, ELIZABETH, *The Psychology of Behavior* (New York: Dodd, Mead, 1920).

SHERMAN, MANDEL, *Basic Problems of Behavior* (New York: Longmans, Green, 1941).

SHERRINGTON, SIR CHARLES SCOTT, *The Brain and Its Mechanism* (New York: Macmillan, 1937).

SHULL, AARON FRANKLIN, *Evolution* (New York: McGraw-Hill, 1936).

SINCLAIR, UPTON, *Mental Radio* (New York: Albert and Charles Boni, 1930).

SKAGGS, ERNEST BURTON, *Human Psychology* (Ann Arbor, Mich.: Edwards Bros., 1939).

SKINNER, CHARLES EDWARD, editor, *Readings in Psychology* (New York: Farrar and Rinehart, 1935).

SMITH, STEVENSON, and E. R. GUTHRIE, *General Psychology in Terms of Behavior* (New York: D. Appleton, 1921).

SMITH, T. V., and MARJORIE GRENE, *From Descartes to Kant* (Chicago: Univ. of Chicago Press, 1940).

SMUTS, JAN CHRISTIAN, *Holism and Evolution* (New York: Macmillan, 1926).

SPEARMAN, CHARLES, *The Abilities of Man* (New York: Macmillan, 1927).

——— *The Nature of "Intelligence" and the Principles of Cognition* (London: Macmillan, 1923).

——— *Psychology Down the Ages* (London: Macmillan, 1937).

SPENCER, HERBERT, *The Principles of Psychology* (New York: D. Appleton, 1914).

SPRANGER, EDWARD, *Types of Man*, tr. from the 5th ed. by Paul J. W. Pigors (Halle: Niemeyer, 1928).

SPROTT, WALTER JOHN HERBERT, *General Psychology* (New York: Longmans, Green, 1937).

STARCH, DANIEL, *Controlling Human Behavior* (New York: Macmillan, 1936).

STERN, WILLIAM, *General Psychology from the Personalistic Standpoint* (New York: Macmillan, 1938).

STOUT, GEORGE FREDERICK, *A Manual of Psychology,* rev. by C. A. Mace (London: University Tutorial Press, 1938).

STRECKER, EDWARD ADAM, *Discovering Ourselves* (New York: Macmillan, 1931).

STROUD, JAMES BART, *Introduction to General Psychology* (New York: Prentice-Hall, 1938).

SULLY, JAMES, *Outlines of Psychology* (New York: D. Appleton, 1888).

——— *The Human Mind* (London: Longmans, Green, 1892).

TAYLOR, JAMES GARDEN, *Popular Psychological Fallacies* (London: Watts, 1938).

TERMAN, L. M., *The Measurement of Intelligence* (New York: Houghton, Mifflin, 1916).

THORNDIKE, EDWARD LEE, *Animal Intelligence: Experimental Studies* (New York: Macmillan, 1911).

——— *Human Learning* (New York: The Century Co., 1931).

——— *Human Nature and the Social Order* (New York: Macmillan, 1940).

THOULESS, ROBERT HENRY, *General and Social Psychology* (London: University Tutorial Press, 1937).

THURSTONE, L. L., *The Nature of Intelligence* (New York: Harcourt, Brace, 1924).

TISCHNER, RUDOLF, *Telepathy and Clairvoyance,* tr. by W. D. Hutchinson (New York: Harcourt, Brace, 1925).

TITCHENER, EDWARD BRADFORD, *A Beginner's Psychology* (New York: Macmillan, 1918).

——— *Experimental Psychology of the Thought-Processes* (New York: Macmillan, 1909).

——— *Systematic Psychology: Prolegomena* (New York: Macmillan, 1929).

TOLMAN, EDWARD CHASE, *Purposive Behavior in Animals and Men* (New York: The Century Co., 1932).

TROLAND, LEONARD THOMPSON, *The Fundamentals of Human Motivation* (New York: Van Nostrand, 1928).

——— *The Mystery of Mind* (New York: Van Nostrand, 1926).

——— *The Principles of Psychophysiology,* 3 vols. (New York: Van Nostrand, 1929–32).

VALENTINE, WILLARD LEE, *Experimental Foundations of General Psychology* (New York: Farrar and Rinehart, 1941).

Van de Woestyne, P. F. Zachary, *Psychologia* (Mechlin: 1925).
Vaughn, Wayland Farries, *General Psychology* (New York: Doubleday, Doran, 1939).

Wait, Wallace Theodore, *The Science of Human Behavior* (New York: Ronald Press, 1938).
Walker, L. J., *Theories of Knowledge* (London: Longmans, Green, 1924).
Wallin, J. E. Wallace, *Minor Mental Maladjustments in Normal People* (Durham, N. C.: Duke Univ. Press, 1939).
Warcollier, René, *Experiments in Telepathy* (New York: Harper and Bros., 1938).
Wasmann, Erich, *Comparative Studies in the Psychology of Ants and of Higher Animals,* tr. by J. Gummersbach, 2nd ed. (St. Louis: B. Herder, 1905).
——— *Instinct and Intelligence in the Animal Kingdom* (St. Louis: B. Herder, 1903).
——— *Modern Biology and the Theory of Evolution* (London: K. Paul, Trench, Trübner, 1910).
Watson, John Broadus, *Behavior: An Introduction to Comparative Psychology* (New York: H. Holt, 1914).
——— *Behaviorism* (New York: W. W. Norton, 1930).
——— *Psychology from the Standpoint of a Behaviorist* (Philadelphia: J. B. Lippincott, 1929).
Weismann, August, *Essays Upon Heredity and Kindred Biological Problems,* tr. by Poulton, Schönland, and Shipley (Oxford: Clarendon Press, 1891).
——— *On Germinal Selection as a Source of Definite Variation* (Chicago: Open Court Publ. Co., 1896).
Weiss, A. P., *A Theoretical Basis of Human Behavior* (Columbus, Ohio: R. G. Adams, 1925).
Weld, H. P., *Psychology as Science* (New York: H. Holt, 1928).
Wertheimer, M., *Drei Abhandlungen zur Gestalttheorie* (Erlangen: Verlag d. phil. Akad., 1925).
Wexberg, E., *Individual Psychology,* tr. by W. B. Wolfe (New York: Cosmopolitan Book Corp., 1929).
——— *The Science of Psychology,* 2nd rev. ed. (New York: Thomas Crowell, 1940).
Wickham, Harvey, *The Misbehaviorists* (New York: L. MacVeagh, The Dial Press, 1928).
Willis, J. C., *The Course of Evolution* (Cambridge Univ. Press, 1940).
Wilson, E. B., *The Cell in Heredity and Environment,* 3rd rev. ed. (New York: Macmillan, 1935).

WINDLE, B. C. A., *The Evolutionary Problem as It Is Today* (New York: Wagner, 1927).

——— *What is Life? A Study in Vitalism and Neo-Vitalism* (London and Edinburg: Sands and Co.; St. Louis: B. Herder, 1908).

WOOD, LEDGER, *The Analysis of Knowledge* (Princeton Univ. Press, 1941).

WOODWORTH, ROBERT SESSIONS, *Contemporary Schools of Psychology* (New York: The Ronald Press, 1931).

——— *Experimental Psychology* (New York: H. Holt, 1938).

——— *Psychology* (New York: H. Holt, 1937).

WUNDT, WILHELM MAX, *Outlines of Psychology,* tr. by Ch. Hubbard Judd (New York: G. E. Stechert, 1902).

YOUNG, PAUL THOMAS, *Motivation of Behavior* (New York: J. Wiley and Sons, 1936).

ZILBOORG, G., and G. W. HENRY, *A History of Medical Psychology* (New York: W. W. Norton, 1941).

INDEX